❖ A STERNER PLAN FOR ITALIAN UNITY

THE ITALIAN NATIONAL SOCIETY
IN THE RISORGIMENTO

God reigns, and let earth rejoice!
  I bow before His sterner plan.
Dumb are the organs of my choice;
He speaks in battle's stormy voice,
  His praise is in the wrath of man!

—from "Italy" by John Greenleaf Whittier,
written in 1860

A STERNER PLAN
FOR
ITALIAN UNITY

THE ITALIAN NATIONAL SOCIETY

IN THE RISORGIMENTO

BY RAYMOND GREW

PRINCETON, NEW JERSEY

PRINCETON UNIVERSITY PRESS

1963

Publication of this book has been aided by
the Ford Foundation program to support publication,
through university presses, of works in the humanities
and social sciences

Printed in the United States of America by
Vail-Ballou Press, Inc., Binghamton, N.Y.

✤

TO MY MOTHER AND FATHER

WHO HAVE DEDICATED

MUCH MORE TO ME

CONTENTS

CONTENTS

INTRODUCTION

✤ IT IS A WRITER'S VICE to find the importance of his subject proved by the bulk of his words. The historical importance of the Italian National Society, however, is attested to in others' words as well; for nearly all who write on the Risorgimento find the Society important to their tale. Even those who describe in one great sweep the epic of Italy's unification usually honor the National Society by making its name the title of one of their chapters. The things the Society did are central to that story, and one's understanding of the National Society will do much to determine his interpretation of the Risorgimento.

This book is, first of all, a roughly chronological history of that organization itself; but the excitement of the topic is that it permits, simultaneously, some study of the political, intellectual, and social history of the period in which Italy became a nation. As a political history, this work attempts to analyze the organization and effectiveness of those nationalists who won—those who favored unification with monarchy. It means to assess and explain the way they conducted their political battles and the kind of institutions they helped to establish. It argues that their political roots were shallow and their support limited but that they were even more cautious than they need have been. It contends that they came from fear as well as realism to rely on diplomacy, Piedmont's army, and the state rather than on revolution and popular participation to effect Italy's unification.

As an intellectual history, this book deals with the unsystematic and not very profound ideas of propagandists. But it argues that, taken together, the ideas and values of the National Society interlocked more effectively than its sponsors knew, that they reflect the historical significance of these years of the Risorgimento, and that they moved with inner necessity from concern for liberty and justice to an emphasis on unanimity and the strength of the state.

As a social history, this book treats men of little fame—the members of the National Society, who were the new Italy's most ardent supporters. It discusses their relative strength in different periods, province by province, and, insofar as evidence allows, says something of the classes from which they came. This study means to provide a sense of how the process of unification was understood and what it felt like in practice to the local leaders who made it possible; it attempts to describe the spirit of these years while arguing that the core of the movement was the professional men who out of social habit, liberal hope, and political fear entrusted themselves and Italy to the nationalist gentry.

How these themes are touched upon and how they relate to the Risorgimento as a whole can be explained in terms of what the Society was and what it did. Above all, it was a movement of opinion. Its formation was the most dramatic sign that republicans were turning to Cavour, that nationalists would accept unification under Piedmontese monarchy, that the era of Mazzini was really over. Because it drew increasingly close to Cavour and even claimed to be an instrument of his policy, the history of the National Society becomes an important measure of what Cavour's policy really was. Nearly every argument about the nature of Cavour's nationalism or about the skill and intent of his political manipulation rests in some part on one's view of the Society.

From 1857 to 1862, the Society published a newspaper, first a weekly, then a daily. Its circulation was national, for even before the war of 1859 it was smuggled across the borders into the petty states it sought to eliminate. The Society had, in addition, connections with other influential newspapers; it published a number of pamphlets which were distributed in thousands of copies, and its committees issued hundreds of manifestoes. It was the Society, more than any other agency, which developed and broadcast the dominant ideas of the "high" Risorgimento. In the National Society one finds the ideology of the Risorgimento in practice, the set of ideas—just below the level of political theory—in terms of which Italian nationalists conceived the unification they were bringing about.

Organized through local committees across the Peninsula, the Society's membership provides an indication of who Italy's monarchical nationalists were, where they were numerous and how they were effective.

The Society played a vital part in the great movement of volunteers who came from all of northern Italy to fight with Piedmont in 1859. It was largely its committees which led the revolutions in town after town of central Italy as the Austrian and Papal armies retreated. The same men then formed the interim governments which demanded annexation to Piedmont with such persistence and skill that diplomacy could not prevent it. In 1860 the Society was deeply involved in Garibaldi's expedition to Sicily and Cavour's invasion of the Papal States. The history of the Italian National Society includes most of the great events which led to Italian unification. It provides some insight into the kinds of acts which made Italy and the policies, ideas, and interests which prompted them.

The Society also had a central role in the plebiscites and elections which followed unification. At times it was an agency for recruiting the new bureaucracy; on occasion it served as an auxiliary to government itself. As something like a political party, it lasted into 1864. The study of the Society tells something, finally, about the nature of Italy's political system.

Perhaps the reader of a book so big deserves some more specific guidance. The dates after each chapter title indicate the period intensively treated, though some topical material often overflows these artificial termini. The text is thick with proper names, many of which will be familiar and informative to those who have previously encountered the Risorgimento. But the argument can be followed without such erudition, for individuals and places are more fully introduced where the argument requires it. Although the Society's doctrine is the topic of Chapter Five, its further development is treated in parts of Chapters Nine, Fourteen, and Fifteen. This is a study of the National Society as a whole and not the series of regional histories it could be, but it often makes fairly extended assessments of the Society in each of Italy's provinces. The non-specialist may understandably choose not to immerse himself in these sometimes detailed additions to a complicated subject. This warning applies especially to Chapter Eleven but also to parts of Chapters Eight, Fourteen, and Fifteen. The terms for Italy's regions are, incidentally, used primarily as the Society understood them and as the relations among its committees reflected them (Pontremoli, for example, is usually treated as part of the Duchies).

In a book meant to be read, some apology may be due for the length of the footnotes. No history of the National Society has ever been written, and most of the evidence on which this study ultimately rests has not been unearthed before. Its arguments modify and sometimes consciously contradict interpretations long respected. Pedantry may never be appealing but it can be an aid to others' scholarship and a pressure for precision in one's own. The notes are meant to suggest where problems merely touched on here can be in part pursued and to provide a fuller sense of the quality of the argument, where the pillar of evidence is so tall as to raise interpretation almost to truth and where the evidence is so peripheral as to reduce assertion to mere guess. The nature of the subject makes the footnotes long. Much of this study is concerned with attitudes, always hard to document; at many points it deals from a different viewpoint with incidents and issues much disputed and on which a new stand demands a full display of evidence. Occasionally, facts uncovered which did not earn a place in the text seemed useful enough to be crowded into the notes. The reader of any book must, after all, make his own map through it; he can choose the bypaths he wants to follow.

A study of the Italian National Society can claim, then, more than the historian's minimal comfort—that it fills a gap. Its subject is, to be sure, the most important and best organized, the most successful and best known political movement of the climactic years of the Risorgimento. But the Risorgimento itself, too often treated simply as one of the great and colorful stories of the nineteenth century, has a wider significance.

Nationalism, the growth of the state, the desire for representative government, and the dream of prosperity loom large in modern history; the unification of Italy provides a valuable case for studying what these abstractions mean in practice. Italy, with her ancient and rich culture, had been deeply affected by the experiences of the French Revolution and Napoleonic rule. She was no mere backwater, and her educated classes could readily accept and apply Western technology and ideas. At the same time, Italy was politically weak and divided, long subject to the domination of other powers; she was, even in the north, economically and institutionally behind England and France although close to them in spirit. Italy's leaders thought in terms of ideas which flourished in these countries while operating under conditions quite different. In the next century those ideas would spread to far more alien environments. The attempt to accommodate them to different conditions has become a common theme of history. It is the effort to make that accommodation in Italy in the middle of the nineteenth century which produced the Italian National Society.

The following abbreviations are used in the notes:

ASF	Archivio di Stato, Firenze
ASR	Archivio di Stato, Roma
AST	Archivio di Stato, Torino
BCT	Biblioteca Civica, Torino
BSMC	Biblioteca di Storia Moderna e Contemporanea
HCL	Harvard College Library
ISR	Instituto per la Storia del Risorgimento
MCRB	Museo Civico del Risorgimento, Bologna
MCV	Museo Correr, Venezia
MNRG	Museo Nazionale del Risorgimento, Genova
MNRM	Museo Nazionale del Risorgimento, Milano
MNRT	Museo Nazionale del Risorgimento, Torino
MRF	Museo del Risorgimento, Firenze

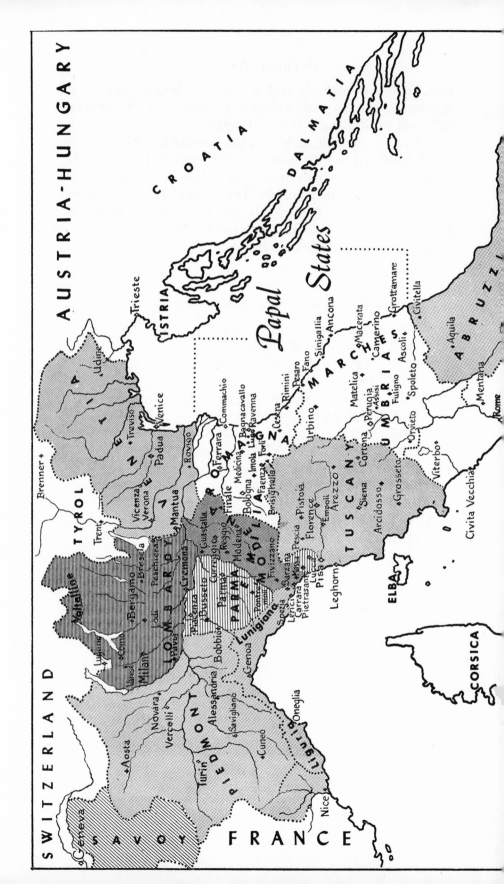

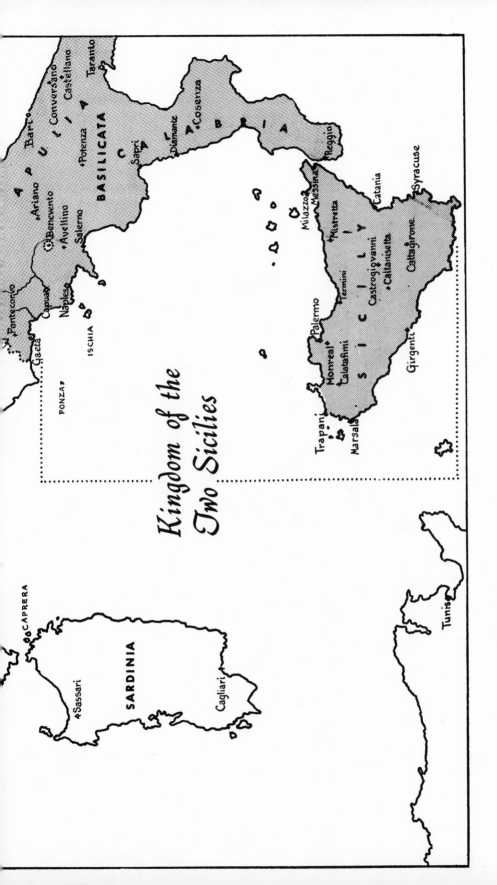

Kingdom of the
Two Sicilies

I ✦ BEGINNINGS

CHAPTER ONE

POLITICAL PROGRAMS CENTER ON PIEDMONT
(BEFORE THE CONGRESS OF PARIS)

THE MOST COMMON consolation for defeat is the claim that it has made men wiser. By 1850 the political leaders of Italy had great need of such solace. The revolutionary miracles of 1848 were over. Then the hope and enthusiasm of revolt had leaped from capital to capital, and Italians had shown themselves part of the European mainstream as they had not been in the long generation since Napoleon or perhaps in the centuries since the Renaissance. The barricades of Paris had not been better built than those of Milan; the constitutions of the North had not been more liberal than those of the Peninsula. In all Europe there was no greater hero than Garibaldi; nowhere had there been greater civic courage than in Venice. At last in history's vanguard, the revolutionaries of Italy, like their brothers elsewhere, had then been defeated. Italians watched their heroes become martyrs, their leaders, exiles. Intense activity devoted to remaking the world had left it appearing dramatically unchanged. Austrian troops reconquered Lombardy and Venetia. The Dukes of Modena and Parma and Tuscany, the Pope, and the King of the Two Sicilies returned to their thrones now more nearly Austrian puppets than ever. Charles Albert had shown that a king, at least in Piedmont, could be a patriot—and had had to abdicate.

The Italian revolutions of 1848 brought together many movements and a variety of demands. The romantic secrecy of the *carbonari* had largely given way to the more sophisticated propaganda and utopian visions of Giuseppe Mazzini. Among the liberal gentry, scientific congresses and agrarian societies had for years campaigned about the need for reform. The benefits of railroads and tariff unions as well as of representative government were widely understood in Italy. The revolutions themselves had begun with rather moderate constitutional demands. But the agitation grew in vigor. Too hesitant in their concessions

3

to inspire confidence, most of the local regimes toppled one by one. The question of local, domestic reform had quickly become a question of the form of government. The national issue, the demand that each government support the cause of freedom in the rest of Italy, drove a further wedge between mild reformers of the old regimes and those who dared to call themselves democrats.

The revolution became more radical. Rome without the Pope became militantly republican. Venice, more in the name of ancient glory than future prospects, declared itself again a republic while not quite closing the door to protection from Piedmont's King. Tuscany, too, finally proclaimed a republic, though with still greater hesitance; and Lombardy accepted union with Piedmont but with open misgiving. Still, revolutions are as well remembered for their actions as their programs. The citizens of Milan had driven one of Europe's most respected armies out of town. The Roman republic under Mazzini kept amazing order and under Garibaldi fought the French with surprising heroism. Venice, hopelessly isolated, held on with stirring tenacity, the last to fall and only then to the blockade around her and the plague within. Disunited and internally divided, these regimes were soon defeated. The Neapolitans helped to crush revolt in Sicily only to lose the concessions they had won at home. Elsewhere, it took foreign armies to cut down the new regimes; and Italy was left a legacy of decent constitutions untried and valor unforgotten.

If Piedmont twice went to war against the Austrians in 1848 and 1849, it was never certain whether her policy was an old dynastic one or a new national one. When the Pope and the King of Naples had turned away from the nationalist cause and from the reformers who looked to them, Charles Albert, the King of Piedmont, was thrust into a role of national leadership. He could not play it with confidence. Piedmont displayed some selfishness, indecisiveness, and sheer incompetence in going down twice to defeat. The very magnitude of that defeat emphasized, however, the chivalric qualities of Piedmont's stand. The little kingdom of Savoy gained the credit of having fought, and her policy became more nationalist in defeat than it had been in earlier victory.

In Italy the failures of 1848 and 1849 seemed to clarify political issues. They suggested that local reform required national support. They ended neo-Guelph programs for Italian federation under the Papacy and greatly weakened any claims for federalism. They established that all of Italy's crowned heads except possibly Piedmont's new King, Victor Emmanuel II, were anti-nationalist. They effectively taught many that Italy's future depended on the policies of France and England as well as those of Austria. The framework within which any program for political change in Italy would have to be considered was by 1850 better defined than ever before. But questions of which program of change or how to effect it were still far from answered.

More than before, Italian reformers had become Italian nationalists, but Mazzinians still vied with other republicans and both groups opposed the monarchists. Some thought in terms of military cooperation and political federation; some were outright unitarians. If all were willing to pay greater attention to Piedmont than in the past, the ultimate direction of Piedmont's own policy was far from certain. After the overwhelming defeat of the revolutionaries, while the newly restored regimes were still reacting with vengeance, the prospects for an independent Italy were dim. The "Italian problem" was somewhat clearer, but that was bound to seem a rather empty gain.

Italians by the hundreds, too fully implicated or too much committed by the revolution to be able to stay in Italy, left the country, the greatest number going to France, which claimed still to have kept its republic. Everywhere they engaged in discussing the past, trying to justify their part and to learn the lesson that would give meaning to defeat. These debates reflected the fact, however, that the faith which had fired revolutions largely remained. The dreams of a decade were no less stirring for having been nearly fulfilled, and men practiced in dreaming and used to failing could not now accept defeat as final. When in the 1850's Italian patriots in Paris or Turin or London analyzed the recent past, they were at the same time stating the promise of the future.

Italian political discussions in this period were in part a continuation of the discussions which had preceded 1848; for the meaning of the events of that year was sufficiently ambiguous to permit the revival of many of the old competing programs. The tenor of the debate had changed, however. In one sense the disappointments of 1848 and 1849 were less great in Italy than elsewhere because the successes which preceded them had been more surprising. Thus there was in the 1850's less rhetoric about Italian nationality than before; its existence had been established, its possibilities outlined. That national sentiment had deep roots and that popular enthusiasm could be rallied around it had been demonstrated, and in a sense Mazzinian urgings now seemed less relevant because Mazzinian faith had in part been vindicated. Italian nationalists could, more than those of any other country, view their defeat as simply the result of an external military force. They therefore emphasized the need of adding better armies and more careful organization to all they had achieved before. To many, it seemed necessary only to modify their previous course, not to reject it. This was the more true because the revolutions in Italy had shown little of the class conflict which frightened France and had produced little of the shock to the social structure that rigidified Prussia.

Because the defeats seemed hardly less miraculous than the triumphs they wiped out, it was easy to think in terms of next time, to recognize that then no forces could be wasted. The awful international circumstances which had made isolated defeat possible might change, and then close cooperation and coordination of all forces would assure success. The emphasis on coordination came naturally to the men who now led the discussion of Italian politics, for they were no longer the men of the secret societies but men who had held posts in government, who had savored the practical challenge of making a political system operate. Similarly, especially in exile, talk of concord and unity among Italian patriots came easily not only because they were now politicians but because they had come increasingly to realize their interdependence and to feel their closeness against an enemy which had fooled them by seeming to disappear only to return stronger.

From the first, then, the political discussion centered on a program for the establishment of an independent Italy; and since most of Italy's recent leaders were now in exile, it was from the exiles that the program was expected to come. As the most experienced exile and the most vocal nationalist, Mazzini, who had returned to London, assumed immediate leadership for himself. His *Associazione Nazionale* published its *programma* in 1850. In keeping with the spirit of the exiles as well as Mazzinian doctrine, it was a mild program, stressing the need to work together and the brotherhood of those who accepted its principles.[1] As a kind of patron saint, Mazzini still had prestige; an influential group of the new exiles, for example, protested to the French press against the charge that Mazzini was plotting the assassination of some prominent European figures. It was not, they explained, that they always agreed with Mazzini, but the honor of Italy required that they defend his high personal character.[2]

Such respect for his person proved, however, to have been a sort of kindly farewell to the prophet. His program, despite its mildness, had stressed the need to prepare for action and talked of the collection of arms as a first step; most of the exiles in Paris would no longer respond to the old call for the courage of suicide. It was not long before Mazzini was bemoaning that others should act as leaders when they had lost all hope. And it was not long before the Piedmontese press could make an impressive list of the names of those not now at Mazzini's side.[3] Mazzini's efforts to form an association acceptable to a wide range of Italian nationalists had failed, and his republican declaration in August 1851, only moved him farther from the other exiles and further diminished his ranks. The new exiles in Paris had shown their difference from the old one in London. If they were to establish a program for the liberation of Italy, it would not be Mazzini's. One of the possibilities was being eliminated.

Thus the exiles in Paris began to seem the likely source of a new program. The leaders to provide one were not lacking. There was Daniele Manin, the great leader of the Venetian republic,

[1] *Edizione Nazionale degli scritti editi ed inediti di Giuseppe Mazzini*, XLIII (Imola, 1926), 185–88.

[2] *Ibid.*, XLII (Imola, 1925), 214n–15n. Gioberti to Pallavicino, 24 August 1850, B. E. Maineri (ed.), *Il Piemonte negli anni 1850–51–52, lettere di Vincenzo Gioberti e Giorgio Pallavicino* (Milan, 1875), 33. Those signing the letter to *La Patrie* included Montanelli, Manin, Aurelio Saliceti, Giuseppe Mazzoni and Michele Amari. Gioberti was horrified by it.

[3] Mazzini to George Sand, 10 October 1850, and memorandum to the letter of 7 October, *Scritti di Mazzini*, XLIV (Imola, 1926), 106, 249. *Opinione* noted that Montanelli, Pepe, Manin, Garibaldi, Niccolò Tommaséo, Carlo Cattaneo, La Farina had left the Master. *Ibid.*, 264n–65n. The paper called for the election of a council among the emigrants to operate under a common banner.

and Giuseppe Montanelli, who had been a triumvir of the Tuscan republic, a beloved democrat, unable either as minister or author of a constitution to further unity among the Italian states. There was Guglielmo Pepe from Naples, an old *carbonaro* prominent in constitutional agitation there, who had been the general of the Neapolitan troops sent to fight the Austrians. When the King of Naples recalled his army, Pepe had stayed on to fight for Venice and then gone into exile. There was Vincenzo Gioberti, priest, philosopher, Premier of Piedmont in the first months of 1849. And there were scores of lesser figures. They must have seen a fair amount of each other; [4] yet the lack of even the most general of manifestoes from such men, in the age of manifestoes, suggests either uncertainty or disagreement. There was something of both. Montanelli, with his stress on the "European democratic principle" was too radical for the others.[5] He tried, without success, to bring Gioberti and Manin closer together; the Piedmontese philosopher distrusted Montanelli as too much a poet and disliked Manin as "prosaic in excess." [6] Pepe wanted the exiles to meet to discuss their common concerns, but the meeting seems to have led to nothing. Among those who looked to Piedmont as the basis for Italian independence there was uncertainty as to whether first to attempt to win the exiles to Piedmont or the King to a more national policy. There was even some talk of sending a representative to Victor Emmanuel to tell him "all the truth," but that too came to nothing. All the truth lacks something as a political program.[7]

Still, some sort of accommodation with Piedmont made obvious sense. Piedmont still flew the flag of the revolution; it had kept the cautious constitution Charles Albert had granted in

[4] Mario Brunetti, Pietro Orsi, and Francesco Salata, *Daniele Manin, intimo* (Rome, 1936), 356–57. Anna Koppmann Pallavicino (ed.), *Memorie di Giorgio Pallavicino*, II, *dal 1848 al 1852* (Turin, 1885), 275ff., 297, 390–400ff.

[5] Montanelli to Pallavicino, 9 October 1850, *ibid.*, 265–66. Montanelli was tempted by Lamennais's French-Spanish-Italian Democratic Committee which Pallavicino objected to as republican and Mazzini opposed as federalist. Memorandum by Pallavicino for the Government in his letter to Aurelio Bianchi-Giovini, 9 July 1851, *ibid.*, 403. Mazzini to Pietro Cironi, 18 [August 1851], *Scritti di Mazzini*, XLVII (Imola, 1927), 26–7.

[6] Montanelli to Pallavicino, 3 October 1850, *Memorie di Pallavicino*, II, 261. Gioberti to Pallavicino, 7 December 1850, Maineri, *Piemonte*, 60.

[7] Gioberti to Pallavicino, 23 January and 3 February 1851, *ibid.*, 100, 105. Pallavicino would have been the representative.

1848; it still had an army, even if it had been defeated. The man who sought single-mindedly to join the aspirations of Italian nationalists and the power of Piedmont was not an exile from Italy but a Lombard who lived in Turin, an aristocrat who believed himself a democrat. Giorgio Pallavicino Trivulzio was a wealthy marchese who had once been attracted by Joachim Murat and then became a follower of Confalonieri. As a "martyr" of the Spielberg (he was careful not to let the title die), where he had been sentenced with Confalonieri for his part in the revolutionary plots of 1821, his nationalist credentials were excellent. His fear of communism and distrust of the revolutionary excesses of the French had made it easy for him to become a supporter of Charles Albert. He was not an original thinker, but more than any man he was the father of the Italian National Society. Political influence does not, after all, often depend on originality. It was less his reputation, his perseverance or persuasiveness than his personal connections which allowed his influence to be deeply felt. Though they themselves seemed but rarely aware of it, the leaders of Italian nationalist efforts were a rather small group of men; and the Marchese, with his social and political contacts in Turin and Paris, knew most of them personally.

The belief that the winning of independence required the sacrifice of hopes for a republic came early to Pallavicino; indeed, for the Marchese, it was something less than a sacrifice. In a brief pamphlet in 1849, he had stated the argument: as much as "the most fervid republicans [we want] free institutions, institutions largely democratic; but we want at the same time, we want above all, not the republic but Italy!" [8] For a decade the argument would always start in the same place, always proceed on the same pragmatic basis. I want, he would explain, "independence above all; and so long as Piedmont preserves the tricolored flag, in Piedmont I see Italy." To spread republican propaganda in Piedmont, to create difficulties there seemed to him "a felony against Italy." [9] It was not that he found monarchy inherently good; indeed, with that clear view of the future common to his

[8] Giorgio Pallavicino, *Ai Lombardi* (n.d. [1849]), 1. He signed it "Pallavicino-Spielberg."
[9] Letter of Pallavicino's, January 1850, *Memorie di Pallavicino*, ii, 183.

time, he conceded that "the republic will be the last scene of the last act of that providential drama which we see being played in our hemisphere." His argument was only for the present, valid so long as one could not say how many such acts that drama would have.[10]

Such inexorable historical processes in fact provided an argument against the republic—"the best of governments possible on earth" when, that is, "the times permit it." That it would be good for our children did not mean that it was, "in this moment also good for us." [11] The requirements for a republic, one gathered, were pretty high; the Marchese doubted that men who grew up "in the malign influences of a corrupt government" could be republicans of good faith.[12] The example of Belgium, not France, should be followed; in the present circumstances constitutional monarchy was the best government to be hoped for —and besides the difference was not really great. There was something of the best of both worlds in his cry for a union of North Italians "under the republican scepter of Carlo Alberto." [13]

If Pallavicino could hold these views before the final failures of 1849, it is hardly surprising that he maintained them afterward. The emphasis upon Piedmont as the answer to Italy's military needs fitted well with the increased concern for practical considerations of force. "To defeat cannons and soldiers, cannon and soldiers are needed. Arms are needed, and not Mazzinian pratings. Piedmont has soldiers and cannons: *therefore I am Piedmontese.*" By habit and tradition Piedmont is monarchical; "*I therefore am not republican.*" Pallavicino saw his stand with syllogistic simplicity as a case of first things first. "First independence, then liberty: first I want to live, about living well I will think later." [14] If only, Pallavicino sighed, Italians would accept Piedmontese hegemony, then Piedmont would be strong enough to defeat Austria.[15]

[10] Pallavicino to Montanelli, 21 June 1851, *ibid.,* 328.

[11] Giorgio Pallavicino, *Anzitutto il Ben Pubblico,* a pamphlet (probably of 1849) reprinted in B. E. Maineri (ed.), *Daniele Manin e Giorgio Pallavicino, epistolario politico (1855–1857)* (Milan, 1878), 319.

[12] *Ibid.,* 321.

[13] *Ibid.,* 322.

[14] Pallavicino to Girolamo Pepe, 18 November 1851, *Memorie di Pallavicino,* II, 438.

[15] Letter of Pallavicino's, 14 January 1852, *ibid.,* 460.

In his correspondence with Italian exiles Pallavicino strove to lead them to his views. Everyone, he wrote, looked to Victor Emmanuel; and the King ached for revenge against Austria.[16] The Marchese assumed the role of representative of Victor Emmanuel's inner thoughts and reported the King's belief in constitutions, his bitterness when speaking of the Italian reactionaries, and his milder comments on the republicans.[17] He wrote that the Ministry, too, had decided to support liberal principles and that now "all the moral forces of the peninsula" were centering on Piedmont.[18] Pallavicino's correspondence had become propaganda, and all his unquenchable hope sings through his account of the celebration in Turin on Constitution Day.[19]

The leaders of Piedmont could not, however, always be counted upon to see things with the same clarity as the Martyr of the Spielberg, and Pallavicino's campaign carefully included them. He explained to Massimo d'Azeglio, then Prime Minister, that there were two republican parties, that of Mazzini and that centered about Manin. The latter, not hostile to Piedmont, would not propagandize within the Sardinian state and could indeed even be looked to for support if Piedmont chose to lead the revolution. At first, the Marchese felt he was being listened to with understanding by both King and Minister.[20] Still, the Government seemed not to rise to its opportunities. Pallavicino made sure it received a memorandum analyzing the political situation. "There is today in Italy," he explained, and the statement marks a further development in his thought, "an Italo-Sardinian party. The advancement of this party must be promoted with money, with the press, with secret societies, and, when the opportunity presents itself, even with insurrection." And as if to overcome any possible ministerial qualms, he added, "any means is good to obtain the most holy goal of our independence." [21] Pallavicino had come to view nation-wide respect

[16] Pallavicino to Manin, 12 July 1850, *ibid.*, 217.

[17] Pallavicino to Bianchi-Giovini, 30 September 1850, *ibid.*, 254. See also his letter to Manin, 19 May 1853; *ibid.*, III (*dal 1852 al 1860*) (Turin, 1895), 31.

[18] Pallavicino to Pepe, 21 December 1851, *ibid.*, II, 455.

[19] Pallavicino to Manin, 19 May 1853; *ibid.*, III, 31.

[20] Pallavicino to Vincenzo Gioberti, 2 December 1850, Maineri, *Piemonte*, 53-4.

[21] Memorandum included in Pallavicino to Bianchi-Giovini, 9 July 1851, *Memorie di Pallavicino*, II, 401-403. Cf. his letter to Gioberti, 16 July 1851, Maineri, *Piemonte*, 146.

for Victor Emmanuel as evidence of an inchoate political party.

There was in Pallavicino's thinking a human proportion of vanity and even ambition. He had been made a citizen of Piedmont and been named *Cavaliere dei SS Maurizio e Lazzaro*; he was elected to parliament from Turin to the seat held by the famous Balbo until his death. He saw himself as uniquely situated, close to the King, with the sympathy of both the aristocracy (as a marchese) and the democrats (as the Martyr of the Spielberg).[22] Anxious to play some active and important part in the drive for Italian independence, he hoped to use his position as a bridge between these major factions of nationalist sentiment. When about to make a trip to Paris, he offered to undertake for d'Azeglio any secret mission he might desire. The Prime Minister, however, proved either less imaginative or more cautious; and the Marchese who heard nothing more about his offer turned to the King, from whom he seems in fact to have received some assignment.[23] He was, Pallavicino felt, born a diplomat just "as Alessandro Manzoni was born a poet"; and he entertained hopes of being named Ambassador to Paris (even the republicans would welcome the appointment, Montanelli assured him). It was not, however, sheer fondness for the title which motivated him; he would willingly accept the task of secret agent to promote in France the interest of Piedmont— even at his own expense.[24] When Piedmont proved unwilling to venture even this, he made propaganda on his own, informing French friends of his pride in seeing "in a corner of my dear Italy, a *petit peuple* which gives lessons in political wisdom to a large part of Europe. *Le spectacle est beau, il est magnifique!*"[25]

Pallavicino's ideas and hopes had become a program. Experienced in many of the attempts since Joachim Murat's to transform programs into parties and a party into a political force, Pallavicino was not unequipped for his self-appointed task. He had earlier shown a natural attraction to the committees and societies whose heroic manifestoes and subsequent failures had

[22] Pallavicino to Gioberti, 9 February 1851, *ibid.*, 111.

[23] Pallavicino to Gioberti, 9 and 18 February, and 26 March 1851, *ibid.*, 111, 117, 143.

[24] Pallavicino to his wife, 28 October 1850 and 24 May 1851, *Memorie di Pallavicino*, II, 279, 282–83.

[25] Pallavicino to C. Flandin, May 1853, *ibid.*, III, 31.

such a large part in the Risorgimento.[26] He had a real flair for the use of the press, and he saw that Piedmont's papers publicized noted exiles' conflicts with Mazzini and reprinted articles favorable to his cause which had appeared in the French press.[27] He planted articles in the influential *Indépendance Belge* and managed to have his views reflected in such important Parisian journals as the *Presse* and *Siècle*.[28] By assuming the debts of the *Opinione* of Turin, he was pleased to have made it "the interpreter of my sentiments." [29] But more than anything else Pallavicino's influence was the result of his relations with the important group of exiles in Paris. Almost unaccountably, he managed to maintain a view of them as essentially one group, really on the verge of accepting his own clear position. On occasion he claimed to be their spokesman, and his relations with them remained close even when they disagreed.[30]

It was in Vincenzo Gioberti that Pallavicino found the most responsive chord and to him that he turned more and more hopefully. Gioberti's *Primato d'Italia* had been one of the great statements of confidence in Italy's destiny; his appointment as Prime Minister of Piedmont late in 1848 had been a guarantee of the monarchy's nationalism. His brief period in office had, however, reflected in microcosm all the disappointment of that disappointing year. His omniscience produced discord, his opportunism led to confusion and dissatisfaction. After a turn as Ambassador to Paris, he had become an exile more from bitterness than necessity. Yet much remained of his nationalist faith and his political skepticism to which Pallavicino's optimism and heavy realism appealed. Despite grave differences, the two men felt they shared a common conviction as to the means of Italy's

[26] See in *ibid.*, II, 27, 110, 627–28.
[27] Pallavicino to his wife, 1 and 12 November 1850 and 27 April 1851, *ibid.*, 18, 284, 296, 369.
[28] Pallavicino to Bianchi-Giovini, 16 February 1850, *ibid.*, 185; and letter of October 1853, *ibid.*, III, 61.
[29] Letter of Pallavicino's, 16 December 1851, *ibid.*, II, 453; and Pallavicino to Gioberti, 17 January 1852, Maineri, *Piemonte*, 218.
[30] He announced, for example, that he spoke in the names of Pepe, Montanelli, and Gioberti in opposing any Piedmontese alliance with Austria: Pallavicino to Bianchi-Giovini, 12 March 1850, *Memorie di Pallavicino*, II, 211. He saw Enrico Cernuschi, Manin, and Montanelli as a Parisian triumvirate who respected Victor Emmanuel: Pallavicino to his wife, 20 April and 8 May 1851, *ibid.*, 366, 375. Yet he maintained his friendship with Montanelli despite their disagreements, Montanelli to Pallavicino, 20 July 1853, *ibid.*, III, 57.

13

salvation. Indeed, at times they felt themselves to be the responsible leaders of a party.[31]

Gioberti's great contribution to their common campaign was the publication of his vast essay, *Del Rinnovamento Civile d'Italia*. For Gioberti, the Risorgimento had died with his defeat; and he now called for a renewal which was to be a turning away from the dreams of the past into a more practical path, which was to build on the resurgence already experienced. The core of his book is the historical mission it foresees for Piedmont, and that was something of a triumph for Pallavicino. For Gioberti had written in this vein despite his apparent conviction that the republic was the governmental form of the future. He had resisted the Mannesian and Saint Simonian influences he found so tempting. The optimistic note of *Del Rinnovamento* is more like Pallavicino's letters to Gioberti than the latter's replies, which expressed deep pessimism and lasting doubts even about Piedmont's chances of survival.[32] There was reason, then, to congratulate Pallavicino on having won the match with those of Gioberti's friends who had wanted him to come out in favor of the monarchy and those who had sought his support for a republic.[33]

Del Rinnovamento was probably more important as a symptom than for whatever direct influence it may have had. In form and manner a part of the earlier Risorgimento, it is a confusing mixture of philosophical categories, awesome assumptions about the processes of history, and very specific political polemic. The great stretches of the book devoted to a defense of Gioberti's policies as Prime Minister created the most discussion at the time. And there was much in the book that should have made Pallavicino uncomfortable; for Gioberti wrote ambiguously of

[31] See, for example, Gioberti to Pallavicino, 21 January 1851, in which he wants the Marchese to write Pepe "to keep him in the faith," Maineri, *Piemonte*, 157. Also Gioberti to Bianchi-Giovini, *ibid.*, 225.

[32] Vechietti notes that Gioberti never really overcame these doubts: Tullio Vechietti, "Tre momenti dell'evoluzione Giobertiana," *Rivista Storica Italiana*, v, ser. 5 (1940), 48. Anzilotti reads this contrast between Gioberti's letters and *Rinnovamento* as evidence that the latter was conscious propaganda: Antonio Anzilotti, *La funzione storica del Giobertismo* (Florence, 1913), 408–10, 412. See also Widor Cesarini-Sforza, "Appunti sulla politica di Gioberti," *Rassegna Storica del Risorgimento*, II (1915), 747–49.

[33] As Montanelli did in his letter of 20 November 1851, *Memorie di Pallavicino*, II, 439.

a new and altered Piedmont, of French hegemony in a new Europe, and of faintly federalist programs. Still, the strong attacks on Mazzini and *"i puritani,"* and on conservative weakness and municipal egoism were part of an effort to carve out a broad center coalition of nationalists in support of Piedmont; and the confidence in her destiny made quibbles about her policy seem petty.[34] In that forest of words Gioberti was seeking a path that would not deny the Romantic sense of destiny or the categorical ideals of his generation while meeting the practical challenge of the post-1848 political terrain. Gioberti's remained a great name, and his position in support of the Piedmontese monarchy, taken so deliberately and prolixly, was a major moment in the battle of ideas. The former leader of those who had looked to the Papacy and federation as the answer to Italy's problems now rejected those solutions. This abandonment of neo-Guelphism was the burial of a body long dead, but it added to the impression that the political alternatives before Italian nationalists were narrowing. With his death in 1852, *Del Rinnovamento* became Gioberti's testament; and more and more men began to suspect that, among his many prophecies, some had been correct.

Another of Pallavicino's correspondents was the important exile, Daniele Manin, whose role in the Venetian revolution had made him a European liberal hero. As part of a campaign to win Manin to the Piedmontese monarchy, Pallavicino's letters described with familiar fervor the nationalism of the King, his popularity with his subjects.[35] He hoped to have Manin come to live in Piedmont; and the Government, despite a certain coolness, was readier than Manin for the change.[36] Moved by Manin's

---

[34] Maineri, *Piemonte*, 266–316. Anzilotti, *Gioberti*, 14–15. Adolfo Omodeo, *Vincenzo Gioberti e la sua evoluzione politica* (Turin, 1941), *passim*, esp. 100–101. In *Rinnovamento* see especially Book I, Chapter XII and Book II, Chapters I–II, IV.

[35] The correspondence with Manin in this period was more sporadic than with Gioberti but see, for example, the Marchese's letters of 12 July 1850 in *Memorie di Pallavicino*, II, 217–18; and of late 1851 in Maineri, *Manin e Pallavicino*, xl–xli. Pallavicino's later claim that Manin accepted his idea and that he was no mere subordinate has usually been ignored: letter to C. Belgioioso, 16 January 1860, *Memorie di Pallavicino*, III, 563.

[36] Pallavicino had Bianchi-Giovini speak to d'Azeglio in 1850, and several years later he himself spoke to Cavour about the matter. He won from Manin the statement that he would accept Piedmontese hospitality if not her citizenship: Pallavicino to Manin, 12 July 1850, *ibid.*, II, 218; and 19 May 1853, *ibid.*, III, 30–1.

poverty and the ill-health of his children, Pallavicino collected
funds in the Venetian's behalf only to have them staunchly refused.[37] Still, the Marchese comforted himself with whatever
signs he could find that Manin was coming around.[38] Primarily
occupied in tending his sick daughter and mourning the death
of his wife, Manin remained politically independent and a figure
of the first rank. Interspersed among appointments to give Italian
lessons were meetings with many of the most prominent men in
Paris. He talked with Mazzini, "King Jerome" Bonaparte, and
Lamartine and dined with Victor Hugo. He savored the power
of the moderate when, in the same day, he had dinner with the
Archbishop of Paris and meetings with such men as Cavaignac,
Lamoricière, and Montanelli.[39] Among such company, Pallavicino's influence was limited at first; it was not until the entry in
Manin's agenda of June 3, 1852, that Pallavicino's name was cor-
rectly spelled.[40]

Manin remained, first of all, a republican and one with strong
federalist sympathies at that.[41] He refused a seat in the Piedmontese Chamber when Cavour offered it to him,[42] and it seems
quite clear that the principal reason for the refusal, like that for
his reluctance to move to Piedmont, was the strength of his
republican sentiments.[43] But Manin was also a firm political

[37] Pallavicino's efforts had found little support: Bianchi-Giovini to Pallavicino,
20 July 1851, and Pallavicino to Manin, *ibid.*, 407, 413. The Austrian police
still thought Manin had absconded with great funds and that he lived well,
Italo Zingarelli, "Italiani a Parigi dopo il 1848," *La Cultura*, xi (1932), fasc. ii,
279–81, 283.
[38] Pallavicino to his wife, 24 October 1850, *Memorie di Pallavicino*, ii, 275.
[39] Manin's agenda for 23, 24, 26 May 1850; 7 June 1850; and 27 February
1851 is in Brunetti, *et al.*, *Manin*, 355–56. He had appointments, too, in 1851
with Saint-Beuve, H. Say, d'Adda, Carnot, Quinet, Michelet, and Napoleon.
Manin was important enough, too, for the Austrian agents to watch him and
even intercept his mail, Zingarelli, "Italiani a Parigi," *Cultura*, 283–85.
[40] It appeared as "Pallavicini" before, Brunetti, *et al.*, *Manin*, 355–58.
[41] The sensitive Austrian police had, however, already heard rumors of his
rapprochement with Piedmont: Zingarelli, "Italiani a Parigi," *Cultura*, 291. But
see: Antonio Monti, *Un dramma fra gli esuli* (Milan, 1921), 25; and F. Planat
de la Faye, *Documents et pièces authentiques, laissé par Daniel Manin* (Paris,
1860), i, 265, 265n. Manin defended the declaration of a republic in Venice
in a letter to the *Constitutionnel* of 10 November 1853, *ibid.*, ii, 424–25, 430.
[42] Gallenga says that Cavour made the offer to both of them when they visited
Manin: Antonio Gallenga, *Episodes of My Second Life* (London, 1884), 236.
Manin's agendum notes the visit on 28 September 1852, Brunetti, *et al.*, *Manin*,
358.
[43] Levi, *Manin*, 52–56. Raffaello Putelli, *Daniele Manin in esilio* (Venice,
1917), 18, suggests it was Manin's concern lest the republicans gather around

realist. As a man who was said to have replied to the praise that he would be the Redeemer of his country by asking, "With or without crucifixion?" [44] he had no easy visions of triumphant revolutions. He had early recognized that the liberation of Venice would have to come from outside,[45] and he began to take a more active part in the discussions of the exiles at a time when international realities weakened the chances for any Italian republic. France was ruled by an Emperor, and there was now in the European concert a liberal (and ambitious) Italian monarchy. Piedmont had preserved her constitution and under Cavour seemed daily to grow stronger. There were, in the fall of 1853, already rumors about a war in the east and the role Piedmont might play in it.[46]

The exiles in Paris had established their disagreement with Mazzini; but while he propagandized and organized, they remained inactive except for occasional pieces in the French press.[47] Thus international politics, developments in Piedmont and France, the activity of Mazzini and the ineffectiveness of his Paris opponents all gave Manin reason to take a public stand and become once again a political leader. There is the excitement of a man re-entering politics in his comment, in the fall of 1853, that soon "grave events might call us again to serve our country." [48] It was in this climate that Manin moved toward

him and embarrass the Government rather than his own distaste for monarchy which kept Manin from going to Piedmont. The explanation seems too subtle.

[44] Cited in Levi, Manin, 11–12.

[45] Emilia Manin to Regina Coen Arbib, 7 April 1850, Levi, Manin, 60; and a letter without date in Adolfo Mangini, "Ricordi di Daniele Manin dal 1840 al 1852," Risorgimento Italiano, Rivista Storica, I (1908), 613.

[46] Adolfo Omodeo, L'opera politica di Conte di Cavour (Florence, 1945), I, 279. In defending his actions in Venice Manin had stated his reliance on French aid, letter to the Constitutionnel, 10 November 1853, Planat de la Faye, Documents par Manin, II, 430.

[47] For Manin's reaction to the confusion among the Paris exiles, see Levi, Manin, 82. Mazzini, too, was somewhat confused as to the political positions of noted patriots. He hoped to win funds from Pallavicino: Mazzini to Grilenzoni, 22 November [1852], Scritti di Mazzini, XLVIII (Imola, 1927), 61. He knew that Manin and Montanelli would like "to kill my influence" and feared for their effect on Garibaldi: Mazzini to Aurelio Saffi, November 1853, ibid., L (Imola, 1928), 152; and Mazzini to Emilio Visconti-Venosta, 5 April 1853, ibid., 50. Manin, on the other hand, was probably impressed by the fact that Garibaldi had made the trip to London and that Mazzini had tried (and apparently learned nothing from) another revolt in Lombardy.

[48] Manin to Lione Serena, 9 October 1853, Brunetti, et al., Manin, 325. Manin continued to meet and talk with Englishmen and Frenchmen of note in this

some declaration of intent.[49] He had seen in Mazzini, in local reaction, and in foreign diplomacy the enemies of his aspirations for Italy; and he had told Pallavicino they must combat all three.[50]

On March 22, 1854, the anniversary of the revolution in Venice, there appeared in the *Presse* a public declaration by the leader of that heroic revolt.[51] Daniele Manin had entered the debate on the future of Italy. His statement in the *Presse* was a letter of reply to Lord John Russell who had declared to Parliament that there was hope of Austrian reform in Lombardy if the Italians were only quiet for a bit. Manin expressed shock that so eminent a statesman could so miss the point; but while informing the Foreign Minister of the goals of Italian patriots, he was in fact attempting to establish what those goals should be. Austrian humanity or liberalism, even if possible, could not, he argued, interest Italians; they could make no concessions from their demand for complete independence and union throughout the Peninsula.

In the same tone of reporting a universal attitude, Manin went on to state his program. The questions which divided Italian patriots were lesser ones and wholly secondary. On these they would make the concessions which circumstances required. The voice of the Manin of Venice rang out in declaring resignation cowardly counsel, but Manin the moderate balanced it with a promise of restraint. "If you tell us, if you proved to us that the moment for action has not yet come, we would wait" while steadfastly preparing. In the best tradition of diplomacy, the promise (that revolutionary outbreaks could be halted) was matched by a threat: "the Italian question is from now on a

---

period and to think in international terms. See his agenda for January and February 1854, *ibid.*, 359; and the letters to him from C. A. Clericetti in England, 16 and 24 February 1854, mss. in the Museo Correr, Venice (hereafter MCV), bxxii/142.

[49] The death of his daughter, despite the despair it caused him, had left time for political matters. The meeting of a number of republicans, Manin among them, to discuss their common concerns caused a stir in Piedmont, the presence of Plonplon, Prince Napoleon, making it almost ominous. Marchese Salvatore Pes di Villamarina to Giuseppe Dabormida, January 1854, cited in Omodeo, *Cavour*, ii, 241.

[50] Manin to Pallavicino, 23 December 1850, Maineri, *Manin e Pallavicino*, xl.

[51] Levi, *Manin*, 72, points out the anniversary; the date of publication may, however, have been a coincidence. The letter itself was dated March 19.

European question of the first order. It must be resolved in a way which conforms to our indomitable national aspirations." Until it was, Italy would always be a *"foyer de trouble,"* an *"occasion de guerre"* threatening the peace of Europe.[52]

Manin had chosen his moment with care, and in the patriotic act of explaining the demands of nationalism to the British Foreign Minister, he probably hoped to win many of the exiles to his views.[53] By assuming the unity he hoped to create, he had made his threat to the Minister more effective. The threat might in turn lead diplomacy in a direction that would both aid Italian nationalist dreams and bring about that unity among the nationalists themselves which Manin described. He was playing against each other two forces, neither of which he controlled.

He may really have hoped to win something from English diplomacy by his subsequent trip, in June, to Great Britain. His fame is well measured and the potential of his influence excitingly indicated by the very list of names of the men he saw.[54] With politicians, however, two weeks is not enough time in which to triumph with talk. They say, Manin wrote, "that in politics the useful is just; and I reply that the just is useful . . ."; but pragmatists with power are hard to convince.[55] Gladstone later remembered that it was from Manin that he had had his "first lesson in Italian unity as the indispensable basis of all effectual reform. . . ." At the time, however, he noted simply that Manin, too, was wild.[56] And Manin also learned a lesson: the wind is not propitious. Not that he felt the trip to have been useless. "It is always useful to sow; there can come favorable

[52] The famous letter is cited in many works on the Risorgimento. The uncut version may be found in Maineri, *Manin e Pallavicino*, 323–25.

[53] See Manin to Serena, 21 March 1854, Brunetti, *et al., Manin*, 334. This first statement, then, seems not to have been written at the behest of Pallavicino. Indeed, Manin assures Serena that it is *"quello che mi hai domandato,"* although Serena seems to have been asking more for personal counsel than a public statement. Manin had, of course, long been under pressure from many to make himself heard. See Zingarelli, "Italiani a Parigi," *Cultura*, 284. Even Mazzini accepted Manin's statement of the things on which patriots could not compromise, but see his letter to Giuseppe Sirtori, 6 April 1854, *Scritti di Mazzini*, L, 341.

[54] He moved among Lords Clarendon and Minto, Beaumont, Granville, Shaftsbury, and Lansdowne; he saw Palmerston and Gladstone, Henry Reeve and Antonio Panizzi, Lacaita and Cobden. Brunetti, *et al., Manin*, 359–60.

[55] Manin to Planat de la Faye, 24 June 1854, *ibid.*, 335.

[56] John Morley, *The Life of William Ewart Gladstone* (New York, 1911), I, 402.

conditions that from the seed give plant and fruit." [57] Yet to sow with so little hope of harvest is not the attitude with which to build a party.

Manin was left with little to do in a position only partially defined. In his letter to Russell, Manin had warned that Italian agitation would continue, but what sort of agitation he favored was not clear. He was against any call to revolt until he could be sure that success was likely.[58] He still tended to hope for a republican federation in Italy. A monarchical federation would be, he felt, a denial of unity altogether, but he recognized that unity under the King of Piedmont was an acceptable and the most likely solution.[59]

Manin was a sufficiently important figure for an English newspaper to wonder in print what he was doing. But his reply had more charm than content: I teach Italian in Paris, he began; and he may have meant by that more than the language. I am waiting ("to begin again the battle"), and I prepare. In explaining how he prepared, Manin tried again to suggest he represented a position without exploring its implications. He kept himself in touch with the most distinguished men of the various shades of liberal opinion; he tried to increase sympathy for the Italian cause, to correct errors and prejudices about it and to convince all "that the solution of that question in terms of our national aspirations is of the highest interest for England, for France, and in general for the cause of civilization, of progress, of durable peace and of the true European equilibrium." He was against all attempts which had no serious chance of success, adverse to all appeal to cruel or savage instincts. He was preaching that one does not "regenerate a nation by corrupting it." He was trying to rally all patriots under one flag with a program

---

[57] Manin to Planat de la Faye, 24 June 1854, Brunetti, *et al.*, *Manin*, 335.
[58] Manin to Serena, n.d., *ibid.*, 334.
[59] These statements are from an interview with Manin conducted, apparently on May 13, 1854, by the author of "The Continent in 1854," *North British Review*, xxvi (February 1855), 319–25. Described as "one of the wisest and honestest, and therefore one of the most moderate, of the Italian patriots" (p. 319), Manin is quoted as feeling that tradition required the Roman States to be a republic. Savoy he recognized as French. As for what to do with Sicily, his answer was, "Not let *you* have it." (p. 235). Charles Albert had, he felt, greatly hurt the national cause by making a war of aggrandizement. (pp. 323–24).

(independence and union) which had, he thought, "been accepted by all the most important and esteemed men of the Italian nationalist party." [60]

The very fact of his statements implied, however, that such acceptance had not been gained and that even if it had he would not be ready for any dramatic action. In fact, he was conceding that revolution alone was not enough; the force required to unify Italy would have to come from the outside. His own arguments were leading him to look more to diplomacy and (a step he had not yet taken) to seek for nationalism a permanent military ally. Italians needed both a common program and foreign friends; the efforts of patriots, if Manin was the example, should be directed through propaganda to those ends. It was not a very clear program and hardly heroic.

One can understand Mazzini's shrewd disgust: ". . . what in the devil do they think, say and want? Do they believe in Piedmontese initiative? Do they want to descend to the tail of a decembrist battalion? Are they waiting for Murat? Do they expect Austria to go away by herself [*naturalmente*]? Have they a program, idea? Do they state it? Do they claim to have influence? Do they recognize that influence acquired constitutes a duty?"

Too much the idealist to admit that political action does not always require that all such embarrassing questions be answered, Mazzini could not understand the phenomenon before him, that the record of failures (many of them his own) had made men lower their sights. He put his finger on the difference between them when he complained that others only loved Italy "*intellectually*"; my love is a "*religion*"; theirs is "*philosophy*." [61] Manin's ideas were not yet a philosophy, but they stressed a flexibility which was lacking in that Mazzinian religion intended to correct this world.

Mazzini could recognize much that was his in Manin's statements; and although he at first denied that Manin's letter was a program, he strove hard to win support for his own "program of universal concord, that was then hinted at in Manin's let-

---

[60] Letter to *The Leader* cited in Levi, *Manin*, 80.

[61] Mazzini to Giuseppe Mazzoni, 26 July 1854, *Scritti di Mazzini*, LIII (Imola, 1929), 8–9.

ter." [62] But impatience for that final call to revolution obscured his insight. Convinced that Piedmont would be a "traitorous ally," Mazzini did not see the abyss that separated him from Manin.[63] He honestly meant to sacrifice all to prevent division, to win support of Manin and Montanelli and then perhaps of all others to a call for immediate action. He bombarded Paris with appeals and emissaries, but he got no answer.[64] In Paris they knew the differences they had not fully defined. The exiles there would give not a cent, not a gun. They are, Mazzini declared, "men of the day after." [65] He could not be expected to realize that 1848 had been his day. This was the day after.

Pallavicino, at least, had reason to be well pleased with Manin's public stand. When Manin told him of articles in the *Times* and *Siècle* which saw Piedmont as the hope of Italy, that good news matched the Marchese's mood.[66] He looked forward to a militant attack upon clerical privilege from the approaching session of Parliament, and the growing talk of war added to his excitement. His faith, he insisted, was not in French or English liberalism but in Providence; but his letters show a faith in Piedmont, too.[67] He dramatically reported to Paris ". . . news that will seem to you unbelievable. It seems that Italians want to raise a single banner in the peninsula—the banner of independence—*of independence at any price!* The Sardinian king would be the captain of the undertaking and would receive as the great guide of the Herculean work, the crown of Italy." It is said, he added, that the emigrants in Piedmont, with the exception of the Mazzinians, accept the program. "The thought is beautiful and generous; it is the thought of [eighteen] twenty-one; it is my thought!" [68] Pallavicino's optimistic reports and Manin's state-

[62] Mazzini to Sirtori, 26 July [1854], *ibid.*, L, 341; and to Mazzoni, *ibid.*, LIII, 8.

[63] Mazzini to Sirtori, 6 April [1854], *ibid.*, L, 340.

[64] Letters to Nicolao Ferrari and Cironi, *ibid.*, LII (Imola, 1929), 78, 113, 306; to Dall'Ongaro, *ibid.*, 115; and to Mazzoni, *ibid.*, LIII, 9.

[65] Mazzini to Sirtori, 6 April [1854], *ibid.*, L, 343.

[66] Manin to Pallavicino, 9 November 1854, ms. in Museo Nazionale del Risorgimento, Torino (hereafter MNRT). The articles were in the *Times* (London) of 21 and 22 September; Manin even sent along the clippings.

[67] Pallavicino to Flandin, 21 August 1854, and to Montanelli, 15 October 1854, *Memorie di Pallavicino*, III, 83, 86–87.

[68] There were, he boasted, four newspapers which wrote in this sense, Pallavicino to Montanelli, 28 October 1854, *ibid.*, 91.

ments spurred on their friends in Paris. An impressive group of exiles met in long conferences to draft an agreement on "the idea that would govern an Italian movement."

Their program called for Italians to rise at the "first favorable occasion." Questions of monarchy or republic, federation or union would be postponed until the war was won, with anyone who, during the war, sought to force a particular solution to these issues being considered an "enemy of the nation." War government would stem from an assembly (one deputy for every 50,-000 inhabitants in free territory). Piedmont could either send deputies to the assembly or simply be allied with it. If the King initiated the revolution, the Paris exiles were willing that he do as he liked; but they clearly expected action to begin with "the people." To then give leadership to the King would be the "negation of nationality." If the King contributed enough, the people might vote him their ruler. Honest democrats, they insisted on a legal expression of the popular will and believed that only this would prevent further divisions.[69] Their hopes for national unity still contained dreams of popular risings and assemblies.

The program thus accepted Manin's definition of secondary issues, and a copy was sent Pallavicino for his comments. He found it far from the corrective to the errors of 1848 he had been insisting upon. Even if it could guarantee agreement on matters political (and experience made that more than doubtful), such a program offered no solution to the military and tactical problems upon which the outcome of any war would depend. This was not the program of independence at any price which Montanelli claimed it to be, but rather of unity among the exiles at a price Piedmont would not pay. The exiles in Paris were so diligently learning the lessons of 1848 that they were prepared only for history to repeat.

Pallavicino's reply to this program was one of his finest moments. It was the reply of a man who sees truth clearly, whose tact and grace could scarcely hide the pleasure of shocking unrealistic friends. His heart, Pallavicino began, accepted their proposals; but his stubborn head did not. With this hint as to the

[69] Manin, Montanelli, Girolamo Ulloa, Sirtori, Amari, Maestri, Leon Pincherle, Guilio Dragonetti, Mazzoni, Guerrieri and others took part. These names and the program are in Montanelli to Pallavicino, November 1854, *ibid.*, 91–93. He insisted the Marchese's opinion would carry great weight with them all.

nature of his case, the Marchese's argument began with a dangerous premise: to want independence is to want the means of gaining it. Its means are Piedmont's army. Thoroughly monarchical,
the army will be friend or foe according to its captain. Therefore, said Pallavicino, it was not his concurrence which counted
but that of Victor Emmanuel. His first objection, then, was that
theirs was not a program meant to woo a king. He, too, must
be assured of his reward. Pallavicino admitted that Victor Emmanuel probably would not take the initiative in redeeming Italy,
but he saw in this no argument for an assembly which would
also be "composed of men with their passions—of Italians with
their old prejudices of town and party." It was true that all
now wanted the nation, but it was true, too, that each wanted
it at the time and in the way which would aid his old banner.
The Marchese pictured men motivated only by self-interest;
and under the pressure of his argument, even his democratic
instincts began to wilt; he feared demagogues as well as discord.

The "profession of faith" with which he closed was largely a
summary of his previous letters, and the best of his phrases were
carefully transplanted. He published it without even waiting
for a reply from any of his correspondents. Pallavicino apologized for adding one more to the plague of programs, but he
promised to be as positive as a mathematician, as calculating as
a banker. Such positive calculation quickly led to acceptance of
Piedmontese (and monarchical) hegemony. It was not liberty
but independence which allowed a nation to live (the Turks
and Russians were once again cited as evidence), and once again
the desire for independence made the monarchy's potential usefulness outweigh any theoretical distaste for it. The Marchese
saw two forces, "the opinion of Italy and the army of Piedmont,"
which must be brought together; each impotent alone, combined
they could make that armed nation which must precede freedom.

In rejecting the idea of an assembly, Pallavicino stressed the
importance of efficient wartime leadership, and he went a step
farther in calling for "the dictatorship of a soldier" (Victor
Emmanuel). He did state the case for Piedmont as a liberal
government (and therefore acceptable to all) and for the King
as a trustworthy nationalist (for that was where his interest lay);
but these, too, now seemed secondary issues. Might not Victor

Emmanuel be "the elect of Providence to complete the great work of our national redemption"? [70]

Pallavicino had gone beyond Manin to call for the unification of Italy under the Piedmontese monarchy. The moderate nationalists were not agreed. Montanelli insisted on an assembly, treating it as the means of satisfying both King and people (he pointedly saw them at antipodes). But his reply was surprisingly weak; circumstances made it painful to argue against Piedmont.[71] Their disagreement lay less in programs than in the tone with which each spoke of King and people.

Encouraged by the reception his program had received in the press of Turin, Pallavicino presented his ideas to Cavour and reworked them as a new attack on Mazzini. He wrote with renewed confidence in his position and in Piedmont. "Republicans of Italy," he demanded, "be Italians!" [72] The polemic had become repetitious; even the debate with Montanelli ceased.[73] Pallavicino had strongly stated the argument for supporting Piedmont; and that argument, general and pragmatic, had proved difficult to refute. It would in the following years be much repeated but only slightly changed.

Pallavicino now, like Manin, waited for others to recognize his victory in debate. Manin had described a reasonable position all patriots should be able to adopt; Pallavicino had shown the logical need to turn to Piedmont. But both had argued for an attitude without proposing a policy. They had nowhere to go. At times Pallavicino had hoped for some European revolution or war to spawn from a crisis the action his own program did not provide.[74] Short of that, he could find little to say. He found it

---

[70] Pallavicino to Montanelli, 6 November 1854, *ibid.*, 93–5. The profession of faith was printed in *Unione*, 14 November 1854, and is reprinted in Maineri, *Manin e Pallavicino*, 326–28. Mazzini, too, saw the hopelessness of asking the King to accept an Assembly. See his letter to N. Fabrizi, 18 October [1854], *Scritti di Mazzini*, LIII, 212.

[71] Montanelli was not convinced that Piedmont was truly Italian; partial fusion with Piedmont, state by state, he saw as the fatal error of 1848, Montanelli to Pallavicino, 17 November 1854, *Memorie di Pallavicino*, III, 98–101.

[72] He thought the Prime Minister not displeased, *ibid.*, 101–102. Pallavicino's "Un italiano alla Giunta Nazionale d'Azione" appeared in *Unione*, 24 November 1854, and is cited in Maineri, *Manin e Pallavicino*, 329–31. It was a reply to Mazzini's "La Giunta Nazionale d'Azione agli Italiani."

[73] Montanelli to Pallavicino, 10 January 1855, *Memorie di Pallavicino*, III, 112.

[74] He could also imagine help from Napoleon III or Palmerston or aid from America. See his letters and comments in Maineri, *Piemonte*, 96; *Memorie di*

difficult to develop his theoretical position because he distrusted both Piedmont's policies and her ministers. Diplomacy, with its ambiguities and caution, disgusted him, and he saw it as a force bent upon preventing the needed revolution. He rejected the Crimean alliance as cooperation with Austria for Piedmontese rather than national ends and dismissed any claims for the value of alliances in general.[75] "I do not believe possible," he had written, "the brotherhood of peoples in the Nineteenth Century." [76]

His speeches and articles soon labeled him an enemy of the Government.[77] Pallavicino, who knew little about the administration of a state, could not establish any practical path from the daily decisions of the present to the goal he sought. He knew that patience was required of the politician, and he tried to have the necessary minimum. While he anticipated war, the Chamber debated details which bored him; and he could not understand why the Government did not declare itself by openly and fully adopting a national policy.[78] Never did he find the ministry to satisfy him.[79]

The Marchese's plans for a certain future thus nearly floundered on his confused view of the present. He was asking others to support a Government whose leaders he doubted and demanding that the Government eschew diplomacy as a major part of policy while fulfilling its heavy role as the only nationalist Italian state. Confident of the King, he took comfort in the

Pallavicino, II, 530ff.; *ibid.*, III, 11, 22, 53. Montanelli had not been out of sympathy with these dreams, Montanelli to Pallavicino, 11 September 1853, *ibid.*, 57.

[75] See Pallavicino's introduction to Maineri, *Piemonte*, viii, and his letter to Flandin, 21 August 1854, *Memorie di Pallavicino*, III, 83.

[76] Pallavicino to Pietro Romeo, 30 September 1851, *ibid.*, II, 429.

[77] *Ibid.*, III, 113–16, 122–23.

[78] See his speech of 14 January 1854 to the Chamber, *ibid.*, 66; and his letters to Montanelli, 1 January and 17 March 1854, *ibid.*, 64–5, 74.

[79] He thought d'Azeglio adequate for quiet times: Pallavicino to Manin, 12 July 1850, *ibid.*, II, 217. Also, Pallavicino to Gioberti, 5 March 1852, Maineri, *Piemonte*, 283. He hoped first that Gioberti, then Manin would be called to office but comforted himself that Cavour might have an Italian head despite a Piedmontese heart and at times thought that he could influence him. For Pallavicino's views of Cavour: letters to Victor Emmanuel, 3 November 1852, Luigi Chiala, *Lettere edite ed inedite di Camillo Cavour*, v (Turin, 1886), 280; to Scipione Giordano, 18 November 1852, *Memorie di Pallavicino*, III, 2; to his wife, 24 May 1852, *ibid.*, II, 543; to Ferdinand de Lasteyrie, October 1853, *ibid.*, III, 59. Cf. his earlier comment to Gioberti, Maineri, *Piemonte*, 283, and his letter to Cavour, *Memorie di Pallavicino*, III, 85.

monarch's assurance that he would, when dissatisfied with his ministers, have them changed—strange solace for a democrat.[80] Manin, who had gone less far in publicly supporting Piedmont, was in no better position. After a lapse of more than a year, he published another letter in May 1855. But it only insisted again that Austria was incapable of reform and appealed to the liberal Western powers, promising popularity to any power who made itself Austria's enemy.[81] The Dictator of Venice, whose long silences had already been effectively noted by Mazzini,[82] had nothing new to say.

It was the Muratist threat which led Manin to amplify his old position. Joachim Murat had been one of Napoleon's gifts to Italy, and the reign of another Napoleon in France was bound to revive thoughts of a Murat in Naples. Whatever the deficiencies of Lucien Murat, the current claimant, his freedom of clerical influence was attested to by his position as a Masonic Grandmaster; his promise as a reformer was supported by the contrast between the policies of the French Emperor and the Bourbon King. The long-anticipated campaign in behalf of Murat gathered new force in the fall of 1855 with the publication of the pamphlet, *La question italienne, Murat et les Bourbons.*[83] At a time when the ambitions and daring of the French Emperor were yet unmeasured, the Muratists posed a real problem for those nationalists who held unity the prime goal. Like Lord Russell on Lombardy, the Muratists promised an immediate improvement in local conditions. It could not be denied that life in the Neapolitan Kingdom would be pleasanter under Murat than under the Bourbons.

The Muratists won some significant support. Among the

[80] Pallavicino to Bianchi-Giovini, 30 September 1850, *ibid.,* II, 254–55. For Pallavicino's relationship with the democrats see his letters, *ibid.,* II, 553; III, 47, and Luisa Fiori, "Il Marchese Giorgio Trivulzio-Pallavicino (1796–1878)," *Rassegna Storica del Risorgimento,* XIII (1926), 575–76.

[81] The letter, dated 20 May, was to M. Havin, editor of the *Siècle* and published in *Estafette,* 26 May 1855. It is reprinted in Maineri, *Manin e Pallavicino,* 332.

[82] Mazzini to *Italia e Popolo,* 27 October 1854, *Scritti di Mazzini,* LI (Imola, 1928), 305.

[83] On the campaign of the Muratists see *Memorie di Pallavicino,* III, 51 (for Pallavicino's view) and Fiorella Bartoccini, *Il Murattismo, speranze, timori e contrasti nella lotta per l'unità italiana* (Milan, 1959), 3–82. On the authorship of the pamphlet see Maria Vittoria Gavotti, *Il Movimento Murattiano dal 1850 al 1860* (Rome, 1927), 85–8, 92ff.; and Bartoccini, *Murattismo,* 92–7.

exiles there was some doubt as to where Manin would stand, and perhaps even some effort to win him to the further compromise of Murat.[84] Manin had to issue another statement. A model of brevity, it declared "independence and unification," the banner to which Manin remained faithful, and went one step further than he had gone before to declare that if Italy must have a king it could only be the King of Piedmont.[85] Manin's letter was followed by a flood of pamphlets and declarations; Italian patriots seemed almost grateful for this excuse to debate again their destiny. Here were practical alternatives for the near future, a King and a pretender who offered the promise of power. Imminent action as well as general principle was involved. Manin's letter won the enthusiasm of many Italians, applause in the British press and silence in the French.[86] At the same time there were continued signs that the promise of reform in Italy—even under foreign influence—was deeply attractive to men who had so recently failed at revolution.

The reception he had received and the need of combating Murat spurred Manin to issue another statement just four days after the last. The most famous of his letters, it announced his conditional support of Piedmont.[87] "The republican party, so bitterly calumniated, commits," he announced, "a new act of

[84] According to Manin, Montanelli, Dragonetti and Sirtori asked him to join them in supporting Murat: Manin to Pallavicino, 24 December 1855, Maineri, *Manin e Pallavicino*, 30; Pallavicino to Manin, 17 January 1856, *ibid.*, 44. Bartoccini, *Murattismo*, 89, finds it unlikely they could have hoped for so much.

[85] Dated September 15 and published in the *Siècle*, September 20, 1855, the letter is reprinted in Maineri, *Manin e Pallavicino*, 411. It began by citing with approval an earlier letter opposing Murat written by Giuseppe Ricciardi, an exile living in Tours who, like Manin, had been reported to have accepted Murat. Manin's letter was widely republished in Britain, France, and Piedmont.

[86] Gavotti, *Movimento Murattiano*, 100ff.; Bartoccini, *Murattismo*, 90ff. Note the equally vigorous but less effective opposition of Mazzini to Murat, *Scritti di Mazzini*, LV (Imola, 1929), 81–8, and the development of La Farina's position in his letter to Ricciardi in Ausunio Franchi (ed.), *Epistolario di Giuseppe La Farina* (Milan, 1869), I, 563.

[87] Reprinted in Maineri, *Manin e Pallavicino*, 333. It also probably reflected the influence of Pallavicino, who was then in Paris. See Manin to Pallavicino, 24 December 1855, *ibid.*, 30. Tommaséo's cynicism confuses his chronology when he sees the impetus for this declaration in Manin's trip to London, taken "not without an understanding with someone in the Imperial Household [*casa*]," I. del Lungo and P. Prunas (eds.), *N. Tommaséo e C. Capponi, Carteggio inedito dal 1833 al 1875*, IV (Bologna, 1923), 398. Tommaséo was perceptive, however; and Manin's decision to issue another statement was certainly influenced by his concern for the international aspects of the Italian Question and by his own international connections.

abnegation and sacrifice to the national cause." Once more Manin's personal position became by self-appointment a party pronouncement:

"Convinced that above all Italy must be made, that this is the first and most important question, it [the republican party] says to the House of Savoy: Make Italy and I am with you.—If not, not.

"And it says to the constitutionalists: Think about making Italy, and not of enlarging Piedmont, be Italians and not munici-palists, and I am with you.—If not, not."

"I, a republican, plant this unifying standard." If all who want Italy to exist gather around and defend it, then *"Italy will be."* Having declared with pride that the republican party was the truly national one, Manin had added with sorrow that its day was past. Having declared all questions but unity to be secondary, Manin had come to see but two "camps of opinion" —"unifying nationalist" and "separatist municipal." He did not assume that a national policy on the part of Piedmont was in-evitable. More experienced in politics than Pallavicino, he was not surprised by vacillations in Piedmontese policy; [88] he re-quired the monarchy only to act in self-interest. Union of all patriotic parties would simply present a prize which Victor Emmanuel could not refuse.[89]

Piedmont and the republicans would cooperate, motivated by parallel promises (to Piedmont of an Italy under the House of Savoy and to the republicans of an Italy united) and parallel threats (to Piedmont that those she did not lead would be her enemies and to the republicans that the price of disunion was continued failure). Piedmont would be followed if she led in the right direction—if not, not. The conservatives were warned and the republicans assured that their concession was conditional. Seven years earlier in Venice, Manin had declared that the only "political color" which a provisional government should have was that of opposition to the enemy. Now once again it was

[88] He had predicted them in his letter to Pallavicino, 23 December 1850, Maineri, *Manin e Pallavicino*, xxxix–xl.

[89] Gen. Carlo Alberto Radaeli remembered Manin as having expressed this view in 1855 while sitting in his study where the King's portrait hung among those of Italian patriots. Cited in Umberto Ferrari Bravo, "Daniele Manin," *L'Ateneo Veneto*, xxx, Vol. II (1907), 275n–76n.

time for the provisional. Manin had taken his stand for the union of all the parties, and he offered the republicans the glory of another sacrifice. Few responded.[90]

Pallavicino leaped to capitalize on Manin's declaration by publishing, in November, no less than three articles commenting upon it. He stressed the weight of Manin's influence, noting the support he had won in the British and French press and describing the retreat of the Muratists. And he used that success to apply pressure on Piedmont: their press must be as Italian as that of England and France; their Government must abandon any temptations to a kingdom merely of northern Italy.[91] Manin joined in the effort to keep their program before the public, sending a letter to the French press challenging it to match the sympathy shown in England. Hardly the most interesting of Manin's letters, it was very widely reprinted in England, France, and Piedmont.

The letter was an extraordinary success. Manin was coming to be recognized as the leader of an important movement, and he was finding wide opportunities for influencing opinion.[92] In Piedmont itself Pallavicino saw signs that they were gaining recognition in high circles. The King, he reported, had thanked them for their "ultimatum"; and one of the ministers had astonished their townsmen by taking the Marchese by the arm and walking with him under the porticoes. Cavour assured them of his sympathy; d'Azeglio seemed ready to accept their stand. Even Depretis might be won, for Pallavicino keenly saw that "Depretis [the] deputy, is republican; Depretis [the] minister, will be monarchist." [93] By direct appeals and personal flattery,

[90] Levi, *Manin*, 35, 117. Tommaséo to Capponi, 25 March 1859, del Lungo and Prunas, *Tommaséo e Capponi*, iv, 402.

[91] The three articles, published in *Il Diritto* on 17, 20, and 24 November 1855, are reprinted in Maineri, *Manin e Pallavicino*, 442–53. They also stressed the disinterestedness and consistency of Manin's policy, a favorite theme of Pallavicino's. See his letter to Manin, 20 November 1854, *ibid.*, 10. Later in the month Pallavicino replied with great vigor to the moderate Muratism of Bianchi-Giovini.

[92] The letter, dated 10 December 1855, was published in the *Presse* on December 14. It is printed in *ibid.*, 489–91. In England the *Times*, *Morning Advertiser*, and *Morning Post* printed it; the *Leader* and *Globe* were expected to. Forthcoming articles favorable to Manin were promised in the *North British Review*, *Morning Post*, and *Economist*. In France, *Estafette*, *Siècle*, *Unione* also printed it; and the *Journal des Débats* cited it, Manin to Pallavicino, 24 December 1855, *ibid.*, 27.

[93] Pallavicino to Ulloa, 28 December 1855, *Memorie di Pallavicino*, iii, 173–74; Pallavicino to Manin, 20 November 1855, Maineri, *Manin e Pallivicino*, 9–10.

the Marchese hoped to win others to their cause.[94]

Manin and Pallavicino had made themselves heard, but once again they were at a loss for more to say. Pallavicino continued writing article after article attacking the Muratists and the Mazzinians and defending Manin. He quoted men of note, coined phrases, and repeated himself. Attacks on Piedmontese policy he answered by declaring it ridiculous in this "atheist and prosaic century" to depend for salvation on an idea without an army. These articles all have an air of tiredness, for his was becoming a hollow realism that doubted its own cause. As the Congress of Paris approached, all his old fears of selfish Piedmont bent on piecemeal aggrandizement, trapped by diplomacy between two emperors, came again to the fore. The first in his series of articles had ended with doubt that the King's ministers wanted to make Italy; the last began with self-pity that his warnings had been ignored.[95] Manin now found him "discouraged and discouraging," and that staunch defender of the House of Savoy cried in return, "martyr, I have the faith of martyrs: but you said it, and I repeat it to you: *'if not*, NOT!!!' " They might, Pallavicino suggested, have to pass to the republicans.[96]

Yet Pallavicino's faith in Italy's destiny was strong. Sensing that he had reached a stalemate, he had pleaded with Manin to take the field with him and amplify his stand.[97] Manin, ever

The Marchese hoped Cavour and Manin might build on Cavour's reassurances when the Prime Minister was in Paris, but Manin doubted that Cavour would call on him and had no intention of taking the first step: Manin to Pallavicino, 25 November 1855, *ibid.*, 13. Their other gains (including that of some army colonels and Sebastiano Tecchio, as soon as he understood their stand) are listed in Pallavicino to Manin, 18 November, 7 and 24 December 1855, and 24 and 25 January 1856, *ibid.*, 7, 23, 26, 32, 48. The comment on Depretis, with a complaint that Angelo Brofferio was less malleable, is from the letter of 1 December 1855, *ibid.*, 16–17.

[94] Note Pallavicino's desire that Manin greet Francesco Govean in Paris: letter of 17 January 1856, *ibid.*, 45 and 45n; and his letter to Francesco Carrano in December 1855, *Memorie di Pallavicino*, III, 166, and to Alphonse Peyrat, 29 December 1855, *ibid.*, 174–75. The letter to Peyrat is especially surprising in view of Manin's distrust of him, which is partially excised from Manin's letter to Pallavicino, 24 December, as printed in *ibid.*, 28–9, but clear indeed in the original ms. in MNRT.

[95] The articles appeared in *Il Diritto*, December 6 and 13, 1855, January 2 and 20, 1856. They are reprinted in Maineri, *Manin e Pallavicino*, 544–57.

[96] Manin to Pallavicino, March [6, date from ms. in MNRT] 1856, *ibid.*, 63; Pallavicino to Manin, 14 March 1856, *ibid.*, 64–5. His renewed distrust of Cavour and disappointment in Piedmont shows in Pallavicino's letters of 10 December 1855 and 25 January 1856, *ibid.*, 26, 47.

[97] Pallavicino to Manin, 1 and 7 December 1855, and 17 and 25 January 1856, *ibid.*, 15, 25, 44, 47–8.

cautious, waited; perhaps he would rather have said no more until the outcome of the Paris conference was known. He was worried, however, by the Marchese's despondency and by their failure to win firm support from many others.[98] It was necessary to define more fully what they demanded of Piedmont. Manin sent off another statement to *Il Diritto*.[99]

He presented his views as somewhat tentative and this statement as only a partial exposition of them. In Manin's hands the great national party would remain free to develop in the way circumstances required. As spokesman for a view now widely held, he offered himself as an example of the sacrifice for unity he was asking others to make. He wanted, *"a priori,"* a federal republic; but as a political man, he felt he must seek what was "practically possible."

Once again he was addressing the "true patriots," those "republicans who love Italy more than the republic," those monarchists who "love Italy more than any dynasty whatsoever." He insisted, more firmly than in the past, that the issues which divided nationalists were secondary ones and that unification and independence were inseparable goals. If others offered a better means of uniting all the "forces" of Italy, Manin modestly promised to accept it; but he stressed two "facts." Piedmont was a great national force which it would be folly to alienate or render ineffective; and she had a monarchy. "It is therefore necessary that a concession be made to the monarchical idea. . . ." Having made his concession, Manin returned to the warning that if Piedmont failed in this mission, he would look elsewhere.

So far he had ably summarized the position he and Pallavicino had previously taken, but he knew the next step was the crucial one. You will ask, he said (and he may have been thinking of Pallavicino), how "the Piedmontese monarchy should conduct herself to fulfill her mission." It was on the answer to this question that Pallavicino had floundered, and Manin's answer would determine whom they could win to their banner. The monarchy, he said, must make independence and unification its goal, be

[98] Manin to Pallavicino, 25 November 1855, 21 February and 6 March 1856, *ibid.*, 13, 60, 63.

[99] The letter to Lorenzo Valerio was dated February 11, 1856; it and the statement it prefaced are printed in *ibid.*, 501–506.

vigilant against all that might impede the realization of that goal, maintain itself as the "center of attraction of Italian nationality," prevent the establishment of other such centers, and— when the time came—take resolute part in the national battle. It would have to be willing, without hesitation, "TO LOSE THE THRONE OF PIEDMONT TO CONQUER THE THRONE OF ITALY." Manin was insisting on a certain attitude but he knew the wisdom of giving the government leeway in fulfilling his aims. It must continue to do, but more clearly now, what it seemed to him to have done since 1848. Later it must be willing to do more.

By implication he had warned it not to support competitors, such as Murat. Specifically he warned against any pact that would be a "divergent" or "retrograde step." The Government must not tie its hands by making any treaty with the "perpetual enemies of Italy, Austria and the pope." It must avoid any treaty confirming or recognizing "that territorial and political position which it is called to destroy. . . ." Manin, too, was worried about the outcome of the Congress of Paris. While warning Piedmont and assuring republicans that his support of the monarchy was not unconditional, he had left Piedmont a good deal of room in which to follow its own interests and still appear nationalist. Manin's position had remained moderate and general. He asked that it be discussed with "good faith," "sympathy" and "calm." [100]

The statements of Manin and Pallavicino assumed that nationalists of good faith and Piedmontese of good sense would be forced to accept their position. When that did not happen, at least not clearly enough, they found it hard to say more. They insisted that theirs was a practical program, but it is hard for practical men to write programs. If theirs predicted the future, its practicality often required that they wait for events. The crucial test of such a program was less what it demanded of Piedmont than what Piedmont did. After all their claims, it was Piedmont's role at the Congress of Paris which shaped their practical stand into a political movement.

[100] From Manin's covering letter to the newspapers, dated February 12, 1856. Maineri, *ibid.*, 507, prints it as sent to *Opinione;* but the same letter appears in Eduardo Zabban, *Due lettere d'illustri italiani* (Florence, 1877), 5. He undoubtedly sent it to a number of papers.

CHAPTER TWO

MANIN AND PALLAVICINO FORM A PARTY
(MARCH 1856—JUNE 1857)

THE CRIMEAN WAR was badly fought for unclear ends. It grew out of a quarrel in which both France and Russia asserted rights over the Turkish Empire to protect Christians in Jerusalem, but the issue quickly became one of the balance of power in the Near East with Great Britain the leader in opposing Russian claims. In more general terms it represented a breakdown of the old European concert and the recurring irritant of nationalism; it suggested the increasing role of public opinion in diplomatic matters and a growing willingness to resort to force. But when, in March 1854, France and England declared war on Russia, they found themselves unprepared and uncertain where to fight. Anxious for allies, the two Western powers tried hard to win Austria, with her indispensible geography, to their side. Austria energetically hesitated, and by January Britain and France were happy to have the help of a small Piedmontese contingent. The participation of Piedmont was expected to pressure Austria into joining the alliance; but Austria, as she often would, proved invaluable to her enemies. She did not enter the war in which Piedmont fought well.

After Russia had been sufficiently humiliated to satisfy her opponents and the war proved indecisive enough to make peace attractive, the European powers met at the Congress of Paris, in February 1856. The atmosphere of the Congress was relatively relaxed, in part because the war had produced so few triumphs, its issues were so complex, and suspicions among the powers were so numerous. Having effectively denied Russia's effort to extend her influence, the delegates turned to other matters of general concern. It was in the course of this discussion that Lord Clarendon, the British representative, spoke with sympathy of Italian aspirations. That speech, mildly seconded by the French and deeply resented by the Austrians, was Austria's punishment and Piedmont's reward.

34

The Italian Question had been publicly noted and duly labeled a matter of European concern. Count Cavour was recognized as a statesman of international importance. A hope for the future of Italy was suggested in Austria's isolation and in the striking fact that the representative from the little Kingdom of Savoy was allowed to sit with the men who represented Europe's great powers. Cavour, who had hoped for much more, was disappointed. Italian nationalists, who had feared much worse, were grateful. Piedmont fought a war in which she had no interest and reminded Europe that she had an army. She risked having Austria as her ally and appeared with England's aid the representative of all Italy.

Even Pallavicino came to admit that the Crimean alliance had had "its good side." After the Congress of Paris, he felt, as did nearly everyone else, that Piedmont had acted as the champion of Italy and that her hegemony was assured. He was still far from understanding Cavour's policy; indeed, he saw any conversion more as the Prime Minister's than his—Cavour would, he hoped, be going back to Piedmont "a little more revolutionary" than when he came to France.[1] A bit pompously, the Martyr even reopened "negotiations" with the Government, offering the loyal support of the "Italian party" provided that its leaders had really "ceased to [have] hope in diplomacy" and that they would give a guarantee (necessary, he hinted, considering the past) in deeds, not words.[2] But Pallavicino supported the plan to present the Conte di Cavour with a petition of gratitude for his part at the Congress of Paris, because the Count had "this time, shown himself Italian." [3]

In such an atmosphere it was easier to find supporters. To be sure, Pallavicino had earlier claimed Cosenz, a leading Neapolitan exile, and Garibaldi himself as among "ours," and Manin had believed that his support in radical Genoa had grown.

[1] Pallavicino to his daughter, 17 April 1856, *Memorie di Pallavicino*, III, 214. See also his letter to La Farina, 27 April 1856, *ibid.*, 215.

[2] The deed he had in mind was maintenance of the Anglo-Italian Legion which had been formed during the Crimean War. He presented the plan as that of Ulloa and Manin, but it bears the stamp of his optimism: Pallavicino to Rattazzi, 3 May 1856, *ibid.*, 217. Rattazzi's warm reply of May 10 committed him to little, *ibid.*, 218–19.

[3] Carrano to Pallavicino, 27 April 1856, and the Marchese to his daughter, *ibid.*, 214, 216.

La Farina, once somewhat in doubt, was already safely in the fold.[4] By spring the names of those whom Pallavicino claimed as supporters were impressive enough to be used to win others. Rattazzi, Govean, Garibaldi were all informed of the movement's new strength; and if some of those claimed were still doubtful, the usefulness of claiming them was not. To dare thus to cite some twenty-three men, most of them politically prominent, as adherents of their movement was itself a mark of real progress.[5] Pallavicino could scent victory in the simple fact of being no longer alone. With understandable exaggeration, he boasted, "Today an Italian party exists, and this party is a *power!*" [6] His claim would be severely tested.

With similar optimism, Manin, in May 1856, launched a whole series of letters to "Caro Valerio" which were published in *Il Diritto* and widely reprinted elsewhere. We now know, he declared (and the sigh of relief was barely concealed), that the monarchy made no concessions but rather established the right of Italy to be heard in diplomatic councils. It caused Austria shame and embarrassment and brought to European attention the bad government and intolerable conditions under which so much of Italy suffered. The monarchy's claim to the "recognition and faith of the Italian national party" had increased as

[4] Pallavicino to Manin, 1 December 1855, 21 and 28 February 1856, Maineri, *Manin e Pallavicino*, 16, 59, 61. Manin to Pallavicino, 10 January and 13 February 1856, *ibid.*, 41, 55. La Farina even suggested that they found a paper in his letter of April 15, 1856, *Memorie di Pallavicino*, III, 213. The Marchese, more than twice burnt by journals, was unwilling to join in such a venture while he still had commitments to *Il Diritto*: Pallavicino to La Farina, 27 April and 13 May 1856, *ibid.*, 215, 222. The letter from Paris of May 13 was later used by Buscalioni as evidence of La Farina's pre-eminence in founding the National Society, in *La Discussione, Piccolo Corriere d' Italia*, supplement to *Bollettino Settimanale* No. 42, published 23 October 1863. (Bulletin No. 42 was published October 18.)

[5] Tommaséo, Ulloa, Ruggiero Settimo, Giuseppe Del Re, Carrano are all mentioned in Pallavicino to Manin, 14 March 1856, Maineri, *Manin e Pallavicino*, 65. He feared that others, however, wanted merely to use Manin's prestige. He listed, in addition to these, Garibaldi, Enrico Cosenz, Sirtori, Amari, Vincenzo Malenchini, Carlo Fenzi, La Farina, and Vincenzo Fardella di Torrearsa in his letter to Rattazzi, 3 May 1856, *Memorie di Pallavicino*, III, 217. The list had grown to include Avesani, Domenico Piraino, Gattina della Petrucelli, and Milo di Campobianco when he wrote to Govean, 17 May 1856, *ibid.*, 222. Valerio, Govean, Costantino Reta, Dragonetti are added in the letter to Garibaldi, *ibid.*, 225n (dated 23 May 1856 here, it is 1 June 1856 in the ms. in Istituto per la Storia del Risorgimento [hereafter ISR], busta 48, n. 15).

[6] Pallavicino to Govean, 17 May 1856, *Memorie di Pallavicino*, III, 223. He made a nearly identical claim to La Farina, 13 May 1856, *ibid.*, 222.

had its prestige and moral influence. Supported by public opinion at home and by gratitude and applause from elsewhere in Italy, the monarchy would, Manin predicted, find it easy to go on from this first step and, "I hope and believe *impossible to retrogress.*" To support Victor Emmanuel was, more clearly than ever, the "present practical application" of the principle of independence and unification.[7]

In any case, he argued, the national party would continue with its work. What that work should be, however, was never wholly clear. Manin hotly denied that he allowed no initiative to those outside the Government, and he repeated his call for "agitation." But when he came to define "agitation" more fully, Manin displayed his innate conservatism. Agitation was not, he explained, insurrection; it was preparation for insurrection and was to be manifested in many ways according to "circumstances of time, of place, of occasion. . . ." There would be, for Manin's national party, no commands from abroad. Mazzini's errors would not be repeated. Agitation, cautious yet energetic, would prepare the enemy for the larger wounds of open battle. It would provide "a healthful gymnastic, that reveals, educates, reinvigorates the intellectual and moral forces of the future combatants. . . ."[8] There was, after all, a Mazzinian concern for the moral regeneration of Italy in Manin's call. With joy, he noted that it would not take much to set off a revolution; yet he warned vaguely against an untimely disturbance. While French troops remained in Rome, a clash with them must be prevented "at any cost."[9] Already the national party spoke with the serious responsibility of one in power.

Such emphasis on restraint led easily to Manin's next and most controversial blast, his attack on the "theory of the dagger." He called assassination and the belief in it a great enemy to be fought by the national party. Opposition to such tactics would win the support of the best men and applause from "all civilized Europe."[10] Manin did not argue primarily on a moral plane

[7] From the first and last letters of the series, published on May 11 and May 29, 1856, reprinted in Maineri, *Manin e Pallavicino*, 507–509, 511–12.
[8] Quotations are from the letter of May 23, *ibid.*, 510. Agitation was also discussed in the letter printed May 20, *ibid.*, 509–10.
[9] From the letter published May 8, 1856, *ibid.*, 511.
[10] The letter, dated 25 May 1856, first appeared in the *Times*; Manin's tact in attributing most assassinations to partisans of the "Austro-Clerical despotism"

(where, he noted, the skilled dialectic of the "Jesuit reverend fathers" could justify even assassination). The attack was a dangerous one. While openly appealing to the moderates, Manin had adopted the ancient charge hurled by the right against the left. He admitted to Europe that Italian politics were not only volatile in practice but bloody from principle. European conservatives had often seen Italian patriotism in just this light. Pallavicino himself had been accused of supporting the doctrine of assassination.[11] Manin's first political statement from Paris had been to defend Mazzini from the very charges he himself now leveled—and there was no mistaking this—at Mazzini. Manin meant to establish that Italian patriots were politically mature, dependable allies, worthy of the support of the London *Times*, which he saw as "the key" to the immense publicity he had gotten.[12] He may have meant to reassure Cavour, to overcome the fears of Napoleon, and to instruct his own party in restraint.[13] But in doing this he had also conceded the bitterest charge made by the enemies of Italian nationalism, and had injured that Italian patriotic pride to which he had previously appealed. Furthermore, to disavow assassination "in whatever time, in whatever place and for whatever motive" was to move surprisingly far from talk of revolution.[14]

---

was hardly noticed. Yet others of the exiles in Paris had shared Manin's view. Countess Cristina Trivulzio di Belgioioso had been asked by some refugees (perhaps through Manin's influence) to protest the *patente di assassini* of the London exiles and hoped Montanelli would take the lead. See her letter to him, "domenica sera" 1856, in Alessandro d'Ancona, "Spigolature in archivi privati dal carteggio G. Montanelli," *Nuova Antologia*, iv (1910), 11.

[11] In 1848. See *Memorie di Pallavicino*, ii, 40–2.

[12] He said that he had thereby gotten publicity in England, Germany, America, Spain, Portugal, and thus in France and Italy, Manin to Valerio, 4 June 1856, Maineri, *Manin e Pallavicino*, 507–18.

[13] Cavour had talked with Manin in Paris where they achieved some mutual sympathy, if not agreement. See Pallavicino to La Farina, 27 April, and to Rattazzi, 3 May 1856, *Memorie di Pallavicino*, iii, 215, 216. Putelli sees Manin's attack on the "theory of the dagger" as deliberate aid to Cavour, *Manin nell' esilio*, 21. Cf. Omodeo, *Cavour*, ii, 157. Manin may also have genuinely feared some imminent Mazzinian move, see Levi, *Manin*, 112–13.

[14] Manin resented this criticism when T. Mamiani raised it, replying that if he really could not tell assassination from revolution, he was not capable of understanding a political discussion: Manin to Pallavicino, 29 June 1856, Maineri, *Manin e Pallavicino*, 111. The problem, however, was never clarified. Mazzini, earlier than Manin, had seen that the latter's willingness to look for something from diplomacy separated him from the cause of revolution, ". . . consequently [he] refuses all cooperation with men of revolutionary action." Mazzini to George Sand, 1 October 1850, *Scritti di Mazzini*, xliv, 106.

Manin had calculated the advantages of a public break, dramatic and definitive, with Mazzini. But the hopes of Italy were too
easily reduced to political good sense in the Imperial calm of
Paris. From a small, dark apartment in a foreign city, Manin
had sent his statement in a foreign tongue to the newspaper of
still another foreign country. In Italy it sounded like a slur on
Italians.

Mazzini replied effectively, reminding Manin that revolution
had brought him his fame and noting a lack of clarity or real
political doctrine in Manin's program.[15] But being opposed to
Mazzini had some value; in the ensuing argument the conservative *Il Risorgimento* and the clerical *L'Armonia* arrayed
themselves more or less on Manin's side.[16] The opposition of
old friends, however, was upsetting. Valerio had wanted not to
print the letter and felt that at least a statement should be added
to it implying that the condition attacked had never really
existed.[17] Degli Antoni, who had held an important place in
Manin's circle of political friends, warned that Manin's letter
would have the wrong effect; when his prediction proved essentially correct, he was not above saying he had told them so. He
advised Manin to keep quiet for a while and to abandon his
"epistolary system." [18] He reported that everyone at the *Caffè
Nazionale* greatly disapproved of Manin's letter and that some
could not believe it genuine. The embattled Manin could not
trust himself to reply.[19]

[15] "A Daniele Manin," *Scritti di Mazzini*, LV, 147–75. Levi feels that Mazzini
so clearly had the better of the exchange in both argument and dignity that
Manin failed to reply because he could not justify himself: Levi, *Manin*, 124. According to La Farina, some contemporaries felt much the same way, La Farina
to Pallavicino, 30 June 1856, Maineri, *Manin e Pallavicino*, 337.

[16] Pallavicino to Manin, 10 June 1856, *ibid.*, 74–9.

[17] Valerio to Manin, 29 May 1856, *ibid.*, 516. Valerio's caution had bothered
Pallavicino before: Valerio to Manin, 4 December 1855, *ibid.*, 20. *Armonia*
publicly enjoyed this devision among its enemies: Pallavicino to Manin, 10 June
1856, *ibid.*, 78. *Civiltà Cattolica* also made the most of Manin's plight, ser. 3,
III (issue of 28 June 1856), 104.

Manin had, of course, been attacked before; note Bianchi-Giovini's "Le proteste de futuro," printed in Maineri, *Manin e Pallavicino*, 454–61; and his article
of the following month printed in *Memorie di Pallavicino*, III, 697–98. See also
Fiori, "Pallavicino," *Rassegna Storica*, XIII, 750.

[18] Angelo Francesco Degli Antoni to Pallavicino, 30 May and 13 June 1856,
Maineri, *Manin e Pallavicino*, 411; and to Manin, 29 May 1856, ms., MNRT.
He had acted as intermediary between Manin and Valerio.

[19] Manin to Pallavicino, 15 June 1856, *ibid.*, 89; Maineri omits Degli Antoni's
name. The letter referred to here is probably that from Degli Antoni to Manin

Manin's efforts to restate his position were no better received. La Farina, whose *Piccolo Corriere* had ignored the whole affair, advised that Manin would do well to write as little as possible and that not one person would defend him.[20] Even the truth, Cosenz noted, can at certain times do more harm than good.[21] Pallavicino's wife did not exaggerate in reporting from Turin that everyone "is against the declaration."[22] And the *Times* noted Manin's unpopularity in Turin declaring with journalistic assurance, "The fact is, M. Manin has always been more esteemed by his countrymen for his honesty of purpose than for his discretion or talents." This might be, the paper kindly conceded, proof of the adage about a prophet having no honor in his own country. Manin recalled a Venetian proverb: "If everyone says you are drunk, go to bed."[23]

Undoubtedly, his prestige had been dimmed; yet Manin's movement survived this serious setback. It did so because he had been right to see a growing body of opinion and the turn

---

dated 11 June 1856 and printed in *ibid.*, 522–23. In his letter to Pallavicino of 9 June 1856, Manin refers to the first of these two letters from Degli Antoni, saying that a copy is being sent; the copy, not printed by Maineri, is part of the ms. of Manin's letter in MNRT. In it Degli Antoni explains that the edition of Manin's letter attacking the "theory of the dagger" on which everyone was commenting was that printed in *Opinione*, June 4, along with the comments of the *Times*. Manin had refused to answer this letter, too, fearing "some word a little hard" would escape, and finding Degli Antoni's conduct *"poco conveniente"*: Manin to Pallavicino, 6 June 1856, Maineri, *Manin e Pallavicino*, 69. The ellipses and initial "A" hide the name of Degli Antoni, cf. ms. in MNRT.

Their rift had apparently been smoothed over somewhat by the time of Manin's letter to Degli Antoni of 28 July 1856, in Brunetti, *et al.*, *Manin*, 349. Degli Antoni may have earlier begun to waver. He had written to Pincherle, 28 March 1856, mentioning Bianchi-Giovini's latest article (which disagreed with the program of Manin and Pallavicino)with the comment that it was not without interest, ms. in MCV, Documenti Manin, bxxiii/192.

[20] La Farina to Pallavicino, 30 June 1856, Maineri, *Manin e Pallavicino*, 336–37.

[21] Cosenz to Pallavicino, n.d., *ibid.*, 339. Degli Antoni now found things worse, commenting *"peggio per te,"* from Manin's copy of Degli Antoni's letter of 12 July in the ms. of Manin's letter to Pallavicino, 17 July 1856, MNRT.

[22] The Marchesa's comment is quoted in Pallavicino to Manin, 12 June 1856, Maineri, *Manin e Pallavicino*, 80. For further reaction to Manin's declaration also see *ibid.*, 522–23. Note Leonida Balestreri, "Patrioti veneti nella storia del giornalismo genovese," *Rassegna Storica del Risorgimento*, xliv, fasc., iii (October–December 1957), 608.

[23] *Times* (London), 25 June 1856. Manin referred to the article in a letter to Pallavicino, 27 June 1856, Maineri, *Manin e Pallavicino*, 111. The clipping of it is still to be found with the ms. of the letter in the MNRT. The proverbial admonition is cited in Manin to Pallavicino, 18 July 1856, Maineri, *Manin e Pallavicino*, 134.

of events themselves as favoring his position; it did so because his movement was developing new militancy and organization. Manin's ideas were not just his, and they were not really new. The movement he led was deeply rooted in a tradition of many prophets, and they were not all without honor. His writings and those of Pallavicino had built on that tradition. The insistence that monarchy was acceptable, that unity was necessary, that the division of parties should be overcome, that foreign alliances (particularly with France) should be encouraged—these things could all be found in Gioberti's *Del Rinnovamento*.[24] And Cesare Balbo had expressed ideas much like them.

There is much in Manin that echoes Mazzini. One of the great teachers of the nineteenth century, Mazzini more than any other had made credible Italy's claim to be a nation and had made a political force of that belief. It was he who had first cried "if not, not" to a Piedmontese king, and he had frequently expressed a willingness to subordinate the question of a republic to that of unity. In 1854 he, too, had been thinking and talking of a movement to unite all parties. Indeed, one may wonder to what extent the rest of Mazzini's doctrines, for all their high moral content, their optimism and beauty, ever won many supporters. Certainly many of his followers remained, despite the Master's teachings, easy prey to the offer of another compromise as the price of national unity.[25] Many republicans had begun to waver as sympathy for Piedmont grew.[26] Like Bertani, they grew tired of optimism and inadequate preparation.[27] An older romantic vision faded before the not wholly dissimilar promises of the "realists," who could add military statistics to their arguments.

The ideas of Manin and Pallavicino were part of a mainstream; other contemporaries came to stress the importance of accepting

[24] See Giovanni Gentile, "Gioberti," *I profetti del Risorgimento Italiano* (Florence, 1923), 113–14, 141–42; Anzilotti, *Gioberti*, 379–81, 400–401.

[25] Gaetano Salvemini, *Mazzini* (Florence, 1925), 117–34, 140–42. Omodeo notes the elements of Mazzini in Manin and a general decline of the appeal of romanticism, *Cavour*, II, 161, 222–27

[26] This wavering is well shown in Attilio Bargoni, *Memorie di Angelo Bargoni* (Milan, 1911), 49–94. Louis Viardot, for example, disliked Mazzini's articles on Manin. See Mazzini to Emily Hawkes, 25 May 1856, *Scritti di Mazzini*, LXI (Imola, 1932), 235.

[27] Jessie White Mario, *Agostino Bertani e i suoi tempi* (Florence, 1888), I, 270–76.

Piedmont (and her army) as a means to unity and to treat that goal as distinct from and even above other aims. Cattaneo had shrewdly recognized that Italy wanted independence rather than revolution, that she was *"innamorata"* of unity in which strength was believed to lie.[28] Garibaldi, with military concreteness, had noted that ". . . an army of forty thousand men and an ambitious king . . . are elements of initiative and success." Fed up with cries for futile uprisings, he was ready to follow a battle cry from Piedmont.[29] Even while trying to stir up a few revolts in the south, Cosenz denied that any "divergence of opinion" still existed in Italy; he thought it necessary to spur Piedmont on a bit, but he did not imagine unification without her. His plans, he felt, did not conflict with Pallavicino's program.[30] Similarly, Tommaséo, despite his well-publicized doubts about the intentions of the House of Savoy, admitted that Italy would need military force, that a republic was out of the question. Even that Venetian skeptic conceded that, should Piedmont work openly for unification, they must all support her. He too could feel gratitude for Cavour's role in Paris, while insisting on more proof that Piedmont could be trusted.[31]

Symptomatic of this change in the tide of opinion and of the utmost importance for the later history of Manin's national party, is the strange odyssey of Giuseppe La Farina. An experienced polemicist and a leader in the Sicilian revolution of 1848, La Farina began his period of Parisian exile by accepting the

[28] Quoted in Monti, *Fra gli esuli*, 59.
[29] Garibaldi to Jessie White Mario, 3 February 1856, in Jessie W. Mario, *Vita di Garibaldi*, I, 149–50. Garibaldi notes that the idea of fighting with Piedmont against Austria was not new to him: *Le Memorie di Giuseppe Garibaldi*, Edizione Nazionale degli scritti di Garibaldi, II (Bologna, 1932), 341. Curatolo makes a similar point, Giacomo Emilio Curatolo, *Il dissidio tra Mazzini e Garibaldi* (Milan, 1928), 161–62.
On similar grounds, Pallavicino could claim General Pepe as one of theirs. See his article of 2 January 1856 in *Diritto* in Maineri, *Manin e Pallavicino*, 551; and Pepe to Pallavicino, 19 December 1852, *Memorie di Pallavicino*, III, 4.
[30] Cosenz to Pallavicino, n.d., Maineri, *Manin e Pallavicino*, 398.
[31] Tommaséo to Pallavicino, 31 May 1856, *Memorie di Pallavicino*, III, 230. See also in Niccolò Tommaséo, *Il Secondo Esilio* (Milan, 1862), II, 237, his letter to Corfù, 4 January 1856; and his letters of 16 February (1854 is printed here but this is probably an error; 1856 would seem to be the correct date), 24–41; and May 1856, 294–97. Note also *ibid.*, 42–86. Even Franceso Guerrazzi was tempted by Manin's program, Armando Sarpori, "Il Guerrazzi e la politica unitaria del Cavour," *Rassegna Storica del Risorgimento*, XI, fasc., I (January–March 1924), 164–67.

role of Mazzini's principal agent there.[32] At that time, his few qualms were minor; yet the seeds of his political evolution lay in his assurance that he was and always had been unitarian and republican, and that while the two positions seemed inseparable he was "unitarian above all." [33] A vigorous fighter against federalism, he found the wind taken from his sails by Gioberti's *Del Rinnovamento*; the lessons he had learned from 1848 did not differ greatly from those made more famous by the philosopher and by Montanelli. Within a year still another mutation was apparent. His *Storia d'Italia* concluded with a discussion of Italy's future in which neither monarchy nor republic was found to be intrinsically good or bad. Whichever most effectively gathered the needed force should be preferred; the times would determine which form was best.[34]

La Farina had arrived at the point of needing only proof of Piedmont's intent to be convinced by her power. Still, the full conversion came slowly. At first, believing that the King's ministers lacked energy and then that they wanted only territorial aggrandizement, he nevertheless came to see some promise for Italy in the Crimean alliance.[35] The Congress of Paris he interpreted as a great gain for Italy; and if he still thought in terms of stirring things up in Tuscany, the Duchies, and Sicily, it was all to be done under the banner of "independence and Italian unity; out with Austria and the Pope." [36] La Farina

[32] Mazzini to La Farina, 29 November 1850 and 24 May 1851, Franchi, *Epistolario di La Farina*, I, 380–83, 412–13. Also La Farina to Mazzini, 3 June 1851 and n.d., *ibid.*, 415–18, 418–25. He denied that he was a partisan of the House of Savoy in a letter to Nicola Fabrizi, 5 January 1851 [T. Palamenghi-Crispi], "L'Evoluzione alla Monarchia di un repubblicano," *Risorgimento Italiano*, VIII (1914), 243–44.

[33] La Farina to Ricciardi, 10 January 1851, and to Mazzini, n.d. and 3 June 1851, Franchi, *Epistolario di La Farina*, 390, 424–35, 415.

[34] La Farina to Maurizio Giugoni, 19 and 22 November 1851, *ibid.*, 437, 439. Giuseppe La Farina, *Storia d'Italia dal 1815 al 1850* (Turin, 1852), IV, 655–65 but especially 659–60.

[35] For his view of the ministers see his letters to Ernesta Torti, 5 February 1855, and to Raeli, 17 September 1855, in Franchi, *Epistolario di La Farina*, I, 531, 557. His view of the Crimean alliance was expressed in a letter to Torti, 13 March 1855, *ibid.*, 535, and in an article for the *Rivista Enciclopedia Italiana* quoted in Ausunio Franchi (ed.), *Scritti politici di Giuseppe La Farina* (Milan, 1870), II, 347–53.

[36] La Farina to Oddo, 29 April 1856, Franchi, *Epistolario di La Farina*, II, 11. His letter to Fabrizi, 24 May 1856, is even more striking evidence of conversion [Palamenghi-Crispi], "L'Evoluzione alla Monarchia," *Risorgimento Italiano*, VII, 244.

joined in an expression of appreciation to the Prime Minister which contained the ambiguous statement that, "the future will show that you made every effort to avoid the evils of a revolution." [37] Of his old revolutionary ardor only the ardor was left. When he fully joined Manin's party, it was as its most enthusiastic supporter of Cavour. His excellent anti-Muratist pamphlet of July 1856 could already be called a document of the national party—indeed, much of its argument was a repetition of Pallavicino's earlier statements.[38]

It was not, however, merely the famed figures of Paris and Turin who reflected the movement toward a program such as Manin's. In the provinces of Italy there were men who read similar evidence in the same way, many of whom would later become leaders in the Italian National Society. Bartolommei, a noble and a nationalist, had early found Piedmont attractive and begun to publicize his views in Tuscany.[39] Former Mazzinians in Rome and the Marches had, like Manin, begun to ask, "why so many forces dispersed?" Their search for a program of maximum agreement also led toward Piedmont. They, too, made contributions for the medal given Cavour; so did some future members of the National Society in the Duchies.[40] In Bologna a small "Piedmontese party" grew up among the students under a leader, Casarini, who would later dominate the Society there.[41] Under the influence of Gaspare Finali, the Mazzinian society of Cesena added an amendment to its *statuto* swearing to aban-

---

[37] The public letter was dated 26 April 1856, and the loyal Franchi says La Farina wrote it; certainly he signed it. Franchi, *Epistolario di La Farina*, II, 10.

[38] Giuseppe La Farina, *Murat e l'unità italiana* (Turin, n.d.). The pamphlet is reprinted in Franchi, *Scritti politici di La Farina*, II, 67–79. This is true even to the phrasing in his arguments about the dependence of the House of Savoy on a national policy, p. 7, and to a less extent in his emphasis on the divisiveness of Muratism, p. 2. His argument against reform as a sound first step is essentially Manin's, p. 2. His view of the international complications of Muratism was better balanced and wiser (and of course more up to date) than Pallavicino's.

[39] Indeed, Puccioni says he was active as early as 1852. Piero Puccioni, "Ricercando negli archivi del ministro dell'interno della Toscana avanti e dopo il 27 aprile 1859," *Rassegna Storica del Risorgimento*, XXIII (1936), 1085.

[40] From the manifesto by Cesare Mazzoni, 9 April 1853, cited in Giuseppe Leti, *Roma e lo Stato Pontificio dal 1849 al 1870* (Ascoli Piceno, 1911), II, 120. See also *ibid.*, 133, and Giovanni Canevazzi, *Francesco Selmi* (Modena, 1903), 229.

[41] Ernesto Masi, "Camillo Casarini e la Società Nazionale Italiana," *Fra Libri e Ricordi di storia della rivoluzione italiana* (Bologna, 1887), 82; note also, 102–103.

don the republic and follow Piedmont should she attempt the winning of independence.[42] Committees of correspondence had grown up among liberals in the Romagna who sought Italy's salvation in acceptance of Piedmont and who felt themselves the followers of Gioberti, d'Azeglio, and Balbo.[43]

Similarly, those close to the Government, well aware that the republicans were now on the defensive, were willing to let Manin and his like see what they could do.[44] Urbino Rattazzi, now in the cabinet as Cavour's political ally, might have a mediocre opinion of La Farina, be wary of Manin, and lack confidence in either "the capacity or . . . the character" of Pallavicino, but he himself was being won to their dreams of uniting Italy. Cavour might be uncomfortable before the tears of Pallavicino, but he knew he could now have his support.[45] As he explained to Rattazzi, "I had a long conference with Manin. He remains a little utopian; he has not given up the idea of a purely popular war; he believes in the efficacy of the press in stormy times; he wants the unity of Italy and other foolishness; but nonetheless when it comes to the practical step, he could be used." [46] The men in power might still watch such efforts with condescension, but they no longer opposed them. It was now

[42] Tullio Zampetti-Biocca, *La Società Nazionale nella Marca* (Ascoli Piceno, 1911), 31; Zampetti-Biocca, however, confused such moves with the formation of the Society itself, *ibid.*, 28–9. *Civiltà Cattolica* claimed that similar movements took place in the Marches in 1852 with the support of Piedmont, ser. 5, XII (issue of 3 October 1864), 166. Cavalletto remembered most of the former Mazzinians convicted by the Austrians as having accepted Manin's program after the Crimean War, Alberto Cavalletto to Luigi Zini, 10 October 1867, ms. cited in the catalogue of the Libreria Antiquaria L. Bonzi, *Risorgimento italiano, uomini e fatti* (Bologna, 1960), 9.

[43] Alberto Giovanni, "Luigi Tanari e la Società Nazionale Italiana," *L'Archiginasio*, VIII (1913), 265. The Bologna group had ties with most areas of the Papal States: Giovanni Maioli, "Luigi Tanari e il suo *memoriale* ad Ernest Masi sulla *Società Nazionale* in Bologna e nelle Romagne," *ibid.*, XXVIII (1933), 60–61. Men like Minghetti and Luigi Carlo Farini at first opposed forming an organization but finally agreed even to that: Marco Minghetti, *Miei Ricordi* (Turin, 1890), III, 131. Their slogan was to have been "Nationality, Independence, Unification," from a handwritten note by Tanari among the ms. of Carte Tanari, I, in Museo Civico del Risorgimento, Bologna (hereafter MCRB).

[44] See, for examples, the letters of d'Azeglio, 11 April 1855 and 12 April 1856, in *Cavour e l'Inghilterra, carteggio con V. E. d'Azeglio* (Bologna, 1933), I, 449, 457.

[45] Mme. M. L. Rattazzi, *Rattazzi et son temps*, I (Paris, 1881), 338. It is her view that Cavour and Rattazzi were just becoming mildly nationalist at this time, *ibid.*, 320, 338.

[46] Cavour to Rattazzi, 12 April 1856, *Cavour e l'Inghilterra*, I, 463.

understood than Manin was "very benevolent toward Piedmont which he intends to serve in his own way." Cavour had, after all, once before in speaking to Manin recognized that Italy could use friends anywhere she found them.[47] Inevitably, this growing body of opinion [48] was reflected in print. Declarations and manifestoes, pamphlet after pamphlet, by men unknown and by men whose fame had been won in other causes, appeared in Piedmont. An anonymous pamphlet offered at length the familiar arguments that the distinction between monarchists and republicans, if maintained, would keep Italy in her present state for another millennium, that Piedmont was Italy's greatest military and moral force, and that Victor Emmanuel's concern for his throne was the patriot's guarantee.[49] The league of newspapers formed by *Il Diritto* stressed similar ideas.[50] One of the earlier leaders of the revolution of 1848 in Rome posthumously conceded that independence, unity, and the republic were separate questions, and important in that order. Better Piedmont than disunity, he argued, while admitting that the Piedmontese at least had found an honest king.[51] Mauro Macchi established in some two hundred pages that he had been with Pallavicino, Manin, and La Farina for some time.[52] There

[47] Cavour to Giovanni Lanza, 28 February [1856], *ibid.*, 227; Gallenga, *Second Life*, ii, 236.

[48] An interesting summary of this trend is in the report done for Cavour by Cesare Correnti on Lombardy-Venetia, 1858–59. After the Crimean War, he says, there was a rush to join political groups; but, he adds, it was "not poetic and sentimental as at other times but reflective and knowledgeable and [came] from various parts of Italy. Those of thoughtful and independent opinion tried to form on a practical base, beyond questions of forms and ideas, a strong and solid national party." He seems not, however, to have been referring to any particular movement. The report was attached to Cavour's letter to Costantino Nigra, 7 January 1859, and is printed in *Il Carteggio Cavour-Nigra, 1858–1861* (Bologna, 1926), ii, 267. Omodeo, *Cavour*, i, 179–90, 180n, discusses this movement of opinion. The appeal of Piedmont to the middle-class advocate of representative government can be seen in the parallel development in American opinion, Howard R. Marraro, *American Opinion on the Unification of Italy, 1846–1861* (New York, 1932), esp. 206–21.

[49] *Non più partiti* (Genoa, 1855). Manin recognized his ideas in the seventy-two page work and wanted Pallavicino to give it greater circulation, but the Marchese objected to its literary style.

[50] See *Memorie di Pallavicino*, iii, 693–701.

[51] Livio Mariani, *L'Italia possibile, considerazioni storico-politiche* (Turin, 1857), 270, 157. The pamphlet bore an introduction by Antonio Morandi and, interestingly enough, was edited by Giuseppe Del Re, one of Manin's early supporters.

[52] Mauro Macchi, *La conciliazione dei partiti* (Genoa, 1857).

were many others.[53] Even those who went to press to state their differences with Manin, tended to show a large measure of agreement with him.[54]

There had been some real basis, therefore, for that sense of strength which had enabled Manin to launch his attack on the "theory of the dagger"; and he defended himself with vigor.[55] If he had overestimated the extent of his support, the current of opinion favorable to his ideas kept that setback from being a major defeat. As the reverberations of Manin's statement died, however, his moderate program was faced with a new and more subtle challenge. As talk of imminent war lessened in the summer and fall of 1856, rumors of imminent revolts increased. Mazzini insisted that any city in Italy could be the starting point for a general uprising; [56] and if such a view was excessive, Mazzini was closer to the temper of Italy than his opponents cared to admit. Manin himself came to believe the rumors of boiling discontent in Naples and Sicily and to accept the suggestion of the English press that his own calls to "agitate" had played a part in creating it.[57]

[53] Among them: Marco Stucki's address calling for all to unite behind Cavour which first appeared in the Revue de Genève (and gained seven printings in the Gazzette de Savoie), Pallavicino to Manin, 8 June 1856, Maineri, Manin e Pallavicino, 72–3. Giuseppe La Masa, Della guerra insurrezionale in Italia (Turin, 1856), closely followed (and sometimes cited) the arguments of Pallavicino and La Farina. Mazzini recognized the importance of such propaganda and his need to offset "the insidious theses of the moderates," Mazzini to Dall'Ongaro, 28 May [1856], Scritti di Mazzini, LVI (Imola, 1930), 251.

[54] Ricciardi wrote Il Diritto, 25 February 1856, insisting that his slogan, "Indipendenza e Sovranità Nazionale," had preceded Manin's and was preferable to it. Still unable to give the monarchy an evviva, he admitted he would support it if it led Italians on the field of action: Maineri, Manin e Pallavicino, 334–35. Giacoma Sega, L'Italia possibile (Nizza, n.d. [1857]), argued for federalism and opposed Manin in a prolix style studded with historical example; but he, too, clearly accepted Manin's concern for unification and granted Piedmont's probable role in gaining it. Pietro [?] Sterbini's position is outlined in Maineri, Manin e Pallavicino, 582–85.

[55] He demanded that Il Diritto publish the declaration, insisting that the preaching of assassination was well known: Manin to Valerio, 4, 5, and 15 June 1856, ibid., 517–21. Pallavicino printed 2,000 copies of it and Manin tried to have it published in Siècle despite the protest of some Italians in Paris: Pallavicino to Manin, 10 June 1856, and Manin to Pallavicino, 29 June 1856, ibid., 79, 113. The name of Léon Plée, who informed Manin of the angry deputation, is omitted in the printed text but appears in the ms., MNRT.

[56] The letter, dated 2 July 1856, is reprinted in Scritti di Mazzini, LV, 174. See also Mazzini's personal letter to Antonio Mordini, 17 August [1856], ibid., LVII, 20.

[57] This interpretation of the Neapolitan unrest is striking evidence of Manin's

The rumors of great unrest in Milan were repeated and apparently believed by men close to Manin.[58] Despite their belief in moderation and their hope for Piedmontese leadership, the dream of a great revolution was too deeply a part of these nationalists to go ignored. From Paris Ulloa was advocating that his Neapolitan countrymen bring off a revolution under no banner and no name, a Mazzinian compromise with clear dangers for those who accepted Piedmont's hegemony.[59] La Farina found the revolutionary promise for his beloved Sicily irresistible. Convinced that revolution in the south was imminent, he felt it was time to agitate and "rise up," a facet of agitation Manin had tried to exclude for the time being.[60] Without revolution, said La Farina, nothing could be gained; "all true lovers of the *patria* want the revolution." [61]

With time, expectations did subside somewhat. Cosenz was willing to wait a bit in preparing his expedition to Sicily with the aid of a "power"; yet things had gone so far that he dared ask Pallavicino for financial help.[62] Garibaldi, whose seduction by the call to action Pallavicino had greatly feared, preferred

importance in the eyes of the British press. Manin cites the *Daily News* in a letter to Salazaro, 14 August 1856, in Salazaro, *Cenni sulla rivoluzione*, 17. He refers to the *Times'* article in a letter to Pallavicino, 19 August 1856, Maineri, *Manin e Pallavicino*, 168; the article is adequately summarized in *ibid.*, 561. With the ms. of the August 19 letter in MNRT there is a clipping of the article, which stresses the moderate aspect of the agitation there and repeats the distinction between agitation and revolution. The article is datelined Naples, August 13.

[58] Pallavicino quotes Anna on this in his letter to Manin, 21 June 1856, Maineri, *Manin e Pallavicino*, 99. Degli Antoni wrote to Pincherle, 28 March 1856, that people coming from Milan report "ferment" in every class and express fear of "another 6 February," ms. in the MCV, Documenti Manin, bxxiii/192.

[59] Manin to Pallavicino, 19 June; Pallavicino to Manin, 26 June and 5 July 1856, Maineri, *Manin e Pallavicino*, 96–7, 105–106, 120.

[60] La Farina to Vincenzo Cianciolo, 19 July and 3 August 1856, and to Ricciardi, 6 August 1856, Franchi, *Epistolario di La Farina*, ii, 16, 17, 18. La Farina to Nicola Fabrizi, 24 May 1856, ms., ISR, busta 523, n. 56. The supplement to the *Bollettino Settimanale* No. 42 of *La Discussione*, 23 October 1863, says the 20 June 1856 issue of La Farina's *Piccolo Corriere* called for a Sicilian rising. La Farina envisioned it spreading to all of Italy: La Farina "ad un amico—Palermo," n.d., Franchi, *Epistolario di La Farina*, ii, 27–30. See also Gen. Ignazio Ribotti to La Farina, 5 January 1857, *ibid.*, 30. La Farina, who had once hoped for English aid to Sicily, now looked to Piedmont. Bartoccini's suggestion that this was a Cavourian policy, *Murattismo*, 139, 175, seems unlikely.

[61] La Farina to Cianciolo, 23 November 1856, Franchi, *Epistolario di La Farina*, ii, 26.

[62] Cosenz to Pallavicino, 11 June 1856 and n.d., Maineri, *Manin e Pallavicino*, 400–401, 397–98. Ulloa to Pallavicino, 22 June 1856, clearly refers to Cosenz, *ibid.*, 379–80.

that plans be postponed until the following spring. Garibaldi even seemed to be under the influence of Cavour. Yet while declaring that the push toward action should come from Piedmont, he was planning an expedition to rescue Poerio, the liberal hero of Naples, from jail. Garibaldi would soon be asking the national party to furnish him arms for a great spring campaign.[63] Its nominal supporters kept asking what was being done by "our Italian national party," fearful it had left the field to men with more extreme programs. As talk of revolution continued, some wondered if the followers of Manin and Pallavicino were being left out.[64] They were not less tempted by the thought of revolution just because on questions of action their position was unclear. When one of them wrote about the need for revolutionary organization, arms, and Governmental support, Manin felt that this was essentially his program, too.[65] Manin spoke to a Polish count about persuading the exiles of his country to make common cause with Italy, and Pallavicino found it hard to resist stories of Austria's preparations for war and Sicily's for revolution.[66] Manin contributed to Mazzini's fund for 10,000 rifles; Pallavicino gave financial aid to a Sicilian rising and spoke with warm approval of an organization to teach "the people" to use guns.[67]

[63] Pallavicino to Manin, 17 June 1856, ibid., 92; Felice Foresti to Pallavicino, 26 July, 15 August (which mentions Garibaldi's meeting with Cavour), and 15 September 1856, ibid., 355–56, 357, 360–61. Foresti to Pallavicino, 7 August 1856, Memorie di Pallavicino, III, 289. Garibaldi and Foresti expected Pallavicino to win the Government's aid in the purchase of three merchant ships to serve as the center of their military operations, Foresti to Pallavicino, 27 February 1857, Maineri, Manin e Pallavicino, 363–64.

[64] Foresti, in the Genoese environment, was especially concerned that the national party "judiciously" infiltrate among the conspirators of revolution and not abandon its revolutionary heritage. Foresti to Pallavicino, 26 June, 8 and 26 July, 24 August 1856, Maineri, Manin e Pallavicino, 351, 353–54, 356, 359–60; and 7 August 1856, Memorie di Pallavicino, III, 289.

[65] Memorandum of Foresti to Pallavicino, Maineri, Manin e Pallavicino, 529–31; also Manin to Pallavicino, 18 July 1856, ibid., 134.

[66] Manin to Pallavicino, 5 August 1856, ibid., 154–55. The Count's name, omitted here, is nearly illegible in the ms., in MNRT; it may be Ritschervski. Pallavicino to Manin, 2 November and 2 December 1856, 18 January and 5 May 1857, Maineri, Manin e Pallavicino, 230, 243, 267–68, 310.

[67] Manin to Pallavicino, 27 November 1856, and Pallavicino to Manin, 10 and 16 December 1856, ibid., 242, 249–50, 251–52. Manin contributed to the fund for rifles in order, he rationalized, to show his independence of Piedmont and deprive Mazzinians of any excuse for not contributing to the hundred cannon at Alessandria. Pallavicino gave 7,000 lire for a Sicilian revolt, and La Farina was among those thanking him for it: ibid., 249n, 549. The request for

But leaders of a party must offer more than hesitant support for the plans of others. Their plans were a challenge Manin had to meet with his own program of action. His attempt to do so resulted in two of his strangest letters. The first dealt with the agitation in Naples, the second with that in Sicily.[68] His argument was simple. Intricate disputes about reform in Naples were unnecessary, for the Neapolitan constitution was still legally in effect. It forbade the collection of taxes without the consent of parliament. Taxpayers, therefore, should not pay taxes. The government could thus be forced without "violence [but by] legal and calm resistance" to call a parliament. Similarly, in Sicily Manin objected to petitions calling for the Constitutions of 1812. To insist instead on the Constitution of 1848, which had never been repealed, would demonstrate that any separatist ideas had been abandoned. Sicilians then should demand the "reign of laws," and that could be done by a declaration. By warning that every functionary would be held responsible henceforth for any violation of the law and every tax collector for sums illegally collected, the good citizens of the Bourbon Kingdom would quietly capture the state. Either, Manin promised, Poerio would become Prime Minister "without the shot of a gun" or a revolution would make Victor Emmanuel King of Italy.

These letters reflected the peaceful bourgeois' horror of violence and his respect for the officials of the state. They showed a faith in civic courage as optimistic and perhaps as naïve as anything in Mazzini. Even in a land of town meetings it is easier to achieve sporadic, angry outbursts than to maintain calm, unanimous but private opposition to the established powers. Moved in part perhaps by recollection of his own successes in Venice, Manin appeared to have mistaken the Venice of 1848 (a phenomenon which never recurred even along the Grand Canal) for all of Italy. He feared, from experience, the results

---

funds had the impressive backing of Tommaséo, Cosenz, Vare, Giovanni Interdonato, Gemelli, Mordini, and La Masa. Although Manin distrusted these men, he assured Pallavicino that his heart had counseled him well, letter of 18 December 1856, ibid., 253.

[68] The first was dated July 1, 1856; the second, July 3. They were sent to the Times and are reprinted in ibid., 527–29. Manin stuck to his view of the legality of the Venetian Republic in a letter of 10 November 1853 to Le Constitutionnel: Planat de la Faye, Documents par Manin, xii, 425. Levi, Manin, 96.

of revolution ill-timed and ill-prepared and felt any revolution at that time would be both.[69] He wanted to educate Italians to a steady and effective expression of their will and to make their political acts respectable. Aware that the national party might be accused of opposing all action, he wanted to gain sufficient influence among the activists "to prevent errors."[70] His new program had the further advantage of not implicating the government of Piedmont. To do so now, he knew, would either endanger Piedmont abroad or necessitate a denial which would lessen her prestige in Italy.[71] Indeed, Manin felt he had solved his problems so excellently that he planned to issue similar statements for Rome and Lombardy.

Once again, however, the reaction to Manin's pronouncements was far from favorable.[72] Coming on the heels of his attack on Mazzini and at the height of hope for a revolution in the south, his suggestions had seemed too much a surrender to diplomatic respectability. Still, as time passed and the revolution did not take place, his proposal became less offensive to men of the left. It may in fact even have won some support in both Sicily and Naples.[73] In Tuscany the idea of legal agitation won general acceptance (even from Malenchini and Montanelli), and with a quieting in Naples (and the formation of a relatively moderate committee of Neapolitan exiles in Turin) opposition to Manin's declaration quieted, too. This was after all a time of preparation; revolution might have to follow a Piedmontese declaration of

[69] Manin to Pallavicino, 6 June 1856, Maineri, *Manin e Pallavicino*, 71.
[70] For the same reason he did not want Ulloa to give an outright refusal to Cosenz' request for aid for his "project." Manin to Pallavicino, 29 July 1856, *ibid.*, 150.
[71] Manin to Salazaro, 5 August 1856, Salazaro, *Cenni sulla rivoluzione*, 15.
[72] Prof. E. Franceschi reported to Pallavicino that the *Presse* of Turin would not even distribute the letters on separate fly sheets and that La Farina, Pasquale Stanislao Mancini, and Antonio Scialoja all disliked the statement. He feared that Manin would yet "lose that halo which surrounds him," 7 July 1856, Maineri, *Manin e Pallavicino*, 408–409. Cosenz thought such agitation in Tuscany might make sense but not in the south: Cosenz to Pallavicino, n.d., *ibid.*, 399. Even Salazaro took some convincing: Manin to Salazaro, 14 August 1856, Salazaro, *Cenni sulla rivoluzione*, 17. See also Francesco Crispi, *I Mille*, T. Palamenghi-Crispi (ed.) (Milan, 1927), 67–8.
[73] This is, at least, the import of an unidentified note thought to have been written to Manin, ms. in the MCV, bxxix/10. See also Pallavicino to Manin, 7 August 1856, Maineri, *Manin e Pallavicino*, 156.

war.[74] Agitation, then, remained an admired form of preparation but for a distant future.[75]

The sort of agitation more suited to the moment was suggested by Govean in his *Gazzetta del Popolo*. When parliament appropriated money for the fortifications of Alessandria, he opened a public subscription for one hundred cannons there. This was a demonstration in which people all over Italy could take part with as much or as little notoriety as they wished. Not a substitute for revolution but a declaration of faith in Piedmont and of enmity for Austria, it won wide support. It advertised Piedmont's military potential and Italian unity while serving a specific, practical end. Manin quickly sent his contribution to the fund—five francs he could ill afford to lose. Pallavicino soon followed (and was a bit bothered when his name did not appear among the contributors). By now perhaps a bit uncertain as to how his efforts would be received, Manin asked Govean if he might collect additional sums in France from both emigrants and Frenchmen.[76] The collection for the hundred cannons became closely associated with the movement he led.

This demonstration would, Manin declared to the Parisian press, prove the unanimous concern for their nation which motivated Italians.[77] Associated with no single party or government, it had that quality of universality Manin desired. He saw it as essential that Italians from all provinces contribute and that foreigners join in. He hoped to establish a center for public collections in every French village which had a sizable number of emigrants. The *Daily News*, he announced, would accept contributions in London; he would take charge of the collection in Paris. Like fund-raisers ever since, he insisted that the size of the donation did not matter but that "whoever wants Italy freed of

[74] See Ulloa to Pallavicino, 22 June 1856, *ibid.*, 379–80. A firm convert to legal agitation, Ulloa reported that the majority of Neapolitan liberals now agreed with Manin although they did not yet dare refuse to pay taxes. He even interpreted the silence from the south, somewhat optimistically, to explain the lack of acclamations for Victor Emmanuel; in Naples they stood for legality. The important thing was to increase Piedmont's strength, Ulloa to Pallavicino, 11 September and 5 July 1856, *ibid.*, 383, 382.
[75] La Farina, too, conceded revolution would have to wait, La Farina to Giuseppe Oddo, Franchi, *Epistolario di La Farina*, ii, 24.
[76] Manin to Pallavicino, 6 March and 2 August 1856, Maineri, *Manin e Pallavicino*, 62, 151; Govean to Pallavicino, 20 August 1856, *ibid.*, 406.
[77] Dated September 1, 1856, and printed in *ibid.*, 419–21.

foreign domination" should give something. He sent out form letters and saw to it that those people he knew to be sympathic to his movement contributed.[78] He made sure that the collections made in France were publicized in Italy as evidence of European sympathy.[79]

The subscription for one hundred cannons appealed to conservatives such as Minghetti and to the more radical nationalists of Rome.[80] La Farina's *Piccolo Corriere* supported the collection of these funds with vigor. Indeed, its part in the demonstration marks a major step toward its becoming the official organ of Manin's movement; and the style of propaganda it then found so effective would be used again and again. The reports of sizable contributions from Tuscany, Venice, Rome, from Algiers, Mexico, California made this the demonstration of which Manin had dreamed.[81] Although French government officials did not always favor the subscription, Manin could point to the fact that it was not prohibited in France as a sign of official interest in Italy.[82] The collections did in fact go surprisingly well there, and they won Italy some permanent friends of importance.[83] By

[78] One such form, dated 10 October 1856, is in the Bibliothèque Nationale, Paris, 22953/149. Two drafts of another letter to the same purpose are among the Documenti Manin of the MCV, bii/168. An example of Manin's concern for particular individuals' contributions is the pressure he put on Foresti. See Pallavicino to Foresti, 4 October 1856, Giovanni Maioli, "Il Fondatore della Società Nazionale," *Rassegna Storica del Risorgimento*, xv (1928), 22; also Manin to Pallavicino, 21 October, Maineri, *Manin e Pallavicino*, 225; Pallavicino to Manin, 22 October, *ibid.*, 226; and Foresti to Pallavicino, 14 October, *Memorie di Pallavicino*, III, 336.

[79] Manin to Pallavicino, 11 February 1857, Maineri, *Manin e Pallavicino*, 282. Note Govean's surprise at this support, Govean to Pallavicino, 30 August 1856, *ibid.*, 406.

[80] Minghetti, *Ricordi*, III, 132; Leti, *Roma e lo Stato Pontificio*, II, 127. Mazzini recognized in the demonstration a threat to his position: Mazzini to Caroline Stansfield [24 August 1856], *Scritti di Mazzini*, LVII (Imola, 1931), 32–33; Pallavicino to Manin, 22 September 1856, Maineri, *Manin e Pallavicino*, 199–200.

[81] For example, the *Piccolo Corriere* of 1 February 1857 reported 2,219.87 lire from Tuscany (Florence, Arezzo, Pistoia, Grosseto, and many small *paese*) and 1,640.15 lire from Venice. The issue of 8 February listed 325 lire sent from Algeria, and 1,000 from Mexico and 1,235 from Rome were reported in the issue of 10 May 1857. The news that $1,000 (5,000 lire) had been given the Piedmontese Consul in San Francisco was reported in the issue of 26 July 1857.

[82] Manin to Pallavicino, 19 September 1856, Maineri, *Manin e Pallavicino*, 195; and Dr. P. Pirondi to Pallavicino, 24 October 1856, *ibid.*, 404–405. Manin was careful to let the English press know of his French success: see his letter of 21 September, *ibid.*, 421.

[83] A newspaper clipping attached to the ms. of Manin's letter to Pallavicino of 19 September 1856 says he had received 612 francs from 206 persons (at 2 fr.

contributing for cannons at Alessandria, Italians were able to demonstrate their patriotism and nationalists could show their sympathy for Piedmont without implying commitment to her policies. Manin was so closely associated with the campaign for cannons that its success reflected well on his party. In the last year of his life Manin's still unorganized movement was gaining in prestige.

When next he launched a statement on his own, Manin took a safer tack. He denounced the Swiss mercenaries who served the King of Naples, contrasting their liberty at home with the brutality of their task abroad. In the south, he cried, the Swiss were not soldiers but *sbires*. By warning that the rights of one nation depend upon those of others, Manin ran little risk of dividing Italian nationalists.[84] He drew Europe's attention again to the Kingdom of Naples; and this was, in terms of propaganda, Italy's strongest card. He offered, too, an attractive chance to subvert the enemy. La Farina soon entered actively into the preparation of a further attack upon the Swiss (which Manin outlined) to be distributed among Neapolitan soldiers.[85] There was some restiveness in France at this raising of international complications on the part of immigrants, but Manin scored neatly by noting that in a country ruled by an exile it was not good taste to make of the word an insult.[86] The national party spoke once more for most Italian nationalists. Soon Manin would be referring to his old "plan of campaign," and Pallavicino would

---

each) in Bordeaux, MNRT. The first 20 lists published in *Siècle* totaled 5,282.50 francs, and unpublished contributions brought the total to 7,834.30: Ulloa to Degli Antoni, 30 October 1857, ms. in MCV, bxliii/43. The following month de la Forge gathered 300 francs more: Ulloa to Degli Antoni, 17 November 1875, ms. in MCV, bxliii/121.

Anatole de la Forge and de Lasteyrie were two of those in France who became active in support of Italian causes: de Lasteyrie to Pallavicino, 8 January 1857, *Memorie di Pallavicino*, III, 365; and to Manin, 7 January, *ibid.*, 742–45. Also see the *Piccolo Corriere*, 11 January 1857.

[84] The letter was dated December 30, 1856 and is reprinted in Maineri, *Manin e Pallavicino*, 604–607. It led to the kind of debate in which Manin excelled: Manin to Pallavicino, 31 December 1856 and 2 January 1857, *ibid.*, 261, 263. The Marchese had again been demanding that Manin write something, letter of 25 August 1856, *ibid.*, 173–74.

[85] Manin to Pallavicino, 31 December 1856, and Pallavicino to Manin, 7 January 1857, *ibid.*, 261, 265.

[86] This thrust was sent to *La Patrie*, dated 18 January 1857 and is printed in *ibid.*, 617.

speak again of the importance of Piedmont's armed strength, of the great tasks before a little state.[87] They were aided in regaining their old position by the continuation, through the fall of 1856 and well into 1857, of their old polemics against Mazzinians and Muratists. It was not that Manin's thinking ever underwent the fuller development he had promised, but the repetition of old arguments made the distinctions between groups grow sharper and the position of Manin and Pallavicino thus seem clearer. And old arguments can win new converts. Furthermore, these printed debates did force the leaders of the national party to define far more carefully their relationship with Piedmont, the weakest part of their program.

Although many of their friends did not agree, Manin and Pallavicino still saw Mazzini as the archenemy. They had fought him too long (and too often measured the depth of his influence) not to feel the need of fighting him incessantly.[88] They were well aware of Mazzini's deep appeal to those who ached for action. They knew that Mazzini's call for a "neutral banner," —the postponement of political decisions about the form of government until after a successful revolution—sounded dangerously like their own demands for compromise. They might, especially if a revolution did break out, be squeezed between Mazzini's promises and Cavour's hesitance.[89]

When Mazzini hammered away at the opportunism of the so-

[87] Manin to Pallavicino, 10 February, and to the Marchese's daughter, 14 March 1857, ibid., 281, 619. Speech of Pallavicino's in the Chamber of Deputies, 19 June 1857, and cited in ibid., 628–29.

[88] La Farina argued that fighting Mazzini only prolonged his political life: La Farina to Pallavicino, 13 August 1856 and 5 July 1857, ibid., 165, 339. Degli Antoni in a letter to Pallavicino, 13 June 1856, ibid., 413, and Valerio in a letter to Manin, 25 June 1856, ms. in MNRT, took a similar stand stressing Mazzini's impotence. Yet Manin and Pallavicino continued to watch Mazzini's every move with concern. See the Marchese to Manin, 11 and 26 June, 23 and 28 July, 4 October 1856, and Manin's replies of 27 September and 23 December 1856, Maineri, Manin e Pallavicino, 80, 106, 110, 144–45, 147, 216, and 205–206, 257. Also Pallavicino to his wife, Memorie di Pallavicino, III, 260.

[89] What they feared from Mazzini is discussed in Manin to Pallavicino, 22 and 29 June, 3 July, 5 August, 27 September 1856, and Pallavicino to Manin, 15 June, 28 July, and 4 October 1856, Maineri, Manin e Pallavicino, 101, 113, 116, 155, 206, and 86, 147, 215–16. See also Degli Antoni, 14 August 1856, and Foresti, 15 September 1856, to Pallavicino, ibid., 403, 360. Degli Antoni's assurance that the Mazzinians are a "party dishonored by assassins" who recruited "vagabonds and mendicants" is omitted in the printed text. See ms. in MNRT. For Mazzini's side see his letters to Caroline Stansfield, 24 August 1856; to Grilenzoni, 9 September 1856; and to Mordini, 1 January 1857, Scritti di Mazzini,

called national party, noted how much they had stolen from his ideas and slogans, and insisted that Piedmont was unwilling to accept the great role they were thrusting upon her, Pallavicino found it hard to answer.[90] Gradually, he shifted ground somewhat. It was not necessary that Piedmont's policy be deliberately national; her interests would enable them to "compromise the King." Like Manin before, he no longer insisted that Piedmont's government accept their program. Pallavicino was led to a new argument for monarchy. Unification, to be "understood by the multitudes" must be "translated into a thing and incarnated in a name." The national party was moving closer to Piedmont. There was much in Mazzini's case that was true and touching, but his arguments wore the tiredness of repetition. The names of those Mazzini asked to rejoin his fold bespoke his weakness. Yet it was less that he was losing the debate than that he lost his following as the debate lost its relevance. Few movements could have borne the burdens which befell his: the inglorious failure of Pisacane's expedition which was supposed to spark revolution throughout the south, the outrageousness of his party's disturbances in Genoa, and the sensational revelations of previous plots to assassinate the King. Manin appeared vindicated as Mazzini failed.[91]

Muratism represented a position as venerable as Mazzini's though far less tangible, and it dangerously supplemented the Mazzinian attack on Manin and Pallavicino. They were accused by both groups of being unwilling to compromise for the national

---

LVII, 34, 88, 265. He still hoped for some *rapprochement* with Garibaldi, letter of 11 September 1856 to Jessie White Mario, *ibid.*, Appendice v (Imola, 1941), 145–46.

[90] Mazzini to Pallavicino, 2 August 1856, was published in *Italia e Popolo* and is reprinted in Maineri, *Manin e Pallavicino*, 540–43. Mazzini's subsequent attacks were published in *Italia e Popolo* October 21 and 31. The former is reprinted in *ibid.*, 414–17; the latter in *Memorie di Pallavicino*, III, 726–34. Pallavicino confessed his difficulties to Manin in letters of 4 and 21 August 1856, Maineri, *Manin e Pallavicino*, 170–71, 186–89; his formal reply, *Non bandiera neutra!*, is reprinted in *ibid.*, 586–88.

[91] The sense of success and the reactions to Mazzini's latest failures are discussed in Pallavicino to Manin of 23 September and 4 October 1856, *ibid.*, 205, 215; and Manin to Pallavicino, 9 October and 17 November 1856, 12 January 1857, *ibid.*, 222, 237–38, 267. Foresti found Pallavicino's reply "beautiful, noble, frank and wise": Foresti to Pallavicino, 15 September 1856, *ibid.*, 360. Fabrizi gave up hope for a republican rising: Fabrizi to La Farina, 7 August 1856, ms., ISR, busta 523, n. 57. Ausunio Franchi would soon turn a convert's wrath on Mazzini. The revelations about assassination were those of the famous Gallenga incident.

56

good and insisting on Piedmontese supremacy. Muratists, too, spoke in terms of secondary issues which should be postponed, placing the national reform above immediate unification.[92] Lacking a forceful leader or even many proponents who would admit they were Muratists, the movement had a ghostly quality that made it more frightening. Pallavicino feared their dominance among Neapolitan exiles, and rumors of new converts to Muratism circulated with a speed usually restricted to light opera.[93] To combat Muratist rumors and "lies," Manin issued an abnormally unequivocal statement in which he insisted that Italy be unified under one head, concluding: *"he who supports Murat betrays Italy."* [94] To exclude a whole group from the national party in itself suggested growing strength.

It was the position of Piedmont, however, which made Muratism so embarrassing. There were some signs that even Cavour might compromise with Murat, and there was nothing to prove Piedmont would oppose him. As rumors spread, Manin sought (and indirectly got) some assurances from the Government.[95]

[92] Manin to Pallavicino, 27 September, 21 October, and 17 November 1856, Maineri, *Manin e Pallavicino*, 205–206, 225, 238. Also Pallavicino to Manin, 25 June, 7, 9, and 21 August, 19 September, and 29 October, *ibid.*, 105, 132, 157–59, 197, 211, 229. See also the statement of Fabrizi, *ibid.*, 538–39; Carrano to Pallavicino, 12 March 1858, *Memorie di Pallavicino*, III, 455; Gavotti, *Movimento Murattiano*, 108.

[93] Manin heard that Cesare Correnti, La Farina, and La Masa had been won to Murat: Manin to Pallavicino, 29 August and 27 November 1856, Maineri, *Manin e Pallavicino*, 181, 242. Ulloa knew that Carrano, G. S. San Donato, Carlo Mezzacapo had had a secret rendezvous with Saliceti, a leading Muratist, and that Valerio had attended a Muratist conference: Ulloa to Pallavicino, 11 September 1856 and 10 July 1857, *ibid.*, 384, 386. Sirtori himself claimed Lombardy-Venetia as a Muratist conquest: Manin to Pallavicino, 27 November 1856, *ibid.*, 238. The Paris correspondent of *Unione* named Manin as a Muratist, the *National* of Brussels so named Pallavicino; Mazzini nearly believed it, letter to Mordini [20 October 1856], *Scritti di Mazzini*, LVII, 169. On the effectiveness of such rumors see Manin to Pallavicino, 27 November 1856, Maineri, *Manin e Pallavicino*, 242, and Gavotti, *Movimento Murattiano*, 159. Note Pallavicino's comment [about La Masa, whose name is omitted here, but this is clearly a reply to Manin's letter of 27 November] in his letter to Manin, 2 December 1856, *ibid.*, 244.

[94] Manin's statement of 4 November 1856 was sent to the *Unione* and is reprinted in *ibid.*, 590–91. Pallavicino seconded it in a letter to the *National*, 17 November, cited in *ibid.*, 592–93. He had earlier attacked Muratism in answering Bianchi-Giovini with arguments very much like those he used in *Non bandiera neutra!*, which was printed in *Il Diritto*, not *Unione* as stated in *Memorie di Pallavicino*, where it is reprinted, III, 355–56.

[95] Ulloa, full of dark news about Cavour, favored this move: Manin to Pallavicino, 25 July, 19 and 22 August 1856, Maineri, *Manin e Pallavicino*, 142, 168, 178. Manin to Tecchio, 22 August 1856, Isotto Boccazzi, *Lettere inedite di Daniele Manin* (Venice, 1904), 318–19.

La Farina, probably quite on his own, wrote Cavour directly. He showed understanding of the Government's difficult position but pointed out the impossibility of his own if the Government favored Murat. He asked only for personal assurance, nothing public, adding dramatically that if the Government was Muratist he had one more "favor to ask, that of a passport for Paris." Cavour replied by asking La Farina to come see him; the Sicilian never needed his passport.[96] Still, there remained no public proof of the Government's intent, and Pallavicino was bitter that Cavour and Rattazzi felt they could not oppose Murat.[97] The Republicans made the most of these uncertainties, arguing that at least the national party should demand a new ministry. Pallavicino nearly fell for the bait.[98]

The Muratist polemic had some of the amorphousness of the movement itself, and this caused Manin and Pallavicino particular anguish. Pamphlets would appear making little or no mention of Murat but stressing the value of reform in the south, the impossibility of immediate unification, or the separation of the Neapolitan Question from the Italian Question.[99] Commenting on the author of one such work, Pallavicino said, piling insult on insult, "I knew that Sirtori was a *priest*, but I did not know that he was a *Jesuit*." [100] Their strange friend and frequent rival, Montanelli, wrote the article which most infuriated Manin and Pallavicino.[101] He traced, with relative fairness, the debates among the exiles down to 1851, suggesting that unanimity had

[96] La Farina to Cavour, n.d., Franchi, *Epistolario di La Farina*, II, 22–3, and Cavour's reply, *ibid.*, 22n. Omodeo, *Cavour*, II, 143–44, suggests La Farina's anti-Muratist pamphlet was written under Cavour's inspiration.

[97] Massari, among others close to Cavour, seemed friendly to Muratism: Gavotti, *Movimento Murattiano*, 120. Cavour seems to have hoped for British support against Murat, see his letter to Conte Corti, 8 September 1856, Chiala, *Lettere di Cavour*, II, 391.

Pallavicino said Cavour and Rattazzi told him they could not oppose Murat: letter to Manin, 7 August 1856, Maineri, *Manin e Pallavicino*, 155. Pallavicino's bitterness shows in his comments on T[ecchio]: letter to Manin, 19 September 1856, *ibid.*, 197. Manin refused to believe, however, that Cavour had committed himself to Murat in writing, letter to Pallavicino, 9 October 1856, *ibid.*, 222.

[98] On Pallavicino's difficulties with republican arguments, see his letter to Manin, 13 November 1856, *ibid.*, 234–35. A bit from *Italia e popolo* of November 2 in this battle of syllogisms is printed in *ibid.*, 565–68.

[99] Francesco Trinchera was one of the few open Muratists. His nine-point summary of Muratist claims is printed in *Memorie di Pallavicino*, III, 737–39, from the *Unione* of November 14, 1856. See Gavotti, *Movimento Murattiano*, 114–16, 142–43. These arguments are made in the articles by Bianchi-Giovini and Sirtori.

been prevented because some had insisted on a Piedmontese dictatorship. However, Montanelli happily reported, Piedmont had saved Italy from Piedmontism; she did not wish Italian states to remain under tyranny just so she might seem their savior. Montanelli then shrewdly presented Manin's call for legal agitation as part of a new current; the national party, having become truly national, recognized that each region had its own problems and traditions. Each, while admiring the liberalism of Piedmont, would act for itself.

So effective that it sowed still greater confusion, the article nevertheless went unanswered. Pallavicino and Manin dared not say in print what Piedmont would do, but at the same time, they had reason for growing confidence. The debate over Muratism had led to many articles and pamphlets arguing against Murat, and these writings were usually more effective than the propaganda they answered.[102] Furthermore, alliances are always strengthened by common enemies; the national party appeared to be growing. Manin could hope that pamphlets by Gherardi and La Farina would be published under the heading, *"partito nazionale italiano."* [103] These debates with old opponents had

---

[100] Pallavicino to Manin, 23 March 1857, Maineri, *Manin e Pallavicino*, 285. He was especially angered by Sirtori's requesting that he use his influence in behalf of the pamphlet, *La Questione Napolitana.* For Sirtori's resentments over the treatment he received, the ambivalence of his position, and his relations with Manin, see Carlo Agrati, *Giuseppe Sirtori* (Bari, 1940), 141–63.

[101] It appeared in the *Revue de Paris* in the issues of 1 and 15 July, and 1 August 1856 and was reprinted as a pamphlet, Giuseppe Montanelli, *Le parti national italien, ses vicissitudes et ses espérances* (Paris, 1856). For their reaction, see Manin to Pallavicino, 5 August 1856 and 11 February 1857, Maineri, *Manin e Pallavicino*, 155, 282; Pallavicino to Manin, 10 December 1856, *ibid.*, 250; and Ulloa to Pallavicino, 11 September 1856, *ibid.*, 384. Ulloa quit seeing the Montanellis socially.

[102] Among the most effective rebuttals to Muratism, in addition to La Farina's in July, was that of Francesco De Sanctis in October (see Cavour's comment in his letter to Conte Giulio di Groppello, 5 October 1856, Chiala, *Lettere di Cavour*, VI [Turin, 1887], 42). For an excellent discussion of this debate, the diplomatic aspects of Muratism, and its decline, see Bartoccini, *Murattismo*, 93–214.

[103] Manin to Pallavicino, 29 August 1856, Maineri, *Manin e Pallavicino*, 179. He knew the value of such publicity even though he thought Gherardi's effort no *"gran cosa"*: letter to Pallavicino, 3 October 1856, *ibid.*, 213. Pallavicino paid for printing 3,000 copies of La Farina's pamphlet: Pallavicino to Manin, 31 August and 3 September 1856, *ibid.*, 182–83, 185; it had grown out of a request of Pallavicino's. La Farina's reply to *Italia e popolo* on Muratism, 10 October 1856, is printed in Giuseppe Biundi, *Di Giuseppe La Farina e del Risorgimento Italiano dal 1815 al 1893, memorie storico-biografiche* (Palermo, 1893), II, 528–31.

made that party's position seem better defined, its purposes clearer, its following larger. The vigorous round of propaganda had lessened the need for other and more decisive activity. The sense of an organization doing battle had developed from the correspondence of Manin and Pallavicino. Their letters were often affectionate and sometimes contained such catalogues of aches and pains as only good friends could exchange. But always they were intensely political. They regularly traded the flattery on which lonely men who foresee the future must feed; they exhorted each other to courage hundreds of times and in dozens of ways. There was warm camaraderie in Manin's assurance that they were now underway and in his jaunty afterthought, "we may break our necks." Manin was often tired and sometimes despondent. Pallavicino seemed to rush from ecstatic confidence to despair. But they shored each other up, Manin finding the Marchese ardent and prudent, *caro* and *valoroso*; Pallavicino reminding the Dictator of Venice that he was Italy's Achilles—it was for him to do battle.[104] In the round of polemics with Mazzinians and Muratists, through the disappointing reception of many of their statements, Manin and Pallavicino expressed a growing militance. Manin addressed himself to his "lieutenant"; Pallavicino spoke of having carried out his "commissions." There was no doubt who led the movement, and their vocabulary, vibrant with military analogy, expressed their confidence in their cause.[105]

They weighed the effect of their every printed word and assayed the attitude of each noted political leader. Thus they saw nearly every event in their lives as skirmishes in the larger battle. When Pallavicino's *Spielbergo e Gradisca* was published (it was meant to remind Italians of the evils of Austrian oppression and to refurbish the Marchese's status as a martyr), Manin had it published in French. The world of letters, however, proved as disappointing as that of politics; the *Revue des Deux Mondes*

[104] Manin to Pallavicino, 13 June, 21 and 29 July, 21 October 1856, Maineri, *Manin e Pallavicino*, 84, 136, 150, 224. Pallavicino to Manin, 11 and 15 June, 10 and 26 July, 25 August, 2 and 13 November 1856, *ibid.*, 80, 85, 124, 145, 174, 230–31; also, 10 August 1857, ms. in MCV, bxxvi/459.
[105] The military titles had appeared as early as 1855: Pallavicino to Manin, 6 November and Manin to the Marchese, 24 December 1855, *ibid.*, 14, 27–8. Pallavicino even refused to comment on a pamphlet which had been sent him until he got in touch with Manin, Pallavicino to G. La Cecilia, 15 January 1856, ms., ISR, busta 550, n. 42.

gave it an unfavorable notice.[106] Manin rushed to confer with the offending critic (who proved contrite), and Pallavicino was surprisingly widely defended. The leaders of the national party found themselves less alone than they had feared, and Manin looked forward to making use of the friends they had uncovered.[107]

There is a striking modernity in this sensitivity to the press and in the importance attached to public opinion. When Manin found passages in George Sand's *La Daniella* which he deemed offensive to Italian character, he encouraged his friend, de la Forge, to protest against it. Even the indomitable George Sand seemed a bit taken aback by this new controversy, but Manin persisted. Anxious to let no chivalric French gestures to Italy go unacknowledged, he then made a demonstration of thanking de la Forge. But their friends found it hard to take such subtle matters of propaganda so seriously. With great difficulty Pallavicino succeeded in winning twenty-three signatures for Manin's letter of appreciation to Italy's French defender.[108] Most of those who signed were later the founders of the National Society; the sensitive militance of Manin and Pallavicino was extending beyond them.[109]

[106] In all, three French editions were published. Pallavicino's intent in publishing it and the crisis over the critic who viewed it as an apologia for Pallavicino's conduct is discussed in Pallavicino to Manin, 7 December 1856, 30 January, 1 April, and 24 May 1857, Maineri, *Manin e Pallavicino*, 247, 275–76, 289–90, 311, and Manin to Pallavicino, 22 January 1857 (as dated on the ms., MNRT, Maineri has it 27 January), *ibid.*, 273.

[107] Pallavicino to Manin, 7 December 1856, 31 January, 1 and 17 April, 5 May 1857, Maineri, *Manin e Pallavicino*, 271, 277, 289–91, 299–300, 308–309. Manin to Pallavicino, 17 and 23 April, *ibid.*, 300, 305. Tommaséo in *Diritto*, Felice Mornand in *Illustration*, La Farina in his *Piccolo Corriere* praised the pamphlet; San Donato was ready to, in *Indépendance Belge*.

[108] The resistance Manin met was such that he imagined Montanelli and Maestri having, with the aid of *Il Diritto* in Turin and *Le Courrier Franco-Italien* in Paris, "organized a numerous Italian coalition in favor of him who abuses Italy and against him who defends her. . . ." They had even, he added, sent instructions to that effect to "their correspondents" in Genoa. The difficulty of Manin's personal position is suggested in his description of how ". . . the friends of Sig. de la Forge laugh at him and say: see what one gets for taking the side of the Italians." All this, from the ms. of Manin to Pallavicino, 11 April 1857, in the MNRT, is omitted in Maineri, *Manin e Pallavicino*, 293–95.
Mauro Macchi must also have opposed the effort; for Manin declared unconvincingly, "*m'è indifferente l'opinione di Mauro Macchi che copiò fedelmente a Genova la parte rappresentata da Pietro Maestri a Parigi*": Manin to Pallavicino, 14 April 1857. The names of Macchi and Maestri, omitted in *ibid.*, 295, appear in the ms., MNRT.

[109] They were Salvatore Tommasi, Francesco Carrano, Piersilvestro Leopardi,

In such matters they worked together well. But Pallavicino could not by temperament provide his chief with the precise information, the reports on public opinion or politics, that Manin wanted. Pallavicino never supplied the answers *"categorically, point by point,"* for which Manin pleaded. Once, Manin asked with some pain if Pallavicino still had his letters; and the Marchese replied sweetly that he kept them "like jewels" and did his best to follow their counsel.[110] If these differences in temperament kept Manin from being as informed as he wished to be, they had some advantages. Pallavicino's enthusiasm gave the movement a broader tone than Manin's legalisms were likely to; and their very differences of approach disguised, often from them, differences in program. Pallavicino thought a popular revolution much less likely than did Manin, and Manin felt far less commitment to the House of Savoy than his lieutenant.[111]

It was not possible, however, for them to ignore their differences over Cavour. Pallavicino had no use for diplomacy; he found Piedmont dangerously parochial in outlook (and Cavour *piemontesissimo*).[112] Manin commented gently, "My kind lieutenant has a vivacity, a boldness, an effervescence really youthful." After warning against impatience he added more pungently, "It would be unfair to require that a *government* speak and work as we who are *revolution*." [113] It was a distinction with which

G. S. di San Donato, Giuseppe La Farina, Paolo Emilio Imbriani, P. di Cambello, Carlo Mezzacapo, Enrico Cosenz, G. Tofano, G. Pisanelli, P. S. Mancini, Cesare Oliva, M. Casaretto, G. Bianchi, Cristoforo Moja, Ernesto Migliara, Augusto Paselli, Tommaso Villa, G. de Pasquale, A. d'Ancona, N. Rosci, Castellani-Fantoni: Pallavicino to Manin, 7 April 1857, Maineri, *Manin e Pallavicino*, 292. Only Foresti signed from Genoa, Manin to Pallavicino, 14 April 1857, *ibid.*, 295.

Manin's relief at this success shows in his letter to Pallavicino, 11 April 1857, *ibid.*, 294.

[110] Manin to Pallavicino, 25 November 1855; 29 July, 17 November, 18 December 1856; and 23 April, 5 May 1857, *ibid.*, 13, 147, 236–39, 254, 305, 309. See also Pallavicino to Manin, 4 December 1855, *ibid.*, 20.

[111] Pallavicino warned Manin against "copying Mazzini" with regard to revolution and argued against omitting any reference to the Cross of Savoy as part of their banner; it came with the King: Pallavicino to Manin, 10 and 24 August, 10 September 1856, *ibid.*, 158–59, 172, 192–93. He took a somewhat different tone with other friends. Cf. his letter to Foresti, 4 October 1856, Maioli, "Il Fondatore," *Rassegna Storica*, xv, 22.

[112] Pallavicino to Manin, 1 and 4 October 1856, Maineri, *Manin e Pallavicino*, 212, 215.

[113] Manin to Pallavicino, 23 December 1856, *ibid.*, 257; he had to repeat the argument in his letter of 30 January 1857, *ibid.*, 274. Salazaro needed to be re-

Pallavicino was never happy. In June 1856 the Marchese seemed to have established fairly good relations with Rattazzi; the minister even promised to try to place some of their articles in the newspapers he denied controlling. But the continued coolness of the pro-Government press and the doubts about Cavour raised by fears of Murat quickly reawakened Pallavicino's distrust [114]— a distrust that was shared by many of the Marchese's friends. He came to see Cavour's diplomacy as an instrument to be used against revolution, after revolution had been used against Austria. His distrust became personal and bitter. "More than Mazzini, more than Murat, I fear Camillo Cavour. . . ." [115]

Manin made a firm effort to calm his lieutenant. Experienced in political office, he knew the pressures on a government. They must, Manin argued, mold public opinion to create a pressure on their behalf. He recognized Cavour's ability and the value of his European fame; it would be a loss not to have him as an ally, still worse to have him an enemy. Cavour, Manin said, should be prodded not overthrown. ". . . I think Cavour too intelligent and too ambitious to deny himself to the Italian undertaking when public opinion imperiously asks it." [116] Manin had hoped Pallavicino would use his influence in the Chamber of Deputies to further their cause and explore members' views. Instead, he had become labeled as an opponent of the Government and felt himself isolated. Tempted by proposals that they

---

minded of the same point, letter of 5 August 1856, Salazaro, *Cenni sulla rivoluzione*, 15.

[114] Pallavicino's intimate relationship with the Government during this period can be followed in his letters to Manin of 12, 15, 18, 19, 22 June, and 5, 17, 24 July 1856, Maineri, *Manin e Pallavicino*, 80, 85-7, 95, 97, 103, 119, 121, 130-31, 140; in his letter to Tommaséo, 20 June 1856, *Memorie di Pallavicino*, III, 252; and the letters of Rattazzi to him, 23 July 1856, *ibid.*, 276, and 31 July 1856 (setting an appointment for August 1), ms., MNRT. Manin's attack on the "theory of the dagger" had seemed to leave the Government friendlier.

[115] Ulloa resented the treatment accorded him: Ulloa to Pallavicino, 22 June and 29 September 1856, Maineri, *Manin e Pallavicino*, 380, 384-85. Cosenz thought Piedmont merely opportunist: letter, n.d., to Pallavicino [post-June 11, 1856], *ibid.*, 398. Foresti suggested preparing for the negative solution to Manin's "if not, not": letters to Pallavicino, 26 June and 8 July 1856, *ibid.*, 351, 353. Pallavicino's views are expressed in his letters to Manin from August 10 through December 2, *ibid.*, 159-250, and in his letter to his wife, June 1856, *Memorie di Pallavicino*, III, 258. Cf. Rattazzi to Pallavicino, 28 September 1856, *ibid.*, 327-28.

[116] Manin to Pallavicino, 27 September 1856, Maineri, *Manin e Pallavicino*, 206.

ally themselves with the parliamentary left, Pallavicino began to dream of the new Government they might support.[117] But Manin was firm. "Loyal opposition," he pleaded, would try to see what, from Cavour's position, was possible; "the Sardinian minister is not on a bed of roses."

The national party, Manin said, must preserve "freedom of action"; it would support whoever accepted its program but not become embroiled in secondary issues by allying with any group.[118] Gradually, Pallavicino backed down. He even defended the Government on occasion, hoping to demonstrate that Cavour felt sympathy for a national program. Cavour, the careful calculator of his own interests, must be shown "with mathematical proof" the strength of their party. The Marchese was returning to a position closer to Manin and now felt they could best win the shrewd Prime Minister by influencing public opinion.[119] Pallavicino's retreat was already a bit late. His view of Cavour was not entirely wrong, but it led him to actions ill-designed to win the Prime Minister. Pallavicino had shown his displeasure publicly just as Cavour was displaying signs of renewed interest in Manin's views.[120] Pallavicino's opposition and Manin's death prevented the national party from attempting to establish with the Government the rapport which might then have been possible and under terms quite different from those of the later relationship between Cavour and La Farina.

Pallavicino, too, was paying a price for supporting Piedmont.

[117] Manin to Pallavicino, 25 November 1855, ibid., 13; Pallavicino to Manin, 18 and 21 January, 4 February 1857, ibid., 268, 270–71, 278–79. He was cut by Cavour's reply to his speech at the January 25 session, reprinted in ibid., 610–14. Brofferio to Pallavicino, 2 January 1857, ms., MNRT, suggests that the Marchese's joint attack with the spokesmen of the left may have been planned.
[118] Manin to Pallavicino, 30 January 1857, Maineri, Manin e Pallavicino, 275–76.
[119] La Farina's influence played a part in this: La Farina to Pallavicino, 12 July 1857, ibid., 341. Cf. Pallavicino to Ulloa, 16 July, Memorie di Pallavicino, III, 399. On June 19 he spoke in behalf of a Government measure for increasing the army, managing in the course of it to score off "piedmontists." Interestingly, this speech was reprinted as a pamphlet under the heading of the Italian National Party. It is reprinted in Maineri, Manin e Pallavicino, 628–32. The Marchese also tried to soften some of the resentment of the Government's harsh anti-Mazzinian measures. See his letters to La Farina, 7 April and 1 September 1857, Memorie di Pallavicino, III, 385, 424; and to Foresti, 3 December 1857, Maioli, "Il Fondatore," Rassegna Storica, xv, 34–5.
[120] Cavour noted well Pallavicino's opposition. See his reply cited in Chiala, Lettere di Cavour, II, cciii. He still recalled it in the session of June 8, 1860; Pallavicino's rather embarrassed reply to this is in Maineri, Manin e Pallavicino, 423–30. On Cavour's interest in treating with Manin, see his interesting letter

He must accept ministries he did not like just as Manin had relaxed his reservations about monarchy. If Piedmont's policy were national, they had promised to support her, "if not, not." They found it comforting to have made their support conditional, but their own arguments left them with only one alternative to faith in Piedmont—despair. Thus there was little reciprocity in their relations with the Government, and Manin had understood that they could only lose by becoming involved in Piedmontese politics. So in a sense the national party supported Cavour, as they had applauded him at the Congress of Paris, less for what he did than for the destiny they saw foreshadowed in him. The changes they wanted in the policies of Piedmont would come with time and the development of public opinion. They could wait for time to pass, and they could propagandize to mold public opinion.

There were other reasons for an emphasis on propaganda. As nationalists and enthusiasts, these supporters of Piedmont preserved the tradition that made agitation and revolution good words. La Farina especially insisted that he was devoting himself to agitation to prepare the way for that revolution without which Italy and Piedmont would be lost. But his agitation consisted largely of writing articles which reminded Italians of their destiny, and he quickly came to see that the revolution he wanted must be controlled by Piedmont.[121] Revolution came to mean only a little more than Italy's predestined change. As realists, these men knew that revolutions were not easily ordered; as advocates of monarchy, they were wary of what revolution might bring. Manin had moved in the same direction with his advocacy of legal resistance in the Kingdom of the Two Sicilies. He hoped to achieve the benefits of revolution, that is the effective expression of a national will, without the risks that accompany violence. His proposal was stillborn because it managed to be neither inspiring nor practical. The next best thing had proved to be demonstrations, the collection of money for cannon in Alessandria or a letter of gratitude to the critic of George Sand. These

---

to Conte Ercole Oldofredi, 19 March 1857, Chiala, *Lettere di Cavour*, II, 264.
    [121] See his letters to Fabrizi, 24 May 1856, n.d., and 8 September 1856 [Palamenghi-Crispi], "L'Evoluzione alla Monarchia," *Risorgimento Italiano*, VII, 245–46, 248–49, 250–51. Cf. his letter to the editor of *Il Risorgimento*, 8 September 1856 and published September 10, cited in Franchi, *Epistolario di La Farina*, II, 560–61.

demonstrations were so satisfying because they ran no risk of dividing patriots or embarrassing diplomats. They expressed an attitude of patriotic unanimity which seemed itself a foretaste of Italy's destiny.

Concerned with the creation and spread of this attitude, the men of the national party allowed their theoretical republicanism to fade. Manin's attack on the "theory of the dagger" had thus not merely established his respectability and his separation from Mazzini, it had implied the abandonment of judicious indifference between republic and monarchy in favor of monarchy. Like the call for legal agitation or the initial acceptance of Piedmont, it meant these men were willing to surrender the promises of a democratic revolution in order to be rid of its dangers.[122]

The national party, then, could have no effective part in the Piedmontese parliament; it could not agitate for revolution in the old sense. Yet it must be active; it must do something to remain alive as a recognizable and attractive political position.[123] This was the third reason for emphasizing propaganda—it was what the national party could safely do. Furthermore, the general propositions of the party had won support. Its opponents had helped, for in the debates over Italy, the Mazzinians had demanded too much of men and history, and the Muratists (dependent on another power and offering reform only) had not promised enough. Nearly all could see, in general terms—the terms, that is, of propaganda—that Manin's national party moved with destiny. Thus propaganda was the core of Manin's movement, but to propagandize efficiently it would organize, and the organization of a party would become the best of demonstrations. The spread of their propaganda, the founding of an organization, the staging of a demonstration, would all be accomplished through the incarnation of an attitude in the Italian National Party.

---

[122] Alfredo Oriani, *La lotta politica in italia, origini della lotta attuale* (Bologna, 1943), II, 345, makes this point in reference to Garibaldi.

[123] Simply being "active" was extremely important for the prestige of one's movement. Indeed, many still felt, as Montanelli had in his exchanges with Pallavicino, that that party which was simply most active would win the most support. Similarly, Carlo Pisacane felt that action by the Mazzinians was the way to defeat Murat, Domenico Di Giorgio, "Il 1860 in Calabria e Benedetto Musolino," *Historica*, I (1948), fasc. 5–6, 128.

CHAPTER THREE

THE ORGANIZATION AND SPREAD OF THE NATIONAL SOCIETY

(MAY 1856—NOVEMBER 1858)

HAVING DECIDED that revolution would break out by itself when "the hour to rise up is really come," and that Piedmont would not take up the sword until "the national idea is generally . . . accepted," Manin's party was dedicated to the spread of that idea.[1] With a goal so broad, Manin was bound to find that ". . . our own political doctrine is not yet sufficiently widely expounded, unfolded, discussed, diffused. Thus the neophytes cannot be numerous enough, nor sufficiently instructed in the faith that they are disposed to embrace." More than neophytes, he wanted "apostles" (and he had his eye on La Farina).[2] Pallavicino hoped to find support among the "inflammable material" at the university by making himself "*simpatico*" to the students.[3] For the most part, however, they looked to propaganda to spread their ideas. Their concern was more to provoke discussion of Italy as a nation than to convince with heavy argument. If the press of Piedmont could be made to discuss the Italian Question, that would be a great gain.[4] Wide circulation became more important than wise content. Once their general propositions were commonly discussed, they would certainly prevail.

At first, it was largely to newspapers that these propagandists looked. Manin saw to it that articles favorable to Italy were reprinted in the Italian press and that Italian gratitude was made known abroad.[5] They carefully observed, reported on, and tried

[1] Manin to Pallavicino, 30 June 1856, Maineri, *Manin e Pallavicino*, 114–15.

[2] Manin to Pallavicino, 27 September 1856, *ibid.*, 207.

[3] Pallavicino to Manin, 10 and 16 December 1856, *ibid.*, 248, 251.

[4] Pallavicino to Salazaro, 17 September 1856, *Memorie di Pallavicino*, III, 317. Manin to Pallavicino, 6 June and 12 August 1856, Maineri, *Manin e Pallavicino*, 69 and 162. Foresti took a somewhat different view, letter to Pallavicino, 15 August 1856, *ibid.*, 357.

[5] *Il Diritto*, 27 February 1856, for example, quoted from the article in the *North British Review*, cited in *Memorie di Pallavicino*, III, 203–207. Manin to

to gain influence with some thirty Italian newspapers and about as many in the rest of Europe, especially in France, Britain, Switzerland, and Belgium. Through friends, they maintained regular journalistic contacts in Turin, Genoa, Brussels, Paris, and Britain. Manin achieved the useful privilege of seeing the proofs of articles on Italy that appeared in the *Presse* of Paris. Papers in Spain, Switzerland, and Britain had agreed to disseminate their views.[6]

By the fall of 1856, they had established a system of propaganda that was working impressively. The occasional notice by an agency such as the *Agence Havas* and the contemporary habit

Pallavicino, 5 and 24 December 1855, 10 January and 16 February 1856, Maineri, *Manin e Pallavicino*, 22, 28, 42, 56. Pallavicino to Manin, 18 and 20 November 1855, and 17 and 25 January 1856, *ibid.*, 6, 11, 43, 47. Manin to Degli Antoni, 13 February 1856, Brunetti, *et al.*, *Manin*, 348.

[6] With lapses they loudly lamented, the *Diritto*, *Gazzetta del Popolo*, *Risorgimento*, and (at first) *Unione* in Piedmont; the *Estafette*, *Presse*, and *Siècle* in Paris; the *Times* and *Daily News* in London printed their material. Degli Antoni had acted as their liaison with the press of Turin until Manin's attack on assassination. Canuti became their paid agent for French and Belgian contacts: Degli Antoni to Pallavicino, 20 May 1856, Maineri, *Manin e Pallavicino*, 411, and to Manin, 29 May 1856, ms., MNRT, and Canuti to Manin, 5 August 1856, ms., *ibid.* Salazaro acted as agent for the publication of their letters in Brussels and Paris and later in Genoa: Pallavicino to Manin, 2 January 1856, Maineri, *Manin e Pallavicino*, 39. In Genoa he established relations with the *Corriere Mercantile* and *Movimento*: Salazaro, *Cenni sulla rivoluzione*, 8, 15. Manin dealt with him as a kind of press agent in his letter of 28 July 1856, *ibid.*, 14. Cf. Manin to Pallavicino, 6 July 1856, Maineri, *Manin e Pallavicino*, 123.

Manin's contacts with the editor of the *Indépendance Suisse* prompted the latter to ask Pallavicino to send some articles from Turin. Manin also reported the conquest of a French paper on the Italian border: Pallavicino to Manin, 13 November, and Manin to Pallavicino, 17 November 1856, *ibid.*, 234, 239. Manin saw a great many French journalists: Brunetti, *et al.*, *Manin*, 262–63. He won assurances from the Spanish minister in Paris that the liberal press of that country would support them, and *Las Novedades* began printing his letters with favorable comment, Manin to Pallavicino, 6 and 29 June 1856, Maineri, *Manin e Pallavicino*, 70, 111–12.

Manin was frequently pleased by his friend, W. R. Greg, who presented their ideas in the *North British Review*. Greg also wrote in the *Economist:* Manin to Pallavicino, 18 August 1856, *ibid.*, 165. Cf. Mazzini's comment in his letter to Saffi, 10 [September 1857], *Scritti di Mazzini*, LVIII (Imola, 1931), 285. When the *Times* correspondent in Turin seemed too closely to reflect the views of the Piedmontese Government, Manin suggested Pallavicino get to know him: letter of 17 November 1856, Maineri, *Manin e Pallavicino*, 239. They had been pleased, however, by the three long articles the *Times* devoted to Manin's attack on the "theory of the dagger": Manin to Pallavicino, 6 July 1856, *ibid.*, 122. Pallavicino used his influence with Peyrat to win Manin the chance to comment in advance on articles in the *Presse:* Manin to Pallavicino, 25 November and 24 December 1855, 10 January 1856, and Pallavicino to Manin, 17 January 1856, *ibid.*, 13, 26, 40, 43.

of reprinting in one paper items of interest from another increased the value of each printing their ideas received.[7] A literate follower of Italian affairs would have been unlikely not to know that Manin and Pallavicino were up to something. But casual encounters with occasional letters are not likely to convince a man of the truth of a doctrine or even of the strength of a movement. Far from content with what they had achieved, Manin and Pallavicino strongly felt the need of an official organ or at least of a paper that would regularly represent their position. One by one, friendly papers in Piedmont had proved disappointing. There had been disagreements with the *Unione* and then the *Diritto*; Pallavicino's pleadings with Rattazzi for more sympathetic treatment in the ministerial press had produced little change in the *Espero*, and the Marchese's rather naïve hope for the *Risorgimento* had come to nothing. He came to see journalists as a "race of vipers" willing to sacrifice truth to money. He despaired of finding a "good" paper in Piedmont.[8] Influence with some foreign papers was no substitute for a solid base in Italy.

The Italian press was tiring of letters from the same two men, and they in turn found little new to say as each communiqué passed into journalistic oblivion within a few days. Manin had

[7] Pallavicino's *Non bandiera neutra!* was printed in four Piedmontese papers (*Tempo, Movimento, Pontida, Gazzetta Militare*) and commented on in five (*Espero, Opinione, Risorgimento, Armonia, Italia e Popolo*), not always entirely favorably: Pallavicino to Manin, 29 October 1856, Maineri, *Manin e Pallavicino*, 227. Manin's anti-Muratist letter of November had been printed in six Piedmontese papers (*Diritto, Risorgimento, Gazzetta Militare* in Turin and *Corriere Mercantile, Movimento, Cattolico* in Genoa), and Pallavicino sent it to a dozen more, Pallavicino to Manin, 13 November 1856, Maineri, *Manin e Pallavicino*, 232.

Manin sent his letter on the Swiss mercenaries to papers in England, Belgium, and Switzerland as well as France and Italy: Manin to Pallavicino, 31 December 1856, *ibid.*, 261. Pallavicino's latest effort appeared in France in *Campanone, Univers, Estafette*; and *Siècle*, which had recently become more friendly, promised to print it, Manin to Pallavicino, 29 June (where the *Agence Havas* is mentioned) and 27 August 1856, Maineri, *Manin e Pallavicino*, 113, 176. The *Gazzetta Popolare* of Cagliari is an example of a paper giving the movement good publicity on the basis of items first appearing elsewhere, Pallavicino to Manin, 14 March 1856, Maineri, *Manin e Pallavicino*, 67.

[8] Bianchi-Giovini's *Unione* had reflected its editors' sympathy for Muratism; Valerio balked at putting his *Diritto* at their disposal as Manin's concern for diplomacy and Pallavicino's trust in the King made them seem to move to the right; he clashed with them over Manin's attack on assassination. The cautious *Risorgimento* had treated Manin well on that issue but could hardly support their whole program. None of the Piedmontese press had printed Manin's letter on the hundred cannon although there were many later references to it.

tried to counteract this by his use of the foreign press. Comments on Italy in major French or English papers were in themselves news in a country sensitively feeling its untested nationality. Therefore, he frequently sent his own writings first to a British or French paper; he also supplemented them by seeing that other items favoring his program were republished in Italian papers. Harder to transplant than to find, some articles were at Manin's behest reprinted in Piedmont.[9] Some of the items were, of course, initially placed by Manin or his friends, which gave him partial control of the tone and content and some indication of how the article would be treated when printed. But for the most part he was dependent on what others said.[10] Indeed, he added a subtle touch to his technique by arranging for direct exchanges between sympathetic papers in France or England and Piedmont, and by having friends appointed as the Italian correspondent of British or French papers.[11]

[9] They were from the *Times, North British Review, Economist, Siècle* and *Estafette*. The effort this required was immense. The *Times* article (which so paralleled Manin's arguments as to make one wonder who wrote it) is referred to in Manin to Pallavicino, 19 June, 3 and 25 July, 5 August 1856; and La Farina to Pallavicino, 13 August 1856, Maineri, *Manin e Pallavicino*, 96, 118, 142–43, 153–54, 165. The *North British Review* article is discussed in Manin to Pallavicino, 9 October and 17 November 1856, *ibid.*, 221, 238.

The *Economist*'s contribution was mentioned in Manin to Pallavicino, 1, 6, 17 and 19 June, 14 and 22 July 1856, *ibid.*, 69, 70, 92, 96, 127, 138. To savor the complications even so simple a task can raise, see Pallavicino to Manin, 19 and 24 July 1856, *ibid.*, 135, 138; and Rattazzi to Pallavicino, 23 July 1856, *Memorie di Pallavicino*, III, 275–76. The article is summarized in Maineri, *Manin e Pallavicino*, 526.

On the *Siècle*, Pallavicino to Manin, 10 July 1856, *ibid.*, 124; for the *Estafette*, Manin to Pallavicino, 30 July 1856, *ibid.*, 151.

[10] Dragonetti wrote for the *Economist*; his letter to Pallavicino, 19 August 1856; and the Marchese's reply, 26 August 1856, *Memorie di Pallavicino*, III, 299, 303. Manin sent for publication, for example, the letter of a Sicilian jurisconsult: Manin to Pallavicino, 27 July 1857, ms., MNRT; Salazaro tried to place the work of a Tuscan exile: letter of Manin to Salazaro, 18 September 1856, Salazaro, *Cenni sulla rivoluzione*, 23. Manin also made a French translation of La Farina's anti-Muratist article for circulation in that country, Manin to Pallavicino, 19 September 1856, Maineri, *Manin e Pallavicino*, 196.

[11] For the exchanges arranged, see Manin to Pallavicino, 22 July 1856; and Pallavicino to Manin, 10 December 1856, *ibid.*, 135, 250. The foreign papers mentioned here are the *Leader* and *Estafette*.

Foresti was named correspondent of a northern British paper, "the first in influence" (probably the *North British Review*). This was arranged through Greg: Manin to Pallavicino, 18 July and 18 August 1856; and Pallavicino to Manin, 28 July 1856, *ibid.*, 133, 165–66, 146–47.

La Farina seems to have filled the same role successfully with *La Presse* although he did not write French: Manin to Pallavicino, 23 December 1856 and

However effective such techniques may have proved, they tended to disassociate the movement from its propaganda, which was the work of many pens, sporadically published in a variety of papers. During Pallavicino's visit to Paris in April and May, the two men apparently agreed that it would be useful to publish their writings on fly sheets.[12] And their first small four-page folder, neatly printed on thin paper, was soon followed by a second and similar brochure. Published in Paris, apparently while Pallavicino was there and probably with his money, the two contained some of Manin's most important letters.[13] Through these folders they could achieve independence of editorial vagaries, and Manin suggested that three more sets of pamphlets be planned. This time he wanted all three pamphlets to bear the heading:

Partito Nazionale Italiano
Indipendenza   *Unificazione*

Their party would be promoted to capital letters and given a kind of corporeal form. These folders could then, Manin sug-

---

2 January 1857; Pallavicino to Manin, 28 December 1856, *ibid.*, 257, 262, 259; and Manin to La Farina, 3 March 1857, Franchi, *Epistolario di La Farina*, II, 34.

    There were, however, great complications, see Manin to Pallavicino, 10 February 1857, Maineri, *Manin e Pallavicino*, 281. M. Yvan, who asked Manin to procure a correspondent, apparently lacked authority from his editor; and Manin raged against Yvan for such thoughtlessness. The tirade, indeed, is so strong that Maineri omits it: Manin to Pallavicino, 11 April 1857, ms., MNRT. His tone suggests that La Farina had gone unpaid; Manin says his items did great good.

    The system worked so well that Pallavicino was ready and waiting with a correspondent for the *Courrier de Paris*: Pallavicino to Manin, 20 April 1857, Maineri, *Manin e Pallavicino*, 303. Manin, however, would not take the hint when Valerio asked for a cheap Paris correspondent for his paper, Pallavicino to Manin, 22 July 1856, *ibid.*, 138.

[12] References to sending copies appear, without prior explanation, in Manin to Pallavicino, 11 May and 6 June 1856, and Pallavicino to Manin, 8 June 1856, *ibid.*, 68, 69–70, 73.

[13] The first folder contained Manin's letter of 22 January 1856 to *Il Diritto* (which amplified his ideas and made a distinction between the *uomo politico* and *pensiero*) and that of 11 February 1856 in *Opinione* which asked that this be openly discussed. The second contained Manin's letter printed 15 September 1855 to *Il Diritto* (the Italian translation of the "If not, not" letter to the *Times* in which Manin made unification and independence the two central points of his program).

    Printed by Felix Maltest et Cie., copies of both may be found in the Bibliothèque Nationale, Paris, or the Biblioteca Civica, Turin. How many were printed is not known, although Salazaro alone was to get 200, and by June Manin was talking of a new edition: Manin to Pallavicino, 6 June 1856, Maineri, *Manin e Pallavicino*, 69–70, 79. (See Chapter Two, note 55.)

71

gested, be distributed to a paper's subscribers if its director preferred not to print their statements. Free of some unsympathetic editor's comments or deletions, Manin's short letters would gain a permanence newspapers could not give them. Taken together, under their party label, they would have the effect of that longer statement of doctrine Manin had never written.[14]

Their propaganda in this form achieved increasingly great importance in their minds. Manin's pamphlets were followed by reprints of Pallavicino's writings and by statements others had written. Ulloa was asked to contribute something, and Dragonetti's pleas for Papal abnegation added to what Manin came to call their "library" of nationalist writings. An article from the *North British Review*, one by Tofano against the Muratism of Bianchi-Giovini, and La Farina's contributions to the attacks on Swiss mercenaries soon followed. Manin also hoped to see writings of Gherardi and Valerio and his old "if not, not" appear under his banner.[15] But it was the association of other names with that banner that mattered most.

These publications themselves must have done a good deal to give the impression of the National Party as a large and thriving organization. They may even have helped to win official supporters with the tempting bribe of getting their works in print. They also tended, however, to becloud much of the Party's already imprecise program. Tofano's rather ineffective anti-Muratist statement was in line with Manin's earlier stand, but La Farina's plan for Piedmontese annexation of Sicily was not. In the two pamphlets offered by Dragonetti they suffered their greatest descent from intellectual respectability.[16] The first, A

[14] The three sets of pamphlets would contain his "Caro Valerio" letters of May 1856, letters he planned to write the *Daily News* (on non-payment of taxes in the south) and subsequent letters to be sent Valerio: Manin to Pallavicino, 13 and 17 June 1856; and Pallavicino to Manin, 14 October 1856, *ibid.*, 83–4, 94, 223.
[15] Ulloa complained that he was not a man of letters: Ulloa to Pallavicino, 5 July 1856, *ibid.*, 381; and Pallavicino to Ulloa, 19 August 1857, *Memorie di Pallavicino*, III, 417. Also Manin to Pallavicino, 19, 27 and 29 August, 21 October 1856, 11 February 1857, Maineri, *Manin e Pallavicino*, 170, 177, 189, 225, 282. Manin, a talented propagandist, was as concerned about presentation as content and worried about the quality of translations, letters to Pallavicino, 9 November 1855 and 16 February 1856, *ibid.*, 4–5, 55.
[16] For the background of these pamphlets, which were anonymous, see Manin to Pallavicino, 29 June, 6 July, 7 August 1856, *ibid.*, 113, 121, 156. They were hardly the memorials from Neapolitan and Papal exiles which Manin had wanted:

Sua Santità Pio IX, P.M., was an impassioned plea for the Pope to renounce his temporal power in his own interest; the second called on the Papacy to evacuate to Jerusalem, where its presence would unite both branches of the Church, convert the Jews and Arabs, and enable it to escape the tide of rationalism then sweeping over Europe. Only the clear fervor of its author kept the pamphlet from being good satire. If Marchese Dragonetti's efforts were not well received, these publications as a whole undoubtedly did aid the party.[17]

All in the same format, the first printings of these various pamphlets varied from 300 to 3,000 copies, with most editions nearer the latter figure.[18] They were distributed in a number of ways. The simplest, most obvious, and perhaps most effective way was to send them off to a long list of private acquaintances. Thus the King and each minister received Pallavicino's collected political writings as did his friends in Paris. Foresti's friends in Genoa were also sent copies. Manin sometimes used the same method, which had the advantage of requiring some sort of acknowledgment from those who received the pamphlets.[19] A

---

see Manin to Dragonetti, 28 February [1856], Marchese Guilio Dragonetti (ed.), *Spigolature del Carteggio letterario e politico del Marchese Luigi Dragonetti* (Florence, 1886), 321–22. Dragonetti's second pamphlet was based on an article by the Abbé Michon.

[17] Pallavicino to Manin, 19 and 22 September 1856, Maineri, *Manin e Pallavicino*, 196, 202–203. Mazzini did not miss the easy target Dragonetti offered, letter to Pallavicino, 31 October 1856, *Memorie di Pallavicino*, III, 734.

[18] At first only 300 copies were printed of Manin's letter on the Swiss mercenaries: Pallavicino to Manin, 18 January 1857, Maineri, *Manin e Pallavicino*, 268. Some 1,000 copies of his anti-Muratist statement were printed: Pallavicino to Manin, 13 November 1856, *ibid.*, 232. There were 1,500 copies made of his letter to the *Daily News*: Pallavicino to Manin, 15 July 1856, *ibid.*, 129. The second set of Manin's letters was printed in an edition of 2,500, the first in one of 3,000: Pallavicino to Manin, 21 June 1856, and Manin to Pallavicino, 17 June 1856, *ibid.*, 98–9, 93. In a rush of enthusiasm, 3,000 copies were also printed of Dragonetti's first effort: Pallavicino to Manin, 31 August 1856, *ibid.*, 182. (There were 3,000 and 2,500 copies printed of La Farina's anti-Muratist pamphlet and of Pallavicino's *Spielbergo e Gradisca*, respectively, Pallavicino to Manin, 3 September 1856 and 7 January 1857, *ibid.*, 185, 265.)

[19] Pallavicino to Manin, 19, 22, and 27 September 1856, 17 January 1857; Foresti to Pallavicino, 24 August 1856, *ibid.*, 197–98, 201–202, 208–209, 265, 359; Pallavicino to Gen. Enrico Cialdini, September 1856, *Memorie di Pallavicino*, III, 326.

Manin to Pallavicino, 27 January 1857, Maineri, *Manin e Pallavicino*, 273. See also Ulloa to Pallavicino, 29 September 1856, *ibid.*, 385; and Mamiani, 31 December 1856 and de Lasteyrie, 8 January 1857, to Pallavicino, *Memorie di Pallavicino*, III, 306, 365.

73

second technique was to send the folders to scores of newspapers; if they did not want to reprint a given letter, its handsome format might at least induce them to refer to its having been published. A few agreed to distribute the pamphlets to some of their subscribers.[20]

As every effort was made to give these pamphlets the widest distribution, friends were called upon to act as agents. While Pallavicino was taking the waters in Aix-les-Bains, his wife made arrangements for sending out their literature. Franceschi helped with these shipments, especially those for distribution in Tuscany and the Papal States, and La Farina also took an active part. Salazaro and Foresti served in Genoa; Pirondi sent forth their material from Marseilles, and Manin himself actively distributed pamphlets from Paris.[21] Getting these pamphlets across borders, past hesitant or hostile officials presented a problem. Pallavicino managed to get most of his shipments into France by sending them as packages in light wrappers. For a while bundles of pamphlets were sent from Turin through the private channels

[20] Pallavicino sent his fly sheet on the Italian Question (probably the single article of August 15 and not his full *scritti politici*) to all the newspapers of Piedmont and asked Manin to send it to some papers in Germany and Spain in addition to the *Times, Daily News, Economist, Siècle,* and *Estafette,* Pallavicino to Manin, 24 August 1856, Maineri, *Manin e Pallavicino,* 173.
The *Risorgimento, Tempo* (Casale), and *Corriere Mercantile* distributed the letter on the "theory of the dagger;" Pallavicino quotes his wife on this in his letter to Manin, 26 June 1856, Maineri, *Manin e Pallavicino,* 109. The *Movimento* (Genoa) distributed 100 copies of Manin's letter to the *Daily News,* and Salazaro also distributed 300 copies in Genoa, an important center for the discussion of southern affairs: Pallavicino to Manin, 22 July 1856, Maineri, *Manin e Pallavicino,* 138. Six Piedmontese papers distributed 1,500 copies of one set of Manin's letters (probably the *Altri scritti di Manin*). The *Gazzetta del Popolo* distributed 500 copies, *Opinione, Unione, Risorgimento, Tempo* (Casale) 200 each. The *Gazzetta dei Tribunali* agreed to include copies of the Party's literature in its shipments to Sardinia. Pallavicino to Manin, 26 July and 13 November 1856, Maineri, *Manin e Pallavicino,* 145, 234.
[21] Pallavicino to Manin, 17 July 1856, *ibid.,* 138; La Farina to Pallavicino, 24 August 1856, *Memorie di Pallavicino,* III, 338; and to Oddo, 8 September 1856, Franchi, *Epistolario di La Farina,* II, 20–7. C. A. Clericetti in Tunbridge Wells, Kent (and later in Brighton) and W. R. Greg in London also distributed a few. Foresti was expected to circulate some in the United States: Manin to Pallavicino, 19 August and 17 November 1856; and Pallavicino to Manin, 31 August and 27 September 1856, Maineri, *Manin e Pallavicino,* 170, 238, 182–83, 208. Salazaro adds that Casimiro De Lieto, whom he calls the "Nestor" of the exiles, worked with him: Salazaro, *Cenni sulla rivoluzione,* 17–18. Salazaro distributed large numbers of particular pamphlets in Genoa. (See above, note 20.) Foresti circulated their literature among his influential friends and in the University there, Foresti to Pallavicino, 24 August 1856, Maineri, *Manin e Pallavicino,* 360, and of 25 June 1856, ms., MNRT.

of the *Assicurazione Generale* to its agent in France, who then turned them over to Manin. This system eased border difficulties and cost the party nothing; but after a few months of being so used, the company backed out.[22]

Still, Manin found many people, especially from the Italian provinces, who had not even heard of his writings.[23] Pallavicino insisted that he was working hard and that Piedmont at least was flooded as, indeed, it must have been; the Marchese's several hundred electors and the National Guard of Turin received 1,300 copies of his writings. A great deal of their material was sent to Naples and Sicily where it was distributed through friends or left at café tables to be grabbed, it was believed, by eager citizens. Impressive numbers went into Tuscany and the Papal States.[24] In Sardinia the supply of their publications may well have exceeded demand; Manin's writings, at least, reached the

---

[22] Manin to Pallavicino, 29 June 1856, Maineri, *Manin e Pallavicino*, 111. The name of Léon Pincherle, the agent, is not in the printed text but in the ms. in MNRT. See also Manin to Pallavicino, 6 July 1856, Maineri, *Manin e Pallavicino*, 121. Degli Antoni had used this system, too. In September the Marchese found four of their packets sitting in the Turin office still unsent, Pallavicino to Manin, 6 September 1856, *ibid.*, 190.

[23] Manin to Pallavicino, 21 October 1856, *ibid.*, 225. He himself gave out hundreds of copies; his letters from September 1, 1856 to January 1857 are full of requests for more copies of their literature, *ibid.*, 183–275. Less than two weeks before this complaint, for example, he had asked for 400 to 500 copies of his letter on the fund for the hundred cannon, Manin to Pallavicino, 9 October, *ibid.*, 220.

[24] Luigi Cora did this bit of distribution in Turin: Pallavicino to Manin, 22 September, 1 and 29 October 1856, *ibid.*, 201–202, 212, 226. Pirondi seems not to have distributed the 3,000 copies throughout Italy he had said he would, but he must have sent out several hundred folders: Manin to Pallavicino, 17 January 1856, *ibid.*, 93. Pallavicino mentions 200 copies in his letter to Manin of 26 July and 300 in that of 31 August 1856, *ibid.*, 145, 182–83. Pirondi mentions another 30 in his letter to Manin, 24 October 1856, *ibid.*, 404. See also Pallavicino to Manin, 7 August and 13 November 1856, *ibid.*, 156, 232.

From Genoa, Salazaro seems to have been the principal agent for shipments to the south: 300 copies are mentioned in the letter of Pallavicino to Manin, 22 July; 100 in that of 26 July; 400 in that of 7 August; 300 in that of 24 August; and 100 in that of 7 December 1856, *ibid.*, 138, 145, 156, 173, 247; 80 in Foresti to Pallavicino, 15 January 1857, ms., MNRT. See also Pallavicino to Manin, 29 June, 8 and 26 October, 13 November 1856; and Manin to Pallavicino, 30 July 1856, Maineri, *Manin e Pallavicino*, 109, 215–16, 226, 232, 151.

Salazaro, *Cenni sulla rivoluzione*, 17–18, 17n, recalls "thousands" being sent into central Italy and gives the names of four ship captains who carried their material to the south. Written after these events, which are seen through the haze of final triumph, this account is, of course, liable to inaccuracies. Cf., however, Pallavicino to Salazaro, 17 September 1856, *Memorie di Pallavicino*, III, 317; and Pallavicino to Manin, 29 March 1857, Maineri, *Manin e Pallavicino*, 287.

Marches, where they were recirculated in altered, local versions.[25]

Thus from Turin, which had been saturated, their writings flowed through Piedmont, circulated in France, and trickled into the other Italian provinces, into Switzerland and Belgium, into England, the United States, even to Algiers and Malta.[26] Most of such propaganda may have quickly found a wastebasket; but at a time when those who counted politically were few, a broader awareness of, some sympathy for, a few conversions to their movement were worth a great deal. For these pamphlets were not only propaganda for a doctrine but advertisement for a party; and advertisements need not be closely read to have effect. Having decided to depend on propaganda, Pallavicino and Manin had not done it badly. They had made their ideas widely known; they had established a movement and made it into a party. It was no small accomplishment to have made the words *Partito Nazionale Italiano* bring to mind their writings, the pleadings and the hopes of Daniele Manin and Giorgio Pallavicino.

Finally, in 1857, the Party did in effect acquire a journal. La Farina's *Il Piccolo Corriere d'Italia*, which had seemed to Pallavicino to be the only paper on which they could really depend, joined wholeheartedly in the campaign against the Swiss mercenaries. Manin had already pronounced the paper "very well done"; [27] and as La Farina entered more fully into their circle, he brought his paper with him. The very conception of the paper fitted well with the ideas of Manin and Pallavicino. Dedicated to discussion of one overriding issue, the *Piccolo Corriere* made no pretense of covering affairs unrelated to the problem of unification. It was presented primarily as a digest of other papers, and in its selection from them it gave a picture (like that Manin

[25] On Sardinia see Pallavicino to Manin, 26 June and 13 November 1856, *ibid.*, 109, 234. The statement concerning the Marches is based on such strange documents as that printed in Alessandro Alessandrini, *I fatti politici delle Marche* (Macerata, 1910), II, 1–11, which is a hodgepodge of those letters of Manin's collected in his first two PNI pamphlets but here treated as one letter though still under the PNI label. Similar indications that the PNI writings were known in the Marches, but not always clearly identified, can be found throughout this volume and in that of Zampetti-Biocca, *La Società Nazionale nella Marca*, *passim*.

[26] Manin to Pallavicino, 17 November 1856, Maineri, *Manin e Pallavicino*, 239.

[27] Pallavicino to Manin, 27 September 1856, *ibid.*, 208; and Manin to Pallavicino, 19 September, *ibid.*, 194. *Piccolo Corriere*, 11 and 25 January 1857.

had tried to paint) of Italians united in the national cause. In this case the technique had the further advantage of freeing La Farina from full responsibility for the invective he quoted.[28] Like the National Party's propaganda, the paper was aimed particularly at nationalists beyond the borders of Piedmont. The strong sentiments for union within Piedmont and the affection for Piedmont in other states could, however, be more effectively conveyed as news in the *Piccolo Corriere* than by the bald statements of a party pamphlet. It did not take Pallavicino long to see in that paper one of the best means of reaching into the provinces of Italy.[29]

The acquisition of a newspaper, like the National Party's other successes, tended to diminish Manin's role as the Party's director. The movement's adherents now extended beyond Manin's personal friends; few men could be expected to feel the loyalty of a Pallavicino. The effort to win and keep the support of men influential in their own right required that they be consulted, and thus Manin found himself discussing his plans for the Party with a growing circle of men.[30] At times even sharp criticisms had to be simply ignored, though not all those who accepted Manin's program tried to influence his subsequent statements.[31] Sometimes a new "convert" was sufficiently dis-

[28] He attempted to mollify Fabrizi with this excuse: La Farina to Fabrizi, 24 May 1856, and n.d. [July 1856] [Palamenghi-Crispi], "L'Evoluzione alla Monarchia," *Risorgimento Italiano*, VII, 245–46, 248–49. The paper's purpose is discussed in the *Piccolo Corriere*, 8 February 1857, and in La Farina to Signora Torti, 27 August 1856, Franchi, *Epistolario di La Farina*, II, 20. It was claimed in nearly all issues that the paper reached into every corner of Italy, a claim repeated in the supplement to *Bollettino Settimanale* No. 42 of *La Discussione*, 23 October 1863.

[29] Pallavicino to Manin, 18 January 1857, Maineri, *Manin e Pallavicino*, 269.

[30] Manin was, of course, anxious to find "new auxiliaries, new apostles of our faith": Manin to Pallavicino 3 and 9 October, 17 November 1856, *ibid.*, 213, 222, 239. They exchanged many reports on their successes in this regard, Pallavicino to Manin, 22 September, 2 and 14 October 1856, *ibid.*, 207, 217, 222. Manin asked the advice of Valerio, Pier Carlo Boggio, and Govean (all, significantly, the editors of important papers), of Depretis, Foresti, and La Farina. The opinion of the last two was given particular weight. In Paris Manin consulted Dragonetti, Ulloa, and even Montanelli when he could: Manin to Pallavicino, 3, 18, and 29 July and 2 August 1856; 14 April 1857, *ibid.*, 118, 134, 148, 151, 295–96. La Farina was not always delighted to be so implicated, Pallavicino to Manin, 24 July 1856, *ibid.*, 140–41.

[31] Manin at one point told Pallavicino to ignore the *pusillanimi* objections of La Farina and Franceschi to the Marchese's strong reply to Mazzini: Pallavicino to Manin, 22 September and 22 October 1856, and Manin to Pallavicino, 9

liked to be no threat; but when, as in the case of La Farina, he was said to speak for "his political friends" (and when Rattazzi, Cavour, Valerio and an "infinity [of] others" were among these friends) then his influence was necessarily felt.[32] More than anything else, it was La Farina's accession to Party councils which most dimmed Manin's authority. Although the Sicilian was becoming closely associated with the National Party and particularly with Pallavicino, he carefully maintained his independence. He did not submit his writings for Manin's imprimatur; yet his prestige was such that the Party happily put its label at the head of his pamphlet.[33]

Pallavicino, too, acted with increasing independence of Manin. This was in part inevitable. Nearly all the money for the Party's publications came from the Marchese's pocket. As the sole judge

October 1856, *ibid.*, 202, 219, 222. Maineri omits the proper names, in the ms. of Manin's letter in MNRT.

Garibaldi took no part in their debates on policy; Degli Antoni, now somewhat forgiven for past harassments, was considered a well-meaning political incompetent. Valerio, it was felt, could be brought into line with sufficient pressure, and Manin continued to send him warm greetings and to declare his dependence on him (see postscript of Manin to Pallavicino, 31 December 1856, omitted in Maineri, ms., MNRT). Also Pallavicino to Manin, 29 June, 19 and 22 July 1856, Maineri, *Manin e Pallavicino*, 113, 134–37, 138. Foresti, who held views close to Manin's, remained personally loyal, Manin to Pallavicino, 18 July and 17 November 1856, and Foresti to Pallavicino, 26 July 1856, *ibid.*, 134, 239, 355.

[32] Ulloa, for example, had considered La Masa a discredited *"cagliostro"* who could do no good for their cause: Ulloa to Pallavicino, 7 January 1856, *ibid.*, 377. The name, only partially printed here, is apparent in Pallavicino to Manin, 1 January 1856, *ibid.*, and is probably that to which Ulloa refers, ms., MNRT. Pallavicino to Manin (noting La Farina's opposition to Manin's program for non-payment of taxes), 10 August 1856, and Manin to Pallavicino, 18 August 1856, Maineri, *Manin e Pallavicino*, 158, 167.

[33] For La Farina's relationship with Pallavicino, see the Marchese to Manin, 10 and 17 July, 3 September, 24 and 28 December 1856, *ibid.*, 124, 131, 185, 258, 259; and La Farina to Pallavicino, 24 August 1856, and 12 July 1857, *ibid.*, 338, 340.

La Farina's pamphlet calling for the union of Sicily and Piedmont was written without consulting the Party's leaders, and Manin feared it would be seen as a concession to Muratist strength. La Farina's second pamphlet on the subject, *Sicilia e Piemonte, lettera ad un amico in Sicilia* (Turin, n.d.), nevertheless bore the PNI label. See Manin to Pallavicino, 17 November 1856, and Pallavicino to Manin, 2 December 1856 and 7 January 1857, Maineri, *Manin e Pallavicino*, 237, 244, 256. According to the *Piccolo Corriere*, 12 April 1857, the pamphlet was given wide clandestine circulation, which would suggest La Farina was already exploiting his Italian contacts. Omodeo, *Cavour*, II, 158, notes that La Farina's idea was a revival of the democratic program of 1849 for the assimilation of exiles—a view that fits well with La Farina's later ideas and activity.

of what he could afford, he was in fact deciding what should be published.[34] Pallavicino's independence reflected, too, his sense of the Party's success and his response to the environment of Piedmont, from which Manin was so far removed. He suddenly informed Manin that he was publishing anonymously a pamphlet of his own which, should Manin later approve it, could be reprinted under the PNI heading. It called simply for revolution in the name of Victor Emmanuel without the intermediary step of a national assembly, a democratic compromise to which Manin remained attached. Pallavicino explained that he had talked with men of importance in Piedmont (including ministers) and that no one wanted anything to do with a national assembly. Loyally, Manin professed to find the pamphlet excellent except for that one point, and he remained sure that it would do great good. For the time being, Manin added, his opinion would remain "independent." It was an important reversal of roles. Pallavicino's pamphlet soon appeared as one of the statements of the *Partito Nazionale Italiano*; the issue which had been so much discussed four years before was being resolved in favor of Pallavicino's original stand.[35]

The Marchese was ready to push on to new triumphs. They should "organize at Turin our wasted party, independently of the will of the Sardinian ministers." [36] You are, Pallavicino wrote

[34] Pallavicino refused to publish Gherardi's article, apparently because of its style, and he delayed one of Dragonetti's as inopportune: Pallavicino to Manin, 3 September, 14 October, 2 November 1856; Manin to Pallavicino, 27 August 1856, Maineri, *Manin e Pallavicino*, 184–85, 223, 230, 177.

The payments to Canuti had also come from Pallavicino, although he had hoped Canuti might earn the money as correspondent of *Il Diritto*. He sent 300 francs through a Mme. Grouchy, and Manin asked that he write Canuti directly: Manin to Pallavicino, 5 and 27 August, and Pallavicino to Manin, 11 August 1856, Maineri, *Manin e Pallavicino*, 152–53, 176, 161. Manin's receipt indicates the money was actually sent by the Marchesa, dated 23 August 1856, in the Bibliothèque Nationale, Paris, ms. 9625/84. She was concerned that too much was spent on patriotic causes (half of the 50,000 francs they had after expenses, she said), but she herself sent Manin a check for 2,000 francs, ms. MCV, bxxxi/455. The letter, dated 12 October 1856, is unidentified, but the signature as "*implacabile nemica*," Manin's nickname for the Marchesa Pallavicino, leaves little doubt. Cf. Pallavicino to Manin, 18 January 1857, Maineri, *Manin e Pallavicino*, 269.

[35] Pallavicino to Manin, 7 and 9 August 1856, and Manin to Pallavicino, 12, 19, 27 August 1856, *ibid.*, 156–57, 162, 169, 176–77. Foresti was also bothered by this question, see his letter to Pallavicino, 24 August 1856, *ibid.*, 359.

[36] Pallavicino to Garibaldi, 23 May 1856, *Memorie di Pallavicino*, III, 225; Pallavicino to Tommaséo, 20 June 1856, *ibid.*, 252; and to Manin, 10 July and

Manin, "captain of a large army, but do not yet know your soldiers. . . ." He had a plan. They should print about one hundred copies of a simple declaration of their political faith: independence above all, unification under the King of Sardinia (or without him if he did not do his part). The names of Manin and Pallavicino would be printed at the bottom, and the statement would then be circulated among the emigrants for their signatures. Pallavicino had made his proposal at the peak of his irritation with Cavour; he wanted the Party to make its "forces" known. But Manin was still looking toward that spontaneous unanimity which would make parties unnecessary. In his mind their ideas themselves had not yet been widely enough circulated and Mazzinians and Muratists remained a threat. Publishing names would establish the limits of their party as well as the extent of its success.

Pallavicino had to put aside his dream of meeting Cavour "armed" with their list of supporters, able to demand "the frank execution of the national program," but he kept in mind the stronger position an organized party would give them.[37] When, early in 1857, La Farina agreed with Pallavicino, Manin was at last overruled. They would publish a credo and, by shunning equivocation, gain greater authority. It was not even necessary to win many signatures for the National Party provided those they got came from men of influence. La Farina's arguments were strikingly different from those of Manin or Pallavicino.

Italians, he argued, were used to conspiring "with the forms and hierarchies of the Secret Societies." Secret committees formerly in touch with Mazzini were "now in relation with us." The argument for organizing the National Party was thus put on a new basis. "I have in hand," La Farina boasted, "all this correspondence, but I do not doubt at all that my words would acquire greater authority when I could speak not in my name only but in the name of a committee." He knew of the prestige that comes from organization and from a correspondence conducted with "official regularity" on printed stationery. He was

26 July 1856, Maineri, *Manin e Pallavicino*, 125, 144–45. Ulloa to Pallavicino, 11 September and 22 June 1856, *ibid.*, 383, 379–80.
    [37] Pallavicino to Manin, 23 September and 1 October 1856; 21 January 1857, *ibid.*, 204–205, 211–12, 271–72; Manin to Pallavicino, 27 September 1856 and 20 January 1857, *ibid.*, 205–207, 274.

convinced that "the revolution is not in those people who read, who write, and who argue politics." Rather, it depended on a class without sufficient instruction "to be able to think for itself." That class "needs a collective which thinks for it and imposes its thoughts on it." La Farina was asking the National Party to join him. He did so because of the nature of the men they must lead, because "the prestige of authority, of organization, of force, is worth much more for them than a good reason. . . ." [38]

The agitation La Farina proposed was not what Manin had wanted; the revolution La Farina expected was not the one Pallavicino waited for. Yet there was in this a realistic note that made sense. As one professional to another, Manin congratulated La Farina on the political experience and perception reflected in his proposal. Still, Manin objected to a "directorial committee" to "give impulse to action." He did not feel up to directing conspiracies; it would be especially awkward from Paris; he was not sure they really agreed on a plan of action. He must have sensed, however, that La Farina would not insist that such activity be directed by Manin or from Paris. Manin quickly added that he was not refusing, just hesitating.

He, who had objected to publishing a list of their adherents, was now asked to support illegal action, to risk the divisions, the failures, the animosities of a half-secret party. The hero of Venice bowed out gracefully. Afraid that some of La Farina's proposals did in fact conflict with his own writings, he sent his pamphlets to La Farina with the hope that any new declaration would not contradict his published views—views which, he modestly added, had been "tacitly accepted by the national party." If they still felt it "necessary and urgent" that such a declaration be issued and signed, they might go ahead; he could sign it later. [39]

As soon as his health permitted, Pallavicino wrote Manin

[38] Pallavicino to Manin, 26 January 1857, *ibid.*, 50 (the date given here, 1856, is clearly an error); and 4 February 1857, *ibid.*, 279. La Farina to Pallavicino, n.d., *Memorie di Pallavicino*, III, 376n–77n; for more of his view of "agitation" see his letter to Oddo, 8 September 1856, Franchi, *Epistolario di La Farina*, II, 21.
[39] Manin to Pallavicino, 10 February 1857, Maineri, *Manin e Pallavicino*, 280–81; and to Pallavicino's daughter, 14 March 1857, *ibid.*, 619. Pallavicino to Manin, 17 February 1857, *ibid.*, 284; and Manin to La Farina, 3 March 1857, Franchi, *Epistolario di La Farina*, II, 34–5.

agreeing to "what you say." The *Credo* would be published; Manin could sign it when he wished.[40] Thus while Manin sought signatures for his letter of gratitude to M. de la Forge for having defended Italian character against George Sand, Pallavicino sent off the Party's *programma* to Genoa, where Foresti was to collect the signatures of their political friends. Their success would be largely determined in Genoa, for located there were the men of action who had turned from Mazzini but not yet to the King.[41] The names of such men would impress the Government, hurt Mazzini, and add to their Party's prestige.

The *programma* did not commit its signer to a great deal.[42] It said that the *Partito Nazionale Italiano*, which had already collected "numerous and notable adherents in all the provinces of Italy," subordinated every issue of political form and local interest to the "great principle" of independence and unity. It supported the House of Savoy "so long as" the House of Savoy was for Italy "in all the extension of the reasonable and possible." It accepted any ministry that favored Italy (and kept itself out

[40] Manin had favored a conference among the PNI's supporters, but this fell through: Pallavicino to Manin, 23 March 1857, Maineri, *Manin e Pallavicino*, 285. In this same letter Pallavicino informed Manin that *"unificazione"* rather than *"unità"* would be part of their slogan; earlier in September the Marchese had resisted any change from the word Manin had adopted in 1855 before he had come to prefer *unificazione*: Pallavicino to Manin, 10 September 1856, *ibid.*, 192. Perhaps La Farina had favored the change in September, and Pallavicino's statement that *"unificazione"* was being used "in agreement with La Farina" may have meant to show the latter's faithfulness to Manin's concepts. In any case, it was probably this discussion which led to the impression that La Farina was the one who had hit on that fortuitously ambiguous word. See Gaspare Finale, "I partiti politici in Romagna," in Leone Carpi (ed.), *Il Risorgimento Italiano*, IV (Milan, 1888), 301.

Historians traditionally see the importance of the word in its implied acceptance of successive annexations as a means toward unity. See Omodeo, *Cavour*, II, 168. It is true that when Tofano asked if *"unificazione"* meant that small steps toward unity were to be accepted, La Farina replied that any such step was to be welcomed: La Farina to Pallavicino, 19 August 1857, ms., MNRT. This passage is omitted from the letter in *Memorie di Pallavicino*, III, 148. Pallavicino, however, never accepted a policy of piecemeal Piedmontese annexation; and it is unlikely that such subtle foresight was behind the slogan. Manin chose the word to avoid debate on federation versus central union.

[41] The signatures of Garibaldi and Medici in particular were hoped for: Pallavicino to Foresti, 22 March 1857, Maioli, "Il Fondatore," *Rassegna Storica*, XV, 24; and to Manin, 29 March, Maineri, *Manin e Pallavicino*, 287.

[42] It was printed on a single sheet of paper over the name of Pallavicino and ended with the word *"Italia"* and a blank for the date and signature. A copy is in ISR, busta 593, n. 52. The *programma* was later reprinted in several party publications.

of the domestic politics of Piedmont). It believed popular action necessary to Italy's unification. Finally, the *programma* declared that the National Party did not hold itself the "infallible depository of the truth" and was neither intolerant nor exclusive.

Such a party dare not be otherwise, Foresti felt; the reaction from Genoa was not encouraging. He suggested this might not be the time to publish their statement.[43] But under Pallavicino's prodding, Foresti loyally tried again to find them supporters. With skillful timing, he presented the program to a group of emigrants who were drinking a toast to the martyrs of the Spielberg—and found them willing to support Piedmont once she challenged Austria but unwilling to declare themselves in advance or on paper. They wanted to be "free to act with the first party that moves." Foresti sent the *programma* back—without a signature.[44]

He could not put pressure on Cavour, Pallavicino complained, when he was "abandoned by my political friends." Writing directly to Garibaldi, the Marchese protested this refusal to join the PNI from those who claimed they agreed with it. After all, he argued, Manin's "if not, not" kept them free. When Manin asked how their efforts were going, Pallavicino had to confess that the project had "completely failed." Manin suggested they again devote themselves to the "propagation of the faith, the erection of pulpits and the multiplication of apostles." [45]

Then Garibaldi answered, and the project was saved. The good-hearted General did not know that he was the third man to join the Party; but even aside from his penchant for supporting worthy causes, his action was not surprising. More than a

---

[43] Foresti wrote that Garibaldi was at Caprera and that Medici and Amari were disinclined to sign, Foresti to Pallavicino, 24 March 1857, ms., MNRT.

[44] Pallavicino to Foresti, 27 March 1857, Maioli, "Il Fondatore," *Rassegna Storica*, xv, 26. Foresti also wanted them to make Cavour offer some guarantee of his policy, but he reacted against the intransigence of the Genoese patriots, Foresti to Pallavicino, 31 March and 12 April 1857, Maineri, *Manin e Pallavicino*, 367–68, 369–70.

[45] Pallavicino to Foresti, 7 April 1857, *Memorie di Pallavicino*, iii, 385. Pallavicino quotes his arguments to Garibaldi in his letter to Manin, 17 April 1857, Maineri, *Manin e Pallavicino*, 301–302. It is interesting that he also adopted La Farina's argument about the need for being visible to be strong among the "multitudes": Manin to Pallavicino, 11 and 23 April; and Pallavicino to Manin, 17 April and 5 May 1857, *ibid.*, 295, 305–306, 300, 309–10. Foresti assumed Pallavicino had had better luck, letter to Pallavicino, 12 April 1857, *ibid.*, 370.

year before, he had been clear in his support of Manin.⁴⁶ He had come to look toward Piedmont (and her army) as "elements of initiative and of success," and an interview with Cavour had impressed him with the Prime Minister's nationalist intent. Garibaldi, with characteristic exuberance, was ready to commit himself to more than Manin could.⁴⁷ Indeed, the Party's previous failure to use his prestige effectively suggests the validity of Pallavicino's argument for his *programma*; in the next two years Garibaldi's name proved one of the Party's greatest strengths.⁴⁸

As soon as he received Garibaldi's letter, Pallavicino returned to the project whose failure he had conceded. He asked that Manin and Ulloa sign the *programma*, envisioning youth won to their banner, Muratists defeated, the Government prevented from abandoning revolutionaries. Once the Party was formed, he promised, Manin could lead them to battle in accordance with his plan; but Manin, sick and discouraged, seemed unable to make up his mind. Such uncertainty, the lieutenant told his leader, was "paralyzing our action." ⁴⁹ Pallavicino insisted they were recruiting a general staff, not an army, but he clearly wanted the signature of any man of moderate note. He wrote some fifty or sixty letters; La Farina, Foresti, and Ulloa recruited too; the Party's membership form received wider circulation.⁵⁰

⁴⁶ Garibaldi to Pallavicino, 20 May 1857, *Memorie di Pallavicino*, III, 389. In Garibaldi to La Cecilia, 27 January 1856, ms., ISR, busta 547, n. 88, Garibaldi wrote, "*Dunque sono con lui* [Manin] *e con voi*," although he seemed to have in mind some kind of direct action. He had also offered his full support to Pallavicino, Pallavicino to Garibaldi, 23 May and Garibaldi to Pallavicino, 5 July 1856, *Memorie di Pallavicino*, III, 269.
⁴⁷ Garibaldi to Mario in Mario, *Garibaldi*, I, 149; Foresti to Pallavicino, 15 August 1856, Maineri, *Manin e Pallavicino*, 357. Salazaro attributes great importance to a conversation of the General's with Pallavicino, but errors in chronology cast doubt on the whole episode: Salazaro, *Cenni sulla rivoluzione*, 29. Curatolo, *Mazzini e Garibaldi*, 162, contrasts Garibaldi's adherence "*senza condizione di sorta*" to Manin's conditional acceptance of Piedmont.
⁴⁸ The importance of having Garibaldi's support had been recognized: Manin to Pallavicino, 22 July 1856; and Ulloa to Pallavicino, 7 January 1856, Maineri, *Manin e Pallavicino*, 138, 378. Garibaldi's name was particularly influential in the Romagna. See Minghetti, *Ricordi*, III, 125; Masi, "Camillo Casarini," *Fra libri e ricordi*, 103.
⁴⁹ Manin feared that some of the resistance they had met was directed at him personally: Pallavicino to Manin, 27 May and 19 June 1857; and Manin to Pallavicino, 23 April and 28 May 1857, Maineri, *Manin e Pallavicino*, 312–13, 314, 306, 313.
⁵⁰ Pallavicino to Foresti, 20 July 1857, Maioli, "Il Fondatore," *Rassegna Storica*,

The response was still not encouraging. Ulloa reported that emigrants in Paris had become skeptical and that there was a general reluctance to commit oneself to any party.[51] Foresti found the men of Genoa willing to be led in action but not in signing. Medici proved too consistent a democrat to follow Garibaldi's example; for he could not think with pleasure of an Italy formed by the force of one province and the policy of a few men. Nor could he accept their omission of "national sovereignty," the will of the people, as the determinant of disputed issues.[52] Cosenz seemed to agree with them but was unwilling to declare his faith in Piedmont and, Pallavicino thought, thus antagonize his Mazzinian friends.[53] Tommaséo had said that the men who form societies to unite Italians deserve praise and gratitude, but he demanded clearer evidence that Piedmont had the force and Cavour the will to effect that unity before he would sign. Montanelli may have read "with pleasure" the new organization's proposals, but he did not join.[54] For the most part, La Farina and Pallavicino had to content themselves with the signatures of closer friends.[55] Yet these were worth something, and, added to Garibaldi's signature it was a great deal. If their party had more sympathizers than members, it had relatively few declared enemies.

In the efforts at organization which followed, La Farina played his part so prominently that Pallavicino's friends had to be reassured. The Party's efforts, Pallavicino insisted, were as much

xv, 32; to Ulloa, 16 July, 10, 17 and 29 August 1857, Memorie di Pallavicino, III, 398, 410, 417, 423; to La Farina, 25 August 1857, ibid., 422; to Tommaséo, August 1857, ibid., 422; to Giordano, 21 August 1857, ibid., 418. Also Foresti to Pallavicino, 10 June 1857, ms., MNRT, and 12 August 1857, Maineri, Manin e Pallavicino, 375; and La Farina to Pallavicino, 12 and 20 July 1857, ibid., 341, 343. The extent of this circulation is probably exaggerated in Luigi Zini, Storia d'Italia dal 1850 al 1866, I¹ (Milan, 1866), 838–39.

[51] Ulloa to Pallavicino, 21 July and 17 August 1857, Maineri, Manin e Pallavicino, 387, 388.

[52] Some Neapolitan emigrants were at least interested in establishing contact with the party, Foresti to Pallavicino, 12 August 1857, Memorie di Pallavicino, III, 408–409.

[53] Pallavicino to La Farina, 1 September 1857, ibid., 423.

[54] Tommaséo, Secondo Esilo, II, 127; Tommaséo to Pallavicino, 30 August 1857, Giovanni Sforza, "Niccolò Tommaséo e la Società Nazionale Italiana," Il Risorgimento Italiano, I (1908), 505–507. Montanelli to Pallavicino, 27 December 1857, Memorie di Pallavicino, III, 437.

[55] La Farina to Pallavicino, 20 July 1857, Maineri, Manin e Pallavicino, 343; and Pallavicino to Giordano, 21 August 1857, Memorie di Pallavicino, III, 418.

his and Manin's as La Farina's.[56] When La Farina wrote a preface to Pallavicino's *programma*, a new sense of authority was already apparent. Members of the National Party now contracted to pay dues of 50 *centesimi* a month (toward printing costs) and bore the "moral obligation" to propagate the Party's principles and publications. With corporate militance the Party would unite the efforts of "the good [men] which are lost and sterilized in isolation. . . ." Mazzini would be met on ground more like his own.

La Farina also suggested that their Party change its name to *Associazione Nazionale Italiana* so there might be no confusion with the Mazzinians, who often referred to themselves as the national party. He was thinking, La Farina said, in terms of an association comparable to the British Anti-Corn Law League. Manin had thought of his party in the vaguer sense of a growing consensus, but La Farina envisioned a directoral committee and various subcommittees, including clandestine ones outside Piedmont. Pallavicino, who accepted the change willingly, soon began referring to the *Associazione Nazionale*, refusing to discuss again matters already decided by "the directoral committee." The change that had taken place was concisely reflected in a postscript. Sign your *schede*, Pallavicino instructed Manin, and send it to La Farina.[57]

With La Farina's ascendancy, the movement's attitude toward the Government of Piedmont was altered. La Farina's declaration noted that the Party was possible because of the freedom Piedmontese law allowed. Quick to hint that their

---

[56] Foresti wrote warning of La Farina's unpopularity: Foresti to Pallavicino, 27 August 1857, Maineri, *Manin e Pallavicino*, 375. Pallavicino's trust of La Farina shows in his instruction to ". . . do as you said; we are completely agreed": Pallavicino to La Farina, 9 July 1857, *Memorie di Pallavicino*, III, 398. It was on the basis of such a relationship that the Marchese naïvely declared that La Farina does nothing "without my consent": Pallavicino to Ulloa, 29 August 1857, *ibid.*, 423. In this letter of praise La Farina was first called the "*anima*" of the party, a judgment raised to a cliché by subsequent historians. *La Discussione*, supplement to *Bollettino Settemanale* No. 42 (23 October 1863) printed a letter from Pallavicino to La Farina, 12 September 1857, asking who was on their directoral committee and if their friends could be assured that the Marchese shared with La Farina the responsibility for their publications.

[57] La Farina to Pallavicino, 5 and 12 July 1857, Maineri, *Manin e Pallavicino*, 339–40, 340–43; Pallavicino to Foresti, 28 July 1857, Maioli, "Il Fondatore," *Rassegna Storica*, IV, 32; to Ulloa, 16 July 1857, *Memorie di Pallavicino*, III, 400; to La Farina, 17 August 1857, *ibid.*, 416; to Tofano, 22 August 1857, *ibid.*, 419. Pallavicino to Manin, 10 August 1857, ms., MCV, bxxvi/459.

very existence was evidence of the Government's sympathy, he felt that a general awareness of such sympathy would have great effect. He informed Pallavicino that the Government had seen his declaration and offered no objection; even the Marchese admitted that was significant. In return he thought the National Party should state that it favored the House of Savoy not "so long as" but "because it has faith that" the House of Savoy is for Italy. He reported that this was suggested by "our friends"; they, too, were now close to La Farina and relatively out of touch with Pallavicino.[58] He referred to the coming elections in terms which implied some covert understanding with the Government, and he put rather unsubtle pressure on the Marchese, warning that some said Pallavicino "almost always" voted against the Government.[59]

La Farina similarly took charge of forming a directoral committee of the Association, and he reported on that at a "meeting of a good number of friends." All wanted Pallavicino to serve as treasurer. You have, he pleaded, done much for Italy; do this much more "at least for the first period of the Association." That they sought his prestige not his judgment was made clear; one Le Piane would do most of the real work in his name.[60] The

[58] Maineri, *Manin e Pallavicino*, 342; La Farina to Pallavicino, 23 August 1857, *ibid.*, 347. La Farina to Pallavicino, 20 July and 1 August 1857 (Tofano, Imbriani, Nicola Le Piane, Clerici were the friends named), *ibid.*, 343, 345. Pallavicino to La Farina, 26 July 1857, *Memorie di Pallavicino*, III, 405; the suggestion ended in compromise, La Farina to Pallavicino, n.d., No. 24, ms., MNRT.

[59] La Farina reported that Cavour feared Pallavicino might be defeated in Turin and wanted him to run in Genoa: La Farina to Pallavicino, 20 July 1857, Maineri, *Manin e Pallavicino*, 343–44. By the change, Cavour could probably have gained a stronger supporter in Turin and lost a surer opponent in Genoa. La Farina also hinted that the Marchese's opposition to the government was making him unpopular (except with the forgiving Prime Minister). At the same time La Farina seemed to agree with Pallavicino's criticisms of the Government and to be willing to present them to the ministry, La Farina to Pallavicino, 16 October 1858, ms., MNRT.

La Farina's most effective support of the Government was often in his apparently objective reports to friends, as when he assured Ulloa that the ministry was doing its best to make up for its harsh treatment of some exiles in Piedmont or when he sent word to the young Manin that the suggestion for a statue of his father in the public gardens had come from Cavour: La Farina to Ulloa, 18 October 1857, Doria, *Ulloa*, 342–43. Even his friends sensed a change in the tone of the *Piccolo Corriere*, La Farina to Natoli, 11 and 26 July 1857, Biundi, *La Farina*, I, 528, 535–36.

[60] In July La Farina had suggested Le Piane for secretary: La Farina to Pallavicino, 12 July 1857, Maineri, *Manin e Pallavicino*, 341, 343; and of 1 August 1857, ms., MNRT.

"meeting of friends" was, of course, a meeting of directors; they were acting without the Marchese. Ill and absent from Turin, Pallavicino had allowed the leadership of the National Party to slip from his hands. Either too conscientious to take a post he would not fill or too proud to accept so subordinate a title, Pallavicino must have refused, for when La Farina's declaration was finally published, it named Le Piane treasurer. And where, in the draft sent to Pallavicino it had been signed "for the management, the secretary," the printed form precisely put it, "for the Committee, Giuseppe La Farina." He would always in the public mind be the Association's primary figure.

Daniele Manin lived long enough to sign the membership blank of the organization he had both fathered and opposed. He died in time (September 22) not to see the National Society develop most of the strengths and weaknesses of the sects he had hoped to make obsolete. Poor, lonely, often despondent, he had in exile earned still another chapter in the history of the Risorgimento. A devout liberal, Manin came closer than do most such men to building political success on his faith in man's good nature and on his belief in the efficacy of a printed mixture of logic and utopia for creating those unspectacular civic virtues which he himself epitomized.

In its printed version La Farina's declaration of August 1, 1857, had referred to the "Society founded by us"; and by the end of the month, it had officially become the *Società Nazionale Italiana*. Thus Manin's movement to unite all who desired Italy's unification became La Farina's political Society. If it failed to attract so many of those authoritative names as Pallavicino had anticipated, it set a pattern for its future activity in quickly organizing around men of lesser fame but equal fervor. La Farina's *Piccolo Corriere d'Italia* became its official organ; the National Society was founded.[61]

Manin's signature on a membership blank had given the National Society the belated blessing of its spiritual father. Serious organization was underway, and by the end of August between twenty and fifty men had signed the Society's forms.[62]

[61] Biundi, *La Farina*, I, 363–64. The *Piccolo Corriere* became the official paper of the Society on August 1 also.
[62] Ulloa, Livio Zambeccari, Bianchi-Giovini, Tommasi, Carrano, and Col. Oliva are listed as having returned signed forms: La Farina to Pallavicino, 19 August

La Farina was always willing to exaggerate the extent of his successes, but the Austrian agent who reported that the Sicilian had not won a single signature was guilty on his side of greater optimism than La Farina on his.[63] It was even something of a tribute to Manin's years of propaganda and to La Farina's organizational skill for the Society already to have earned a mention by the Austrian police. When on Sunday, December 27, 1857, the Society's "council of promoters" met in Pallavicino's Turin home, La Farina, Tofano, Zambeccari, Tommasi, Bianchi-Giovini were among those present.

For a meeting in the capital of Piedmont, and one held just as the deputies were returning for the opening of the Chamber, it was not a very impressive turnout. They listened to a report, undoubtedly by La Farina, on the "results obtained" during the previous year, unanimously approved it and proceeded to the election of officers. There could not have been much in that report on which to disagree, but the belief that the National Society was already established seems to have been stoutly maintained.[64] This time Pallavicino was elected president, Cora made

1857, ms., MNRT. Buscalioni later listed eleven men as having signed by August 17; but since the list was part of a polemic meant to establish the minor part played by Manin and Pallavicino in the Society, it may not have been complete: supplement to *Bollettino Settimanale* No. 42 of *La Discussione*, 23 October 1863. He gave them as follows: Bianchi-Giovini, d'Ayala, Zambeccari on August 10; Carlo Ariento and Pallavicino, August 11; Ulloa on August 12; Carrano on the 16th; Enrico Brizzolari, Antonio Greco, Gaetano Braglia, Enrico Wagner, and Becchi on the 17th.

Salazaro rather hazily recalls the following men simply as having been early to join: Tecchio, Bianchi-Giovini, Gherardi, Mamiani, San Donato, Ulloa, Petruccelli, Interdonato, Gemelli, Montanelli (which is clearly wrong), Sirtori, Foresti, Tommaséo (another certain error), Malenchini, Guerrierio, Sterbini, Macchi, "and others," Salazaro, *Cenni sulla rivoluzione*, 11.

Maineri, *Manin e Pallavicino*, 422, prints a partial list of subscribers to the *Piccolo Corriere* for "the first" quarter (although not necessarily, as he assumes, for the first quarter of the paper's existence; it might be May–July 1857, the first quarter of the second year). In any case, these 30 men were all in contact with the Society's leaders and as subscribers to its paper were likely to have been early members of the Society itself. Sbarbaro and G. B. Michelini may also have been among the early signers, Giuseppe Mazza, *Sulla vita e sulle opere di Pietro Sbarbaro* (Scansano, 1891), 13.

[63] Lina Gasparini, "Rapporti della polizia segreta austriaca in Piemonte nel 1857 e 1858," *Rassegna Storica del Risorgimento*, xxv (1938), 1709.

[64] La Farina had word that their circular had reached Sicily, that signatures had arrived from Modena and Lucca, and that a committee at "L." [Livorno?] had been formed in case "F." [Firenze?] did not respond to their call: anonymous letter to La Farina, 12 August 1857, Maineri, *Manin e Pallavicino*, 347–50. He claimed to have committees in Leghorn, Ancona, and Rome, and to hope for

treasurer, and La Farina kept as secretary. Garibaldi and Ulloa were offered posts as vice-presidents. Delighted to find the establishment of a society such an easy matter, Pallavicino was sure they were now an important part of ". . . that irresistible force which must one day make Italy." [65] Garibaldi, for whom such dreams of Italy were simply familiar truths, accepted his honorary office (while declining to pay dues); they had won the name that would "add prestige." Ulloa decided to be merely their Paris representative.[66]

The Sunday meetings at Pallavicino's house became almost a weekly occurrence. There La Farina would report on the Society's new conquests; plans and pamphlets would be discussed, a common aspiration shared. One of the minor members of that group later recalled how those men "grown gray in prisons and exile" had sat about talking of the "public spirit and of the progress of the Society in their native provinces." The talk could not have been very specific if, as he proudly remembered, they

one soon in Calabria: La Farina to Pallavicino, 19 August 1857, ms., MNRT. He reported that the *Gazzetta di Milano* had spoken favorably of them, that Bianchi-Giovini had joined them, that there was nothing to fear for the spread of the Society except in Genoa where, because of the temper of the city, he opposed the formation of a committee: La Farina to Pallavicino, 23 August 1857, Maineri, *Manin e Pallavicino*, 346. Foresti had suggested a committee in Genoa in his letter to Pallavicino, 12 August 1857, *ibid.*, 375. Pallavicino declared that committees "of correspondence and cooperation" were being formed "throughout the peninsula": Pallavicino to Foresti, August 1857, *Memorie di Pallavicino*, III, 409. Few of these committees, however, were ever heard from again.

It is possible that the circular which Olper said was circulating among the most important Roman exiles and which he himself seemed to favor was the Society's, Samuele Olper to Giacomo Dina, 26 October 1857, ms., MNRT.

[65] The excuse for electing new officers was, apparently, the death of Manin, who was now said to have been their first president—an honor of which he may never have known. *Piccolo Corriere*, 3 January 1858; Pallavicino to Garibaldi, 9 January 1858, *Memorie di Pallavicino*, III, 441; to Degli Antoni, 28 December 1857, ms., MCV, bxliii/70; to Foresti, 29 December 1857, Maioli, "Il Fondatore," *Rassegna Storica*, xv, 35–6.

[66] Garibaldi to Pallavicino, 22 January 1858 (only partially printed in *Memorie di Pallavicino*, III, 441–42), ms., MNRT, and Ulloa to Pallavicino 15 January 1858, *Memorie di Pallavicino*, III, 442–43. Jessie W. Mario says that Garibaldi gave himself entirely to the SNI, *Garibaldi*, I, 151. Ulloa feared too many famous names suggested either the need to advertise the few they had or the formation of a potential government. Pallavicino kept his new title from the public, apparently from fear the Austrians might confiscate his property in Lombardy. Salazaro adds that the Marchese did not want to be deprived of those means "necessary for the redemption of the *patria*": Salazaro, *Cenni sulla rivoluzione*, 20; Pallavicino called it "prudence" in his letter to Ulloa, 11 January 1858, *Memorie di Pallavicino*, III, 442.

made it a point never to mention names in order to protect those members beyond the borders of Piedmont. At first, there were probably few men to mention, few names known. Eighteen, a dozen, more often far fewer, would attend; and not many of them were the famous exiles or the men of power in Piedmont. Yet those sessions served their purpose; those present were assured that theirs was an important task and that they were not alone in carrying it out. That they met to direct the Society helped of itself to create an organization, and the fact of their meetings tended to convince others that success had already been achieved.[67]

Pallavicino continued to try to win new recruits for their Society through his correspondence with the noted men he knew.[68] These letters of pleading and wheedling, of argument and flattery, became less important, however, than the letters of La Farina. His were sent more often to shopkeepers or bureaucrats who had expressed interest in the Society. Letters to smaller men, they dealt with smaller things: monthly reports and dues, the winning over of local citizens to the Society. La Farina was, to be sure, capable of the heaviest flattery, but most of his correspondents did not expect it. Rather, he gave them instructions that they might play well a small part in a great organization. By February he had developed an impressive set of directions.[69] Local committees were 1) to correspond directly with him, 2) to send a report at least once a month on the public spirit in their area, together with a list of their new members and any other information of use to the Central Committee. They were 3) to put themselves in touch with other parts of Italy, informing

[67] Pallavicino to Ulloa, 27 January 1858 (says 18 attended the third meeting of *soci promotori*); and La Farina to Pallavicino, 6 February 1858, *ibid.*, 447, 448–49; Alessandro d'Ancona, *Varietà storiche e letterarie, prima serie* (Milan, 1883), 327–28 (he noted the absence of the *pezzi grossi* among the emigrants); Tommaséo to Capponi, 26 May 1858, del Lungo and Prunas, *Tommaséo e Capponi*, IV¹, 233. La Farina said their committee was made up of 30 members, half Piedmontese and half from other provinces, La Farina to Bartolomeo, 25 April 1858, Franchi, *Epistolario di La Farina*, II, 56.

[68] See Pallavicino to Mamiani, 4 August (". . . it does not seem to me that our Society has the right to call itself the Italian National Society when you are not part of it.") and to Tecchio, 6 August 1858, *Memorie di Pallavicino*, III, 466, 467.

[69] For an example of La Farina's flattery, see his letter to Bartolomeo, 25 April 1858, Franchi, *Epistolario di La Farina*, II, 56. The instructions are in his letter to Barigozzi (in Pallanza), 8 February 1858, *ibid.*, 43.

the Central Committee of their activity but keeping names secret. They should try 4) to have their program adopted by the local press and to win its support of the Society. While being conciliatory at all times, they were 5) to use all means of honest propaganda, 6) spreading the Society among all classes of citizens. If asked about the intentions of the Government, they should state 7) that the Society favored the House of Savoy, that, using the liberty granted in Piedmont, it was wholly legal, its existence a public fact. Of course, it was explained, the Government could not explicitly support the Society for fear of compromising itself.

A somewhat vaguer but similar set of instructions was printed a few weeks later in the *Piccolo Corriere*. It was clearly hoped that a smoothly running, highly centralized organization could be established. Members were reminded to pay their dues promptly; [70] there was a hint of some exciting plan in the request for reports on local conditions. The references to the Government's position were a triumph of delicacy. La Farina's mastery of the statement that said little but implied much would prove one of the Society's greatest assets.

The establishment of the Society encouraged great optimism among its directors; Pallavicino especially was moved by the feeling of growth which organizing produced. The National Society was, he believed, ". . . still weak in Piedmont, but vigorous in the other parts of Italy, and especially in the Duchies, Tuscany, the Romagna and Sicily." It is perhaps significant that he found the Society weakest in the areas he knew best, but he cited new proselytes "from all classes" to justify his optimism. There was always a tendency to think of one correspondent as representing a militant committee, to greet the news of a new committee as if it meant the conversion of a community. If this estimate of their own strength was not very precise, at least their opponents, too, tended to exaggerate their numbers.[71]

[70] The instructions were in the *Piccolo Corriere*, 21 February 1858. Ermanno Buscalioni was the new treasurer; dues could be paid at the office of the *Unione*. Their burden was lightened by permitting five members together to pay the one lira a month required. This soon became a simple reduction in dues to 20 *centesimi* for *artigiani*, *Piccolo Corriere*, 17 January, 14 February, 12 April 1858.
[71] He reported that Ariento, Carrano, the young Marchese d'Angrogna, Sena-

At first, particular attention was paid to the formation of committees in Piedmont. The *Unione* pointed out that success here would stand as evidence of Piedmont's nationalism and (a rather provincial appeal in a nationalist cause) that only strong organization in Piedmont would keep Turin the Society's center when, at the outbreak of war, the exiles returned to their native provinces. La Farina let it be known that there were already 36 committees in the Kingdom, and much of those Sunday meetings at Pallavicino's was devoted to talk of the need for committees in "the principal cities of Piedmont, Cuneo, Alessandria, Nice, etc." In February three men were placed "in charge" of various areas of Piedmont, presumably to see to the formation of committees there; and in the following months the establishment of committees in nine other Piedmontese towns was announced.[72] When one of his acquaintances went to Lerici, La Farina asked him to form a committee there, adding as inducement, "you could be president." [73] At first, the Society appeared to be spreading in Piedmont with extraordinary speed. Even Genoa seemed conquered. Rumor had it that the Workers' Association there wanted to break off relations with Mazzini, and Pallavicino thought their Society might step into the breach. Degli Antoni also brought good news from that republican center, and Pichi not only joined the SNI but agreed to form a Genoese committee

tor Audifredi, *avvocato* Levi, a few students and even some women had joined the SNI: Pallavicino to Garibaldi, 9 January; to de Lasteyrie, 26 January; and to Ulloa, 27 January 1858, *Memorie di Pallavicino*, III, 441, 444–46, 447. Mario, *Bertani*, I, 278, says the SNI gained converts "by thousands and with marvelous speed." *La Discussione*, supplement to *Bollettino Settimanale* No. 42 (23 October 1863), cites correspondence in the *Piccolo Corriere* from such cities as Modena, Siena, etc., as evidence that the SNI was organized in those places.

[72] The *Unione* is cited in the *Piccolo Corriere*, 17 January 1858. Pallavicino to Ulloa, 27 January 1858, *Memorie di Pallavicino*, III, 447. Bianchi-Giovini was given charge of Alessandria, Voghera, Acqui, and Savona; a Signor Chersi for Novara and Vitale for Mondovi: La Farina to Pallavicino, 6 February 1858, *ibid.*, 448–49. Committees in Dogliani, Vercelli, Arona were mentioned in *ibid.* The *Piccolo Corriere*, 28 February 1858, named Pallanza, Dogliani, Sarzana, and Arona as the sites of committees, adding Cava, San Martino, Siccomario and Zeveredo to the list in its issue of 7 March 1858.

[73] La Farina to Pietro Poggi, 8 July 1858, Franchi, *Epistolario di La Farina*, II, 70. He let Pallavicino believe, however, that a request to form a committee had come from Lerici: La Farina to Pallavicino, 6 July 1858, ms., MNRT. La Farina also wrote Francesco Betti in Lerici, 14 June 1858, arguing for the importance of organizing, ms. described in the catalogue of the Libreria Antiquaria L. Bonzi, *Risorgimento italiano* (Bologna, 1960), 21.

of "three influential citizens." Soon he was complaining that he had not been sent enough membership blanks, and La Farina declared that Pichi had worked "miracles." [74]

The National Society's records are incomplete, and many others may have meant to join it; many other committees must have been proclaimed and planned. To sign a membership blank, however, is only to declare an intent; the promise it implied was not often fulfilled. The National Society's Genoa committee was not heard of again until a new one was established a year later. A committee in Sarzana was twice announced in the *Piccolo Corriere*; yet a month later La Farina had to apologize to the committee's supposed founder for having been premature, and three months after that he was assuring him that even three members would be enough for a start. Quality, La Farina developed the habit of saying, should not be sacrificed for size; it was enough to have a few men of "probity, zeal, prudence, activity." [75] The Society's newspaper had to remind the committees that sending in signatures was not enough; they were expected to keep in touch with the Central Committee. It was impossible, the paper pleaded, that there should be nothing to report.[76] But the Italian National Society never established so firm a base in Piedmont as it had hoped for.

Lombardy presented the Society with a challenge of a different kind. Economically and socially it was one of Italy's most advanced areas; but, despite Pallavicino's hopes, the democratic groups in Milan refused to unite with the SNI.[77] One of the

[74] Pallavicino to Foresti, 2 and 8 January 1858, Maioli, "Il Fondatore," *Rassegna Storica*, xv, 36–7; La Farina to Pallavicino, 4 February and 26 July 1858, mss., MNRT (the passage referring to Degli Antoni is omitted in *Memorie di Pallavicino*, iii, 461–62); Foresti to Pallavicino, 4 February and 9 April 1858, mss., MNRT (cf. *Memorie di Pallavicino*, iii, 466n). There were, apparently, separate forms to be filled out by those who undertook to be the Society's agents for further organization: Pallavicino to Foresti, 7 August 1858, Maioli, "Il Fondatore," *Rassegna Storica*, xv, 42. Of those Pichi got to join the Society, La Farina seems to have been particularly pleased about a Robertson who owned a plant that had 400 employees: La Farina to Pallavicino, 21 July 1858, ms., MNRT. Pallavicino had particular hope for success among Genoese officers and students, Pallavicino to Foresti, 15 March 1858, Maioli, "Il Fondatore," *Rassegna Storica*, xv, 40.

[75] *Piccolo Corriere*, 28 February and 7 March 1858; La Farina to Giuseppe Capitani, 28 March and 14 June 1858, Franchi, *Epistolario di La Farina*, ii, 52, 65; La Farina to Poggi, 8 July 1858, *ibid.*, 70.

[76] *Piccolo Corriere*, 7 June 1858.

[77] Ermano Barigozzi attempted the negotiations: La Farina to Pallavicino, 16

Society's members in Carbonara remembered the committees of Milan, Mantua, and Cremona as having operated with perfect coordination; but there is no other evidence for this tale told by a veteran recalling his part in a battle since become famous.[78] If its organization in Lombardy was weak, the National Society did, however, have important contacts there. Many of the most influential exiles then in Turin were from this area; and through them, particularly the younger men among them, the Society did exert its influence in Lombardy. Homodei, a friend of La Farina's, was especially active in the Society's behalf; and he managed to establish some committees there and in the Duchies. Luigi Zini refused to join the National Society out of distaste for all such groups, but he, too, undertook various tasks in Lombardy at La Farina's behest and persuaded some others to join. Visconti-Venosta, then a young exile in Turin, similarly won others to the Society and worked closely with it without becoming a member himself.[79] Some Lombard nationalists at least sent someone to "confer" with La Farina but their emissary struck the secretary of the National Society as "a little too prudent for his age." Their fourteen committees in Lombardy of which Pallavicino was so proud may have been only that many enduring contacts, but that was something.[80]

October 1858, ms., MNRT. New members, outside Piedmont, were not expected to sign their names if some member of the Central Committee knew them personally. This was still a society of friends, La Farina to Gaetano Dovidi, 5 April 1858, ms., ISR, busta 61, n. 35.

[78] Ing. Mai to the Central Committee of the SNI, dated Pavia, 16 October 1863, ms., ISR, busta 717, n. 21.

[79] It was Francesco Homodei who first contacted Mai, although the date he gives, July 1857, is probably a year too early, *ibid*. Correnti reported to Cavour, however, that moderate pro-Piedmontese ideas (very much like those of the Society) had rapidly gained in Lombardy. See his *Memoriale* in *Cavour-Nigra*, II, 263–86. Luigi Zini, "Memorie dei casi che condussero il mio commissariato a Modena nel giugno 1859 . . . ," n.d., ms., MNRT. It was his friends Francesco Selmi and Manfredini, both active in the Society and vigorously pushing its organization in the Duchies, who put Zini in touch with La Farina. Pagani saw Visconti-Venosta in May 1858, about working with the Society. Giovanni Visconti-Venosta, *Ricordi di Gioventù, cose vedute e sapute, 1847–1860* (Milan, 1904), 455–56.

[80] La Farina to Pallavicino, 18 September 1858, ms., MNRT; Pallavicino to Garibaldi, 19 June 1858, *Memorie di Pallavicino*, III, 460; Maineri, *Manin e Pallavicino*, 432–35. Massari, a bitter opponent of the Society, exaggerated in comforting himself that in Lombardy the SNI was considered a "ridiculous thing": entry for 4 August 1858, Giuseppe Massari, *Diario 1858–60 sull'azione politica di Cavour*, Licineo Cappelli (ed.) (Bologna, 1931), 3. La Farina failed

The rulers of the Duchies were among the most unpopular in Italy, and the Society seems to have had little difficulty in establishing committees in the cities there. Once again it was particularly fortunate in having the help of some exiles of great influence, men such as the educator and scientist, Francesco Selmi and the playwright Paolo Ferrari.[81] La Farina reported in February that the committee in Parma was already growing, and the *Piccolo Corriere* boasted that the police in Massa were trying to break up the committee there. The committees in Sarzana and Lerici were in close contact with Massa and Carrara, and Selmi's brother in Piacenza was already experienced at sending on into the Duchies material from Piedmont.[82]

In Tuscany, which had the strongest autonomist tradition and, after Piedmont, the most liberal government in Italy, the National Society did not meet with such clear success. In 1856 Pallavicino had claimed Malenchini and Fenzi for his party; a year later La Farina announced the formation of a committee in Florence, and the year after that the *Piccolo Corriere* declared that the Society's progress in Tuscany was "marvelous." La Farina repeatedly instructed SNI committees along the border of Piedmont to maintain contact with Tuscan towns; and at least twice during this early period, agents of the Society were sent into Tuscany to make contacts and report on conditions there. Yet there is little evidence of any firmly established committee in Tuscany until early in 1859. Certainly the Society was already in touch with those men who would be its Tuscan leaders,

---

to win over a democratic society in Milan, La Farina to Pallavicino, 16 October 1858, ms., MNRT.

[81] See above, note 79. A particularly interesting example of how these contacts worked is offered by Ferrari who, traveling from city to city to direct performances of his plays, became friendly with the members of the SNI in Turin and Bologna and then himself became a leader of the Society in his home city, Modena, Vittorio Ferrari, *Paolo Ferrari* (Modena, 1899), 137, 141, 149.

[82] La Farina to Pallavicino, 6 February 1858, *Memorie di Pallavicino*, III, 441; *Piccolo Corriere*, 18 October 1858. La Farina to Capitani, 14 June; to Pietro Poggi, 8 July; and to Ottavio Mazzi, 8 July and 7 September 1858, Franchi, *Epistolario di la Farina*, II, 65, 70, 72, 78. Lina Gasparini, "Relazioni della polizia politica austriaca nel 1857–9 della Svizzera, Parigi, Londra, Toscana, Bologna e Parma," *Rassegna Storica del Risorgimento*, XXIX (1942), 789; the note on Selmi is dated 26 May 1857. An earlier Piacentino committee came over to the SNI: Fermi and Ottolenghi, *Manfredi*, 44. It may soon have had hundreds of members, *ibid.*, 46.

but as yet there was not much readiness in Tuscany to take very seriously the formation of committees or the payment of dues.[83]

In the Romagna, where clandestine political activity was almost a way of life, the National Society eventually achieved its strongest organization; but even there success took time. A group of the SNI was formed in Bologna; but Luigi Tanari, who finally became president of that committee, would not join the Society until he himself had been to Turin to see just what it was supposed to do. By the fall of 1858, however, the National Society could boast committees in most of the larger cities of the Romagna.[84] After Pietro Inviti made a staunch stand against the Mazzinians of Ravenna (at a café there), the Society spread to that Adriatic city; soon a committee was formed in Imola and the one in Bologna expanded. Tanari had reason to say, even before

[83] Pallavicino to Govean, 17 May 1856, Memorie di Pallavicino, III, 222; La Farina to Michelangelo Castelli, n.d., ms., MNRT (the letter was written between 12 July and 1 August 1857; that is, after dues were set at 50 centesimi but while the party was called the Associazione Nazionale); Piccolo Corriere, 7 July 1858. The Tuscan police, resolutely missing the point, reported that a subscription for the "Republican Manin" had been sent from Leghorn: entry of 21 January and 12 April 1858 in Prefettura Segreta, in Archivio di Stato, Firenze (hereafter ASF), busta 1, ins. 16 and busta 5, ins. 73; La Farina to Omero Mengozzi, 8 February; to Mazzi, 14 April and 8 July; and to Poggi, 8 July 1858, Franchi, Epistolario di La Farina, II, 42, 65, 70–1. Castelli made the trip in May: Foresti to Pallavicino, 1 May 1858, ms., MNRT; and Salazaro had been there before: Salazaro, Cenni sulla rivoluzione, 31. La Farina wrote Pallavicino, 6 February 1858, of the "definitive" formation of a committee in Florence and of a comitato succursale in Leghorn: Memorie di Pallavicino, III, 448. Carlo Boncompagni, although he encountered the Piccolo Corriere in Tuscany, was much more impressed by the gentlemen of Biblioteca Civile than by the SNI: his reports to Cavour of 16 March, 9 April, 6 May 1858, mss. in Lettere ministri, Legazione in Toscana, Archivio di Stato, Torino (hereafter AST). See also Raymond Grew, "La Società Nazionale in Toscana," Rassegna Storica Toscana, II (1956), 81–9.

[84] The Society's origin in the Romagna stemmed from Paselli's letters to Camillo Casarini; Luigi Tanari's hesitance may have been due in part to the fact that he had been planning a similar organization of his own: Alessandro Paselli to Casarini, 18 June, 2 July and 31 August 1858, in Giovanni Maioli, "La Società Nazionale in Bologna e nelle Romagne," Saggi e documenti di storia del risorgimento italiano (Bologna, 1933), 73–4, 75–6, 80–2; Giovanni Maioli, "Luigi Tanari e il suo memoriale ad Ernesto Masi sulla Società Nazionale in Bologna e nelle Romagne," Archiginasio, XXVIII (1933), 50. A line of communication through Piacenza and Parma was set up and competing groups headed off. La Farina spoke of a "Committee of Ferrara" in a letter to Pallavicino, 6 July 1858, ms., MNRT; Foresti wrote the Marchese, 9 April 1858, of a young Romagnol he met in Genoa who promised to found some committees in his native province, ms., ibid. Grew, "Società Nazionale in Toscana," Rassegna Storica Toscana, II, 87.

he joined it, that the National Society was having a good effect in the Romagna.[85]

These were the areas of the Society's real successes. Elsewhere its propaganda won some influence; some firm friends were made, but the committees and regular communications of an organized movement did not appear until the war or even later. In the summer of 1858 Degli Antoni undertook a secret mission to Venice on behalf of the Society, and his report that Manin's principles were universally accepted fit with what La Farina had heard of the gains made by their program in Manin's city. There is, however, no evidence of further National Society activity there; nor were many of the noted Venetian exiles in Turin close to the leaders of the Society.[86] In Rome the Society had the same kind of initial paper success with little evidence of accomplishment afterward. It was announced in July that the *Comitato Nazionale Romano* adhered to the program of the SNI; but the formality and careful qualification of the statement suggest a negotiated agreement rather than simple acceptance. The Roman group did advocate policies that were on the whole consonant with those of the National Society, but beyond that it seems to

[85] Men like Giacchino Rasponi of Ravenna and Benvenuto Pasolini of Faenza, who would soon head SNI committees, were already frightening the Tuscan police by their trips to that quieter province: Alberto Dallolio, *Le spedizione dei mille nella memorie bolognese* (Bologna, 1910), 10. The Ravenna committee was formed during a meeting at Rasponi's house, 8 December 1858: Giovanni Maioli, "La Società Nazionale in Ravenna," *Il Commune di Ravenna*, 1 (1938), 6; Romeo Galli, "La Società Nazionale e il Conte Anton Domenico Gamberini," *La Romagna*, xvi (1927), 396. Gabriele Rossi, a member of the SNI in Bologna, thought the committees in the Romagna were formed early in 1859 (the period of expansion when he joined the Society): "Memoriale a Signora Tanari," 4 September 1868, ms., MCRB. Massari, *Diario*, 21, entry for 24 August 1858; Cerutti, he admitted, agreed with Tanari's estimate of the important influence of the SNI on public opinion in the Romagna.

[86] Degli Antoni to Pincherle, 6 August 1858, ms., MCV, bxliii/152; La Farina to Ferdinando Molena, 16 June 1858, Franchi, *Epistolario di la Farina*, ii, 65–6. The committee for the Veneto formed in Turin and headed by Tecchio seems to have been as much a fraternal or charitable organization for Venetian exiles as an active political group. The few remaining documents of the committee make it clear that it had no formal connection with the SNI; the largest group of papers referring to this group are in the ISR.

Tommaséo's opposition to the SNI is well known, but Pincherle, too, held it in contempt. He especially resented Degli Antoni's informing a Venetian committee (SNI?) which supported Manin's program of the existence of some funds belonging to the Venetian Republic which Manin brought from Venice with him (and which Pincherle apparently controlled), Pincherle to Degli Antoni, 2 September 1858, and Degli Antoni to Pincherle, 6 August and n.d. (his copy of his reply to the above), mss., MCV, bxliii/152.

have maintained no very close contact with the larger Society.[87] It was similarly through antecedent local committees that the ideas of the Society spread in the Marches. By 1857 some of these groups were consciously adopting Manin's program, often in addition to a strange mixture of Mazzinian concepts and Masonic ritual. Such groups should not, however, be conceived of as a formal part of the SNI; probably their only contact with it was through some members of the Society in Tuscany and the Romagna.[88] When it came to Naples, even La Farina's vigorous optimism left him. There is no evidence of any local organization of the Society there before 1860. The "timidity" on the mainland seems to have come as no surprise to this Sicilian, but about his native island he was more sanguine. He could even wonder about the prospects of a successful revolution there, and he won from the distinguished Ruggiero Settimo, who in exile had moved down the Mediterranean to Malta, some hesitant support for the National Society. Despite La Farina's many friends on the island, however, there is no evidence of an active committee of the SNI in Sicily before the arrival of Garibaldi.[89]

Outside Italy, too, the Italian National Society was sometimes organized into local committees. After becoming a member himself, Costantino Reta set about forming a committee of other Italians in Geneva, a city always important to Italian national movements. And like a true believer, he stoically confessed, "We are a little persecuted by the *signori Mazziniani*. . . ." [90] There

[87] La Farina wrote Pallavicino, 6 July 1858, of the agreement defining unification as the desire to unite all forces for independence with political unification an eventual goal if "events don't counsel otherwise," and accepting the Society's *Credo* as the correct statement of its doctrine, etc., ms., MNRT. Records of the Roman committee for this period are scanty, but the copies of its publications (in the Biblioteca di Storia Moderna e Contemporanea, hereafter BSMC) make no mention of the SNI. See Chapter Fifteen, note 36.

[88] A committee in Costanza informed their brethren in Camerino, 25 January 1857, that Manin's was "precisely our political faith": Zampetti-Biocca, *La Società Nazionale nella Marca*, 29; a Fano committee similarly acknowledged Manin, 8 November 1857: Alessandrini, *I fatti*, ii, 17. Both authors persist in seeing all pro-Piedmont activity in the areas as the work of the SNI, a view which would have the Society formed there before it was in Turin.

[89] La Farina to Filippo Bartolomeo, 25 April 1858, and Settimo to La Farina, 10 June 1858, Franchi, *Epistolario di La Farina*, ii, 56–8, 64. His subsequent letters, however, were full of assurances that all went well in Sicily. But see Francesco Guardione, "La Società Nazionale in Sicilia dal 1856 al 1860," *Il Risorgimento Italiano*, v (1912), 898–901. Also Crispi, *I Mille*, 13–17, on earlier organization in Sicily.

[90] Reta to Pallavicino, 3 February 1858, Maineri, *Manin e Pallavicino*, 392.

was no limit to La Farina's ambition for the Society. When a group of Italians in Mobile asked for some of the publications of the SNI, the secretary replied suggesting they form a committee there. Mobile, he explained to Pallavicino, is in the *"stato d'Ala presso la Florida e la Luissiana."* For the most part, however, Foresti, who had taught at Columbia and was the American Consul in Genoa, was relied upon to put the SNI in touch with the New World.[91]

The National Society was always greatly concerned about opinion in France, and it quickly became associated with the solicitations there for a monument to Manin. The *Piccolo Corriere* also vigorously supported the fund from the start. La Farina got those most concerned to agree that the monument should symbolize Manin's great concept: unification and independence. Pallavicino tried to coordinate the French and Italian committees who were collecting funds. When a kind of victory banquet was held in Turin for members of both groups, a good number of those who attended were members of the Society, and all there were reminded that the SNI was the inheritor of Manin's program. From all this the National Society gained in both members and prestige; for as a demonstration, the collection for a monument to Manin was a great success. Leading Frenchmen spoke of their sympathy for Italy (and donated money to prove it); their Italian counterparts replied by speaking of France as a second *patria*. Manin would have been overjoyed to know his program had achieved so much.[92]

Collecting funds for the monument to Manin also proved an

His letters to Pallavicino, published here, are an interesting comment on the exiles in Geneva. Reta himself had been associated with Cavour on the *Risorgimento*: see Guido Bustico, *Giornali e giornalisti del Risorgimento* (Milan, 1924), 89–128. The president of the committee in Geneva was Marchese Bossi, a Milanese noble who, like Pallavicino, had been associated with Federico Confalonieri, Alphonse de Candolle, *Elogie di Marquis Begnaio Jerome Bossi* (Geneva, 1870).

[91] La Farina to Pallavicino, 6 July 1858, ms., MNRT; Pallavicino to Foresti, 22 January and 7 August 1858, Maioli, "Il Fondatore," *Rassegna Storica*, xv, 38, 42. The Sardinian consul in Algiers promised to circulate their *Credo* there, Pallavicino to La Farina, 30 July 1858, *Memorie di Pallavicino*, iii, 463.

[92] Tommaséo, Mezzacapo, and Tecchio initiated the project for a monument to Manin: *Piccolo Corriere*, 4 and 11 October 1857, and 24 May 1858. Also La Farina to Pallavicino, 26 July 1858, ms., MNRT (the rest is in *Memorie di Pallavicino*, iii, 461–62; La Farina complained that he was supported only by Frenchmen in his effort to make the monument a tribute to Manin's ideas as well as to the man); and La Farina to Pallavicino, 28 July 1858, *ibid.*, 462–63.

effective demonstration in Italy. Deputies, cabinet members, and the city council contributed from Turin; 4,000 francs were collected from Venice; funds came from Tuscany and other provinces; Italians in Egypt and England sent sizable sums. La Farina was able to point to the Prime Minister's interest in the monument as evidence of Cavour's trustworthiness, and his own efforts won him the confidence of Manin's friends in the Society.[93] Fresh from these successes, the leaders of the Society talked of joining other demonstrations or staging a lottery. They even allowed themselves to engage in some quasi-military operations and to confer about the possibilities of revolution in Lombardy.[94]

Increasingly the Society reflected the personality of La Farina. It was Pallavicino himself who had not wanted it announced that he was president of the Society; but as a result, his name nearly disappeared from the columns of the *Piccolo Corriere*, which in

---

Tecchio, Mezzacapo, Sineo, Valerio, Zambeccari, Tofano, Degli Antoni, Annoni, Lanfrey, de Lasteyrie were among the 32 men at the banquet.

Also see, *ibid.*, 437–39. The *Siècle, Presse*, and *Courrier de Paris* supported the subscription. The French committee collected 13,387 francs from 23,000 contributors. Planat de la Faye not only formed the SNI in Paris but pledged himself to see that Manin's principles were propagated by the French press: Planat, *Vie de Planat de la Faye* (Paris, 1895), 633–34. Maioli has suggested that the activities connected with raising this money were meant to enlarge the SNI as well, Maioli, "Il Fondatore," *Rassegna Storica*, xv, 9–10.

La Farina's gain in prestige as a result of this project is shown in the attitude of Ulloa: Ulloa to Pallavicino, 7 January 1858, Maineri, *Manin e Pallavicino*, 389; Pallavicino to La Farina, 3 August 1858, *Memorie di Pallavicino*, iii, 465.

[93] *Piccolo Corriere*, 18 October 1857 and 21 March, 9 May, 26 July 1858; La Farina to Ulloa, 18 October 1857; G. Doria, "La vita e il carteggio di Girolamo Ulloa," *Archivio Storico per le Provincie Napoletane*, n.s., xv (1929), 343; Pallavicino to La Farina, 3 August 1858, *Memorie di Pallavicino*, iii, 465.

[94] La Farina felt they should have an ostentatious part in the presentation of a medal to the King: letter to Pallavicino, 18 October 1858, ms., MNRT; Pallavicino favored a lottery: letter to La Farina, 30 July 1858, *Memorie di Pallavicino*, iii, 468; and to Foresti, 7 August 1858, Maioli, "Il Fondatore," *Rassegna Storica*, xv, 41–2.

La Farina obtained a military map of Piacenza and environs which he presented to General Alphonso La Marmora: letter to Pallavicino, 6 July 1858, ms., MNRT. Ing. Mai recalls a conference on revolution in Lombardy as having been held in March 1858, to talk, significantly, about action in the spring of 1859. The conversation, however, was probably less formal and more general than he remembered: Mai to Buscalioni, 16 October 1863, ms., ISR, busta 717, n. 20. Emilio Della Noce, a dealer in arms, says he made some ten shipments (partially at his expense) to Sicily in 1857–58 after having even earlier (when an agent for the English insurance company, Gresham) procured plans of the Gulf of Baja, Lake Agnano, and the fort of San Elmo, in his brief autobiography accompanying a request for the insignia of a Cavaliere dei Santi Maurizio e Lazzaro, ms., n.d. [1860?], ISR, busta 555.

November had hailed the Marchese as the man who more than any other stood for the National Society. Now, however, he was identified only as one of "our political friends" or merely as a "deputy from Turin." Official announcements of the SNI were made by a nameless president and the "secretary, Giuseppe La Farina," and it was he who came to be identified with the Society. The quip that Pallavicino was "a man *segretariabile*" must have expressed a general impression.[95] Indeed, the Marchese's function in the Society had become largely ceremonial; La Farina was making the day-to-day decisions. So basic a document as the National Society's *Credo politico* was not only written by La Farina but had begun appearing in print six weeks before it was given the usual reading before and was approved by the Central Committee.[96]

A prodigious worker with a genius for organization, La Farina was skilled in polemic and knew how to communicate that sense of importance and of militance which would help hold his Society together. His warnings, for example, to members of the SNI who lived in Austrian territory not to sign letters with their real names can hardly have been needed. But such advice suggested in one electric sentence Austria's fear of the Society, the hazardous business of its members, and the professional skill of the Central Committee. In those dull moments when doctrine needed no explication and specific instructions would have said only to create no great disturbance, it was a useful substitute to declare that "from a part of Italy, which we think it not wise to name, we are advised that some persons, who call themselves emissaries of the Italian National Society, [by] misusing authoritative names are inciting untimely and senseless risings and promising the aid of arms and ammunition. The Central Committee is entirely convinced that this is a police trap in order to catch the incautious in the net and discredit our Society." It may be that the Society did "have in hand proof that the pretended emissaries

[95] *Piccolo Corriere*, 15 November 1857, 28 February, 25 April, 3 January 1858.
[96] When, for example, a painting was presented to the Society, Pallavicino was asked to thank the donor (our treasurer who is incompetent in such matters, La Farina noted, thinks it beautiful): La Farina to Pallavicino, 6 July 1858, ms., MNRT. The *Credo Politico* began appearing in installments in the *Piccolo Corriere* with the issue of 3 January; it was formally approved 21 February 1858. Salazaro, a good friend of Pallavicino's, is the only person to maintain that the Marchese really controlled the Society, *Cenni sulla rivoluzione*, 20.

are in the service of the Austrian police," but such a statement did not depend on accuracy for its effectiveness. Members of the SNI had been well warned to do nothing rash and simultaneously assured of their organization's alertness.[97]

This air of militance was maintained with equal vigor in the *Piccolo Corriere*. The reply to the *Nord de Brusselle* for having said the National Society was preparing the ground for the Mazzinians declared the *Nord* to be an organ of Russian politics. Its article, the *Piccolo Corriere* reasoned, must have been the work of a Cossack. When the *Staffetta* wrote of reforms being planned for Lombardy with the famous Cesare Cantù scheduled to be made minister of public instruction, the Society's paper retorted heavily that the *Staffetta* had done well to leave the item in French; for in Italian it might cause death from laughter.[98]

The *Piccolo Corriere* was not dull reading, and it showed at least equal skill in latching on to the most unlikely bedfellows. Recently published letters of De Maistre, for example, were quickly annexed to the nationalist cause. Passages showing that arch-conservative's dislike for Austria were emphasized and his statements painted as upsetting to the Austrians and a great blow to the clericals. Even he referred to the King of Italy; even he declared that a nation's greatest shame was to obey a foreign power.[99] From the opposite camp, Orsini's anti-Mazzinian letters and statements provided excellent propaganda. Readers of the *Piccolo Corriere* learned in detail how Mazzini had left Orsini stranded in jail, how he objected to a collection being taken up to aid poor Pisacane's daughter. Orsini, who had come to see the light only through the bitter experience of failing to assassinate Napoleon III, knew what he was talking about when he said that the Mazzinian party must be destroyed. For Mazzini was more than cruel; his talk of omnipresent Piedmontese agents was treacherous; his reference to Victor Emmanuel as a foreign king (while calling on the Neapolitans to revolt), treachery. Since nearly every issue of the Society's paper gave further evidence of the death of Mazzinianism, there remained the question of why he kept trying. "*It is certain*," La Farina explained, that Mazzini

[97] La Farina to someone in Cremona, 28 March 1858, Franchi, *Epistolario di La Farina*, II, 53; *Piccolo Corriere*, 2 May and 7 June 1858.
[98] *Piccolo Corriere*, 26 July and 7 September 1858.
[99] *Ibid.*, 30 August, 13 and 20 September 1858.

sought not so much his own success as the disorganization of the SNI; "we have clear proof of it." [100] Even Mazzini could be understood in terms of the National Society.

A favorite point of polemic in the *Piccolo Corriere* was the threat from the Church. In its anticlericalism the paper followed closely the prejudices of its editor; and the dangers of the black menace, of Jesuitical reasoning, of "clerical impudence" were frequently outlined in its pages. One of the Society's members wrote and got La Farina to print a pamphlet on the administration of justice in the Papal States which was so extreme that it raised opposition from thoroughly secular sources. The *Piccolo Corriere*, however, defended itself not by accepting responsibility for the pamphlet but by striking a new anticlerical note. The SNI was not a Jesuitical society where all had to think with the minds of their superiors; having no infallible authority, it allowed individual opinions.[101]

Clearly, the life of the National Society was centered in the written word. If money could be found elsewhere, it did not matter that by July only eight to ten members of the Society outside Piedmont had sent in their dues—provided there were men to receive the National Society's communications. These there were. La Farina's correspondence flourished, the Society's pamphlets were distributed by the "thousands," the circulation of the *Piccolo Corriere* had risen to from three to four thousand.[102] La Farina's letters dealt primarily with the problems of the Society

[100] *Ibid.*, 28 March, 5 and 12 April 1858; La Farina to Mazzi, 16 August 1858, Franchi, *Epistolario di La Farina*, II, 74.

[101] The pamphlet, entitled *Administrazione della giustizia nello Stato Pontificio*, may have been that sent to La Farina by the "committee" of Ferrara. The authors had served in the papal police. La Farina himself had had sufficient doubts about the pamphlet to print it without the heading of the SNI (which was still blamed for it, however); he had to defend it even to Pallavicino whom he assured that it had created a fierce "schism" among papal defenders, La Farina to Pallavicino, 6 and 28 July 1858, ms., MNRT. *Piccolo Corriere*, 17 January, 2 and 23 August 1858.

[102] La Farina to Pallavicino, 6 July and 18 September 1858, ms., MNRT. La Farina estimated the requests for copies (whether of pamphlets or the newspaper is not clear) at 3,000 in his September letter. The Supplement to *Bollettino Settimanale* No. 42 of *La Discussione* (23 October 1863) gives the number of pamphlets circulated outside Piedmont as over 50,000 but this may be for the entire prewar period and in any case is not necessarily reliable. The *Espero*, 6 January 1861, says that the *Piccolo Corriere*, which it succeeded, first had a circulation of 500 which "soon" became 4,000 and that 12,000 copies of the *Credo* alone were circulated. This distribution of the newspaper appears, however, not to have been very efficient. See *Piccolo Corriere*, 18 October 1857;

as an organization. They assured local groups of the SNI that they were an important part of an active movement, alertly directed from Turin by men who knew things local members could not guess, a movement with myriad mysterious connections and a clear central role in Italian affairs. The pamphlets published by the Society in this period were primarily summaries of its program and interests, intended apparently to win new friends and members. The crucial task of maintaining a common outlook among members on current, concrete political events fell to the *Piccolo Corriere*. With the same militant certitude with which it fought its ideological opponents, the paper presented a simple picture of Italy on the threshold of unity, preparing to fight beside Piedmont.

From a quarter to a half of each issue of the paper was devoted to letters from the provinces of Italy; most of them purported to be reports sent to the Society, although their impressive consistency in style and content suggest at least the editorial hand of La Farina. The reader of the *Piccolo Corriere* thus knew that Lombardy was not so prosperous as she might appear; heavy taxes carried her wealth to Vienna and bad administration left her people miserable. Blindly, Austria was depending more and more on military rule while her subjects' hatred grew. All possible pomp had failed to get the populace of Milan to celebrate the birth of a new heir to tyranny; and the lonely Archduke had to recruit three shopkeepers and a cobbler in order to have someone attend his salon. The few still willing to cooperate with their rulers were harshly ostracized by the great majority who felt a new unity—and a deep gratitude to the *Piccolo Corriere*. Everyone in Brescia was looking to Victor Emmanuel; in Cremona all honest men of all classes "including a few good nobles" had read and approved the Society's latest pamphlet.[103]

The Duchies were seen as in even greater turmoil. The Government of Parma was dangerously ineffective; Piacenza rocked with demonstrations in favor of Piedmont. The picture of Modena, where Jews and Protestants were persecuted and the Gov-

---

subsequent issues contain further confessions of failure to get the paper to all its subscribers.

[103] *Piccolo Corriere*, 10 and 24 January, 14 February, 5 April, 9 and 30 August, 27 September, 11 and 25 October 1858.

ernment corrupt, was the blackest of all. The *Piccolo Corriere* devoted three long articles, in addition to its usual correspondence from Modena, to the horrors of this state where the only reform was a relaxation of the laws against begging, where the schools were run by Jesuits who taught logic with solecisms, some Latin and Greek but little Italian. It was hardly surprising that the Duke lived in terror of the National Society or that in Massa and Carrara, where atrocities were a way of rule, only his hirelings would enter church on the day of his *festa*.[104]

The news from Tuscany was, fittingly, calmer; but it was easy to prove that the Grand Duke's government was not really liberal, that as an Austrian pawn he allowed an unpopular German to control his army. After all, he had even sent delegates to Marshall Radetsky's funeral. Tuscan liberals were now united; the Society was even growing there.[105] Oppression and heavy taxes, peculation, incompetence and Papal unpopularity were the almost traditional themes of the reports from Rome. The general tone, however, was one of slander. The paper wondered at length about the source of Cardinal Antonelli's wealth and added for good measure some speculation about the Mastai family. The *Piccolo Corriere* was careful to note whenever its views were supported by the foreign press, and stories of brigandage in the Romagna or the maltreatment of Jewish children were conscientiously recirculated. Political conditions were summarized by the story of the rabbit seen racing from the forest. The lion had outlawed all horned animals, and the rabbit feared that zealous police might find offense in his long ears. The parables of the *Piccolo Corriere* were not complex.[106]

The Kingdom of Naples provided the easiest, but in some respects the least satisfactory, of targets. There was, of course, never a lack of atrocity stories; it was possible to declare the whole state a prison without fear of contradiction. One correspondent reported the country to be divided into only two classes—the robbers and the robbed. It could be entertaining to examine in

[104] *Piccolo Corriere*, 21 February, 14 March, 5 July, 16, 23, and 30 August, 6 September, 11, 18, and 25 October, 1 November 1858.
[105] *Ibid.*, 17 January, 21 March, 21 June, 19 and 26 July, 16 August, 1 November 1858. Also see Grew, "Società Nazionale in Toscana," *Rassegna Storica Toscana*, II, 88–9.
[106] *Piccolo Corriere*, 17 January, 12 April, 14, 21, and 28 June, 19 July, 23 and 30 August, 7 and 20 September 1858.

detail the cost of casting statues of Ferdinands I and II and of transporting them from Rome to Messina. The lack of serious political unrest, however, proved embarrassing. It was necessary to see silence as the sign of moral revolt, inaction as proof the wise were waiting for Victor Emmanuel.[107] For Sicily the problem was reversed. Demonstrations of discontent were frequent but to establish that they were nationalist in nature was difficult. The Society's newspaper, however, assured its readers that the Piedmontese consuls were often cheered, that the tricolor frequently flew during Sicilian demonstrations.[108] Through the *Piccolo Corriere* patriots throughout the Peninsula could be sure they were not alone. They must also have felt that political progress was being made, for what had been reported as a sign of discontent in February was seen as planned political action in August.

An equally important change was evident in the five pamphlets published by the Society during this first year.[109] Four of them were written by La Farina. As one might expect, the anticlerical and anti-Mazzinian strains were more biting than they had been in the earlier writings of Manin and Pallavicino. The basic difference, however, was in the kind of argument they contained. The *Partito Nazionale* had addressed a relatively careful argument to the politically well-informed, stressing the necessity for a specific political compromise if Italy was to be united. These newer pamphlets rested their case solidly on the old arguments, but they emphasized more strongly the benefits unification would bring and the need for every Italian to be a nationalist. The SNI was more positively presented as the one real way to achieve the nationalist goals. These pamphlets had the air, in short, of being addressed to men who might have escaped politics before. Despite their varied and interesting titles, they contained essentially the same didactic message. They spoke more than their predecessors of a military alliance with France, speculated more on Russia's role as Austria's enemy, and referred less to England.

---

[107] *Ibid.*, 3 January, 7 June, 2 and 9 August, 20 and 27 September, 18 October, 8 and 29 November 1858.

[108] *Ibid.*, 14 February, 5 April, 5 July, 30 August, 13 September 1858.

[109] The pamphlets were *Italia e Piemonte; Credo politico della Società Nazionale Italiana; La Rivoluzione, la dittatura e le alleanze; Le forze liberatrici d'Italia*, all by La Farina; and, by Biagio Caranti, *Catechismo politico pei contadini piemontesi*.

The emphasis now was on diplomatic relations rather than foreign public opinion.[110] The Society's view of itself ranged widely. It was variously presented as a natural expression of nationalist sentiment, a coordinator of militant action, an organized pressure group, a political party. Whatever it was, the Italian National Society took itself seriously. An organization with members in most of Italy, producing its own newspaper and pamphlet after pamphlet, it permitted no doubt of its own importance. It expressed its trust in Piedmont unequivocally.[111] Should she attack Naples, it was explained, that would be a nationalist not a civil war. Indeed, the talk of war was far more prominent in these statements than in any of Manin's. The thought of dramatic action in cooperation with Piedmont was once again becoming common.[112]

[110] This was, of course, a shift of greatest significance from the dream of revolution to the *Realpolitik* of Cavour; the Society itself still showed some uncertainty. It opposed, for example, the extraordinary laws in France following the Felice Orsini affair: *Piccolo Corriere*, 28 February 1858. Crispi could expect to win its readers' sympathy by explaining why he was expelled from France: Crispi to La Farina, 28 November 1858, Crispi, *I Mille*, 86–8. Like Crispi, the more moderate Medici also felt that Italy's future lay with revolution in France: Medici to Garibaldi, 30 September 1857, ms., ISR, busta 47, n. 23. Thus the Society's general attitude toward France marked its position in the political spectrum. The radical Guerrazzi had been attracted by the general program of the SNI, but he could not accept Piedmont's policy toward France: La Farina to Pallavicino, 6 February 1858, *Memorie di Pallavicino*, III, 449. Guerrazzi to La Farina, 31 March 1858, Franchi, *Epistolario di La Farina*, II, 53–4. Armando Sarpori, "Il Guerrazzi e la politica unitaria del Cavour," *Rassegna Storica del Risorgimento*, XI, fasc. 1 (January–March 1924), 164–67.

[111] In *Italia e Piemonte*, which was prepared for the opening of the Chamber of Deputies, La Farina even involved the Society in Piedmontese politics. He called for unity among liberals to fight the clericals; and while claiming the SNI supported no ministry, he called it a crime to fight the Government then in office since there was no one to replace it. His desire to defend the actions of that Government had been apparent earlier. See his letter to Ulloa, 18 October 1857, Doria, "Ulloa," *Archivio Storico, Provincie Napoletane*, n.s., XV, 342. The *Piccolo Corriere* had tried to present even Pallavicino as ministerialist and had stressed the outcome of the elections as a Government victory: *Piccolo Corriere*, 18 October and 22 November 1857. Castelli may have had the SNI in mind when he wrote Minghetti, 30 November 1857, of the necessity for liberals to be as well organized as the clericals, adding ". . . e ciò sarà fatto, e sin d'ora si organizza sullo stesso piano dei clericali un Associazione liberale che si estenderà in tutte le provincie," cited in Chiala, *Lettere di Cavour*, II, ccxxxi.

[112] Typical of such thought was La Farina's plan for an address to Italian troops in Austrian, Ducal, Papal or Neapolitan armies calling on them to desert rather than risk fighting their Italian brothers: La Farina to Pallavicino, 26 July 1858, ms., MNRT. See also the Party's pamphlet, *Le Forze liberatrici d'Italia* (Turin, 1858), approved by the Central Committee on November 14, 1858.

II ❖ PREPARATION FOR WAR

CHAPTER FOUR

CAVOUR AND LA FARINA: THE IMMINENCE

OF WAR (TO FEBRUARY 1859)

✤ A SOCIETY advocating Piedmont's leadership of the national movement had sooner or later to establish some understanding with Piedmont's Government. To know precisely what Cavour asked of the National Society, to know the extent to which he was in turn influenced by it, would throw a great deal of light on the intentions and plans of both Government and Society. The evidence, by the very nature of the situation, must be slight; but the tradition of reading it as proof of the fullest conspiratorial cooperation has been generally accepted. Not only does such a relationship, on the whole, make sense, it serves the writer well who wishes to establish Count Cavour as a farseeing nationalist with the threads of destiny skillfully in hand. It establishes unification as not just the product of the Prime Minister's diplomacy but as a popular movement well organized through a National Society which was shrewdly moderate and secretly in cahoots with Cavour. The case for the close connection between the National Society and the Government is usually reduced to the question of the relationship between La Farina and Cavour (two men whose political methods made the problem doubly enigmatic). The picture then painted is so attractive indeed that Massari, no admirer of La Farina, was almost alone in complaining that the rapport of Sicilian and statesman had been greatly exaggerated; yet even he conceded that their contacts "had their useful side." [1]

The argument for extensive cooperation between the two men is usually based on two things: a famous interview between them (their first in fact), and La Farina's having begun, in the fall of 1858, authoritatively to predict war for the following spring. There are such doubtful elements about both, however, that they do not make even very convincing circumstantial evidence. In the interview Cavour is said to have expressed faith in eventual

[1] Giuseppe Massari, *Il Conte di Cavour, ricordi biografici* (Milan, 1935), 135.

Italian unity but doubt that Italians were ready for it, to have admitted ignorance of the political atmosphere elsewhere in Italy and fright that association with the National Society would be used against him to the detriment of their common cause. Then he is said to have offered some hope and to have told La Farina to form the National Society, to visit him when he wanted but at an hour when he would be unseen. If he should be "questioned in parliament or diplomatically (he added smiling), I will deny you like Peter, and I will say that I do not know you." An anecdote which asks to be believed, this story conveys the atmosphere of the doubts and fears of the prewar years; it presents an appealing picture of the somberly realistic, yet witty, Cavour. It has won the endorsement of most scholars and been so often repeated that scholarly apparatus is hardly appropriate.[2]

The story first appeared publicly in the newspaper of the National Society on 24 January 1862 in an article written by La Farina. The date of the interview was given only as the first time La Farina saw Cavour, which has universally been placed as the meeting of 12 September 1856, which Cavour asked for in his letter of the day before.[3] This much alone seems improbable. Would the cautious Cavour confess so much and so commit himself to this ex-revolutionary who had entered Piedmont with difficulty but two years before? Then, Cavour had considered La Farina to be a dangerous radical; and the radical had had to recruit aid even to be sure of obtaining a visa.[4] The meeting had

[2] So excellent and careful a scholar as Omodeo says the story has all the elements of *attentabilità* and suggests it as an example of Cavour's system of alliances without written treaties, Omodeo, *Cavour*, II, 167–68.

[3] The paper, a daily, was then called *Espero, il Piccolo Corriere d'Italia*. Cavour to La Farina, 11 September 1856, Franchi, *Epistolario di La Farina*, II, 22n. In a letter, 14 October 1860, to Pietro Sbarbaro, who was preparing a biography of him, La Farina wrote that his relations with Cavour from 1856 to 1859 were completely unknown even to the Count's friends but that he had seen him nearly every day before dawn. He seemed to see the meetings as having been important primarily for their influence on winning Cavour to a nationalist view and as having led to the meeting with Garibaldi. Written at a time when La Farina was still smarting over his expulsion from Sicily, this stress on his own nationalism (and his good influence over Cavour) must be read with caution. The more colorful anecdote of 1862 was not repeated here, *ibid.*, 426–27.

[4] Francesco Selmi, *Giuseppe La Farina*, n.d. (extract from *Rivista Contemporanea Nazionale Italiana*, April 1864), 13; La Farina to Giovanni Ventura, 13 July 1854, Franchi, *Epistolario di La Farina*, I, 509–10; Montanelli wrote Pallavicino, 15 July [1854], asking him to use his influence in behalf of La Farina whom he did not know and assuring him that La Farina was not a Mazzinian, ms., MNRT.

come about, after all, as a result of La Farina's letter to the Prime Minister asking about rumors that the Government might support a Muratist movement in Naples—the discussion would have to have gone a long way to lead to such a provocative understanding.

The specific reference to the SNI makes at least the accepted chronology of the statement impossible; the term *Società Nazionale* was not used for another year, and at this time La Farina's part in the *Partito Nazionale* of Manin and Pallavicino was peripheral. Just three days before this interview, La Farina wrote a friend that his faith in Piedmont's eventual role in unification rested not on the men of the Piedmontese Government but on the inexorable logic of the situation. He added that he did not know Rattazzi and had seen Cavour but once.[5] A month later, he printed a statement to the effect that Cavour, like the Piedmontese, was cold and cautious, that if asked about national questions his answers would be ambiguous, uncertain and obscure not from artifice but from the disturbed state of his soul— not a very grateful response to even a circumspect welcome.[6]

After relating their dialogue, La Farina went on in that article of 1862 to state that for four years thereafter he saw Cavour nearly every day. This statement, which has nearly won the acceptance of the anecdote that preceded it, is frequently cited as evidence that Cavour in fact directed the Society while La Farina informed him of political attitudes and conditions in the provinces. If La Farina wished to suggest that their relationship continued until Cavour's death, that would place this interview in 1857, a more likely date. It is not altogether surprising that little evidence is left of the conversations between these men, but it is disturbing that there is so little indication of what, regarding the National Society before 1859, they could have found to talk about even on a weekly basis. The Society was not so well organized nor Cavour's plans so well formulated that they could have exchanged very specific information and instructions. In

[5] La Farina to Fabrizi, 8 September 1856 [Palamenghi-Crispi], "L'Evoluzione alla Monarchia," *Risorgimento Italiano*, VII, 251. He had pursued a policy quite independent of Cavour as recently as the fall of 1855: La Farina to Signoa Torti, 17 November 1855, Franchi, *Epistolario di La Farina*, I, 569. See also Chapter Two, note 35.
[6] La Farina to *Il Diritto*, 27 October 1856 (printed 3 November 1856), cited in *ibid.*, II, 577.

this statement of 1862, La Farina made no claims about the nature of the meetings, citing them only as evidence that the sentiment for unity was once so dim that Cavour had to be cautious about seeing a man who talked of unification. The accomplishment chiefly claimed for these meetings is the presentation of Garibaldi to the Prime Minister in 1858.

The time of the meetings, "two or three hours before dawn," is suggestively emphasized by La Farina and has been stressed by later writers, who usually accept the less arduous hour of six o'clock mentioned in Cavour's September 1856 note. The Prime Minister, however, frequently entertained visitors at that hour; and one could compile a list of many besides La Farina who remember of their meetings with Cavour the dark and cold of early morning in Turin and the strangeness of secret stairways.[7] What a writer of La Farina's skill writes about Cavour, six months after his death, in the effort to make a political point about something else is inadequate evidence on which to interpret an important element in Cavour's policy.

That in the fall of 1858 La Farina assured all in public and private that war would come with spring is a more substantial piece of evidence. The prediction proved, after all, to be correct; and it is likely that it was at least partly based on what La Farina had learned from circles close to Cavour. As such, however, it proves nothing about the degree of closeness between the two men. La Farina's predictions are too easily explained on the basis of his doctrine; the confidence with which he made them was part of his personality. Insisting that Italy was ready for unity, the Society had to maintain that war was necessarily near; it had for years been publicizing evidence, diplomatic and domestic, to prove its point. Francesco Selmi remembers La Farina telling a group of friends in December 1858 that their dream was about to be realized; their joy and La Farina's fervor would be enough to endow the moment with something of the official, the in-

---

[7] Pallavicino saw Cavour one morning in August 1856: Pallavicino to Foresti, 7 August 1856, *Memorie di Pallavicino*, III, 298. Paolo Ferrari, a less important figure, saw him at five a.m.: Ferrari, *Ferrari*, 151. La Farina repeated essentially the same account in the Chamber of Deputies (during a debate on the dissolution of Agostino Bertani's Emancipation Committees), stressing that Cavour was prepared to disband the Society and that Rattazzi (with whom he was then at odds) had been even cooler to the founding of the SNI, 16 June 1863, *Atti parlamentari, Discussioni*, Leg. VIII, Sess. 1863–64, 1 (Rome, 1886), 362–63.

formed.[8] But rumors of war were on everyone's lips. A treaty with France, increased Austrian ire, English sympathy, Italian discontent—these had been the stock in trade of nationalists for months. Spring was a likely time for warfare to begin; and La Farina had been known in the past to see the future as certainly as he did now.[9]

This is not to argue that Cavour may not have told La Farina much (as he did others); [10] his was, after all, a secret it would have been folly to keep. One must simply read with caution the meaning of La Farina's predictions of war; he was a man who had lived by faith before and spoke from necessity now, who was saying only more firmly what he had said for years. He may have learned from Cavour that war was likely in the spring, but he remained more certain of it than the great diplomat.

These two mainstays of the traditional proof of La Farina's closeness to Cavour do not, then, of themselves furnish very strong evidence; but their significance can be almost wholly salvaged. That the two men were in close contact is not merely a tale told by later writers but a conviction shared by the political observers of the time. Even in August of 1856 Pallavicino referred to Cavour and Rattazzi as among La Farina's political friends, and no one seems to have doubted that the basis for a fruitful relationship existed. Tommaséo, in May of 1858, characteristically accused La Farina of being a spy in Cavour's control (with Castelli the intermediary so that Cavour would be free to deny everything). In June Paselli wrote his Bolognese friends about the Society newly formed in Turin "under the official protection of the Government."

[8] Selmi, La Farina, 17.
[9] He had once known for sure that Murat would soon be given Naples and Sicily, decorating his prediction with instructions to "remember my words, not as the news of journals, or as a supposition, but as a positive fact . . .": La Farina to Ricciardi, 31 October 1855, Franchi, Epistolario di La Farina, i, 567. For other examples of La Farina's appetite for secret "information" from high circles, see his letters to Amari, 9 January, to di Torrearsa, 16 September, to Raeli, 17 September 1855; and to Oddo, 29 April, and to Cianciolo, 19 July 1856, ibid., i, 525, 545, 548; ii, 10, 16. He wrote Fabrizi, 24 May 1856, that England and France had promised Piedmont aid against Austria [Palamenghi-Crispi], "L'Evoluzione alla Monarchia," Risorgimento Italiano, vii, 144. He predicted the war in 1859 even before Plombières, La Farina to Capitani, 14 June 1858, Franchi, Epistolario di La Farina, ii, 65.
[10] He seems, for example, to have informed the Dandolo brothers of the agreements of Plombières, Visconti-Venosta, Ricordi di gioventù, 457.

Writing years later, Zini remembered that La Farina had been in some relation with the Government, "perhaps in full accord." Even in 1860 Salazaro printed an account of La Farina as having been Pallavicino's representative to the Prime Minister. (Cavour showed himself "on many occasions" willing to "second" their work although he left the Society "all freedom of action" and reserved the right to "deny" them.) Manfredi recalled that in his circle the "secrets of the policy of the Conte di Cavour [were] known by means of La Farina." *Civiltà Cattolica* believed it had evidence that Cavour's Government aided the SNI through its consuls, "corrupting officials, setting up Committees, selling consciences. . . ."[11] There was also a widespread belief in La Farina's influence over the Prime Minister. D'Azeglio listed him among "those who surround Cavour," and expressed the hope that his influence would not lead to *"imbrogli."* A Swiss major promoting his "revolutionary" ideas of war, or Garibaldi wanting Cavour to have faith that the revolutionary forces would support Piedmont—both first got in touch with La Farina.

If—as the evidence suggests—La Farina and Cavour had some steady relationship by July 1857, it was hardly a secret.[12] There is always in politics the tendency to see a coincidence of interests as cooperation, cooperation as conspiracy. The connection between La Farina and Cavour was probably not very precisely defined (certainly not before the fall of 1858). What matters is not how often they met but that a general awareness of some

[11] Cavour wrote Sbarbaro, 20 May 1858, noting that La Farina recommended him: Mazza, *Sbarbaro*, 20. Pallavicino to Manin, 10 August 1856, Maineri, *Manin e Pallavicino*, 158; Tommaséo to Capponi, 26 May 1858; del Lungo and Prunas, *Tommaséo e Capponi*, IV, 224–25; Paselli to Casarini, 18 June 1858, Maioli, "Società Nazionale in Bologna," *Saggi e documenti* (1933), 73; Zini, *Storia d'Italia*, I², 10 (earlier and in private he was more reserved: Zini, "Memorie dei casi che condussero il mio commissariato," ms., MNRT); Salazaro, *Cenni sulla rivoluzione*, 19–20; from an article by Manfredi published 15 January 1910, cited in Stefano Fermi and Emilio Ottolenghi, *Giuseppe Manfredi, patriota e magistrato piacentino* (Piacenza, 1927), CLXXVIII–CLXXIX (he himself had gone to Turin to get direct encouragement from Cavour, *ibid.*, CLXIV); *Civiltà Cattolica*, ser. 5, XII (1864), 165. See also Chapter Six, note 1.

[12] D'Azeglio to Nigra, 24 January 1859, *Cavour-Nigra*, II, 23; the major, August Viande, reached La Farina through Lorenzo Festi (which suggests that the undated letter may have been written in 1860), ms., ISR, busta 718, n. 86; Garibaldi to La Farina, 22 December 1858, Franchi, *Epistolario de La Farina*, II, 99. On La Farina's relations with Cavour in July 1857, see Chapter Three, notes 58 and 59. Cavour's own political difficulties in the fall of 1857 may have led him to take greater interest in La Farina.

relationship was to the advantage of both. Through this publicized sympathy for the National Society, Cavour established himself as worthy of nationalist confidence and made it easier to meet with important members of the Society. He could influence specific actions of the SNI when he wished, and the National Society was always there (as an excuse for policies adopted or a warning of the pressures he was under) to show to foreign diplomats.[13] That Pallavicino, never a convinced Cavourian, ceased at least his open opposition to the Prime Minister "from December 1857 to April 1859"[14] must have been a result of this new light on Piedmont's policy.

Certainly, there was no easier way for Cavour to arrange a visit from Garibaldi. In later years, as the meetings of these two so different men came to seem the very symbol of Italian unity, the supporters of La Farina rather usurped for their hero the honor of having first presented the two. Cavour and Garibaldi had managed to meet before without the aid of the Society; but the SNI probably deserves the more important credit of having presented a Garibaldi well disposed to Cavour's plans. Immediately after the Plombières meeting, in August, Garibaldi was told through Foresti and Pallavicino that Cavour would like to see him any day at 6 a.m. Thereafter such matters appear to have been handled through La Farina, and Massari records having one morning encountered La Farina and Garibaldi sitting in Cavour's anteroom.[15] La Farina, observed by his Neapolitan antagonist while acting as the visible link between Italy's two greatest leaders, must have had few greater moments.

It was similarly through the men of the Society that Cavour won the services of the exiled General Ulloa or made sure Kossuth did not dangerously influence Garibaldi.[16] The Prime Min-

---

[13] That Cavour also used the Society in this more subtle way is suggested in the acceptance by Hudson, the British Ambassador, of the statement in the *Times* that La Farina and Pallavicino were typical of the emigrants who were prodding Piedmont to war. See Massari, *Diario*, entry of 24 January 1859, 174–75.

[14] So Pallavicino claimed in 1860, Maineri, *Manin e Pallavicino*, 424.

[15] On their earlier meeting see Pallavicino to Manin, 24 August 1856, *ibid.*, 172; and to Foresti, 7 August 1856, *Memorie di Pallavicino*, III, 298; Cavour to La Farina, 26 November 1856 and 24 December 1858, Chiala, *Lettere di Cavour*, II (Turin, 1883), 354, 362; Massari, *Diario*, entry for 3 March 1859, 218.

[16] Pallavicino to Manin, 11 August 1856, Maineri, *Manin e Pallavicino*, 161;

ister must have thought of the National Society when he assured Louis Napoleon that he could at any time secure petitions of complaint from Massa and Carrara.[17] Certainly it was most comforting to Cavour to have someone who would effectively warn against precipitous action or excessive demonstrations. His letters to La Farina repeat the same warnings over and over, and he would have been reassured to know how fully La Farina's letters echoed the theme. The National Society could not prevent convinced revolutionaries from plying their trade or hotheads from getting angry; but at the very least, its letters to its members must have made waiting more bearable for the impatient and inaction seem part of a plan.[18]

Cavour, however, was never one to depend solely upon one policy or upon one agency to carry it out; and his dependence upon the National Society can be easily overstressed. He was too clever, there was too much at stake, and the situation was too complex to allow the SNI a role in which it might call the tune. Most of the men close to Cavour (Massari, Minghetti, Farini, Boncompagni) were outside the Society and somewhat suspicious of it. As late as January 1859, Boncompagni, Piedmont's ambassador in Tuscany, seems not to have known what the SNI was.[19] Cavour wrote that he had had "L" [La Farina?] *and others* try to calm things down in Lombardy, and Farini spoke of how fine it was that La Farina and others were doing so much for the volunteers arriving in Piedmont.[20] But Farini, ignoring the Society, sent his own instructions to Malenchini, its leader in Leghorn; both d'Azeglio and Castelli apparently felt

---

two letters of Cavour to La Farina, n.d., and one from La Farina to Medici, 24 December 1858, Franchi, *Epistolario de La Farina*, II, 100, 136.

[17] Nigra to Cavour, 1 October 1858, and Cavour's project for Massa and Carrara, *Cavour-Nigra*, I, 157, 184. A. J. P. Taylor points out the importance in the plans of Cavour and Napoleon III of finding a "respectable" cause for war: *The Struggle for Mastery in Europe* (Oxford, 1954), 104. The SNI would have been a great comfort at this point.

[18] See Cavour to La Farina, n.d., Franchi, *Epistolario di La Farina*, II, 134, 151.

[19] Boncompagni wrote Cavour, 8 January 1859, of the writings of the "National Committee directed by La Farina" then circulating in Tuscany saying "probably under these words a republican concept is hidden . . . ," ms. in Lettere Ministri, Legazione di Toscana, AST.

[20] Cavour to Nigra, 8 December 1858, *Cavour-Nigra*, I, 233; Farini to Cavour, 28 March 1859, Luigi Rava (ed.), *Epistolario di Luigi Carlo Farini*, IV (Bologna, 1935), 244.

that *they* had been given particular responsibility to represent the Prime Minister among the Tuscan liberals.[21] Cavour wrote directly to such local leaders as Ricasoli, Ridolfi, Bartolommei or Casarini.[22] And when men of regional prominence came to Turin, they were certain to talk with Cavour himself.[23]

Within Cavour's own circle there were others who kept him in touch with the National Society. D'Ancona remembered Farini and Castelli as having been the intermediaries between the Society in Turin and the Prime Minister. It was Bardesono who presented Casarini, well coached, to Cavour; and it was Castelli who presented Tanari (then a potential recruit to the Society) to La Farina and perhaps he who introduced La Farina to Cavour.[24] The Prime Minister, then, had many strings to his bow, and his relationship with the Society must have been very much like that he advocated for Minghetti: constant contact with it while preserving full freedom of action. It was with the same attitude that he answered one of Massari's attacks on the Society. "Nevertheless it is useful to make use of it: in a symphony many instruments are needed, the shrill [*acuti*] and the deep [*profondi*]; in the Italian symphony the Association is a shrill instrument: that too is needed." [25] Cavour had no doubt as to who was conducting the orchestra.

The role of subordinate, however, could not have come easily to La Farina. No amateur in politics, he was motivated by more

[21] Farini to Malenchini, 20 March 1859, *ibid.*, 241; W. K. Hancock, *Ricasoli and the Risorgimento in Tuscany* (London, 1926), 189; Luigi Chiala (ed.), *Ricordi di Michelangelo Castelli* (Turin, 1888), 226.

[22] Cavour to Nigra, 18 February 1859, *Cavour-Nigra*, II, 18; and Cavour to Cosimo Ridolfi, 11 April 1859, cited in Sergio Camerani, "La Toscana alla vigilia della rivoluzione," *Archivio Storico Italiano*, CIII–CIV (1945–46), 168; Cavour to Bartolommei, 19 February 1859, Matilda Gioli, *Il Risorgimento toscano e l'azione popolare* (Florence, 1905), 239 (other communications to Ferdinando Bartolommei from the Prime Minister through such men as Enrico Lawley and Carlo Pellati are apparent in the Carteggio Barolommei, mss., Museo del Risorgimento, Firenze, hereafter MRF); Bardesono to Casarini, 3 April 1859, Masi, "Casarini," *Fra Libri e Ricordi*, 113–14.

[23] Alberto Dallolio, "I Colloqui di Camillo Casarini col Conte di Cavour," *La Strenna delle colonie scolastiche bolognese*, XXXVII (1934), *passim*; Alessandrini, *I fatti* II, 22; Camerani, "La Toscana alla vigilia," *Archivio Storico*, CIII–CIV, 143–46.

[24] D'Ancona, *Varietà storiche*, 328–29; Masi, "Casarini," *Fra Libri e ricordi*, 108; Paselli to Casarini, 31 August 1858, Maioli, "Società Nazionale in Bologna," *Saggi e documenti* (1933), 81; supplement to *Bollettino Settemanale* No. 42 of *La Discussione*, 23 October 1863.

[25] Minghetti, *Ricordi*, III, 136; Massari, *Diario*, entry of 1 March 1859, 216.

than admiration for Cavour or faith in his policies though he led the SNI to become more and more the Prime Minister's instrument. His agreement with Cavour had not, in fact, come automatically. La Farina's attachment to the idea of an insurrection in Sicily was deep; he had been displeased by Boncompagni's homages to the Pope and had expressed his displeasure in print. We have never, he wrote, believed in diplomacy as an answer to the Italian Question; and he argued that Piedmont's support of a national policy would result from necessity more than intent. As late as October 1858, he agreed with Pallavicino that the Society should bring pressure on the Government to make it modify its policy. He found it useful even in the spring of 1859 to declare the Society free of any official ties which might hinder the development of its program throughout Italy.[26]

La Farina, who had once thought the "present ministers" really interested only in territorial aggrandizement and who had hoped to communicate his ideas to the King without their knowledge,[27] nevertheless labored hard to assure the Society's followers that Cavour was a convinced nationalist. His letters hinted that the Prime Minister's acts were all part of a plan for Italian unification; the *Piccolo Corriere* gave Cavour restrained but favorable publicity. By dropping frequent hints of his relationship with Cavour, La Farina certainly gained in personal prestige. Not a modest man, this in itself must have appealed to him; a consummate politician, he was able to use such prestige to great advantage. This as well as his great vigor led him to overshadow Pallavicino in the Society. More and more within its councils La Farina could claim additional information which made his views prevail. The authoritative tone is hard to resist in the statement that, "I have had an interview with the friend for three and a quarter hours. Things go excellently, however this fall we will have to work." [28]

Necessarily such prestige was carried over to the Society itself; La Farina's letters are full of references to the things that he dare

---

[26] *Piccolo Corriere*, 17 May, 26 July and 1 August 1857; La Farina to Pallavicino, 16 October 1858, ms., MNRT; La Farina to Cipriano Conti, 30 March 1859, Franchi, *Epistolario di La Farina*, II, 156.
[27] La Farina to Reali, 17 September 1855, *ibid.*, I, 557.
[28] La Farina to Pallavicino, 8 August 1858, photostat in MNRT.

not say in writing, of assurances that an article in the *Piccolo Corriere* can be considered as "official" or at least "semi-official."[29] The instructions and opinions of a small group of hopeful men, often proved wrong in the past, were far more impressive with the shadow of Cavour behind them.

The Society profited from this relationship in another way, too. One may doubt La Farina's account of Cavour's confession, at their first meeting, that he knew little of affairs outside Piedmont; but it probably is an accurate statement of La Farina's opinion. As Cavour used the Society, it was the Society's men with whom he increasingly came into contact. His correspondence with Bartolommei and Casarini, his relations with Zini, the discovery that Garibaldi was not necessarily an enemy of his policy—these things were bound to have some influence upon him of the very sort that Pallavicino felt to be necessary. Cavour's few statements about what he requested of the SNI suggest he tended to accept La Farina's view of it as a highly organized, militant unit. La Farina's reports of conditions beyond the border seem to have been taken seriously even if Cavour knew better than to depend upon them wholly, even if they sometimes contained nothing he did not know: "I am informed of the happenings in Tuscany," he wrote La Farina with a touch of impatience.[30] Equally important, La Farina's loyalty won him Cavour's confidence, a fact which enabled the Society to withstand the dislike for it felt by many of those closest to the Prime Minister.

Prior to September 1858, La Farina seems not to have claimed knowledge of information which "it would be the greatest imprudence, even a crime, to reveal."[31] Not until November is there any sign that Cavour has begun corresponding frequently with La Farina. Cavour may not have been telling the whole truth in August when he told Massari he did not know the leaders of the National Society, only that they were opposed to Mazzini; that he could have expected the knowledgeable Massari to believe him suggests that his relations with the Society had been

[29] La Farina to Mazzi and Filippo Amadori, 24 January 1859, Franchi, *Epistolario di La Farina*, II, 121, 119.
[30] Cavour to La Farina, n.d., *ibid.*, 151.
[31] La Farina to Mazzi, 7 September 1858, *ibid.*, 78–9.

limited.[32] It would have been unlike Cavour to establish any close policy of cooperation with the Society until he knew when and how he might use it and what the risks of the relationship might be. These things he could feel sure of only after the secret meeting at Plombières in July 1858, where he and Louis Napoleon plotted their war against Austria. This suggests that only in the fall of 1858 did Cavour and the SNI begin active cooperation. There is no real evidence to the contrary.

Then, however, there was a flurry of activity; the Society published predictions of imminent war; small secret missions were undertaken for the Government and more exciting ones planned; new committees were established and the Society itself more strongly organized. The Italian National Society was preparing for great events.

In October the *Piccolo Corriere* carried an article entitled, "Where are we going?" The answer was not precisely given, but it was clear that something was coming; everyone was arming; Italians must ready themselves. La Farina began writing the committees of the SNI that war was scheduled for the spring.[33] The Society's newspaper emphasized the growing unrest throughout the Peninsula. In Parma and Milan, among Hungarian troops in the Austrian army, smoking had ceased; and this sacrifice to deprive the enemy of more revenue had, it was confidently reported, gotten on Austrian nerves. The theaters of Lodi, Carrara, Palermo rang with patriotic demonstrations; pictures of Victor Emmanuel, Cavour, La Marmora were selling well in Lombardy. Everywhere the walls were covered with patriotic slogans. The carnival in Reggio was boycotted; balls in Venice and Como went unattended. The girls of Piacenza—and the article made it clear they were the most desirable ones—were said to have formed a league, agreeing not to marry any boy who did not fight for Italian independence; the *Piccolo Corriere* could imagine no "more serious, more sublime, more significant demonstration." [34] Despite foreign oppression, despite the fact that war would be won with arms and foreign aid, the people

[32] Massari, *Diario*, entry of 25 August 1858, 23.
[33] *Piccolo Corriere*, 25 October 1858; for example, La Farina to Felice Bolognini (Lerici), 20 October 1858, Franchi, *Epistolario di La Farina*, II, 81.
[34] *Piccolo Corriere*, 6 and 20 December 1858; 3, 10, 17 January, 7 and 14 March, 28 February 1859.

of little power and modest courage but deep conviction were playing their part, too.

In January Victor Emmanuel gave his speech from the throne with its electrifying reference to "the cry of suffering" that came from much of Italy and was heard in Piedmont. The response rose from every hamlet to fill pages of the paper. The ferment in Lombardy, Venice, Modena grew; Reggio was excited by talk of war; the people of the Romagna and Tuscany were united by the very thought of it. And war was not far away.[35] Above all, there was promise for the future in the support won by the National Society's program. A long battle between the two newspapers of Savona was ended when both adopted that program, and a committee of the SNI had "with great solemnity" been established there. The Piedmontese press in general praised the Society's publications, and three more papers adopted its program.[36] The *Credo politico* of the National Society had become a part of the student songs in Pavia; its other pamphlets were widely read and praised from Palermo and Naples to Tuscany and Piacenza. Even beyond Italy, the Society could boast new journalistic conquests; for the *Messaggero d'Egitto* (before the Austrian consul forced its closing), the *Italiano* (Lima), the *Corriere Italiano* (New York), and the *Corriere Italiano di Grecia* (Athens) were all using its materials.[37]

Seen through the eyes of the National Society, the international situation further justified exhilaration. Thanks to the Society, the Italian Question raised no issues of liberty, only those of independence; Louis Napoleon and Tsar Alexander had nothing to fear. Indeed, the third Napoleon was seen as a great boon for Italy, for now France was united and strong, ruled by a man of action who knew Italy well. The Bourbons had supported Metternich; the Second Republic had sent troops into Rome (the part of President Bonaparte was conveniently forgotten). Any other regime in France now would be a socialistic one, trying to export to Italy the kind of revolution for which

[35] *Ibid.*, 17 and 10 January 1859; 22 and 29 November, 27 December 1858.
[36] The papers were *Il Diario di Savona* and *Il Saggiatore di Savona: Piccolo Corriere*, 10 January 1859. The praise had come from *Unione, Espero, Tempo* (Casale), *Indipendente Casalese: ibid.*, 29 November 1858. *Il Messaggero di Novi*, the *Costituzione Bellereze, Stella d'Italia* (Turin) adopted the program, *ibid.*, 24 January 1859.
[37] *Ibid.*, 6, 20, 27 December 1858; 31 January and 21 February, 4 April 1859.

Italians lacked the necessary "elements and convictions." [38]
The French press was extensively quoted as evidence of spontaneous sympathy for Italy and (in a dictatorship) of official policy. Austria was France's greatest enemy, and to aid Italy was in her own best interest. Reports of France's growing armed strength, signs even of mobilization, and the talk of war there were hailed by the Society.[39] Not all French actions, however, were consistent with the Society's view of her intent. Her refusal to withdraw from Rome even at Cardinal Antonelli's request, and the rumors that Prince Napoleon was out of favor were causes of alarm· To many throughout Europe La Guerronière's officially inspired pamphlet, *Napoléon III et l'Italie* was shocking and bellicose, but the Society hoped for so much more that talk of a Papal federation came as a serious setback. Many in France, it was explained, opposed Italian unification, and the pamphlet was written to prepare them. We prefer, the *Piccolo Corriere* declared, the authority of Napoleon I, who looked to Rome as the basis of a renascent Roman empire.[40]

Good news from abroad did not stop with France. Russia, the old enemy of the Crimean War, was now the friend who used Sardinian ports. Her "natural" conflict with Austria led her to look kindly on Piedmont, and the *"Gazzetta di San Pietroburgo"* was quoted as predicting a great part for Piedmont in Italian history, ominously declaring that treaties could be changed. Prussia, jealous of her German neighbor, added to Austria's isolation. British public opinion was seen as solidly behind Piedmont; Lord Derby's *Morning Herald* warned of Austria's shaky position, and Lord Palmerston's *Morning Post* foresaw Victor Emmanuel inevitably following the example of Charles Albert in attempting to unify Italy.[41] All these nations were preparing for war; and France, Great Britain, and Russia who had previ-

[38] *Ibid.*, 13 December 1858; *Italia, Francia e Russia* (Turin, 1859), 7; *Le forze liberatrici*, 5, 9.

[39] *Piccolo Corriere*, 20 September 1858; 10 January and 7 February 1859; *Italia, Francia e Russia*, 7; *Piccolo Corriere*, 12 July, 20 September 1858; 24 January, 14 and 21 February 1859.

[40] *Ibid.*, 29 November 1858; 14 February 1859; 25 October, 15 November, 13 December 1858; 31 January and 7, 14, 21 February 1859; *Italia, Francia e Russia*, 7–8.

[41] *Piccolo Corriere*, 27 September and 15 November 1858; 20 September and 20 December 1858; 11 January and 21 February 1859.

ously joined to establish the freedom of four million Greeks would surely do as much for ten million Italians. Great Britain and Prussia were warning Austria; France and Russia were near an agreement similar to the one between France and Piedmont. The Papal nuncio had shown real insight by nearly fainting when Louis Napoleon, at his New Year's Day reception, expressed regret to Ambassador Hübner that Franco-Austrian relations were not better.[42]

Austria, too, was busily arming; but the *Piccolo Corriere* proved to its own satisfaction that of the 600,000 troops she claimed it would be possible to put no more than 150,000 on the battlefield in Lombardy. Victory was as certain as war. Nor did the Society allow any doubt as to who the enemy was. Parma and Tuscany had relatively mild governments, but they were as anti-national as any other. Talk of their allying with Piedmont was ridiculous; the follies of 1848 would not be repeated.[43] Best of all, Piedmont was actively preparing. The King promised his soldiers they would smell dust again in the spring, and a willing parliament granted him a war-loan. Cavour, who had shrewdly brought Piedmont to the center of European politics, was promisingly vague when asked if that loan might be used for an offensive effort. Garibaldi, who did not take his association with the SNI lightly, had come to Turin to prepare for action.[44]

With so much so imminent, excitement ran high; and in that heated atmosphere the Society thrived. Never was it closer to achieving its ambition of uniting all but the political extremes than when Pallavicino could write Ulloa worrying lest some reckless revolt upset the "well-meditated" plans of Cavour; or when the Marchese could assure Garibaldi that the Government had at last recognized its dependence on popular forces. Piedmont would prepare her army and placate diplomacy, he said, while the National Society conspired.[45] And never was the

[42] *Ibid.*, 15 November and 27 December 1858; 17 January and 7 and 28 February 1859; 10 January 1859.
[43] *Ibid.*, 12 September, 22 November, 20 and 27 December 1858; 10 January, 7 and 14 February 1859.
[44] *Ibid.*, 29 November, 6 and 13 December 1858; 10 January, 7 and 14 February 1859.
[45] Pallavicino to Ulloa, 29 November; and to Garibaldi, 13 November 1858, *Memorie di Pallavicino*, III, 477-78, 475-76.

Society closer to winning the Government to the conspiracy of which La Farina had dreamed than in that fall and winter of 1858.

In October the Society's secretary wrote out and presented to Cavour a plan for the revolutionary action which would extend the war with Austria into areas under nominally independent Italian governments.[46] The plan was intended to keep war and uprisings separate (on the grounds that regular armies weaken revolution and local bands ruin military discipline) and to restrain the revolution it sponsored. Deserters would be absorbed into the regular army. The rest of the plan would go into effect only where revolution broke out spontaneously. Once the revolution was won, a state of siege should be declared, with supreme judicial authority given to special war councils. No newspapers, only an official bulletin would be allowed. The revolution, in short, would be used, controlled, ended. Meant to require a minimum displacement of Piedmontese troops, the plan's other advantages were declared to be that it centered on the areas of the Society's greatest strength, did not require that each single uprising succeed, and would in the eyes of all establish the need for Piedmontese intervention.

The plan itself, however, bore fewer marks of such caution, and the thinking of the professional agitator showed through. Upon the outbreak of revolution in Massa and Carrara (May 1 was the hypothetical date), some 300 men, gathered by the SNI and under Garibaldi, would march from Sarzana and Lerici to their aid. Enlarged by union with another group from Varese, they would on the third day attack Parma. In case of resistance

[46] The plan, "approved after long discussion the evening of 19 October," is printed in Franchi, *Epistolario di La Farina*, II, 82–6. The discussion, Biundi says, was with Cavour and one of his personal secretaries; but he gives no evidence. It seems unlikely that Cavour would at this date formally agree to so extensive a plan, and "accepted" may well refer to discussions within the Central Committee of the SNI. It is unlikely that Cavour would promise to send the Piedmontese fleet to Tuscany, or to give Garibaldi the free hand the plan leaves him, or even to contribute so substantial an amount of arms. La Farina, on the other hand, could not have conceived of carrying out the plan without Cavour's knowledge and approval of it; and its emphasis on Massa and Carrara fits well with the Plombières agreement. The plan, which well reflects the Society's thought, can probably be taken as the maximum to which Cavour might have agreed. Its very conception suggests extensive rapport with the Government.

"our friends there" were to capture the arsenal, which in itself was expected to be enough to discourage Ducal troops. If victorious, Garibaldi would continue on toward Reggio and Modena, if not, he could retreat to the Apennines where he would be strengthened by the rebels from Fivizzano, Pistoia, and other parts of the Lunigiana. Piedmontese troops would meanwhile have taken Massa and Carrara and the two Apennine passes— under the pretext of defending them against Austria—in order to aid the efforts in Parma. In a "bolder and perhaps more decisive" alternative, Garibaldi might attack Modena from Massa and Carrara.

After pondering such successes, there was no stopping. The Piedmontese fleet would enter Leghorn supposedly to prevent Austrian intervention and this, coupled with activities in the Lunigiana, would be enough to make the Grand Duke depart; Tuscan troops would not resist. If all went well, Garibaldi could then turn toward Bologna. "Our friends" in Lombardy-Venetia would have begun a guerrilla harassment (cutting telegraph wires and so forth); and in the likelihood that Lombardy and Venetia should rise up, a force led by Ulloa could march from Bologna across the Po while Garibaldi threw himself into the Marches. Austria and France, the international prestige and influence of the Papacy, the military weaknesses of untrained bands were all forgotten.

The plan ended with an imposing list of what would have to be provided in the way of arms (600 carbines and pistols by November 1; 12,000 by March) and money (400 francs a month until March to pay spies and reimburse their commissaries for travel expenses). This was cheap enough for a plan that would place the Austrians between two fires and open the way into Tuscany and the Romagna for the Piedmontese army, enabling it to turn the Quadrilateral. Mazzini could not have done better. Like so many of its predecessors, the plan had developed an intoxicating power of its own; unspecified numbers of men became "forces"; battles were replaced by uprisings and "fires." It is a measure of the height to which hopes had risen that such a plan was committed to paper. One must doubt that Cavour very seriously depended upon it; but it does seem to

have been the background against which the Society's preparations for war were made. These preparations unfolded more
slowly than the plan had allowed. But Garibaldi was contacted;
Massa and Carrara remained the points of initial focus; various
members of the Society did cross the border for consultations;
some weapons were ferreted into border towns and instructions
were sent out for the cutting of telegraph wires and the blocking
of highways. For a moment the Society showed again its radical
antecedents and its older determination to influence Cavour.

There were signs indeed that in matters of smaller scale the
National Society had taught the Government to see the utility
of its conspirings. Its committee in Sarzana was repeatedly called
upon to produce detailed complaints—La Farina asked that they
be concrete—on conditions in Massa and Carrara for use by the
Government in a diplomatic note. He wanted a list of instances
in which laws were violated or injustices committed, an enumera-
tion of political trials and of emigrants departing.[47] When the
Government of the Duke demanded the extradition of some of
its citizens in Carrara, the SNI sent out instructions that a
statement from the friends and relatives of the men concerned
should be sent Cavour. The instructions left no doubt as to the
form this statement should take. The events leading to the
emigrants' arrests should be given a "political color"; there could
be references to the injustices and "wickednesses" committed
there, and it should be made clear that the arresting police were
all notorious *sanfedisti*. The petition itself should be dated as
of the previous month, in order, apparently, that the discontent
would seem of longer duration and the petition more spontaneous. It would, La Farina promised, give the Government of
Piedmont a good chance "to molest" the Duke. Even the Society's penchant for petitions took a conspiratorial turn. La
Farina suggested in December that some of the members of the
National Guard in the Piedmontese border town of Sarzana
should request permission to form a company of troops [*bersaglieri*] which the "youngest and most courageous" could enter.
There would thus be, he hinted, a corps organized and instructed
for all possible "occurrences." Once their petition, which should

[47] La Farina to Mazzi, 16 August, 7 September, 22 December 1858, *ibid.*, 74,
79–80, 98. See also note 17 above.

not contain any revolutionary phrases, was sent to him, he would attempt to gain the necessary permission.[48]

Toward the end of the year some steps were taken to gather arms for an insurrection in the Duchies,[49] and in February Zini was asked through the Society to make a tour of Tuscany, the Duchies, and Bologna to report on the political temper of the public there. He was briefed about the trip by La Farina in a room belonging to the Ministry of the Interior, and the trip itself appears to have been paid for by the Government. Zini was later assured that his report, which he had given to Boncompagni, was in the hands of Cavour.[50] Marchese Tanari came from Bologna to talk of organizing for action and to commit the Government to some mutually acceptable plan.[51]

Great things were afoot, and in November Pallavicino and La Farina again asked Garibaldi to come to Turin. The General, too, anticipated important activity, and he put Medici in charge of organizing troops for his part in that action. He was, he declared, only waiting for the instructions of La Farina or "*il Conte*"; everything else he was willing to leave up to La Farina or Pallavicino. For even Garibaldi had come to praise Cavour; and he assured all of them that they need not worry about any suggestions which might come to him from London.[52] For his part, Cavour was coming to feel that Garibaldi showed political "good sense" beyond all praise; the Government, Cavour noted with pride, asked no one about his political past. The Prime Minister was anxious that measures meant for Mazzinians not

---

[48] La Farina to Mazzi, 23 November 1858 (the date he suggests for the petition is October 30), *ibid.*, 87–8. Cavour's concern for the matter is shown in his letter to Giovanni De Foresta, November 1858, Chiala, *Lettere di Cavour*, II, 353. La Farina to Mazzi, 22 December 1858, Franchi, *Epistolario di La Farina*, II, 98.

[49] How extensive these preparations were is far from clear, but Della Noce wanted credit for some part in them, Della Noce, autobiography, ms., ISR, busta 555.

[50] It was Selmi who first asked him to come to Turin from Lombardy to discuss the matter, Zini, "Memorie dei casi che condussero il mio commissariato," ms., MNRT.

[51] Massari, *Diario*, entries for 21 and 24 August 1858, 21. Tanari's emphasis on local revolutions and his thought of one in France, too, could have done nothing to increase Massari's confidence in the Society.

[52] Pallavicino to Garibaldi, 13 November 1858, *Memorie di Pallavicino*, III, 475–76; Garibaldi to Pallavicino, 11 and 30 January 1859, mss., MNRT; Garibaldi to La Farina, 15 November and 21 December 1858, 8 and 30 January 1859, Franchi, *Epistolario di La Farina*, II, 91, 97, 110, 124.

be applied by zealous officials to "the party of union represented by La Farina . . . our friends."[53] Such concord represented the very achievement which the Society had claimed to represent.

This concord was, however, based on the belief in imminent action; and the delays which came instead strained that mutual confidence. Cavour postponed until late December his meeting with Garibaldi and in the meantime worried about other influences on the General. Pallavicino himself took pains to assure Garibaldi that the Government had not changed its plans as malicious rumors might suggest. Garibaldi hinted that perhaps Cavour was not sufficiently convinced of the support he had from the revolutionary elements, and he suggested quite gently that La Farina use his influence to assure the Prime Minister that, given an Italy rich in men and money, they could achieve their goal by themselves. It bothered Garibaldi that "our enemies" might still accuse Cavour of doing nothing. By March, Pallavicino's confidence in Cavour's policy had slipped a bit, though he assured himself Cavour was and would have to remain "with us."[54]

The November optimism had also led to an organizational strengthening of the SNI. In Turin the National Society set up its own office, which was open from two to four every afternoon, and dues were raised from one to one and a half lire a month. It was announced that the Central Committee felt it necessary to redouble its propaganda, and the old practice of sending five copies of the *Piccolo Corriere* to each member was dropped in favor of sending an unlimited number on demand, but otherwise only two.[55] A committee was finally established in Genoa where it was still worthwhile even for the SNI to stress its "ab-

[53] Cavour to Cesare Cabella, 14 March 1859, Chiala, *Lettere di Cavour*, III (Turin, 1884), 44–5; and to Castelli, February 1859, Luigi Chiala (ed.), *Carteggio politico di Michelangelo Castelli* (Turin, 1890), I, 173.

[54] Cavour to La Farina, 26 November 1858 and n.d., and La Farina to Medici, 24 December 1858, Franchi, *Epistolario di La Farina*, II, 91, 100, 101; Pallavicino to Garibaldi, 29 December 1858, 9 January and 2 March 1859, *Memorie di Pallavicino*, III, 484, 486, 503–504; Garibaldi to La Farina, 22 December 1858 and 30 January 1859, Franchi, *Epistolario di La Farina*, II, 99, 124.

[55] *Piccolo Corriere*, 22, 15 and 8 November 1858; artisans could still pay dues of only 20 *centesimi*. Pallavicino may have assumed a more active role in the Society during this period; note, for example, his letters in *Memorie di Pallavicino*, III, 480ff., and the more frequent references to him in the *Piccolo Corriere*, 3 January, 7 February, 7 and 14 March 1859.

solute independence of Governmental influence." [56] By spring the Society could claim 94 local committees in various parts of Italy.[57]

The increase in the number of committees was less important however than the strengthened lines of communication within the Society. Local committees probably held formal meetings rarely, and whether members met in a private *palazzo* (Florence and Piacenza) or in the back of a bookstore (Modena) or in a café (Bologna and Imola) they were usually personal friends probably meeting more to maintain good spirits than to settle policy.[58] Indeed, La Farina had to remind his committees that anyone who agreed with them on central matters should be welcomed as a member. Furthermore, these local committees varied greatly in temper and size (from a very few members to a score or more); they kept their own funds and were highly autonomous.[59] If the committees were to perform functions other than those of propaganda, their capacity to do so would depend on the closeness of their connection with the Central Committee in Turin.

Within Piedmont itself, however, the problem of communication was immense. Complaints were often received that not even the correct number of copies of the *Piccolo Corriere* arrived on time.[60] Once formed, local committees demanded attention; Sarzana's, important as it was, had to be scolded for sending a dramatic telegram which, wrote La Farina, made the telegraph

[56] Announcement of organization of the Genoa committee, 31 January 1859 (signed by Domenico Doria Pamphili, Luigi Centurini, Angelo Pichi, Emanuele Bignone, Daniele Morchio, G. Galleano Rosciano, Prospero Padoa), in the Carte Morchio, Museo Nazionale del Risorgimento, Genova (hereafter MNRG). The new committee actively sought further members as evidenced by its "*catalogo provvisorio dei componenti*," ms., *ibid*. See also Pallavicino to Doria Pamphili, 15 January 1859, *Memorie di Pallavicino*, III, 494.

[57] Selmi, *La Farina*, 19; the figure seems to be taken from the Society's announcement of its reorganization, 20 October 1859.

[58] Gioli, *Risorgimento Toscano*, *passim*; Fermi and Ottolenghi, *Manfredi*, CLXIV, Manfredi admitted that the committee of Piacenza almost never met; Ferrari, *Ferrari*, 150; Masi, "Casarini," *Fra Libri e ricordi*, 105; Galli, "Società Nazionale e Gamberini," *La Romagna*, XVI, 399, 406.

[59] La Farina to Morchio, 9 March 1859; to Mazzi, 18 October 1858; and to Conti, 30 March 1859, Franchi, *Epistolario di La Farina*, II, 144, 86, 156; Maioli, "Tanari e il suo memoriale," *Archiginasio*, XXVIII, 64.

[60] La Farina to Amilcare Carlotti, January [1859; the date given here, 1856, is clearly in error]; and to Morchio, 9 March 1859, Franchi, *Epistolario di La Farina*, II, 11, 149.

carriers laugh and Count Cavour furious. Telegrams, he reminded them, are quasi-public. The committee of Pallanza was reprimanded for sending a letter unstamped, apparently thinking to take advantage of deputies' franking privilege; the Society's affairs were declared too grave, too important for such forgetfulness. Such matters were not very serious, but the time they required was. La Farina complained that the Central Committee now dealt with letters not in the dozens but in the hundreds.[61]

La Farina alone handled nearly all the correspondence with local committees; only in this way, he said, could the secret "which has been the desperation of the police," be kept. The burden was a heavy one, and the Society's secretary again and again had to begin letters by apologizing for his tardiness. The only remedy developed was to have letters copied by their first recipient and sent on to others, but this was hardly satisfactory. The main strength of the Society as an organization had come to depend upon the personal relations of each committee with the Society's secretary. He made the smallest tasks seem part of a plan important to the whole nation. To be in touch with La Farina was to see things from the top, even to receive hints about the future. It was no small encouragement to learn that your last letter had been read by "C,"whom La Farina had never seen laugh with such delight as at the anecdote you told.[62]

Outside Piedmont, the problem was to deliver letters, papers, and pamphlets once they were written. Copies of the *Piccolo Corriere* and pamphlets or letters intended for the Lunigiana were apparently smuggled across the border from Sarzana and Lerici. Packets seem to have been regularly sent by sea from Genoa to Mengozzi in Leghorn who then distributed them to others in Tuscany. The long border with Lombardy and the frequent travel across it made communication in that direction

---

[61] The Sarzana committee had apparently been greatly excited by rumors of troop movements across the border. La Farina reminded them that the political situation could be better judged in Turin than Sarzana and added cruelly that the committee in Cava-Carbonara, near 20,000 Austrian troops, remained calm. La Farina to Mazzi, 15 March 1859; and to Barigozzi, 24 January 1859 and 17 December 1858, *ibid.*, 149–50, 119–20, 94.

[62] La Farina to Mazzi, 24 January; to Bolognini, 13 January; to Mazzi, 2 February; to Bartolomeo, 30 March; to Conti, 11 March 1859, *ibid.*, 121, 114, 125, 155, 147. The Romagna offered something of an exception in that local groups usually wrote to the Bolognese committee.

easier.[63] It was, in addition, always possible to use code names and send apparently uncompromising letters through the regular mail.[64]

The Society's best organized system of underground communications was along the Via Emilia through the Duchies and into the Romagna; the conveniently small *Piccolo Corriere* as well as letters and pamphlets were sent down that route in quantity. Some of the officials along the way were willing to close their eyes; some of them may even have been members of the SNI. In any case, the border inspections were probably not very difficult hurdles for a resourceful courier, and years of plots and suppression must have made resourceful couriers not hard to come by. From Stradella these packets went to Piacenza where Manfredi would pass on information to those in his immediate area and distribute Piacenza's quota of the *Piccolo Corriere*; the other copies he might send on to Cremona or into the Veneto, but usually they went to Parma. There Armelonghi, who appears to have handled the most traffic, performed the same function, and so on to Reggio, Modena, and Bologna. A number of Manfredi's acquaintances would carry his parcels between Stradella and Piacenza, although sometimes Armelonghi could find someone making the whole trip to Stradella. The Society in Modena had its own contacts with Genoa, and a cheese peddler carried its material between Modena and Reggio. In Turin La Farina continued to receive help with such shipments from Francesco Selmi who was a friend of Conti's in Stradella and had other friends all along the line, particularly in Modena.[65] Such a system

---

[63] Omero [Mengozzi to Piero Puccioni, it seems certain], 12 April 1859, ms. in the possession of the Puccioni family in Florence. La Farina mentioned that 400 copies of one of Pallavicino's pamphlets had been sent into Lombardy, and he often referred to reports from there: La Farina to Barigozzi, 25 February; and to Carlotti, January 1856, Franchi, *Epistolario di La Farina*, II, 135, 118.

[64] La Farina referred to the *"nome convenzionale"* of a friend in Verona in a letter to Pallavicino, 10 January 1859, ms., MNRT; but Miani complained that a letter which reached him in Modena through the regular mail was compromising indeed, Enrico Terrachini to Selmi, February 1859, in Canevazzi, *Selmi*, 214.

[65] Fermi and Ottolenghi, *Manfredi*, 37, 37n, 38n, 47–8, 48n, 52, 54; CLXIV; Canevazzi, *Selmi*, 23–4, 41n, 202, 210, 213–14, 229; Prospero Padoa to Selmi, 18 February 1859, *ibid.*, 220; Ferrari, *Ferrari*, 150; La Farina to Giacomo Pelucchi, 27 November; to Leonzio Armelonghi, 27 December 1858; to Morchio, 27 March 1859, Franchi, *Epistolario di La Farina*, II, 92, 102, 153. Paselli told Casarini in July that the route to Parma from Turin was "secure," Paselli to

had its obvious weaknesses, the failure of one man could break the chain; and La Farina had to ask those along the way not to hold up the material they received. Yet, on the whole it did work; and when the Modena committee asked for 50 more copies of the *Piccolo Corriere*, they clearly expected to get them.[66]

The Society was further strengthened by the fact that nearly all its committees were headed by men of position in their communities, usually men long active in moderate politics. Their contacts with patriots of all stripes, with the old aristocracy as well as the new leaders of Piedmont, almost automatically placed them in that middle position the National Society sought to hold. They were sure to know men in nearly any city—and especially in Turin—who could send them political news. Furthermore, they were likely to know each other. Marchese Bartolommei (Florence), Conte Rasponi (Ravenna), Marchese Tanari (Bologna), Conte Gamberini (Imola), soldiers of note such as Malenchini (Leghorn), emigrants in Turin such as Professor Selmi—each of these men had dozens of contacts important to the Society. Because there was a social and often personal basis for their relations with each other, the Society had less need to be highly organized.

In its messages—whether printed in its newspaper or written in a small hand on thin paper, tightly folded and carried in a shoe—the Society continued to promise and predict that war was near. The event for which it had long been the herald was at hand; yet the instructions sent to local committees seem barely to have changed. Everywhere the word was to work, be

---

Casarini, 2 July 1858, Maioli, "Società Nazionale in Bologna," *Saggi e documenti* (1933), 76.

[66] La Farina said he sent out packages every Monday, asking that each man send them along quickly: La Farina [to Tanari], 28 February 1859, ms. in the Carte Tanari 1, MCRB. He explained in another letter that "the person who was to make the trip via L. [Lodi?] was unable to make it." He hoped, however, that they would get the "bundles sent you by way of P." [Parma?, he mentions "friend A." who might be Armelonghi]: La Farina to Bologna committee, n.d., ms. in the Fondo Dallolio, Carteggio Casarini, MCRB. Terrachini wrote to Selmi in February that since the departure of the pharmacist in Reggio, who was apparently a key link in their chain of communications, they had been completely without word from Turin: Canevazzi, *Selmi*, 211–12. Pietro Menozzi asked for the additional newspapers in a letter to Selmi, 20 December 1858, *ibid.*, 199.

prepared, stimulate zeal.[67] The sense of urgency in La Farina's letters must have been exciting to men already anxious to believe; but if they finished rereading the glowing promise from Turin and turned to act, they must have wondered precisely what one did to prepare for so great a coming. Occasionally a somewhat more specific note crept in: in Varese they were to agitate actively among the Pontremolese and to keep spirits high; Siccoli was pointedly reminded that Tuscany must not remain an "inert spectator" to the war of liberation; Lerici was urged to extend its relations beyond the borders as much as possible.

But on the whole, less was being said about seeing that everywhere revolution broke out simultaneously and to one cry.[68] The talk was more of "agitation" and "forces" which were to be redoubled or increased or sometimes merely maintained. These were statements designed more for effect than to instruct. Yet even they were accompanied by a note of warning. What really mattered, La Farina wrote, was to remain united and agreed; members were to "prepare," but they were also to be conciliatory, tolerant.[69] To the extent that such instruction referred at all to revolutionary action, to be prepared meant to be unsurprised when something happened; to maintain concord was to attempt nothing not tried before.

Yet the very maintenance of a political organization requires that it do something. The members of the National Society were too well aware of their strength, too sanguine of the future to be content with a vague and passive role. Everywhere there were signs of restiveness. Ulloa wrote Pallavicino that the publication of statements by him and by Garibaldi would have great effect, but Garibaldi himself was awaiting only a word from La Farina. Medici wrote saying he would be glad for some instructions; in Tuscany, too, there was doubt as to what to do next. A member of the Genoa committee felt he should do more than sell the

[67] La Farina to Pelucchi, 27 November; to Molena, 3 December, and to Amadori, 17 December 1858, Franchi, *Epistolario di La Farina*, II, 92, 93, 95.
[68] La Farina to Amadori, 24 January 1859, and to Bolognini, 12 November 1858, *ibid.*, 107, 88–9; La Farina to Stefano Siccoli, 30 December 1858, ms., ISR, busta 382, n. 33.
[69] La Farina to Molena, 3 December, and to Giuseppe Clementi, 21 December 1858, Franchi, *Epistolario di La Farina*, II, 93, 95; *Piccolo Corriere*, 20 December 1858.

Piccolo Corriere.[70] The committee of Modena, divided on what course to take, was on the verge of schism. One group favored the assassination of Duke Francis V, and Ferrari finally conferred with Cavour on the matter, who seems somehow to have settled the dispute by recommending "prudent audacity!" Others wrote from the Duchies asking for instructions, even news.

In the confusion the moderate faction grew to fear their more conspiratorial brethren, even to wonder who really was the director of the Society in their area and if they belonged in it at all. The policy of concord was beginning to take its toll. There was all that talk, too, of imminent action and firm discipline; and some feared they could not maintain that "blind obedience" which the Society would require.[71] The important Bologna committee was divided, though more in terms of personalities than politics. There was fear that Farini, who was always close to Cavour, was making plans for the Romagna which ignored the Society; and it was thought that Marchese Pepoli, a cousin of Napoleon's, was trying to capture control of the SNI in Bologna. Concerned to know if the Society even had a program for the Romagna, Casarini went to Turin. There he seems to have gotten the assurances he wanted from Cavour and La Farina. He returned home comforted by the knowledge that Garibaldi was to have a big part to play, warned of the importance, difficulty, and danger of the Society's task (preserving unity in the Romagna) and instructed that an agreement with the party of action would be a good thing provided the SNI had the "advantage." [72]

[70] Ulloa to Pallavicino, November 1858, *Memorie di Pallavicino*, III, 476–77; Garibaldi to La Farina, 30 January 1859, Franchi, *Epistolario di La Farina*, II, 124; Medici to Pallavicino, 5 January 1859, *Memorie di Pallavicino*, III, 487; Ermolao Rubieri, *Storia intima della Toscana dal 1 gennaio 1859 al 30 aprile 1860* (Prato, 1861), 26–7; La Farina to Francesco Terasona, January 1859, Franchi, *Epistolario di La Farina*, II, 118.

[71] Ferrari, *Ferrari*, 151–52; Pietro Menozzi, 30 December 1858, and Terrachini, February 1859, to Selmi, Canevazzi, *Selmi*, 199, 211–13.

[72] Dallolio, "I Colloqui di Casarini col Cavour," *La Strenna delle colonie scolastiche*, XXXVII, 12–14, 19–20; Maioli, "Tanari e il suo memoriale," *Archiginasio*, XXVIII, 67–69; Masi, "Casarini," *Fra Libri e ricordi*, 107–10. The meeting with Cavour was apparently useful to the Prime Minister, too, for he mentioned to Nigra that a leader of the Romagna's "militant party" had been to see him to reach an agreement on future action and cited the latter's estimate of public opinion there, Cavour to Nigra, 28 February 1859, *Cavour-Nigra*, II, 45.

There was a need for clear instructions, then, not only so members of the Society would know what to do but as evidence that their Society and they personally would count for something in the events ahead. Doubts spread easily in silence, and it fell to La Farina to send out a steady succession of reassurances —an impressive tribute both to his organizational skill and his inventiveness. At first, La Farina stressed the necessity for a well-coordinated national movement, the not unpleasant implication being that other areas of Italy lacked the maturity of the one to which he was then writing. He spoke authoritatively of the "general design" in which each city had its part. But, he told them, before you are informed of your part, other cities of Italy must complete their tasks. Piedmontese troops would be concentrated at Alessandria within eight days, but time was still needed to be ready in all provinces. One week it was the Milanese who were not yet ready, but two weeks later it was explained that the Government might seem somewhat reserved because of its fear of a premature outbreak in Lombardy-Venetia.[73]

Such explanations must have begun to pale as the propaganda poured out from Piedmont telling of nationalist fervor throughout the Peninsula and as volunteers streamed in, providing tangible evidence of it. The Government was waiting only for an external event to justify action, La Farina explained; and he asked the committee in Sarzana to keep quiet in order to divert the enemy's attention from that area of imminent and important activity.[74] Even La Farina, however, showed signs of tiring. It is a difficult thing to explain why the culmination of decades must wait another week. You have been sent no particular instructions, he once confessed, because they would be useless in your location—a strange admission of the Society's plans for so strategic a position as Voghera. With disarming honesty (if I have been silent it is simply because there is nothing to tell you) and doubtful flattery (the reason you have not been sent instructions is that a person like you does not need them) he tried to lessen that great difficulty which, as he confessed to

---

[73] La Farina to Mazzi, 7 September; to Clementi, 21 December 1858; to Bolognini, 13 January; to Medici, 7 January 1859, Franchi, *Epistolario di La Farina*, II, 78, 95–6, 113, 108.
[74] La Farina to Terasona, 12 February; and to Mazzi, 2 February 1859, *ibid.*, 129, 125–26.

Medici, lay in the fact that "things go slowly." In all the arsenal of the Society's ideas, of its propaganda and promises, there was nothing to explain why such things should go so slowly. It was faith which enabled La Farina to add, "but well." [75]

[75] La Farina to Carlotti, January [1859]; to Mazzi, 2 March; to Carlotti, 8 March; to Medici, 11 February 1859, *ibid.*, 117, 137, 143, 126.

CHAPTER FIVE

THE IDEOLOGY THAT EVOLVED

(TO THE WAR, APRIL 1859)

THE NATIONAL SOCIETY had been founded on a political program so simple that "Unification and Independence" had been not just a slogan for it but a summary of it. In the task of defending that program in a weekly newspaper and in pamphlet after pamphlet, however, it was necessary to relate it to the real world of current events and to defend it in a variety of ways. Even as a matter of propaganda, it was soon apparent that a coherent statement of doctrine was a useful thing. In the course of its writings the National Society evolved that doctrine. Its leaders were not philosophers, and their ideas lack that formal relationship and their statements that terror of contradiction that mark the man primarily concerned with ideas. Much of what the Society wrote had the quality of a family argument, with a great deal assumed, a lot obliquely said. In their separate reasonings, these men disagreed more often than they knew. As propagandists, they were anxious to score immediate points, many of which did not rest comfortably with other points previously made. Yet even when the criterion for selecting an argument was a belief in its effectiveness more than its truth, it was necessary to avoid the most obvious contradictions. The very estimate of what would be effective reflected the judgments and aspirations of those who made it. Most of the Society's pamphlets, after all, did bear the assurance that they had been "unanimously approved"; many of them wore the serious label of Program, Creed, or Catechism.

The ideas the Society thus put forth proved satisfying to many of the men most important in the unification of Italy, but they should be neither stated nor studied as if formally derived from stands clearly taken. Having evolved from arguments made in the heat of debate, they were a natural reflection of the attitudes and values of the men who proposed them. Once stated, those ideas led further (and fit together better) than the men of the

Society seem ever to have realized. The argument began simply. Just as the artist or scientist must set up his goal of ideal *bellezza* or absolute truth, La Farina once reasoned, so too the political man must establish his direction. The Society's slogan of unification and independence was meant to serve that purpose.[1] In that slogan unification was the word of weight, for "above all Italy must be made."[2] The cry for unification rested, of course, on the assumption that Italy was a nation; characteristically, this fundamental point was rarely made a matter of explicit argument. After generations of nationalist agitators and writers, it was too natural an assumption to need further debate; Mazzini had done his work too well. Italy was conceived of as a geographical entity which, although less diverse than England, France, or Germany, had lost its independence.[3] A common language, common customs, religion, and interests—these were points used only to prove the obvious to peasants or foreigners.[4] There was little further consideration of the nature of a nation or the role of the state in European society. Garibaldi had recognized their aim as being that of Dante, Petrarch, and Machiavelli;[5] a concept with such roots needed no defense.

The first task, then, of the Society's propaganda was to prove that under present conditions unification was both a possible step and the necessary one for the realization of other goals. The *Piemonte* saw in such a dream the "castles in air" of another sect, and the *Opinione* viewed it as utopian. Tommaséo suspected this too was another *romanza;* Cavour's doubts are famous.[6] The Society sought to meet such skepticism—and this, too, is typical of its temper—not with theoretical statements but

---

[1] Giuseppe La Farina, *Sicilia e Piemonte* (Turin, n.d. [1857]), 1. This pamphlet appeared under the label of the PNI.

[2] [Pallavicino], "Programma della Società Nazionale Italiana" (always printed with the *Credo*).

[3] [La Farina], *Credo Politico della Società Nazionale Italiana* (Turin, 1858), 7, 20.

[4] [Biagio Caranti], *Catechismo politico pei contadini piemontesi* (Turin, 1858), 11; article in the *North British Review*, February 1856, as printed in Maineri, *Manin e Pallavicino*, 550.

[5] *Memorie di Garibaldi*, 341.

[6] The *Piemonte* is quoted in Pallavicino to Manin, 1 December 1855, Maineri, *Manin e Pallavicino*, 16; the *Opinione*, 14 June 1858, is cited in Zini, *Storia d'Italia*, I², 839n–840n; Tommaséo to Pallavicino, 30 August 1857, Giovanni Sforza, "Niccolò Tommaséo e la Società Nazionale Italiana," *Il Risorgimento Italiano*, I (1908), 506. See Omodeo, *Cavour*, II, 164–65.

with arguments based on its reading of the political situation, with detailed analyses of relative military strengths and international alliances.

That unification was the necessary condition for the fulfillment of other Italian aspirations was the point most firmly made. Italy could not defend herself from foreign enemies nor could the way of life in the Peninsula be improved without unification. Italian "genius" was of no avail when so divided, when its very expression was a crime in four-fifths of Italy.[7] Italy's betterment was not in Austria's interest nor within the power of the smaller states. This was an issue on which the Society would not compromise; reform without unification was a chimera. Since it made them possible, unification was even "more important than independence itself or than liberty." It would be better to have a little less liberty guaranteed by an Italian army than to continue to suffer division and foreign domination.[8] Seven years before, Pallavicino had made this kind of distinction by declaring that ". . . first I want to live, of living well I will think later." The phrase was much repeated in the Society's literature, and the implication had gradually grown that unification itself was "living well." The National Society was arguing for the simplest nationalism; even "Amleto" was cited to show that the only question was whether to be or not to be.[9]

All other issues were labeled as secondary. Potentially divisive, they could be postponed. The National Society could therefore justify its vagueness on specific policy, a vagueness which tended to become a hallmark as well as a political tactic. By putting its "great principle of Independence and Unification" over any "predilection" for political forms or issues, the Society was free to develop its doctrine as circumstances warranted. The very choice of the word unification had been an example of this intentional imprecision for a pragmatic purpose. When ideas of federation were still strong, federalists were not to be antagonized by that firm word, union. Officially, then, the propaganda of the Society could deny responsibility for any stand on "secondary" issues. Arguments, however, have a momentum of their

---

[7] *Credo*, 4, 6, 11, 13, 17.
[8] [La Farina], *Italia, Francia e Russia*, 11–12.
[9] *Programma; Credo*, 5.

own. The Society's political program in fact led to an anti-federalist position.[10]

Similarly, the National Society claimed that its strong support of monarchy was not a matter of political principle. Indeed, Manin conceded that as a "thinker" he preferred the republican form of government; La Farina said he had always found it the "most logical regime," and Pallavicino considered it "the best of governments possible on earth" and thought it might prove good for his children or grandchildren. The contention was simply that a republic was not then possible, the implication, that it might come later. The argument was not for the good but from the possible. "In practical politics," said La Farina, "the impossible is immoral."[11] Governmental forms simply did not matter. "We are not such children that the name of king upsets us. . . ." One could be free under a prince or slave under a republic. Even revolution and a prince's rule were not necessarily incompatible.[12] The neat distinction between supporting a monarchy as a practical necessity and advocating monarchy as a form of government, between looking to Piedmont from need and looking to her ministers with admiration proved difficult to maintain. So delicate an argument allowed men to remain theoretical republicans while working for the monarchy, but it did not for long describe the SNI's position.

It was declared axiomatic that the making of Italy would depend on both Victor Emmanuel and on revolution. The concept was particularly dear to Pallavicino, and his bitterest complaint against the Piedmontese Government was that it did not point its policy more clearly toward an Italian revolution. Manin, too, was pleased that Europe was coming to realize that an Italian revolution was "necessary and legitimate," and the *Piccolo Corriere* hotly denied the charge that the Society opposed revolution.[13] But revolution too was a secondary dream,

[10] The *Piccolo Corriere* was filled with the strongest attacks on Cattaneo and Ferrari; the issue of 10 May 1857 showed in detail that the American experience with federalism would not apply to Italy. Pallavicino, too, rejected federalism, letter to Tofano, 22 August 1857, *Memorie di Pallavicino*, III, 419.

[11] Manin's letter of 22 January 1856 in Maineri, *Manin e Pallavicino*, 502; Pallavicino, "Anzitutto il ben pubblico," *ibid.*, 319; La Farina to *Italia e Popolo*, 5 October 1856, Franchi, *Epistolario di La Farina*, II, 566.

[12] *Credo*, 21; *Italia, Francia e Russia*, 9.

[13] Maineri, *Manin e Pallavicino*, 587, 614; Manin to *Il Diritto*, 11 May 1856, *ibid.*, 509; *Piccolo Corriere*, 7 September 1858.

important only as it might contribute to unification. It could not be called a good thing in itself; the circumstances would determine "the justice, the necessity, the opportunity" of such a move. These very considerations made revolution a doubtful weapon. Any revolution the Society favored must not lead to new division among Italians; it could, therefore, invoke "no question of liberty or social structure." Under French influence, the argument ran, revolution had been associated with the desire to eliminate feudal abuses and to reconstitute society. Now, however, Italy was moving away from French influence, and national independence was her goal.[14] It was agreed that Italy must have no revolt which was not directed toward independence and unification, and that there must be reasonable expectation of its success. Revolution would only be legitimate when necessary, possible when based on a majority will for independence and unification, beneficial when not the work of a sect but intended only for the "glory of the nation." [15] Even Pallavicino came to define revolution merely as armed uprising, thereby suggesting local cooperation with a Piedmontese army rather than popular effort at social change.

Such a revolution, it was recognized, could not be planned, and revolution so viewed lost its vitality. It ceased to be a matter of central concern to the National Society which was content with the statement that it opposed revolution in Piedmont and favored it elsewhere. The uprising for unification and independence, it was added, would be the last one.[16] The concept of the Risorgimento was being changed from a revolution that would remake society to a merely political change brought about by the force of arms. Pallavicino did not effectively answer the Mazzinians when they demanded to know what sort of regeneration this was to be.[17]

[14] *Ibid.*, 13 December 1858; [La Farina], *Le forze liberatrici d'Italia*, 4. This, too, was a publication of the Society.

[15] La Farina, *Sicilia e Piemonte*, 1; Giorgio Pallavicino, *Non bandiera neutra!* (Turin, 1856), 1 (a publication of the PNI); [La Farina], *La rivoluzione, la dittatura e le alleanze* (Turin, 1858), 7, 10, a pamphlet of the SNI; *Credo*, 23.

[16] Pallavicino, *Non bandiera neutra!*, 3; *Piccolo Corriere*, 10 May 1857, 28 February 1858.

[17] Pallavicino to *Il Diritto*, 2 January 1856, Maineri, *Manin e Pallavicino*, 551. This slighting of concepts previously important to Italian nationalists did not go unnoticed by contemporaries. Finali did not join the Society because of its omission of the word "liberty" from its slogan, *Memorie di Gaspare Finali*

From insisting on the principle of unification the Society found itself opposing federalism, supporting monarchy, discounting revolution. A single clear political goal rather than a moral and social reformation became the Society's aim as its reasoning tended to separate ends from means. The Italian National Society rejected no element of force, no "honest means" from "books to rifles, from diplomatic notes to cannon shots" to free the *patria*. La Farina instructed the head of one of the Society's committees that if "prudence counsels it, we must keep quiet about part of the truth." Pallavicino willingly confessed that in the moment of revolutionary storm he would not be "too tender of legal forms." [18] It did not matter whether Victor Emmanuel led them in his own interest or as a result of their votes. It did not matter what regime was in power in Piedmont, provided it was nationalist. It would be the greatest folly to wait for popular suffrage before proclaiming Italy one and united.[19]

There was in this a dangerous circle of reasoning. The postponement of all issues save one kept concern for the kind of Italy that should be made from influencing its creation; even ideas tended to be measured primarily in terms of their present usefulness. The pen was adopted to make possible the use of the sword.[20] Yet the one goal toward which all was to be directed was not an absolute one; "there are no perfect [*ottimi*] governments . . ." but only those which best meet the needs of their people. If conditions changed, the Society would change its program.[21] In saying this, however, the SNI conceded that the nature of the goal would after all be determined by the path to it. Having declared the politically impossible to be immoral, the Society was dangerously close to declaring the possible moral.

(Faenza, 1956), 118; and Guerrazzi believed revolution to be anathema to the Society, Guerrazzi to La Farina, 22 May 1858, Franchi, *Epistolario di La Farina*, II, 60.

[18] *Credo*, 19; Franchi, *Scritti politici di La Farina*, II, 188; La Farina to Luigi Tanari, 13 May 1859, ms. in the Carte Tanari, MCRB; Pallavicino, *Come vivremo* (Turin, 1856) also published as Part V of his "La Questione Italiana," in *Scritti politici di Giorgio Pallavicino* (Turin, 1856), a PNI pamphlet.

[19] Pallavicino to Foresti, 12 September 1856, Maioli, "Il Fondatore," *Rassegna Storica*, XV, 18; [La Farina], *Italia e Piemonte*, 1; *La rivoluzione*, 12.

[20] The phrase is Pallavicino's, letter to Ulloa, in Doria, "Ulloa," *Archivio Storico, Provincie Napoletane*, n.s., XV, 340.

[21] *La rivoluzione*, 7; Pallavicino to Foresti, 12 September 1856, Maioli, "Il Fondatore," *Rassegna Storica*, XV, 19.

This emphasis on the possible was meant to give the Society's program broad appeal. It would allow all Italians to unite in doing what could be done instead of sharpening their differences on abstract argument. The Society's moderate program held out hope (in the future) for reformers and reassured the conservatives with its limited aims. For it had long been recognized that only a program which stepped on few toes could gain the support it would need.[22] Their program was meant to make unification possible, but the meaning of "unification" soon extended beyond the merely territorial. The men of the Society felt it necessary to "gather the forces and attitudes of the nation, temper and harmonize them, subordinating them to a common thought." [23] Like many contemporaries, they saw "the secret of victory . . . in the concord of all thought, of all wills, of all desires. . . ." [24] Discord was the primary cause of the present woes of Italy; if Italians could just cry out with one voice, that united will would overcome all obstacles.[25] It was because the Society sought to create a general will even more than specific agreement that this party was not a sect, that it claimed to be a step on the path to Italian redemption. The Society would "combat prejudices, broadcast healthy doctrines, preach concord." [26]

Thus unity was sought on all levels and among all groups. The "marriage of the Italian insurrection to the army of Piedmont" stood in the Society's eyes as its greatest achievement,[27] but it also strove for unity of opinion among the various provinces and with republicans. It demanded positive participation not the peace of passivity; and exiles were criticized for living in seclusion, for not taking part in the work of conciliation. The Society's instructions called not only for the avoidance of

[22] Salvatorelli notes this of d'Azeglio's "Proposta di una programma per l'opinione nazionale italiana," Luigi Salvatorelli, *Il pensiero politico italiano dal 1700 al 1870* (Turin, 1949), 240.
[23] *Credo*, 11.
[24] Angelo Brofferio, *I Miei Tempi*, vii (Turin, 1859), 289; Gioberti had made, of course, a similar plea for overcoming party division, see Anzilotti, *Gioberti*, 379–81.
[25] Announcement of Organization of the *Comitato di Genova*, 31 January 1859, in the Carte Morchio, MNRG; Pallavicino to *Diritto*, 17 and 27 November 1855, Maineri, *Manin e Pallavicino*, 444.
[26] Letter of Manin, 22 January 1856, *ibid.*, 504–505; Pallavicino to Foresti, 4 July 1856, *Memorie di Pallavicino*, iii, 265.
[27] The SNI's announcement of dissolution in the *Unione*, 21 April 1859, cited in *Memorie di Pallavicino*, iii, 511.

all religious or social issues which might spread discord but for efforts to maintain concord among citizens of all classes and from all provinces. In its propaganda to the Piedmontese peasants the Society even managed to subdue its anticlericalism, to put in a good word for a hypothetical priest. (A fervent nationalist, if somewhat lax in the cure of souls, he respected his parishoners' convictions as they did his.) [28]

Such unity was spiritual strength, for "the unanimous will of a nation of twenty-five million cannot be contained by any material force." The establishment of that unanimous will was in fact the Society's primary goal. Less controversial even than talk of unification under a king, this gathering of the "living forces of the nation" was a wish undiluted by compromise. It was a cry to Italians to have faith in themselves; those united "forces" would then bring about political unification.[29] The Society came to view itself as the representative, almost the embodiment, of this will. In such a concept popular participation in Italian regeneration need not entail the risks of revolution.[30] Sects represented a single aspect of the multiform idea which made up the nation, but the National Society spoke for all. Its high goal of national unanimity required, however, that the SNI ". . . labor to extinguish every local jealousy, every petty passion, every fierce egotism, every extreme doctrine, every irrational ambition, which stands in the way of perfect harmony of feeling *now* and of what would mar harmony *then*." "Mischief makers" would have to be silenced.[31]

The leaders of the Society had pointed to the vagueness in their program as evidence of un-Mazzinian tolerance; but tolerance, too, was a tactic. They had stated a minimum program to make it possible for the widest range of nationalists to join together. Having made agreement so easy, they tended to find disagreement unforgivable. Too much was at stake; Victor Em-

[28] *Italia e Piemonte*, 5–6; *Piccolo Corriere*, 21 February 1858; La Farina to Mazzi, 30 July 1858, Franchi, *Epistolario di La Farina*, II, 73; Franchi, *Scritti politici di La Farina*, II, 187; *La rivoluzione*, 2; *Catechismo pei contadini*, 27–8.

[29] Manin to *Il Diritto*, 29 May 1856, Maineri, *Manin e Pallavicino*, 512; *La rivoluzione*, 4; *Italia, Francia e Russia*, 13; *Credo*, 6.

[30] It is noteworthy that Pallavicino sometimes talked of uniting the Sardinian army and Italian opinion rather than the army and revolution. See his 2 January 1856 statement in Maineri, *Manin e Pallavicino*, 554.

[31] "Italian Characters and Italian Prospects," *North British Review*, XXIV (1856), 549.

manuel as dictator and war with Austria—this was the only possible cry. "Any other question is an encumbrance; any other formula is real treachery to the Italian cause." It was a corruption of heart and mind to cry prudence in times demanding fervor. It was a crime to oppose the present ministry so long as a better was not possible. Lovers of the *patria* must defend the government in every way; the measure, after all, of "true patriots" was their willingness to make "any sacrifice to *make Italy*." [32] The concord for which the SNI strove must be "true not feigned"; it would mean the forgetting of "past discords, not weak tolerance of sowers of new discords." Even a touch of intolerance might be the price required if all "the thoughts, the sentiments, and the acts" of Italians were some day to be "gathered into one bundle [*fascio*]." [33]

Such concern for unanimity led to more determined support of Piedmont. Italy could have but one center, Pallavicino reasoned; there must therefore be "fusion with Piedmont." Italian emigrants, defining the dreams which made exile bearable, had argued heatedly by what means Italians should declare their acceptance of Victor Emmanuel's rule. The Marchese, however, would not risk the dangers and confusions of untried assemblies or new constitutions. In his solution there was no such red tape: ". . . at the first rumble [*rumore*] of the Italian people asking the *Kingdom of Italy with the Dynasty of Savoy and the Piedmontese charter*, the parliament and army in Piedmont will raise the same cry: and there you are, Italy—[a] living political person." [34]

To advocate fusion with a state is high praise of it; as propagandists, the men of the Society had to justify that praise. Articles and statistics on Piedmont's wealth were long and frequent. The great freedom the Piedmontese enjoyed, the strength of their nationalism, were consistently stressed. All the arguments that realistically Piedmont was Italy's one hope were repeated again and again. Still, even the Society had to admit that further

[32] La Farina to Bartolomeo, 12 May 1859, Franchi, *Epistolario di La Farina*, II, 173; La Farina, *Murat e l'unità italiana* (Turin, n.d.), 7; *Italia e Piemonte*, 4, 5; Maineri, *Manin e Pallavicino*, 503.
[33] *Italia, Francia e Russia*, 14; *Credo*, 22.
[34] [La Farina], "Dichiarazione," always printed with the *Credo*; Tofano to Pallavicino, 22 August 1857, *Memorie di Pallavicino*, III, 420; Pallavicino, *Come vivremo*.

reform would certainly increase Piedmont's claim to national leadership. Such reform need not be demanded immediately, however, when seen as the inevitable "work of progress." [35] Now on the right path, Piedmont could hardly be criticized for what it was when it was so promisingly clear what it would become. Piedmont was the "true and only representative of liberal ideas in Italy," of those "new ideas" of which the new Italy would be made. Like men of similar mind in England, the Society saw Piedmont's material progress as placing her next to Rome among ancient nations and after England among modern ones. There was in Piedmont's willingness to undertake her national mission even something of the magnanimous.[36]

Having argued for Piedmont as the means to unification, the Society learned to avoid responsibility for Piedmont's specific policies. In the years following the Crimean conference it was hard to establish that Piedmont was seriously preparing to meet her destiny,[37] but the publications of the SNI insisted that she was, that she had kept the bargain Manin had struck. She had remained "for Italy"; she had maintained the constitution, not become an Austrian vassal, and kept "high and honored the standard of Italian independence." Many nationalists, however, blamed the Government for not having done more. "We can," one pamphlet of the SNI confessed, "in our souls deplore the errors, the hesitancies, the temporizings, the lack of foresight of the ministry and parliament . . . ," but the implication was strong that even such deploring should be done in private. In La Farina's hands the last sting was taken from the Society's graceless threat to support Piedmont only if its policy was nationalist, "if not, not." To say this, he argued, would be to take an impatient and myopic view and to assume that a national war could be begun and the national question resolved when and how one wanted. The ashes of Carlo Alberto, the men fallen

[35] One series in the *Piccolo Corriere* on Piedmont's economy ran from 17 May to 14 June 1858; in the issue of 31 May it was noted that per capita meat consumption was higher in Piedmont than in France; *Italia e Piemonte*, 6; Franchi, *Scritti politici di La Farina*, II, 187; *Piccolo Corriere*, 28 February and 7 March 1858; 17 January 1859.

[36] Pallavicino, "La Questione Italiana, III," in Maineri, *Manin e Pallavicino*, 553; *Daily News* quoted in the *Piccolo Corriere*, 24 May 1857; Franchi, *Scritti politici di La Farina*, II, 187.

[37] Omodeo points out the difficulty Cavour faced because his policies had not produced "concrete fruits," Omodeo, *Cavour*, II, 171.

on the fields of Lombardy, the constitution and free press, the honor of the prince and of his dynasty, the tricolor—all this the Society saw as "that part of life and death that ties the dynasty and the Sardinian Kingdom to Italy. . . ." [38] A merely mistaken policy would not dissolve that tie.

The Society was, as Tommaséo complained, asking that "[we] oblige ourselves to do or not to do while others are obliged to nothing. . . ." The SNI guaranteed Piedmont's policy while having no clear hand in determining it. Thus it first insisted that there should be no revolution in Rome while French troops were there and then that there should be no revolutionary action anywhere until Piedmont was armed and ready (something only the government could judge). Early interest in supporting some local uprising quickly faded; and by the spring of 1859, the Society found one of its principal tasks to be that of holding back the overeager, of warning against "inopportune" moves.[39] The policies of the National Society were subordinated to those of Piedmont even before being wholly formulated.

Their arguments had taken the men of the Society farther than they meant in argument to go. But had they recognized that their support of Piedmont was now nearly unconditional, they would not have been altogether disappointed. The men of the National Society saw in Piedmont the virtues they valued most, and these "least poetic, most sensible people of the Italian peninsula" held great attraction for them. Sicilian that he was, La Farina hoped for an early union between his native island and adopted state; he felt that the "alpine coldness" of the Piedmontese would have a good effect on the Sicilians. He was glad that their ardor would be tempered with Piedmontese prudence. The last to enter Italy's national life, Piedmont was "the youngest, most robust," possessing a steadier "nerve and pulse." It was readily conceded, that Piedmont lacked "Lombard culture, Tuscan grace, Roman magnanimity, Neapolitan acumen, Sicilian fervor"; and this was a graceful concession to other local prides. To these practical men of politics, however, such merits

[38] La rivoluzione, 9–10; Franchi, Scritti politici di La Farina, II, 192; Italia e Piemonte, 12.

[39] Tommaséo to Pallavicino, 30 August 1857, in Sforza, "Tommaséo e la Società Nazionale," Risorgimento Italiano, I, 506. Omodeo, Cavour, II, 168; Memorie di Pallavicino, III, 511; cf. Salazaro, Cenni sulla rivoluzione, 56–60.

paled before the fact that "here the people is not softened by suspicious and cowardly tyranny, here the ministers and the courts are not public markets where justice is bought and sold. . . ." If the Piedmontese imagination was less lively, "the practical sense is stronger"; if their wit was not so quick, the spirit was "solider and more constant."

It was with this spirit that Italy would be united. The Society admired more the qualities associated with Western liberals than those traditionally attributed to Italians. Since liberation "is [a] work more of arms than of congresses," Piedmont was best suited to undertake it. It was their duty to defend her. Thus "each member of the *Società Nazionale Italiana*, whatever be the province and city of his birth, will regard himself as a citizen and soldier of Piedmont . . ." until, it was understood, "Piedmont fails in the great mission with which fate has entrusted her." [40] The conditional clause made the request seem modest, but the leaders of the Society knew that soldiers rarely fight provisionally.

Similarly, the National Society came to make an argument for monarchy in practice it would not recognize in theory. Its leaders were more men of 1848 in the terms they used than in the values they held, and it soon became clear that monarchical leadership had its own appeal for these theoretical republicans. There were, after all, advantages in having a single leader when one sought the fullest possible unity among all Italians. With this as the goal, history was found to teach a monarchical lesson. France and Spain under monarchs had become powerful and unified states while Italy remained divided. Holland, to regain her independence, had had to sacrifice the republic; even the Roman republic had not been able to unify Italy. It might well be wise then to look toward a frank and loyal king, "on horseback, holding in his fist the ancient sword of Savoy." [41]

Determination to avoid the errors of 1848 lent added merit to monarchy; for during war, Italy would need a dictator. The

---

[40] Pallavicino to Manin, 18 November 1855, Maineri, *Manin e Pallavicino*, 7; *Sicilia e Piemonte*, 6; *Italia e Piemonte*, 9–10. Omodeo notes that a strong hint of regionalism was present in the acceptance of Piedmontese hegemony, Omodeo, *Cavour*, II, 193.

[41] *La rivoluzione*, 7; Pallavicino to *Il Diritto*, 18 December 1855 (Part II of "Questione Italiana"), Maineri, *Manin e Pallavicino*, 550.

King would most naturally fill this role, giving Italy that central command which was the prime requisite for the success of a nation divided into seven states with diverse laws and militias. Decisions in war must be immediately made and surely followed. So promising did this picture seem that the Society even ceased to care for those "certain guarantees" which parliament might demand before granting a dictatorship. With so loyal a King no guarantees were needed; to limit the extent of the dictatorship would be to change its nature. It was not with a tone of regret that the Society proclaimed, ". . . we need a hand of iron to guide the vigorous, push forward the resolute, drag the refractory." [42]

Implicit in all these arguments was the assumption that history had its own movement, each period its own needs. In its view of history lay the Society's justification of its program, the roots of its faith. The National Society did not view its program as a set of general ideas but as a practical reading of that "real order" of things against which man could do nothing except adapt himself, making use of "the fatal laws that guide human necessities." This was an "atheist and superlatively prosaic century," and for this reason the Mazzinians were wrong to place such faith in the words God and People. The charge against them was that they were out of phase with history as, in their way, were the clericals whose demands "are incompatible with civil progress. . . ." [43] Thus pragmatism was not a compromise with ideals but just good sense. One could believe in a republic for the future if he wanted, but ". . . there is a time of republics and a time of principalities; to want to found a republic when it is the time of principality is [a] mad and tyrannical work. . . ." [44] Values, then, were not permanent, even liberty was only "good according to the times." [45] Similarly, it was false

[42] *Piccolo Corriere*, 28 February and 7 March 1859; *La rivoluzione*, 12.

[43] *Ibid.*, 4–5; Pallavicino, Part I, "Questione Italiana," to *Il Diritto*, 6 December 1855, Maineri, *Manin e Pallavicino*, 545; *L'Italia e Inghilterra* (an article from the *North British Review* as reprinted in *Il Diritto*, a PNI publication), 4.

[44] La Farina to *Italia e Popolo*, 5 October 1856, Franchi, *Epistolario di La Farina*, I, 567; in this view, as in so many others, the Society was a legitimate heir of Gioberti who while supporting the monarchy had been sure that a republic was inevitable, that "Providence is Red." See Widar Cesarini-Sforza, "Politica di Gioberti," *Rassegna Storica*, II, 749.

[45] *Credo*, 23.

to try to create or plan a revolution. Not contraband to be smuggled in, "true revolutions are like the great phenomenon of nature surrounded by shadow and mystery." Thus the Society was not surrendering its initiative but only being wise when it did not plot a revolution, did not attempt more than man could do.[46]

There was, however, an inexorable progress in history, a series of stages through which each nation must pass. Piedmont's economic progress was thus a visible guarantee that she was in fact in the mainstream of the future. The heart of the nation already beat within her; destiny had given Piedmont the position in Italy held by England in India, France in Africa, Prussia in Germany [47] —a set of comparisons not very flattering to the other Italian provinces. The dream was no longer of an Italy different from or better than the other European states. The goal was to see that she caught up with her sisters; it was simply expressed in the Society's frequent exhortations to Italians to prove their "maturity." If this reading of history made Italy's future seem less glorious, it made it more certain. In every field of human endeavor there was a movement toward great unity. It was because "no great undertaking is any longer possible without having in common the intelligence, the study, the capital and the labor of a great nation" that the Society strove to create a unanimity of will. History was on its side; "the spirit of the century tends toward unity. . . ." In this movement Piedmont was the snowball that would become an avalanche.[48]

Salvation was not only inevitable; it was also imminent. The day of the great rising neared; the moment for action was advancing; fortune, which had almost turned its back after 1848, was again smiling.[49] This was the conviction which sustained ardor year after year and justified sacrifices on "secondary issues."

[46] Credo, 21, 23; Pallavicino to Flandin, 17 October 1854, Memorie di Pallavicino, III, 89; Piccolo Corriere, 12 April 1857.

[47] Maineri, Manin e Pallavicino, 320, 612; Italia e Piemonte, 11. Omodeo mentions Gioberti's concern for being in the current of the future, Omodeo, Gioberti, 17, 100.

[48] Credo, 13; Pallavicino to La Farina, 17 August 1857 and to Mamiani, 4 August 1858, Memorie di Pallavicino, III, 416, 496; La Farina to Molena, 16 June 1858, Franchi, Epistolario di La Farina, II, 66.

[49] Italia, Francia e Russia, 10, 12–13; Pallavicino to Manin, 4 October 1856, Maineri, Manin e Pallavicino, 220.

The Society viewed the present in terms of explosive metaphor: the war of liberation might break out at any moment; only a match was needed to set off the flames; the revolutionary volcano was burning even if its flames were invisible.[50] Thus it was the Society's task to prepare men and keep them ready "for any event"; once the time came, any misstep would be fatal. History moved at its own pace, and men must grab their moment before it passed. Until then, it was no surrender of independence to allow Piedmont's policy to determine the Society's action. Until war broke out, action would include "warmly" exhorting "our friends . . . to remain tranquil." The Society saw itself as the "civil militia of the nation" not a "gang of conspirators." [51]

In its view of the historical process, as in its dependence on Piedmont, the National Society deprived itself of any real capacity for political initiative.[52] To place decision in others' hands, whether the firm hands of Cavour or the subtle ones of time, is to prepare for the acceptance of those decisions as others make them. In fact, the men of the National Society thought they knew rather well the sort of Italy to which Victor Emmanuel would lead them, and they had convinced themselves it was what they wanted. Their logic had only led them where their attitudes pointed.

Two of these attitudes are worth singling out; the National Society was making of nationalism a religion and, in its respect for force, approaching militarism. The leaders of the Italian National Society certainly deserve to be called nationalists. They followed Gioberti in declaring the nation an "immutable law of nature" (provinces were the "arbitrary work of men"), and they declared anti-national governments illegitimate even if through "ignorance . . . corruption . . . cowardice . . . despair" they had the support of their people. Before the interests of the na-

[50] Pallavicino to Manin, 25 January 1856, *ibid.*, 45; and Manin to Valerio, 28 May 1856, *ibid.*, 511. This apocalyptic sense did not dim in the following years. See *Italia e Piemonte*, 14; or Paselli to Casarini, 31 August 1858, Maioli, "Società Nazionale in Bologna," *Saggi e documenti* (1933), 82.

[51] *Piccolo Corriere*, 21 February 1858; Pallavicino, "Non bandiera neutra!" in Maineri, *Manin e Pallavicino*, 588; La Farina to Bolognini, 13 January 1859, Franchi, *Epistolario di La Farina*, II, 113; declaration of the SNI on its refounding in 1860 undoubtedly by La Farina, a copy is in ISR, busta 382, n. 42.

[52] Omodeo notes the fact of this lack of initiative: Omodeo, *Cavour*, II, 170–71; and Mazzini predicted it as the result of attempting a "fusion" of parties, Mazzini, "Il partito d'azione," *Scritti di Mazzini*, LI, 98.

tion ". . . municipalities and provinces, individuals and sects, traditions and hopes, dynasties and liberties" all must yield. All other issues, even social questions, were to be kept separate from the overriding concern—the nation.[53] The men who wrote these stark statements of the place of the nation in their political values did not, however, build a political theory upon such doctrine. Rather, these declarations were themselves a reflection of their nationalism, a more formal expression of something they felt, of their fervor and indeed their faith, "for without faith nations are not redeemed." [54]

To the National Society ". . . the love of the fatherland is a religion." It was teaching its own doctrine when it told the peasants to love the *patria* above all, after God. This was why unity and independence were proclaimed "more sublime and holier" than lesser questions. The men of the Society knew they sought a holy goal,[55] and they saw their propaganda as no ordinary political statement.

"An apostolate of a few years, conducted with faith and perseverance, [it] will educate opinion, remove doubts, excite new convictions, dissipate prejudices, weaknesses, fantasies, and make the concept of the nation shine in all hearts. A conspiracy in daylight, holy in ends, holy in means, energetic in activity, moderate in aspirations and judgments, will gain for us even the public opinion of Europe." [56]

Love of the *patria* was only a special application of the admonition to love thy neighbor, and it carried with it high moral requirements. Mazzini's "theory of the dagger" had, it is true, been attacked primarily in terms of its unfortunate political effects, but even then Pallavicino had decried this fall from that "moral purity" which "constitutes the living and true strength of each religion." The virtues which this "religion" most valued were catalogued by Pallavicino when he wrote of a "disinterested, fervent, holy love" of public affairs, of "the religion of sacrifice," of men with the "strongest convictions" and "immaculate" lives,

[53] *La rivoluzione*, 10–11; *Piccolo Corriere*, 13 December 1858.
[54] Franchi, *Scritti politici di La Farina*, II, 187.
[55] *Catechismo pei contadini*, 31, 35; La Farina to *Il Diritto*, 3 November 1856, Franchi, *Epistolario di La Farina*, I, 567; two early references to the "holy" goal are in Manin to the *Opinione*, 12 February 1856; and Pirondi to Pallavicino, 24 October 1856, Maineri, *Manin e Pallavicino*, 507, 404.
[56] Reta to Pallavicino, 21 February 1858, *ibid.*, 392.

of that "civil heroism . . . that faces long martyrdom. . . ." [57]
Such standards were strengthened by a strong sense of duty.[58]
It was the "moral obligation" of members of the Society to
propagate its doctrines. It was an Italian's duty "to promote the
independence and greatness" of Italy, and his most ardent vow
should always be "to be able to see, before dying, my fatherland
independent and united, and to be able to contribute to its
risorgimento, even with the sacrifice of my life, if that should
occur." [59] Sacrifice was the highest moral act, an outward and
visible sign of inner dedication. Thus the movement of volunteers
to Piedmont had something of the spiritual in it; almost "more
sublime, more solemn, holier" than voting, it showed a willingness to risk all. Selflessness was the real mark of the liberal, and
the men of the Society were pridefully certain that "history will
take note of our sacrifice and of our abnegation. . . ." By contrast, the souls of others seemed small.[60] The republicans, after
all, were being asked only to perform a reasonable, moral obligation when the Society called upon them to make a further sacrifice for the national cause.

The battle-scarred, practical men who made the National Society had defined their goal in limited political terms and weighed
the chances of achieving it with hearty realism. Yet they approached these mundane matters with the ardor and the sense
of dedication that man brings to his religion. This is not hyper-
bole, for theirs was a personal faith. On the death of his mother,
Pallavicino consoled himself with the thought that "yet a mother
remains to us here below: Italy. Let us love Italy." [61] The crown
of Italy had been the "greatest of honors on the brow of Caesar,
Charlemagne, Napoleon . . . ," but the Society looked to Victor Emmanuel to earn a "holier and more splendid crown, that

---

[57] *Catechismo pei contadini*, 31; Pallavicino's defense of Manin's stand against
Mazzini is in Maineri, *Manin e Pallavicino*, 514; Pallavicino, "Anzitutto il ben
pubblico," *ibid.*, 321.
[58] Manin wrote Valerio ". . . I have faith that we will succeed. If not, we
will have the comfort of the knowledge of having done our duty," cited in a
letter of 11 February 1856, Maineri, *Manin e Pallavicino*, 502.
[59] "Dichiarazione"; *Catechismo pei contadini*, 35–6.
[60] *Piccolo Corriere*, 15 April 1859; *Italia e Piemonte*, 9; La Farina, *Murat e
l'unità italiana*, 7. Salvemini sees this view of sacrifice as "the sole virtue" as part
of the Mazzinian heritage, Salvemini, *Mazzini*, 187.
[61] Pallavicino to Tommaséo, 20 December 1858, *Memorie di Pallavicino*, III,
479.

of redeemer of the most glorious of nations." Their own efforts, too, received a kind of sanctity because the "noble and sacred goal" of the "*risorgimento* of our dear fatherland" was "entrusted" to them. The feeling was naturally expressed by a member of the Society in dedicating a pamphlet to "Marchese Giorgio Pallavicino, nearly the last and venerated relic of the martyrs of the Spielberg. . . ." [62]

The Society itself was highly conscious of this religious simile. Even Manin had spoken of winning numerous "neophytes" and of the need for "propagation of the faith" and "multiplying apostles." In explaining that the Society could exclude no one who wished to belong, La Farina noted that "no church is closed to him who recites the symbol of the faith." The image was fulsomely worked out in a pamphlet explaining that "the doors of our temple are open." Whoever wants to enter need not "subject himself to initiations, to baptisms, to swearings." But if he enters from "curiosity to know the mysteries of the sanctuary" he will be disillusioned; he "will find on the altar" only "that sacred image of Italy that he saw on the pediment, and [he] will read there only that *Credo Politico* that he had already read on all the corners of the streets." [63]

This was a far cry from the rituals of the *carbonari* or Masons, but it was a natural way of expressing the fervor of a faith, the wholeness of a vision. It has been suggested that Mazzini began to lose followers with the decline of "mystic romanticism," and certainly the Society did not believe in resting its case or setting its goals in terms of anything either mystic or romantic. But if the Central Committee could declare the tricolor to be holy with the blood of martyrs for liberty, there was a great deal of room for local committees to attach either a Mazzinian morality or the most sacrilegious ritual to their expressions of the common

---

[62] *La rivoluzione*, 9; Pirondi to Pallavicino, 24 October 1856, Maineri, *Manin e Pallavicino*, 404; Biagio Caranti, *Delle nuove speranze d'Italia* (Turin, 1859), 1; such religious terminology was, of course, more easily used by a generation raised on romanticism. Still, Degli Antoni viewed his trip to Venice in 1858 as "sacrosanct," not merely because he was carrying out Manin's wishes but because its ultimate purpose was national, Degli Antoni to Pincherle, 6 August 1858, ms., MCV, bxxvi/459.

[63] La Farina to Mazzi, 30 July 1858, Franchi, *Epistolario di La Farina*, II, 73; *La rivoluzione*, 4.

faith.[64] Not many could have sworn that "I believe in the first Napoleon, omnipotent Creator of the French Empire and the Kingdom of Italy and in Napoleon the third, his nephew and our sole Savior." Still, it is important to remember that the faith of the National Society could move at least some simple soul far from Turin to pray: "Our Father who art on the Field as the first Soldier of Italian Independence, hallowed by Thy name, O Victor. Thy peaceful kingdom quickly come, Thy will be done under our heaven, that is on Italian earth; Give us again this day our liberty; make our nationality respected as we respect that of others; lead us to enjoy peace but deliver us from the infamous Austrian." [65]

Faith and militance are easily associated, and the men of the National Society were as fond of referring to their organization in military terms as they were of referring to their doctrine in terms of religious faith. Manin and Pallavicino conferred the ranks of lieutenant and general on each other with a good deal of playfulness, but they seriously thought of themselves as doing battle. They talked of "descending into the arena" and of their friends "fighting in our file"; they felt they were becoming an "army." The Society stressed the need for Italians to "make themselves soldiers," and saw in discipline "the basis of strength." [66] Historical examples from Rome to the present were used to establish the concept that order and discipline were the qualities of success and worth almost any price. The Society even envisioned itself as contributing to that "iron" and "military" discipline which Italy so badly needed.[67]

This emphasis was part of the Society's vaunted realism, a "realism" that had roots in an attitude deeper than the arguments for accepting monarchy or compromising on "secondary issues." It was not just that these men saw politics as an "ex-

---

[64] Omodeo, *Cavour*, II, 222–27; *Italia e Piemonte*, 11.

[65] Cited in Zampetti-Biocca, *La Società Nazionale nella Marca*, 59. See also Documents Nos. 2 and 5 in Alessandrini, *I fatti*, II.

[66] Anna Pallavicino was given temporary rank as lieutenant-colonel, aide-de-camp: Pallavicino to Manin, Maineri, *Manin e Pallavicino*, 286; Pallavicino to Manin, 29 October 1856, *ibid.*, 226; and to Mamiani, 4 August 1858, *Memorie di Pallavicino*, III, 406. *Le forze liberatrici*, 11.

[67] *Italia, Francia e Russia*, 14; La Farina to Bolognini, 16 August 1858, Franchi, *Epistolario di La Farina*, II, 75; *Piccolo Corriere*, 3 January 1859.

perimental science" in which one began with things as they are; the realism of the National Society went beyond that realism widely shared by Risorgimento thinkers.[68] Determined to learn from their past defeats, the men of the SNI developed a deep respect for sure, solid, military force.

"Religion," the Society's *Credo* acidly remarked, "sanctifies martyrdom, but politics requires triumph; for religion it is enough to die, for politics it is necessary to win." These men had had enough martyrs,[69] and the lesson they learned was that "honesty alone is not enough in times in which right is nothing without the aid of force." "Providence" they knew to be "always the friend of the strong. . . ."[70] The Italian Question was, to be sure, a "question of justice at the tribunal of God," but it was a "question of force, *solely* of *force* before [the] tribunal of men." The great solutions, Pallavicino suggested, were not effected with the pen; and if, La Farina explained, ". . . we believe in the force of ideas, we believe also in that of cannon."[71]

Theirs was a dim view of human nature, and Pallavicino's epigram that without Paradise there would be few saints expressed a basic theme in their thought. Experience, they believed, had taught "that egoism dominates the world, that the sympathies of the people are inert and barren, and that interests alone make for efficacious and constant impulses. Thus are men made. . . ." Anyone who believed it to be otherwise would only ruin himself and his country.[72] With good men, with those used to freedom, reason would be enough; but force was the way to reason with the "evil," with those debilitated by servitude. The good order was that which "put people in need of being good"

---

[68] Macchi contrasted the realism of the SNI with Mazzinianism, in Macchi, *La conciliazione dei partiti,* 155–57; Omodeo noted the growth of a doctrine of "realism" around Cavour: Omodeo, *Cavour,* II, 164. On realism in Gioberti," see Gentile, "Gioberti," *I profeti del Risorgimento,* 114. Cf. Salvatorelli, *Pensiero politico,* 24–44.

[69] *Credo,* 22; *Memorie di Pallavicino,* III, 485.

[70] La Farina to Molena, 3 December 1858, Franchi, *Epistolario di La Farina,* II, 93; *La rivoluzione,* 10.

[71] Pallavicino, *Come vivremo,* Maineri, *Manin e Pallavicino,* 613; Franchi, *Scritti politici di La Farina,* II, 187.

[72] Pallavicino to Montanelli, 6 November 1854, *Memorie di Pallavicino,* III, 94; in arguing that the King would have to be appealed to on the basis of his interests, the Marchese commented that ". . . even he is a son of Adam." *La rivoluzione,* 13–14.

not the one without power to combat evil.[73] This was what had come of considering "men, principles and people, not as they ought to be, but as they are." [74] These dour successors to the dreams of Mazzini knew all too well what men were. To be sure this time of hitting some target, they had lowered their sights. The *risorgimento* would be brought about by the good men with a few leaders under one king.

The Italian state would be forged in victorious war; the lessons of 1848 and the tenets of realism made that apparent. This war had become the "only thought of every Italian," and it was natural to add, "Long Live the Sardinian Army!" The National Society placed great store by that army, and its leaders were particularly pleased by signs of support for their program among the military.[75] Here belief and "realism" met: "I have faith," said Pallavicino, "in muskets and cannons." If Italy focused all her force on the one great cataclysm, she would surely triumph. This sense of drama burst forth in Foresti's cry to "*Arms!* Blessed [are] the *carbines of death* of the American arsenals! blessed [are] their *Cott's* [sic] *revolvers* of four, six and more shots!" The promise of modern weapons was deeply felt. "Yesterday," La Farina wrote, "I was at the arsenal, and I assure you that tears of tenderness fell from my eyes, when I saw the immeasurable [goods] of war that are being prepared." [76]

Clearly, through all these views of the National Society there runs a broad set of values, values which were those of the people to whom the Society mainly appealed. The practical as the standard in politics, the desire for reform but ambivalence toward revolution, concern for discipline and order, willingness to compromise, moderation seen as the mark of the wise man, respect for "virile work"—these were the attitudes of the Italian middle class. The men of the Society genuinely wanted to "amalgamate

[73] *Le forze liberatrici*, 12; *Italia e Piemonte*, 3; there was even a reference to the use of terror against such evil men, *La rivoluzione*, 12.
[74] *Credo*, 8.
[75] *La rivoluzione*, 13; La Farina, *Murat e l'unità italiana*, 7, and Pallavicino to Manin, 29 October 1856, Maineri, *Manin e Pallavicino*, 227; Pallavicino to Manin, 10 December 1855 and 13 November 1856, *ibid.*, 26, 235.
[76] Pallavicino to Manin, 10 July 1856, *ibid.*, 126; "memorandum" of Foresti to Pallavicino, mentioned in Pallavicino to Manin, 15 July 1856, *ibid.*, 128, and cited in *ibid.*, 531; La Farina to Filippo Bartolomeo, 1 September 1858, Franchi, *Epistolario di La Farina*, II, 78.

every political color," but they naturally thought most of "cultivated men, industrialists, traders, capitalists, property holders, artisans, artisans of the city and artisans of the country. . . ." [77] Their writings betrayed an intense class consciousness. They had accepted the King, but they had little sympathy for the privileges of rank. The Society was combating "the aristocracy, which wants to make itself master of society" as well as demagoguery. They observed with a strong note of uncertainty, a trace even of fear, how "the great figure" of the people "again rises huge." [78] They worried that "the multitudes" might easily be seduced by false doctrine, that for the masses their own idea of concord would prove "a bit abstract." Communism already rang in their ears as a word of horror. [79]

The Society's view of the peasantry (and the literate peasantry at that) was so transparent as to impair its propaganda. The *Catechismo politico pei contadini piemontesi* was not only dedicated to the "honest country men" but bore a footnote warning the "reader furnished with that cognition which the peasants generally do not possess" not to look here for "purity of language" or "sublimity of thought." Its seven little stories, in that "figurative language" which, it was explained, was all the country folk could understand, portray peasants learning of Italy and of their responsibility to her. If they read those lessons well, however, the Piedmontese peasants would have learned something else from their ideal exemplars, who, in these stories, always depended on the judgment of their betters (after taking off their hats to them and "respectfully" greeting them). "Good harmony" between rich and poor was a recurrent theme, and the peasants were frankly instructed to be "honest and industrious and not to aspire for things too much above your status." [80]

[77] Garibaldi to Caranti, 15 June 1858, ms., ISR, busta 547, n. 83; *Italia e Piemonte*, 13. Though stated somewhat more harshly, these values are strikingly similar to those found in the previous generation of Lombard liberals by Kent Roberts Greenfield, *Economics and Liberalism in the Risorgimento: A Study of Nationalism in Lombardy, 1814–48* (Baltimore, 1934).

[78] *Credo*, 19; Foresti to Pallavicino, 26 June 1856, Maineri, *Manin e Pallavicino*, 351.

[79] Pallavicino to Manin, 17 April 1857, *ibid.*, 302; *Catechismo pei contadini*, 28–9; Pallavicino, "Anzitutto il ben pubblico," in Maineri, *Manin e Pallavicino*, 321.

[80] *Catechismo pei contadini*, 5n; 29, 7, 18, 5–6.

Goodness and docility, sincerity and simplicity were virtues the Society easily confused.

Its leaders, aware of the danger of "servitude" under democratic or socialist veils and suspicious of revolutionary calls to "cruel and savage instincts," directed their efforts toward "the most distinguished men of the different nuances of the liberal party. . . ." [81] Their followers were, for the most part, like them —practical men of moderate success who saw the need for tax reforms and freedom of conscience as part of the reason for being a nationalist.[82] Minghetti felt the Society performed a function of the moderates in attempting to overcome class antagonisms; and the Society in turn shared Cavour's fear that social questions, problems of capital and labor, might complicate the central national question.[83] The National Society would show the world that Italians "can be moderate as well as enthusiastic, resolute and patient as well as insurgent and impulsive. . . ." [84] They knew the importance of their role because in revolution "the few dare, the many follow, all applaud. . . ." [85]

Self-conscious liberals, the Society's members closely associated such benefits as an independent judiciary and freedom of the press with liberties of commerce and industry, but it was in their emphasis on the latter that they most clearly represented their class.[86] Politics today, they declared, "is mercantile," and they were speaking for themselves when they added that the "need most felt by a people in modern times is the complete development of its own economic forces." To be sure, the magnanimous and generous" might want unification for the "love

[81] Le forze liberatrici, 5; Manin to the Leader, 29 July 1854, Levi, Manin, 79. It is interesting that Mazzini, too, sought local leaders among the middle class. See his letter to Mordini, 17 August [1856], Scritti di Mazzini, LVII, 20.

[82] At the time it supported the SNI, the journalistic league headed by Il Diritto listed part of its program as financial reform, more equitable distribution of taxes, freedom of conscience, administrative simplicity, greater legal equality for all citizens, cited in Memorie di Pallavicino, III, 693–96. Mamiani supported the Society because it strove for nothing too far from the practical, Mamiani to Pallavicino, 29 August 1858, ibid., 468–69.

[83] Minghetti, Ricordi, III, 131; Massari, Diario, 58–9.

[84] This quotation from "Italian Characters and Italian Prospects," North British Review, XXIV, 550, undoubtedly reflects some English prejudices; but it was an authorized presentation of Manin's views which he endorsed.

[85] Credo, 23.

[86] Italia e Piemonte, 2; Piccolo Corriere, 3 January 1858.

of liberty," but they were thinking of the men they knew best in declaring that to make the desire universal it would be necessary to "demonstrate its utility for commerce, industries, for the well-being of the greater number." True to their word, they argued at length that one railroad or cotton mill or foundry would economically more than offset the losses from the abolition of a local court, which owed its wealth to taxes. Provincial officials were assured that they would find a more profitable career in a national bureaucracy.[87]

Of all the arguments for unification, this was the clearest, that Italian industries, commerce, fleets could not prosper (nor public instruction meet the need of the times) without it. It was a great state's economic virility that the National Society most envied; and no member of the Manchester School could have written more glowingly of the fruits of "the association of capital, talent, and work" that had "made possible the construction of those stupendous networks of railroads which connect London and Paris with the manufacturing cities and seaports of England and France; that has founded in those nations the great institutions of credit, that has organized the great navigation lines, that has multiplied the workshops, introducing great numbers of machines into them, dried swamps, built embankments along rivers, dredged ports, made the most sterile land fertile." [88] In discussing economic, educational, and administrative reforms, the SNI could be quite specific. The political system which might accompany unification was still ill-defined; but about the economic benefits it would bring, there was no doubt.

It was the nature of their liberalism as much as their realism which led them to depend so heavily on Piedmont. When applied to specific issues, their ideas and attitudes frequently led to a deep ambivalence. Most such issues were, of course, "secondary" ones on which the Society could feel free to enjoy the luxury of ambiguity. When circumstances required a clear stand, however, the Society's leaders intended to find their model in the existing institutions of Piedmont. How well that model fit the sum of the Society's ideas is shown in three of the specific issues on which the SNI was forced to take a stand, one a

[87] *Italia, Francia e Russia*, 5; *Credo*, 11; *Le forze liberatrici*, 7–8.
[88] *Credo*, 1, 11, 16.

question of its very program, another a policy of action, and the third the expression of a basic prejudice. The politically active men of the Italian National Society distrusted the ambitions and disagreements to which politics gave rise. Their view of self-interest as the sure motivation of men led them to suspect others in politics of only wanting to become deputies and professors, and they often felt the need to repeat that they were without such ambitions.[89] Devoted to unity in the fullest sense, they feared the divisiveness of discussion. It upset them that free speech allowed statements that were "manifest incitements to civil war." [90] Thus they came to oppose any assembly as a first step toward unification. Yet these men were genuinely devoted to representative government, and they looked upon Piedmont's parliament as a major factor in her claim to Italian leadership. The resolution of the conflict was, therefore, simply that Piedmont's parliament should become Italy's. It was certain to grant Victor Emmanuel a wartime dictatorship; the dangers of dissensions would be minimized but the institutions preserved.

The National Society was associated with no greater manifestation of national sentiment than the movement of military volunteers from the provinces of Italy to Piedmont. But the Society, with its respect for discipline and fear of repeating the failure of the amateurs in 1848, was uncertain as to what role these volunteers should be given. The solution had been sought, of course, in the fusion of the volunteers with Piedmont's army; but the Society was concerned that this Piedmontese institution remain inviolate. When in fact the volunteers did arrive, the SNI waited for the government's response before declaring its own policy toward them.[91]

The problems raised by their anticlericalism were resolved in much the same way. Most of the members of the Society seem to have agreed that "Catholic tyranny" and "Papal legions" were major enemies. La Farina once cited among the high qualities

[89] Paselli to Casarini, April 1859, Maioli, "La Società Nazionale in Bologna," *Saggi e documenti* (1933), 85; *Italia e Piemonte*, 1; Maineri, *Manin e Pallavicino*, 451.
[90] La Farina to Cianciolo, 23 November 1856, Franchi, *Epistolario di La Farina*, II, 26; letter to Signora Torti, 17 February 1857, *ibid.*, 33; *Italia e Piemonte*, 3.
[91] Pallavicino to Rattazzi, 3 May 1856, *Memorie di Pallavicino*, III, 217; La Farina to Macchi, 15 January 1856, Franchi, *Epistolario di La Farina*, II, 5.

of a member of the Society that he was a "most learned anti-clerical," and Pallavicino worked actively in the Chamber of Deputies for the abolition of clerical privileges.[92] It was conceded, however, that religion was a "social necessity"; and the members of the Society were, of course, anxious not to antagonize any possible sympathizer. The limits they drew to their anticlericalism are significant; separation of church and state (a choice between Christ and Torquemada, said Pallavicino) was the most demanded, that priests be subject to civil penalty, the least. The state remained their central concern and the policies of Piedmont their model.[93]

Thus the National Society had evolved a program meant to appeal to all except those on the political extremes, to teach Italians to say to each other, "to whoever loves Italy I am friend and brother." While propagandizing with revolutionary vigor, the Society could cite its support of the monarchy to "reassure the prudent"; for Piedmont did not make revolution but prevented it. Like Gioberti before them, these men meant to combine the practicality of conservatives with the hopes of idealists. To some, the result seemed too diversified a collection of men around too vague a set of ideas;[94] yet it did hold together. Their realism led to the abandonment of much of the idealism of the earlier Risorgimento; their fervor even gave a kind of moral justification to such a "sacrifice." Like moths, partially blinded perhaps but beating their wings with growing enthusiasm, they circled ever closer around the cool light of Cavour's success. They were thus both expressing their views and serving his ends as they insisted that, when war came, there should be "no circles, no assemblies, no provisional governments, no untimely disputes, no

[92] Pallavicino to de Lasteyrie, 9 December 1854 and 26 January 1858, *Memorie di Pallavicino*, III, 106, 444–46; Manin to Pallavicino, 23 December 1856, Maineri, *Manin e Pallavicino*, 257; La Farina's recommendation is cited in Teodor D. Onciulescu, "Un assiduo della Società Nazionale Italiana e di quella neolatina: Il Torinese Giovenale Vegezzi-Ruscalla," *Rassegna Storica del Risorgimento*, XXVII (1940), 253.

[93] Pallavicino to Flandin, 17 October 1854, *Memorie di Pallavicino*, III, 90; Pallavicino's speech in the Chamber, 9 March 1854, *ibid.*, 73–4; *Credo*, 19; *Italia e Piemonte*, 4; La Farina, *Murat e l'unità italiana*, 3.

[94] Manin to *Opinione*, 12 February 1856, Maineri, *Manin e Pallavicino*, 507; Anzilotti, *Gioberti*, 379; Tommaséo to Pallavicino, 30 August 1857, Sforza, "Tommaséo e la Società Nazionale," *Risorgimento Italiano*, I, 506.

undisciplined bands: [a] single army, [a] single supreme command, military dictatorship, councils of war that reassure the good and check-rein with inexorable justice factious men." Bit by bit the ideas and attitudes, the hopes and fears which the National Society represented had interacted to produce a far fuller program than its leaders realized.

Its view of the present and the program it advocated had lost nearly all that flavor of democracy, moral improvement, and social reform which had once moved Italian nationalists. Beyond the present, the Society protested, it did not theorize. Its view of history, nevertheless, maintained the promise that Italy, once unified, would then become liberal, strong, and prosperous.[95] That a nation of 25 million citizens with a wit and courage to which history testified, with glorious traditions from the past and a firm faith in the future—that such a nation should be strong there could be no doubt. Italy would have an army powerful enough to preserve her independence and a fleet sufficient to protect her coastline and commerce. Indeed, the Society looked forward to an army of 300,000 men and cited no less an authority than Napoleon to the effect that she could support 400 warships, that the proximity of Syria, Greece and Egypt assured the future of Spezia, Taranto, and Venice as great ports.[96] Nor was there doubt of Italy's potential prosperity; for freedom and prosperity like poverty and slavery went together. Under the new dispensation, agriculture, industry, commerce, and the arts would all flourish. The "most fertile and beautiful region of the world," located halfway between East and West, the land which produced the wealth of the city-states, the progenitor of two civilizations that gave the world Caesar and Buonoparte [sic]—such a past was surely a promise that it was only unity which Italy lacked.[97] No more would Italians, who had taught agriculture to the world, pay dearly for fruit while it rotted in Sicily. The added promise of a Suez Canal pointed to Italy's becoming a maritime power without equal in Europe. Nor would culture lag behind. For once unified, Italians would

[95] *Italia, Francia e Russia,* 10–12.
[96] *Credo,* 17–19, 10–11; *La rivoluzione,* 14.
[97] *Le forze liberatrici,* 9; *Credo,* 11, 1, 4–5.

reap the benefits of their Galileos, Voltas, Galvanis. With a national market, publishing would thrive, writers prosper and editors, booksellers, printers, even bookbinders flourish.[98]

All this would come with unification, and the National Society had shown that that goal was within reach, that it depended neither on revolution nor diplomacy but only on unanimous support of Piedmont. To arrive at so simple a solution to Italy's complex problems, the Society had stripped plans of reform from talk of resurgence and concern for present liberty from questions of politics; it had surrendered most of its own political initiative and tended increasingly to conceive of unification as an enlargement of Piedmontese territory. This seemed a most reasonable "sacrifice," because it guaranteed that

> A vita novella
> Rinasce più bella
> L'Italia che fu.[99]

[98] *Ibid.*, 9–10, 13, 8, 16; *Catechismo pei contadini*, 32; *Le forze liberatrici*, 8.
[99] "To a new life the Italy of old is reborn more beautiful," poem of Pallavicino's included in his letter to Montanelli, 28 December 1858, *Memorie di Pallavicino*, III, 482–83.

CHAPTER SIX

THE HOPE FOR ACTION AND THE HABIT

OF CAUTION (JANUARY—MARCH 1859)

✤ DISCOURAGEMENT was dangerous for the National Society, but popular exuberance could threaten Cavour's whole policy. The great fear was that the propagandistic thunder of several months might produce its own lightning. Cavour warned La Farina in November that irritation in Lombardy-Venetia must not grow to the point of any disturbance "*di piazze*"; he asked that word be gotten to Guerrazzi warning against "thoughts of disordered moves, provisional governments and other follies in the manner of [18]48."[1] Letter after letter from La Farina, page after page of the *Piccolo Corriere* echoed these warnings.

Characteristically, the Society presented the danger as coming from counterplots. Sanfedists and Jesuits were trying to bring about a communist uprising, *agents provocateurs* skillfully attempting to mislead local committees. Only those orders bearing the signature of La Farina or his agents should be honored.[2] Mazzinians were declared to be no less wily, and La Farina showed particular concern for their influence in Genoa, Massa and Carrara. With the ease of habit, warnings against Mazzinian agents were passed back and forth between committees in the Romagna and in the Marches. The Modena committee detected an effort to make of Parma a Mazzinian center, and even Gari-

[1] Ferrari had left an interview with Cavour convinced that the SNI and the Government were in full accord: letter of Selmi, 2 March 1859, in Canevazzi, *Selmi*, 233. The best evidence of that accord lies in its transmission of Cavour's warnings, Cavour to La Farina, 26 November 1858 and n.d., Franchi, *Epistolario di La Farina*, II, 91, 134.

[2] *Piccolo Corriere*, 24 January 1859; La Farina to Mazzi, 14 March; to Morchio, 27 March 1859, Franchi, *Epistolario di La Farina*, II, 151, 153. Biagio Caranti wrote the Genoa committee, 23 January 1859, warning them not to confuse the SNI with the newly formed *Società Nazionale per l'Indipendenza d'Italia*; official communications to them would, he said, bear his and La Farina's signatures, ms. in the Carte Morchio, MNRG. La Farina declared the new society's members to be "all Mazzinians or ex-Mazzinians," letter to Mazzi, 24 January 1859, Franchi, *Epistolario di La Farina*, II, 122.

baldi referred to the Mazzinian influence on one of his followers.[3] These plots took advantage of the *"allarmisti"* (fortunately, said the *Piccolo Corriere*, that is not an Italian word) who insisted that the plans had been called off, who claimed that Piedmont no longer looked to war, and who liberally spread "false news." [4] The Society strove so hard to prevent "alarmist" rumors from spreading that for a moment it found itself left behind by the Government. The speech from the throne, cautioned the *Piccolo Corriere*, while very Italian, would be no trumpet blast; for it might prove fatal to overencourage the provinces. Afterward the Society's paper had to concede that it had been pleasantly surprised [5]—an embarrassing admission from men who claimed to know the Government's every move. It was a difficult task to maintain political temperatures without raising them.

There is in La Farina's repeated warnings an almost frenzied note which suggests he was not quite sure of his own Society. Instructions not to take orders from strangers and not to start a revolt demonstrate how little he knew what his followers were like or of the extent to which they would be followers. Yet three of the great military heroes of 1848 were now behaving like the best of moderates. When hints of military preparations came to him from Genoa instead of Turin, Ulloa informed Pallavicino. Garibaldi warned against "inopportune movements" in Lombardy and Tuscany at "whatever cost." And Medici was so concerned by talk of agitation in Lombardy that he went to the frontier himself to meet with local leaders and counsel moderation.[6] The National Society had been more successful than La Farina knew.

Inactivity, however, was an unsatisfactory success, and the So-

---

[3] La Farina to Mazzi, 7 September; to Medici, 29 December 1858 and 11 February 1859; to Morchio, 27 March, *ibid.*, 78, 104, 127, 153; Alessandrini, *I fatti*, ii, 28; Terrachini to Selmi, February 1859, Franchi, *Epistolario di La Farina*, ii, 124; the follower, "B.," is sometimes guessed to have been Bertani. Cavour seems to have accepted Casarini's report that the Mazzinians were the only alternative to the moderates in the Romagna who wanted union with Piedmont, Cavour to Nigra, 28 February 1859, *Cavour-Nigra*, ii, 45.
[4] *Piccolo Corriere*, 24 January, 7 February 1859; La Farina to Amadori, 24 January 1859, Franchi, *Epistolario di La Farina*, ii, 119.
[5] *Piccolo Corriere*, 27 December 1858; 3 and 10 January 1859.
[6] Ulloa to Pallavicino, 23 December 1858, *Memorie di Pallavicino*, iii, 479; Garibaldi to La Farina, 22 December 1858, Franchi, *Epistolario di La Farina*, ii, 99; Medici to Pallavicino, 5 January 1859, *Memorie di Pallavicino*, iii, 487.

ciety called vigorously for "demonstrations," which would make good propaganda at home and throughout Europe without endangering the Government's policies. Instructions for a demonstration were directed particularly at Tuscany and came directly from Cavour. The Prime Minister wanted a great deal. He asked for a demonstration based more on ideas of nationalism and independence than on those of liberty. One which would not commit the future, it should be carried out in such a way that all liberals of whatever faction could take part in it and the military could accept it without loss of honor. It was not to be a revolution, and any conflict with soldiers was to be avoided. Specifically, he suggested that Tuscans present their Government with petitions which would demand the dissolution of any treaty with Austria and insist on diplomatic and (if need be) military union with Piedmont. Demonstrations might then follow.[7]

It is an indication of Cavour's respect for the National Society that after writing Boncompagni of the usefulness of a demonstration, he should spell out the details to La Farina. It is a measure of the Society's subordination to Cavour that, although his initial note asked for La Farina's opinion, the Society's secretary, in sending his "instructions" to Bartolommei, only paraphrased Cavour's statement and, good organizer that he was, made it more urgent. He fired letters off to "all our friends in the principal cities of Tuscany" with similar instructions, telling them that "the die is cast," that petitions, demonstrations, clandestine publications all would be good, just so they did something. "Infuse," he pleaded, "a little of your industriousness in the others. . . . To do nothing would be damaging and shameful." [8] Never one to leave things solely in the hands of others, Cavour wrote directly to Bartolommei and Ridolfi suggesting they come to Turin to confer and stressing that what mattered was the demonstrations in themselves, not whether they changed the Grand

[7] Cavour to La Farina, n.d., Franchi, Epistolario di La Farina, II, 127n.

[8] Cavour to Boncompagni, 20 January 1859, Beniamino Manzone, "Cavour e Boncompagni nella Rivoluzione Toscana del 1859," Il Risorgimento Italiano, Rivista Storica, II (1909), 209. La Farina to Bartolommei, 12 February (Gioli, Risorgimento Toscano, 238, gives the date as 2 February); to Mario Rizzari, 20 February 1859, Franchi, Epistolario di La Farina, II, 128, 132–33. La Farina to Siccoli, 21 February 1859, ms., ISR, busta 382, n. 33.

Duke's policy.[9] Always one ready to work on a grander scale, La Farina extended the idea to the Romagna and wrote Tanari asking if, as in Tuscany, there could be some sort of demonstration there.

The men of the Society were more cautious than their leaders; the demonstrations did not take place. La Farina was bitterly disappointed. "It looks," he said, showing some regional bias, "as if the beautiful designs conceived by the Po are dissipated on the Arno." [10] D'Azeglio, worried by La Farina's orders for demonstrations, revived the idea of raising some of the new Government loan among Tuscan investors; and it is indicative of the temper of the Society in Tuscany that this demonstration of "i piccoli capitali" was more successful.[11]

Nevertheless, nationalist thought was in fact widespread, and Piedmont was its focus. The movement of volunteers to Turin from all parts of Italy established that. It overshadowed the disappointments the SNI had known and left the Society all but swamped by one of the great demonstrations of the Risorgimento. Here was the orderly sense of practical sacrifice of which a nation could be made. And the Italian National Society led the movement, although it had not anticipated nor even advocated the kind of demonstration which developed. As early as July 1858, the Society had tried to face the question of whether it should support the training of small secret militias and the forma-

[9] Cavour to Bartolommei, 19 February, Gioli, Risorgimento Toscano, 239–40; and to Ridolfi, 19 February 1859, Cavour-Nigra, II, 19.

[10] La Farina to Tanari, 25 February 1859, ms. in Carte Tanari I, MCRB; La Farina to Morchio, 9 March 1859, Franchi, Epistolario di La Farina, II, 144. Sergio Camerani, "Lo spirito pubblico in Toscana nel 1859," Rassegna Storica Toscana, II (1956), 106, cites some interesting police reports as evidence that the January-February lull in nationalist activity in Tuscany was so general and synchronized that it must have been the deliberate policy of the SNI. This tends, however, to attribute to the Society greater precision of organization than it had. It is more probable that after long waiting nationalists were tired and discouraged in Tuscany as elsewhere. La Farina's disappointment still must be explained as well as the fact that in the letter to Morchio cited above he said that "authoritative" persons who had come to Turin from Tuscany had agreed to the plan for a demonstration.

[11] D'Azeglio to Nigra, 24 February 1859, Cavour-Nigra, II, 23; and of Malenchini to Tommaso Corsi, 27 February 1859, Valentino Soldani, Pasqua di liberazione (Florence, 1909), 52. Pietro Adami and Fenzi were the important bankers involved; the idea was not new, see Piccolo Corriere, 21 June, 19 and 26 July 1858. After this, Cavour's thoughts turned to the possibility of a demonstration nearer home, in Genoa, Cavour to William de la Rive, 20 March 1859, Chiala, Lettere di Cavour, II, 47.

tion of volunteer corps. Respect for the discipline and dependability of the Piedmontese army determined its answer. Men without previous military experience who wished to serve would have to be trained in the regular army. Deserters from the other armies of Italy could, in contrast, be added immediately to Piedmont's strength. The dangers of undisciplined troops (and their possible effect on the regulars) would thus be avoided; Italy would have one national army. La Farina's October plan had reflected this conception.[12] Piedmont could look forward to an increase of power without a loss of control.

It soon became clear that conscripts newly called up would be more likely to desert to Piedmont than men already established in a military career; for the conscripts, the local levy could be made the last straw of discontent. Having once been liable to military service, they would be more willing to serve in Piedmont's army. And Austria would find Piedmont's acceptance of them highly provocative. Nor would the proportion of dangerous radicals be likely to be so high among conscripts as among volunteers. Their coming to Piedmont would make an effective demonstration, simultaneously strengthen her, and weaken the enemy. When in January rumor had it that Austria might call up two groups of conscripts, La Farina sent out word that mass desertion among them should be encouraged. Ambitiously, he added that the arrival of a few hundred men could prove an embarrassment to the Government and be of little use to Piedmont; but two, three, or four thousand men would make a magnificent national protest which might even precipitate something more.[13]

Lombard conscripts quickly began to arrive in number. A committee had to be set up to handle them, and La Farina showed an increasing absorption in this activity. Caution reigned, however. At first, La Farina did not want such success announced publicly, and he repeated more and more the importance of sending deserters rather than volunteers, who were too likely to be "mature men, undisciplined and undisciplinable." Conscripts,

---

[12] *Piccolo Corriere*, 12 July 1858; Franchi, *Epistolario di La Farina*, II, 81–2.
[13] La Farina to Clementi, 21 December 1858, *ibid.*, 96; La Farina had also hinted, however, that the gathering of volunteers should be held up because "counsels of prudence come from Paris," in a letter to Medici, 1 January 1859, cited in Chiala, *Lettere di Cavour*, III, xviii. See also Cavour to Nigra, 13 December 1858, *Cavour-Nigra*, I, 240.

committees were reminded, should have a "decided will" to serve in Piedmont's army and understand that "for the moment" there was no volunteer corps.[14] The *Piccolo Corriere* even offered a formal defense of the Society's view of volunteers arguing, early in January, that despite the heroism of such men in 1848 an army of 200,000 regular troops in place of 500,000 volunteers might have made for Italian victory. Volunteers, it was concluded, had been needed to start the revolution, but iron discipline was needed now. The article must have surprised and offended many, and the Society was forced to explain that it had not meant to deprive those not in the army of their chance to fight for Italy.[15] The National Society's policy toward volunteers was not yet clear.

There were, however, yet other reasons for the Society's objections to them. The fear remained that a movement of volunteers might prematurely precipitate revolution or war. The Society wanted even conscripts to wait until the end of February before coming to Piedmont and to come then in such a way that the Government need not officially be aware of them.[16] As their numbers grew nevertheless, in large part because of the work the Society had done before, there developed the further fear that active nationalists would be siphoned off to Piedmont leaving the provinces in less nationalistic hands. La Farina sent off frequent warnings during the months of February and March to exercise care lest the countryside be "despoiled . . . of those elements which may later prove necessary." [17]

Necessary in the provinces, they could be a danger in Piedmont, for the men who volunteered were likely to be optimisti-

[14] La Farina to Clementi, 8 January 1859, Franchi, *Epistolario di La Farina*, ii, 110; and to Mazzi, 29 January 1859, ms., ISR, busta 110, n. 22 (the passages relevant here are omitted in Franchi). See also La Farina to Armelonghi, 3 January; to Bolognini, 13 and 30 January, and to Barigozzi, 18 January 1859, Franchi, *Epistolario di La Farina*, ii, 107, 114, 125, 117.

[15] *Piccolo Corriere*, 3 and 17 January 1859. Ulloa's long protest betrays a deeper resentment than its argument which stressed that men beyond military age could see service only as volunteers, Ulloa to Pallavicino, 9 January 1859, *Memorie di Pallavicino*, iii, 488–90.

[16] La Farina to Medici, 1 January; and to Bolognini, 30 January 1859, Franchi, *Epistolario di La Farina*, ii, 109, 125.

[17] La Farina to Bolognini, 17 February 1859, *ibid.*, 132; letter [La Farina to Ferrara committee?], 28 March 1859, ms., ISR, busta 61, n. 35. Mai recalled this concern for Lombardy in his letter of 16 October 1863, *ibid.*, busta 717, n. 20.

cally impatient and politically radical. Many of them might be Mazzinians; and even if not, they were likely, once banded together, to develop political goals of their own. Such fears were not without foundation,[18] and Cavour was concerned over rumors that youths were being encouraged to fight under Garibaldi rather than in the regular army. The SNI cared too much for its relationship with the Government not to be influenced by such concern; it is understood, La Farina warned Medici, that "we would assume in the eyes of the government a kind of moral guarantee for the political opinions of the components of these groups." [19]

The mass desertions which La Farina had envisioned did not take place; instead, men began arriving from Lombardy and the Duchies in a steady, growing stream. La Farina himself could not help being impressed, and he was too good a propagandist not to try impressing others. When the Society published a small "appello clandestino," it found no better call to action than citing the 400 Modenese who had come to serve Piedmont's army (where they would be trained to operate as a unit). The Piccolo Corriere, from the last weeks of February on, described the daily arrival of men from all classes and in such numbers as to make this one of the "most beautiful and notable of events." Prior to the end of February, the Society's paper had not made a great deal of this movement; but from then on each issue noted the progress of the great demonstration. The youth of Italy now knew how to "show our enemies and all Europe that you fight and die for the common fatherland." Cavour too was impressed.[20] Such dramatic activity was also an effective spur to local committees, and La Farina's letters were filled with accounts of the 460 men from the Duchy of Modena (such figures

[18] Mazzini himself looked for support from the volunteers and tried to propagandize among them. See Mazzini to Saffi, May and June 1859, Scritti di Mazzini, LXIII (Imola, 1933), 248–49, 264–65. Brofferio claimed that most of the volunteers were university students who received their political education from the republicans, Brofferio, I Miei Tempi, VII, 292.

[19] Cavour to La Farina, n.d., Franchi, Epistolario di La Farina, II, 151; La Farina to Medici, 23 December 1858, ibid., 100.

[20] The appello, a single printed sheet dated 24 February 1859, is in the ISR, busta 5, n. 47; Piccolo Corriere, 28 February 1859; Cavour to d'Azeglio, 7 March, and to Cabella, 14 March 1859, Chiala, Lettere di Cavour, III (Turin, 1884), 38, 45.

were always a bit flexible), the 164 who arrived yesterday, the hundreds who come daily from Lombardy.[21] La Farina still hoped for the desertion of some company (with arms and baggage) stationed at Massa or Carrara; the Society still favored union of the Tuscan and Piedmontese armies. Volunteers, however, made better propaganda than deserters, and the *Piccolo Corriere* began to use this more effective term. "We speak of volunteers," La Farina wrote Tanari, "but you know that most are conscripts." [22] To call previous arrivals volunteers only made certain that future arrivals in fact would be. Pressure for accepting volunteers was increased by the magic of Garibaldi's name. Despite La Farina's denials, rumors that the SNI wanted volunteer corps in the style of 1848, to be led by Garibaldi, had been sweeping Lombardy since November. Garibaldi was thinking in similar terms; and he put Medici in charge of the formation of *bersaglieri* of the National Guard. It would, he thought, make a "powerful auxiliary" to the Piedmontese army; but La Farina had in mind something rather different from Garibaldi's optimistic plans.[23]

The Government, genuinely embarrassed by the continued arrival of volunteers, was forced to establish some policy. Simply calling them "interned political immigrants" would fool no one and was offensive to men who had left home with visions of doing battle for Italy. Finally, it was decided to expand the National Guard with divisions of volunteers under 36 years of age. Such volunteers were still expected to be men fit for service "who want to enter the army." Given regular training, they were to enlist for eight years. The National Society was no longer in the embarrassing position of having to discourage volunteers, nor did it have to worry much about radicals among those enlisting for

[21] La Farina to Bartolommei, 12 February; and to Torti, 17 February 1859, Franchi, *Epistolario di La Farina*, ii, 128, 130; La Farina to Mazzi, 29 January 1859, ms., ISR, busta 110, n. 22.

[22] La Farina to Mazzi, 19 March; and to Rizzari, 21 February 1859, Franchi, *Epistolario di La Farina*, ii, 152, 133; to Siccoli, 21 February 1859, ms., ISR, busta 382, n. 33; to Tanari, 28 February 1859, ms. in the Carte Tanari i, MCRB.

[23] Garibaldi wanted La Farina to "enlarge upon" the arrival of some students from Pavia and expected funds to be provided for his *bersaglieri*; La Farina only agreed to the formation of companies of *cacciatori* or youths from the National Guard: Visconti-Venosta, *Ricordi di gioventù*, 461; Garibaldi to La Farina, 21 and 22 December 1858, 30 January 1859, Franchi, *Epistolario di La Farina*, ii, 97, 99, 124. La Farina to Terasona, 11 January 1859; to Medici, 23 December 1858, *ibid.*, 112, 100.

eight years. If the *Piccolo Corriere* continued to encourage mass desertions, it admitted that volunteers would be received and then treated like regular soldiers.[24]

On foot, in trains, by ship from Leghorn, volunteers kept coming. Depots were set up in Cuneo and Savigliano to receive them. These men were not always welcomed by the regular army men (or by General La Marmora in particular), and it was one of the Society's important functions to see that the new arrivals were decently treated and adequately provided for, to prevent, in Farini's words, "*le marmorazioni.*" The committee officially in charge of assigning and outfitting these men was in close touch with the SNI, and La Farina was already seeking capable officers to lead them.[25] By March, however, the number of volunteers (and their own clear wish) made it certain that Garibaldi could not be kept separate from the volunteer movement. It was agreed that the hero of two continents could lead a special corps.[26] By thus recognizing the pressure of opinion, the cautious Government and the confused Society purchased a large gain in propaganda with a small concession. Garibaldi's corps was to be made of the men then forming in Cuneo where, as Pallavicino had told the General before learning of his assignment, the "less vigorous" were sent.[27] The idea (expressed in the October plan) of giving Garibaldi only an "unofficial" role had proved impossible; but, as Tommaséo shrewdly noted, Garibaldi had been deprived of the freedom to choose his own men.[28]

The impressive numbers of volunteers and conscripts brought the Society and the Government closer together. At first, border authorities were supposed to allow volunteers simply to pass

[24] La Farina to Mazzi, 24 January and 6 February, to Carlotti, 17 February 1859, *ibid.*, 121, 125, 131; La Farina was consulted on implementation of the law: Cavour to La Farina, 13 February 1859, *ibid.*, 128. *Piccolo Corriere*, 28 February 1859.

[25] La Farina to Mazzi, 19 March, and to Terasona, 18 January 1859, Franchi, *Epistolario di La Farina*, II, 132, 116; Rava, *Epistolario di Farini*, IV, 241.

[26] Cavour to Nigra, 9 March 1859, *Cavour-Nigra*, II, 74; and La Farina to Bartolommei, 9 March 1859, Franchi, *Epistolario di La Farina*, II, 143 (this simultaneity suggests that La Farina warned of the decision as soon as it was made). Cavour to Garibaldi, 17 March 1859, Giacomo Emilio Curatolo, *Garibaldi, Vittorio Emanuele, Cavour, nei fasti della patria* (Bologna, 1911), 22.

[27] Pallavicino to Garibaldi, *Memorie di Pallavicino*, III, 503.

[28] He also noted La Farina's part in securing an arrangement so to the Government's advantage. Tommaséo to Capponi, 25 January 1859, del Lungo and Prunas, *Tommaséo e Capponi*, IV¹, 392.

without seeing them; but this arrangement, although it gave La Farina another chance to suggest that the Government was supplying him with secret instructions, seems not to have proved very satisfactory. By the end of the month, orders were sent out to give volunteers *foglie di via*. Still, things did not always go smoothly at the border, and local committees tended to appeal directly to La Farina when difficulties arose. Indeed, as local members of the SNI came to feel their quasi-official position, La Farina had to remind them not to make unnecessary noise.[29]

Even the Government felt the excitement. As one member of the Society commented, those volunteers gave Cavour the evidence he needed that the Italians were mature. The Prime Minister's letters referred frequently to the great demonstration before him. And he found not only their number extraordinary, for he assured d'Azeglio that they were from the best families. Cavour continued his advocacy of volunteers until late June, and La Farina could write a committee that he was authorized to congratulate them on the volunteers they had sent, not just by the Central Committee but by the Conte di Cavour as well.[30]

Once comfortably backed by the Government, the Society began to see more in the movement of volunteers than it had noted before. It was "a true crusade," holy and sublime (especially when combined with generous subscriptions to war-loans). The accounts in the *Piccolo Corriere* not only made the most of those who had come but encouraged more to follow, and there were stories of fathers sending all their sons and of sons refusing to accept commissions.[31] Each week there were new arrivals to announce, and the achievements of one province were made a spur to the next. All the while, the National Society was gaining greatly in prestige. Farini watched this demonstration with in-

[29] La Farina to Medici, 1 and 7 January; to Mazzi, 29 January; and to Bolognini, 30 January 1859, Franchi, *Epistolario di La Farina*, ii, 105, 109, 122–23, 125.

[30] Letter of Selmi, 2 March 1859, in Canevazzi, *Selmi*, 233 (Selmi, *La Farina*, 17, notes the extent to which La Farina and Cavour were surprised by the movement unleashed by the call for conscripts). Cavour to d'Azeglio, 10 March, Chiala, *Lettere di Cavour*, iii, 38; and 14 April 1859, *ibid.*, vi (Turin, 1887), 388; to P. O. Vigliani, 27 June 1859, *ibid.*, iii, 98. Cavour to Nigra, 14 March 1859, *Cavour-Nigra*, ii, 97. La Farina to Armelonghi, 4 April 1859, Franchi, *Epistolario di La Farina*, ii, 158–59.

[31] La Farina to Armelonghi, 6 March 1859, *ibid.*, 140; *Piccolo Corriere*, 7, 21, 28 March and 15 April 1859.

creased interest, and he gave La Farina his due. Even Massari took the trouble to note in his diary when Malenchini arrived from Leghorn with several hundred volunteers, and the skeptical Tommaséo saw the large numbers of volunteers as a good sign, though he attributed much of the movement to the threat of Austrian service and the "lying promises" of the SNI.[32]

The confusion which was inevitably part of such a movement made the number of volunteers seem even greater than it was. La Farina thought 100 a day were arriving in March and twice as many a month later. A precise number was hard to come by; for excitement is contagious, and even so cautious a man as Cavour within one day changed his estimate of the total number of volunteers from ten to twelve thousand.[33] The *Piccolo Corriere* announced that by the 10th of March the committee for volunteers (established in February) had received 2,365 men, over half of them from Lombardy-Venetia. Neither the geographical nor professional distribution of this group is surprising. The areas closest to Piedmont, where discontent was strong and the numbers of students and small tradesmen high, sent the most volunteers in those early months. Largely from the lower-middle class, nearly one-half of them worked in crafts or trades. There were twice as many professional men and students as peasants.[34] Only a week later, however, it was reported that the number of arrivals from Parma and Piacenza had tripled. The most reliable figure for the total number of volunteers who

[32] Farini to Cavour, 25 March; to Malenchini, 20 March; to Boncompagni, April 1859, Rava, *Epistolario di Farini*, iv, 244, 241, 246–47. Massari, *Diario*, entry for 18 April 1859, 297 (he said there were 800 men under Malenchini although the number is more commonly given as 600. A manifesto boasting of Malenchini's efforts, dated 15 April, gives the number as 700, described in the Catalogue of the Libreria Antiquaria, L. Bonzi, *Risorgimento Italiano* [Bologna, 1960], 48). Tommaséo to Capponi, 25 March 1859, del Lungo and Prunas, *Tommaséo e Capponi*, iv¹, 390.

[33] La Farina to Carlotti, 8 March; and to Torti, 8 April 1859, Franchi, *Epistolario di La Farina*, ii, 142, 161; Cavour to d'Azeglio, 16 April, and to Nigra, 17 April 1859, *Cavour-Nigra*, ii, 163, 167.

[34] *Piccolo Corriere*, 14 March 1859, gave the following breakdown of this group: from Lombardy-Venetia, 1,331; Parma and Piacenza, 576; Modena, 408; Tuscany, 34; the Romagna, 8; Hungary, 3; Sicily, 2; Switzerland, 2; Corsica, 1. By profession (apparently with some duplication): 1,037 were in crafts and trades; 454 were *laureati* or students; 409 in the professions and liberal arts; 443 were peasants and laborers; 409 property holders; 58 of undetermined status. The Society later claimed to have spent half a million lire on 50,000 volunteers, *La Discussione*, supplement to *Bollettino Settimanale* No. 42, 23 October 1863.

arrived in Turin between January 15 and March 25 is 19,656 of whom 5,000 were incorporated into the Piedmontese army.[35] Militarily, even this figure is not tremendously significant. As a demonstration, however, the number is impressive in itself, still more so when one remembers the hazards and expense of the journey. For a man to leave his *paese* and his home, risking encounters with unfriendly police to join the army of another state, requires a high degree of fervor. For every one who made the trip, there must have been several left at home who shared at least his enthusiasm. To the unemployed, this trip may have been indistinguishable from the traditional migratory search for work; but what we know of the occupations of the volunteers suggests that in general this was a conscious demonstration of convinced nationalists.

Although the active "recruiting" of conscripts and volunteers began first in Lombardy, it was probably never so highly organized there as in the other northern provinces. The trip to Turin was, after all, not arduous; and although Austrian border guards sometimes made it difficult, the border was long and places for slipping men or goods across it were frequent and well known. In Milan a fund was set up to pay the way for those who could not otherwise afford it, and the Central Committee of the Society claimed to have spent a good deal in bringing Lombards across the border. In fact, it was because of such expenses that the Society insisted its committees along the frontier of the Duchies should from their own treasuries meet the costs created by the hundreds of volunteers who passed through their hands. In the Duchies themselves the situation seems to have been comparable to that in Lombardy, and as much as 50,000 lire may have been raised in Parma alone to pay the expenses of volunteers.[36]

[35] Comando del Corpo di Stato Maggiore, Ufficio Storico, *La Guerra del 1859 per la indipendenza d'Italia*, I, *narrazione* (Rome, 1910), 117. By province: 7,244 from Lombardy-Venetia; 3,890 Tuscany; 3,708 Duchy of Parma; 2,448 the Romagna; 1,974 Duchy of Modena; 392 the Two Sicilies.

In May La Farina estimated that 26,000 volunteers had arrived of whom 20,000 were incorporated into the army, La Farina to Bartolomeo, 19 May 1859, Franchi, *Epistolario di La Farina*, II, 175.

[36] Visconti-Venosta, *Ricordi di gioventù*, 461–67; statement of Mai, 16 October 1863, ms., ISR, busta 717, n. 20. La Farina to Mazzi, 29 January 1859, *ibid.*, busta 110, n. 22; and to Conti, 30 March 1859, Franchi, *Epistolario di La Farina*, II, 156. *Piccolo Corriere*, 18 April 1859.

Tuscany was much slower to respond, and the Society was not alone in showing concern for what seemed to be an excess of the famed Tuscan "mildness." Gradually, however, the sending of volunteers to Piedmont grew to be a great project, so great in fact that even the inefficient Tuscan police were well aware of it. Bartolommei played a major organizing role (which included contributions from his own pocket), and Malenchini even began giving large groups of men some preliminary training in Leghorn—interesting evidence that locally many in the Society thought more in the terms of 1848 than did their Central Committee. The highlight of the Tuscan movement was Malenchini's shipment of nearly 600 men in March; sizable groups continued to arrive into May. The effect of all this on the Society in Tuscany was extraordinary. Its organization developed, and its prestige increased; new committees appeared, and correspondence flourished. Collections in Lucca and Florence raised sizable sums. Many not previously part of the Society, not even entirely sympathetic to it, now joined in the common effort.[37]

The Romagna, which no one accused of lacking interest, was slower than Tuscany in responding to the call for volunteers. When Casarini was in Turin, La Farina told him of the importance of having men from his area; there need not be many of them, he explained, this was a demonstration. He prodded the Bologna committee again and again in his letters, and Paselli seconded him effectively, citing the large number of men from Tuscany.[38] The Bologna committee, however, seems to have been afraid of stirring up too much, and to have been thinking of forming some militia of its own. The Bolognese appeared uncertain as to whether the Central Committee really wanted armed men ready there or volunteers in Turin. As late as April, Pepoli wrote asking if Cavour wanted many or few volunteers;

[37] With regard to Malenchini's group of volunteers, note the effort to keep it as a unit: Corsi to Castelli, 14 April 1859, Chiala, *Carteggio di Castelli*, I, 190–91; figures for the amount of money raised in Florence go as high as 100,000 lire. Grew, "Società Nazionale in Toscana," *Rassegna Storica Toscana*, II, 91–3. D. Tonarelli [to Puccioni] from Grosseto, 15 April 1859, ms. in the archives of the Puccioni family.
[38] Dallolio, "I Colloqui di Casarini col Cavour," *La strenna delle colonie scolastiche*, XXXVII, 20; La Farina, 28 March 1859, ms. in the Carte Tanari II, MCRB; and n.d., in Masi, "Casarini," *Fra libri e ricordi*, 114–15; Paselli to Casarini, 9 April 1859, ms. in Carteggio Casarini, I, MCRB; and April 1859, in Maioli, "Società Nazionale in Bologna," *Saggi e documenti* (1933), 84–5.

we can, he boasted, send another 2,000.[39] Gradually, activity throughout the Romagna increased, and many deserters from Lombary-Venetia went to Bologna where they were given a meal and helped on their way to Piedmont through Tuscany. From April through June the Bologna committee gave such aid to over 1,800 men.[40] In addition, the leaders of Romagna committees of the SNI made trips of their own into Tuscany, leading small groups of volunteers.[41] The National Society in the Romagna played its part.

The sending of volunteers was organized even in the Marches and Rome although activity there was on a fairly small scale. An effort was made among those in the Marches sympathetic to the SNI to require that prospective volunteers have certificates of birth, vaccination, and good health and that they swear to the reliability of their political doctrines. The documents such caution required, however, proved embarrassing to men stopped at the border; and the requirements seem to have been dropped. In Rome organization for the sending of volunteers was slight, but some did make the long trip; and a committee of emigrants from the Roman states was set up in Turin to aid them on their

[39] Dallolio, "I Colloqui di Casarini col Cavour," *La strenna delle colonie scholastische*, xxxvii, 20; Masi, "Casarini," *Fra libri e ricordi*, 110; Maioli, "Tanari e la Società Nazionale," *Archiginnasio*, viii, 270; Maioli, "Tanari e il suo memoriale," *ibid.*, xxviii, 70. Pepoli to Castelli, 9 April 1859, Luigi Chiala (ed.), *Carteggio politico di Michelangelo Castelli* (Turin, 1890), i, 188.

[40] The Bologna committee spent about 2 lire per man on meals; it aided 270 men in April, 1,313 in May, 225 in June. Seventy-two volunteers from Forlì, 29 from Faenza, and 26 from Imola are noted on a scrap of paper in the Carte Tanari ii, MCRB; Galli says Imola sent 156 volunteers and 65 deserters between March and June and that over 4,000 lire was collected to pay for the cost of this: Galli, "Società Nazionale e Gamberini," *La Romagna*, xvi, 403. The figures and expenses (693.20 *scudi* for the period 23 April–4 June) of deserters aided by the Bologna committee are given in "Spesa per spedizioni dei volontari Lombard-Veneti e desertori pel Piemonte," ms. in the Carte Tanari ii, MCRB.

[41] The reports of the Tuscan police refer to many such trips. Pietro Beltrami brought some volunteers: report of 24 March 1859 in Prefettura Segreta, busta 8, ins. 160 in ASF. Count Bizzi led 12 volunteers from Forlì, a dott. Negrigioli brought 5 from Rimini and 3 more traveled on their own from Ravenna to Leghorn: report of 5 April 1859, *ibid.*, busta 8, ins. 181. Achille Laderchi brought 11 volunteers from Faenza (and had to swear they were all subjects of the Pope): report of 11 April 1859, *ibid.*, busta 8, ins. 188. Beltrami and Laderchi were particularly active in their respective committees of the SNI. The police could not discover what Tanari, Eugenio Romagnoli (a member of the SNI in Forlì) or Laderchi (on a second visit) were up to, reports of 3, 8 and 20–24 April, *ibid.*, busta 13, ins. 302 and 303; busta 3, ins. 308.

arrival.[42] Italy had never known a more national demonstration. Nor could the National Society have participated in a movement which would do it greater credit. Here at last was the demonstration all Europe had to note, one which stood as proof of national popular support for Piedmont. As a propaganda agency, the Society could have asked for nothing better. Although the SNI did not by any means direct the entire movement, the arrival of each volunteer was a feather in its cap. Its organizational structure (and its ideas) made it so ideally suited for such a movement that most of those interested in the SNI found themselves cooperating with it. Its fame as the promoting agency spread, and many an individual who wished to volunteer wrote directly to its Central Committee.[43]

At last given something specific (and exciting) to do, local committees flourished as they had not before. The increased contacts from province to province, the collections of money for the expeditions all greatly strengthened the Society as an organization. The movement's popularity and success increased the prestige of the SNI in the eyes of the Government while necessitating greater cooperation between them. Here was the practical compromise between the Society's willing dependence upon the Government and its aspirations for activity, its fondness for agitation. The great movement of volunteers resulted more from the SNI's propaganda than its plans, but it established the National Society as a success and bode well for national unity.

By March the signs of the Society's success were visible for all to see. The King made La Farina a citizen; the Central Committee moved to a new office which would now be open from ten to four. Cavour was delighted to think that radical Romagnols would, as he told them, take instructions from no one but "the committee of La Farina . . . the man Mazzini detests the most." He seems to have felt that through the SNI even repub-

---

[42] Zampetti-Biocca, Società Nazionale nella Marca, 61; Alessandrini, I fatti, 25-6. Giuseppe Mazzatinti, "Contributo alla storia del 1859," Archivio Storico del Risorgimento Umbro, I (1905), 69; Farini to Cavour, 28 March 1859, Rava, Epistolario di Farini, IV, 244; Piccolo Corriere, 15 and 18 April 1859.
[43] Manfredini to Selmi, 11 February 1859, Canevazzi, Selmi, 190-92; La Farina to Conti, 30 March 1859, Franchi, Epistolario di La Farina, II, 156.

licans could be made useful and prevented from being dangerous. This was the time when La Farina and Garibaldi went together to see Cavour, and the Prime Minister's contentment with the General was especially great.[44] It was not hard to sense that important plans were underway. All the signs indicated an important part for the National Society. Cavour wrote La Farina asking that Pallavicino be "invited" to inform Ulloa that his presence in Piedmont would be useful; and the Society's secretary characteristically let it be known that "today, by dispatch, I am calling Ulloa from Paris." For three years Pallavicino had looked forward to the time when Piedmont would use Ulloa; now at last all were drawing together for the great moment at hand.[45]

On the first of March the Society printed its secret instructions which, with great warnings about keeping them really secret and in the hands of only the most trustworthy, were apparently sent to all the committees of the SNI outside Piedmont.[46] The instructions themselves, signed by "the president," Garibaldi, and La Farina, contained fifteen points of which just over one-half had to do with the organization of a government once revolution was successful. The rest were the instructions for revolution, and they represented the Society's grand entry into the attractive area of revolutionary conspiracy. As tradition required, the revolutionary cry was first established. Once war began, the local committee was to rise to the cry of *"Viva l'Italia e Vittorio Emanuele! Fuori gli Austriaci!"* If insurrection proved impossible in "your city," members should go to the nearest one where success was likely, the city nearest Piedmont being given preference.

Such revolution was advocated primarily as an aid to the mili-

[44] *Piccolo Corriere*, 14 March 1859; Cavour to Nigra, 9 March 1859, *Cavour-Nigra*, II, 74; Cavour to Cabella, 14 March 1859, Chiala, *Lettere di Cavour*, III, 45.

[45] Cavour to La Farina, n.d.; La Farina to Mazzi, 2 March 1859, Franchi, *Epistolario di La Farina*, II, 136–37; cf. Pallavicino to Manin, 11 August 1856, Maineri, *Manin e Pallavicino*, 160; to La Marmora, 20 January 1859, *Memorie di Pallavicino*, III, 494–95. Sterbini hoped to get the exiles in Paris to leap on the Society's bandwagon, letter to Ricciardi, 1 March 1859, in *Liberazione del Mezzogiorno*, V, 270.

[46] La Farina to Mazzi, 2 and 4 March; to Armelonghi, 6 March; to Carlotti, 8 March; to Amadori, 14 March 1859, Franchi, *Epistolario di La Farina*, II, 137, 138–39, 141, 142, 148. The Society's instructions are reprinted in *ibid.*, 137n–39n.

tary. Everything possible should be done to disorganize the Austrian troops: communications interrupted, bridges broken, telegraph lines pulled down, supplies burned. Those high in the service of the enemy should be kept in "courteous hostage." Every means to induce Italian and Hungarian soldiers to desert to the Italian flag should be used, and those who did desert were to be welcomed as brothers. The regular troops among them should immediately be sent to Piedmont. Nor did the Society expect too much. Should there be no revolution, it added, then the committees should adopt every means to show their aversion for the present regime, their devotion to independence, and their faith in the House of Savoy and the Government of Piedmont. In a final warning the old note of caution reappeared: avoid conflicts, avoid isolated and inopportune moves. Nevertheless, revolution was now the official policy of the Italian National Society. The promised word had been spoken.

La Farina seems to have been thinking in terms of his October plan. The March instructions of the Society, which were heavily distributed in the Lunigiana, echoed many of the phrases of the older plan; and La Farina's letters are larded with references to cities in the Duchies. The meetings with representatives from the committees of Sarzana and Parma, which La Farina had requested so they might learn things that could only be told *a voce*, had been postponed from December or January, to late January, to the end of February; but perhaps they did take place then.[47] The British Consul in Carrara sadly reported that a formerly tranquil population was, by February, on the verge of revolution; and he declared that some respectable citizens were in constant correspondence with La Farina's committee and that they intended to prepare the population to accept Piedmont's troops while preventing any demonstrations until Piedmont was ready. At the proper time, they planned to disarm the few Ducal troops and invite the Piedmontese in on pretext of the need to maintain order.[48]

La Farina's requests, during the winter, for information on

[47] La Farina to Mazzi, 4 March 1859; and to Armelonghi, 13 September 1858 and 3 January 1859; to Mazzi, 18 October 1858, *ibid.*, 137–38, 80, 107, 86.
[48] This interesting report, dated 12 February 1859, suggests the Consul, Mr. W. Walton, had gotten wind of La Farina's October plan. It is printed in Chiala, *Lettere di Cavour*, III, lvn; no source is given.

the military garrison in Parma and for weekly accounts of troop placement in the Lunigiana suggest that the thought of action there had never died. Selmi sent the Society's secretary a list of those in the Duchy of Modena who "would descend into the piazza" if need arose, and Armelonghi in Parma was instructed to help Modena (which seemed a bit cool) when the time came. If things went badly, he was to fall back on the Apennines and on down to Massa and Carrara—another echo of the October plan. The Parma committee was also told to prevent the Duchess and the young Duke from leaving unless they went in the direction of Lombardy; even then the Duchess should be treated with all respect.[49] The committee of Piacenza had gathered some arms of its own, and in April La Farina appears to have had some weapons and supplies ready. Some 4,000 rifles manufactured by Della Noce in his Turin home were smuggled into Lombardy and the Duchies and were stored along the border of Massa and Carrara.[50] La Farina was also in fairly close touch with General Cialdini.

Yet, a number of signs suggest that there was no coordinated, comprehensive plan. The projected activities of the Bologna committee were extremely diverse. Cavour sent word to take orders for any demonstration from La Farina; the committee itself was organizing a local battalion and, through La Farina, communicated with Cialdini. The General, on the other hand, seemed rather impatient with the committee's military plans. As late as February the Bologna committee requested (on orders from Turin, it said) a census of the arms and men available in the various parts of the Romagna. In April it was asked how long a warning it would need before being able to lead two or three battalions to some rendezvous in the Romagna where arms would be gathered, and La Farina instructed

[49] La Farina to Armelonghi, 15 November 1858; to Clementi, 13 January, and to Mazzi, 24 January 1859; La Farina to Armelonghi, 18 April, and to Monteverde, 2 April 1859, Franchi, *Epistolario di La Farina*, II, 90, 113 and 113n, 122, 166, 157–58. Giovanni Sforza, "Esuli estensi in Piemonte dal 1848 al 1859," *Archivio Emiliano del Risorgimento nazionale*, II (1908), 110.

[50] Fermi and Ottolenghi, *Manfredi*, 51; La Farina to Armelonghi, 18 April; to Dr. Emilio Broghera, 14 April; and to Mazzi, 2 March 1859, Franchi, *Epistolario di La Farina*, II, 166, 162, 136. Della Noce ms., ISR, busta 555 (those kept along the border were apparently used by Ribotti).

the Society in Bologna to plan both on going to the aid of Modena and on initiating an uprising in the Marches.[51]

The Society did far less planning for the important areas of Tuscany and Lombardy. La Farina's declaration in January that Tuscany must revolt with the outbreak of war had by April grown less specific; Tuscany should, once the Duchies and the Romagna rose up, "complete the work so well begun." Bartolommei was believed by the police to have collected a few weapons, and there was talk of keeping in Tuscany some of the volunteers gathered at Leghorn under Malenchini, in case they might prove useful there. But Cavour himself, through Ridolfi and Boncompagni, took the lead in Tuscan affairs; the Society's role there was secondary.[52] La Farina's talk of planning a revolt in Milan and lesser Lombard cities was dropped; he requested and apparently got the plans of the fortifications of Pavia, but the 400 rifles he promised the committee of Carbonara were never sent or needed.[53]

The overeager Mazzi had to be reminded that a revolution in Massa and Carrara was only to be thought of as a "cog in a great machine"—a machine which would be not the Society's plans but the Franco-Piedmontese war effort. Groups of volunteers were being gathered in Sarzana and Lerici by the SNI committees there, but they would be led not by Garibaldi (as the October plan had suggested) but by General Ribotti. The activity of the National Society in preparation for local revolutions reflected an urge, a hope. But if this activity was based

[51] Cesare Bardesono (acting as Cavour's secretary) to Casarini, 3 April 1859, Masi, "Casarini," *Fra libri e ricordi,* 113; Paselli to Casarini, 9 April 1859, ms., Carteggio Casarini, MCRB. The evidence for the census is on a small bit of paper dated February 1859 from the committee of the *"provincia";* it is signed with a code symbol, ISR, busta 5, n. 47. Paselli to Casarini, April 1859, Maioli, "Società Nazionale in Bologna," *Saggi e documenti* (1933), 84; La Farina to Tanari, 15 April 1859, ms. in the Carte Tanari 1, MCRB.

[52] La Farina to Siccoli, 10 January 1859, ms., ISR, busta 382, n. 33, and to Ridolfi, 11 April 1859, in Camerani, "Toscana alla vigilia," *Archivio Storico* (1945–46), 167. Prefettura Segreta, report of 30 March 1859, ASF, busta 8, ins. 158. Cavour to Boncompagni, in Manzone, "Cavour e Boncompagni," *Il Risorgimento Italiano,* II, 209–16; to Ridolfi, 18 February 1859, *Cavour-Nigra,* II, 47; and Farini to Malenchini, 20 March 1859, Rava, *Epistolario di Farini,* IV, 242.

[53] La Farina to Carlotti, 8 March; and to Broghera, 14 April 1859, Franchi, *Epistolario di La Farina,* II, 142, 163; Prefettura Segreta, ASF, busta 8, ins. 171 and 180; Ing. Mai, 16 October 1863, ms., ISR, busta 717, n. 21; he says the plans were wanted by the Ministry of War.

on some general plan, it was one never very fully worked out. The Society's relation to the Government, its ambiguous view of revolution, its organizational weaknesses prevented it from doing more. If local revolutions occurred, they would depend on the initiative of local committees. Those "secret instructions" of March were general ones, applicable everywhere. The National Society was simply asking for revolution "wherever you can."[54]

The Society's primary concern was to prepare minds rather than soldiers; and in the months before the war that was a time-consuming task, for anticipation is the mother of rumor. In addition to battling rumors, the SNI had to explain a frightening fact. In March and April a European conference on the Italian Question appeared inevitable. The National Society's last great prewar propaganda effort strove to convince all nationalists that they need not fear such a conference. It cannot, the *Piccolo Corriere* reasoned, tell the Austrians to get out of Italy; and it cannot tell us to tolerate domination. The paper's cry was strident as it insisted that a conference might postpone but could not prevent a war, that it was too late for anyone to turn back. The Society issued a throwsheet citing Cavour's record and had letter after letter written showing that war was never more certain.[55] Meanwhile, the French friends of the Society were publicizing Manin's ideas and Austria's villainy in an effort to sway public opinion.[56]

It was not, then, quite yet time for action; and the Society returned to its call for demonstrations, a call made with a pre-

[54] La Farina to Mazzi, 15 and 21 April; to Bolognini, 21 April 1859, Franchi, *Epistolario di La Farina*, II, 166–68.

[55] As an example of the battle against rumors see La Farina to Bartolomeo, 30 March 1859, *ibid.*, 154; the Society began sending out letters of "notizie e istruzione"; *Piccolo Corriere*, 28 March, 4 and 11 April 1859.
[La Farina], Società Nazionale, "Notizie e istruzione," No. 2, 14 April 1859, ms., ISR, busta 5, n. 47; *Appello Clandestino*, 24 February 1859, *ibid.*; Alessandrini, *I fatti*, II, 26–7; Paselli to Casarini, 2 April 1859, Dallolio, "I Colloqui del Casarini col Cavour," *La strenna delle colonie scolastiche*, XXXVII, 26–7.

[56] Charles-Louis Chassin, *Manin et l'Italie* (Paris, 20 February 1859), reprinted a number of Manin's political letters in addition to a laudatory introductory biography. *L'Autriche dans le Royaume Lombardo-Vénitien, ses finances, son administration* (Paris, 1859), three anonymous letters "from Milan" dated 13, 16 and 20 February (the first was published in *Siècle*, 5 March) with *avant-propos* by H. Martin and H. Planat de la Faye, dated 18 April 1859. The letters faithfully echo the arguments of the SNI with detailed statistics on conditions in Lombardy. Both these rare pamphlets are in the Bibliothèque Nationale, Paris.

cision lacking in the talk of revolution. Agitation was the cry: petitions by the hundreds of thousands, protests, meetings, the sending of volunteers—these would show Europe that all Italians supported Piedmont, that a conference of Powers was helpless to prevent her unification.[57] The Society followed Cavour and Farini in stressing the need in Tuscany for the collection of signatures on Bianchi's *Austria e Toscana* and for legal agitation in the Romagna. Petitions demanding independence should be collected in Parma, as well as in Massa and Carrara and in the Romagna. Indeed, the SNI even sent along forms bearing the petitions so that the Romagnols merely needed to affix their names. They were to join the Civic Guard if the Pope should reinstitute it, and they should try to do what was being done in Tuscany—but that was not spelled out. These calls for agitation, like their predecessors, stressed the need to limit demonstrations to protest against Austria's position in Italy and to avoid conflict of any sort with local armies. "It is understood," La Farina added, "that we do not do this without the support and encouragement of him who has in his hand the rudder of our ship." [58]

On the eve of war, authority was slipping away from the National Society. Pepoli, whose connections made him quite independent of the SNI, was acting increasingly as though he were its leader in the Romagna, subordinate only to the Government of Piedmont. In Tuscany Cavour's friend and ambassador, Boncompagni, was more and more assuming leadership of those who supported Piedmont. He in turn looked toward the influential moderates of the *Biblioteca Civile*, to men like Ricasoli, Bianchi, Ridolfi, rather than to the "*Lafariniani.*" Boncompagni's authority extended also into the Romagna, where he had direct contact with Pepoli. A special commission for Lombard affairs was established in Turin to advise the Government, but it was composed of men who had no connection with the SNI al-

---

[57] Farini to Boncompagni, 25 March 1859, Rava, *Epistolario di Farini*, iv, 243; Cavour to Boncompagni, 22 March 1859, Chiala, *Lettere di Cavour*, vi, 376; Bardesono to Casarini, 3 April 1859, Masi, "Casarini," *Fra libri e ricordi*, 113–14. "Notizie e istruzione," No. 2, ms., ISR, busta 5, n. 47.
[58] La Farina to Tanari, 15 April 1859, ms. in the Carte Tanari i, MCRB; La Farina to Armelonghi, 3 April; and to Morchio, 6 April 1859, Franchi, *Epistolario di La Farina*, ii, 158, 160.

though many of them were on good terms with it.[59] Cavour had never depended solely upon the National Society to make his wishes known or to carry out his program, but the Society had come to depend solely upon Cavour for its policy. It had so strongly supported the Prime Minister that most of its members were quite ready to take their orders directly from the Government.

The Italian National Society had done its task. Its "secret" instructions of March 1 had given more space to the organization of provisional governments than to the call for revolution itself. In bequeathing revolution to its local committees, the Central Committee carefully reminded them of the intent with which revolution should be attempted. Concerned that discipline be maintained and that the luxuries of freedom not be overdone, these hard-headed instructions concentrated on the political and military task at hand. Within that focus there was no time for talk of the joys of liberation, no need felt for representative councils. Each local committee of the Society was to create order, to gain authority in its area and then present its gains to Piedmont. The provisional government itself should strive to aid the war effort. Men between 18 and 25 were to be conscripted (in the ratio of 10 for every 100 population), those between 25 and 35 to be accepted as volunteers. A complete accounting of public funds, arms, and munitions available in the city and province should be sent to Victor Emmanuel; requisitions of money, horses, carts, boats, and wine could be made when needed. Revolution was to be firm and orderly. A permanent council of war should judge and punish, without regard to rank or class and within 24 hours, any effort against the national cause or the life or property of peaceful citizens. No political group or journal should be allowed; an official journal would give those "facts which it is important to bring to the attention of the public." All magistrates and employees averse to the "new order of things" should be removed from office, and "the most severe and inexorable" discipline should be maintained among

[59] Cavour to Boncompagni, 3, 14 and 17 April 1859, Manzone, "Cavour e Boncompagni," Il Risorgimento Italiano, II, 214, 217–18; Giacchino Pepoli to Castelli, 9 April 1859, Chiala, Carteggio di Castelli, 1, 189; Visconti-Venosta, Ricordi di gioventù, 312–13.

all militia (with military law applied to them while the war lasted). Deserters should be treated "inexorably" and "the most severe orders [given] with regard to their dependents."

Yet the National Society was concerned that these juntas avoid revolutionary excesses. Men were to be removed from office only provisionally and then with "prudence and secrecy." The council of war was to condemn no one for political acts committed before the revolution; requisitions were to be made only when necessary and with written receipts. There should, in short, be a minimum of change although the new order might make itself attractive by abolishing the family and poll taxes and all the hated taxes on bread and milling. The criterion by which such reforms should be made was as clear as their purpose. Provisional governments would do well to remove "in general all the burdens which do not exist in the Sardinian States." Then, military and civil command having been assumed by him "who most enjoys the public esteem and faith," his title would be "Provisional Commissioner for King Victor Emmanuel"; and he would hold his post until the arrival of a commissioner sent by the Government of Piedmont. Where revolution broke out, there would be an early injection of that Piedmontese austerity of which the new state would be made. If the instructions asked that a great deal be done with only trust in Piedmont as guarantee, the faith that such sacrifice was worthwhile showed in the dateline those instructions bore—"*Italia, 1° marzo 1859.*"

On April 26 the Central Committee met for the last time in Pallavicino's home. With the outbreak of war, the Italian National Society announced its dissolution. This was in part a confession that the Society had not really intended to be a conspiratorial organization; in part it was the recognition that revolutions do better without direction from distant offices. Primarily, it was acknowledgment that Italy's hope lay this time with war; and wars are won by armies. The things the Society had done best—spread ideas, created hope, maintained faith—would now be done by the events themselves. As Pallavicino pridefully said in that romantic imagery which had made good propaganda: "We have wished to reunite the living forces of Italy, marrying the Italian insurrection to the army of Piedmont.

The wedding is consummated; the dictatorship by us proposed was decreed by the representatives of the nation. Our task is finished." [60]

When re-established after the war, the Society looked back upon this dissolution as an "example of abnegation perhaps unique in history. . . ." [61] But the abnegation had been implicit in its very conception; it had chosen a specific political goal that now seemed nearly achieved. If the Society was successful, an intermediary between the Government of Piedmont and believers in unity was no longer needed. In time of war only one source of instructions was wanted. Pallavicino's faith had become pompous when, "in the name of this committee," he entrusted "the outcome of Italy to the government of the Honest King." [62] It was just this that the Society had for years been asking others to do.

The local committees of the National Society did not disband, and their members, left without instructions at a time when there was no choice but to act, suddenly assumed a position of decisive importance in Italian history. One may sympathize with the contemporary who wrote that "the National Society is dissolved, and this is a great good, inasmuch as these Societies, whether National or anti-National, are the plagues of human Society." [63] But he had missed the point of his pun; the one society requires these others.

[60] As printed 27 April 1859 in the *Indipendente e Patriota*, the paper sent to the *Piccolo Corriere*'s subscribers after its suspension of publication, cited in *Memorie di Pallavicino*, III, 511.

[61] Proclamation of the SNI dated 20 October 1859, among the Siccoli papers, ISR, busta 382, n. 22. Massari and others of those close to the Government who distrusted the Society insisted that it must disband on the outbreak of war and claimed to have La Farina's promise that it would, Massari, *Diario*, entries of 10 and 12 April 1859, 275–84.

[62] Statement in *Memorie di Pallavicino*, III, 511.

[63] A letter from a man named Ranuzzi to a friend, written from Bologna, 30 April 1859, ms., ISR, busta 550, n. 94.

III ❖ CONSOLIDATION IN THE NORTH

CHAPTER SEVEN

THE SOCIETY'S CONTRIBUTION TO A GOAL

PARTLY GAINED (APRIL—AUGUST 1859)

THE CENTRAL COMMITTEE'S announcement of its dissolution won pleasant obituaries from the newspapers in Turin, and soon the only trace of the committee was the group of women who met at the Marchesa Pallavicino's to prepare bandages for the front.[1] Yet the meaning of the Society's dissolution, wherever its program became a "governmental fact," was characteristically ambiguous. Where Piedmont held power the Society was not to become a pressure group with an independent policy. But what of the local committees? Would they receive instructions? Should they continue on their own?

Many, of course, were sure they saw through it all. The Society was disbanded in that it no longer published a paper or held meetings, Tommaséo commented, ". . . but the ranks that move in other *paesi*, remain in the hand of La Farina, who is secretary to Cavour."[2] In quasi-official tones Minghetti explained to the confused Romagnols that the dissolution of the Central Committee "was fitting, even necessary," but the SNI would continue. He conceded merely that the lack of a single center would modify its mode of operation. The Society should, in short, continue to send volunteers from the Romagna into Tuscany, but Minghetti did not disavow insurrection as a possible "political manifestation."[3] Like the Italian National Society's own propaganda, such interpretations helped to obscure the fact that the SNI would give no secret orders for revolt. Perhaps it never intended to. In any case the French army made such risks unnecessary. Still, the Society would remain the focus of local desires for action, and it was to be prepared—when troops were close at hand—to give them orderly support, even to take over power.

[1] *Piccolo Corriere*, 11 April 1859; *Memorie di Pallavicino*, III, 508–14.
[2] Tommaséo to Capponi, 22 May [1859], in del Lungo and Prunas, *Tommaséo e Capponi*, IV², 27.
[3] Minghetti to Tanari, 7 May 1859, ms. in Carte Tanari, MCRB.

La Farina presented the Society's dissolution as a clarification of its position. "Now," he explained to the Tuscans, "the veil is removed and all must know that the National Society ceases, or to say it better, identifies itself with the Government." [4] Almost by habit, La Farina continued to make much of his closeness to Cavour, picturing himself as reluctantly chained to a desk by a promise he had made the Count "when nearly everyone was ignorant of my personal relations with him." Many noted his "promotion." And in his correspondence during May La Farina showed himself to have lost none of his concern for the intricacies of secret activity, none of his ability to imply far more than he said. He did, then, remain in touch with the local committees of the SNI and may have hoped for more from them than the Government planned. But as in the past, he gave more encouragement than instructions.[5] The part played by the Italian National Society in the liberation of northern Italy would depend primarily on the initiative taken by local committees.

For the Society as a whole there did emerge a general policy during the early weeks of the war. It was, first of all, to wait for decisive military action or at least for the proximity of Piedmontese troops before attempting any revolutionary coup against Tuscan or Ducal authorities. In the meantime, activity was to focus on the continued recruitment of volunteers (and the continued enrollment of deserters), a policy Cavour would still be encouraging even in late June.[6] This meant that the direction of local action tended to rest primarily on the nearest military commanders whether they led units of the Piedmontese army or of volunteers. The leaders of the Society were encouraged to take their cue from men such as General Ribotti or the Mez-

[4] La Farina to Ridolfi, 24 April 1859, cited in Camerani, "Toscana alla vigilia," Archivio Storico, CIII-CIV, 117.

[5] Franchi, Epistolario di La Farina, II, 169–77. See especially his letters to Conti, 14 May 1859, ibid., 174, where he speaks of the need to "conspire officially" and to Lafond, 11 May 1859, ibid., 171. Bianchi-Giovini wrote of La Farina's "promotion": letter of 26 April 1859, ms., MNRT. Tommaséo summarized this general view in commenting that La Farina was operating with "one seal more": letter to Capponi, 9 June 1859, del Lungo and Prunas, Tommaséo e Capponi, IV², 79. By May La Farina even saw military victory as a necessary prelude to a successful rising in the Duchies, an area for which he had once had much more daring plans, La Farina to Selmi, 10 May 1859, Franchi, Epistolario di La Farina, II, 170.

[6] Cavour to P. O. Vigliani, 27 June 1859, Chiala, Lettere di Cavour, III, 98.

zacapo brothers. Such cooperation with the military lessened the dangers of independent political action and placed initiative more in governmental hands.

The third general point of the Society's policy was to further cooperation and unity. By its very existence, the Society helped provide a sense of some general plan in which each local group was to find its place. As a means of communication, it continued to pass along encouragement, to present local patience as essential to the fate of the nation as a whole. Furthermore, great effort was made to prevent the inevitable development of factions. The Society in the Romagna cooperated with Bonapartists and ex-Mazzinians. In Tuscany it followed the careful lead of Boncompagni; and when La Farina heard that Montanelli was planning to return there, a whole campaign was launched to dissuade him lest he become a center of dissension.[7] Thus from the outbreak of the war the Society was being used to prevent the danger of division and the risk of revolution. At the same time, there was hope that it would, at the right moment in each area, provide evidence of popular enthusiasm for the national cause. The extent to which its role was being limited was probably never fully understood even by its leaders; perhaps it was simply incapable of the more radical action many expected of it.[8]

Still, the National Society—or more correctly now—many of its members, remained very active. Despite the call for dissolution, the Genoa committee made an attempt, which floundered, at reorganizing and establishing new committees in neighboring Ligurian towns.[9] The Society's position in Lombardy, where it

[7] La Farina to Pallavicino, 30 April 1859, ms., MNRT; Tito [Menichetti] to Malenchini, 8 July 1859, in Assunta Marradi, *Giuseppe Montanelli e la Toscana dal 1815 al 1862* (Rome, 1909), 242–44. Cf., however, his letter of [15] July in Piero Gerini, "Candidature di autonomisti all'Assemblea costituzionale toscana," *Risorgimento Italiano*, II (1909), 222–23. See also Malenchini to Montanelli, in d'Ancona, "Carteggio Montanelli," *Nuova Antologia*, CLI, 385.

[8] Cavour to Farini [3 July 1859], *La Liberazione del Mezzogiorno e la formazione del Regno d'Italia*, V (Bologna, 1954), 435. Federico Comandini, *Manfredo Fanti* (Verona, 1872), 293, says that both Farini and Fanti had been misled into expecting too much from local committees.

[9] The newly appointed president for a committee in Sestri Levante accepted the post but expressed concern over the omission of others who had formerly belonged, from the list of prospective members, letter of 11 May 1859 to Doria Pamphili, ms., Carte Morchio, MNRG. Centurini, in a letter to Morchio, 5 May 1859, ms., *ibid.*, had felt they should follow Turin's example and disband.

had never been strongly organized, was equally confused. La Farina may really have had plans for an insurrection to be staged by the committees of Varese and Como, but the 2,000 rifles he wanted to send them never arrived. They were finally given to Garibaldi instead. Whatever his intent, La Farina kept in touch with Lombardy through a few individuals, although Cavour's connections, which included some men also in touch with La Farina, were clearly more important. Members of the Society may have engaged in some sabotage against the Austrians and often have provided the Piedmontese with guides through local hills. They were undoubtedly among the most vocal as Piedmont's troops marched through the streets. Many of the newly appointed administrators were members of the SNI. But there is little evidence of political activity there by the Society as such.[10]

In Tuscany the Society was relatively well organized and had been increasingly active in the months before the war. Yet even there distributing propaganda and making such demonstrations as the sending of volunteers remained its main activities. Its manifestoes to the troops had been circulated "even to the drummers"; and from all over Tuscany the police reported oc-

---

However, Doria Pamphili was named president and efforts were made to call a meeting; most of the committee apparently failed to come and some (Paganini and Padoa; Luigi Coccarini expected more to follow) resigned, Coccarini to Morchio, 3 June 1859, ms., *ibid.*

[10] Decio was in contact with Varese and Como for La Farina and encountered Bernadino Bianchi who apparently also had instructions to encourage an insurrectionary movement: Giulio Decio, "Una missione del Conte di Cavour nell'alto Novarese all'inizio della guerra del 1859," *Bollettino Storico per la Provincia di Novara*, xix (1925), 87–94. In May he became the commissioner for administrative and political matters attached to Garibaldi. One Cordiglia recalled, on La Farina's death, having been part of a vast spy system organized by the Society and operating out of Arona: letter, ms., n.d., in ISR, busta 543, n. 45.

Giuliani, acting as Cavour's agent, had a dominant influence in Milan, where, according to Massari, he found La Farina's "lines" to have fallen into Mazzinian hands: Massari, *Diario*, entry of 7 May 1859, 328. On preparations in Lombardy and the contacts of La Farina and Cavour there see "Il Memoriale di Cesare Correnti sulle condizione di Lombardo-Vento nel 1858–1859," in *Cavour-Nigra*, ii, 263–86; Maineri, *Manin e Pallavicino*, 432–35; Carlo Pagani, *Milano e la Lombardia nel 1859* (Milan, 1909), 106–10; Visconti-Venosta, *Ricordi di gioventù*, 498–514; Ausano Labadini, *Milano ed alcuni momenti del Risorgimento italiano* (Milan, 1909), 108–109; Zini, *Storia d'Italia*, i², 215; and Mario, *Bertani*, i, 337, where the aid is acknowledged with credit given, however, to Pallavicino. Rossignoli reported from Milan but only on general conditions, ms., 18 March 1859, in ISR, busta 719, n. 17.

casional encounters with its propaganda.[11] Increasingly concerned, the police were fearful that some of the money collected for the volunteers was being kept for more revolutionary uses.[12] Yet in the confused excitement of April, as Tuscan nationalists listened to rumors and talked of action, the National Society could offer no clear plan; its members seem not even to have been dominant among nationalists.[13]

At three a.m. on the morning of April 27, the day the Grand Duke departed, one of the Society's leaders could still complain of the anarchy, *"non di piazza ma di accademia"*; yet this same man also worried about the dangers from "speculators in liberty, popular effrontery, the intrigues of pro-Austrians." Revolution is not an easy task for men with such concerns. The ambivalent position of the Society was nicely expressed by its committee in Grosseto, which published a circular assuring the rich that a revolution would not rob them of their wealth and promising the poor it would at least improve their lot.[14] Some members

[11] Mengozzi to Puccioni, 23 April 1859 (Yorick [the pseudonym of Ferrigni] was reported as having done the distributing): cited in Mario Puccioni, "Il Risorgimento italiano nell'opera, negli scritti, nella corrispondenza di Piero Puccioni," *Rassegna Storica del Risorgimento*, xvi (1929), 458. Puccioni says other pamphlets were printed locally by the Society, *ibid.*, 446, 455, 460; the "Pubblicazione del Partitio Nazionale No. 2" filed by the police in Prefettura Segreta, ASF, busta 8, ins. 191, was probably the work of the SNI. Farini offered to have published anything they could not print in Tuscany, Farini to Malenchini, 20 March 1859, Rava, *Epistolario di Farini*, iv, 242.
Some references by the police to the Society's propaganda are cited by Camerani in "Lo spirito pubblico in Toscana nel 1859," *Rassegna Storica Toscana*, ii (1956), 1–2, 105–107. See also *Piccolo Corriere*, 5 July 1858. The Society actively collected signatures in support of Bianchi's pamphlet, *Austria e Toscana*, a demonstration which made it appear a more radical manifesto than its author had intended: Ciro Cannarozzi, *La Rivoluzione toscana e l'azione del Comitato della Biblioteca civile dell'italiano* (Pistoia, 1936), 252–53. Farini wrote of the importance of this demonstration to Cavour, 25 March, and to Boncompagni, 28 March 1859, Rava, *Epistolario di Farini*, iv, 242–43.
[12] Report of 20 March cited in Puccioni, "Piero Puccioni," *Rassegna Storica*, xvi, 443; Camerani, "Lo spirito pubblico," *Rassegna Storica Toscana*, ii, 107–109, 115–16.
[13] For reports, sometimes conflicting, on the discussions and confusions of this period, see Camerani, "Toscana alla vigilia," *Archivio Storico*, ciii-civ, 80, 168–73, 183; N. Corsini di Laiatico, *Storia di quattro ore* ([Florence?], 1859), *passim*; Rubieri, *Storia Intima*, 44–6; Gioli, *Risorgimento toscano*, 248–49; Rodolfo Della Torre, *La evoluzione del sentimento nazionale in Toscana* (Milan, 1916), 60–6; G. Cecconi, *Il 27 aprile 1859* (Florence, 1909), 59–63; L. Assing, *Vita di Piero Cironi* (Prato, 1865), 166.
[14] Mengozzi to Puccioni, 27 and 21 April 1859, in Puccioni, "Piero Puccioni," *Rassegna Storica*, xvi, 669, 455. The Grosseto circular is cited in Puccioni, "Ricercando negli archivi," *ibid.*, xxiii, 1090–91.

of the Society talked of preventing the Grand Duke from escaping to Elba, some may really have expected the Piedmontese fleet to arrive off Leghorn (as called for in the October plan). And a great tricolored flag was sewn together on the eve of the 27th in the Palazzo Bartolommei.[15]

What took place the next day, however, was less a revolution than an evacuation. On the second day of the war the Grand Duke of Tuscany left Florence. The Tuscan nationalists had, by their demands for an alliance with Piedmont, done a good bit to precipitate the Duke's departure. They had striven in every way to make his cause appear as hopeless as he now saw it, but even those activities had been largely directed by Boncompagni. Piedmont's ambassador to Tuscany had become the director of nationalist activity there. Naturally, members of the Tuscan National Society looked to him for instructions. Boncompagni, however, preferred to work with the respectable moderates of the *Biblioteca Civile* and "principally those of them in whose honesty I most trust." They, he expected, would in turn cooperate with various groups in the provinces, "if need be with La Farina." [16]

The most important contribution of the National Society to the events in Tuscany, then, was in the attitudes it encouraged rather than the acts it committed. It had helped in Cavour's desire to frighten the Grand Duke and leave the ground open to the "national party." The well-known fact of its existence constituted a pressure on the more conservative men, such as those of the *Biblioteca Civile*, to take a stronger stand against the Government while encouraging those inclined to more open opposition, men like Dolfi or Rubieri, to wait. The Society's willingness to subordinate itself to Boncompagni meant that the

[15] Mengozzi to Puccioni, 21 April 1859, Puccioni, "Piero Puccioni," *Rassegna Storica*, xvi, 455; Ferrigni to Puccioni, 23 April 1859, *ibid.*, 459; A. Lombardi, *Ferdinando Bartolommei* (Florence, 1889), 31. The Carteggio Bartolommei contains a list of possible contributors to their cause in case of war, ms., MRF, busta 8, n. 1.

[16] Boncompagni to Cavour, 17 April 1859, Manzone, "Cavour e Boncompagni," *Risorgimento Italiano*, ii, 218. His reports to Cavour of 16 March and 9 April also reflect his admiration for the *Biblioteca Civile*, mss., AST. Cavour wrote Ridolfi, 24 April 1859, that Boncompagni had the Government's instructions: cited in Camerani, "Toscana alla vigilia," *Archivio Storico*, ciii-civ, 177. La Farina had ordered the Society to put pressure on the Grand Duke while avoiding either any commitment to him or any conflict with his troops, Manfredini to Teresa Bartolommei, 28 February 1859, ms., MRF.

various shades of nationalists were in fact working together; and its propaganda made that unity seem greater than it was. Leopold's despair, the military might of Piedmont and France, the propaganda of the Society—all this had made unnecessary the kind of revolution the SNI feared. Even at the last minute it was not pressure from the Society but word from Cavour which stiffened the demands made of the Grand Duke.[17]

When, after the Grand Duke's departure, the three provisional governors of Tuscany were selected by Boncompagni, he chose Malenchini as one of them.[18] The men of the National Society were politically important. Of the seven regional commissioners named by the new government, at least two were members of the SNI and two others men often associated with it.[19] Bartolommei became *gonfaloniere* of Florence as did Cecconi of Leghorn; Antonio Ricci, head of the SNI in Siena, was on the governing council there; Toscanelli, prominent in the Society in Pisa, was one of three counselors to Pisa's prefect. In Pistoia the Society's committee temporarily assumed direction of affairs; and Tonarelli, a member of the committee in Grosseto, replaced the prefect there (at Puccioni's direction). The importance of the Society was increased as its men often sought fellow members for important interim posts.[20]

[17] Cavour to Boncompagni, 11 April 1859, Manzone, "Cavour e Boncompagni," *Risorgimento Italiano*, II, 215; Vincenzo Salvagnoli, Bianchi, and Ricasoli worked closely enough with Bartolommei in sending volunteers that the police believed them to be his subordinates in the same organization, Prefettura Segreta, report of 27 March 1859, ASF, busta 8, ins. 158. Chiala, *Carteggio di Castelli*, I, 272–73; Chiala, *Ricordi di Castelli*, 226–27. For the negotiations leading to the demands made of the Grand Duke, see Camerani, "Toscana alla vigilia," *Archivio Storico*, CIII-CIV, 150–52 and 177ff., and Corsini, *Quattro ore, passim*.

[18] Boncompagni to the municipal government of Florence, 27 April 1859, in Zini, *Storia d'Italia*, II², 120. Peruzzi and Ermolao Rubieri were the others; the latter was certainly friendly to the Society and is usually named as a member. For the argument against this view see Grew, "Società Nazionale in Toscana," *Rassegna Storica Toscana*, II, note 49, page 86. Similarly, Dolfi should not be thought of as belonging to the SNI, see *ibid.*, and Mario, *Bertani*, II, 138.

[19] Puccioni was named commissioner for Siena-Grosseto, Tito Menichetti for San Miniato. Agostino Bianchini, commissioner for the Romagna, and Rubieri, for Prato, are the other two who were close to the SNI.

[20] Puccioni named at least three members of the Society as *gonfalonieri* of towns in his jurisdiction (Giuseppe Becchini in Arcidossa, Gaspare Petriccioli in Pitigliano, and Emilio Nardelli in Manciano): Grew, "Società Nazionale in Toscana," *Rassegna Storica Toscana*, II, 98. For Grosseto, see Giovanni Mazzei, *Ricordi della vita e dei tempi del Leopoldo Mazzei* (Florence, 1901), 175. From 8 to 11 of the 42-man consultative council named by Boncompagni in Florence

Such men in such positions were important not only because of their willingness to cooperate with Piedmont (and Boncompagni) or their useful contacts with other provinces (particularly the Romagna), but because of their strong nationalism and their experience in attempting to influence public opinion. Boncompagni found a strong Tuscan desire for autonomy, and d'Azeglio attributed the demonstrations there in favor of annexation entirely to the "old *pasticcio*" of the Society, a mixed company of the "liar and fool."[21] However exaggerated such views, it clearly mattered that there was in Tuscany a corps, at least loosely organized, of convinced nationalists. On the one hand, La Farina could explain to d'Ancona that he favored administrative independence for each province but that it was imperative that arms and diplomacy be centrally controlled. On the other, Puccioni could assure militant members of the SNI that Tuscany's policy was not regional but precisely what Cavour wanted and then call for more and more petitions demanding unification.[22] In Tuscany the Society took seriously its role as custodian of public opinion, and it found a powerful weapon in the newly established newspaper, La Nazione, whose founders were all members of the SNI.[23] With no clear program of its own, the Society contributed importantly to the functioning of the provisional government of Tuscany, to the acceptance of Boncompagni's policies, and to the preservation of an atmosphere of apparent

---

were members of the SNI. The council is listed in Zini, *Storia d'Italia*, ii[2], 232–33; Adami, Bartolommei, Corsi, Del Re, Fenzi, Malenchini, Luigi Nobili, Antonio Ricci were certainly members of the Society; Rubieri, Atto Vannucci and Angelo Zanetti may also have been. Although Ulloa was named by Cavour as Commander of the Tuscan Army in large part as a result of his membership in the Society, he does not seem to have had strong contacts with the Society in Tuscany; and the appointment was in many respects unfortunate.

[21] Boncompagni to Cavour, 14 June 1859, AST; d'Azeglio to avv. Giovanni Batta Giorgini, 14 June 1859, in Mario Puccioni, *Cinquantasette lettere di Massimo d'Azeglio* (Florence, 1935), 101.

[22] La Farina to d'Ancona, 25 May 1859, Franchi, *Epistolario di La Farina*, ii, 177 (Cavour used a similar vague promise with Bianchi: M. Gioli, *Il Risorgimento toscano e l'azione popolare* [Florence, 1905], 276); and Puccioni to Ricci, 15 and 17 June 1859, in Mario Puccioni, *L'unità d'Italia nel pensiero e nell'azione del Barone Bettino Ricasoli* (Florence, 1932), 75, 77.

[23] Fenzi, Puccioni, Leopoldo Cempini, Bartolommei, and Menichetti were "promoters and proprietors," d'Ancona was "administrator," G. Barbèra, *Memorie di un editore* (Florence, 1883), 162.

concord. Cavour had reason to view the Tuscan revolution as the "splendid justification" of his policies.[24]

It was for the Duchies that the Society had once held its most daring visions; but when Austria relieved Cavour of the need to invent an excuse for war, those plans were never wholly revived. In the Duchies, however, there were not, as there were in Tuscany, important groups outside the Society prepared to pursue Piedmont's policy. Thus a great deal of independent action fell to the SNI. Communications between the Society's leaders in Massa and Carrara and Piedmont had always been strong; when the representatives of the Duke of Modena withdrew from those cities, on April 27 and 28, the leaders of the Society there quickly took charge of local administration.[25] The Tuscan pattern was repeated, but here Piedmontese troops were able almost immediately to add their stabilizing presence. Vincenzo Giusti, a leader of the Society who had assumed control in Massa, was soon named royal commissioner, a role he must have filled with some vigor; for he was credited with having put down "two reactionary attempts." [26]

A few days before the war broke out, La Farina had suggested to his friend Selmi, who already had instructions to promote revolts wherever he could, that he go to Parma. He gave similarly broad advice to Zini with equally clear hope for revolution.[27]

[24] Cavour to Boncompagni, n.d., Manzone, "Cavour e Boncompagni," *Risorgimento Italiano*, II, 225.

[25] Although all commentators agree that Vincenzo Giusti in Massa and Enrico Brizzolari in Carrara led a bloodless revolt, aided by their followers in the SNI (for example, Sforza, "Esuli estensi," *Archivio Emiliano*, II, 127; Zini, *Storia d'Italia*, I², 96), it is difficult to establish the precise role of the Society in these events. It is stated in Corpo di Stato Maggiore, *Guerra del 1859*, narrazione II (Rome, 1912), 31, that Bolognini and Poggi (both prominent in the SNI) prepared the revolt from Lerici. The picture is further complicated by Cesare Cantù's claim that Cavour ordered the revolt by a telegram to Massa saying simply, "*insorgete*": cited in Carlo Tivaroni, *L'Italia degli italiani*, II (Turin, 1896), 101. It is probable that whatever planning there was took place in conjunction with the nearby Piedmontese garrison.

[26] Selmi to Chiesi, 24 May 1859: cited in Sforza, "Esuli estensi," *Archivio Emiliano*, II, 122. Even at this date he viewed opinion in Massa as uncertain with most people waiting to see how events turned out. Brizzolari of the SNI directed the police in Carrara, *ibid.*, 127.

[27] La Farina talked with Selmi on April 24 and with Zini on April 26. Zini had begun his trips into Tuscany, the Duchies, and the Romagna at La Farina's request in March: Zini, "Memorie dei casi che condussero il mio commissariato," ms., MNRT. Canevazzi, *Selmi*, 25n, 27n, 29n. Maria Miani, "Un pattriotta

When the Duchess of Parma made her frightened departure, the National Society acted immediately. Apparently at Selmi's instigation, it presented the Government which the Duchess had left behind with a demand for union with Piedmont. The Government then resigned, and on May 1 the SNI in Parma proclaimed a provisional government in the name of Victor Emmanuel. The new junta's request, however, that Modena and Reggio follow suit went unanswered; and the troops of Parma remained loyal to their Duchess.

When, on May 5, the army took advantage of discontent with the provisional government and presented counterdemands, the Society's regime fell as easily as its predecessor. The Government of Parma ruled once again in the name of Maria Luisa and her son. The National Society had had neither the arms nor the will of a revolutionary government. Prepared to fill a power-vacuum with orderly patriotism until Piedmont could take over, it had mistaken incompetence and indecision for such a vacuum. It was precisely the kind of mistake the Society had meant to avoid. Massari almost gloated at the Society's debacle, and La Farina stated the lesson they all had learned: they would await a military victory over the Austrians and then, ". . . profit from the enthusiasm that will spread over all Italy to free ourselves of the dukes." [28]

Selmi returned to Massa where, by mid-May, he and Zini were accredited to General Ribotti, who was in charge of a small corps of volunteers. After that, revolution moved with the army. Selmi remained in touch with La Farina, sending reports on local con-

---

modenese; Francesco Selmi," *tesa di laurea* (University of Bologna, 1951), 85, 90. (I am indebted to Signorina Miani for making her thesis available to me.) Selmi had refused in January to head a committee of the Society, letter to Buscalioni, 9 January 1859, ms., ISR, busta 719, n. 17.

[28] The May 1 proclamation by the provisional government (signed by Armelonghi, Miani, A. Garbarini, and Salvatore Riva—the first three certainly and the last probably members of the SNI) and the May 5 declaration of its successors are printed in Zini, *Storia d'Italia*, II^2, 100–101; Massari, *Diario*, entries of 6 and 8 May 1859, 327, 330; Sforza, "Esuli estensi," *Archivio Emiliano*, II, 112–13. La Farina's reaction can be seen in his letters to Conti, 3 May, and to Selmi, 10 May 1859, Franchi, *Epistolario di La Farina*, II, 169–70. Cavour's pleasure in the lack of disorder caused by the Parma coup proved premature: letter to E. d'Azeglio, 2 May 1859, *Cavour e l'Inghilterra*, II, tomo I, 328. Manfredini had heard in February that affairs were well ordered for some move in Modena, letter to Marchesa Bartolommei, 28 February 1859, ms., Carteggio Bartolommei, MRF, busta 93, n. 6.

ditions (he found many *"duchisti"* still in Massa) and enemy troops. He reported the public spirit to be good in the larger towns, poor in the country and asked authority to remove local officials as necessary. As Ribotti moved toward Fivizzano, he requested further instructions. Zini energetically attempted to stir things up in the cities of the Apennines, seeking the cooperation of members of the SNI as General Ribotti's troops approached.[29]

But it was only after the Duke of Modena had chosen to retreat behind Austrian lines and the Austrian troops themselves evacuated Modena, that the Society made any overt move in that important city. Then on June 13 a crowd marched on the town hall, where a provisional government dominated by men of the SNI was announced. Two days later Zini arrived to act as dictator; six days after that Luigi Carlo Farini, named official commissioner by Cavour, took over his duties.[30] When there

[29] Selmi arrived in Massa on May 16, Ribotti took Fivizzano on May 23: Sforza, "Esuli estensi," *Archivio Emiliano,* II, 113, 121–22. Selmi and Zini, with Ribotti, asked for more troops on the 18th, *ibid.,* 118–20. Selmi may have gone first to Turin: Canevazzi, *Selmi,* 25n–26n, 29. But La Farina's letter to him of May 10 makes it clear that Selmi was earlier thought to be in close touch with Ribotti; it also establishes a striking lack of prior planning, for La Farina urges that Ribotti organize a pair of companies and promises to send limited amounts of arms: Franchi, *Epistolario di La Farina,* II, 170–71. Ribotti seems in fact to have been aided largely from Tuscany; just as Zini's Tuscan friends helped prepare proclamations for various Apennine towns, Canevazzi, *Selmi,* 28n, 29.

There is also a lack of clarity as to the position held by Selmi and Zini. Canevazzi, *Selmi,* 27n, 234–36, implies an official position of great latitude but Miani, "Selmi" 96–7, suggests they were given a mandate less clear than they wanted, with La Farina concerned as always for the inevitable differences in local conditions. Evidence of Selmi's constant contacts with La Farina may be found in Bianchi to Selmi, 19 April 1859, *ibid.;* La Farina to Conti, 3 May, and to Selmi, 10 May, Franchi, *Epistolario di La Farina,* II, 169–70; Canevazzi, *Selmi,* 235–36, and Sforza, "Esuli estensi," *Archivio Emiliano,* II, 128–30.

[30] The Duke left on June 11 as Ribotti approached; the Austrians followed in the next two days. The manifesto published by the Modena group and signed by Giovanni Montanari, Pietro Muratori, Giuseppe Tirelli, Egidio Boni, and Emilio Nardi is in Zini, *Storia d'Italia,* II², 174. Only about Montanari do I have clear evidence of membership in the SNI, but they are all usually viewed as having been *soci.* Ferrari, *Ferrari,* 158–59, certainly gives the impression of the Society's having been dominant in the movement, and the quickness with which these men abdicated in favor of Zini further suggests it (Ferrari claims credit for convincing Zini he should resign in turn).

Zini's proclamation on assuming governmental authority made it plain that as few changes as possible would be made: cited in Zini, *Storia d'Italia,* II², 175–76 (cf. Farini's, *ibid.,* 177–78). Zini did find it necessary to make some appointments, see Selmi's apologetic telegram, Sforza, "Esuli estensi," *Archivio Emiliano,* II, 130.

really was a vacuum, the Society had held the fort; it had preserved order and prevented any effort at instituting the sudden social changes which would have embarrassed Cavour. Indeed, Zini may have been overzealous in imprisoning ". . . persons whom he knew [to be] the most turbulent of the vulgar base"; but, despite some unpopularity, he hung on. And, although he apparently enjoyed his brief reign, he was easily persuaded to resign in favor of Farini. Selmi was sure that Zini's dictatorship had "saved all"; certainly it had smoothed the way for Cavour. Still, things had not gone so easily in the Duchies as had been hoped, and there were signs in Turin of a growing distrust of La Farina's agents there.[31]

In similar circumstances provisional governments were proclaimed in Reggio and in Parma and Piacenza. The men who led Parma's second attempt at union with Piedmont appear not to have been connected with the SNI, but in Reggio and Piacenza members of the National Society were prominent in the new governments.[32] In less than a week these provisional governments gave way to another royal commissioner sent from Piedmont. As it had done in Tuscany, the Society immediately disappeared as a political bloc; but its members filled many of the most important posts of the new regime. They were picked, and in Piacenza frankly preferred, as commissioners, as intendants, and as editors of official newspapers; and La Farina used his

[31] Canevazzi, Selmi, 29n, 30n; Ferrari, Ferrari, 158–61; Adolfo Colombo, "La missione di Luigi Zini a Modena nel 1859," Rassegna Storica del Risorgimento, XIX (1932), 285–86. Selmi felt it necessary to go to Turin in June to justify Zini's administration even though La Farina had written in April, on the Government's stationery, that any provisional government which might include Selmi and Zini would be viewed with pleasure in Turin.

[32] The Reggio junta consisted of Enrico Terrachini, Ferrari, Gherardo Stucchi, and Carlo Baroni; the first was president of the SNI there and the others may have been associated with it. On the revolt in Reggio see Umberto Dallari, Il 1859 in Due Ducati dell'Emilia (Reggio e Guastalla) (Reggio, 1911), 14–19, and Andrea Balletti, Storia di Reggio nell'Emilia (Reggio, 1925), 724.

In Piacenza the junta consisted of Manfredi, Mischi, and Gavardi, the first two leaders of the SNI; indeed, the provisional government is treated as exclusively an affair of the SNI in Fermi and Ottolenghi, Manfredi, 59n and 66. Manfredi had provided the province with most of its information about nationalist plans and activities until forced to flee in mid-May, ibid., 52–7; he apparently returned with the Piedmontese. See also F. Giarelli, Storia di Piacenza, II (Piacenza, 1889), 399. Stucchi (of the Reggio junta) and Tirelli (of the Modena junta) had, months before, been named by Selmi in a list of reliable men for a movement di piazza, Sforza, "Esuli estensi," Archivio Emiliano, II, 110.

influence to make of participation in the SNI a qualification for a place in the new government.[33]

The Italian National Society in the Duchies had by its propaganda and the very rumors of its presence strengthened the defeatists within the old regime; it had enabled Piedmontese control to come quickly and from apparent local demand; it had provided the new government with a corps of local supporters. And all of this happened with such speed that in retrospect the very hesitance and confusion within the Society seemed proof of hidden but brilliant coordination. The Society in the Duchies had failed to stir that great surge of popular sentiment its propaganda had predicted, but it could hardly have been more useful to Piedmont.

The situation in the Romagna was far more confused. The National Society there had always had a conspiratorial air; it was not even certain through whom Piedmont's wishes would be made known. When the Romagnol members of the Society had attempted direct communication with Cavour or Cialdini, it had been made clear that they should expect their instructions through La Farina.[34] Figures like Minghetti or Farini, however, could not be expected to accept such authority over their native provinces. Minghetti was a man of great political influence both in Turin and in the Romagna, and he had always looked some-

[33] Selmi was put in charge of public instruction under Farini; Zini became commissioner of Guastalla; Ferrari directed the official newspaper in Modena, *ibid.*, 140; Ferrari, *Ferrari*, 164 and 172. Diodato Pallieri, the royal commissioner in Piacenza, seems in particular to have favored men from the SNI. Three of his first appointments went to members of the Society's local committee. Armelonghi was put in charge of internal affairs and Mascaretti made intendant in Piacenza. La Farina himself pointed out Manfredi, declaring on the official stationery of the Ministry of the Interior that Cavour wanted Pallieri to know that Manfredi was one of those who had done most for the national cause. Pallieri in turn was soon writing the Ministry of Foreign Affairs in praise of Manfredi's role in the SNI. In his various administrative posts, Manfredi similarly favored men of the Society—making the *Gazzettina Piacentina* the official paper, for example, because of the services its editors had rendered the Society: Fermi and Ottolenghi, *Manfredi*, 45, 64, 76-7, 96; La Farina to Pallieri, 30 June 1859, *ibid.*, 75, and Pallieri to Ministry of Foreign Affairs, 3 July 1859, *ibid.*, 59.

The Society was useful in other ways; the electoral committee which in July and August argued so vigorously for annexation and gave the elections a certain democratic vitality included most of the Modena committee of the SNI; the electoral committee is listed in Canevazzi, *Selmi*, 32n.

[34] Bardesono to Casarini, 3 April 1859, in Masi, "Casarini," *Fra libri e ricordi*, 113; and Paselli to Casarini, 9 April 1859, ms. in Carteggio Casarini, MCRB.

what askance at the Society. Its members could only hope he would be brought in line with the SNI by Cavour himself.[35] Similarly, it had been feared that Farini was attempting to increase his personal influence in the Romagna, although in April he had joined a group of 32 Romagnols in Turin who endorsed the Society's program. After war was declared and the Central Committee disbanded, Farini suggested that all correspondence with regard to the Romagna should go through Boncompagni's hands, thus skirting La Farina.[36] The Bologna committee was further upset when Mezzacapo, as the head of a corps of volunteers in Tuscany, began acting on matters related to the Romagna without consulting the SNI. Finally, Tanari, accompanied by Scarabelli from the Imola committee, made a trip to Tuscany to achieve some coordination with leaders there.[37] The National Society in the Romagna was learning the need to act on its own.

If competition among political leaders led to confusion, the dissension among nationalists generally made any plans for action risky. Marchese Gioacchino Napoleone Pepoli, a cousin of Napoleon III and a leading figure in Bologna, was a major source of such dangerous division. He had in the past proved useful to Cavour for various diplomatic assignments; and when in April he returned from Paris with a "pallid protest" about conditions in the Romagna all written out and ready for the nationalists to issue, the Prime Minister could only make sure that La Farina had the SNI accept it. Pepoli then went to see La Farina who, in the Marchese's presence, wrote a letter to the Bologna committee, the effects of which he would later try to

[35] Paselli to Casarini, April 1859, Maioli, "Società Nazionale in Bologna," *Saggi e documenti* (1933), 84. Massari seems to have had an important part in the communications between the Romagna and Cavour. He kept Minghetti informed of the unfortunate effects of the Society's actions and was in touch with Pepoli, Ercolani, and E. Rasponi as well. He felt, in May, that Casarini wanted to know too much of the Government's plans, Massari, *Diario*, entries of 6 May, 17 May, 19 June, and 18 July 1859, 327, 344–45, 393, 427.

[36] Paselli to Casarini, 9 April, ms. in Carteggio Casarini, MCRB. La Farina to Pietro Inviti, 11 April, Giovanni Maioli, "La Società Nazionale a Ravenna e in Romagna," *Studi Romagnoli*, III (1952), 119; and Farini to Boncompagni, 11 May 1859, Rava, *Epistolario di Farini*, IV, 260. Cavour had already made use of Boncompagni's Romagna contacts, Cavour to Boncompagni, 22 March 1859, Chiala, *Lettere di Cavour*, VI, 370.

[37] Maioli, "Tanari e il suo memoriale," *Archiginnasio*, XXVIII, 69–70; Masi, "Casarini," *Fra libri e ricordi*, 118; Galli, "Società Nazionale e Gamberini," *La Romagna*, XVI, 404. On later dealings with Mezzacapo see Corpo di Stato Maggiore, *Guerra del 1859*, Documenti II (Rome, 1912), 118, 190.

soften. Pepoli, La Farina explained, had been sent to him by Cavour. He found that the Marchese completely accepted the Society's principles (except for reservations about Naples!) and complained only that certain groups in the Romagna were being excluded from the SNI. La Farina assured the Bologna committee that their authority remained great, but he pointedly added that their course "must be like the *misericordia* of God." In the name of forgiveness, Pepoli, who had previously tried to form a competing society, must be accepted into the circle of the SNI in Bologna. Cavour was pleased to have established concord between the potentially dangerous Pepoli and the Society; and Massari was, to his distaste, given the task of helping pass word of the agreement. It was a tribute to the Society that it could be expected to swallow so much; the effort cannot but have weakened its sense of revolutionary purpose.[38]

The National Society in the Romagna thus cooperated with a noted Napoleonid, an aristocrat of great influence who had long been the object of personal and political suspicion in the close society of Bologna. The National Society proved still more seriously restive when La Farina called for cooperation with Eugenio Valzania. A noted Mazzinian with a talent for guerrilla warfare, Valzania had long been regarded as an enemy by the leaders of the SNI. They were shocked when La Farina announced that Valzania would direct military arrangements in Ravenna and Forlì and form a battalion in his native Cesena. They resented, too, the sudden authority he seemed to be given within the Society. He brought a message from La Farina to

---

[38] Some 1,000 copies of Pepoli's manifesto to which La Farina claimed at least to have added the phrase "national independence" were printed in Turin for distribution in the Papal States (although Pepoli complained that they did not arrive: Pepoli to Castelli, 9 April 1859, Chiala, *Carteggio Castelli*, 189; in the same letter he, significantly, sent greetings to Ercolani, Farini, and Massari as well as to La Farina).

La Farina's letters were to Inviti, 11 April 1859, Maioli, "Società Nazionale a Ravenna," *Studi Romagnoli*, III, 118–19; and to Casarini [?], n.d., ms. in Carteggio Casarini, MCRB. See also Maioli, "'Tanari e il suo memoriale," *Archiginasio*, XXVIII, 68–9, and Massari, *Diario*, entries of 11, 13, 14 March and 25 June, 237–38, 393. Cavour informed Boncompagni of the understanding in letters of 5 and 14 April, Manzone, "Cavour e Boncompagni," *Risorgimento Italiano*, II, 214, 217. Minghetti also wrote of the importance of cooperating with Pepoli: letters to Malvezzi, 29 April (actually written by Carolina Tattini Minghetti) and 6 May 1859, Aldobrandino Malvezzi, "Intorno all origine della Lega dell'Italia Centrale nel 1859," *Rassegna Storica del Risorgimento*, XLV (1958), 380.

the Bologna committee, and the Rimini committee complained because Valzania boasted that in Turin La Farina had shown him letters they had written attacking their new ally. Yet even the Rimini committee concluded its complaint by citing one of the Society's pamphlets on the need for concord. While insisting that they were the "legitimate representative" of the Marches and the area around Rimini, they accepted the need to cooperate with Valzania. The Society was making plans which seemed most promising.[39]

How this understanding and the organization it implied were to be used nevertheless remained unclear. La Farina continued to imply the possibility of great and important activity by the Romagnol patriots. He urged them to be ready at least for a demonstration, informing them of the demands to be made in Tuscany for cooperation between Tuscan and Piedmontese troops. He reminded them again of the need to eliminate all questions of liberty and reform from their program. When in mid-April the threat that an international congress might forestall war arose, the Society's secretary came as close as he ever did to assigning a precise role to the SNI in the Romagna. If the congress was held, great numbers of signatures on a nationalist manifesto (he enclosed a suitable sample) must be collected. If war did break out, the Society must be prepared for revolt; and he had suggested they move on Modena where they should be met by other forces of the SNI. In case of defeat there, they could retreat across the Apennines to Massa and Carrara. He even included coded phrases which could safely be sent by telegraph giving the order to rise up or to remain quiet, to move toward Modena or to the south. The rest of their orders, he had

[39] The instructions stating that Eugenio Valzania and the SNI should work together were strengthened with the assertion that this was Garibaldi's wish, too: La Farina to Valzania, 4 March 1859, in Maioli, "Società Nazionale a Ravenna," *Studi Romagnoli*, III, 117–18; copies of letters of La Farina to the Bologna committee, 28 March and 19 April 1859, mss., Carte Tanari II, MCRB; Rimini committee to the Bologna committee, 18 and 27 April 1859, mss. in Carte Tanari I and Carteggio Casarini, MCRB.

See also Alberto Dallolio, "Eugenio Valzania e la Società Nazionale," *La strenna delle colonie scolastiche Bolognese*, XXXVI (1933), 36–42; Maioli, "Tanari e il suo memoriale," *Archiginasio*, XXVIII, 65–6. Note Mazzini to Cesare Turino, August 1859, *Scritti di Mazzini*, LXIII, 327. In the fall Valzania was arrested for planning a revolt in the Marches, but La Farina gave a deposition in his favor, Alfredo Comandini, *Cospirazione di Romagna e Bologna nelle memorie di Federico Comandini* (Bologna, 1899), 237.

added, were in the secret instructions of the Society, which gave general and cautious advice about where to revolt and the kind of order to establish. He authorized two men "to prepare means and ways to stimulate" a war.

By mid-May the Romagna had had no revolution, and La Farina's instructions took a quite different tone. He repeated the importance of eliminating all questions except that of unity; but he spoke vaguely of the need the Government now felt for "some major regard for form." It would still be willing, he assured them, to send a commissioner and intendants wherever requested and thus to achieve union by *fait accompli*. The effects of a revolution were still to be won, but the implication was strong that the risks of revolution were to be avoided.[40]

Without firm orders from beyond the Romagna, the Society there was in no position to act. As late as March, the committees of the SNI in the Romagna had been debating the nature of their connection with La Farina and the Society in Turin, wondering if they should not have some direct communication with Cavour as well and debating the kind of organization they wanted to maintain. Pepoli, Valzania, and others were still distrusted; and they in turn complained that they were not kept fully informed. The committees were not sure whether volunteers were still wanted or if they were to form their own battalions, or if they were expected to attack retreating Austrian troops.[41] Uncertain as to what to do, anxious to play their roles, they continued doing what they had done well before. They continued recruiting volunteers and sending them into Tuscany. Minghetti encouraged them, noting that it was better to have

[40] La Farina's orders can be found in his letters to Conti, 2 April 1859, Franchi, *Epistolario di La Farina*, II, 156–57; to the Bologna committee (a copy), 28 March 1859, ms. in Carte Tanari II, MCRB; an unsigned letter in a style and hand like La Farina's, 28 March 1859, telling local committees to cooperate with Bologna, ms., ISR, busta 61, n. 35; to the Bologna committee, 13 April and 13 May, mss. in Carte Tanari I, MCRB. La Farina's authorization to stimulate war was sent to Beltrami and Adolfo Spada, dated 19 April 1859, in Maioli, "Società Nazionale a Ravenna," *Studi Romagnoli*, III, 119–20. Bardesono had also written Bologna expressing approval of the formation of a special battalion in the Romagna, 3 April 1859, in Masi, "Casarini," *Fra libri e ricordi*, 113.

[41] Rasponi to [Casarini?], 7 March 1859, ms. in Carteggio Casarini II, MCRB; Pepoli to Castelli, 9 April and n.d. April 1859, Chiala, *Carteggio di Castelli*, 189, 192; note from Pepoli, n.d. [to Casarini?], ms., Carteggio Casarini, misc. I, MCRB; Medicina wrote, 8 May 1859, of its distrust of Cesare Simoni who had been given some important mission, ms. in *ibid.*

"soldiers armed and instructed than insurgents unarmed and disordered." Understandably, Valzania complained that the revolutionary army he was attempting to forge was being undermined. The Rimini committee found itself receiving, resentfully, what seemed like orders from the new Tuscan provisional government; the direction of military affairs fell more and more into the hands of Mezzacapo.[42]

The local committees maintained their underground communication through the *trafila;* but their communiqués were more debates as to what should be done than reports on what they were doing. Many of their letters were lost, and the abbreviations they used were so primitively transparent that they were right to fear that the Papal police could be ready for any move they made. They were left with the nucleus of a revolutionary program, with enthusiasm and doubts but little more. Laderchi of the Faenza committee wrote his superiors in Bologna using, with conspiratorial care, his secret symbol; but he wrote in the first person of the crowd that angrily shouted "Laderchi" over and over when they thought the Papal *gonfaloniere* had placed a leader of the SNI under arrest. In fact, he was released after letting about a hundred armed citizens into the room and threatening the *gonfaloniere* with arrest. It was, Laderchi proudly reported, *"un orgasmo tutto romagnolo";* yet he feared the people had learned too well of the weakness of the government.[43] So close to revolution did the Romagna come and

---

[42] Minghetti to Tanari, 7 May 1859, ms. in Carte Tanari I, MCRB; Valzania to Bologna committee, 25 April 1859, Dallolio, "Valzania e la Società Nazionale," *La strenna delle colonie scolastiche,* xxxvi, 39–40. The papers of the Society in this period reflect the attention paid to volunteers; especially letters of the Faenza committee, 28 May (complaining of the 600 *baiocchi* they had spent on volunteers from Lombardy and Venetia), and the Rimini committee, 18 and 27 April, mss., Carte Tanari II and Carteggio Casarini, MCRB. On the sending of volunteers from Imola see Galli, "Società Nazionale e Gamberini," *La Romagna,* xvi, 402–404. Tanari felt men rejected for military service should be issued papers proving they had volunteered; then they could face their townspeople: letter to Mezzacapo, 17 May 1859, Ugo Pesci, *Il Generale Carlo Mezzacapo,* 70. On Mezzacapo's growing authority, Masi, "Casarini," *Fra libri e ricordi,* 118, notes his tendency to work through personal acquaintances rather than the SNI; La Farina concedes the General's authority in a letter to Bologna, 13 May, ms., Carte Tanari I, MCRB. This volunteer corps and its poor organization and preparation is discussed in Mazzatinti, "Contributo alla storia," *Archivio Storico Umbro,* I, 74–5, and Corpo di Stato Maggiore, *La Guerra del 1859,* narrazione II, 23–5.

[43] Letters of the Rimini committee, 18 April, ms., Carte Tanari II, and 21 April, ms. in Carteggio Casarini, complain of delays of nine days, lost letters,

so far removed from revolution was the temper of the good men of the SNI.

They did make plans for revolt. As early as April 10 delegates from the committees of Forlì, Faenza, Ravenna, Lugo, Rimini, and Cesena met to discuss plans for a simultaneous uprising and to inform their friends in Bologna and Turin of their views. The Bologna committee itself drafted a complicated plan for revolution, dividing the city by districts and marking the spots for barricades. Boys were even assigned to ring the bells at the appointed hour, and the committee received reports from night-watchmen of the plans of Papal authorities. The movements of Papal and Austrian troops were carefully noted; and after the Florentine rising, Boncompagni arranged almost immediately for the Romagnol committees to inform the Tuscans of any movement of troops to their border.[44]

Yet throughout their plans and discussions, doubts about revolution were evident; the Rimini committee could not forget the "unpardonable crimes" that would come with revolt nor the inadequacy of a few hunting rifles against an army. The Ravenna committee felt their plans had not been sufficiently coordinated. And Tanari, who claimed a "prudent" relationship with the Papal police, may not have been altogether disingenuous in convincing Cardinal Milesi that the National Society would be useful as an instrument of order should the troops depart. When the Parma committee, about to fall from power, called upon Romagnol committees to rise up, there was no response from the Romagna.[45] Such a call from Turin might have had a quite different effect, but none came from there.

and the danger of their signs and abbreviations being recognized. Laderchi's letter, 26 May, ms. in *ibid.*, expressed similar fears. A list of "conventional phrases" and meanings is in *ibid.* All in MCRB.

[44] Notes of the April 10 meeting to discuss Bologna's plan for revolt in the Romagna, and the plan for revolution in Bologna are mss. in Carte Tanari II and Carteggio Casarini respectively. Reports from the *pattuglia* dated 13 May and 7 June and some undated reports on troop movements including one from Ferrara, 31 May, are also in the Carteggio Casarini. There is a receipt, 4 May 1859, for the purchase of 32 guns in Carte Tanari II. All in MCRB.

Pietro [Beltrami] to Marchese [Pepoli or Tanari?], 27 April and telegram of the same day from Beltrami to Ballerini, are in Carteggio Casarini. He refers to "il Sig. Cav.," whom I take to be Boncompagni, as suggesting they arrange conventional phrases to warn of Austrian troop movements. Cecconi to Ulloa, 2 May 1859, in Soldani, *Pasqua di liberazione*, 155, suggests the system was fairly extensively used.

[45] Letters of Rimini committee, 27 April (commenting on a circular from

The failure of the Romagnols to demonstrate their sentiment with the heroic simplicity of revolution was a grave disappointment to many, and Cavour commented acidly that it had proved to be soldiers, not patriotism, that produced success for their cause. He was indignant that the popular enthusiasm promised by Minghetti, Beltrami, and Farini was not forthcoming. When the caution of the Romagnols became an embarrassment, Cavour could not recognize that they, in part at least, had learned it from him. Minghetti himself had insisted that no move should be made until the Austrians left and that Turin was to be called on only in the name of maintaining order.[46] Patriots in the Romagna were now as responsibly careful as those in Turin.

Finally, on June 12, the enemy soldiers left Bologna. Immediately, the leaders of the National Society declared themselves a provisional government and added two men from outside the SNI to broaden their appeal.[47] There was no doubt, however, of the Society's dominance; Pepoli took over the ministry of finance, Casarini that of war, and Tanari the ministry of the interior.

In town after town similar governments appeared behind the retreating Austrians, usually in a matter of hours. Sometimes these juntas were made up wholly of members of the National Society, and in every case, members of the SNI were predominant. This influence had shown itself in the quiet quickness

Forlì); and Ravenna committee, 8 May 1859, mss., Carteggio Casarini in MCRB. Maioli, "Tanari e il suo memoriale," Archiginasio, xxviii, 66–7; Rossi confirms the relationship to the police in his Memoria, 4 September 1868, to Signora Tanari, ms. in MCRB. The request from Parma, dated May 5, was addressed first to Modena and passed among the Romagna committees.

[46] Casarini's trip to Turin, when Massari felt he wanted to know too much, Diario, entry of 17 May 1859, 344–45, may have been meant as a further effort to get firm orders and support from Turin. The disappointment of Gaspare Finali and Minghetti is cited in Giulio del Bono, "Bologna e la Romagna durante la guerra del 1859," Memorie Storiche Militare, v (1911), 46. Cavour's comments, including the accusation that with the departure of the Austrians, 3,000 Swiss were holding down 3,000,000 people, are in his letter to Farini [3 July 1859], Liberazione del Mezzogiorno, v, 434–35. Minghetti to Malvezzi, 29 April 1859 (by Carolina Minghetti) and 6 May 1859, A. Malvezzi, "Lega dell'Italia Centrale," Rassegna Storica del Risorgimento, xlv, 380–81.

[47] Conte Malvezzi, who had headed the National Guard in 1849, was chosen because of his police contacts and reputed popularity with the artisans. Professor Montanari, a former minister of Pius IX, was added at the last minute, apparently for the reassuring respectability of his name. The preparations for the coup and assignment of important offices are described in Rossi, "Memoria a Signora Tanari," ms. in Carteggio Casarini, MCRB.

with which such governments appeared (Cesena was a partial exception) only after the Austrians left and in the consistency with which local juntas followed the pattern of the SNI in declaring their subordinance to the provisional government of Bologna.[48] For a month the Romagna was ruled by these men. Acting in time of war, with the status of their regime in doubt, indoctrinated with the ideas of the SNI, their primary concern was to maintain order.

On its first day in power the Bologna group banned all political writings and newspapers except for its official paper. The old bureaucracy was maintained in office but given ten days to obtain the seals of the new government; then at least the symbol of office would change. The local police organization was disbanded, but its replacement included all former policemen willing to swear allegiance to the provisional government. Most of them kept not only their jobs but their seniority, and it was explained to the public that the police were now to be trusted. Committees to collect contributions for the war effort and to enroll volunteers were established; the Piedmontese military code was adopted, and deserters were repeatedly warned that they would be tried under the "rigors" of military law. The old administrative divisions were efficiently maintained. Small grants were provided for families with men in arms, and political prisoners were freed (on June 21). By the end of June the only major administrative changes had been the lifting of some of the restrictions on the export of farm animals and the acceptance of lire as legal tender at a fixed rate.[49]

[48] The smaller towns close to Bologna declared their loyalty to the new junta on the 13th and 14th. The more important cities and the dates of their formal adherence to the Bologna junta follow. 13 June: Faenza; 14 June: Budrio, Fossignano, Lugo; 15 June: Bagnacavallo; 16 June: Medicina; 17 June: Fano (thus spreading into the Marches; only one of the men involved here, Civilotti, appears to have been in the SNI and he may have joined it later); 18 June: Imola (also given as the 14th); 19 June: Ravenna (the date of 13 June is also given); 20 June: Forlì; 24 June: Ferrara. Originali degli atti di seduta, Bologna, Giunta Provvisoria di Governo, ms., in Atti e decreti, Bologna, AST, Nos. 85, 94, 98, 102–103, 112, 125, 129, 130. Many of the names of the members of those governments are given in Domenico Valente, *La guerra d'Italia del 1859* (Naples, 1860), 294–95, 298–99, 308. For the slight exception of Cesena, see Finali to Valzania, 11 July 1859, in Maioli, "Società Nazionale a Ravenna," *Studi Romagnoli*, III, 111. Alfredo Grilli, "Imola nel Giugno 1859," *Il Risorgimento e Luigi Carlo Farini* (Faenza, 1959), I, 153–54, says that Inviti of the Bologna committee sent word to local committees telling them to revolt.

[49] The Bologna junta asked Boncompagni for arms so that citizens could be

The National Society was rapidly disappearing as an independent force. The official delegation which journeyed to the front to present Victor Emmanuel and Louis Napoleon with a petition asking the King to become their dictator was almost exclusively composed of members of the SNI; and when another international congress seemed likely to threaten Piedmont's annexation of the Romagna, the Society prepared, in its name, instructions to Cavour pleading the case for unification.[50] But the Bologna junta looked to men such as Minghetti and Mezzacapo in Tuscany, and Farini in Modena rather than the SNI for its policies. It arranged a public welcome for Mezzacapo when he arrived to head Romagna's military forces and with apparent joy handed over full authority to d'Azeglio when he came, on July 14, as military governor. Cavour had chosen d'Azeglio, but he had not dared to name him royal commissioner as nationalists had hoped. It was, however, in keeping with the Society's spirit to present the Romagna as a gift to the King with such insistent finesse that Cavour's delicate policies would not be endangered.

Once d'Azeglio arrived, little was required of the National Society beyond abnegation. His appointments went to Piedmontese deputies and quieter, more conservative Romagnols. Despite some personal disappointment, the Society's men, who had been able to accept Valzania and Pepoli, could be content with d'Azeglio. Though shunted aside, except in city governments where they were still predominant, their personal influence in part remained; when d'Azeglio retired, Minghetti and

---

prepared to help maintain order, a task apparently requiring more force than had their "revolution": letter of 13 June 1859, Malvezzi, "Lega dell'Italia Centrale," *Rassegna Storica del Risorgimento*, XLV, 375. Its acts, published as proclamations, are in the volumes for 1859 of the collection of proclamations, edicts, and documents concerning Italy with special emphasis on Bologna in the library of the Harvard Law School. Most of them (with some omissions and additions) are printed in *Raccolta degli atti governativi nelle provincie delle romagne e dell'Emilia del 12 giugno 1859 al 18 marzo 1860* (Bologna, 1860).

[50] Pepoli, Casarini, Count Cesare Albicini (from Forlì and the only one of the group who may have had no connection with the Society at the time), Count Rasponi (from Ravenna), Professor Gherardi (from Ferrara) were the delegation. The statement to Cavour, *Istruzioni per i Sig. Deputati dal Partito Nazionale Italiano a S. E. Sig. Conte di Cavour a Torino*, n.d., ms. in Atti e decreti, Romagna, AST.

[51] Masi, "Casarini," *Fra libri e ricordi*, 128–30. Of the fifteen councilors of

214

Massari would have to oppose a local effort to name La Farina his successor.[51]

These were the areas of the Society's successes, but in the Marches and Umbria it played at times a tragic part. Various committees of the Society in these provinces were in touch with those in the Romagna and with nationalist leaders in Tuscany. From the Bologna and Rimini committees in particular, nationalists in the Marches and even in Umbria got word of the Society's policies, of the program for volunteers, and news of the events of April and May.

Some of the committees in the Marches had sent representatives to a council in which general plans for organization and insurrection were agreed upon. Men such as Giulio Cesare Fabbri traveled to Florence (where he came to believe that Mezzacapo and Boncompagni would support revolts in the Marches after a rising in Bologna) and then went through the Marches urging committees to action. Valzania's troops had been meant for use across the mountains of Feltre, and there were promising rumors about them. On June 15 and 16 many towns of the Marches tore down the Papal flags and raised the tricolor of Piedmont, despite warnings from Rimini against any uprising. Fano even declared its loyalty to the Bologna junta and began a local program of remaking their laws on Piedmontese models. When support from the outside did not arrive, the patriots of the Marches felt an understandable resentment. One by one the Piedmontese flags came down, local nationalists went into exile or quietly home. There was, at least, a minimum of bloodshed. In the long run the great contribution of the National Society in the Marches and Umbria would be its part in preserving the desire for unification and faith in Piedmont after the frustration of such unheroic defeat.[52]

---

state appointed by d'Azeglio only Tanari and Salvoni were certainly members of the SNI although Malvezzi and Scarabelli probably were. Of the provisional government, only Pepoli and Malvezzi kept high administrative office. Tanari was one of those who later advocated La Farina's appointment, Biundi, *La Farina*, I, 425; Massari, *Diario*, entry of 18 July 1859, 427.

[52] Alessandrini, *I fatti*, II, 26–7, 50; Zampetti-Biocca, *Società Nazionale nelle Marche*, 61–5; Mazzatinti, "Contributo alla storia," *Archivio Storico Umbro*, I, 69–74; [Camillo Franceschi], *Relazione del Comitato Nazionale di Fano* (Fano, 1861), 10–17. Tommaséo to Capponi, 12–13 July 1859, del Lungo and Prunas, *Tommaséo e Capponi*, IV², 109.

The bloodier tragedy of the defeated revolt in Perugia reflects similar weaknesses. The Society was sufficiently widespread that local nationalists could feel themselves part of a general movement and be keenly aware of plans for revolts elsewhere. The knowledge of many such committees, and the excited conversations with men such as Mezzacapo and Boncompagni in Tuscany led to the belief that revolt in Perugia would be followed by uprisings throughout Umbria and the Marches which would then be supported from Tuscany and the Romagna. Perhaps such promises were really given. In any case, these committees were not well enough organized nor sufficiently prepared for an independently successful revolt. The dissolution of the Society's Central Committee led to greater confusion everywhere; the Bologna committee refused to take authority for Umbria, and Boncompagni held neither the principles nor the position from which to coordinate a large conspiracy. Just enough a part of the Society to feel compelled to act and to be deeply influenced by the example of the Romagna, the nationalists of Perugia staged a revolt which momentarily succeeded. Then, ill-equipped and isolated, they had to withstand the well-organized fury of the Papal army. They could not. In defeat they gave a testament of the Society's faith by exonerating Piedmont for not aiding them and by not implicating the monarchy in their foolhardy enthusiasm. Yet Tuscan leaders, at least, had been involved; and the tragedy of Perugia was a major failure of a Society which could bring itself neither to forego the dream of revolution nor deliberately to accept the preparation it required and the diplomatic dangers it ran.[53]

It was in Venetia that La Farina's energies were to be given full play. Named commissioner there in July, he hurried to Ferrara well provided with funds and the promise of troops. He hoped, apparently, to instigate some local risings and to organize a battalion of deserters, but Napoleon's disenchantment with the war came too soon. The National Society's leader did not manage to do in Venetia what the Society had just succeeded in doing in the Romagna. Cavour's efforts to promote the kind

---

[53] Giustiniano Degli Azzi, *L'Insurrezione e le stragi di Perugia del giugno 1859* (Perugia, 1909), 17, 20–1, 31–3; Beatrice Raschi, *Movimento politico della città di Perugia dal 1846 al 1860* (Foligno, 1904), 95, 205–206, 238–43.

of rising he wanted came too late. The truce of Villafranca found La Farina with nine-tenths of his funds unspent and his part in the politics of Ferrara his only tangible achievement. He had helped to prepare the town's citadel for a siege and had seen to the expulsion of the Jesuits. (As a good anticlerical, he searched their papers finding them, of course, a bit erotic but disappointingly unpolitical.) [54]

The relative quiet in the Kingdom of the Two Sicilies while war raged in the north was equally disappointing to La Farina. Some refugees from the south had agreed to support the program of the SNI, and La Farina repeatedly urged a revolt in Sicily and Calabria. He pointed to the sacrifices being made in Piedmont and argued for the need to demonstrate enthusiasm. He even implied that Napoleon was sure to support their demands for unification once their seriousness was shown by revolution. But Sicily did not proclaim Victor Emmanuel its dictator. If there was any basis for the claim that the *"lafariniani"* prevented a more radical revolt in Sicily later that fall, one can only conclude that even there the men of the Italian National Society were more adept at preventing than initiating revolution.[55]

From the outbreak of the war until the truce of Villafranca, the Society had cooperated in important ways with others who favored the nationalist cause, and everywhere it had been a consistent source of support for Cavour's policies. In Parma it had dared and failed; in many places it accomplished less than the Prime Minister had hoped. But in Tuscany it had provided a useful pressure for stiffer demands on the Grand Duke and against the greater caution of many Tuscan leaders. In the

[54] Cavour informed Farini of La Farina's appointment in a letter of 3 July 1859, *Liberazione de Mezzagiorno*, v, 435. La Farina had spent only 2,000 of the 20,000 lire he was given. What can be found in printed and manuscript sources about this venture is collected in Benito Vittorio Gallea, "La missione di Giuseppe La Farina a Ferrara nel 1859," *Bollettino del Museo del Risorgimento*, II (Bologna, 1957), 224–32. La Farina had some earlier contacts in Venetia: see his letter to Cipriano Conti, 14 May 1859, Franchi, *Epistolario di La Farina*, II, 174. Farini, who hoped for a few more days that the truce did not mean peace, offered La Farina 15,000 men, Farini to La Farina, 15 July 1859, *ibid.*, 189.

[55] La Farina to Bartolomeo, 19 May, 16 and 28 June 1859; and to Giuseppe Giunti, 28 June 1859, Franchi, *Epistolario di La Farina*, II, 175, 181–84. Rosolino Pilo to Salvatore Calvino, 10 November 1859, in Curatolo, *Garibaldi, Vittorio Emanuele, e Cavour*, 51.

Romagna it had been the very backbone of the provisional governments which did finally take power. Nowhere had Cavour depended upon the Society exclusively; he did so most nearly, perhaps, in the Duchies and least so in Lombardy, but in both areas the march of armies was decisive. Always Cavour worked most closely with and more directly through the leaders of volunteer corps, such as Ribotti and Mezzacapo, or agents of his own, such as Boncompagni in Tuscany, or men he knew and trusted who themselves had important connections, such as Minghetti, until finally he had his own appointees, such as d'Azeglio and Farini, with whom to deal.

The members of the Society gave way to men of greater note naturally as well as out of loyalty to Cavour. The Society's were the local men, the men on the scene, but they were willing that greater authority be held in other hands not merely because of modesty or because their Society had taught them to have confidence in Piedmont. What the interim governments demanded was precisely what the Society had preached; if the SNI gave way before Boncompagni and d'Azeglio, Boncompagni and d'Azeglio were now for the first time acting like members of the Society. Their dictatorships stressed the maintenance of order, both as their primary concern and as the justification for their existence. They insisted on avoiding controversy, shunting aside talk of federalism in Tuscany or social reform in the Romagna. They were intent upon assimilating local laws to those of Piedmont as quickly as possible, as Farini did in the Duchies. Yet they recognized the importance of capitalizing on every manifestation of popular support for these policies. The things which Cavour's agents did in central Italy were precisely what the Society had called for and, where possible, had done.

Thus even after the truce of Villafranca the men of the Society remained an important source of support for these regimes. Inevitably, such men received important preferment in local posts even if they fell from the ranks of policy makers.[56] Representative institutions dedicated to quick and complete unification

[56] Massari could complain, even in Lombardy, of the preferment given men of the SNI, *Diario*, entry of 10 July 1859, 413. See note 33 above about the special place given Manfredi. A report from Bologna listing those who had participated in the citizen guard of the local committee shows how on the lowest level such men were noted for special favor, ms., n.d., in Sezione del Interiore, Romagna 1859, AST.

with Piedmont, the special assemblies called in these provinces had particular appeal for the Society. As men of established patriotism, members of the Society were frequently elected deputies; about one in seven of the delegates to these assemblies belonged to the SNI.[57] Their role in the various commissions and as proponents of important resolutions was somewhat greater than their numbers. When these assemblies avoided issues (often crucial ones) which were likely to create division and passed with monotonous unanimity resolutions for annexation, they represented the triumph of the National Society's program.

Beyond the assemblies themselves, there were further discernible echoes of the Society's influence. Like so much in which the Government of Piedmont had acquiesced, the truce of Villafranca was a bitter disappointment to Italian nationalists. Cavour's resignation, which accompanied it, added to the frightening uncertainties of the last six months of 1859. But the attitudes which the Society had helped to develop prevented disappointment from leading to new divisions and to demands for new policies. The men who had promulgated those attitudes were busy once again, and along the network of confidence created by the Society there went the words of encouragement and explanation which could hold nationalists together. La Farina insisted that nothing had really been changed by the truce; and Garibaldi, despite his personal resentment at the minor part he had been given in the war, issued a proclamation recognizing Italy's debt to Napoleon and declaring that the correct slogan was still "Italy and Victor Emmanuel." That important statement, from the man who could easily have been the focal point for serious discontent, represented another success for the SNI.[58]

[57] Precise or complete records of membership in the SNI do not exist, but by checking the names for which we have evidence—or at least an indication—of membership in the Society against the lists of delegates, my estimate would be: 9 or 10 of the 73 delegates to the assembly of Modena and Reggio were in the SNI; 3 to 8 of the 65 in the Parma and Piacenza assembly; 18 to 25 of the 122 in that of the Romagna, about 26 of the 172 in the Tuscan assembly. It was in Parma, where the Society had known the disaster of excessive zeal, that the fewest of its members were elected deputies. The purposes of the assemblies are discussed in Domenico Demarco, Le 'Assemblee Nazionali' e l'idea di costituente alla dimane del 1859 (Florence, 1947), 210; the natural acceptance of the importance of parliamentary representation is noted in Domenico Zanichelli, Studi di storio costituzionale e politica del Risorgimento italiano (Bologna, 1900), 27.

[58] Some of La Farina's post-Villafranca letters are in Franchi, Epistolario di

In the months that followed, members of the Society were prominent among delegations to the King and the Emperor, in the regional assemblies, in local government, and on many of the newspapers which defended the policies of Cavour. The attitudes the Society had sponsored also lent support to the specific policies of the new regional governments, all of which now acted with a decisiveness that greatly extended their authority. Many of their acts were of doubtful constitutionality and presented grave problems for the doctrinaire liberal. The men of the Society, however, were not doctrinaire. They argued from necessity for censorship and limited suffrage, insisting in tones the Society had made familiar that strength, not justice, was Italy's immediate concern.[59] Thus the Society had a major part in the events which made a revolution out of the retreat of Dukes, which made the keeping of order the revolution's major aim, and caused reform to mean the enactment of Piedmontese law. La Guerronière's pamphlet, *Napoléon III et l'Italie*, had distinguished sharply between subversive and national revolutions. The men of the National Society had understood the Emperor's warning and preserved that distinction. Tommaséo enjoyed the paradox in stating that La Farina was attempting to combine the roles of conspirator and police agent.[60] Their relative success in that somewhat unattractive position was La Farina's and the Society's great contribution to the Risorgimento.

La Farina, II, 190–93; Garibaldi's proclamation of 23 July 1859 is printed in Zini, *Storia d'Italia*, II², 299. He later made clear his resentment against the Government in a letter to Pallavicino. Malenchini strove to make sure the General was kept in the fold. See Pallavicino's letter of 17 July 1859, *Memorie di Pallavicino*, III, 536–37, and Delle Torre, *Sentimento nazionale in Toscana*, 291.

[59] Teodosio Marchi, *Le luogotenenze generale, 1848–1915, nel diritto costituzionale italiano* (Rome, 1918), 39–43, 67–9; Gaetano Arangio Ruiz, *Storia costituzionale del Regna d'Italia (1848–1898)* (Florence, 1898), 115–21. The president of the Society's committee in Milan, a lawyer, published a detailed and intelligent if somewhat tortured argument for the necessity of treating liberty exactly as Cavourians had: Pietro Castiglione, *Della Monarchia Parlamentare e dei diritti e doveri del cittadino secondo lo statuto e le leggi del piemonte* (2 vols., Milan, 1859). See especially: I, 277–83; II, 68–72, 203–33. The statements of the editors of *La Nazione* in Florence on censorship and justice are characteristic: Puccioni, *Ricasoli*, 107, from editorial of 20 August 1859. Cempini, Fenzi and Puccioni to Ricasoli, 5 July 1859, Mobile and Camerani, *Carteggio di Ricasoli*, VIII, 292.

[60] "*gl'imbrogli del cospiratore con quelli dell'uomo di polizia*," Tommaséo to Capponi, 12–13 July 1859, del Lungo and Prunas, *Tommaséo e Capponi*, IV², 109.

CHAPTER EIGHT

THE NATIONAL SOCIETY RE-ESTABLISHED

(AUGUST 1859—APRIL 1860)

IN THE FALL OF 1859 the Italian National Society announced its existence once again. A flurry of hortatory letters and the reappearance of the *Piccolo Corriere* on November 1 marked the event, but for months La Farina had been discussing, even advertising, the revival. The decision to re-establish the Society was La Farina's personal decision, and the reasons for it were first of all personal ones. He had meant to accept the armistice of Villafranca stoically, planning only to go "where the wind will send me." But he could not maintain such passivity even for a sentence; he expected that wind to send him "where there will be something to do," where he would need "to keep our banner high." [1] Images of militant activity were part of La Farina's view of life, and he had begun almost immediately to think of a revitalized Society. He knew that he had many enemies and that those in power would treat him more seriously if he represented a political movement. After Cavour's angry resignation in July over the armistice, he was anxious to establish his influence with the new government led by Rattazzi. And he was wistful about lost chances for positions of importance. Above all, he saw Italy threatened by disorder and himself as the man to save her. [2]

La Farina was always sensitive to the wants and even more to the fears of an important element of Italian opinion. Lombardy was now joined to Piedmont, and Tuscany, the Duchies, and the Romagna might yet be if Italians used the proper skill. But Venetia, the Papal States, and the Kingdom of Naples were for the moment lost. There was widespread uncertainty about Rattazzi's policies, and the intentions of France could not be known.

[1] La Farina to Francesco Homodei, 17 July 1859, Franchi, *Epistolario di La Farina*, II, 190.
[2] His reference in July to a "new program" for the Society followed a complaint about Boncompagni's unfriendliness: La Farina to Vincenzo Giusti, 26 July 1859, *ibid.*, 193; letter to Canevazzi, 30 August 1859, *ibid.*, 207.

For men used to the firm direction of Cavour, Rattazzi's hesitance and his penchant for intrigue were frightening. The spirit of self-sacrificing nationalism had faded, and wartime unanimity was lost. As political issues became more specific, disagreement grew more bitter, and doubt gave way to distrust between groups and provinces.[3]

Worse still, the Society's old enemies began to show themselves again. The "democrats" disliked a monarchy which was a mere extension of Piedmont. Some complained of being hounded by former friends who had been given power by the SNI. Brofferio, perhaps Italy's most effective publicist, described how the republicans of Modena, the Romagna, or Tuscany were no better treated than under the old regimes. Yet La Farina feared the Government itself was sponsoring Brofferio's activities. Returning troops expected more than public gratitude and were reported dangerously tempted to independent action. Even a former leader of the National Society complained of that "moderate party" which did nothing but oppose all action while Mazzini restated with unreal enthusiasm his arguments for a national revolution.

But democrats were not the only danger. Clerical influence was reported strong; La Farina, watching Cipriani's activity in Bologna and the number of Bonapartists around him, put them on his list of feared opponents. When the committee in Sissa was re-established, it would add *legittismo* to *mazzinianismo* and *gesuitismo* as the rampant dangers it must combat.[4] The Italian

---

[3] Note Massari, *Diario*, 525, and Malvezzi, "Lega d'Italia Centrale," *Rassegna Storica del Risorgimento*, XLV, 406; and La Farina's letters from Bologna, Parma, and Florence in this period, Franchi, *Epistolario di La Farina*, II, 193–215.

[4] Michele Di Piero, *Storia critica dei partiti italiani* (Rome, 1946), 12–13; Primo Uccellini, *Memorie di un vecchio carbonaro ravegnano*, Tommaso Casini (ed.) (Rome, 1898), 112; Angelo Brofferio, *I miei tempi*, XIII, 285–307; XIV (Turin, 1860), 1–129. La Farina to Manfredi, 30 August, and to Franchi, 24 September 1859, Franchi, *Epistolario di La Farina*, II, 205, 210. La Farina was particularly caustic about the Romagna: letter to Farini, 10 July 1859, in Gallea, "La Missione di La Farina," *Bollettino del Museo del Risorgimento*, Bologna, II, 231. Brofferio's popularity caused Ricasoli some embarrassment, too: Ricasoli to Ricci, 14 September 1859, in Puccioni, *Ricasoli*, 218; cf. Tommaso Casini, "Garibaldi nell'Emilia nel 1859," *Archivio Emiliano del Risorgimento Nazionale*, I (1907), 300–301. Report of the intendant of Ravenna, ms. in Sezione dell'Interno, Romagna, indici al protocolo generale della giunta provvisoria del governo, 9 September 1859, AST (Cipriani also received unsigned reports stating that the provisional junta had lost public confidence, *ibid.*, Emilia). Marco Ballelli, Faenza, to Casarini, 23 October 1859, ms. in Carteggio Casarini, MCRB; pam-

National Society had disbanded in the spring, confident not merely of Piedmont's success but of the triumph of Cavourian nationalism. The confidence did not now seem justified.

Other, less restrained organizations might possibly take the place of the SNI. In the Romagna, among the leaders of the Society itself, there was extensive planning for an invasion of Venetia and the Marches.[5] Among men closer to Mazzini, there was much talk of revolution in Sicily.[6] Elsewhere, from Rome to Milan, new political societies were being formed and old ones revived. Some of them frankly opposed the policies of Cavour; some, like Garibaldi's Million Rifles Fund, offered a vague promise of action which won the support of many, including former leaders of the Society.[7]

Not by nature a pessimist, La Farina saw in the resolutions for unification which passed the assemblies of central Italy in August and September proof that the Society's program was in fact

phlet of Sissa committee, n.d., by A. Bellantini, p. 2. See Mazzini's "Il Moto italiano e i moderati," *Scritti di Mazzini*, LXIV (Imola, 1933), 114–19; and his letter to Adriano Lemmi, 5 September, *ibid.*, LXV (Imola, 1933), 160. Zini, *Storia d'Italia*, II², 381ff.

[5] A note was sent to Rinaldo Simonetti, 19 October 1859, about 4,000 rifles being sent them, ms. in Posizione Simonetti, MCRB. A Veronese soap manufacturer proposed a plan for hiding rifles among his stores of soap and offering some of his profits to the cause. The plan was seriously discussed among such officials as the Inspector of Public Security and the vice-director of police in Bologna until Buscalioni, in December, was able to put them in touch with Simonetti, representing the SNI: Pietro Santarelli, Verona, to vice-director of police, Bologna, n.d., and Buscalioni to Luigi Marchi, Inspector of Public Security, 5 December 1859, ms. in *ibid.*; letter of Marchi, n.d., ms. in ISR, busta 719, n. 17. Chiala, *Lettere di Cavour*, III, cclv, cites Corandini to the effect that committees of the SNI were preparing a rising against the "*papalini*," and similar plans circulated vigorously in the Marches, Alessandrini, *I fatti*, II, 108–109; Zampetti-Biocca, *Società Nazionale*, 77–82.

[6] Crispi, Fabrizi, and Pilo were involved in the Sicilian plans in which Farini and Tanari also seem to have had some part: Crispi to Fabrizi, 16 September, and Fabrizi to Crispi, 9 November 1859, Crispi, *I Mille*, 98–101; see also Chapter Ten, note 34. La Farina found the idea tempting, too, letter to Franchi, 24 September 1859, Franchi, *Epistolario di La Farina*, II, 212.

[7] The Associazione per l'Annessione dell'Italia Centrale al Regno Subalpino is a good example of a parallel organization with a slightly more radical tinge: Carlo Agrati, *Giuseppe Sirtori* (Bari, 1940), 186. Garibaldi's fund was supported in New York by the Society's founders: Howard R. Marraro, "Documenti italiani e americani sulla spedizione garibaldina in Sicilia," *Rassegna Storica del Risorgimento*, XLIV (1957), 39–40; Puccioni collected for it in Tuscany: Puccioni, *Malenchini*, 114–15; and it proved a threat to unity among nationalists in Imola, Galli, "Società Nazionale e Gamberini," *La Romagna*, 31–2; Pallavicino supported it vigorously, Pallavicino to Belgioioso, November 1859, *Memorie di Pallavicino*, III, 550–51.

the "will of 13 million Italians." The SNI could use Garibaldi's popularity while keeping the quixotic general in check, and Garibaldi himself was sympathetic to La Farina's plans.[8] Italian patriots were once again arguing what course to take as they had been when Manin first spoke out. Once again the National Society could provide a common program, spare Italy the divisive enthusiasms of radicals, and push the Government to stronger action for unification.

As early as July, word had reached Pallavicino of La Farina's ambitions for reviving the SNI. The Marchese was opposed. Those behind the treachery of Villafranca, he argued, would not permit the propaganda of the National Society. Its dissolution had been no mistake. He feared the Society would have to be frankly governmental as, in his eyes, it had not been before. And now he liked Piedmont's policy less. When La Farina formally asked Pallavicino to join him, arguing somewhat falsely that the Society already existed in Sicily and Venetia and that demands for its reactivation were coming in from all over the north, the Marchese held firm. He told La Farina to go ahead; this time he would not be president. In La Farina's view, Pallavicino's absence was no serious loss.[9]

His request for Cavour's approval was a more important matter. La Farina wrote him on September 27, carefully presenting his case. It was, he began, his travels in central Italy which had made him think of re-establishing the Society. He gave four reasons for doing so: to satisfy the demands of Sicilians and Venetians (he had told Pallavicino the same day that the Society was already established there), to prevent the formation of other societies which was already taking place in the Romagna and Lombardy, to establish relations with the Ger-

[8] Garibaldi to La Farina, 8 August, and La Farina to Bartolomeo, 23 August, to Canevazzi, 30 August, and to Franchi, 26 August and 24 September 1859, Franchi, *Epistolario di La Farina*, II, 201–202, 207, 204–205, 211. This view became a permanent part of the Society's propaganda; note La Farina to the editor of *Il Pugnolo*, 10 December 1859, *ibid.*, 581–83.

[9] Pallavicino, 21 July and 4 October (to La Farina) 1859, *Memorie di Pallavicino*, III, 540–42. La Farina to Pallavicino, 27 September 1859, ms., MNRT. La Farina here wrote fulsomely of his fondness for the Marchese, but he assured others that his invitation had been *pro forma*: La Farina to Giusti, 1 October, and to Homodei, 6 October 1859, Franchi, *Epistolario di La Farina*, II, 214–15, 220; La Farina to Cavour, 27 September 1859, Chiala, *Lettere di Cavour*, VI, 445–46. Rossignoli apparently acted as agent between the two men during their negotiations.

man National Society which was modeled on the SNI and wished to be in touch with it, and to combat the effects of anti-national propaganda. He reported that things were going well everywhere save in the Romagna, where he credited the Society with already having prevented disaster. Pallavicino insisted that Cavour would oppose the Society, La Farina said, so now he wrote the Count. Good liberal and skilled politician that he was, Cavour replied suggesting that such societies should not be needed where the press was free. For the moment he was against re-establishing the SNI; but his note was friendly, and he asked to hear from La Farina again.

He did—in a letter which matched the tone of the Count's and was filled with expressions of loyalty and admiration. To Cavour, who felt deeply the disappointment of Villafranca and the loneliness of the politician out of office, that letter must have been a welcome one. Its business remained the National Society, and La Farina's arguments acquired a disturbing edge as he amplified them. He wrote a bit more bluntly now of the source of strength the Society had been for the Government and of the need to check others who have "neither our good sense, nor our good faith." With a dogmatism hardly flattering to Italy, La Farina insisted that many would welcome a dictatorship which the *Piccolo Corriere* proposed while rejecting one advocated by *Opinione* (which supported Rattazzi). He confidently predicted that for another fifty years there must be a conspiracy either for Victor Emmanuel or for Mazzini. He had, La Farina added, perhaps with a touch of warning, consulted Rattazzi who thought the Society could do no harm, but he would not act until Cavour declared La Farina's arguments convincing.

On the same day, he wrote Farini that the Society was being re-established. La Farina had few doubts that Cavour would be convinced; and the Count, reluctant still to acquiesce in writing, replied in comradely tone with the suggestion that they meet at "the old hour" to exchange views and begin again their work.[10] The new Society would in fact be closer to Cavour than had the old. Its tone would be less one of conciliation than one of ex-

[10] La Farina to Cavour, 27 September and 3 October, and Cavour to La Farina, 2 [September, in *ibid.*, III, but given as 2 October in *ibid.*, VI, 446*n*] and 6 October, *ibid.*, VI, 445–46, 454–56, and III, 134–35, 139. La Farina to Bardesono, 3 October 1859, ms., MNRT.

clusion for any who did not accept the program already established. Its new members would be not merely those who had shared its dreams in 1858 and its activity in 1859 (many of whom were now disillusioned) but rather those now convinced that safety lay in continuing the course marked out by Cavour. Pallavicino, who felt the old Society had never been adequately appreciated, was hurt to see so many "reaping who have not sown." Soon La Farina was once again urging on local committees and mentioning, in suggestive confidence, that the decision to revive the Society had not been made without getting "the opinion of the *conte di C.* and of *Comm*. *R.*" [11]

There remained another name as important to the Society's success as these. Garibaldi's support would preserve for the SNI the claim of representing all honest nationalism. His flattering letter in August had undoubtedly encouraged La Farina. In mid-October Garibaldi accepted the presidency of the Italian National Society. It was a major triumph, and he wrote of his decision with the ring of a proclamation. His regret that Pallavicino could not be president obscured the fact that the Marchese's absence measured a change in the nature of the Society. His call for Italians not to lay down their arms had an irrelevant militance which gave a spark of hope and a sense of purpose to the Society.[12]

On October 20, the day after Garibaldi agreed to be president, La Farina signed a manifesto announcing that the Society was re-formed. It caused little surprise. Even Bianchi-Giovini, after noting the unattractiveness of "revived corpses," conceded that the National Society might still be useful. He naïvely asked that Garibaldi choose another aide; La Farina had made too many mistakes and antagonized too many groups.[13] An impossible request, it was a useful warning.

Soon the Society was in full swing. Garibaldi's manifesto was circulated on a fly sheet. La Farina suggested that money for

[11] Pallavicino to Ulloa, 20 November 1859, Doria, "Ulloa," *Archivio Storico per le Provincie Napoletane*, n.s. xv, 376; and La Farina to Canevazzi, 28 October 1859, Franchi, *Epistolario di La Farina*, ii, 225.

[12] Garibaldi to La Farina, 8 August and 19 October 1859, *ibid.*, 201, 221–22. To someone like Fabrizi, of course, it was clear that Garibaldi had been fooled again, Nicola Fabrizi to General Ribbotti, 21 October 1859, Curatolo, *Garibaldi, Vittorio Emanuele, e Cavour*, 33.

[13] Bianchi-Giovini, "Associazione e programmi" in *Unione*, 21 October 1859, reprinted in *Memorie di Pallavicino*, iii, 545–46.

the Million Rifles Fund be placed with the SNI.[14] The re-establishment of the Society was presented as the "logical" result of Villafranca; the previous months' revolutions, plebiscites, and assemblies were seen as the universal acceptance of the Society's program. Indeed, it was claimed that each of the SNI's "94 committees" had played a part in the great events of spring and summer, that its men had "captained the first moves" and then disposed of their power with "marvelous civic modesty." It all sounded like the Society of old, and in fact many phrases came from previous publications.

But the call for concord could now be made in a voice filled with experience and success; now, the Society argued (thanks to the French), Italy was in a position to proceed on her own. Yet the discerning eye might have noticed a slight hesitance in the profession of support for the present governments and a stronger emphasis on anarchy rather than apathy as Italy's greatest danger. Some may have wondered at the efficacy of the simple order that all local committees "will be reconvened." Even the least informed reader knew that all was not well when the fourth issue of the *Piccolo Corriere* had to explain Garibaldi's resignation of command in the army of central Italy.

Garibaldi's position there had been ill-defined. His presence was a promise that action was possible in the Marches. His popularity made him a political force in the Romagna. But his relations with General Fanti and Farini, who represented the regular military and civil authorities, were always delicate. Talk of starting a revolt across the border in Papal territory or merely aiding one already begun brought Garibaldi into conflict with the regular army and led to major disputes through September and October. At the end of October Garibaldi went to Turin relying on the King, as he had before and would again, to resolve these disagreements. In a matter of weeks, when Garibaldi heard (incorrectly) of a revolt in the Marches, the old disputes erupted again—this time to be calmed by Farini.

After a stormy meeting on November 15 during which Gari-

---

[14] La Farina to Garibaldi, 19 October 1859, ms. in ISR, busta 574, n. 27. The Manifesto, dated October 20, was printed as a separate circular, copies of which may be found in the Buscalioni pamphlets in Harvard College Library (hereafter HCL) and in the Siccoli papers in ISR. It became a part of the 1860 edition of the Society's *Credo*. The Society's view of itself is taken from the Manifesto and *Piccolo Corriere*, 1 November 1859.

baldi, Farini, Fanti, and La Farina snarled over the noise of a crowd outside, Garibaldi resigned.[15] La Farina was involved, as he had been before, because Farini believed him to have important influence in the Romagna and because Garibaldi tended to associate his position in the army (as savior of revolution) with his role as president of the SNI. In September La Farina had seen clearly the importance of preventing a break with Garibaldi; in November he sided with Farini and Fanti.[16] As mediator, he had failed.

When forced to face the issue, Farini had to choose the regular army and a policy of restraint. Traditionally, however, the role of the National Society had been to reconcile the caution of government with the aspirations of revolutionaries. Now, instead of a group above parties the Society was becoming a party. To have antagonized Fanti, La Farina argued, would have been to antagonize the officers and "all the rich and intelligent classes"; he fooled himself by claiming that the attitudes of those classes were shared by "the immense majority of the population." Dread of a Garibaldian venture in the Marches had caused international concern, and La Farina's part in preventing it increased his prestige in government circles and brought him closer to Cavour.[17] In the long run, however, it weakened him; he would wield less influence among activists the next time.

Garibaldi accompanied his resignation from the army with a proclamation which complained of the "cunning arts" which had been used against him—a dangerously open acknowledgment of the depth of his resentments. It was Pallavicino who

[15] Casini, "Garibaldi nell'Emilia," *Archivio Emiliano*, I, 282–357; Zini, *Storia d'Italia*, II², 505–506. Gualterio blamed the SNI for the plans for revolt: Gualterio to Ricasoli, 27 October 1859, cited in Puccioni, *Ricasoli*, 151–53. La Farina to Franchi, 23 November 1859, and to Sbarbaro, October 1860, Franchi, *Epistolario di La Farina*, II, 236–37, 431–32. *Edizione nazionale degli scritti di Garibaldi*, IV (Bologna, 1933), 196.

[16] La Farina to Franchi, 24 September 1859, Franchi, *Epistolario di La Farina*, II, 211. Casini, "Garibaldi nell'Emilia," *Archivio Emiliano*, I, 334–35. La Farina to Farini, 19 July 1859, Gallea, "La Missione de La Farina," *Bollettino del Museo del Risorgimento* (Bologna), II, 232; Farini to Castelli, 4 November 1859, Rava, *Epistolario di Farini*, IV, 330.

[17] La Farina to Franchi, 23 November, and Cavour to La Farina, November 1859, Franchi, *Epistolario di La Farina*, II, 237, 235; La Farina to Bardesono, n.d., ms., MNRT. Zini, *Storia d'Italia*, II², 465n–66n. Massari, *Diario*, entry of 11 November 1859, 565; Casini, "Garibaldi nell'Emilia," *Archivio Emiliano*, I, 323–27; Capponi to Tommaséo, 19 August 1859, del Lungo and Prunas, *Tommaséo e Capponi*, IV², 176, give evidence that fear of Garibaldi was widespread.

played the role that had been the Society's by warning that such frankness could hurt their cause. The *Piccolo Corriere* explained that their patriotic sacrifices enabled Garibaldi and Fanti to get along well. But once the threat of Papal attack had passed, Fanti assumed command. Garibaldi could not be made into a "tranquil garrison general."[18] In Bologna the Society's committee assured its fellow citizens that the King and Garibaldi were in complete agreement; the greatest demonstration in favor of Garibaldi would be to maintain order. Garibaldi himself put forth another and milder statement telling the soldiers to stay at their posts. The Society was still an effective force for concord. Its paper promised that no one was to blame for Garibaldi's retirement; it had, La Farina explained to his friends, nothing political about it.[19]

Garibaldi nevertheless became, more than ever before, the symbol of a program which competed with Cavour's. At a time when the Government was hesitant and Rattazzi himself was splashing in intrigue, alternative programs quickly led to a battle for power. The Cavourian press insisted that Cavour be appointed Italy's delegate to the forthcoming international congress on Italian affairs. Cavour made his acceptance contingent upon the recall of parliament (where his supporters were still dominant). Everyone understood that along with all the grave questions facing Italy the political future of Cavour and of his policies was at stake. Brofferio began to mount an increasingly vituperative campaign against Cavour, and in its issue of December 25 the *Piccolo Corriere* replied by accusing a "minimal fraction" of the parliamentary left of making "civil war" in a time of crisis.

Four days later, Italy's favorite hero and the National Society's most popular member resigned its presidency. Garibaldi now saw the National Society as a supporter of the policies and a

[18] *Piccolo Corriere*, 22 November 1859. This version of events aroused Fanti's ire, but Farini insisted that it was for the good of Italy to tell the story that way: La Farina to Bardesono (includes Fanti's letter), 29 November, and Farini to La Farina, 5 December 1859, Franchi, *Epistolario di La Farina*, II, 243–45. On the depth of Garibaldi's discontent see *Scritti di Garibaldi*, II (Bologna, 1932), 401; Carlo di Nola, "Politica e guerra nel 1859–60," *Nuova Rivista Storica*, XLII (1958), 456.
[19] Proclamation of Bologna committee, SNI, 20 November 1859, in Posizione Simonetti, MCRB; *Piccolo Corriere*, 27 November 1859; La Farina to Bartolomeo, 23 November 1859, Franchi, *Epistolario di La Farina*, II, 239.

part of the group he openly opposed. He vigorously endorsed the society of the *Liberi Comizii*, a rival of the SNI established by Brofferio. The National Society had been seriously hurt. It was most severely tested in the Romagna. There, as elsewhere, the Society was for the most part directed by moderate men of the middle class for whom its restraint had a good deal of appeal. Yet its leaders there were keenly aware that they needed to keep the support they had won among the lower-middle class and among some artisans. Their genuine admiration of Garibaldi included a realistic response to their own political situation. With increasing self-consciousness, they distinguished between the "intelligent" and the *"popolo minuto,"* who came to nationalism with "more heart than understanding" and accepted unification from sentiment rather than analysis. Convinced that in politics most people "see with the mouths of others," they acknowledged Garibaldi's influence without accepting his position.[20]

La Farina was shocked by the signs of sympathy for Garibaldi within the SNI. He found himself fighting on several fronts. He argued that Garibaldi had been only an honorary president, but that was evidence more of past weakness than present strength. Now La Farina was elected president of the SNI. Noting that two great names had held that office before him, he accepted with public modesty, but there was fractiousness in his assertion that, whatever gifts he lacked, he had "tenacity." Within the Society, he insisted, nothing had really changed; Garibaldi's defection was the result of personal pique and bad counsel (though not from La Farina). It led him to become the spearhead of a conspiracy aimed not at La Farina but at Cavour, Farini, and Ricasoli. Indeed, in La Farina's mind, the issues soon

---

[20] Garibaldi's resignation from the SNI may also have been connected both with what Crispi told him of its Sicilian activity (Crispi, *I Mille*, 107 [La Farina blamed Rattazzi for this impression: letter to Cavour, 3 January 1860, Franchi, *Epistolario di La Farina*, II, 269]) and with his growing wish for a stronger man at the head of the Government: Garibaldi to Pallavicino, 21 December 1859, ms., MNRT. Carlo Pischedda, "L'Attività politica del Cavour dopo Villafranca," *Scritti vari della facoltà di Magistero di Torino*, II (1950), 25–39, presents an excellent discussion of the events of this period. The Romagna conference met in Faenza, January 5, with delegates from the Society's committees in Bologna, Imola, Cesena, Rimini, and Faenza: Galli, "Società Nazionale e Gamberini," *La Romagna*, XVI, 31–3. The analysis of Garibaldi's appeal to the lower classes is from Gamberini's tactful letter to La Farina, 10 January 1860, *ibid.*, 35, 182–84.

transcended personalities. He saw programs for confederation and separate kingdoms and efforts to prevent unification swirling among his opponents' charges. Once again Mazzinians and pro-Austrians seemed to be working together; Rattazzi's own ministry had better reverse itself or be lost. It was true that Brofferio's attacks raised important issues and that Garibaldi's support plus Rattazzi's encouragement added weight to those attacks. But La Farina presented these issues in a way which enlarged the divisions he described and deplored. It was dangerously intolerant to view as a *coup d'état* an attempt by Brofferio and Garibaldi to form another political society.

La Farina conceded them no chance of success. He repeatedly listed the achievements of the Society in its "six years" [sic] and everywhere found evidence of continued faith in its program. He heard the crowds of Turin, gathered to cheer for Garibaldi but yelling "viva Cavour," and felt that Rattazzi's ministry had lasted largely because of the Society's restraint.[21] Soon the *Liberi Comizii* did falter, and Garibaldi announced a new organization, the *Nazione Armata*. Its more openly military aims were too dangerous; within a week, at the King's request, Garibaldi had resigned from it as well. The siege was over. The varying ambitions of the King and Rattazzi were defeated, too. By the end of January Cavour was asked to form a government.

La Farina could not resist gloating. Garibaldi's reputation was lost, the ministry discredited. Even the General's warmest admirers were reminded of one of the great clichés of the Risorgimento: Garibaldi was not a man of politics.[22] But La Farina saw his triumph as more decisive than it was, more permanent than it could be, and as his own when it was largely Cavour's. If there

[21] La Farina to Selmi, 30 December 1859; to Morchio, 1 January; to Giuseppe Germani, 2 January; to Rossignoli, 2 January; to Mai, 5 January; to Selmi, 5 January; to Maurizio Ghisalberti, 5 January; to the president of a committee in the Romagna [Gamberini?], 13 January 1860, Franchi, *Epistolario di La Farina*, II, 263, 265–68, 271, 273, 282. La Farina to Gamberini, 7 January 1860, Galli, "Società Nazionale e Gamberini," *La Romagna*, XVI, 181–82. La Farina to the *Corriere Mercantile*, 2 January 1860, ms., MNRG. *Piccolo Corriere*, 25 December 1859 and 8 January 1860. La Farina's fear of Mazzini had some basis, note Mazzini to Cuneo, 6 January 1860, *Scritti di Mazzini*, LXVIII (Imola, 1934), 33.
[22] La Farina to [Gamberini?], 7 January; to Ghisalberti, 10 January; and to Braglia, 18 January 1860, Franchi, *Epistolario di La Farina*, II, 275–76, 278, 285. *Piccolo Corriere*, 8 January 1860. *Memorie di Pallavicino*, III, 557; Ghisalberti, 7 January, and Homodei, 10 January 1860, to La Farina, mss. in ISR, busta 716, ns. 73, 93.

was in the *Liberi Comizii* much of that imitation which is flattery, there was also a serious warning. Its hint of greater action reflected a promise the National Society had once made but not kept. Garibaldi's sincere hope that the *Nazione Armata* might conciliate all nationalists meant that the SNI did not.[23] The failure of Garibaldi's new organizations reflected some disillusionment with all such efforts; but when the chances of action looked better, the Society would meet with new competition.

Cavour had won a major battle against Brofferio, Rattazzi, and Garibaldi; the Society had been his firm ally. La Farina wrote Cavour about the intrigues of their common enemies with less deference, and Cavour recognized La Farina's value in politics more certainly than in the summer before.[24] Their triumph owed much to the division and the excesses of their enemies, to a general dissatisfaction with Rattazzi and with royal meddling. In power, Cavour had new reason to wish to work within parliament and to distrust extraparliamentary political institutions. Nevertheless, the Society, though more dependent on Cavour than ever before, shared the prestige of his victory. It remained the one political organization which extended throughout the new kingdom and into the rest of the Peninsula.

Once again that organization was spreading. Indeed, it showed signs of becoming more extensive in the north than it had been before; no longer dangerous, membership in the SNI might even prove advantageous. In the important cities its leaders were mainly the men who had previously led it. They returned to their tasks from a sense of duty and with the comfort of having done them before. Some found in the Society a political purpose and a personal importance they were anxious to regain. Some showed an attitude that would haunt Italian history in their wish to

[23] Ida Nazari-Michele, *Cavour e Garibaldi* (Rome, 1911), 58–9; Pischedda, "L'Attività politica del Cavour," *Scritti vari*, 26n; Garibaldi to Malenchini, 9 January 1860, Puccioni, *Malenchini*, 117; *Scritti di Garibaldi*, II, 402–403.
[24] Cavour to La Farina, 2 January 1860, Chiala, *Lettere di Cavour*, III, 159–60 (dated as in *ibid.*, VI, 524n); La Farina did efficiently publicize the comments of the British press on Cavour's appointment as the Count requested: La Farina to the *Corriere Mercantile*, 2 January 1860, ms. in Carte Morchio, MNRG; *Piccolo Corriere*, 8 January 1860. Massari, *Diario*, entries of 29 and 31 December 1859 and 1 January 1860, 609, 612, 614. La Farina to Cavour, 3 January 1860, Franchi, *Epistolario di La Farina*, II, 269. Cavour to Farini, 2 and 3 January, and Farini to Cavour, 3 and 14 January 1860, *Liberazione del Mezzogiorno*, V, 441–48. Cavour to Boncompagni, 11 January 1860, Manzone, "Cavour e Boncompagni," *Risorgimento Italiano*, II, 231.

recapture the emotions which had once bound patriots together.[25] Strikingly, in a Society so dedicated to opposing federalism, its own organization displayed an increasingly federal character. The social composition of the Society, like its social function, remained essentially what it had been before: it served as a link between the liberal gentry who now wielded power and a middle class of merchants and professional men. The peasants, most of the artisans, and many of the nobles remained outside Italian politics; and those who are silent, whether from apathy or caution, are easily overlooked. The Society soon again counted among its members a significant portion of those who constituted Italian political opinion. It had never succeeded very well among those whose status was secure, among the more austere nobles or men of independent political power. But just below the Ricasolis, Minghettis, and Rattazzis, it was strong. Most of its leaders bore the label of their class: *conte, cavaliere, professore, dottore, ingegnere, avvocato.* Many artisans contributed to the Society, supported its subscriptions and served as its volunteers; but rarely did one sit high on a local committee. The very structure of the Society's bureaucracy tended to be symbolic, in the pattern of the relationship Pallavicino and La Farina had once had. A committee's president was frequently a local noble of note if not pre-eminence, but the work was usually performed by its secretary who would be a young man of the middle class.[26]

In Italy after 1860 membership in the Society increasingly served a social function. Its most enthusiastic members were the lower nobles and the younger professional men who would otherwise have had only a peripheral part in the restricted arena of Italian politics. The National Society allowed many a man who might otherwise have felt left out to see himself as part of Italy's destiny. Now, the Society offered a chance to participate in the "real" politics of power, and it was winning a new group of men. More clearly than before, the Society's rank and file included few who had been active in 1848. To an extraordinary

---

[25] In 1882 Ferrari could ask a favor of a friend by invoking their old relationship in the SNI, Ferrari, *Ferrari*, 150.
[26] In Geneva Marchese Bossi was president, Costantino Reta, a journalist, secretary. The same relative positions were held by Marchese Doria Pamphili and avv. Daniele Morchio in Genoa, Marchese Bartolommei and avv. Piero Puccioni in Florence, Principe Simonetti and avv. Camillo Casarini in Bologna.

degree and throughout Italy, however, its leaders, even in the 1860's, were still the men who had known each other in natural social intercourse and in exile in Tuscany, Piedmont, or Paris. The Society's members on the local level showed a more specific commitment to Cavourian policies. They showed, too, an increased class consciousness, marked by dislike of the upper nobility, discomfort with the artisans, and positive fear of the peasantry. It was this fear which supported their anticlericalism —a practical suspicion of those who were most influential among the peasants. The men of the reorganized SNI displayed more clearly than before the attitudes associated with professional classes. They gave the Society a tone still further removed from Mazzini's as they responded to programs of limited goals to be arrived at through practical means, as they accepted their own limited roles with a bureaucrat's caution and fondness of order, seeing themselves as part of the general triumph of liberalism in Europe.[27]

These subtle changes in the nature of the Society were reflected in its organization. The first issue of the *Piccolo Corriere* had declared simply that the Society was re-established. Accompanied by tales of the SNI's past successes, the announcement implied that nothing more than an order from Turin was needed to revive its vigor. La Farina knew better, and he made some changes. Dues were increased by establishing two categories of membership. *Soci ordinari* were to pay a 5 lire admission fee and one lira a month, but *soci promotori* would pay 20 lire on admission and 5 lire a month, which entitled them to as many copies of the Society's publications as they might want. Furthermore, municipal committees would be subordinate to provincial committees, which would in turn correspond directly with the Central Committee in Turin and send on the dues collected from the entire province.

The *Piccolo Corriere* soon reported even greater success than had been expected, and the flow of money was stimulated by associating the SNI with Garibaldi's rifle fund. When La Farina became president, Carlo Buscalioni stepped up to the secretary's

---

[27] There are striking parallels here with the classes who supported liberalism in Russia, as analyzed by George Fischer in the first two chapters of his *Russian Liberalism, from Gentry to Intelligentsia* (Cambridge, 1958).

post; and his brother, Ermanno, replaced him as treasurer. Vegezzi-Ruscalla, an able linguist with important connections in Turinese academic and political circles, served as secretary for foreign affairs. Soon the National Society opened a new office in downtown Turin; and in January the directors of the Society began meeting there every Sunday.[28] Organizationally, the SNI had never been so impressive.

Reality was less neat than the Society's instructions. Some provinces did not have provincial committees, and the repeated exhortations for all committees to send in their dues and the names of their members contained a hint of frustration. In January a new rank was created, the commissioner. Appointed from Turin to form a committee in a specified area, the commissioner was an admission that in many areas the Society was still not organized. And many a commissioner, of course, did not fulfill his mission; in later years the title would become simply a more attractive way of winning single members. From the first, the creation of commissioners had the ambitions of a chain letter; the very form appointing a commissioner for one area asked that he recommend commissioners for neighboring *paese*. Some did their job, and many committees began to meet again. A fourth edition of the Society's *Credo* was used up and a fifth, of 8,000 copies, announced in February. Few documents in nineteenth-century Italian history can have had wider circulation. Local committees were encouraged to find a local newspaper which would propagate their principles and to distribute the Society's literature in reading rooms and cafés; the *Piccolo Corriere* was again going strong.[29]

As before, then, the Society was successful in distributing its propaganda; but its real success in 1860 would depend more than before on the size and quality of its committees. The concession in April that where "absolutely necessary" commissioners might

---

[28] *Piccolo Corriere*, 8, 15, and 29 November 1859; 8 and 29 January 1860. The latter issue announced the receipt of 718 lire for Garibaldi's fund; La Farina to Ottavio Mazzi, 23 November 1859, Franchi, *Epistolario di La Farina*, ɪɪ, 238. The office at Galleria Natta, No. 2, was open from 8 a.m. to noon. Vegezzi-Ruscalla was the brother-in-law of Costantino Nigra. Ermanno Buscalioni had been treasurer before (see Chapter Three, note 70) but Carlo Michele Buscalioni had held the post since the Society's re-founding.

[29] *Piccolo Corriere*, 11 and 25 December 1859, 29 January and 5 February 1860. The forms appointing commissioners varied from time to time. Copies can be found in ISR, busta 721, n. 87, and in the Buscalioni pamphlets in HCL.

"modify" dues implied some difficulties, but the order creating district committees for each *circondario* (they would stand between municipal and provincial committees) made the Society's organization pretentiously parallel on paper to that of the Government itself.[30] What the Italian National Society was province by province would largely determine its role in the enlarged Italian state.

In Piedmont proper the Society remained relatively weak. This may have reflected La Farina's conviction that the lesson the SNI taught had, in Piedmont, already been learned. By March at least a dozen commissioners had been appointed. The resistance they met, however, was not so different from that in other provinces. As the commissioner of Murazzano explained, in "this *paese* ignorance and superstition still reign." He looked for success among "cultivated persons" for the others simply laughed or showed horror at talk of unification.[31] La Farina himself claimed committees only in Sarzana and Pietrasante, although by May a committee in Lerici was also active. Of them all, the Sarzana committee under Ottavio Mazzi was the most enthusiastic, sending in some dues left over from 1859 and once again proselytizing in Fivizzano.[32]

In Genoa Daniele Morchio, who had been active in the SNI before the war, was prevailed upon to work toward a new committee while La Farina spurred him on with accounts of the Society's growth elsewhere. But adherents other than the loyal Marchese Doria Pamphili proved difficult to win. La Farina suggested some nine men he knew, but only three of them joined; and one soon departed over some clash of personalities.[33] Worse, a competing society of similar views seemed to prosper, but the

[30] *Piccolo Corriere*, 1 April and 29 January 1860.

[31] Letter of Luigi Drocchi, 29 February 1860, ms., ISR, busta 719, n. 1; by August six persons had joined the SNI. Two commissioners were appointed to the Alessandria region, *ibid.*, busta 720. Commissioners were also announced for Saluzzo, Cive, Novara, Bussolino, Mondane, Nizza Marittima, Carmagnola, and Ovada, *Piccolo Corriere*, 19 February 1860.

[32] La Farina to Fenzi, 28 January 1860, Puccioni, *Malenchini*, 114. Pietro Possi, Lerici, n.d., ms., ISR, busta 718, n. 5. Mazzi to La Farina, 7 March 1860, ms., *ibid.*, busta 717, n. 48. La Farina to Mazzi, 1 November 1859, Franchi, *Epistolario di La Farina*, II, 228.

[33] Morchio to Doria Pamphili, 11 November 1859, ms. in Carte Morchio, MNRG. La Farina to Morchio, 21 November 1859, Franchi, *Epistolario di La Farina*, II, 234–35; the names, omitted in the printed text, are in the ms. in

SNI in Genoa resisted the fusion of the two societies which La Farina apparently hoped for.[34] When Garibaldi announced support of the *Liberi Comizii*, La Farina rushed long explanations to his Genoese followers obviously fearing they would not stay in line.[35] They did, though, and by the end of the year the nucleus of a committee was formed. Even before then, the committee in Genoa had with optimistic self-importance printed its own stationery. It issued some circulars and later was important in the formation of an election committee. Morchio proudly reported that this new committee consisted of the "most respectable" citizens from the patriciate, the propertied, the liberal professions, and commerce.[36] La Farina did not need to worry about the political color of the National Society in Genoa.

The organization of the National Society in Lombardy centered on personal acquaintances of La Farina. There was a somewhat haphazard air about the spread of the Society there, and La Farina's frequent statement that the SNI in Lombardy showed few ill-effects from his break with Garibaldi was a bit misleading. When a man in Bobbio asked La Farina's support in getting a government job, La Farina replied with a promise of help and a plea that the applicant establish a committee of the

---

Carte Morchio, MNRG. Cabella, one of those named, later broke with the committee and was not won back despite La Farina's efforts: La Farina to Morchio and Cabella, 5 February 1860, Franchi, *Epistolario di La Farina*, II, 291–92. Morchio's difficulties were such that he offered to resign, letter of 13 February 1860, ms., ISR, busta 717, n. 35.

[34] The founder of the *Nazione* society claimed it had 73 members: letter of Virgilio, 19 February 1860, ms. in ISR, busta 718, n. 90. He hinted at a possible fusion later but La Farina had earlier tried hard to have Virgilio made secretary of the Genoa committee: La Farina to Morchio, 21 November 1859; the printed text refers to "l'avv. V." but the full name is in the ms., see note 33 above. La Farina took up the matter again in a postscript of his letter to Morchio of 1 January 1860, omitted in Franchi, *Epistolario di La Farina*, II, 266, but in ms., Carte Morchio, MNRG. La Farina to Giuseppe Vergara, 18 February 1860, suggests he was giving up on Virgilio, Franchi, *Epistolario di La Farina*, II, 297.

[35] La Farina to Morchio, 1 January 1860, *ibid.*, 264–66. He also wrote the editor of the *Corriere Mercantile* on the same day giving his account of sentiment in Turin, ms. in Carte Morchio, MNRG. Buscalioni nevertheless dunned the committee for its dues: letter of 24 February 1860, apparently a form letter, ms., *ibid.* The penned corrections on the form suggest that the Genoa committee had already halved its dues.

[36] The *Piccolo Corriere* announced the formation of the Genoa committee in its 19 December 1859 issue, after a trip of Morchio's to Turin. The announcements of the Genoa committee are in Carte Morchio, MNRG. Morchio to La Farina, 27 December 1859, ms. in ISR, busta 719, n. 18.

SNI. When in December Garibaldi had visited a friend in Como, La Farina suggested that the General recruit his host for the Society. Around Pavia some old friends could report on local conditions, but the effort to find a sufficiently "influential" figure to head a committee apparently failed. Still, La Farina had a genius for making the most of a little; the death of a member of the Society in Pavia led the *Piccolo Corriere* to carry a flattering obituary which implied great organizational strength.[37]

Much energy was devoted to establishing and supporting a committee in Milan; the results were disappointing. La Farina remembered that men of power there had once derided the SNI, and his efforts to win the important Belgioioso family to the Society failed. As early as November some dues were sent from Milan, but the committee formed there was hurt by serious dissensions between two of its most important members. The political atmosphere was never very friendly. The *Pugnolo* accused the National Society, with effective vigor, of showing no concern for liberty; the competing *Società Unitaria*, which La Farina thought was associated with the *Liberi Comizii*, clearly frightened him even when he insisted that it was no threat.[38] In Milan, as elsewhere, the elections gave the Society new vigor; its committee promoted a special election journal, and several hundred copies of the *Piccolo Corriere* were distributed. Pietro Castiglione, who became president of the committee, wrote a carefully reasoned book which, in two volumes, repeated general arguments for liberty while developing a legal rationale for all the restrictions on freedom Cavour had employed. Something

[37] La Farina to avv. Carlo Francioni, 25 December 1859, to ing. Mai, 5 January 1860, and to dott. Cesare Tamagni, 10 April 1860, Franchi, *Epistolario di La Farina*, II, 261, 270–71, 312. La Farina to Garibaldi, 12 December 1859, ms. in ISR, busta 45, n. 93. [Homodei] to La Farina, 9 December 1859, ms., *ibid.*, busta 719, n. 18. *Piccolo Corriere*, 22 April 1860.

[38] La Farina to Ausonio Franchi, 26 August, 24 September, n.d. October, 20 December; to Felice Tacchini, 7 October and 11 November; to Gaspare Stampa, 10 November 1859; to Morchio, 12 December; and to Teresa Bartolommei, 16 December 1859, Franchi, *Epistolario di La Farina*, II, 205, 211–12, 220–21, 225, 257, 229–31, 253, 254. The debate with *Il Pugnolo* can be traced in *ibid.*, 581–85, and the *Piccolo Corriere*, 11 and 18 December 1859. Vittorio Ricci to Festi, 11 November 1859, ms. in ISR, busta 718, n. 21. [Homodei] to La Farina, 9 December 1859, ms., *ibid.*, busta 719, n. 18; Giulio Porro and Achille Pagano were the members who had a falling out. Homodei to Buscalioni, 6 December 1859, ms., *ibid.* When the Bologna committee attempted to contact the Society's committee in Milan, none, apparently, could be found, L. Gualtiori to Casarini, 7 January 1860, ms. in MCRB.

went wrong, however; and in April the *Piccolo Corriere* announced that the "Provisional Committee" of Milan was dissolved. In Milan the National Society became again a few personal friends of the Society's president.[39]

In the rest of Lombardy, despite La Farina's lists of towns where committees were thriving, the National Society's position was equally uncertain.[40] One hamlet decided not to subscribe to the *Piccolo Corriere* with communal funds; individuals far off in Legnano, or in Gallerate, or Luino occasionally wrote the Society of their enthusiasm, sending money, a patriotic song, or reports on local conditions. There were committees in Busto Arsizio and Lodi, but the one in Como was apparently never formed. Each letter attempted to justify the lack of greater success and in doing so painted a picture of a few patriotic individuals who felt their voices lost amid apathy and the burden of local problems. There were a number of commissioners scattered here and there, but they tended, like the one in Lugano, Switzerland, to complain of local ignorance. (He could only suggest that enthusiasm for annexation to Italy might be strengthened by greater purchases of the tobacco produced in his canton.) [41]

The Society was stronger in towns along a border, where national and international politics had long been intermixed with local affairs. In Lombardy, it was fairly active in Cremona, in Bergamo and Brescia, next to the promise of Venetia. Establishing committees still proved difficult. Though instructed to find some leader "illustrious for social position," La Farina's friends in Cremona were not yet a committee in December. An election committee was founded more easily, and La Farina was reduced to suggesting they declare it to be "of the National Society." The

[39] *Piccolo Corriere*, 11 December 1859, 8 January, 26 February, and 1 April 1860. Vittorio Ricci to Festi, 1 February 1860, ms. in ISR, busta 718, n. 21. La Farina to Tacchini, 4 April 1860, Franchi, *Epistolario di La Farina*, II, 308.

[40] La Farina to Selmi, 5 January 1860, *ibid.*, 273; to Fenzi, 28 January 1860, Puccioni, *Malenchini*, 114.

[41] Letter of the Delegato Communale of Guinzano, 30 January 1860, ms. in ISR, busta 720, n. 4. Luigi Kroni, Legnano, to Buscalioni, n.d. and 12 February 1860, ms., *ibid.* Domenico Guzzi to Ermanno Bangozzi, 30 January 1860, ms., *ibid.*, busta 719, n. 1. Letter of Vita Missaglia, Gallerate, n.d., ms. *ibid.*, busta 717, n. 57. Letter of Federico Bineghi, February and 14 April 1860, mss., *ibid.*, busta 715, ns. 43, 44. *Piccolo Corriere*, 14 February 1860. La Farina to Ghisalberti, 2 August, 7 November 1859; 10 January, 5 February, 18 March 1860, Franchi, *Epistolario di La Farina*, II, 197, 228–29, 271–73, 278–79, 293, 302.

Cremona committee seemed safely in hand when La Farina was stunned to learn it might consider Cattaneo as its candidate for deputy. His strictures on "ultraliberalism" must have been effective; Giuseppe La Farina became their nominee.[42]

In Bergamo the Society had some loyal followers; Homodei, La Farina's friend who had done much in Pavia, now worked hard there. Once again, a suitable president was difficult to find. Hopes focused on a local count, who apparently refused; and then on the *sindaco* himself until he showed too much interest in Garibaldi's petition against the cession of Nice and Savoy. Others continued to pay their dues, sometimes with uncertain knowledge of their Society's precise title. Some commissioners sent in reports. In April a committee was at last formed, and Turin was asked to send copies of the *Credo* (they, too, were troubled by *"retrogradi"* and republicans as well as by rumors that Louis Napoleon intended to split all northern Italy with Austria).[43] If Brescia had no very active committee in this period, some individuals were anxious to be of service, including the editor of the widely read newspaper, the *Sentinella*.[44] For all its weaknesses, the Italian National Society was stronger in Lombardy than it had ever been before.

Tuscany always presented a special problem for La Farina. He had lived there, and he spent some time there again after Villafranca; but he viewed Boncompagni as hostile and Tuscan politics as unfortunate. By December he labeled Tuscany the only area not to understand the SNI's importance, an epithet which came in print to be that Tuscany in the recent past had contributed nothing to the cause of unification.[45] Provided with

[42] La Farina to Giuseppe Germani, 28 October, 5 and 15 December 1859; 2 and 16 January, 24 February 1860, *ibid.*, 221, 250–51, 255–56, 266–67, 284, 297–98. Letter of Nicolo Estran, commissioner in Bonemerse, 12 April 1860, ms. in ISR, busta 720, n. 5.

[43] Mario Piacezzi to Buscalioni, 5 December 1859, and Homodei to La Farina, 9 December 1859, mss. in ISR, busta 719, n. 18; Giovanni Copelli to Buscalioni, 14 January 1860, ms., *ibid.*, busta 720, n. 4. Homodei to Buscalioni, 10 January and 11 April 1860; and to Festi, 18 April 1860, mss., *ibid.*, busta 716, ns. 93, 95. *Piccolo Corriere*, 19 February 1860.

[44] *Ibid.* Fossati to Buscalioni, 26 October 1859, ms. in ISR, busta 719, n. 17. Nicolo Gualstalla to Festi, n.d., ms., *ibid.*, busta 548, n. 45. Luigi Botterelli to Festi, 1 February 1860, *ibid.*, busta 715, n. 55.

[45] La Farina to Giusti, 26 July 1859; and to Gallina, 4 December 1859, Franchi, *Epistolario di La Farina*, II, 246. *Piccolo Corriere*, 18 December 1859.

a list of those to whom the *Piccolo Corriere* should be sent, a follower in Pisa appears to have dutifully distributed it in cafés. After three months, no committee had been formed. The Society's man could refer only to municipal spirit and priestly influences in the countryside; he hoped they might do better in Siena. Leghorn, with the vigorous political traditions of a seaport city, had had an active committee before the war; but by December, the close friend upon whom La Farina relied could point to no success in re-establishing it.[46]

Thus there was a hint of desperation when La Farina wrote directly to Ricasoli, making the case for the National Society. He presented it as a force for unity between Piedmont and provinces, upper and lower classes. He stressed the part it had played in the other liberated provinces and described it none too subtly as the great bulwark against efforts of the left to attack just such men as Ricasoli. That, he urged, was the meaning of his break with Garibaldi. More sympathetic to the redshirts than any prominent moderate, Baron Ricasoli had received other assessments of the SNI; but his reply at least enabled La Farina to combat rumors that Tuscany's great leader opposed the National Society.[47] La Farina also turned to Marchesa Teresa Bartolommei, the wife of the most prominent Tuscan in the Society before the war. With cautious statements of the Society's intent and bold outlines of Italy's needs, he won her interest and through her that of Fenzi, the banker. She used her influence well. In February the establishment of a Florentine committee was announced, with full pomp, in the *Piccolo Corriere*; the Marchesa's husband was its president. The prominent men who joined that committee may, as one of them suggested, have been skeptical of its value, but by the end of the month they had issued a manifesto repeating La Farina's arguments. They expressed, in addition, the wish not to embarrass those then directing Tuscan affairs, but they called for the formation of local

<hr/>

[46] La Farina to Rizzari, 21 and 30 November 1859, Franchi, *Epistolario di La Farina*, II, 234, 244; Rizzari to [Buscalioni?], 26 February 1860, ms. in ISR, busta 718, n. 45. La Farina to Gallina, 17 January 1860, Franchi, *Epistolario di La Farina*, II, 285.

[47] *Ibid.*; La Farina to Ricasoli, 1 and 12 January 1860, Marco Tabarrini and Aurelio Gotti, *Lettere e documenti del Barone Bettino Ricasoli* (Florence, 1888), IV, 133, 157. Gualterio to Ricasoli, Puccioni, *Ricasoli*, 152-53.

committees of influential men in every town.[48] The National Society was launched in Tuscany.

In Leghorn the Society was gradually winning back its former members. Throughout the spring they claimed confusion as to whether dues should be sent to Turin or to Florence, complained that some of their members wanted only personal friends in the Society, or noted simply that Malenchini was out of town. If a committee had not been formed, the men involved had increasingly become those of real political influence. Requests for the *Piccolo Corriere* and for copies of the *Credo* doubled from February to May, at which time fifty copies were not enough. Elsewhere in Tuscany the Society was still feeble; there was a commissioner near Arezzo, an effort to organize in Siena.[49] In general terms La Farina was not wrong to worry about the shallow support the SNI received in Tuscany, but the basis for further organization had been established. The political importance of its members there made its influence potentially as great as anywhere in Italy.

The Society had been most active before the war in the Duchies, and its re-establishment was well received there at a time when the political fate of those provinces was still uncertain. In the Lunigiana in particular, committees of the SNI tended, throughout the Society's history, to be larger than elsewhere. By March there were over a dozen members in Fivizzano and signs of activity in Pontremoli. In the nearby commune of Bagnone a zealous supporter ordered two copies of the *Piccolo Corriere* for each of the town's 22 parishes. If he came to dis-

[48] La Farina to Marchesa Bartolommei, 5 December 1859, ms. in MRF, 105/2; 16 December, 28 January, and 9 February 1860, Franchi, *Epistolario di La Farina*, II, 254, 286, 295. La Farina to Fenzi, 28 January 1860, Puccioni, *Malenchini*, 114. Emilio Cipriani to Stefano Siccoli, 24 February 1860, ms. in ISR, busta 382, n. 10. The *Piccolo Corriere*, 12 February 1860, listed the members of the Florentine committee, in addition to Bartolommei, as Piero Puccioni, secretary, Carlo Fenzi, Tommaso Corsi, Giacomo Cheleschi, and Tito Menichetti. The Manifesto, dated February 27, copies of which are in the Buscalioni papers in HCL and in the Biblioteca Nazionale in Florence, was signed by these men and also by Cipriani and d'Ancona. The covering letter, dated February 28, is in the Biblioteca Nazionale.

[49] Michele Morteo to Buscalioni, 16 and 23 February, 2 March, 11 April, 20 April, 9 May 1860, mss. in ISR, busta 717, n. 70; Omero [Mengozzi] to Puccioni, 4 March 1860, ms. in the papers of the Puccioni family. Letters of M. Redditi, commissioner in Foiano, 17 January 1860, and Eugenio Pelosi (Siena), 12 May 1860, mss. in ISR, busta 718, n. 16, and busta 717, n. 104. Cf. the views of Della Torre, *Sentimento nazionale in Toscana*, 472, and Puccioni, *Ricasoli*, 247.

trust the aristocracy and to believe that most of the *canaglia* opposed Italy's *risorgimento*, he did not lose faith in the effectiveness of the "evangelical words" in the Society's newspaper. He found lively support among the national guard, named a number of commissioners (including one friendly with both Bourbons and liberals), won the assistance of the *sindaco*, as well as some "honorary members" among the bureaucracy.[50] In Massa and Carrara the former leaders of the Society led in its re-establishment. With La Farina's skillful prodding, commissioners grew in number; contacts were made with men of political influence; personal antipathies were overcome, and many national guardsmen were recruited to membership.[51]

As elsewhere, the National Society in the Duchies fared better in the smaller cities and towns than in the great centers. Establishing active committees in Parma and Modena proved difficult. La Farina traveled through the area a number of times in the fall of 1859; he had many personal friends there, and his relations with Farini, who wielded vast power, were excellent. Still, no committee was established in Parma; the Society's great fiasco there in 1859 was not forgotten. In the smaller surrounding towns the SNI did better. Requests for membership came from Guastalla and plans to form a committee came (along with a tract for the conversion of others) from Luzzara; there were some commissioners in Piacenza, and the commissioner in Sissa established a committee which quickly took to issuing long manifestoes.[52]

Despite great claims for the National Society in Modena, La Farina was complaining by the end of 1859 that a committee

[50] Mazzi to La Farina, 7 March 1860, ms. in ISR, busta 717, n. 48. Pietro Zani to Buscalioni, 1 December 1859, 29 January 1860, ms., *ibid.*, busta 720, n. 4. Antonio Bondenari, 28 February 1860, and the *sindaco* to La Farina, 27 February, mss., *ibid.* Zani to Buscalioni, 1 March 1860, ms., *ibid.*, busta 718, n. 95.

[51] Cesare Romoli, a deputy to the Modenese assembly was among those named commissioner; and the communal magistrate of Carrara testified to the Society's importance: fragments, dated 23 November 1859, 4 and 26 March 1860, mss., *ibid.*, busta 720, ns. 4, 5. La Farina to Giuseppe Toretti, 25 December 1859, Franchi, *Epistolario di La Farina*, II, 260.

[52] La Farina to Manfredi, 30 August; to Giusti, 1 October; to Franchi, 23 November; to Selmi, 21 December 1859, *ibid.*, 206, 215, 236, 259. Farini to La Farina, 2 January 1860, *ibid.*, 267. Fabbrio Papazzoni, 12 November and D. Roccalari and Ubaldo Bonanomi, 14 December 1859, to Buscalioni, mss. in ISR, busta 719, n. 18. Gaetano Lasardi to Buscalioni, 5 September 1860, mss., *ibid.*, busta 719, n. 5. Some Sissa manifestoes are in the Buscalioni pamphlets, HCL. The committee was announced in the *Piccolo Corriere*, 19 February 1860.

243

had still not been formed there. "Oh, would God," he moaned, "that all Italy were Piedmont." He wrote his friends, Selmi in particular, over and over; he proposed others who might help. His Modenese friends could not be shamed into action. He warned that other and wilder men would do what they had not. He promised to let a Modena committee keep one-third of its dues. Fear of a plebiscite by universal suffrage may have been the most effective spur. By the end of January Modena had a committee; by March it, too, had printed a manifesto.[53] Reggio showed similar inertia in establishing a committee, but the smaller towns were enthusiastic. With the help of Modena's committee, one was organized in Concordia which quickly grew to some 30 members. Scandiano set up a committee with little apparent difficulty. In such places the SNI became part of the politics of the town itself.[54]

In encouraging a rebirth of the SNI in the Romagna, La Farina had consulted Minghetti and invoked the prestige of Cavour and Rattazzi, while showing his usual preference for dealing with personal friends. His friends, however, were not the men who had dominated the Society in the past. And it was around its former leaders that the SNI in the Romagna re-formed. Prince Rinaldo Simonetti became the president and Camillo Casarini once again the secretary of the important Bologna committee.[55] As, one by one, committees were formed in other

[53] La Farina to Morchio, 21 November; and to Giusti, 5 December 1859, Franchi, *Epistolario di La Farina*, II, 235, 248. La Farina to Selmi, 4 August, 5, 21, and 30 December 1859, 5 and 30 January 1860, *ibid.*, 200, 248–50, 258–59, 263, 273–74, 287–88. La Farina to Zini, 6 March 1860, *ibid.*, 300. Copies of the manifesto, dated 3 March 1860 and signed by prof. Antonio Baschieri, president, ing. Luigi Galli, secretary, are in the Museo del Risorgimento in Milan and the Buscalioni pamphlets in HCL.

[54] Paolo Ottani became the SNI's commissioner in Reggio as the result of merely suggesting that his newspaper exchange with the *Piccolo Corriere*: letters to Buscalioni, 24 November 1859, and 13 February 1860, mss. in ISR, buste 719 and 717, n. 56. A list of the Concordia committee in March 1860, ms., *ibid.*, busta 720; an unidentified newspaper clipping tells of Modena's help, in H. N. Gay newspaper clippings, 1886–1927, in HCL (dott. Ercole Murator, pres., dott. Leonardo Gatti, sec't'y). La Farina to Braglia, 7 November and 5 December 1859, Franchi, *Epistolario di La Farina*, II, 228, 247.

[55] Biundi, *La Farina*, I, 425. La Farina to Giusti, 26 and 27 July 1859, Franchi, *Epistolario di La Farina*, II, 192–93; to Canevazzi, 28 October 1859, *ibid.*, 237; to Braglia, 5 December 1859, *ibid.*, 247; to Terasona, 11 December 1859, *ibid.*, 251. In November he claimed over 8,000 members in the Romagna: letter to Mazzi, 23 November 1859, *ibid.*, 238. La Farina hoped to work through Canevazzi in Bologna, who seems in fact to have served briefly as the committee's

Romagna towns, they corresponded for the most part directly with the one in Bologna rather than with Turin.[56] The organization of the SNI in the Romagna maintained a quasi-autonomous cast.

The first important act of the new Bologna committee was its statement, issued when Garibaldi resigned from the army, that King and General were in full accord. The subsequent news of Garibaldi's resignation from the SNI reached the Romagna just as other committees were being established. It immediately caused a crisis. On January 5 delegates from five Romagna committees met in Faenza to consider what should be done. The programs of the SNI and Garibaldi's *Nazione Armata* were read and, with an amazing lack of commitment, voted on. The National Society's program won unanimously, but it was decided to appoint a committee of four who, in consultation with the SNI in other areas, were to seek means of again making Garibaldi its president. To the patriots of the Romagna, the difficulties of simultaneously following Cavour and Garibaldi would not be apparent for months. If they understood little of the organization to which they belonged, it was important to them to belong to one that was nation-wide. Soon, the news that Garibaldi had disbanded his new society was telegraphed with obvious relief from committee to committee. The Conference in Faenza had speeded the effective regional organization of the National Society.[57]

---

secretary before being replaced by Casarini who had done the job before. Lollini, Giuzzardi, both businessmen, and Marchi were also in the committee, Dallolio, *La spedizione*, 13ff.

[56] When men in Ravenna considered establishing a committee there, they wrote Casarini (who contacted Rasponi, the former leader of the SNI there): Giacomo Camporesi and Augusto Brancanti to Casarini, 10 December 1859, ms. in Carteggio Casarini, MCRB. Buscalioni even communicated to local committees through Casarini: Buscalioni to Casarini, 19 December 1859, ms., *ibid.*, and La Farina expected it to deal with Ferrara, Ravenna, and Forlì, letter to Canevazzi, 25 November 1859, Franchi, *Epistolario di La Farina*, II, 241.

[57] The committees of Bologna, Imola, Cesena, Rimini, and Faenza were represented. They hoped to make contact with committees in Florence, Modena, Parma and Reggio. This whole episode is reported in Galli, "Società Nazionale e Gamberini," *La Romagna*, XVII, 32. The minutes of the meeting are in Carteggio Casarini, MCRB; they indicate that Casarini, Gamberini, Costantino Turci, Alessando Niccolini, and Ballelli cast the votes for their respective committees. Giovanni Galeati, of Imola, Laderchi and seven others of the Faenza committee attended. Ballelli wired Bologna about Garibaldi's latest resignation on 7 January 1860; he had been wired from Modena; Paselli wrote from Rimini about

When such solicitude for Garibaldi was reported to La Farina, he was indignant. He accused the Bologna committee, somewhat obtusely, of inactivity; and he threatened to replace its members with others who would be more active. But Casarini was both skillful and contrite. He apologized for what La Farina called his "long and obstinate silence" and suggested that the Bologna committee would indeed like to hear more often from the Society's directors in Turin. La Farina's explanations of the conflict with Garibaldi were not necessary after all. Calling itself the central committee of the SNI in the Romagna, the Bologna committee sent a circular to all local committees explaining that the General had retired from politics to prepare for action and warning against the activities of agents from competing societies. Canevazzi's dark reports to La Farina had served only to make the Society in the Romagna stronger while it stayed in other hands. La Farina made his peace and promised to send 300 copies of the *Piccolo Corriere*.[58]

The Bologna committee set about broadening its influence. Recognizing that the SNI had no roots among the "popular element," the Society's leaders in Bologna proposed a new plan of organization. Its elaborateness bespoke their optimism—and their fear. Those whom the people trusted were to be elected *capi stradi*; they in turn would elect *capi quartieri*, the "best of whom" would be invited to take part in the committee's discussions of matters having to do with the lower classes. Thus official policies could be explained to the lower classes in their own terms and popular grievances could be safely heard by men of influence. But the system could not succeed because it had

it the next day, mss. in MCRB. New committees in Ferrara and Lugo were very upset at not having been invited to the Faenza meeting, apparently because the others did not know of their existence, Gaetano Forlani, Ferrara, 15 January; Rasponi, Ravenna, 20 January; and Gamberini, Imola, 21 January 1860, to Casarini, mss., *ibid.*

[58] La Farina to Canevazzi, 25 December 1859 and 13 January 1860, Franchi, *Epistolario di La Farina*, II, 261–62, 280–81. Farini to La Farina, 2 January 1860, *ibid.*, 267. La Farina to [Gamberini], 7 and 13 January 1860, *ibid.*, 275–76, 281–82. Cf. Galli, "Società Nazionale e Gamberini," *La Romagna*, XVII, 181–84. La Farina to Casarini, 28 January 1860, ms. in Carteggio Casarini, MCRB; and Casarini to La Farina, 30 January 1860, ms. in ISR, busta 546, n. 35. The promise to send so many papers may not have been kept immediately; Buscalioni repeated it to Simonetti, 7 March 1860, ms. in Posizione Simonetti, MCRB. The Bologna circular, n.d., on printed stationery is in Carteggio Casarini, *ibid.*

no purpose beyond communication. The National Society did not distribute the patronage of an American political machine; it could not allow the revolutionary plans of Jacobins or Mazzinians. The Bologna committee showed prescient understanding of the dangers in Italy's social cleavages and the unconscious arrogance which maintained them. More comfortable with traditional expressions of social obligations, the committee also provided legal aid to some of the poor and took part in establishing a special charity fund for workers.[59]

With similar intent, the Bologna committee hoped to have at least one man in each parish throughout the countryside distribute literature written especially to explain the national movement to peasants. A prime function of this parish propagandist would be to assure his neighbors that the movement in no way impinged on religion. By defining the priest's legitimate influence, he would help them understand that priests should remain apart from politics. There was even talk of printing a biweekly newspaper (to be called *All' Eco del Piccolo Corriere d'Italia*) to aid in enlightening the "minds of the ignorant in current affairs." [60] The fears produced by the imminent plebiscite were creating a sense of mission. In the Romagna in 1860 the National Society came the closest it ever would to being an organization of all the classes.

The Bologna committee itself remained relatively small, and unemployment made it difficult for some men to pay their dues. Plans for the Society in the Romagna to purchase a local newspaper collapsed. Still, the Bologna committee was doing well, and it was in touch with a growing number of committees. When Buscalioni made a tour of inspection at the end of February, he in effect recognized Bologna as the provincial central committee it claimed to be. Soon, La Farina was happily boasting of the 28 Romagnol committees of the SNI.[61]

[59] Bologna's committee to Forlì's, n.d., and Forlì's reply, 31 January 1860, mss., *ibid*. Casarini to La Farina, 2 February 1860, ms. in ISR, busta 546, n. 35.

[60] The plan, announced in a circular of 7 February 1860 in MCRB, was to be under the direction of Taddeo Marti; *soci* were also to be recruited at reduced rates. He succeeded in setting up a number of committees on a trip for which the Bologna committee paid his expenses, Marti to Simonetti, 26 March 1860, ms. in Posizione Simonetti, *ibid*.

[61] Casarini to Buscalioni, 8 and 10 February 1860, mss., ISR, buste 546 and 555. The paper to be purchased was the *Età Presente*; the Bologna and Imola committees purchased 7 shares (at 100 lire each): circular from the Bologna

The committee in Imola was one of the most successful. The first to be firmly re-established, its president had become *gonfaloniere*, and its relations with governing officials were excellent. Its leader, Count Gamberini, was blessed with both the best of social connections and excellent relations with Imola's working classes. An artisan was even included among the committee's officers. More successful than most in attracting some workers to its ranks, the committee was one of the first to systematically lower dues, and it had long taken an interest in the workers' aid societies. By the end of December the committee had nearly 200 members and was still growing; its major complaint was that the rest of the SNI was not so efficient.[62]

The committee in Faenza was re-established much more slowly, but its location made it an important link in the communications among the Romagna committees. No one seems to have noticed that when the Society's conference was held in Faenza, the host committee was only two days old. Uncertain, early in January, as to what a committee did, the leaders of the SNI in Faenza were asking for 100 copies of the *Piccolo Corriere* by the end of the month. By the end of February, with their own system of reduced dues, they had recruited 281 members.[63] Forlì had no committee until the end of January, but

committee, 30 January 1860, MCRB. Simonetti bought 3 additional shares: receipt, 31 January 1860, ms. in Posizione Simonetti, *ibid.* Casarini explained the failure of the plan in a letter [to the Lugo committee?], 22 February 1860, ms. in Carteggio Casarini, *ibid.* Bologna's role between the Romagna committees and Turin is clear in its circular about sending dues and the names of members to Turin, n.d. [between 6 and 8 February 1860], and the ones announcing Buscalioni's visit and its result, 24 and 29 February 1860, *ibid. Piccolo Corriere*, 11 March 1860. Bologna's influence in the Romagna had increased after Villafranca in all political matters: Dallolio, *La spedizione*, 19. La Farina of course attempted to maintain his independent contacts: La Farina to Rodolfo Audinot, 12 March 1860, ms. in ISR, busta 5, n. 17. Livio Zambeccari to La Farina, 23 February 1860, ms., *ibid.*, busta 551, n. 99.

[62] Count Giuseppe Scarabelli became *gonfaloniere*. When Gamberini visited London in September, Minghetti wrote introducing him to Antonio Panizzi: note from Minghetti, 1 September 1860, ms. in Panizzi papers, British Museum, vol. VII, n. 545. Galli, "Società Nazionale e Gamberini," *La Romagna*, XVI, 395; XVII, 19–21. Gamberini to La Farina, 10 December 1859 and 10 January 1860, *ibid.*, XVII, 178, 183. Gamberini to Casarini, 21 January 1860, ms. in Carteggio Casarini, MCRB. By comparison, La Farina said, Bologna should have 2,000 members: letter to Canevazzi, 25 December 1859, Franchi, *Epistolario di La Farina*, II, 262. Buscalioni wrote Gamberini, 7 March 1860, promising 200 copies of the *Credo* and 300 of the *Piccolo Corriere*, Galli, *loc. cit.*, XVII, 185.

[63] Ballelli to Casarini, 3 and 28 January, and 26 February 1860, mss. in Car-

then some 100 citizens met and approved the Society's *Credo* and drastically lowered its dues. They then dutifully waited for La Farina's approval before they announced, in April, their *regolamento*, an amazing constitution of baroque complexity providing for "Sections" and "Companies" headed by the "Committee." [64] The Society's members in Cesena, on the other hand, had not quite succeeded (even by May and despite their intendant's interest) in organizing a committee. [65]

Rimini was strategically located on the border of the Marches, and there had been a well-organized committee of the SNI there before the war. An air of conspiratorial activity had remained in the city, centering around the Committee of Emigration which dealt exclusively with affairs in the Marches. Perhaps it overshadowed the SNI, for by the end of February Count Salvoni, the Society's president in Rimini, conceded that shamefully little had been done. In a meeting on March 2, however, 89 members were signed up. Casarini had expected more. He found this number so disappointingly small that he used his influence to have an army officer who could help the Society transferred to Rimini. The committee became more active. It aided some boys who had "escaped" from Macerata, printed manifestoes about the Marches and the forthcoming elections, and even considered establishing a headquarters with regular employees. Such zeal had its effect. Rimini, the committee boasted, was a town of only 18,000 citizens most of whose youth were away in the army, whose nobles took no part in politics, most of whose artisans were too poor to join, and still it had nearly 400

---

teggio Casarini, MCRB. Casarini wrote La Farina asking for 200 copies of the *Piccolo Corriere*, 30 January 1860, ms. in ISR, busta 546, n. 35; a month later Buscalioni promised to send them: letter to Casarini, 7 March 1860, ms. in Carteggio Casarini, MCRB. *Piccolo Corriere*, 11 March 1860.

[64] G. Tirelli to Casarini, 4 January 1860; [Temistocle Panciatichi? to Casarini?], 31 January 1860, and draft of Bologna's reply, n.d.; Panciatichi to Casarini, 9 February 1860, mss. in Carteggio Casarini, MCRB. Casarini to La Farina, 30 January 1860, ms. in ISR, busta 546, n. 35. The printed *regolamento* is in MCRB. It became a custom in the Romagna to use the term "committee" only for the executive committee of the local Società.

[65] Luigi Nicoletti, *Il Carteggio del Comitato di Emigrazione di Rimini* (Fabriano, 1925), 51–2. Alessandro Serpieri, 16 February 1860; Vincenzo Massacci, 23 February 1860; Turci, 7 March 1860, to Casarini, mss. in Carteggio Casarini, MCRB. Serpieri to Tanari, 14 March 1860, ms., *ibid*. *Piccolo Corriere*, 26 February and 11 March 1860. Casarini to La Farina, 15 May 1860, ms. in ISR, busta 546, n. 35; Casarini to Buscalioni, 7 February 1860, *ibid*.

members by the end of March. Understandably, the *Piccolo Corriere* noted Rimini as an example to all.[66]

The National Society in Ravenna was always dominated by the Rasponi family, and the modesty of its organization there before April may be due to their Bonapartist inclinations. But dissidence within the committee was put down; the prominence of Gioacchino Rasponi in Romagnol affairs kept the committee in touch with its sisters, and the Rasponis' control of the influential newspaper, *L'Adriatico*, obscured any gap in organization.[67] The committee in Lugo, on the other hand, always felt itself slighted by the SNI in Turin and the Romagna. It went unconsulted in January; mail to it was misdirected; even the newspapers to which it subscribed came with suspect irregularity. Nevertheless, by April it had 220 members; in addition to letting dues fall as low as 20 *centesimi* a month, the committee in Lugo maintained its sympathy for Garibaldi and its closeness to the proletariat (it wanted to keep much of the money it received for needy and patriotic families). Yet it was enthusiastic in supporting the plans for a newspaper of the Society in the Romagna, and it was as doctrinally sound as successful when it boasted in April that not a soul in Lugo had signed the petitions opposing the cession of Nice.[68]

On balance, the National Society was extraordinarily successful in the Romagna. Enthusiasm for it showed in the smallest towns where a single individual, members of a town council, or emissaries from a neighboring city would persuade a group of men to form their own committee. By December one had begun in Russi where it would soon be printing election manifestoes.[69]

[66] Ascanio Ginevri-Blasi to Casarini, 18 December 1859; and Vincenzo Salvoni to Casarini, 28 February, 2 and 6 March 1860, mss. in Carteggio Casarini, MCRB. Salvoni to Buscalioni, 8 and 31 March 1860, mss. in ISR, busta 720, ns. 4 and 5. Col. Masi was the officer: Casarini to Buscalioni, 4 March 1860, ms., *ibid.*, busta 546. *Piccolo Corriere*, 15 April 1860. Dallolio, *La spedizione*, 22. Dues here were also lowered with the initiation fee eliminated in the bottom bracket.

[67] Rasponi, 20 January, and Camporesi, 19 February, 23 and 27 March 1860, to Casarini, mss. in Carteggio Casarini, MCRB. Rasponi to Festi, 22 February and 20 March, and to Buscalioni, 21 March 1860, mss., ISR, busta 718, ns. 15 and 14. Casarini to La Farina, 30 January and to Buscalioni, 29 February 1860, mss., *ibid.*, busta 546, n. 35. Clipping from *L'Adriatico*, n.d. [March 1860], in the H. N. Gay newspaper clippings, 1856–1927, HCL.

[68] Letters of Rasponi, 20 January, and of Giuseppe Masi, 2, 17, and 28 February, 9 March, 5, 20, and 25 April 1860; Buscalioni to Casarini, 7 March 1860, mss. in Carteggio Casarini, MCRB.

[69] Aristide Farini to Buscalioni, 15 December 1859 and 11 February 1860,

Neighboring Bagnacavallo then followed this example.[70] Soon Fusignano and then more miniscule Fognano had their committees ready to guide the elections safely.[71] Imola saw to the creation of a committee in Medicina and nearby towns; and the Society spilled out from Bologna to Budrio and Anzola.[72] Ferrara resented being in the shadow of the Bologna committee, but its own was only moderately successful. Little Comacchio found a new use for the Italian National Society when, hurt by severe floods, it called on its sister committees for aid—and received it.[73] Throughout the Romagna the National Society was becoming well organized; its still somewhat cautious connections with the lower classes, its determination to make voting a triumph for the moderates, its ambitions for the liberation of the Marches, its belief that concord among patriots was possible—all this gave it an *élan* it had nowhere else.

The Marches was the only area of Italy in which the National Society may in fact have been stronger than La Farina claimed it to be. Perhaps only Ancona and Fano had committees which belonged to the SNI, but the scores of other patriotic committees throughout the Marches corresponded with the Committees of Emigration in Rimini and Bologna.[74] Headed by liberal nobles

---

mss. in ISR, buste 719, n. 18, and 716, n. 26. Farini to Casarini, 8 March 1860, including copy of the manifesto, ms. in Carteggio Casarini, MCRB.

[70] Cesare Bubani to [Buscalioni?], 21 March and 5 April 1860, mss. in ISR, busta 715, n. 66. Letter of Ludovico Brandi, 28 February 1860, ms., *ibid.*, busta 720.

[71] Cesare Armandi to Casarini, 13 March 1860, ms. in Carteggio Casarini, MCRB; seven *schede*, all February 1860, for Fognano, mss. in ISR, busta 719.

[72] Galli, "Società Nazionale e Gamberini," *La Romagna*, xvi, 37–40; Buscalioni to Gamberini, 7 March 1860, *ibid.*, xvii, 185; Giovanni to [Buscalioni?], 10 April 1859, ms. in ISR, busta 716, n. 75. Dott. Luigi Menarini to Casarini, 2 February and 7 March 1860; Achille Nicolao Leoni to Cassarini, 10 March 1860, mss. in Carteggio Casarini, MCRB. Medicina set up a committee in Castelguelfo and commissioners in Mordano, Dozza, Castel San Pietro, Casalfumanese, Monterenzo, Castel del Rio, Castel Bolognese, Solarolo.

[73] Forlani to Casarini, 15 January 1860, and Giuseppe Prosperi to Casarini, 14 February 1860, mss. in Carteggio Casarini, MCRB. Buscalioni to Gaetano Dondi, 23 January, and Casarini to La Farina, 30 January, and to Buscalioni, 29 January, mss. in ISR, buste 61, n. 36; 546, n. 35. La Farina to Canevazzi, 25 November 1859, Franchi, *Epistolario di La Farina*, ii, 241.

Vincenzo Grondi to [Casarini], 10 January 1860, ms. in MCRB; broadside of Comacchio committee, dated 22 March, and letter, dated 26 March, *ibid.* Giuseppe Vandini to [Buscalioni], 4 April 1860, ms. in ISR, busta 718. Clipping of 22 March 1860 in H. N. Gay newspaper clippings, 1856–1927, HCL. *Piccolo Corriere*, 8 April 1860.

[74] A careful reading of the *documents* in Alessandrini, *I fatti*, ii, and Nicoletti, *Comitati di Emigrazione* (see pp. 79, 84 on Ancona) makes this distinction ap-

who had left the Marches, these Committees of Emigration provided the focus and central instructions for an extensive organization. Separate from the SNI, that organization reflected a local desire for liberation more than a dedication to the national policies of Cavour. In this sense La Farina may have been right to make little claim for the Society's strength in the Marches. Nevertheless, in both Rimini and Bologna the leaders of the Committees of Emigration were leaders of the SNI, too. The two organizations carefully cooperated, and the Society's propaganda was sent throughout the Marches.[75] The Committees of Emigration were active in the fall of 1859 before the National Society, but the distinctions between these two organizations were often lost on contemporaries just as they have been on historians. After their liberation in the fall of 1860, many committees which had corresponded with Rimini and Bologna then continued in the National Society with little awareness of any important change. Among these committees, the talk of and plans for revolution went beyond what the Society had permitted elsewhere; but their ultimate caution bore the mark of the Society's influence.[76] The political program of the Italian National

parent. Camillo Franceschi, *Relazione del Comitato Nazionale di Fano* (Fano, 1861); and Girolamo Orsi, *Relazione del Comitato Nazionale Centrale delle Marche in Ancona* (Ancona, 1861), treat the histories of their committees as continuous within the SNI. Both pamphlets are in HCL. In 1860 Fano had apparently expected its activities to be reported in the *Piccolo Corriere*, Nicoletti, *Comitati di Emigrazione*, 236.

[75] Ginevri-Blasi and Simonetti were active in both organizations. The Committee of Emigration in Bologna promised to forward to La Farina any information of interest to him: letter of 29 February 1860, ms. in ISR, busta 720, n. 4. La Farina, in turn, sent his promises concerning the Marches directly to Simonetti: Casarini to Buscalioni, 4 March 1860, ms., *ibid.*, busta 546; Buscalioni's reply to Casarini, 7 March 1860, ms. in Carteggio Casarini, MCRB, and La Farina's reply to Simonetti referred to by Buscalioni, printed in Alessandrini, *I fatti*, II, 173–74. The Rimini Committee of Emigration kept Salvoni, president of the SNI there, informed of its activities, and considered joining the National Society as a group: Ginevri-Blasi to Simonetti, 24 January 1860, and the Rimini committee to the Bologna committee, 3 March 1860, Nicoletti, *Comitati di Emigrazione*, 51, 173; for other men in both organizations see *ibid.*, 320–21; the Bologna Committee of Emigration similarly felt loyal to the Society's political position, Ionni, n.d., and Simonetti, 7 May 1860, to Ginevri-Blasi, *ibid.*, 447 and 411.

The *Piccolo Corriere* and La Farina's "Ai militi italiani" were distributed by the committees. See the letters in Alessandrini, *I fatti*, II, 197–98, and Nicoletti, *Comitati di Emigrazione*, 116, 197, 288–89, 321; the Rimini committee took "unification and independence" as its slogan, *ibid.*, 248–49.

[76] Augusto Paselli to Casarini, 8 January 1860, ms. in Carteggio Casarini,

Society was sometimes distorted and often confused as it spread through the Marches, but nowhere was it more widely disseminated or less directly challenged. The nationalists in Umbria were in touch with those in the Marches, but the organization of their committees remained largely separate. These Umbrian committees, of which Perugia's was the most active, were, in tone and policy, indistinguishable from the National Society as they warned their compatriots to be prepared but to do nothing rash. After the bloody failures of 1859, Umbrian nationalists were understandably willing to accept moderate direction from the outside. This was provided by the Directoral Commission for the Subject Roman Provinces established in Florence by January 1860. Dominated by exiled Perugians and with strong connections with the Tuscan government, this commission was separate from the National Society and less closely allied to it than were the Committees of Emigration. Like the SNI, it protested the fate of the Papal States in a manifesto to the Powers and collected new evidence of the evils of Papal rule, while exonerating Piedmont from responsibility for their misfortunes.[77] It, too, sent on some of the Society's propaganda.

One of the achievements of the Italian National Society was that its attitudes were adopted by others and that it gained credit then and has since for actions taken independently of it. When in 1860 the committees in Umbria were again thinking of possible revolutionary action, they corresponded primarily with Gualterio, who worked closely with Ricasoli. Gualterio disliked the National Society intensely; yet Umbrian patriots seemed to have assumed they had some connection with the SNI.[78] When they were liberated in the fall of 1860, most of them joined the National Society as a matter of course.

In 1860, then, the Italian National Society was strongest

MCRB; Alessandrini, I fatti, II, 108–109, 122–23; Zampetti-Biocca, Società Nazionale, 77, 92ff.
[77] Nicoletti, Comitati di Emigrazione, 17; Raschi, Perugia, 95–6, 229. Degli Azzi, Liberazione, 6, 16, 61–2; a copy of the January 10, 1860, manifesto of Commission is in MCRB; Zampetti-Biocca, Società Nazionale, 233–34, 236–37.
[78] Dispatch of Conte du Chastel, Netherlands Ambassador to the Holy See, 5 May 1860, as summarized in Alberto M. Ghisalberti, "Documenti sulla caduta del regno Borbonico," Archivio Storico per la Sicilia, IV–V (1938–39), 544. Gualterio to Ricasoli, 27 October [1859 or 1860?], Puccioni, Ricasoli, 151–53.

where politics had been most exciting (and the outcome most in doubt) in 1859. The National Society's connections with the Veneto seem not to have gone much beyond a committee of emigrants in Turin; its association with the *Comitato Nazionale* in Rome remained more ideological than organizational.[79] In Naples the SNI was associated with the *Comitato dell'Ordine*, a quite conservative group of limited influence.[80] In Sicily where, as in the Veneto, La Farina's own contacts should have made the Society strong the SNI was only a little more influential. But his means of communicating with the island were irregular at best and his calls for vigor had results no more tangible than his hope for an uprising.[81] In all these areas the Society's friends were numerous enough that, when it was safe, some could be depended upon to join. In the meantime, propaganda could be smuggled in (La Farina even sent a packet to Malta), and occasional demonstrations could be reported in the *Piccolo Corriere*. But neither the local temper nor the policies of a Society more and more closely associated with the Government of Piedmont allowed it the subversive role it had played in the Duchies or the Romagna.

The international connections of the re-established National Society reflected the changes which had taken place both in the Society's doctrine and in Italy's international position. The old theme of Latin sympathy was still present, but it was stressed less; and no mention was now made of those committees throughout France led by patriotic Italians in exile and supported by generous Frenchmen.[82] Exiles in New York established

[79] For the Veneto, the argument must be from silence, but such silence is impressive. Cf. La Farina to Gallina, October 1859, Franchi, *Epistolario di La Farina*, II, 217, and *Piccolo Corriere*, 5 February 1860. Nazari-Michele, *Cavour e Garibaldi*, 70. The Roman committee sent Cavour a petition of gratitude, 10 August 1859, *Carteggio Cavour-Salmour* (Bologna, 1936), 311.

[80] La Farina to Vergara, 25 March 1860, Franchi, *Epistolario di La Farina*, II, 305.

[81] *Ibid.*, and La Farina to Franchi, 24 September; to Rizzari, 21 November; to Bartolomeo (23 November, for example); to Morchio, 12 December; to Vergara, 24 December 1859, *ibid.*, 212, 234, 238–39, 252–53, 260. Local historians have credited the SNI with a good deal of influence but this seems to mean little more than that local patriots, after Garibaldi's arrival, often formed committees of the SNI. For example, Serafino Privatera, *Storia di Siracusa antica e moderna* (Naples, 1879), II, 437–39; Giuseppe Parlato, *Siracusa dal 1830 al 1880* (Catania, 1919), 120.

[82] *Piccolo Corriere*, 15 January 1860, reported sympathetic items in *Las Novedades*, Madrid, and *Journal de Commercio*, Lisbon; *ibid.*, 29 January and 19 February 1860, reported friendly French attitudes.

a committee there, but when word of Garibaldi's resignation finally got across the Atlantic, it proved fatal for the American branch of the Society. Loyal primarily to the hero of two continents, the committee decided to send funds directly to Garibaldi along with the gift of one hundred revolvers from Colonel Colt of Hartford.[83] Vegezzi-Ruscalla, as the Society's foreign secretary, was soon busy translating manifestoes, reporting on the foreign press, and keeping in touch with exiles from anywhere east of the Rhine. But even his strong interest in Hungarian, Rumanian, and Balkan affairs left within the Society less trace than in 1858 of concern for nationalist movements throughout Europe.[84]

The National Society followed German affairs more closely than those of any other country. La Farina had given the German National Society as one reason for re-establishing the SNI, and the *Piccolo Corriere* viewed the *Deutsche Nationalverein* not merely as a flattering imitation but as an opportunity for sympathetic relations between two groups standing for the same principles and combating the same enemy. And there was in fact some exchange of letters between the two societies.[85] The *Piccolo Corriere* reported a clandestine pamphlet from the German Tyrol, explaining that what mattered was not its stress on German superiority nor the reference to Italians as rebels but the fact that Germans, too, were anti-Austrian. The Society extended its Nordic contacts by formally thanking the Burgesses of Stockholm for having supported the annexation of central

[83] Report of the New York Consul of the Kingdom of Two Sicilies, 24 November 1859, in Marraro, "Documenti italiani e americani," *Rassegna Storica del Risorgimento*, XLIV (1957), 13. Vincenzo Botta to La Farina, 4 January and 27 February, and to Buscalioni, 21 January 1860, mss. in ISR, busta 545, n. 69.

[84] La Farina to Selmi, 30 December 1859, Franchi, *Epistolario di La Farina*, II, 263. Mazzini warned a German friend that Vegezzi-Ruscalla was "*le plus intrigant d'entre les intrigants*," letter to Karl Blind, 1859, Mazzini, *Scritti*, Appendice VI (Imola, 1943), 78.

[85] Cavour was also increasingly struck by the parallels of Piedmontese and Prussian history: Federico Chabod, *Storia della politica estera italiana dal 1870 al 1896, Le premesse* (Bari, 1951), 8. *Piccolo Corriere*, 22 January 1860; a copy of the *Erklärung des Ausschusses des Deutschen Nationalvereins Beschlossen* is in the Buscalioni pamphlets, HCL; a draft of the SNI's earlier reply to the *Nationalverein*, dated 14 January 1860, is in ISR, busta 720, n. 9. The leaders of the *Nationalverein* were less enthusiastic about contacts with the *Società Nazionale* though their organization was in fact inspired by the SNI, Hermann Oncken, *Rudolf von Bennigsen, ein deutscher Liberaler Politiker* (Stuttgart, 1910), I, 339.

Italy.[86] Such gestures had their effect, for the Turin correspondent of the *Tagblatt der Stadt Basel* reported the act in full and commented on other signs of German-Italian friendship. The *Piccolo Corriere* in turn reported the friendly item in the Basel paper. When a Genevan *Arbeiterbildungsverein* sent Garibaldi a letter to which the Society replied, the air was soon full of *"Volksolidarität"* and comparisons of Tasso and Goethe, Rafael and Dürer, Dante and Schiller. Advised that northerners liked that sort of thing, the Society made Bennigsen, who was president of the *Nationalverein*, and some of the Stockholm burgesses honorary members of the SNI.[87]

Domestically, the National Society's influence was further extended by its relations with a number of newspapers. The *Piccolo Corriere* was able to list some eight other papers friendly to the Society, and members of the SNI controlled or were influential in important dailies in Genoa, Florence, and Rimini.[88] Local committees were constantly encouraged to see that the Society's views were represented in local papers and many established special election papers. Lorenzo Festi, a friend of La Farina's and an important member of the Society's Central Committee, served, sometimes apparently without pay, as the Turin correspondent for papers in Florence, Parma, Brescia, Ravenna, Geneva, and for a Paris agency. In addition he used his own connections in Lombardy and the Tyrol to aid the distribution of the *Piccolo Corriere* there. The ideological content of Festi's reporting was apparently high, for even his friends on the *Nazione* in Florence confessed they had had to tone it down. A Genevan paper complained of his strong bias against

[86] *Piccolo Corriere*, 15 November 1859; the 15 January 1860 issue cites a Cologne newspaper and some German Swiss papers. A copy of the letter signed by La Farina and Garibaldi to the Stockholm Burgesses, 23 December 1859, is in ISR, busta 719, n. 18; the *Piccolo Corriere* announced it, 25 December 1859.

[87] *Tagblatt der Stadt Basel*, item dated Italien, 2 January 1860, clipping in the H. N. Gay newspaper clippings, 1856–1927, HCL. *Piccolo Corriere*, 1, 8, and 22 January, 1 April 1860. Commel, Geneva, to Lorenzo Festi, 1, 12, and 19 January 1860, mss. in ISR, busta 715, ns. 102, 103.

[88] *Piccolo Corriere*, 15 January 1860, listed the *Corriere Mercantile* (Genoa), *Espero* (Turin), *Croce di Savoia* (Modena), *Diario Savonese*, *Nazione* (Florence), *Bandiera Italiana*, and *Espérance* (Geneva). Morchio was connected with the *Corriere Mercantile* (see ms. letters in Carte Morchio, MNRG); the founders of *Nazione* were all members of the SNI as was Alessandro d'Ancona, who edited it; the Rasponis controlled *Adriatico*. La Farina, Simonetti, and Canevazzi were in touch with Paolo Tambri when he established his paper, Tambri to La Farina, 30 January 1860, ms., ISR, busta 547, n. 45.

Rattazzi and Brofferio; the agency in Paris noted his biased treatment of Garibaldi.[89] One did not have to read the *Piccolo Corriere* to encounter the views of the National Society. The re-established Society may also have received some ghostly assistance from Italy's Freemasons. By nature a difficult subject, the question of Masonic influences has been further obscured because it inevitably invites a kind of scholarly yellow journalism. The argument for the SNI and Freemasonry as interlocking conspiracies is usually made with so little evidence or judgment that it can be discounted.[90] Yet one is left with the feeling that such acrid smoke must signal some flame of truth. The Ausonia lodge of Turin, which became the base for Italy's Grand Orient, was founded in October 1859, with La Farina as a member. Throughout Italy the lodges, which began to be established at this time, were intensely patriotic; and their members included men of importance in every aspect of Italian nationalist politics. A bitter anticlerical and recently a francophile, La Farina had shown sympathy for Masonry before; and Buscalioni later would become one of the highest Masonic officials. Indeed, Buscalioni's son remembered a family tradition which made the lodges and the SNI equally instruments of Cavour's policy; the history of one, he decided, must include the history of the other. This may reflect only the natural tendency to exaggerate the importance of the organizations to which one be-

[89] Alessandro d'Ancona to Festi, 30 January, 21 February, and 5 May 1860 (Festi's column appeared thrice weekly), mss., *ibid.*, busta 547, n. 5. Luigi Bottarelli, 1 February 1860, and N. Guastalla, n.d., to Festi (for *La Sentinella* of Brescia), *ibid.*, buste 715, n. 55; 548, n. 45. Rasponi to Festi, 22 February and 20 March 1860, *ibid.*, busta 718, n. 15. Antonio Scotti, n.d., and Francesco Scaramuzza, 10 August 1860 (about the *Gazzetta di Parma*), to Festi, *ibid.*, busta 718, ns. 49 and 45. Ducommun to Festi, January, February, and March 1860 (for the *Révue du Genève*), *ibid.*, busta 716, n. 21. Letters of Danjou (for the Bullier agency), March-November (6 in all), *ibid.*, busta 716, n. 9. Vittorio Ricci to Festi, November 1859 to November 1860 (about the Trentino and Tyrol, 21 letters in all), *ibid.*, busta 718, ns. 21 and 22.

[90] A man who sees the Crimean War as a Masonic plot is not to be taken seriously if he finds the Masons behind La Farina's activities, too: Père N. Deschamps, *Les sociétés secrètes et la société ou philosophie de l'histoire contemporaine* (Paris, n.d. [1883]), III, 165, 178–79. *Civiltà Cattolica*, ser. 5, XI (1864), 701, believed the SNI to have been formed by Freemasonry. Some merely insist on a suggestively close connection between the two: Louis Lachat, "La Charbonnerie et la Fr. ∴. Mac ∴. dans le reveil italien," *L'Accacia*, LXI (1929), 495; C. A. Mondell-Nestler, *La Massoneria* (Rome, 1887), 141–43. Lorenzo Di Baroni Leoni, *La Massoneria e le annessioni degli Stati Pontifici*, II (Viterbo, 1893), 3–87, sees the SNI as a frightening conspiracy but establishes no connection with Masonry.

longs, but many historians have accepted it.[91] The Ausonia lodge, at least, may have been established to prevent Garibaldians from dominating Italian Masonry.

The evidence is scanty and often inconclusive. In addition to La Farina and Buscalioni there were others in Turin, men such as Cordova and Govean, who were themselves Masons and who were close to the National Society. When Zambeccari, a member of the Ausonia lodge, moved to Bologna, he founded a lodge there but also reported to La Farina about local political conditions and took an interest in the National Society. Certainly in the Marches and Umbria, and probably in the Romagna, a high percentage of those who were leading the Society in 1860 became active Masons. Much the same was probably true the following year in Sicily.[92] Thus Masonry, as a social institution which drew together middle-class anticlericals, may have helped to spread knowledge of and interest in the National Society. Probably the contacts as often worked the other way: men who had become friendly in the SNI joined the same Masonic lodge. But many of the Masons were, like Nigra and Minghetti, in a sense above the Society; many simply had no connection with it; many, indeed, were Garibaldians.[93]

There is, in short, little evidence of any connection between the two organizations beyond the important fact that some individuals played a significant part in both. The ideas and interests expressed by the two societies were only as similar as their members. In fact, the Masons became well organized later in the 1860's as the National Society declined. Masonry

[91] Buscalione [sic], "Cavour e la Massoneria," *Rassegna Contemporanea*, VII, ser. II (25 July 1914), 234–37. Carlo Patrucco, *Documenti su Garibaldi e la Massoneria nell'ultimo periodo del Risorgimento italiano* (Alessandria, 1914), 12n. (This study is based on Buscalioni papers, the same ones apparently which ended in the ISR.) Adolfo Colombo, "Per la storia della Massoneria nel Risorgimento italiano," *Rassegna Storica del Risorgimento*, I (1914), 58–9, 85–6. Muratism had of course been connected with Masonry; note La Farina's early attitude in his letter to Montanelli, 2 October 1855, Franchi, *Epistolario di La Farina*, I, 565.

[92] Buscalione, "Cavour e la Massoneria," *Rassegna Contemporanea*, VII, 244–45; Zambeccari to La Farina, 23 February 1860, ms. in ISR, busta 551, n. 99. Giuseppe Leti, *Carboneria e Massoneria nel Risorgimento italiano* (Genoa, 1925), 309–54, lists Masons in these areas.

[93] This judgment is closest to the view of Alessandro Luzio, *Massoneria e il Risorgimento* (Bologna, 1925), I, 287–305, 350–51. Cf. the articles in *Civiltà Cattolica* [by P. Pirri?], LXXVII (1926): "La Massoneria e il Risorgimento italiano a propositio del saggio storico-critico di Alessandro Luzio," 107–20; "Camillo Cavour, Costantino Nigra e il rinascimento della Massoneria italiana," 309–24.

had more to do with the later decay of the SNI than with its refounding in 1860. One need not therefore read any secret meaning into the statement made in 1871 by the man who would become Grand Master of Italy's Masons in 1910 that their lodges preserved too much of the tendencies of the National Society, that they were too subservient to Cavourian politics. Nor is much added to our understanding of Italian politics by the appealing theory that the Ausonia lodge was founded by non-Masons in order to weaken that secret organization.[94] So dramatic an exercise of whimsical individual subversion would in any case belong to the history of Italian Masonry, with which it is much more congenial, than to the history of the Italian National Society.

Early in 1860, then, the SNI had committees in every free province of Italy. It included among its members men of national and local influence, men in positions of power, and hundreds of men who did not aspire to either. It had connections, personal, official, and accidental with a score of newspapers. It showed a tendency to be relatively stronger in towns than in major cities. Less useful where politics were already organized, the Society was perhaps too cautious to meet urban needs.

In a given town the Society's success depended upon the personality and influence of the individuals first attracted to it. To be successful, committees needed men whose local roots were deep. Everywhere the leaders of the Society reported difficulty in attracting followers. That difficulty tended to increase their pessimism about their neighbors. The fear of priestly or Mazzinian influences and of simple ignorance was more openly expressed, and it undoubtedly tended to make the Society more conservative, more willing to follow the Government. At the same time, these leaders tended to believe the Society's propaganda, to fear that only their own area lacked the enthusiasm that was sweeping the rest of Italy. This belief would be the cause of many later miscalculations, but for the moment it was an effective spur to action.

Garibaldi's resignation, first from the army and then from the SNI, weakened the new Society and tended to make it less idealistic and less popular than the old one; for no man even of the

[94] Ludovico Frapolli was the Grand Master: Colombo, "Massoneria nel Risorgimento," *Rassegna Storica*, I, 66. Luzio, *Massoneria*, I, 298–305.

moderate left was likely now to join. Yet the National Society survived in Lombardy where its members were usually men of little independent political importance and therefore highly loyal to the Society. It survived in Tuscany where its members were men of such great prestige that the Society's dimmed luster could not lessen their position. It survived in the Duchies, where its men were frequently in the government itself, and in the Romagna where the Society's leaders, however regretful at the loss of Garibaldi, were anxious that political influence should not pass to men of the left. No longer really a revolutionary organization, the Society's relations with the rest of Italy were largely indirect. It lost many of its connections abroad as the Italian Question lost the attraction of a great cause by becoming a half-fulfilled reality. Its relations with Germany, unlike its earlier ones with France, were the limited product of deliberate policy rather than sentiment.

The proddings of La Farina bore fruit. His pleas to friends and former associates, his trips throughout the north saw committees formed in town after town.[95] As things settled down, as even the threat of an international congress passed, the need for day-to-day politics became more apparent. The National Society offered a vehicle of tested moderation and nationalism at a time when political action was both necessary and frighteningly dangerous. The threat to Cavour which Brofferio and Rattazzi represented was in itself reason for reactivating the National Society. At first, who belonged to the Society was more important than how well it was organized; but organizations have needs of their own. By itself, propaganda was no longer exciting enough nor its purposes clear enough to justify the effort a society requires of its members. The forthcoming elections gave the SNI something important to do. Local leaders could call meetings and issue lengthy manifestoes over their names. All were reminded of how insecurely Italy held its recent gains, of how important organization was in a political world. The elections made the National Society a vital association, and in them it played one of its most important roles.

[95] La Farina traveled a number of times to Modena and Bologna; Buscalioni visited Milan, Parma, Modena, Bologna, Ferrara, and Tuscany: La Farina to Franchi, 23 November 1859; to Vergara, 28 February; and to Tacchini, 4 April 1860, Franchi, *Epistolario di La Farina*, II, 236, 298, 308.

CHAPTER NINE

ELECTIONS AND PLEBISCITES: THE TASKS OF
A PARTY TRIUMPHANT
(NOVEMBER 1859—APRIL 1860)

✣ THE LEADERS of Italian politics felt a genuine dedication to the representative system. An election of deputies throughout northern Italy stood naturally as the first symbol of unification. If Cavour was used to having his will dominate, it was through parliament that his domination had been achieved. When, out of power, he had found himself more and more opposed to Rattazzi while still at odds with the King, he made the immediate holding of elections his political issue. That demand was to be a lever with which he would pry Rattazzi out of office, and he looked to the National Society to help make it irresistible. The Society which had so recently triumphed over Garibaldi and the *Liberi Comizii* was to support widespread agitation for the holding of elections.[1] Now, as in the past, Cavour wanted the National Society to provide the agitation which would justify his policies. Insistence upon the importance of such elections came easily to the Society, but it hardly had launched its campaign when Rattazzi fell. With Cavour in office, preparations for an election offered the Society a chance to demonstrate anew its closeness to the Government. La Farina, of course, saw elections as another form of those public demonstrations which the Society had always supported.

Cavour, anxious to consolidate his power, could use all the help he could get; the Society, able to reassert its semi-official position, immediately prospered. Even Farini wrote to La Farina as to a kind of campaign director, and La Farina pushed Ca-

---

[1] Cavour to La Farina, n.d. [December 1859 and January 1860], Franchi, *Epistolario di La Farina*, ii, 264, 289; Biundi, *La Farina*, i, 447. Cavour, of course, never placed himself in the position of depending on one man: see Pischedda, "L'Attività politica di Cavour," *Scritti vari*, ii, 29. La Farina did do his part: see his letters to [Gamberini], 16 December 1859, and Ghisalberti, 5 January 1860, Franchi, *Epistolario di La Farina*, ii, 255, 272; and the *Piccolo Corriere*, 27 November 1859.

vour's own candidacy.[2] So much was made of the governmental connection that the Society had to explain that it supported policies not men, and La Farina took to citing his refusal of a post in the Government as evidence of his independence. In advocating the election of truly independent deputies, however, the National Society made its own position clear; it defined the independents as those willing to support the Government in contrast to those who consistently opposed it.[3]

The Society's vigorous response to the challenge of elections came not simply from self-interest but from genuine fear as well. The effect of Cavour's open break with Rattazzi was still to be measured; and if the Mazzinians were no threat at the polls, the Society shuddered at the candidacies of Cattaneo and Ferrari, Ulloa, Tommaséo, and Guerrazzi.[4] Their vaunted realism made the leaders of the Society recognize that resentments against a government in power were inevitable, and the *Piccolo Corriere* carefully reminded the Lombards that conditions in Lombardy were their own responsibility. No one really knew how the "less cultivated classes" might vote, and the *Piccolo Corriere* warned against election committees made up of professional groups exclusively.[5] It was, after all, idealism more than their realism which had enabled the Society to follow a policy primarily concerned with one class while believing it to be in the interests of all.

With the formation of a *Unione Liberale* among the moderates of the Chamber of Deputies, a step was taken toward drawing together Cavour's supporters. Their refusal to cooperate with the *Liberi Comizii* and the election of Boncompagni as their president and La Farina as vice president had been an important demonstration against Rattazzi and in favor of

[2] La Farina to Bartolommei, 18 February; to Zini, 6 March; to Morchio, 23 March 1860, Franchi, *Epistolario di La Farina*, II, 296, 299–300, 303. Farini to La Farina, 5 January and 2 February 1860, *ibid.*, 267, 290.
[3] La Farina to Conti, 15 March 1860, *ibid.*, 300–301; *Piccolo Corriere*, 5 February (citing the circular letter of the SNI of 3 February) and 23 March 1860.
[4] Vinciguerra, *I partiti italiani*, 52. The *Piccolo Corriere* was filled with attacks on these men (note the issue of 19 February 1860). Cf. La Farina to Germani, 24 February 1860, Franchi, *Epistolario di La Farina*, II, 297–98. Ulloa was now held, at the very least, to be a regional separatist. Guerrazzi reciprocated in print by noting how much La Farina resembled Judas in Leonardo's picture of the Last Supper, *La patria e le elezioni* (Genoa, 1860), 26.
[5] *Piccolo Corriere*, 11 and 18 December 1859.

Cavour. Their program, which was almost a paraphrase of the SNI's, was evidence of how pervasive the Society's influence had become; yet the fact of their formation suggested the limits of the Society's effectiveness. The task of conciliation was better undertaken outside the SNI. Having decided to support a slate of candidates for the Chamber, the *Unione Liberale* quickly became an electoral power. And the Society cooperated with the *Unione* enthusiastically, thereby gaining influence where it was weak and winning supporters it could not have won independently.[6]

Throughout northern Italy local election committees began to spring up. Sometimes they consisted of members of the SNI who "transformed" themselves; sometimes the SNI was only one of several sponsoring groups; occasionally it merely supported a committee established by others, perhaps as an offshoot of the *Unione Liberale*. Such committees sensitively reflected local needs. The Society was only one of several groups supporting the committee in Genoa; and although it could take comfort from the fact that the Genoa committee included the "most respected citizens" (the propertied and men from the liberal professions), that committee strayed so far as to support Garibaldi's candidacy.[7] The committee in Milan emphasized cooperation between the city and the rest of Lombardy.[8] In Bologna the Emigration Committee was active with the SNI in

[6] La Farina to Ghisalberti, 10 January; and to Selmi, 30 January 1860, Franchi, *Epistolario di La Farina*, II, 279, 288. *Piccolo Corriere*, 1 January 1860. Cavour to Boncompagni, 7 February; and to Valerio, 10 February 1860, Chiala, *Lettere di Cavour*, III, 200–201, 208. The program of the *Unione Liberale* is printed in *Memorie di Pallavicino*, III, 852–55; the Marchese could join the *Unione*, however, *ibid.*, 554. Virgilio, for example, could lead his group in Genoa to cooperate with the SNI through the *Unione Liberale*: letter to La Farina, 19 February 1860, ms. in ISR, busta 718, n. 90. Mario, *Bertani*, II, 90, sees the *Unione* as evidence of a decline in the Society's influence.

[7] Morchio to La Farina, 27 December 1859, ms. in ISR, busta 719, n. 18. The *Circolo Commerciale* and the *Associazione Marittima* were also sponsors of Genoa's *Comitato Elettorale Liberale*: see the *Piccolo Corriere*, 18 December 1859; and Antonio Mazzotti [to Buscalioni], 28 February 1860, ms. in ISR, busta 717, n. 49. Memorandum, n.d.; telegrams of Morchio to Garibaldi, and L. Daziani to Cerutti, 21 March 1860, in Carte Morchio, MNRG.

[8] The *Comitato d'istruzione civile e militare della Guardia Nazionale di Milano* also sponsored the Milanese committee, circular by Pietro Castiglione, 6 December 1859, announcing publication of *L'Elettore*, in Buscalioni pamphlets in HCL. Homodei to Buscalioni, 6 December 1859, ms. in ISR, busta 719, n. 18; and Pietro Cordiglioni to Festi, 8 February 1860, ms., *ibid.*, busta 715, n. 87.

the election committee, while in Bergamo the initiative came from the local *circolo politico*.[9] Though on the whole it worked well, this cooperation with other political groups ordered by the Central Committee sometimes left the Society's members confused between friend and foe.[10]

Its own doctrines and its past experience made the National Society desire to meet the challenges of an election with those twin supports of any successful campaign: the widest possible appeal and careful organization. Long in the habit of presenting its program as one all honest men could accept, the Society now attempted to broaden it still further by softening its anticlericalism. The aversion of the clergy to unification, the *Piccolo Corriere* pointed out, should not be exaggerated. And a sharp distinction was drawn between the upper clergy and the lower clergy, who knew the needs and the will of the people. The Modena committee even advocated consulting local priests where they were "honest and liberally inclined."[11] The need for organization fit well with the Society's efforts to re-establish itself. Committees were told to devote themselves to the election and to see that no conflicting political centers grew up among liberals. Since the enemies of unification were pictured as having organized with sinister effectiveness, the Society could once again call for zeal, sacrifice, and discipline—the "discipline of all forces and all wills"; it could once again dream of "a committee in each commune . . . commissioners in each suburb, in each village. . . ."[12]

[9] Most of the 30 men on the Bologna committee were in the SNI: Sarri [to Buscalioni], 6 March 1860, *ibid.*, busta 718, n. 36; clippings of 23 February in H. N. Gay newspaper clippings, 1856–1927, HCL. A. Ramuzzi to Casarini, 30 January, and draft of a letter from [Casarini?] to La Farina, mss. in Carteggio Casarini, MCRB. Mario Piacezzi (Bergamo) to Buscalioni, 5 December 1859, ms. in ISR, busta 719, n. 18.

[10] Paolo Ottani to Festi, 28 February 1860, ms., *ibid.*, busta 717, n. 89. La Farina to Porro, 12 December 1859, Franchi, *Epistolario di La Farina*, II, 253. *Piccolo Corriere*, 5 February 1860, containing La Farina's circular of 3 February.

[11] *Piccolo Corriere*, 4 March 1860; Istruzioni of the Modena committee, n.d., among the Buscalioni pamphlets in HCL. The Bologna committee also took pains to establish that unification in no way endangered religion, circular of 7 February 1860 in MCRB.

[12] *Piccolo Corriere*, 11 December 1859 and 4 March 1860. La Farina to Porro, 12 December; to Teresa Bartolommei, 16 December 1859; to Ghisalberti, 10 January 1860, Franchi, *Epistolario di La Farina*, II, 253, 254, 279. *Croce di Savoia* (Modena), 24 February 1860, clipping in the H. N. Gay newspaper clippings, 1856–1927, HCL.

In January, February, and March of 1860 the Italian National Society won its greatest response among Italy's middle classes. Everywhere, additional members were recruited, new committees formed, and old ones made more active. Local committees sponsored ambitious little election newspapers and thousands of broadsides to be sent through the mail or plastered on walls.[13] In itself a demonstration of fervor and dedication, even of some financial sacrifice, this propaganda met its authors' needs. The list of names at the end of a manifesto stood as a kind of declaration of political self-importance; men filled with the promise of Italy's future had a chance to express their feeling in their fullest *liceo* prose. Long-winded, vague, and often pompous, these statements were the apt expression of a political faith that was deep and sincere whatever its ambiguities. They reflected well the men who wrote them—self-consciously middle class, striving for an imitative eloquence, anxious to impress their betters while appealing to the masses. The broadsides of the National Society created a chorus that echoed from town to town —a chorus of hope and belief, of a sense of mission that helped to create in others the state of mind it expressed.[14]

[13] The most ambitious was that of the Milan committee of the SNI which published an eight-page paper three times a week. Modeled on the *Piccolo Corriere*, it was called *L'Élettore* and cost only 5 lire per quarter: *Piccolo Corriere*, 11 December 1859; printed letter of Castiglione, 6 December 1859, and manifesto of the Milanese committee, n.d., both in the Buscalioni pamphlets in HCL.

The SNI committee in Pavia sponsored a *Bollettino del Circolo Elettore Politico*, first announced on December 29; from a copy of the *Bollettino*, n.d. [March?] in the Buscalioni pamphlets in HCL. On the failure of the Bologna committee's special newspaper see Chapter Eight, note 61. The *Elettore Politico* of Genoa was paid for by the local committee of the SNI, the *Circolo Commerciale, Associazione Marittima, Associazione La Nazione* (Virgilio's), and a Comitato della Reale Marina. Even a Comitato Medico contributed 50 lire; from a bill, dated 29 March 1860, and Gerolamo Boccardi to Morchio, 10 March 1860, mss. in MNRG. The Leghorn committee of the SNI, which began activity independent of the local election committee only on March 11, was one of the last formed in Tuscany, Omero [Mengozzi] to Puccioni, 4 March 1860, ms. in archives of the Puccioni family.

[14] Based on the following manifestoes: Modena (in *Croce di Savoia*, 24 February 1860, in H. N. Gay newspaper clippings, 1856–1927, HCL), and the published letter of the *Società Pattriottica* (by its secretary who was in the SNI) to Cavour, 7 March 1860 (in Buscalioni pamphlets in HCL), manifesto of 3 March 1860 (*ibid.*); Piacenza, 2 February 1860 (*ibid.*); Parma (Fermi and Ottolenghi, *Manfredi*, 144–47); Ravenna, n.d., Faenza, 6 March; Russi, 8 March (MCRB); Rimini, n.d. (Nicoletti, *Comitato di Emigrazione*, 201); Imola (Galli, "Società Nazionale e Gamberini," *La Romagna*, XVII, 157); Scandiano, n.d. (in Broadsides in HCL, 440), and the announcement of the transformation

265

The leaders of the Society intended to influence the elections without running the risks or making the enemies that would result from a stand on specific issues or the nomination of particular candidates.[15] But it is hard to have a part in politics while remaining above them. The Society's own view of the elections as a demonstration requiring sweeping victory, its closeness to the Government, and the interests of its local members soon led it to behave more like a loose political party. The choice of candidates was supposed, then, to fall to local election committees; and most of them seem to have made their selection without great difficulty. The Romagna committees, which suffered more disagreement than most, nevertheless managed to resolve most of their difficulties by themselves. Still, when they devised a plan for doing so, they felt it necessary to communicate with the SNI's Central Committee in Turin.[16]

Local committees were particularly sensitive to the "indirect influence" of local men of note, of doctors and priests, intendants and commandants of the National Guard. These were the men who might succeed in "exciting the less active and instructing the less enlightened." [17] But when the Pavia committee chose Ricasoli as its candidate because of his fame and their desire to make the election of a Tuscan in Lombardy a demonstration of Italian unity, or when the Carrara committee picked General Cucchiari, "who had sustained on the battlefields the principle of annexation," they did so after consulting Turin.[18]

---

of the Tuscan central committee into an electoral committee, *Piccolo Corriere*, 4 March 1860.

[15] *Piccolo Corriere*, 15 January 1860.

[16] The Bologna committee thought of gathering the delegates to the Romagnol assembly to help in selecting a candidate before Mamiani was finally settled upon, leaving only the Imola committee, which had wanted Scarabelli, badly split: Ramuzzi, 14 January; Prosperi (Ferrara), 14 February; Salvoni (Rimini), 15 and 28 February; Serpiere (intendant of Cesena) and Masi (Lugo), 17 February 1860, to Casarini, mss. in Carteggio Casarini, MCRB. Telegram from Gamberini to Casarini, 2 February 1860 (and the latter's note on the back), *ibid.* Copy of a letter of Casarini to La Farina, 20 February 1860, *ibid.* Galli, "Società Nazionale e Gamberini," *La Romagna*, XVII, 158.

[17] Sarri sent a list of such men in the Romagna to Buscalioni, 6 March 1860, ms. in ISR, busta 718, n. 36; Istruzioni, n.d., and manifesto, 3 March 1860, of the Modena committee in the Buscalioni pamphlets in HCL.

[18] *Bollettino del Circolo Elettore Politico*, Pavia, n.d., *ibid.*; Tuscan broadside citing the *Osservatore Pavese* in the Houghton Broadsides, Tuscany, 1859–60, 750, HCL. Manifesto of the Carrara committee, n.d., among Buscalioni pamphlets in HCL; Dell'Amico to La Farina, n.d., ms. in ISR, busta 719, n. 8.

The Society's members calculated that the middle classes would be drawn by a nationally famous name; they saw the political value of having a Venetian or someone from the Trentino as a candidate. When they thought in more than local terms, they tended to look to the SNI's Central Committee for advice and assistance.[19] The candidate from Casalmaggiore even hoped the Society would use its influence to have their *podestà* reappointed so he could help in the elections; the Faenza committee wondered if the Central Committee could give its man some financial aid when he came to serve in Turin.[20]

On the local level, too, the Society came to serve as a political party as one after another of its committees took an active part in the local elections. Some proposed complete slates for local offices, usually including a generous proportion of names from the Society itself. Even that voter's mirage, lower taxes, was held out as a benefit which would come from having the supporters of the new order triumphant at home as well as nationally.[21] In some areas the intendant's cooperation with the Society must have made it seem as much an official party locally as nationally.[22]

Attention centered, however, on the elections to the Chamber of Deputies. During February and March, the *Piccolo Corriere* had reported some of the activities of its various election committees and noted a few candidacies which especially pleased it, particularly those of its own members. Then the issue of March

---

[19] Mai to Buscalioni, 21 May 1860, ms. in ISR, busta 717, n. 21; Antonio Gazzoletti to Festi, 30 January and 11 February 1860, mss., *ibid.*, busta 716, n. 59.

[20] Pietro Cordiglioni to Festi, 8 February 1860, ms., *ibid.*, busta 715, n. 87; and Casarini to La Farina, 27 February 1860, copy in Carteggio Casarini, MCRB.

[21] Participation in local elections, too, was a policy among the Romagna committees: circular of 7 February 1860, and Ballelli to Casarini [15 February 1860], ms. in Carteggio Casarini, MCRB; Galli, "Società Nazionale e Gamberini," *La Romagna*, xvii, 155–56. Manifestoes of the Piacenza (2 February), Pavia (n.d.), Carrara (n.d.), and Reggio (27 April 1860) committees, in Buscalioni pamphlets in HCL. Reports from Bagnacavallo, 21 March, and from Bussetto, 9 April 1860, ms. in ISR, busta 15, ns. 66 and 74. The Reggio committee was fairly typical in its list of candidates for the *consiglio communale* when it included 5 of its own members among the 15 it recommended, manifesto, n.d., in H. N. Gay newspaper clippings, 1856–1927, HCL.

[22] Serpiere, intendant of Cesena, to Casarini, 16 February 1860, ms. in Carteggio Casarini, MCRB; reports of the intendant of Ravenna, 15 and 30 August, about the Society's triumphs in the elections for the communal council of Ferrara, ms. in Indice al protocollo generale della giunta provisoria di governo, Romagna, Sezione del Interno, AST.

23, published two days early so it would reach its readers before the election, listed the candidates preferred by the *Unione Liberale* and the SNI for 122 seats.[23] Preparations for the election had become increasingly professional. Although neither the National Society nor the *Unione Liberale* officially nominated anyone, La Farina had begun early to speak of "our" candidates and to violate his dictum that their choice must be made locally. The widespread concern to prevent two "liberals" from running for the same seat gave the Society an increased role as a kind of clearing house, and soon the president of the SNI was suggesting which famous names it would be wise to run and encouraging the choice of men from other provinces.[24]

Overwhelming victory for the supporters of Cavour, the multiple election of the famous moderates, the election of men outside their native province—all this had become to the Society as important for what it would show at the moment as for what it might later produce in the Chamber. With so much at stake, La Farina necessarily played a part in picking candidates for particular seats. Soon he was questioning whether the man chosen locally could win, applying his full arsenal of argument to persuade Bartolommei to run from Florence in order to assure a safe seat there, using the public pressure of the *Piccolo Corriere* to persuade Scarabelli to be the candidate from Imola, or seeking a seat for Vegezzi-Ruscalla. The Society's Central Commit-

[23] *Piccolo Corriere*, 5 and 12 February, 4, 11, 18 and 23 March 1860. The 18 March issue contained a briefer list of *Unione Liberale* and SNI choices. The list was apparently drawn up by the former, however; for it omitted some selections of local SNI committees (probably because uninformed of them), while including men from a wider political spectrum than the Society was likely to support, such as Garibaldi for a seat from Genoa and one from Nice among many multiple candidacies.

[24] Letter, unsigned, to Morchio, 6 March 1860, on *Unione Liberale* policy, ms. in Carte Morchio, MNRG. La Farina to Gamberini, 16 December 1859, Galli, "Società Nazionale e Gamberini," *La Romagna*, XVII, 179, and, unidentified, in Franchi, *Epistolario di La Farina*, II, 254–55. La Farina to Germani, 2 January 1860, *ibid.*, 266. Manifesto of the Modena committee, 24 February 1860, in H. N. Gay clippings, HCL. La Farina recommended Minghetti, G. Malmusi, or Pepoli to Vergara, 6 February 1860, Franchi, *Epistolario di La Farina*, II, 294. *Piccolo Corriere*, 5 February (praising the nomination of Ricasoli in Pavia and Farini in Milan), 12 February (predicting the good effects of electing Ricasoli from Turin, too; Cavour from Bologna and Brescia and Minghetti from Genoa), 4 March (noting the value of picking emigrants from unliberated areas). The Society nevertheless failed to prevent two of its most prominent members, Armelonghi and Manfredi, from opposing each other in Monticelli (Piacenza), Fermi and Ottolenghi, *Manfredi*, 147–48.

tee may even have contributed funds to the campaign in Tuscany.[25]

The name La Farina most often suggested as a means of demonstrating national sentiment was his own. Occasionally, his suggestion was not well received. He had to be told that there was still resentment in Gallarate for what was felt to have been La Farina's neglect as royal commissioner during the war, and in Luino they reasoned that La Farina's many candidacies might appeal to those wishing to demonstrate something but not to those seeking a candidate.[26] The Society's President, however, continued cautiously to recommend himself to committees having difficulty picking their man, and many clearly considered it an honor to vote for him. By the middle of March he had been offered a candidacy in 10 different electoral colleges, 8 of which he accepted and eventually won. It was only his modesty, the *Piccolo Corriere* reported, which prevented them from listing the places which had so honored him.[27]

This use of multiple candidacies was a device for holding a seat during the first election with the hope that a reliable man of lesser note might be able to win it on the quieter second ballot. It was, La Farina suggested, a strategy he had worked out with Cavour. The president of the SNI would vigorously advocate his personal friends for seats he vacated; and, sometimes with hesitance, the Society's local committee would issue the necessary

---

[25] La Farina to Teresa Bartolommei, 18 February 1860, Franchi, *Epistolario di La Farina*, II, 296–97; *Piccolo Corriere*, 4 March 1860; Pietro Mallegori to Homodei, 1 March 1860, included in Homodei to La Farina, 3 March 1860, mss. in ISR, busta 716, n. 93. Having failed to procure a place for Vegezzi-Ruscalla from Bergamo, he was run from Reggio. Farini, who held a view of the elections similar to La Farina's, wrote to the men of the Society in Leghorn pleading that they block the rumored candidacy there of Brofferio: Puccioni, *Malenchini*, 99–100. [Cempini?] to Puccioni, 5 March 1860, refers to 710 francs from Buscalioni, saying Tito [Menichetti] wanted 200 of it, ms. in archives of the Puccioni family.

[26] Corta to Buscalioni, 1 December 1859, ms. in ISR, busta 719, n. 18. Guzzi to La Farina, 20 January 1860, *ibid.*

[27] La Farina to Selmi, 30 January; to Ghisalberti, 5 February and 18 March; to Zini, 9 February and 6 March; to Braglia, 28 February; to Conti, 15 March 1860, Franchi, *Epistolario di La Farina*, II, 288, 293, 295, 299–302. Casarini to La Farina, 22 February 1860, copy, ms. in Carteggio Casarini, MCRB. *Piccolo Corriere*, 23 March 1860. He was offered the candidacy from Busto Arsizio, Lodi, Cremona, Piacenza, Castel San Giovanni, Scandiano, Guastalla, Fivizzano, Porto Maurizio, and Oneglia. He refused to run in the latter two in order not to be in conflict with other liberals and won in Lodi and Piacenza on a second ballot.

broadsides, assuring voters that this second nationalist offered as attractive an opportunity for demonstrating patriotism as had La Farina himself.[28] The Society was still occupied with finding candidates for some vacated seats in April and May, although previous victories gave the Cavourians every reason for confidence. The greatest scare came from Imola where the Society had already been split during the first campaign. The president of the local committee refused to run, even though he seemed the only one capable of reuniting the factions. When Aurelio Saffi, one of the Roman triumvirs of 1848, announced his candidacy, even the intendant began to worry. But Prince Simonetti of the Society's Bologna committee was rushed into the breach. Still another seat was saved for the supporters of the Government.[29]

The elections were an overwhelming triumph for Cavour, the more impressive for coming immediately after the news that Nice and Savory were to be ceded to France. The limited suffrage, Cavour's own prestige, and the activities of his other followers may have been as important in that victory as the role of the National Society; still, the Society had played its important part in making the elections seem almost like the plebiscite all over again. The Society's standards were so high that the election in Lombardy of two men it opposed had to be attributed to error, faulty organization, inexperience, or lack of discipline. Indeed, the *Piccolo Corriere* could boast that only four men who neither belonged to nor were supported by the *Unione Liberale*

[28] La Farina to Zini, 6 March 1860, Franchi, *Epistolario di La Farina*, II, 299–300. La Farina recommended Vegezzi-Ruscalla (for his role in the SNI) and Ausunio Franchi (an unfrocked priest, for his "religion of the XIX century"): La Farina to Braglia and to Germani, 29 March, and to Franchi, 9 April 1860, *ibid.*, 306–308, 311. Scandiano's manifesto is in the Houghton Broadsides in HCL. Franchi apparently did not choose to run. The *Piccolo Corriere*, 15 April 1860, praised Scandiano and reported with disbelief that a clerical candidate was running in Fivizzano.

[29] La Farina to Giusti, 2 May 1860, Franchi, *Epistolario di La Farina*, II, 314; *Piccolo Corriere*, 29 April 1860. Ballelli of the Faenza committee was convinced that Camporesi, their second candidate, would prove "*inviso*" to two-thirds of the countryside: letter to Casarini, 24 April 1860, ms. in Carteggio Casarini, MCRB. Gamberini, leader of the "left" faction of the Society in Imola had had to resign the seat he won because he was too young; in the ensuing wrangle he could reassure Casarini, however, that they were at least all Cavourians: Galli, "Società Nazionale e Gamberini," *La Romagna*, XVII, 158–60. La Farina to Casarini, 10 May 1860, Dallolio, *La spedizione*, 57; and Finali to Casarini, 29 May 1860, ms. in Carteggio Casarini, MCRB.

or the National Society had been able to win. Only Cavour and Farini were elected from more places than La Farina, and in six constituencies La Farina's election had been nearly unanimous.[30] Some 40 of the newly elected members of the Chamber of Deputies were members of the Italian National Society; 10 of them had been the president of one of its local committees.[31] If some of these were men so prominent that they would have won whether the Society existed or not, there were others who owed their political success largely to the Society. Even some who would have been candidates in any case apparently won because of prestige gained from membership in and the campaign waged by the SNI. And there were those, especially among the deputies elected to seats vacated by more famous men, who owed their presence in the Chamber to the SNI in just the way most backbenchers, whatever their ability, are indebted to their party.[32]

[30] *Piccolo Corriere*, 1 April 1860; 82 of those proposed by the *Unione Liberale* and SNI won on the first ballot, 25 in the *ballottaggio*; 15 other of their men were elected, 5 of whom they had proposed but from other seats, 6 were their own members who for some reason they had not officially endorsed.

In Fivizzano La Farina received 117 of 122 votes (216 were eligible to vote); the votes for him elsewhere: Cremona, 212 of 248 (570 eligible); Busto Arsizio, 305 of 330 (581 eligible); Castel San Giovanni, 245 of 257 (516 eligible); Guastalla, 296 of 304 (442 eligible); Scandiano, 134 of 155 (263 eligible). On the first ballot Farini was elected in 10 places, La Farina in 8.

[31] The figure of 40 members of the SNI elected is from the *Piccolo Corriere*, 1 April 1860. It is, of course, extremely difficult to determine precisely who was formally a member of the SNI; my own lists indicate that about 30 deputies were almost certainly members of the Society and another 35 may have been members or were at least closely associated with local committees. Selmi later remembered 60 or more members of the SNI having been elected, but he is certainly wrong in indicating they were all the most prominent of the Society's following, Selmi, *La Farina*, 22.

The presidents of committees and the location of their seats, where different, were: Luigi Binard, Leghorn; Bartolommei, Florence (Montecatini); Castiglione, Milan (Casalmaggiore); Mai, Pavia; Didaco Maccio, Pistoia (Serravalle); Manfredi, Piacenza (Monticelli); Prosperi, Ferrara; Rasponi, Ravenna; Salvoni, Rimini; Simonetti, Bologna (Imola); Ruggiero Bonghi, president of the electoral committee of Pavia (Belgioioso). Gamberini, Imola, was elected on the first ballot but could not sit.

[32] The pattern of "replacements" is sufficiently interesting to warrant listing some: when Carlo Pepoli, elected from Castel San Pietro, opted for another seat, Gabriele Rossi and then Casarini, of the Bologna committee, replaced him until their elections were annulled on technical grounds. Mai replaced Ricasoli from Pavia when he opted for a seat from Turin. Menichetti replaced Ridolfi from San Miniato when the latter was made a senator. Prosperi replaced Carlo Francesco Mayr, who became intendant-general in Bologna, from Ferrara. A. Salvagnoli replaced his famous brother, who was made a senator, from Empoli. Tanari replaced Cavour in Bologna, and Vegezzi-Ruscalla replaced La Farina

That, even with so limited a suffrage, only about half the eligible voters bothered to cast their ballots may indicate the National Society's failure to stir the response it wanted. But that a plebiscite by universal suffrage could be followed by so limited an election without serious complaint and that the election could be taken as a significant expression of the national will, was at least in part a subtle measure of the success of the Society's propaganda. The SNI seemed to have become a major political power. It had worked closely with Cavour—from the conflicts with Garibaldi and Rattazzi to the crucial elections— and largely succeeded. Within the Chamber, despite his huge majority, Cavour found himself dependent on the newly elected deputies from Emilia and Tuscany, where the Society had been particularly effective, in order to prevent Rattazzi's election as president of the Chamber.

Yet the National Society was less able to behave as a political party in the Chamber than outside it. As always in its history, its very successes in some ways weakened it. Almost lost among Cavour's great majority, the deputies who were members of the SNI left little mark as a political bloc. Having insisted that their program had become the nation's, they had little reason to act as a separate group; the Society which would not oppose Cavour could not admit that it was simply Cavourian. By offering the most general of programs for the widest appeal, the Society had lost the chance to build a platform; and by accepting any safe candidate, it had lost the chance to build its own political identity or to establish how great its electoral strength was. Members of the Society, if aware of an opportunity missed, could only take pride in having been the "pioneers" and, true to their doctrine, in having made another sacrifice of their personal interest.[33]

---

from Scandiano; Tanari could undoubtedly have won without the Society, Vegezzi-Ruscalla perhaps could not have.

[33] Zini, *Storia d'Italia*, I², 559. Cavour to Nigra, 11 April 1860, *Cavour-Nigra*, III, 254–56; he probably exaggerated his weakness somewhat in order to restrain the French. *Piccolo Corriere*, 1 April 1860; Selmi, *La Farina*, 23. Even most of those who ran for the seats vacated by La Farina were not members of the SNI. Two proposals made in the Chamber within this period were sponsored by a significant number of the Society's men—though in neither case were they a majority: one of May 12, providing the grant of citizenship to Italians not born in the present state, had Malenchini, Armelonghi, and Maccio among its 13 sponsors (along with Finali, who was close to the Society, and Rubieri, who has some-

The National Society's participation in the elections was based primarily on its experience in the plebiscites, where the very phrases on the ballot seemed a restatement of the Society's slogans. The decision to have the citizens of central Italy declare at the polls their wish to be annexed to Piedmont had been frankly meant to provide a demonstration which would win the opinion of Europe and disarm Louis Napoleon with his own devices.[34] It was the sort of demonstration in which the Society believed, while the frightening uncertainties of universal suffrage—which the SNI opposed—roused its members to vigorous action. And they tended to be active especially in behalf of those whose "unhappy lack of instruction" might make them easily misled.[35]

For propaganda the Society could use almost unaltered nearly any of its previous statements, but it also developed some new techniques to meet the challenge of popular voting. Committees sent their own men touring the countryside, which they found less "deaf" than they had expected, to stir up nationalist sentiment and organize preparations.[36] Literally tens of thou-

times been mistaken for a member); the other of May 29, calling for a vote by roll call on the cession of Nice and Savoy which was clearly intended to restrict opposition, had Fenzi, Bartolommei, Cempini, and Gualterio (who was close to the Society though not in it) among its 10 sponsors. That they were Tuscan friends may be as significant as the fact that they were in the Society.

[34] Emanuele Marliani to Cavour, 12 and 19 March; and Corti to Cavour, 16 March, Cavour-d'Azeglio, II², 52, 56, 54. There were plans in the Marches to make the plebiscite their demonstration too, with bonfires and special posters, Zampetti-Biocca, Società Nazionale, 107.

[35] Piccolo Corriere, 19 February 1860; Casarini confessed to being "stunned" at the thought of universal suffrage: letter to Buscalioni, 4 March 1860, copy in Carteggio Casarini, MCRB. There was even a certain competition among towns in the issuance of manifestoes: the sindaco of Bagnone to La Farina, 27 February 1860, ms. in ISR, busta 720, n. 4; manifestoes of the Reggio committee, 7 March; the Modena committee, 3 March; the Comitato Nazionale per l'Italia Centrale, 3 March; and the programma of the Comitato Elettorale of Ravenna, 28 February 1860, a joint statement of the Ravenna, Faenza, Castelbolognese, Bagnacavallo committees, among the H. N. Gay clippings (although in fact broadsides) in HCL.

[36] The Bologna committee, which sent four of its men and Major Caldesi through the Romagna, instructed other committees to follow suit: Casarini to Buscalioni, copy, and circular of the Bologna committee, both 4 March 1860, in MCRB. Salvoni toured around Rimini and Galeati and Gamberini around Imola: Salvoni, 7 March, and Gamberini, 5 March 1860, to Casarini, mss., Carteggio Casarini, ibid. Galli, 'Società Nazionale e Gamberini," La Romagna, XVII, 39, 156–57. The Leghorn committee distributed propaganda among the popolani, Omero [Mengozzi] to Puccioni, 4 March 1860, ms. in archives of Puccioni family.

sands of *schede* were printed with the "*Sì*" already marked for easy voting and distributed among the populace.[37] In Lugo, which was unusually well organized, 7,000 marked ballots were printed for the town's 6,500 voters. A festive atmosphere was carefully nurtured. Men's hats were bedecked with tricolored ribbons, slogans for annexations, or the ballot itself. Bands, and sometimes even cool drinks, were provided. If the dignified president of the Society in Rimini found the role of "*Ciarlatano*" distasteful, he nevertheless took pride in the streamers that decorated his city.[38]

Although the National Society was not alone in all this, it was certainly the most active (and perhaps the most inventive) single group which contributed to the happy picture of central Italy on the day of the plebiscite. It had worked hard to see that the piazzas were festooned in red, white, and green and filled with local citizens and country bumpkins, strolling to band music, wearing patriotic ribbons, and clutching their ballots with the "*Sì*" already printed. The members of the SNI were not content to rest their influence on careful explanations to peasants or on the effects of a carnival atmosphere. They made sure that the voting itself proceeded with no casual anonymity. The Modena committee called on the commanders of the National Guard to lecture their men and to encourage the non-commissioned officers "of their own zealous will" to lead their men to the polls. Meanwhile, "influential" men should gather with

[37] La Farina put the figure at "several million": letter to Morchio, 6 March 1860, ms. in Carte Morchio, MNRG. Malenchini worried that the "Guerrazziani" were using the same technique for the opposite result: letter to La Farina, 28 February 1860, ms. in ISR, busta 717, n. 23. The Leghorn committee printed 10,000: Omero [Mengozzi] to Puccioni, 4 March 1860, ms. in the archives of the Puccioni family. The Modena committee instructed its members to provide the printed ballots to voters in its Istruzioni of 3 March 1860: copies among the H. N. Gay clippings, HCL and in the Museo del Risorgimento in Milan. The Bologna committee printed a number and instructed other committees to do the same: Casarini to Buscalioni, copy, and circular, both of 4 March 1860, in MCRB. Imola printed 18,000: Galli, "Società Nazionale e Gamberini," *La Romagna*, xvii, 157. A rich collection of documents on the plebiscite (including the Society's work and that of its members who often directed official municipal activity) is printed in Giovanni Maioli, "Il Plebiscito dell'Emilia e delle Romagna (11 e 12 marzo 1860)," *Atti e memorie, Deputazione di Storia Patria per l'Emilia e la Romagna*, viii (1943), 83–119.

[38] *Ibid.*, and circular of the Bologna committee, 4 March 1860; G. Marchi, 7 March; Masi, 8 March; and Salvoni, 7 March 1860, to Casarini, mss. in Carteggio Casarini, MCRB. Omero [Mengozzi], 4 March 1860, to Puccioni, ms. in archives of Puccioni family.

friends and relatives around the polling places, questioning and instructing others. They were to provide citizens with printed ballots, instructing them in the proper formula if they wished to write it and offering to write for those who were illiterate. As "lovers of liberty," they were "to beware that no one exercise a reactionary influence."

Throughout the Romagna the Society arranged for voting in organized groups. Everywhere the National Guard was particularly important; in Lugo it preceded a group of proprietors who were followed by the local artisans divided into fifteen classes, each holding a banner as it marched to the polls. In Bologna a "corps" of students carrying flags was to precede "corporations" of workers, bricklayers, and so forth. The "corporation of artists" voted en bloc in Ferrara, followed by the laborers en masse. In Faenza each class voted as a group, with the artisans first, then "the most esteemed men" in order to assure that the "*contadini* and *fattori* dependent on them" would do their part. Thus did universal suffrage rest on the Middle Ages, although there was a twentieth-century touch in the provisions in Lugo and Fusignano for women to vote on separate ballots (which could not be counted) in order that the demonstration might be complete. And in all this the Society benefited from the close cooperation of Government officials.[39]

The results of such effort were impressive. The overwhelming triumph of the plebiscites is well known; but the joy, the pride, and the confidence that outcome gave to Italian nationalists became an important element in later elections and in subsequent Italian history. The picture of Italy at last united in spirit, of the sick in the hospital demanding ballots, of the blind going in a body to vote, became part of Italian folklore. The National Society itself bore a new air of victory, of historical vindication. Thus the elections, too, and indeed all of Italian politics must,

---

[39] Istruzioni of the Modena committee, 3 March 1860, in the H. N. Gay clippings, HCL. Masi to Casarini, 8 March; circular of the Bologna committee, 4 March; Prosperi to Casarini, 5 March; Panciatichi to Casarini, 7 March; Armandi to Casarini, 13 March 1860, mss. in Cartegio Casarini, MCRB. In Cesena the preparations for the voting were made in the intendant's office, and the intendant of Forlì reported the results directly to Casarini: Serpieri, 5 March, and the office of the intendant of Forlì, 11 March 1860, to Casarini, mss., *ibid*. In Imola only two priests attempted to oppose the plebiscite, but they were arrested, Galli, "Società Nazionale e Gamberini," *La Romagna*, xvii, 157.

the Society felt, reflect the unanimous will of the nation. The *Piccolo Corriere* singled out 28 committees for special commendation, and the Society formally congratulated itself over and over. In its view, 12,000,000 Italians had made into law the slogan so long held aloft by the *Società Nazionale Italiana*.[40]

Thus the publications of the SNI pictured the Society as having waged a long and lonely battle over the past four (and sometimes even over the past six!) years. Disdained at first, it had succeeded; and that success was attributed particularly to the avoidance of "secondary issues." It was this, La Farina felt, which had kept the Society itself from splitting apart and had enabled it to contribute so much in turn to the unifying of Italy. The Society must not change now. But the argument was self-deluding; the avoidance of controversy in 1860 was in itself a political position. It meant the abandonment of the fruits of unification—liberty, economic growth, social change—as the subject of politics. The Society had not gone so far before; its program was changing after all.

This was reflected in the changed sense of the Society's two favorite words: "discipline" and "sacrifice." Before the war, the call for discipline had emphasized the need for cooperation and restraint among nationalists. Now it meant more. "To do nothing," could still be listed as a civic virtue, but the Society in 1860 also demanded the disciplined will to acquiesce in the policies of the Government. Apparently believing that they had held together a coalition of interests which might fly apart if the enemy disappeared, the leaders of the SNI insisted that their multiple foes were organized and dangerous. Lacking the confidence their successes might warrant and exaggerating the unanimity they had achieved before, they now feared disagreement more than ever. Crucial questions about the administrative organization of Italy or "liberty" itself were with rare explicitness ruled out as not fit subjects for debate. Independence, the Society argued, was still in doubt; and by stressing that Italy was in midstream, that she enjoyed only truce not peace, the SNI justified its own existence. By continuing to exclude all "secondary

---

[40] *Piccolo Corriere*, 18 and 23 March 1860. Circular of the Bologna committee, 13 March, in MCRB. The committees specially cited were all in Emilia and the Lunigiana.

questions," it seemed to broaden its political appeal and to leave its members free to think as they wished on those issues. It was more than coincidence if less than cynicism which made the demand that patriots be disciplined an insistence that the policies of the Government be accepted. The National Society "which had saved Italy" would now "sustain her." [41]

Something was added, too, in the Society's admonitions to "sacrifice." The word had always been used to mean a disregard of other issues and personal tastes in order to unite nationalists. Cavour himself used it in this sense, and La Farina could still expect others to renounce their program and join him. But in 1860 it was necessary to demand the sacrifice of personal and economic interests as well. La Farina boasted that he held no office not merely to prove his independence but as an example to others who would be expected to do without the job they wanted, the taxes or tariffs they advocated, if the Government's policy was contrary. Men who would make such sacrifices were the ideal deputies, and this was why the *Piccolo Corriere* had warned its readers that the Chamber was not an academy; there, too, the willingness to make a patriot's sacrifices was more important than "ability and erudition." [42]

With success the Society grew more intolerant. It viewed the elections as a mandate for its principles and expected its enemies to accept the voice of the people by growing silent. Shrill in its attacks on the "breakers of that concord" which it represented, the Society tended to place its opponents in three categories. As a party in power it expressed a special fear of "intriguers, seekers of employment, malcontents by nature and from personal interest." But those who disagreed from principle fared no better.

[41] La Farina to *Stampa*, 10 November; to the editor of *Il Pugnolo*, 10 December 1859; to Ghisalberti, 5 and 10 January; to Cabella, 5 February; to Conti, 15 March 1860, Franchi, *Epistolario di La Farina*, II, 231, 581–84, 272, 279, 292, 301. *Piccolo Corriere*, 1 and 18 November, 11, 18, and 25 December 1859. Clippings from *Adriatico*, n.d. [January–March 1860], *Croce di Savoia* (Modena), 24 February 1860, in H. N. Gay clippings, HCL. *Proclama agli elettori politici del collegio di Scandiano, Castellarano, e Carpineti*, n.d., in Houghton Broadsides, 440 in HCL.

[42] La Farina to *Stampa*, 10 November; to Germani, 5 December 1859; to Ghisalberti, 10 January; to Clementi, 28 January 1860, Franchi, *Epistolario di La Farina*, II, 231, 251, 279, 287; and Cavour to La Farina, 14 November 1859, *ibid.*, 233. *Piccolo Corriere*, 1 November (La Farina's proclamation of 20 October) and 27 November 1859. Election proclamation of the SNI in Piacenza, 2 February 1860, in Buscalioni pamphlets in HCL.

Opponents from the left were those who would seduce Italians with "impossible proposals." Advocates of unification by some other means were "philosophers and visionaries" who served only to weaken the nation. The *Unione Liberale* had reflected the Society in seeing Cavour's policies as ending "all conflict of opinion in Parliament." Even on Christmas Day, the *Piccolo Corriere* had labeled the maneuvers of Brofferio and others close to Garibaldi as an "attempt at civil war," the result of "senseless policies" and "calumnies collected in the mud of the most vulgar passions." Cattaneo became the target for violent abuse.

The "excesses of Roman theocracy" accounted for the Society's third category of opponents. For although it had, especially in local committees, tried to soften its anticlericalism, to praise nationalist clergy and avoid doctrinal opposition to the Church, the Society continued to see Catholicism behind any opposition it encountered from the right. In combating the "seditious suggestions" of the bishops, the Society extended its attacks to priestly malefactors and the influence of jesuitical arguments. When the *Piccolo Corriere* reported an Irish Catholic demonstration in New York against violations of papal territory, it added the intelligence that there were 44,000 Irish prostitutes in that city, a statistic explained as the natural product of education in bigotry and superstition. There was no doubt as to who was meant in a reference to those who "curse by trade" while dressed as men who should "come to bless." The intolerance of the Italian National Society was doctrinal after all; opposition to the policies of Cavour was simply "counterrevolutionary."[43]

Such attitudes reflected deep doubts felt about the masses and led the Society to defend limited suffrage with conviction. Its claims that even the peasantry were nationalist were made with the tone of those who protest too much. The Society's special pamphlet for the Lombard peasants dripped with condescension; and if the *Piccolo Corriere* reported with pleasure

[43] *Piccolo Corriere*, 18 and 25 December 1859; 19 February, 18 March, and 8, 22, and 29 April 1860. La Farina to Brizzolari and Canevazzi, 28 October 1859; and to Germani, 24 February 1860, Franchi, *Epistolario di La Farina*, II, 228, 297–98. *Programma* of the *Unione Liberale* in *Memorie di Pallavicino*, III, 852–54. *Il Comitato della Società Nazionale alla popolazione del Comune di Sissa* (Sissa, 1860); proclamation of the Circolo Elettore Politico of Pavia, 11 January 1860, in the Buscalioni pamphlets in HCL.

that some workers had joined the SNI, it did so in a way which expressed the great distance the Society's leaders felt between themselves and such men. The fear that public opinion could easily be misled had been a great spur to the Society in the elections, and there was a kind of strength in La Farina's confidence that "the rabble embitter me, but they do not degrade me." But there was only tragedy in his view of the Society's success: now the people "turn to me, but later they will turn to Mazzini, to Garibaldi, even to the devil. . . ." [44]

The views of the National Society in 1860 had earlier been implied in its doctrines, but now they were more inflexibly held. Nowhere was this more evident than in the Society's policy toward the new Italian state. The old arguments for the importance of Piedmont's military strength were, of course, repeated; but if the Society had before stressed the importance of order, it now found it a "duty" to support the Government. Indeed, whereas resentment of the old regimes had been patriotic, continuance of old injustices would not now justify discontent, for the patriot knew that in the reign of liberty all errors would be corrected. Besides, the sacrifices of Piedmont earned Italy's gratitude; and the benefits of unification were just beginning to be felt. Modenese industry and Lombard trade in wine would soon prosper from the abolition of old tariffs; railroads and commerce would blossom. In every respect the tranquil political temper of Turin remained the model.

The National Society could find no basis from which to permit opposition to the Government, and this was almost as true under Rattazzi as Cavour. Cavour's program was the right one, the one that had taken Italy so far toward unification and would carry her the rest of the way. But for all its support of Italy's great minister, the SNI was, as Pallavicino resentfully claimed, fundamentally a party which supported Piedmont's Government as such.[45] There was more sincerity than its critics allowed

[44] *Piccolo Corriere*, 18 December 1859; 4 and 18 March 1860. Manifesto of the Reggio committee, 8 February 1860, in the H. N. Gay clippings, HCL. "Catechismo politico al uso del popolo lombardo," in Biagio Caranti, *Pagine raccolte* (Turin, 1879), 295–312; a copy of the pamphlet, with an introduction dated 12 August 1859, is in HCL. La Farina to Franchi, 16 January, and to Canevazzi, 13 January 1860, Franchi, *Epistolario di La Farina*, II, 283, 280.

[45] *Piccolo Corriere*, 1 November and 11 December 1859; 22 January, 5 February, and 18 March 1860. La Farina to Ghisalberti, 7 November 1859, Franchi,

or historians have recognized in the Society's repeated assertion that it was independent of any particular ministers or ministry. Such independence also explained, in the Society's view, why Cavour did not use the SNI more and why its own support of Cavour should not be called partisan.[46]

The Society's reports of international affairs led to similar conclusions. Presenting the news in such a way as to suggest hidden sources and official contacts, the *Piccolo Corriere* insisted that it had long ago forecast events which the papers of London or Paris had not foreseen. After invoking such prestige, the *Piccolo Corriere* could make its prediction of an imminent European war or the French departure from Rome the justification for demanding that all patriots unite behind the Government. Unanimity was still necessary because the times were still perilous, the war itself was not really over.

Foreign affairs also justified the Society's optimism and answered the charge that Cavour had sold out to France. The readers of the *Piccolo Corriere* were told of Austria's worry when Cavour returned to power. They were assured that even if Napoleon III held the "neo-Guelphist" ideas attibuted to him, the major powers would oppose his plans. Indeed, all the powers favored Piedmont's annexation of central Italy; Germany and Greece were joining the ranks of Italy's friends and even Spain, busy in Morocco, was in no position to aid the papacy. If, however, the Neapolitan Kingdom and the papacy were drawing closer together, they offered the promise of two birds for one stone.[47]

The National Society's program had become more rigid but also clearer than it had ever been before. That clarity would prove a great asset in meeting the crisis which arose with talk of French annexation of Nice and Savoy. After a silence that was becoming noticeable, the *Piccolo Corriere* in its January 29 issue acknowledged some "rumors" by declaring rather weakly that

---

Epistolario di La Farina, ii, 229. *Società Nazionale alla popolazione di Sissa* and Istruzioni of the Modena committee, 3 March 1860. Pallavicino to de Lasteyrie, 23 January 1860, *Memorie di Pallavicino*, iii, 565.

[46] La Farina to the editor of *Il Pugnolo*, 10 December 1859; to Cabella, 5 February; and to Conti, 15 March 1860, Franchi, *Epistolario di La Farina*, ii, 581, 292, 300–301. *Piccolo Corriere*, 11 December 1859 and 5 February 1860.

[47] *Piccolo Corriere*, 1 and 29 November 1859; 22 and 29 January; 5 and 12 February; 4 and 23 March; 1 April 1860.

if the homeland of the House of Savoy wished to become French, the golden rule would require that the Trentino similarly be given a chance to express its feelings. From the first, however, a sharp distinction was made between Savoy and Nice. Vegezzi-Ruscalla's pamphlet establishing that the coastal city was wholly Italian won his Society's full approval. Even on the question of Savoy, the SNI attacked the French press for exaggerating the desire there to become a part of France.

The *Piccolo Corriere* had come close to defining a position quite separate from the Government's; and when the news of Cavour's policy became public and official, the paper could only claim that it had been right all along: the Government would never cede or sell territory although its own principles allowed no objection to a free expression of the popular will. It was not a strong stand, and the Society made no public pretense of supporting the cession. Later, like the supporters of any government which has made an unpopular treaty, the men of the Society would claim they had been taken in. The French had cheated, the Society's paper would explain, describing in anguished prose the tragedy of the *Nizzardi* voting in the presence of French troops. Garibaldi's famous protests were reported with a minimum of editorializing along with simple reports that Savoy would be neutralized, that the election statistics from Nice were impossible, and that the Prussians, Swiss, Belgians, and English were furious.[48]

Such unwonted silence, however, served the Society well. The *Piccolo Corriere* had helped to make it clear that those cessions were the price of annexation in central Italy, but the Society's nationalism had not been tainted. The men of the Society knew how unpopular Cavour's action was; perhaps he was not sorry to have the French know it too. By not pretending to like what realism required, the Society was better able to meet the grumblings in Lombardy or the Romagna. The Bologna committee used the whole arsenal of argument in a circular to the committees under it. Although it feared that those committees would not agree, they did; and they took pride in seeing that the petitions of protest circulated in their towns were not successful. This time the Society's Central Committee was not viewed with

[48] *Ibid.*, 29 January; 5 and 12 February; 1, 8, 15, and 22 April 1860.

suspicion as it had been when Garibaldi resigned from the SNI.[49] In the Chamber of Deputies, where it mattered most, those who were members of the Society began for the first time to meet as a group and to prepare for a favorable vote on the treaty with France, which sanctioned the cession of Nice and Savoy.[50] Cavour could have no better friends than the members of a Society which conducted itself with such political skill. The later tragedy of the Society would be that La Farina did not learn the lesson of the strength that came with subtlety.

With so many triumphs the Society assumed some of the other functions of a successful party. Local committees on occasion cooperated with government officials in intricate projects, or served as semi-official relief agencies.[51] The most important of these functions was a private channel of communication. Cavour could gain information on conditions in the Marches; and La Farina could find out whether the mother of an important official was really in close touch with Rome or related to a monsignor of the same name. He could have the Society check on rumors of corruption in local offices of the finance ministry.[52]

Similarly, membership in the Society offered a means of expressing local grievances with hope that they might be acted upon. The man who reported corruption or ineptitude in the local administration to the SNI was expressing an important confidence both in the new regime and in the National Society.

[49] Homodei [to Buscalioni], 15 April 1860, ms. in ISR, busta 716, n. 95. Circular of the Bologna committee, 14 April 1860; and Rasponi, 19 April, and Masi, 20 April 1860, to Casarini, mss. in Carteggio Casarini, MCRB.

[50] They were to meet every Tuesday and Friday at 8 p.m. in the office of the Society: Piccolo Corriere, 27 May 1860. Simonetti to Casarini, 25 May 1860, ms. in Carteggio Casarini, MCRB. La Farina acted the role of a party whip in making sure Manfredi would be present for the vote, letter to Manfredi, 12 May 1860, Franchi, Epistolario di La Farina, II, 320.

[51] The Modena committee's efforts to get reduced rail fares for émigrées or the projects to aid Comacchio were conceived as facets of the public assistance provided by the regime as a whole: letter of Ferdinando Ferrarini, 8 February 1860, ms. in Carteggio Casarini, MCRB, and clipping of 22 March in H. N. Gay newspaper clippings, 1856–1927, HCL; Piccolo Corriere, 1 April 1860. Ronchietti apparently used his position in the Ministry of War to disseminate the propaganda of the SNI, letter, 28 February 1860, to La Farina, ms. in ISR, busta 718, n. 27.

[52] Ginevri-Blasi to committees in the Marches, 12 January 1860, Alessandrini, I fatti, II, 156; Gamberini to La Farina, 10 December 1859, Galli, "Società Nazionale e Gamberini," La Romagna, XVII, 178; Homodei to La Farina, 11 April 1860, ms. in ISR, busta 716.

The Government of united Italy must have seemed less harshly impersonal to men who could write the Society about their friend who was not promoted or ask assistance for a friend who had some financial dealings with the state. The National Society was in turn a source of important help to the Government when it could assure its members that, despite the rumors they had heard, their intendant was a "good Italian and a good administrator" or when it could promise them generally that unification would be pushed slowly where it threatened to hurt the economy or able bureaucrats were not available.[53]

Inevitably, the National Society tended to act as a channel of patronage. La Farina was well aware of the dangers of such activity, and he reminded his followers that the purpose of their revolution had not been the winning of "rank, employment, or ribbons." He was also anxious not to weaken his position with the Government by asking for too many special privileges. Yet local committees did at times try to influence the selection of their intendant, and others in turn might ask a local committee to recommend, for example, a good anticlerical who could administer the property confiscated from the Jesuits.

La Farina himself found it useful to offer his influence in helping a member's relatives, or to declare that he had spoken a man's praises to his superior in the administration.[54] Such favors were performed, however, more on occasion than with regularity. As a political organization whose cause had won, the National Society necessarily behaved at times like a political party with patronage to dispense. But its own doctrine, like the nature of its organization, prevented its doing so in orderly fashion. The Society's greatest influence in the administration of Italy was therefore one which cannot be determined, the result of personal connections maintained outside the Society but first established within it.

[53] Casarini to Simonetti, 2 June 1860, Maioli, "Ancora della Società Nazionale," *Saggi e documenti del Risorgimento,* 121–22; Pietro Zani [to Buscalioni], 25 April 1860, ms. in ISR, busta 718, n. 95; Homodei to La Farina, 3 March 1860, ms., *ibid.,* busta 716, n. 93; Ghisalberti [to La Farina], 1 March 1860, ms., *ibid.,* busta 716, n. 63. La Farina to Germani, 16 December 1859, Franchi, *Epistolario di La Farina,* II, 256; *Piccolo Corriere,* 22 January 1860.

[54] La Farina to Clementi, 28 January, and to Vergara, 4 April 1860, Franchi, *Epistolario di La Farina,* II, 287, 308–309. Cordiglioni to Festi, 1 March 1860, ms. in ISR, busta 715, n. 87; Galeati to Casarini, 13 April 1860, ms. in Carteggio

With the challenge of elections behind it, the Italian National Society lacked something to do. The political life of northern Italy settled down, and the SNI had fewer functions of a political party to perform. It was opposed to raising controversial issues; yet its own doctrines called for activity. Buscalioni was thus attempting to meet the Society's needs when he suggested that it circulate a petition expressing Italy's gratitude to the SNI. The idea, he said, came from some of the local committees; and he made acting on it easy by listing the Society's accomplishments. The Society had led Italians to concord and helped "to maintain in the population that calm, that order, that full faith in the loyalty of the King, and in the wisdom of his government, that had procured the salvation of Italy and shown her worthy of liberty." A significant confession of the National Society's rather limited aims, it was an impressive claim to gratitude. What Buscalioni sought was another safe demonstration. The committees of the SNI, however, tended to take themselves more seriously than this. The suggestion seemed of little importance, and they rightly wondered at the appropriateness of such a statement's coming from the Society itself.[55] The SNI required more than self-congratulatory make-work.

Anxious to avoid the perils of domestic controversies, the Society therefore returned to an emphasis on propaganda directed to the subject areas of Italy. It had already been involved in some mild demonstrations in the Marches during the plebiscites in the north, and it would be again when the King toured Tuscany. There was even a hint of returning in the Marches to Manin's idea of displaying nationalism by not paying taxes. The silence from Naples and merely tantalizing rumors from Sicily remained disconcerting. Although it assured its "friends" there that their reasons were understood, the SNI called upon them now to get ready to fight. But the promise that the *patria*, like Christ, would honor late workers in the vineyard was more flat-

---

Casarini, MCRB. La Farina to Gallina, October; to Ghisalberti, 7 November; to Canevazzi, 25 December 1859, Franchi, *Epistolario di La Farina*, II, 217, 229, 262–63.

[55] Buscalioni to Casarini, 20 March; circular of the Bologna committee, 22 March; Salvoni, 27 March, Rasponi, 30 March, and Masi, 5 April 1860, to Casarini, mss. in Carteggio Casarini, MCRB.

tering to northern charity than southern fervor.[56] Wishing perhaps to look away from Nice and Savoy, the Society turned to southern Italy in its search for some appropriate activity.

On March 22 the SNI issued a special proclamation to the Bourbon and Papal troops. Similar to Manin's famous appeals to Swiss mercenaries, it represented a return to an older style of general nationalist propaganda. The proclamation emphasized the military strength of the North and warned that public opinion would find it hard to distinguish those who served Italy's remaining tyrants reluctantly from those who did so willingly. If war came, it would be short. While the North fought for the nation it loved, the South would fight for employers they hated. Victor Emmanuel would lead the North; the son of Ferdinand II, descended from a long line of cowards, and "expert in flight and treachery," would lead the South. The proclamation closed with an awesome threat and a simple promise. The memory of those who fought against the nation would be long, falling "on your children and your children's children, like the curse of the fratricide Cain!" But let the cry of "Italy and Victor Emmanuel" rise from their ranks and Italy would be.

With this vigorous appeal, the National Society was hinting at heroic action once again; and the proclamation was distributed by the tens of thousands. Packets went from Genoa to Naples and poured through the Romagna into the Marches and through Tuscany to Rome itself.[57] Once they had sent this propaganda on

[56] La Farina to Teresa Bartolommei, 16 December 1859, Franchi, *Epistolario di La Farina*, II, 254; Zampetti-Biocca, *Società Nazionale nelle Marche*, 86–92, 109–10, 232, 236–37. *Piccolo Corriere*, 11 March and 22 April 1860.

[57] The proclamation "Ai militi italiani al servigio del Borbone e del Papa" is printed in Biundi, *La Farina*, I, 438–40, with only the punctuation changed from the original (in Buscalioni pamphlets, HCL) to make it a bit more elegant. Biundi's estimate, *ibid.*, of hundreds of thousands of copies seems generous. On its distribution: La Farina to Vergara, 25 March 1860, Franchi, *Epistolario di La Farina*, II, 304; letter from the Bologna committee to the one in Rimini, 5 April 1860, ms. in MCRB; Alessandrini, *I fatti*, II, 197–98; Nicoletti, *Comitato di Emigrazione*, 321; report of the Netherlands' Ambassador to the Holy See, 5 May 1860, in Ghisalberti, "Documenti sulla caduta del regno Borbonico," *Archivio Storico per la Sicilia*, IV–V, 544. Zini, *Storia d'Italia*, I², 579–80, suggests the proclamation had some effect. It may also have spurred another one in French to the Swiss troops: Zampetti-Biocca, *Società Nazionale nelle Marche*, 117, 235–36. Chiala sees the proclamation as a change in Cavour's attitude toward the possibility of intervention in the south, *Carteggio di Cavour*, IV, cvii–cviii.

its way, the committees of the SNI had little more to do than believe their own message that another great moment was imminent. As in an earlier period of waiting, the *Piccolo Corriere* took to recounting tales which would show the strength of the national spirit. It told of the grants of money voted in Milan and Lodi and sent as a testimonial to the King, of how in Parma money was collected on Victor Emmanuel's birthday so that rice could be distributed to the poor and the city suitably decorated when next the King arrived. It reported the trip of a Doria to Pisa, returning the chain his ancestors had captured there in 1240. Still something more was needed.

The National Society and Cavour had triumphed; northern Italy was united but Venetia, the Papal States, and the Bourbon Kingdom still remained separate. Nice and Savoy had been surrendered. The petty realities of Italian politics were making themselves felt in every town. So the Society's paper began to list the great changes accomplished since the Congress of Vienna, and it found Italy's "the most fundamental of revolutions," a word it had not much used in the last six months. For Italy's revolution affirmed the right of nations and promised benefits for all the oppressed of the world.[58] The simple clarity of the Society's doctrine, with its self-conscious realism and its promise of very specific gains, was no longer entirely satisfactory. As Italians were asked to be pleased with the present and to wait for a better future, something of Mazzini's more ringing claims returned to the propaganda of the SNI. The National Society could find nothing to do that was both safe and exciting; it pointed, in print, to the south, and it waited.

[58] *Piccolo Corriere*, 11 March; 8, 15, and 22 April 1860.

IV ❖ COMPETITION FOR SOUTH AND CENTER

CHAPTER TEN

GARIBALDI GOES TO SICILY

(MAY—AUGUST 1860)

✤ WITH UNCOMMON RESTRAINT, the *Piccolo Corriere* reported in its issue of April 8 the news of a revolt in Palermo. Subsequent issues added that "Italy and Victor Emmanuel" was the Sicilian battle cry and that revolution had spread to Catania and Messina. A month later, the paper was barely more outspoken, merely noting that these disturbances, whatever their outcome, had had a good effect. They had weakened Austria's major Italian ally and demonstrated, even to Tuscans, the strength of sentiment for unification in the south. It was clear, however, that the National Society viewed these events with all the caution and some of the discomfort of a government. Still juggling the possibility of an alliance between Piedmont and Naples and unwilling to be associated with a revolt which had a slight Mazzinian air and might yet suffer a Mazzinian defeat, the *Piccolo Corriere* was much more at home with news of the "incredible barbarity" with which the Pope had excommunicated those involved in the annexation of the Romagna, much happier with accounts of the frenzied welcome accorded Victor Emmanuel in Tuscany.[1]

Yet such reserve from the Italian National Society was inappropriate; and it became impossible as rumors swept across northern Italy, and imaginations soared.[2] At such a time, the Society's members expected vigorous and dramatic leadership. Particularly in the Romagna, there were complaints that the SNI seemed dedicated to selling subscriptions to the *Piccolo Corriere* and finding multiple seats in parliament for La Farina. The committees in Faenza, Rimini, and Forlì began on their

[1] *Piccolo Corriere*, 8, 15, and 22 April; 13 May 1860. Although they are not always followed here, the classic accounts of Trevelyan remain as impressive for scholarship as dramatic style, G. M. Trevelyan, *Garibaldi and the Thousand* (London, 1910); *Garibaldi and the Making of Italy* (London, 1911); they should be consulted for background to this chapter.

[2] Homodei heard that Garibaldi, La Farina, and La Massa [sic] had already left, letter [to Buscalioni], 21 April 1860, ms. in ISR, busta 716, n. 95.

own to collect funds for aid to Sicily; and a subscription independent of the Society had already been announced in Bologna. Both the Government and La Farina were made aware of the Ravenna committee's desire to aid the Sicilian revolt.[3] The Society's assurances that it would not suffer "the remorse of not having done its duty" were insufficient; on May 6 the *Piccolo Corriere* announced the opening of a public collection for Sicily to be gathered by local committees and sent to the Society's Central Committee in Turin. The same issue of the paper noted the dissolution of the SNI's committee in Nice, but the news from Sicily lessened the sting of the news from Nice.

Once again the National Society was launched on what would become a great demonstration, one quite overshadowing the horse race the Society had planned to sponsor at the celebration of the anniversary of the *Statuto*. Somewhat defensively, the *Piccolo Corriere* explained that its subdued reporting of events was the result of self-censorship, a wish not to endanger their cause the way some others did by showing off the information they had. The Society, it promised, would not act like those "charlatans of revolution" who claim the credit when things go well and blame others when they do not. The virtuous tone suggested a temptation resisted, but an article entitled "The Government and Us" betrayed a further reason for the Society's caution. After carefully explaining the need for the Government to hold itself aloof, the article reasoned that the SNI could act without violating that need. The argument was highly pragmatic; it had turned out to be as imprudent for the Government to impede aid to Sicily as it was for citizens not to act in Sicily's behalf. The Society would claim from the Government only that freedom allowed its enemies; the collections for Sicily were named *Danaro d'Italia* to contrast with the *Danaro di San Pietro* being collected by the Church.[4]

[3] Ballelli [to Casarini], 24 April; Panciatichi had plans so daring they were not suitable for the mails: letter [to Casarini], 27 April. Proclamations of Forlì, 28 April; Rimini, 30 April, and Faenza, 30 April 1860, all in Carteggio Casarini, MCRB. *Monitore di Bologna*, 24 and 25 April 1860, Simonetti, Casarini, and Tanari were among the first contributors. Dallolio, *La spedizione*, 26–7. Conte Guido Borromeo to Farini, 20 April, *Liberazione del Mezzogiorno*, I, 59; Rasponi to Casarini, 19 April 1860, ms. in Carteggio Casarini, MCRB.

[4] *Piccolo Corriere*, 29 April, 6 and 13 May 1860. This formula kept the efforts on behalf of Garibaldi within the law, La Farina to Morchio, 11 May 1860, Franchi, *Epistolario di La Farina*, II, 318.

The fine legalisms of the SNI quickly lost their relevance; during the dark of May 5 Garibaldi and the Thousand sailed out from Quarto. At first, the Society publicly declared only that it had neither counseled nor tried to prevent that expedition, though it claimed four of the seven commanders under Garibaldi as its members.[5] Privately, La Farina made it a point to let his followers know of his part in the expedition even while he waited in tortured ignorance of whether Garibaldi actually intended to land in Sicily or the Papal States.[6] On May 11 the redshirts slipped safely into Marsala, and soon the Society claimed for its committees the "initiative" of a Sicilian revolution and assured its followers that Garibaldi could not have sailed without the help of the SNI.[7] Some of the Society's men remained confused as to their organization's part, but the *Piccolo Corriere* played happily to the hero-worship of Garibaldi. Propaganda is where you find it, and the Society's newspaper compared the General to El Cid, medieval knights, and Napoleon. It found him more like a fable than truth, which was, perhaps, not an unmitigated compliment; but it noted the enthusiasm he had engendered in a "skeptical and materialistic" age.[8] Surprised that the glories of 1848 were not dead, the National Society had nevertheless been implicated in the expedition of the Thousand from the first.

Garibaldi's fabled sailing had been neither sudden nor unexpected. The determination of La Masa, who had planned similar ventures in 1851, 1854, 1856, and 1859, did much to precipitate Garibaldi's trip; he had already been in touch with Cavour, La Farina, Bixio, and Medici among others. Rosalino Pilo had been working for a revolt in Sicily since the fall. Crispi had been at it since September; La Masa and Fabrizi had con-

[5] *Piccolo Corriere*, 13 May 1860; Garibaldi's own attitude to a Sicilian revolt was similar, letter to Malenchini, 3 May 1860, Puccioni, *Malenchini*, 125.

[6] La Farina to Giuseppe Gallenga, 2 and 12 May; to Giusti, 2 May; to Rizzari, 7 May; to Vergara, 11 May 1860, Franchi, *Epistolario di La Farina*, II, 313–14, 319, 315, 317. La Farina to Casarini, 1 and 10 May 1860, Dallolio, *La spedizione*, 39–40, 57. Medici and Amari waited to learn of Garibaldi's destination, too, letters to Malenchini, 12 and 13 May, Puccioni, *Malenchini*, 152, 155.

[7] *Piccolo Corriere*, 20 and 27 May, 3 June 1860. La Farina to Ghisalberti, 17 May 1860, Franchi, *Epistolario di La Farina*, II, 321.

[8] Anonymous letter [to Buscalioni] from Genoa, 9 May 1860, ms. in ISR, busta 720, n. 5; Bartolommei to Puccioni, 5 May, and Puccioni to Teresa Bartolommei, 7 May 1860, mss. in MRF, buste 109, n. 6, and 112, n. 4. *Piccolo Corriere*, 20 May, 10 and 17 June 1860.

sulted Depretis and Rattazzi while the latter was still Prime
Minister. Rattazzi then had used the SNI as an excuse for holding back just as Cavour would later claim that the Society
pushed him on. Even Bertani had encouraged Medici and Bixio
to consult Cavour; Sirtori had talked with him about aid to
Sicily and come away hopeful. In Genoa plans were readily
produced in an atmosphere dank with conspiracy but not
darkened by secrecy.[9]

To have been wholly unaware of such plans would have been
the mark of political ostracism. But these plans went unfulfilled, and disappointed expectations bred resentments. Soon
men like Crispi and Bertani made secrecy from La Farina part of
their plans. In late February excitement had begun to swell
again, and by April Crispi and Bixio were conferring with Garibaldi in Turin. Their guns were called for from Milan. Garibaldi
in turn met with some of Bertani's supporters in Genoa. On
April 16 he decided to go to Sicily and, eight days later, changed
his mind because of bad news of the revolt there. In principle, at
least, he had agreed to lead an expedition; and the unifying
warmth of his personal fervor spread over the conspirators. As
plans advanced, confidence returned; La Farina and others were
again consulted on the plans for Sicily.[10]

In its own way the National Society had been paying more
and more attention to the south. As it did in other unliberated
areas of Italy, the Society tended to rely in particular upon Committees of Emigration; for the men who composed them often
had important connections back home and were usually men of
substance and dignity who were a natural counter to Mazzinian
influences. Early in April a Committee for Aid to Italian
Emigrants was called together in Genoa by the city's vice-
governor. Made up of Cavourians, many of whom were friends
of La Farina, its interest focused heavily on the south and with

[9] [Giuseppe La Masa], *Alcuni fatti e documenti della rivoluzione dell'Italia
meridionale del 1860 riguardanti i siciliani e La Masa* (Turin, 1861), 11. Pilo
to Calvino, 10 November 1859, Curatolo, *Garibaldi, Vittorio Emanuele, e
Cavour*, 51. Crispi to Fabrizi, 16 September, 4 October, 6 and 15 December
1859, Crispi, *I Mille*, 98–106. *Ibid.*, 107, 109–15. Mario, *Bertani*, 11, 1; Medici
to Malenchini, 25 February 1860, Puccioni, *Malenchini*, 110–11. Agrati, *Sirtori*,
189.
[10] Guerzoni, *Garibaldi*, 11, 81, 85; Mario, *Bertani*, 11, 8; Bertani, *Ire d'oltre
tomba*, 51, 57. Pilo to Crispi, 24 February 1860, Crispi, *I Mille*, 115; Chiala,
Lettere di Cavour, vi, cxxv.

an eye to more than charity. At about the same time a committee of some 50 to 80 southern emigrants was formed which then adopted the slogan of the National Society as its program and elected La Farina one of its directors. The chances of a revolution in Sicily was this committee's primary concern, and it sent a number of emissaries to the island.[11]

The National Society was being drawn into the plans for action. Doggedly continuing his preparations for an invasion regardless of Garibaldi's reading of its chances, La Masa approached La Farina for help. He won the promise of arms, munitions, and transportation *for emigrants* at the first sign of revolt. By limiting aid to such men, La Farina lessened the political dangers of the enterprise both domestically and internationally. From a position very different from Crispi's, he found himself also preparing to store rifles in Genoa and waiting for news of the progress of Sicilian revolt. When La Masa ceded his leadership of the expedition to Garibaldi, and the group around Bertani and Crispi began again to consult the president of the SNI, La Farina's preparations came to benefit the Garibaldian effort.[12]

The Society's hesitance and uncertain policy was matched by the Government's. La Masa had spoken with Cavour, and Count Amari was sure they had the Government's sympathy. (It seems even to have been tempted to sponsor an expedition of its own.) Yet Borromeo continued to warn, in official tones, against "imprudences." The Neapolitan Consul had no doubt that La Farina's participation was direct and on orders from Cavour, but the Prime Minister denied it. La Farina may have made Cavour more willing to cooperate with Garibaldi by declaring that the Society's, not Mazzini's, influence was dominant in the plans for an expedition, but he himself was certain not

[11] *Corriere Mercantile*, 30 March 1860, cited in Nazari-Michele, *Cavour e Garibaldi*, 70. Salazaro, *Cenni sulla rivoluzione*, 37, says 84 members were at the meeting of April 9 and that 80 voted. Domenico Di Giorgio, "Il 1860 in Calabria e Benedetto Musolino," *Historica*, 1 (1948), 128, says that 50 men met at Agostino Plutino's house on April 7. They agree that Carlo Poerio, Interdonato, Mancini, Giuseppe [?] Pisanelli, Plutino, and La Farina were among those present. Villamarina to Cavour, 26 April 1860, *Liberazione del Mezzogiorno*, I, 69–70.

[12] La Masa, *La rivoluzione dell'Italia meridionale*, ii–iii; La Farina to Vergara, 4 April, and to Franchi, 9 April 1860, Franchi, *Epistolario di La Farina*, II, 309, 312. Bertani to Garibaldi, 19 April 1860, Mario, *Bertani*, II, 34.

only on April 24 but a week later that no expedition would take place.[13]

The Government, then, neither gave Garibaldi all the aid, even secretly, that it might have nor did it effectively stop him. The interpretation made of the Government's role by contemporaries and by historians has had to rest on their larger view of Cavour.[14] What the evidence overwhelmingly suggests is that the Government had no confident policy. Cavour was probably only exercising the politician's habit of making the truth clearer than it ever is when he protested that he had done all he could to hold Garibaldi back or when he argued that to have succeeded in doing so would have been fatal to his ministry. It was more uncertainty than shrewd dishonesty which made him think of La Farina as an emissary sent to prevent Garibaldi's sailing; just as, when it became necessary that the Government openly sympathize with and even aid the Sicilian venture, he chose to believe that it was really directed by La Farina and those close to the SNI. With the enthusiasm characteristic of his family, the Prince of Carignano spoke to Dolfi about secret governmental aid; but Cavour made it clear that the Prince should deal with the National Society's Malenchini. When he did consult Malenchini, the Prince was disappointed at the vagueness of plans for help from Turin and, with royal naïveté, shocked at the absence of a written document.[15]

[13] Guerzoni, *Garibaldi*, II, 76, 228; Fanti to Ribotti, 6 April 1860, Mario, *Bertani*, II, 23; Count Amari to Michele Amari, 3 May 1860, Luigi Natoli, *La rivoluzione siciliana del '60 e il Conte Michele Amari di S. Adriano* (Rome, 1911) [first printed in *La Sicilia Illustrata*], 11. Borromeo to Farini, 20, 24, and 26 April 1860, *Liberazione del Mezzogiorno*, I, 59, 63; V, 475. La Farina to Cavour, 24 April 1860, *ibid.*, I, 62–3. Barone Giuseppe Canofari to Luigi Carafa, 7 May 1860, *ibid.*, V, 87. Reports of the Neapolitan Legation, 6 and 13 April, of the Russian minister, 19 June, *ibid.*, 79, 255.

[14] A good argument for Cavour's participation is made by H. Nelson Gay, "Cavour und die Tausend," offprint from the *Deutsche Revue*, December 1910. The best recital of the facts and the best case for Cavour's opposition to the expedition is made by Denis Mack Smith, "Cavour's Attitude to Garibaldi's Expedition to Sicily," *Cambridge Historical Journal*, IX (1949), 359–70. An excellent sample of the confusion in the documents themselves is found in Borromeo to Farini, 26 April 1860, *Liberazione del Mezzogiorno*, V, 475. Clearly, Cavour wished that the whole question of an expedition would not come up; but is La Farina promising to put a damper on the planning or insisting that it must continue?

[15] Cavour to Nigra, 12 May and 22 July 1860, *Cavour-Nigra*, III, 294; IV, 94. Cavour to Prince of Carignano, 18 May 1860, *ibid.*, III, 300. Prince of Cari-

The very participants themselves, and La Farina first of all, were not altogether clear as to what was happening or who supported what. Thus the same observer could be struck by the "distrust" between Garibaldi and La Farina on the day the Thousand sailed and remember two days later that they were "perfectly agreed." Later events would determine whether those who organized the expedition would remember a frowning bureaucrat's correctness or a smiling official's leniency as the measure of the Government's position.[16] Garibaldi himself was not one to be worried by subtle political distinctions, and he saw with a general's clarity the importance of maintaining a vigorous center of supply after he had left. Operating in the personal terms within which he was comfortable, he urged many to do what they could. But it was a gentle tribute to the National Society that Malenchini and Tanari were among these. At the moment of departure, La Farina's staying seemed as important as the willingness of many others to go.[17] Both La Farina and Bertani could foresee the fulfillment of their programs when Garibaldi sailed away. If it seemed to produce unity among nationalists, however, the expedition was not the product of real agreement or even understanding. The importance of that fact would become plain in the next few months.

The great effort on behalf of Sicily had barely begun when Garibaldi left. His success would require the collection of great sums of money and the organization of great shipments of men, weapons, ammunition, and equipment. Innumerable committees sprang up across northern Italy to accomplish these tasks. Count Amari had spoken with Garibaldi in April about the need to collect funds for the Sicilians and on April 20 had opened a fund drive for aid to Sicily. Committees formed to

gnano to Cavour, 15 and 20 May 1860, *Liberazione del Mezzogiorno*, I, 104–105, 113.

[16] Zini, *Storia d'Italia*, I², 579n; Nazari-Michele, *Cavour e Garibaldi*, 203–204. Finali to Simonetti, 5 May, and to Casarini, 7 May 1860, Dallolio, *La spedizione*, 42, 53.

[17] Garibaldi to Medici, 5 May, was given wide circulation by the SNI, a copy is in Puccioni, *Malenchini*, 123; Garibaldi to Malenchini, 2 and 3 May, *ibid.*, 124–25; Garibaldi to Tanari, 2 May 1860, in Giovani, "Tanari," *L'Archiginasio*, VIII, 268. Guerzoni, *Garibaldi*, II, 228.

contribute to his fund proved particularly effective in Tuscany and the Duchies, and it was his example which had led to demands that the SNI do as much in the Romagna. Indeed, members of the National Society were among the most prominent of fund-raisers and contributors to Amari's drive. During the first two months after Garibaldi had sailed, most other groups sent their money to the Count; and in all more than 3 million lire passed through his hands, though he himself collected much less. When Garibaldi made him representative to the Piedmontese Government, Count Amari became the channel through which supporters of Garibaldi could aid his efforts while avoiding Bertani; and Cavour himself insisted that contributions should be sent directly to Amari.[18]

The Million Rifles Fund had been founded by Garibaldi much earlier and had been collecting funds longer than any of the others. Profiting by its association with the General, it collected nearly as much money as all the other groups combined. Over half its total of one and one-half million lire came, however, from Lombardy alone; and another one-fifth came from the unliberated areas of Italy, particularly the Veneto, and from other countries, where the glamor of Garibaldi's name was enough to start a fund-drive. The Million Rifles Fund also received many large contributions from municipal governments and from various political and professional organizations.[19] The Central Committee of the National Society received directly, and from member committees, nearly one-half million lire; and Bertani,

[18] La spedizione di volontari per Garibaldi [first printed in the Corriere Mercantile] (Genoa, 1861), 24. Amari collected about 200,000 lire directly: Natoli, Rivoluzione siciliana e Conte Amari, 6. Count Amari to Emerico Amari, 10 April 1860, ibid., 8. Michele Amari to the Count and to the Nazione, 20 April 1860, Alessandro d'Ancona, Carteggio di Michele Amari, II (Turin, 1896), 73–6. The Piccolo Corriere, 24 June 1860, recognized Amari as Garibaldi's agent and advocated sending funds directly to him. The Society had decided, 11 June, to give its own funds to him, ibid., 3 March 1861. Cavour to E. d'Azeglio, 21 June 1860, Cavour-d'Azeglio, II, 85.

[19] Enrico Besana and Giuseppe Finzi, Resoconto di tutta la gestione del Fondo del Milione Fucili (Milan, 1861), gives 1,541,128.03 lire as the total they collected. My addition indicates 801,476.21 came from Lombardy (including 527,830.68 from the province of Milan where the city voted 200,000 and the chamber of commerce contributed 54,226.85). Some 332,384.35 came from unliberated areas of Italy and from abroad, including contributions in dollars from San Francisco, California; Portland, Oregon; $18.50 from "Bear Valley," and $52.50 from "Indian Bar (North-Fork Fealther [sic] River)." The Daily News sent over 5,000 lire collected in London.

who established a *Cassa* of his own and claimed exclusive authority as Garibaldi's representative in all matters of provisioning, collected somewhat more.[20] These figures must be taken as only approximate indications of the contributions of each group. For although the accounts the committees published give every indication of being essentially accurate, their statistics include a good deal of confusing duplications. The statistics tend to slight the role of the National Society in particular. Of these four largest collection agencies, the SNI made the fewest purchases of its own; unlike the others, therefore, it rarely included in its accounts money collected by other groups which it had a part in spending. Furthermore, members of the SNI often actively collected for Amari or the Million Rifles, and all the local committees of the SNI made direct expenditures, much of which is not included in the Central Committee's accounts.[21] Initially, of course, the Million Rifles Fund could provide the most money, and Amari's committee was beginning to receive a steady flow of contributions by the time the first expedition sailed. The National Society's campaign developed quickly, however; and into August the collections of its Central Committee were greater than Bertani's. But the fact that the Society was already organized and had many official connections makes Bertani's success impressive and significant. Nevertheless, from May through August in northern Italy—excluding Lombardy—the Italian National So-

[20] *Piccolo Corriere,* 7 July 1861, in a formal rendiconto lists 451,466.78 as the total received by the SNI's Central Committee. *Cassa Centrale, Soccorso a Garibaldi, 1860, Resoconto di Agostino Bertani* (Genoa, 1860) lists 851,735 lire as the amount collected, but this includes 321,870.06 lire contributed to the first expedition by the Million Rifles Fund which, when subtracted, leaves 529,-864.94 lire. Bertani's accounting also includes 45,000 from the *Società Unitaria* of Milan (which also gave to the Million Rifles Fund) and 36,592.72 lire from Garibaldi himself (which may represent money sent directly to the General).

[21] The Besana-Finzi account includes, for example, 40,000 lire from the SNI in Turin, and they included 10,000 lire voted by the city of Modena to the SNI: Besana to Buscalioni, 16 July 1860, ms. in ISR, busta 545, n. 45. Among the leaders in the SNI who collected for the Million Rifles Fund were ing. Mai in Pavia, dott. Enrico Pontoli in Parma, avv. Luigi Lupi in Piacenza, Simonetti and Tanari in Bologna, and Malenchini in Tuscany, *La spedizione di volontari,* 4. Malenchini was also a heavy contributor to Amari's fund: M. Amari to *Nazione,* 16 May 1860, d'Ancona, *Carteggio Amari,* II, 84; Ersilio Michel, "Vincenzo Malenchini e la Spedizione dei Mille (memoria inedita di Michele Amari)," *Il Risorgimento,* 1 (1908), 990. Bartolommei wrote Puccioni, 4 June 1860, to contribute directly to Amari, ms. in MRF, busta 112, n. 2.

ciety was probably the best known and best organized agency collecting funds for the Sicilian campaign.[22] But this came later. During that April of almost public conspiracy in Genoa, La Farina was welcomed less for the funds he might collect than for the influence he might command. He bustled about negotiating, warning, advising, establishing conditions on which, he was sure to imply, Government support would depend. Officious and earnest, he engendered resentments that for the moment were swallowed while the hope grew of help from Cavour.[23] Then Garibaldi, having decided to go, sent to Milan for some of the rifles stored there by the Million Rifles Fund; but d'Azeglio, who was willing to risk a losing war but never an undeclared one, refused to permit their release. Thus it came about that the rifles Garibaldi took with him came from the National Society, and the teller's prejudices determine whether the point of this oft-told tale is that Cavour overcame the embarrassing squeamishness of d'Azeglio by having La Farina ship cases of rifles innocently marked "books" or that the rifles proved to be rusty former flintlocks, nine-tenths of which would not fire. It is unlikely, however, that even La Farina had the foresight to stash some antiquated weapons in anticipation of a chance to send his rivals to suicide.

The very first expedition, then, left with 1,000 rifles, 5 cases of ammunition, and 8,000 lire from the Italian National Society. This was, apparently, about what La Farina had earlier offered La Masa (his refusal to put up a guarantee for La Masa's ship must have reflected the Society's lack of funds as well as La Farina's recognition of a bad risk). Aid on so small a scale (the

---

[22] *Cassa Centrale, Resoconto* does not break down receipts by province, but 109,715.86 lire in gifts large enough to stand out came from Lombardy and 77,000 lire from abroad. By July the Central Committee of the SNI had received 401,301.49: *Piccolo Corriere*, 1 July 1860. Bertani's fund had 285,166.08 (not counting the 321,870.06 from the Million Rifles Fund). The comparable figures for the end of July are: SNI, 456,156.69 (from *Piccolo Corriere*, 29 July 1860); Bertani's *Cassa*, 389,305.66. For the end of August: SNI, 470,179.05 (*Piccolo Corriere*, 5 September 1860); Bertani's *Cassa*, 484,320.46.

[23] La Farina to Vincenzo Gallina, 2 May 1860, Franchi, *Epistolario di La Farina*, II, 314; Michele Amari to Count Amari, 20 April 1860, d'Ancona, *Carteggio di Michele Amari*, II, 74; Crispi to Pilo, 20 April 1860, Crispi, *I Mille*, 127. Michel, "Malenchini e la Spedizione," *Risorgimento*, I, 991; Domenico Guerrini, "Un documento relative alla spedizione Garibaldiana in Sicilia," *ibid.*, 770.

Million Rifles Fund spent over 300,000 lire on that expedition)
suggests that it came from the Society itself and not indirectly
from the Government. Indeed, that aid implies very little about
Cavour's view of the expedition. La Farina implicated himself
with such caution as to suggest he had no blank check, and an
impressive list can be made of the evidence that Cavour still
rather hoped the expedition could be stopped.[24]

What was important at the time was that, once Garibaldi
sailed, La Farina's participation was taken as a sign of official
sympathy. The Society's importance seemed to grow, and those
preparing expeditions to Sicily never lost the dream of directly
tapping some of the Government's wealth. When Palermo fell,
and the Powers limited themselves to diplomatic protests, the
Government did relax. Garibaldi's cache in Milan was released,
and Cavour gained credit for having allowed it to be gathered
in the first place. By June the Government was giving some direct aid. One of the *rendiconti* in manuscript lists 45,000 lire
"del Governo" as given by the SNI; there was a reference in
August to the Government's sending munitions, and it helpfully
encouraged a steamer service from Genoa to Palermo.

Late in April the Brescia National Guard began negotiations
to pay the Million Rifles Fund 90,000 lire for 3,000 of its rifles;
but the tradition quickly grew that the Government never collected its purchase. The King himself had also contributed to
the Fund. Most contemporaries agreed that much of the huge
sums provided by the Million Rifles Fund for the purchase of
ships in June came from the Government. In all, the Fund spent
nearly 400,000 lire more than it collected; the SNI, nearly 200,-
000.[25] Those in the know felt they knew the source of that sur-

[24] Mack Smith, "Cavour's Attitude to Garibaldi's Expedition," *Cambridge
Historical Journal*, IX, 363–69. *La spedizione di volontari;* Besana and Fenzi,
Resoconto del Fondo del Milione Fucili. La Masa, *La rivoluzione dell'Italia
meridionale,* iii–iv; Mario, *Bertani,* II, 21–31, 40. Bertani insists La Farina arrived
on the scene after the arrangements had been made and that he would not even
make available all the rifles he had, Bertani, *Ire d'oltre tomba,* 35, 45, 52–3.

[25] Alessandro Luzio, "Il Milione di fucili e la Spedizione dei Mille," *La Lettura,*
x (Milan, 1910), 291–93. Medici to Garibaldi, 25 May 1860, Curatolo, *Garibaldi, Vittorio Emanuele, e Cavour,* 103. Count Amari to Michele Amari, 3
May 1860, and to Emerico Amari, n.d., Natoli, *Rivoluzione siciliana del '60,*
10, 14. "Rendiconto Cressini," accounting for the 164,578 lire which he handled, n.d. [the last date is 22 September]; the 45,000 lire is entered as received
August 9, 10, 14, ms. in ISR, busta 719, n. 12. Gay, "Cavour und die Tausend,"

plus; and although the evidence is not conclusive, the fact that neither group showed later signs of suffering from such heavy debts suggests that at some point the Government helped cover these deficits.

Cavour's Government, then, did make important contributions to the Sicilian campaign; but they were hardly enormous, and they came at least largely after Garibaldi's success seemed probable. That so many reasonable men believed the Government had given vigorous and active support, perhaps even all that was wanted, was a result of the tentative presence of the Italian National Society and the now universal conviction that it represented Cavour's well-disciplined conspiratorial arm. Even those close to Bertani came to believe the Government had given nearly 2 million lire for Medici's expedition; and Cavour's supporters would remember nine-tenths of the costs of the Sicilian campaign coming from the friendly Government in Turin. The government of which that was more nearly true, however, was the defeated one in Sicily.[26]

---

from *Deutsche Revue*, 7–13, suggests that Cavour supported the May 24 sailing under Agnetta, but his evidence is not conclusive. Note of Count Amari, 30 July 1860, in *Liberazione del Mezzogiorno*, v, 296.

The price of 30 lire per rifle, for Enfields, is surprisingly low but was used on other occasions as an accounting figure; all of the following assume this was a mere device for aid from the Government: Stefano Türr, *Da Quarto a Marsala nel Maggio del 1860* (Genoa, n.d.), 13; Mario, *Bertani*, II, 74; Nazari-Michele, *Cavour e Garibaldi*, 207, cites *Opinione*, 6 September 1869; Sforza, "Esuli estensi," *Archivio Emiliano*, II, 132n. Besana and Finzi, *Resoconto del Fondo del Milioni Fucili*, indicates their deficit of 397,302.95 lire was met from the arms fund of the National Guard. See also Curatolo, *Garibaldi, Vittorio Emanuele, e Cavour*, 193–94.

Piccolo Corriere, 7 July 1861, lists a deficit of 199,988.32 lire (over 111,000 more than the figure in the issue of 23 December 1860. See Chapter Twelve, note 23); the difference may be what the Government had in fact contributed or merely the result of a more accurate accounting or one meant to make better propaganda. The debt began to accumulate early, but the suggestion that it was based on the "personal obligations" of the members of the Central Committee probably overestimates their wealth as well as their generosity: *Piccolo Corriere*, 27 May 1860. La Farina was worried about it in July: letter to Giuseppe Morelli, Franchi, *Epistolario di La Farina*, II, 380. See also his letter to Vergara, 11 May 1860, *ibid.*, 317.

[26] Alessandro Luzio, "Le Spedizioni Medici-Cosenz," *La Lettura*, x (1910), 481–90. Sirtori and Bixio and even Bertani acknowledged Cavour's aid in the Chamber, 17 and 19 June 1863, *Atti del parlamento italiano*, VIII Legislatura, I (Rome, 1886), 453, 459–61. The energetic Farini added to the impression of Governmental assistance: see Governor of Cagliari to Admiral Carlo Persano, 19 June 1860, Persano, *Diario*, 48. Bargoni to Calvino, 21 June 1860, Bargoni, *Memorie*, 129; G. Nazari to Buscalioni, 16 September 1860, Nazari-Michele,

The two ships on which the Thousand sailed had been seized from the Rubattino Company, but it was impossible to keep procuring transport in this way.[27] Providing a steady flow of men and supplies to Sicily would require fuller organization than had been necessary for the first expedition. Under Medici's direction, an *Ufficio Militare* took general charge of planning expeditions and ordering the necessary stores and transport; most of its funds came through Amari. Bertani's *Cassa Centrale per il Provvedimento* did not limit itself to collecting funds, so that many of its activities overlapped those of the *Ufficio*. By the time Medici himself went south in early June, the *Ufficio* was operating quite independently of the politically suspect Bertani. Cosenz took over this supervising function until he sailed in early July, when he was replaced by Cressini. By then the *Ufficio* had established contacts and even committees of its own throughout northern Italy which dealt primarily with the recruitment and delivery of volunteers to Genoa. Members of the National Society were often the leaders in these committees, except in Piedmont where the Society itself performed these functions; and local committees of the SNI came increasingly to deal directly with the *Ufficio* rather than through their Central Committee.

Not until May 24 did another ship leave to aid Garibaldi. That one, the *Utile* under Agnetta, carrying a few men, 3,000 rifles, and a supply of ammunition, was almost entirely a project of the National Society.[28] The delay of three weeks between the

---

Cavour e Garibaldi, 203. Bertani, in his *resoconto*, lists 5,106.45 lire from Sicily (and 201,632.05 more from Naples).

[27] Fauché, the Rubattino agent who made the seizure of their ships possible, lost his job for his patriotism. G. B. Fauché, *Una pagina di storia sulla spedizione dei mille* (Rome, 1882) [taken from the *Gazzetta d'Italia*, 17 June 1882]; Pietro Fauché *Giambattista Fauché e la Spedizione dei Mille* (Rome, 1905); Amerigo d'Aima, *Giambattista Fauché nell'epoca dei Mille* (Pisa, 1915); Luigi Gasparini, "La verità sulle navi dei Mille," *Nuova Antologia*, LXXXV (1950), 391–99.

[28] The Society issued a circular, 14 July 1860, telling its members to deal with the *Ufficio Militare* with regard to volunteers, *La spedizione di volontari*, 24. Unless otherwise indicated statistics given on the expeditions and expenditures for them are taken from the above (which is a *resoconto* apparently put together jointly by the SNI and the *Ufficio Militare*), from Besana and Finzi, *Resoconto del Fondo del Milione Fucili*, and from the *Cassa Centrale*, *Resoconto* of Bertani. A useful list of the expeditions and the numbers of volunteers on them can be consulted in Trevelyan, *Garibaldi and the Making of Italy*, 316–20.

The *Utile* was rented by Amari, who also paid a deposit against damage to it (it was captured on its second sailing when due to join Medici): Natoli,

first and second expeditions reflected both the lack of prepared-
ness among Garibaldi's supporters and Cavour's determination
not to permit regular shipments until he could be sure it was
safe to do so and that Garibaldi might really succeed. Not until the night of June 9–10 did a really large expedition—some
2,500 men led by Medici, with appropriate supplies—leave the
mainland. This one consisted of three steamers purchased by
the Million Rifles Fund from a French company and christened,
with the blessings of the American Consul, the *Washington*,
the *Franklin*, and the *Oregon*. Not until almost a month later
did another large expedition leave Genoa, this one under Cosenz'
command, with some 2,000 troops. In between, one ship had
gone from Genoa, and expeditions under Malenchini and Langé
had left Leghorn. These latter expeditions were also sponsored
largely by the National Society both in Turin and Tuscany, and
the Society contributed to all the others though far less in each
case than the Million Rifles Fund. For all his activity, Bertani
was overshadowed; and the policy of those willing to trust
Cavour prevailed. There was no attack aimed at the Papal States.

By July the Million Rifles Fund had spent most of its money;
but the requirements for an expedition had changed, too.[29] For
if transport between Piedmont and Sicily was still exciting, it
was now safe enough to be profitable; the available large stores
of supplies had been sent Garibaldi. The greater problem now
was the large groups of volunteers gathering in Genoa. The
solution was to purchase passage for them, in effect renting almost an entire ship. These volunteer armies preserved something
of the society which produced them; the highest officers usually
went first class; lesser officers, second class, and the men, third

---

Rivoluzione siciliana del '60, 6, 19. But the SNI apparently provided the funds
for renting it (30,000 lire) and most or all of the arms it carried. This may be
part of the 66,000 lire the SNI later recalled having given Amari, *Piccolo Corriere*,
3 March 1861.
[29] Sometimes gifts of arms (the City of Florence gift to the SNI of 1,428
Enfields, which were sent with Medici, for example), are listed in terms of their
value in lire among receipts and expenditures, making the National Society's
actual cash expenditures appear a great deal larger than they were. It is clear that
when Medici sailed, the Million Rifles Fund had spent three-fourths of the total
it eventually paid out. Of the money the SNI contributed to Medici's expedition, 8,500 lire was specifically for returning emigrants.
   The Leghorn committee of the SNI spent 16,682.16 lire on Malenchini's expedition and an unspecified amount on Langé's in addition to 15,000 lire from
the Central Committee.

class. Thus there was a shift in the expenditures of the collecting agencies. Instead of vast sums to purchase ships and large amounts of supplies, they tended to equip and book passage for smaller groups or even individual soldiers.[30]

In July and August the National Society spent somewhat more of its money itself instead of sending lump sums to Amari or the *Ufficio Militare*. But it still remained subordinate to the latter in general planning and encouraged its committees to negotiate directly with the *Ufficio* about the sending of volunteers. It purchased weapons from an armorer who was a member of the Society and promised a good rate; like the *Ufficio Militare*, it gave sustenance pay to groups of volunteers through their captain, and even paid—in a gesture that proved futile—for the carrying of Depretis' luggage when he left to become Sicily's prodictator. On occasion it booked passage for particular volunteers or individuals of importance. Sums of a few hundred lire at a time were sent Cressini to pay office expenses and to purchase some revolvers or knapsacks.

Affairs were quieting down a bit, becoming less frenetic and more neatly commercial. But Bertani's persistent efforts began to bring their rewards just when his opponents were running out of money. The volunteers who came to Genoa were increasingly those recruited by his men, and the money sent him by Garibaldi from Sicily gave him new strength. By late July it was his funds which paid for most of the volunteers' passage,

[30] Daniele Cressini to Buscalioni, 14 July and 7 August 1860, mss. in ISR, buste 715; 719, n. 10. In the first he comments on the volunteers piling up and pleads in the second that he be sent no more who are under age or who *lack the means* to get to Sicily; the *Ufficio* was apparently running out of money.

Most of the sailings after June 29 (when the *Medeah* left) were in ships which, like this one, were owned by the Fraissinet Company. The *Isère* made 4 trips and the *Provence* 8, the last of which was September 20! By August, however, volunteers were too few to fill the whole ship. An accounting of these trips, and the numbers of men in each class (the company received a total of 143,668 lire for their passage), in ms., is in ISR, busta 719, n. 12. Valentino Gallino acted as booking agent for most of these trips from June 23 to August 8; he also made the arrangements for sending 500 volunteers, August 16, on the English ship, *Sidney Hall*, for 16,548.49 lire, including food for the men (468.80 for wine!) and 5 horses: rendiconti, mss., ISR, busta 719, ns. 15 and 11. The companies may have required that some first-class passage be booked.

On July 9 and 10 some 2,500 men left on 4 ships with their passage purchased in this way; the ships rented by the Million Rifles Fund also each made another trip. By August, however, Cressini had become so experienced in booking passage that some private individuals simply paid him directly, ms. in ISR, busta 719, n. 16.

a fact probably important in the Government's contribution of 45,000 lire to the SNI.[31] The great expeditions of August were almost wholly sponsored by the intransigent doctor, until toward the end of the month, Cavour, having decided upon an expedition of his own into the Marches, once again cut off shipments to the south.

Although the National Society had taken a relatively small part in the complicated business of organizing these expeditions, it had cooperated effectively with others and contributed importantly to the fact that of the more than 20,000 volunteers who joined the Thousand most were safe from Bertanian influences. By September the Society was spending money on another cost of war, the returning men. It performed an important social service in providing many of them with funds to see them home, the only reward beyond honor most of them would ever get.[32]

Italian nationalists had responded with enthusiasm and surprising efficiency to the opportunities of revolution in Sicily. Spurred by the exemplary heroism of Garibaldi and the popular reaction to it, diverse political factions had been led to supplement each other's activity in a way which suggested again that

[31] From July 2 to September 22, Cressini received 164,578 lire. Over half of this, 86,770 lire, was left at the *Ufficio* when Cosenz sailed. Some 16,800 lire came from the Million Rifles Fund (9,800 on August 13, 4,000 on September 7, and 3,000 on September 22). The only other income after July 18 was 51,408 lire from the SNI, 45,000 of which was from the Government and paid by August 14. Bertani gave only 500 lire on June 19 and 400 on July 22: rendiconti, ms., ISR, busta 719, n. 12. Gallino received 111,032 lire of this for passage for volunteers.

Amari was able to pay for the rent of the *Provence* for the sailing of July 16: *Liberazione del Mezzogiorno*, v, 296; but Bertani paid the costs of transport on the *Franklin* and *Amazon*, July 21, and on the *Isère*, July 23, but told Cressini (who complained to the SNI and asked for 10,000 lire immediately) that he would pay no more: Cressini to Buscalioni, ms., ISR, busta 546, n. 84. The Government's contribution was possibly intended to meet this emergency.

The Society purchased most of its arms from Della Noce (including 5 sabres on August 18). Cressini's and the Society's lump payments (including Oresti Bronzetti's payment of 5 lire for Depretis' baggage) to various captains (from 400 to 1,500 lire), to printers, for telegrams and various travel expenses, are in the disordered array of receipts among rendiconti, ms., ISR, busta 719, ns. 8–16.

[32] Mere organization was expensive; the Million Rifles Fund spent 23,758.39 lire on administrative expenses and the SNI 12,671 lire in connection with volunteers. Bertani purchased 5 ships used primarily for carrying arms (the Society may have bought 2: Biundi, *La Farina*, II, 31). Gallino was still collecting money due him from the Million Rifles Fund in October, and accounts were being cleared until December, rendiconti, ms., ISR, busta 719, ns. 11 and 12.

the unification of Italy was the design of destiny. But from the very first, the aid to Sicily had been a new battlefield for the growing cleavage between the moderates who supported Cavour and their "radical" critics. It was only a few months before that that Brofferio's attacks on Cavour and the National Society had failed, and the resentments which sprang from that defeat were still being aired. Garibaldi, too, had come to feel the deeper division of parties. The cession of Nice added a bitter issue, and he now saw the moderates guilty of treachery as well as timidity. Almost to the moment he sailed for Sicily, he had contemplated an attack on Nice. Even his most temperate followers were sure that only the heavy pressure of public opinion could drag Cavourians to a policy of unification with the south. Men like Bertani and Garibaldi would always remember the Government's hesitance as opposition. The most they hoped for was that the moderates might choose to use them, while ready at any moment to desert and deny them.[33]

The talk of a Sicilian revolt had come to carry implications of an attack on the Cavourians. If La Farina had held hope of a revolution there in the spring of 1859, the radicals had tried to create one in the fall. Their failure they tended to blame on the National Society and its concern for the opinions of Louis Napoleon. Mazzini, with characteristic vigor, raised to the level of doctrine the attitudes which those who distrusted the moderates now shared. With apocalyptic enthusiasm he had hoped for a revolution in central Italy, then one in Venetia,—and even for European war. Now he saw Sicily as the field on which the Party of Action could win out. If the National Society seemed able to defeat them again and again, he argued, the fault must lie in their own lethargy. But now their chance had come. Garibaldi was moving back to them; they could with honesty make his program their own while the moderates and the National Society itself were left helplessly immobile before the pressures of diplomacy. They must prevent La Farina's again making Garibaldi his own instrument. Mazzini was increasingly upset that the Cavourians seemed once more to be stealing the credit for actions only their opponents had been willing to take. But,

[33] Brofferio to Guerrazzi, 26 February 1860, Martini, *Due all'estrema,* 59; Bargoni to Cadolini, 17 May 1860, Bargoni, *Memorie,* 125–26. *Memorie di Garibaldi,* II, 414; Mario, *Bertani,* II, 40; Bertani, *Ire d'oltre tomba,* 45.

Mazzini assured the enemies of Cavour, if they, and especially if Bertani, held firm, their moment of triumph was finally at hand in Sicily.[34] Few of those around Garibaldi were Mazzinians; even Bertani was no dedicated republican. Those who opposed Cavour on less dogmatic grounds, however, similarly tended to see in La Farina their enemy and in Sicily the chance to defeat the moderates.

Cavour, with a clarity no less simple than Mazzini's, had seen the same questions of political hegemony implied in Garibaldi's public acts, his resignations from the Army and the SNI, his bitter hostility to the cession of Nice. Thus on all sides the conspiratorial ferment which preceded Garibaldi's sailing had been watched with partisan sensitivity. With the first rumor that Garibaldi might sail, those close to La Farina were aware that the General's popularity could be used to combat Cavour, and they continued to look with angry misunderstanding for the Mazzinians lurking behind Bertani. The glorious expedition which did so much to win Italy's unification was also a part of the growing division in Italian politics. Whole political philosophies as well as individual careers and the very fate of Italy seemed to be at stake. Increasingly, each side was willing to make of any issue a weapon to use against its opponents, and it was this the Conte de Falloux noticed when he visited Turin. Ends and means were being separated; but only attention to means, he warned with the perception of a man who disliked his century, kept monarchy from despotism and the friends of liberty from demagoguery.[35]

[34] Farini himself had been sympathetic to a revolt in Sicily in the fall. Selmi to [Nicomede Branchi], n.d., Sforza, "Esuli estensi," *Archivio Emiliano*, II, 131*n*–32*n*; Fabrizi to Ribotti, 21 October 1859, Curatolo, *Garibaldi, Vittorio Emanuele, e Cavour*, 33; Pilo to Calvino, 10 November 1859, *ibid.*, 51; Crispi, *I Mille*; Pilo had long blamed La Farina for turning Cavour against him: letter to Bertani, Mario, *Bertani*, II, 280–82. Mazzini to "Fratelli," 21 November 1859, *Scritti di Mazzini*, LXV, 260.

Mazzini to Adriano Lemmi, 5 September 1859; to Saffi, 19 November 1859; to Pietro Zeneroni, 6 December 1859; to Giambattista Cuneo, 6 January; "Ai Siciliani," 2 March; to Grilenzoni, 27 March; to Giovanni Maragoni, 15 May; to Bertani, n.d., June; to Caroline Stansfield, 5 June 1860, *ibid.*, LXV, 114, 249, 301–302; LXVII (Imola, 1931), 33, 144, 200, 313, 374; LXVIII, 16. "I due programma," *ibid.*, LXVI (Imola, 1930), 75–80. Emilia Morelli, "Mazzini nel 1860," *Nuova Antologia*, LXXXV (1960), 9–16.

[35] Cavour to Farini, 2 and 3 January 1860, *Liberazione del Mezzogiorno*, V, 441–43. Homodei to Festi, 7 April 1860, ms. in ISR, busta 716, n. 95; Bartolommei to Puccioni, 8 June 1860, ms. in Puccioni family archives. Carlo Mo-

As nationalists focused on providing aid to Sicily, La Farina and Bertani came to represent the two competing policies for Italian unification. And the position of the National Society was not eased by widespread doubt about its enthusiasm for the whole Sicilian venture. Its slow response was inexplicable to those who saw Garibaldi fulfilling Manin's honored program. Even Mazzini seemed ready to soften his republicanism; and now it was the National Society which, in violation of its own doctrine, appeared too exclusive, too much a wing of the Government. Suspicion and distrust of La Farina were growing (some wondered why this famous advocate of action was not in Sicily), and he was warned that his political reputation had dwindled. The caution of the *Piccolo Corriere* left its readers dissatisfied; some of them carefully maintained relations with both *Lafariniani* and Bertanians.[36] That proved difficult, however, for the general differences between the two camps came to center on immediate and specific issues.

The first great question was whether revolution should be restricted to Sicily or extended to papal territory as well. Somewhat hesitantly, Garibaldi favored the broader vision of a great Italian revolution; but he was in no position to insist effectively after he already had one war on his hands. Bertani had no doubts at all. Intransigently, he insisted on planning an expedition to the Papal States similar to Garibaldi's to Sicily. He was determined not merely to see that international diplomacy no longer dominated Italian politics but anxious to affront it. Bertani's daring had limited appeal against La Farina's hints of help from the Government provided international Catholicism was not involved. The most important supporters of Garibaldi's expedition, men like Medici, Cosenz, Amari, and Malenchini, had learned a good deal of the Cavourian lesson in practicality. If they found Bertani's pretensions in relation to Garibaldi as

---

randi, *I partiti politici nella storia d'Italia* (Florence, 1945), 26. M. le Conte de Falloux, *Itinéraire de Turin e Rome* (Paris, 1865), 112. See Carlo Tivaroni, "Garibaldi e la dottrina della dittatura," *Rivista del Risorgimento Italiano*, II (1897), 668–74.
[36] Pallavicino to Garibaldi, 2 June 1860, *Memorie di Pallavicino*, III, 582–83; Carlo Arnò, "Garibaldi, Cavour e la spedizione dei Mille," *Risorgimento Italiano*, I (1908), 1–12. Mario, *Bertani*, II, 37. Luigi Tanari, Dichiarazione di fatto, ms. in MCRB; Finali to Casarini, 5 and 14 May 1860, Dallolio, *La spedizione*, 47. 65; and *ibid.*, 112–13.

offensive as La Farina's in relation to Cavour, they were driven closer and closer to the National Society by their common fear of recklessness. La Farina could effectively point to Bertani as the "evil genius" of discord.[37]

The Society also succeeded in making the manner of recruiting volunteers an apparent issue between it and the Bertanians. Naturally volatile and an embarrassment to the Government, volunteers worried La Farina; but the Society's official stand became the more popular one which stressed the regular army's importance to Italy. For there was no doubt that enthusiasm for joining Garibaldi threatened to weaken the army, and many in Governmental circles were greatly concerned. The Society talked of imminent war with Austria (the lessons of 1848 were invoked again; it was in the north that the Sicilians had lost their freedom then) and hinted that the Romagnols might be needed elsewhere soon (in the Marches or the Veneto). La Farina even developed a horror story of Austrian and Papal agents who claimed to be recruiting for Garibaldi only to lead their charges to Civitavecchia where they were forced to bear Papal arms. The SNI gained stature as the most responsible of the agencies supporting Garibaldi. It distributed Garibaldi's proclamation against desertion from the army and issued another of its own. Although Bertani also discouraged regular troops from volunteering, the feeling never died that he had been willing to weaken the national defenses for a personal policy.

If La Farina's talk about the danger of the "dissolution of the state" was excessive, it made sense to fear that diabolic reactionaries might put liberals in the position of apparently opposing Garibaldi. There was merit in the Society's argument that volunteers were an expensive form of aid when Sicily had men but needed arms and money. The implication that Bertani wanted volunteers in order to pursue his policies in the Papal States was politically effective. Volunteering proved to have such

[37] Medici to Bertani, 9 May 1860, Mario, *Bertani*, II, 67; Malenchini to Amari, 13 May 1860, d'Ancona, *Carteggio Amari*, I, 83; Medici to Malenchini, 26 May 1860, Puccioni, *Malenchini*, 166; Bertani to Garibaldi, 9 and 17 June 1860, Curatolo, *Garibaldi, Vittorio Emanuele e Cavour*, 48, 121; Mazzini to Bertani, June 1860, *Scritti di Mazzini*, LXVIII, 68; Cavour to Gualterio, 8 August 1860, Chiala, *Lettere di Cavour*, III, 317; Cressini to Fenzi, 1 August 1860, Luzio, "Spedizione Medici-Cosenz," *Lettura*, x, 490. *Ibid.*, 482–84; La Farina to Gallina, 12 May 1860, Franchi, *Epistolario di La Farina*, II, 319. Bertani, *Ire d'oltre tomba*, 59–60, 63, 64–8, 126. On Cosenz' interest in going into the Papal States, see Chapter Thirteen, note 2.

appeal that the Society had to take part. Its own committees were industrious recruiters, and the SNI issued a printed form to encourage the selection of experienced and able-bodied civilians of the right age. Respected in both camps for its vigorous responsibility, the Society gained from the feeling that Bertani's policy was quite different.[38]

La Farina was scoring on Bertani, but their competition horrified nationalists who had accepted the Society's call to sacrifice "personal predilections" and who were anxious that Garibaldi be efficiently supported. There was talk of combining all the collection agencies, and Bertani himself recognized the appeal of reconciliation. Late in May, Luigi Tanari, a marchese, a leader of the SNI in Bologna, and now a member of parliament, undertook a mission for his country. Accompanied by General Caldesi, who had connections in both camps, and Montecchi, who was closer to Bertani, he went to Genoa. There he found others intent on reconciling the two tactless, strong-willed men who had become so prominent among Garibaldi's provisioners. These men met with Bertani. They stressed the tragedy of a split among nationalists and pleaded that all of them wanted to help Garibaldi. Before this fact, they felt, all other considerations paled. They asked that Bertani and La Farina meet in the hope of arranging some scheme for operating jointly. Despite his clear doubts, Bertani agreed; the SNI should give full support to his efforts, and he would not compromise the alliance with France.

When Bertani arrived in Turin, several days after he had been expected, Medici and Cosenz eagerly joined the negotiations. The whole group met in Medici's home, where the steady com-

[38] Francesco Guglianetti to Farini, 25 April; and Efisio Cugia to Cavour, 14 May 1860, *Liberazione del Mezzogiorno*, 1, 66, 101. Medici to Malenchini, 20 May 1860, Puccioni, *Malenchini*, 159. La Farina to Rizzari, 7 May; to Emanuele Tuccari, 10 May; to Vergara and Morchio, 11 May; to Moneta, 17 May 1860, Franchi, *Epistolario di La Farina*, II, 315–18, 322. Finali to Simonetti, 5 May and La Farina to Casarini, 10 May 1860, Dallolio, *La spedizione*, 44, 57. *Ibid.*, 59–60, 63. Casarini to Simonetti, Maioli, "Ancora della Società Nazionale," *Saggi e documenti*, 118.

Piccolo Corriere, 13, 20, and 27 May 1860. The latter included the manifesto "*Inganni*," which, as a single sheet was given a circulation attested to by its presence today in nearly every collection of Risorgimento documents. The Bologna circular was also widely distributed, see Casarini's letter above and clipping from *Espero*, n.d., in H. N. Gay clippings, HCL.

Bertani, *Ire d'oltre tomba*, 35; Trevelyan, *Garibaldi and the Making of Italy*, 38–9. The Society's recruitment form, part of its circular of 22 June 1860, is in the Buscalioni pamphlets, HCL.

ing and going created a disquieting bustle while the amateur ambassadors hesitated to broach their difficult subject. Finally, Bertani arose in disgust to announce he would await La Farina no longer. With some difficulty he was persuaded that the Society's president had never been invited. But then no one dared raise the issue of a subsequent meeting, and it was agreed instead that the Bertanians would draw up an *aide-mémoire* which Tanari could present to La Farina. The next morning, however, Bertani's position was presented all too clearly and too publicly in *Il Diritto*, where La Farina was labeled a "narcoticizer" who drugged the activists.

Bertani, who had never accepted the Society's doctrine that compromise among all nationalists was the path to unity, saw his differences with La Farina as a matter of conviction rather than personality. And he contrasted Garibaldi's program which had awakened Italy with the one that stopped at Villafranca and ceded Nice and Savoy. The hopes of a reconciliation were shattered, but they had never been well founded. Although the tone of the Society's propaganda made differences between the two groups seem petty, they were in fact basic. Even when Bertani promised to recognize the French alliance, he meant only that he would refrain from directly attacking French troops; by full support, La Farina could only mean aid to Garibaldi in Sicily so long as the Government's policy permitted. To talk of the two organizations holding their stores in common but their funds separately, to imagine La Farina resigning from the SNI in order to smooth the way for reconciliation and to make the Society more active was simply to misunderstand the situation. That his supporters could imagine such things was in fact a warning which La Farina missed of how far he had moved from many of them.

Yet the thought of eliminating the strident discord between La Farina and Bertani had so deep an appeal that the disappointment which came with failure would have its own political importance. Bruschi in Genoa and Malenchini in Turin had added their voices to the demands for compromise, and there were many in Tuscany and the Romagna who anxiously awaited the outcome of the negotiations in the capital.[39] Recognizing

[39] Medici to Malenchini, 20 May; and Amari to Puccioni, 29 May 1860, Puccioni, *Malenchini*, 158, 169. Mario, *Bertani*, II, 32, 37, 84, 90–1. Carlo

that La Farina could not reject a real compromise if it was presented to him, Tanari and the others had concentrated their
attention on Bertani. Thus it was on the rocks of Bertani's difficult personality that their efforts had first floundered; almost
unanimously, they blamed him.

The Romagnol negotiators informed their friends that dealing with Bertani was impossible. Almost self-righteously, Bartolommei painted a similar picture for the Tuscan members of
the SNI. In both areas local committees circulated this interpretation as well as expressions of gratitude from Medici and
Cosenz for the Society's aid. Medici wrote Garibaldi that Bertani's "advanced" party and the Mazzinians prevented unity;
and Finzi, Cosenz, and Türr joined in similar warnings that a
break with Bertani might be the price (and they seemed not to
find it an unreasonable one) for the Government's aid. With
the tone of triumph he used so well, La Farina could claim that
all the most important supporters of Garibaldi were agreed with
him and then lament the Mazzinian influence around Bertani.
The dream of unity among the agencies supporting Garibaldi
did not die; but by the end of May La Farina could expect it to
come about through the inevitable demise of Bertani's committee.[40]

Bruschi and others cooperated with Tanari's mission in Genoa; he remembered
the date of the meeting with Bertani there as May 19 and of the Turin meeting as May 28, Tanari, Dichiarazione, ms., MCRB, instead of May 23 and 29,
Dallolio, La spedizione, 106–14. A good collection of the correspondence of the
participants is in ibid., 275–97. Michel, "Malenchini e la Spedizione," Risorgimento, I, 992. There is in ISR, busta 719, n. 8, an unsigned ms., n.d., of a somewhat different (and possibly later) proposal for uniting the two agencies.

[40] Casarini to Simonetti, 26 May and 2 June 1860, Maioli, "Ancora della
Società Nazionale," Saggi e documenti, 118, 122. Tanari, Dichiarazione, ms.,
MCRB; Dallolio, La spedizione, 114. Bartolommei to Puccioni, ms. in MRF,
busta 113, n. 4. The circular of the Bologna committee, n.d., is in MCRB and
contains Medici's statement of June 9 and Cosenz' of June 11; Dallolio, La
spedizione, 116, dates it June 19.

Medici to Garibaldi, 25 May; Finzi and Cosenz to Garibaldi, 11 June 1860,
in Curatolo, Garibaldi, Vittorio Emanuele, e Cavour, 103–105. Medici to
Malenchini, 22 May 1860, Puccioni, Malenchini, 161. Stefano Türr, Risposta
del Generale Türr all'opuscolo Bertani, "Ire d'oltre tomba" (Milan, 1874), 20–1.

La Farina to Casarini, 30 May 1860, Dallolio, La spedizione, 115–16; La Farina
had begun his campaign with a circular of May 19 attacking Bertani's claim to
have sole authority from Garibaldi and noting all the SNI had done, in Buscalioni
pamphlets, HCL. Maineri, "Buscalioni," Carpi, Risorgimento, 671. Bargoni to
Calvino, 21 June 1860, Bargoni, Memorie, 128–29; Michele Amari to Count
Amari, 31 May 1860, d'Ancona, Carteggio Amari, II, 91. Mazzini to Emily
Hawkes, 12 May, Scritti di Mazzini, LXVII, 291.

CHAPTER ELEVEN

THE COMMITTEES CONTRIBUTE TO

THE CAUSE (MAY—AUGUST 1860)

✢ WHEN BERTANI'S COMMITTEES began to operate as a
society called La Nazione, the competition between the
Nazionale and the Nazione added new energy to the collection
of funds and the recruitment of volunteers. La Farina attributed
to Bertani a leakage of information which would put Neapolitan
spies out of business; Bertani suggested that the SNI really opposed the whole Sicilian revolution. The National Society prepared elaborate replies to the Bertanian accusations in Diritto.
Garibaldi was beseeched by Bertani to declare that he alone
was in charge of gathering aid for Sicily. Medici's opposition
was ruining his plans for an attack on the Papal States; "the war
of the Lafarinians" might yet, he feared, leave him "impotent."
Through the summer, however, the collection of men and
money was the main battleground between the parties.

That competition went far beyond the mere rivalry which
sometimes showed itself between the Million Rifles Fund and
the SNI. Bertani warned his friends to see that no money went
to Amari, and Mazzini in turn urged Bertani to hold firm in
the great "war" against La Farina. The National Society had
launched its subscription as another of those great, and politically safe, demonstrations. Indeed, from the Government's standpoint the Society's subscription had been viewed as "less roman-

¹ La Farina to Giusti, 2 May; to Vergara and Morchio, 11 May 1860, Franchi,
Epistolario di La Farina, II, 314, 316–18; Casarini to Buscalioni, 20 June 1860,
ms. in ISR, busta 546, n. 36. Bargoni to Calvino, 21 June 1860, Bargoni,
Memorie, 127; Bertani, Ire d'oltre tomba, 45. Finzi to Valerio, 4 June 1860,
asking him to make sure Como's contribution went to the Million Rifles Fund
because it had done more than either the SNI or Bertani: Luzio, "Spedizione
Medici-Cosenz," Lettura, x, 486–87. Bertani to Crispi, 16 and 23 June 1860,
Crispi, I Mille, 224, 226. Mazzini to Maragoni, n.d.; to Grilenzoni, 26 May
1860; to Bertani, May and June 1860, Scritti di Mazzini, LXVII, 330, 338, 374,
383; LXVIII, 15. Minghetti to Tanari, 10 and 13 May 1860, Mantel, "Tanari,"
174. Bertani even tried to win away some of the Society's Bologna committee:
Tanari [to Simonetti], 18 May 1860, ms. in Posizione Simonetti, MCRB; Dallolio, La spedizione, 98–101. Mario, Bertani, II, 87; Bertani to Garibaldi, 25
and 31 May 1860, Curatolo, Garibaldi, Vittorio Emanuele, e Cavour, 108, 110.

tic" than Garibaldi's expedition and wholly separate from it.[1] So pure a stand proved impossible to maintain, for the political overtones were never absent from the *Danaro d'Italia*. A close analysis of the Society's fund drive and of its recruitment of volunteers becomes, therefore, a significant indication of the political temper of Italy and of the National Society's strength.

Nearly 40 per cent of the entries recorded in the *Piccolo Corriere's* great lists of the contributions it received are from Piedmont.[2] These total, however, to only about 22 per cent of the sum the Society collected; and 60 per cent of that came from the municipal governments of Turin and Genoa. This is the more surprising in that the Society faced in Piedmont the least competition from the other agencies collecting for Garibaldi. Perhaps the Piedmontese viewed their taxes as sufficient contribution; or maybe they were as reserved as their stereotype. These figures suggest both the Society's semi-official position in Piedmont and its relatively weak organization there. Many a town made its official contribution; sometimes its mayor was the collector for the general subscription as well. These contributions from many tiny hamlets were touchingly small, usually less than 100 lire. The number of gifts was large in part because of the accessibility of the Society's headquarters. Four-fifths of them came from individuals, who were then often granted the title of "commissioner" of the SNI; but these commissioners viewed fund-raising as almost their only function, and their number is primarily a measure of how few committees the Society had. Some merely mailed in their neighbors' contributions and refused further responsibilities, one explaining he could do nothing more to combat the influence of the priests.

The committees did somewhat better. Novara's sent in some 5,500 lire; and Oneglia's raised over 2,000—in part, apparently,

---

The Society's circular insisting that La Farina as well as Bertani was charged by Garibaldi with the task of preparing aid is among the Buscalioni pamphlets, HCL.

[2] These percentages must all be taken as approximate; not only are the Society's statistics sometimes incomplete or even the result of misprints (and the total number of contributors for any town is not always given), but the analysis by province, date, and contributors is entirely my own and thus subject to further error. Since publishing lists of contributors was the best publicity for the subscription and the best guarantee that sums collected had reached their destination, they can, however, be safely used in general terms. All comparisons to the Million Rifles Fund are based on Besana and Finzi, *Resoconto del Milione Fucili*; those to Bertani's fund are based on his *Cassa Centrale, Resoconto*.

313

through a special manifesto praising Italian womanhood. Sarzana's committee suffered a schism from those who preferred to support Bertani; but most, like Lerici's, found the subscription an important spur to greater activity. The committees showed a certain pride in the respectability of their members whose titles of doctor, lawyer, engineer, notary, or property-holder decorated their letters and official reports. Often these men could pay the more expensives dues of a *socio promotore*, and this helped to swell their offerings. Yet, when at the end of the year the Society asked for a general accounting from all committees, only four in Piedmont were active enough to reply. And of these, only Oneglia's, which had sponsored two evenings at the theater, could report a sizable sum.

Still, the Society's fame in Piedmont was attested to by the steadiness with which the contributions continued to pour in throughout the summer. In a well-to-do town there would be several gifts of 10 or 20 lire, but those from workers and from the smaller *paese* became increasingly tiny with the occasional exception of one larger contribution which stood out with the ostentation of a great lord's carriage. Some, especially the illiterate, would take the chance to send along a message, like the two men of San Damiano d'Asti who each gave 10 *centesimi* to have themselves entered on the lists as an "old *napoleonide*" and "a poor devil, *viva Italia.*" Sometimes the name, more often merely the title, of a local priest would be included; and the collectors themselves were frequently pharmacists, a measure of their central role in village life. Often whole groups would demonstrate their patriotism, like the Society for Belles-Lettres in Turin or some "Jewish boys" in Saluzzo, a national guard unit or a squad of *carabinieri*. When a name was printed incorrectly, protests were likely to be bitter. Many a newspaper has found the secret of circulation in printing names, and the *Piccolo Corriere* of the summer of 1860 must have gained a wide readership.[3]

---

[3] The Million Rifles Fund collected over 35,000 lire from Genoa but relatively little from elsewhere in Piedmont; Bertani's success was largely limited to Liguria. Gifts of 50,000 lire from the municipality of Genoa were reported in the *Piccolo Corriere*, 10 June; of 10,000 from Turin, *ibid.*, 3 June; and another 5,000 from the capital, *ibid.*, 29 July. The *Corriere Mercantile* contributed 6,000 lire, *Piccolo Corriere*, 3 June. Asti and Vercelli each officially gave 1,000 lire,

The sending of volunteers was an inseparable part of the Society's activity, and it similarly reflected local conditions. The Piedmontese, perhaps because they had an army of their own in which to serve, sent fewer men through the SNI than any other free province of Italy. It was, of course, easier for young men in this area to make their way to Genoa on their own; but the number of volunteers was also related to unemployment. As the Society's commissioner in Asti explained, they would have few volunteers; their men were needed in the fields. Two committees were more active than all the others. The committee in Oneglia may have sent nearly a score of men, and it later provided aid for two who had been wounded. The Lerici committee, with its strategic location, aided some 60 volunteers in getting to Genoa in addition to 10 who came along before Garibaldi had sailed and 20 others who volunteered in the next two weeks. It variously provided food, lodging, or the fare to Genoa by boat or train. By July it had to ask the Central Committee to help meet its expenses.

For all the Society's ambivalence toward volunteers, its fame is registered in the letters from boys in Chivasso or Moncalieri or Alessandria asking to be sent to Sicily. The former captain who wanted to enlist but hoped to keep his rank; the family who did not want their sole provider to be permitted to go; the boy who could not get his papers back from the bureaucracy— all wrote the National Society. Officialdom took the SNI seriously, too. A local mayor and the Minister of Education wrote the Society to recommend a favorite; an official asked to learn the regulations about volunteering, and the stationmaster of Felizzano could think of no better place to direct his complaint

---

ibid., 27 May and 10 June. Places like Piozzo gave 50 or Borgomanero, 90 lire, *ibid.*, 13 and 27 May. The Novara committee reported 1,000 lire, *ibid.*, 20 May, and 4,500 lire, *ibid.*, 3 June.

The Oneglia committee's manifestoes of 14 and 16 May are among, respectively, the Houghton Broadsides, 440, and the Buscalioni pamphlets, HCL. Reports of the Sarzana and Lerici committees, mss. in ISR, buste 718, n. 5; 720, n. 1. The committees of Oneglia, Savigliano, Arquata, and Lerici were the four to report, *Piccolo Corriere*, 23 and 30 December 1860, 27 June and 7 July 1861.

Other data on contributions from Piedmont can be found in the *Piccolo Corriere*, 27 May, 3 June, 29 July, 5 August 1860; and among the mss. in ISR: buste 715, n. 8; 717, ns. 28, 48, 99; 718, ns. 11 and 73; 719, ns. 2, 8, 41; 720, ns. 3, 6, 7, 50.

at seeing volunteers pass through when the boys from his town had been sent back.[4]

Less than 10 per cent of the money collected by the Society came from Lombardy (and less than 20 per cent of the number of contributions). Yet Lombardy contributed far more to the support of Garibaldi than any area of Italy; the Million Rifles Fund received more from Milan alone than the total contributions to the *Danaro d'Italia*; Pavia gave more to the Million Rifles than the Society collected in Lombardy. Bertani got from Lombardy about twice what the SNI did. The activists of Lombardy were too Garibaldian to find the Society very attractive, and it remained weakly organized there. Few Lombards sent contributions directly to the SNI, and not many more were zealous enough to become its commissioners; those who did collect for the *Danaro d'Italia* frequently complained of the competition they encountered. Gifts to the Society from city governments were also relatively sparse. Como made a handsome contribution of 10,000 lire (which the Million Rifles Fund thought was meant for it); Casalmaggiore gave 3,000 lire; Gallarate surrendered funds saved to celebrate the *Statuto*; Camerata and Cantù each contributed 1,000 lire. But even tiny gifts from villages came in infrequently.

In Lombardy, then, the National Society's collections rested primarily on the activities of its committees. Their existence often depended on the enthusiasm of one man, or his friendship for La Farina; but there were more of them than in Piedmont. Formed with a sense of opposing the political atmosphere around them, they tended to be rather narrowly Cavourian. The committee in Lodi boasted that the town council had voted a pension for their member of parliament right after he had supported the cession of Nice and Savoy; funds for the *Danaro* were collected in Bobbio only after the mayor and school inspector had organized an SNI committee because of their distaste for Brofferio and their distrust of Garibaldi's advisers. The Brescia committee, despite the support of the most respected local newspaper, could not really get going until it had added a countess to its roster. Yet some committees had the energy of the one in

---

[4] *Piccolo Corriere*, 23 December 1860 and 7 July 1861. Letters, mss. in ISR, buste 719, ns. 1 and 2; 720, ns. 1, 2, 3, 5.

Busto Arsizio, which in August was still staging marionette shows as a means of making money. But where the National Society did collect sizable amounts, as in Bergamo (which, however, gave more heavily to the other agencies), it had a well-organized and active committee. Generally, the weakness of its committee in Milan hurt the Society throughout the province; by August 1 the *Danaro* had received from the great city of Milan only 765.24 lire and a painting. Complaints about the poor communications with the Central Committee and the irregular deliveries of the *Piccolo Corriere* were common in Lombardy as elsewhere, and they explain a good deal of the Society's general fortune.

Some other characteristics distinguish the contributions the Society collected in Lombardy. The amounts individuals gave were often larger than in other provinces, suggesting that in Lombardy the Society's strongest appeal was among the upper-middle class. Only some 40 men contributed to one of the Society's collections in Milan, but 8 of them gave 20, two gave 40, and one 80 lire. Enough members of the clergy throughout Lombardy contributed to suggest that among the various nationalist associations, the SNI seemed politically the tamest. And finally, there was about the collections everywhere in Lombardy a kind of urban sophistication. Crews of collectors, sometimes including women and priests, would solicit from local merchants and officials. Local organizations often gave as a body; and the employees of a hotel or a courthouse would be canvassed, with everyone from judges to janitor contributing in neat proportion to his rank.[5]

[5] The *Società Unitaria* of Milan contributed additional sums of more than 175,000 lire to the Million Rifles Fund and 75,000 lire to Bertani. In August, after the National Society was again publicly at odds with Garibaldi, its committees were weakened; but it gained new supporters in a number of towns—there was now some reason to support the SNI rather than the other collecting agencies, ms. in ISR, busta 719, n. 1. The proximity to the Veneto was something of a stimulus for the Society, and 2,000 lire from Verona went through Lombardy to Cortes and to the SNI's coffers in July, *ibid.*, busta 720, n. 10.

Some of the towns offering official gifts to the Society were Reda[valle] (20 lire), San Giuletta (50), Piene Albignola (20), Mede (100), Villa Lomellina (158), Garlusco (300) (Homodei and Mai had done a good deal to extend the work of the Pavia committee to the surrounding countryside): *Piccolo Corriere*, 3 June, 1 July, 9 September 1860. The committee in Lodi was largely the work of Ghisalberti, ms. in ISR, busta 716, n. 63; in Legnano of Kroni, *ibid.*, buste 716, n. 98 and 720, n. 5; in Bergamo of Homodei, *ibid.*, buste 716,

If the political atmosphere of Lombardy lessened the Society's effectiveness there in collecting money, the semi-official status of the SNI was sometimes an inducement in the sending of volunteers. The Bergamo committee spent considerable sums providing several hundred volunteers with a meal or two, transportation across the city, their fare to Genoa or Milan, and bread to eat on the way. Homodei hoped to keep these men out of the hands of the "reds" of Milan, but a number of small towns also chose to send their men through the National Society. Como enrolled some 170 men; and the SNI's committee in Carbonara, which had happily cooperated with Bertani's men in recruiting volunteers, depended on the preferred position of the Society to find its men a place when some of their volunteers were turned back.[6]

The contributions which the Society received from the former Duchies were slow to come in and at first rather small in amount. By November, however, they accounted for about 14 per cent of the total number of contributions the Society received and about 10 per cent of the amount of money. When Garibaldi sailed for Sicily, the National Society was nearly moribund in the Duchies (the penalty in part of its weakness in the leading cities); and the contributions it first received were often from groups not officially part of the SNI. A committee of the *Unione Liberale* or autonomous committees for aiding Sicily would ask the Society for advice and send it the money they collected; often, they became the nucleus for a new committee of the National Society itself.

The collection of funds for Garibaldi tended, therefore, to lead to a general reorganization of the Society in this area. In the thin strip of the Lunigiana the SNI had a large number of some-

---

n. 93 and 719, n. 8. The activities of the Bobbio committee can be traced in *ibid.*, buste 716, n. 98; 718, n. 64; 720, n. 5. For the Brescia committee (and the more active one in neighboring Goito) see *ibid.*, buste 716, ns. 39, 40; 717, n. 59; 720, n. 3. For Milan: *ibid.*, buste 716, n. 93; 718, n. 94; 720, n. 2; and the *Piccolo Corriere*, 13, 20, 27 May and 29 July 1860.

Other data on the Society's collections in Lombardy can be found in the *Piccolo Corriere*, 13 and 27 May, 3 and 24 June, 22 July, 12 August, and 30 September; and among the ms. in ISR, buste 716, ns. 39, 48, 91, 93; 719, ns. 1, 3, 57.

[6] The Bergamo committee spent 2,108.49 lire on approximately 300 volunteers. Bobbio sent about a dozen. *Piccolo Corriere*, 9 September 1860; mss. in ISR, buste 716, n. 93; 718, n. 57; 720, ns. 3, 6; and *La spedizione di volontari*.

what inactive members, but organization was feeble. Those concerned with the Society's affairs tended to make individual contacts in Turin or Tuscany as well as in Parma or Modena. By July most of the cities had active committees of varying sizes; but it is likely that in this traditionally radical area Bertani's forces fared better. Elsewhere in the Duchies the organization of the SNI was concentrated in the cities, although Finale's committee, for example, was more active than Modena's. By the fall, the committee in Parma was huge, with over 800 members; and its energy shows in the growth of committees in neighboring cities and towns. Piacenza's committee which was at first independent of the SNI was very active, and it raised more money than Parma's; relatively little was heard from Reggio.

The organization of the Society in this area was erratic then, but the collection for Sicily was a tremendous spur to its development. The donations to that collection vary more widely in amount than in either Piedmont or Lombardy and suggest that the Society here was in touch with both rich and poor. This is confirmed in the committees' membership lists. The huge committee of Parma, for example, was dominated by men from the professional classes; but it included a tailor and a wig-maker, 36 students and 38 "employees" among its members. And it reflected the peculiar traditions of Italy in a membership which included 8 parish priests, curates, preachers, or canons; 4 architects; 5 painters, a sculptor and 6 maestroes. Such disparate membership was in itself an incentive to vigorous propaganda, and the Parma committee issued a number of broadsides which were carefully orthodox in their emphasis on the cooperation between people and Government. Yet, while always keeping aid to Garibaldi in the forefront, the committee was active in many aspects of local affairs, even to helping in the establishment of a workers' association.

With the self-consciousness of their newness, the committees in the Duchies showed particular concern to have their activities recorded in the *Piccolo Corriere*; and in fact they did demonstrate impressive energy in the variety of money-raising techniques they employed. There were lotteries and special evenings in the theater, collections among the national guard, the corps of engineers, marble workers, and young students. Correggio won an excellent response from the girls in a tobacco factory with its appeal to "that inexhaustible treasure of emotions that God has put in that sublime mystery, the Heart of a Woman." Mirandola, with less rhetoric and more organization, averaged receipts of a bit more than half a lire each from 552 women. In Castelnuovo di Garfagnana the committee staged impressive processions until a clash with competing marchers created something of a scandal; but the Society's committee re-established its respectability by coming out firmly for the maintenance of order as a first principle. There were also important demonstrations of patriotism and of political loyalty from municipal governments. Parma's committee contributed 10,000 lire; Piacenza's 6,000; and a score of others offered lesser amounts.[7]

The SNI's committees in the former Duchies spent over 11,000 lire to help more than 1,000 volunteers on their way, although probably only about half of them actually got to Sicily. The initially weak organization of the Society there is reflected in the slowness with which it took part in the movement of volunteers. Only a trickle of men were sent by the SNI in May and

[7] The Million Rifles Fund collected only about twice as much as the SNI from the former Duchies despite its earlier start; many cities in the area sent their first appropriations to Finzi and their subsequent ones to the SNI. Bertani did less well in the area as a whole. The committee of the *Unione Liberale* began the collecting for the SNI in Parma; special committees of aid (probably inspired by Amari's efforts) collected for the SNI in Piacenza, Guastalla, and Borgo San Donnino. There was both a Massa committee and a Massa-Carrara committee although the former was more active. There was also a committee in Castelnuovo di Garfagnana and a smaller one in Fivizzano; Pontremoli had only commissioners at first; in Tresana the SNI seemed to decline steadily; it maintained a sturdy little committee in Correggio. The committees of Busseto, Soragna, Sissa, and Borgo San Donnino were among those active around Modena. The *Piccolo Corriere* announced the dissolution of its Parma committee, 31 May 1860, but a much more active one was almost immediately formed. Some 24,112.04 lire was collected there, and 26,768.91 lire in Piacenza; both committees had large amounts left in their treasuries in November—Parma, 4,155.06 lire and Piacenza, 5,232.68.

Other gifts from municipal governments were: Soragna, 3,000 lire; Cortemaggiore and Busseto, 2,000; Guastalla and Finale, 1,000; Pontremoli, Mulazzo, Besenzone, and Carrara, 500 lire. Many others offered still less.

Evidence of this activity is in the *Piccolo Corriere*, 20 and 27 May; 3, 10, 17, and 24 June; 1, 8, 22, and 29 July; 9 September; 18 November; 23 and 30 December 1860; 21 January; 3 February, and 27 June 1861. Also in ms. of letters in MRF, busta 112, n. 7; ISR, buste 320, n. 110; 716, ns. 13, 25, 62; 717, n. 13; 718, n. 47; 719, ns. 3, 35; 720, ns. 1, 2. Parma broadsides of 14, 18, and 26 June, 4 July; and Correggio broadside of 8 June 1860 in Buscalioni pamphlets, HCL.

June, and only toward the end of July did the numbers become impressive. But many of the Society's leaders felt keenly the shame of lagging behind Bertani's men (who had sent some 300 volunteers from Parma before the Society sent any). One by one, the individual committees were able to organize small corps of local volunteers or to aid groups passing through on their way to Genoa. Carrara's committee was active early in July, and Finale's successes were soon heralded as the best propaganda for the National Society. The Central Committee in Turin used its influence to enable the Piacenza committee to win free passage on the railroads for its volunteers. Modena's committee developed the technique of recruiting only those who could afford to wait the call from Genoa, and Pontremoli's SNI took itself so seriously that it asked permission to grant commissions to some of the men it sent.

Gradually, the Parma committee assumed general supervision for sending the volunteers from most of the Duchies; and it showed great energy in making arrangements through the Central Committee and directly with Cressini in Genoa. By August, however, all the agencies collecting funds, except Bertani's, were running out of money. And Bertani, whenever possible, saw that only the men his committees had recruited were put on the ships he had paid for. Thus committee after committee of the SNI in the Duchies had the heartbreaking experience of seeing the men it had so proudly sent off return from Genoa, unwanted. Often, more money would have to be spent to send those disillusioned patriots peacefully home. The more politically aware began, as they had in May and June, to "desert" from the sponsorship of the National Society to the surer hand of Bertani.

The Parma committee had just succeeded in making all the arrangements to guarantee that men would be accepted on a ship in Genoa, and was proudly printing posters to announce its success, when the Government decreed a ban on any further expeditions to Sicily. Still, recruitment went on. The Society apparently won a dispensation from the Government for the volunteers already gathered in Parma. The Finale committee had already sent some men to Ferrara to join the corps being formed there. Even into October the Society's committees in the Duchies were adding to the volunteer corps attached to Piedmont's army in the Marches. By the fall they were occupied, too, in offering aid to the returning wounded and in seeing that even the healthy but impoverished got safely back to the quieter life of their village. The urgent letters and the painstakingly accurate accounts of those committees testify to the enthusiasm and pride they felt at finding themselves for a moment playing an active role in the Risorgimento.[8]

Garibaldi's expedition evoked great enthusiasm in Tuscany, and the role of the Society's leaders there in collecting aid for Italy's hero earned the SNI a new prominence in Tuscan affairs. Yet by the end of May the *Piccolo Corriere* had reported only one small contribution from Tuscany. Only when aid to the General became a part of Italy's political battle and when it required organization among the masses did the SNI figure importantly. Until the middle of the summer, Tuscan contributions to Garibaldi went primarily through the Million Rifles Fund or were sent directly to Amari. Both agencies did well in Tuscany, better in fact than the SNI; but the prominent patriots who were most active in collecting for or contributing to either fund were in fact usually leaders of the National Society as well. Organizational distinctions simply did not matter at first, although the SNI was clearly the least lively.

Amari himself was uncertain what policies Garibaldi might follow; and, increasingly concerned to cooperate with the Government, he came to rely more and more on members of the SNI for advice. Even Malenchini's early enthusiasm was being tempered by caution. In such circumstances the political reliability of the Society made it more important as an agent for funds and a channel of communication. By June the leaders of the Society had come to recognize a broad political threat from Bertani's influence in Tuscany, and Bartolommei sent out instructions from Turin to withhold funds from Genoa and to win to the SNI new men of action from among "the people and the workers." Dolfi, who had long enjoyed a reputation as the leader of the Florentine lower classes, was now recognized

---

[8] Scaramuzza, of the Parma committee, was the most active of the Society's organizers in the Duchies. Letters, ms. in ISR, buste 719, ns. 1, 2, 5; 720, ns. 1, 2, 3; *Piccolo Corriere*, 30 December 1860, 27 January 1861.

as a Bertanian agent, and Bartolommei wanted the SNI to become so strong that it could squeeze out this dangerous competition. Piero Puccioni, who was secretary of the Florentine committee of the SNI, began actively to serve as the Society's organizational leader for all of Tuscany, a position which may have been implicit in the refounding of the committee in Florence but had not before been pushed with vigor. Among the first fruits of all this was a donation from the Florentine city council, which had previously hesitated to contribute directly to the aid of Garibaldi. In early June it presented to the Society a gift worth 114,240 lire, the largest the SNI ever received and more than one-fifth of the total amount it collected. The divisive politics the Society deplored were part of its strength.

The National Society was already active in a few parts of Tuscany where individual leaders, such as Eugenio Pelosi in Lucca, had seen the importance of keeping its influence strong in the Garibaldian movement. It was he who named a commissioner for Empoli and encouraged the committee in Pistoia (both of them were already issuing proclamations on behalf of Sicily). The SNI was also reported to be doing well in Lucca; yet in so important a city as Leghorn a committee was not established until May 10, and not until late in June would it call on local citizens to show a "faith worthy of the first Christians" as had La Farina, Pallavicino, and Manin.

Puccioni's task was formidable, then; and he named commissioner after commissioner, corresponded with leaders in all parts of Tuscany, revived quiescent committees, and regularly complained to the Central Committee in Turin of its inefficiency. In Florence itself the Society's committee was neither well organized nor very active outside the Palazzo Vecchio (although no less a figure than Cambrai-Digny helped to distribute its literature), and there may even be an element of surrender in the Society's suggestion in August that Dolfi's committee combine with it. But elsewhere, under Puccioni's prodding, the Society flourished. The Pistoia committee approached 200 members and contributed in all nearly 7,000 lire. Frequently, men collecting for the Society became the nucleus for a committee; not merely Siena but Lamporecchio and Sinalunga had committees of their own by the end of the summer. If there were complaints from Lucca that potential donors escaped by claiming to one agency that they had already given to the other, the competition seems on the whole to have been a useful stimulus. Indeed, there was competition among the Society's committees themselves; and those of Pescia or Lucca not only spread their activity to scores of neighboring towns but carefully saw to it that their activity was recognized in Turin and not merely in Florence.

When, in July, the amount the Society was able to collect in Tuscany began to decline somewhat, dozens of small communes voted gifts of 100 or even 300 lire. Increasingly, the SNI seemed to be the dominant political movement in Tuscany. From central Tuscany its organization steadily spread; from Pescia to Pietrasanta; from a somewhat ineffective committee in Pisa to Volterra. By July Leghorn's was the most active committee in Tuscany. It collected over 19,000 lire, and its activity in sending off shipments of volunteers undoubtedly added greatly to the prestige of the SNI throughout the area. The establishment of new committees continued in August, as it did in no other province, so that the committee in Grosseto was enlarged while new and fairly large ones were established in Pitigliano and San Fiora, Manciano and Arcidosso. The committee in Arezzo was particularly active, founding half a dozen committees in nearby towns; the committee of Cortona, however, found Puccioni's leadership so oppressive it switched its allegiance to Bologna until Buscalioni himself had to arbitrate.

By September no province of Italy had more committees of the National Society than Tuscany, and probably in no province did the Society collect so many individual gifts. Even Elba had its committee. The amounts contributed to the Society's funds from Tuscany, however, were small. Most of the gifts were under one lire. If one discounts the magnificent gift from the city of Florence, the Society received only about 3 per cent of its funds from Tuscany. Its organizations enabled the Society there to collect from the lower classes more than it did in most places, but the large gifts from the well-to-do were apparently donated before the Society was well organized and given to the Million Rifles or to Amari. In Tuscany, then, the collections for the *Danaro d'Italia* were in large part a political demonstration in favor of the moderates. Collections were made in cafés and among *facchini*. The *Arciconfraternità della Misericordia e della Morte* in Pistoia gave the proceeds from its annual dinner; donations were made on a kind of installment plan in Lucca. And everywhere special evenings were held in theaters, with sign-painters and ticket-takers as well as performers contributing their services. It was in many ways a magnificent demonstration; perhaps the Tuscans calculated that a political gesture can be as effective when inexpensive.[9]

The sending of volunteers from Tuscany had not originated within the National Society; rather it had been Amari's extensive plans which had prompted the enthusiasm in Leghorn for sponsoring a whole expedition. Malenchini of course dominated such plans; and as the political dangers of the Sicilian venture became more apparent, he was careful to keep in touch with the Cavourians in Turin and Genoa. Soon, the excitement of 1859 was recaptured as once again men came from all over Tuscany to join an expedition under Malenchini. The Leghorn committee prepared to clothe and arm a thousand men; but in an effort to keep down costs some attempt was made to limit the volunteers sailing from Leghorn to Tuscans, and the Society's

---

[9] Teresa Bartolommei, Vannucci, Cheleschi, Crecchi, and Adami, all connected with the SNI, were among the most active in collecting for the Million Rifles Fund; Malenchini, Menotti, and Vannucci collected for and contributed to Amari. At least 8 of the 13 members of the Committee of Emigration in Leghorn were members of the SNI.

Among the city governments which contributed to the Society's fund were: Pistoia, 2,000 lire; Montecarlo, 300; Lamporecchio, 250; Tizzana, Marliana, Vellana, and Uzzana, 100 lire each. The King's tour of Tuscany was also a spur to the Society's organization and to the publication of patriotic proclamations. There were, in addition to those mentioned in the text, active committees in Sinalunga, Empoli, Bagni di Lucca, Massa in Valdimierole, Foiano, San Sepolcro, and Monte San Savino. The last had 55 members in September; the others averaged about a score of members. The contretemps in Cortona centered around the local ambitions of Luigi Diligenti, whose policies and personality antagonized Puccioni.

Evidence of Tuscan activity is taken from: d'Ancona, *Carteggio Amari*, 1, 83–9; Puccioni, *Malenchini*, 129–30, 136, 139–40, 154–57, 205; Michel, "Vincenzo Malenchini e la spedizione," *Risorgimento*, 1, 986–93; Rubieri, *Storia intima*, 372n. Also from ms. letters in the Puccioni family papers; MRF, buste 112, ns. 2 and 5, and 113, n. 4; and ISR, buste 716, ns. 19, 58; 717, ns. 10, 47, 53, 70, 104, 105; 718, ns. 9, 16, 45; 719, ns. 1, 2, 3, 4; 720, ns. 2, 3, 6

Proclamations of the various committees are in the Buscalioni pamphlets and the Houghton Broadsides, 870, HCL. Proclamations, rendiconti, and news of the Tuscan committees appear in the *Piccolo Corriere*: 20 May; 3 and 10 June; 1, 8, 31 July; 12 and 26 August; 9, 16 and 30 September; 7 October; 11 and 18 November; 23 and 31 December 1860; 6, 20, and 27 January; 7 July 1861.

local committees were asked to provide the men they sent with as much of their expenses as possible. The committees of Pescia, Pistoia, and Lucca responded with particular vigor; by June the Lucca committee had already seen some 50 of its men sent back. Although the Society shipped more than 500 volunteers from Leghorn, more men arrived than could be sent to Sicily. The Tuscan committees learned to seek permission before spending their funds on volunteers and, while pressuring Leghorn to prepare other expeditions, they tried to keep informed of how many were actually needed in Leghorn or Genoa.

This organization, and the fact of the Tuscan expeditions from Leghorn, meant that the movement of volunteers led to less frustration within the Society in Tuscany than elsewhere. Local committees were more confident of actual needs and better able to send men the relatively short distance to Leghorn. Committee after committee sent their men, watched their progress with paternal pride, and provided them with further aid when they returned (the Lucca committee alone aided nearly a hundred returning veterans). In the fall committees would encourage enlistment in the Italian army or help emigrants return to their old homes. The sending of volunteers thus gave new meaning to the Society's propaganda in Tuscany and added greatly to its *esprit*. Late in getting established, the Society in Tuscany suffered fewer doubts that its role was major and suffered less from the inadequacies of the Central Committee in Turin. This would later prove a source of strength as would the fact that, having grown in the competition with Bertani, the Society there was content to be self-consciously Cavourian.[10]

More has been written on the contributions of the Romagna to the National Society's fund drive than on those of any other province; yet it remains difficult to compare the activity there with what was done elsewhere. Like Lombardy, the Romagna showed early enthusiasm for Garibaldi's exploits; as in Tuscany,

---

[10] Local committees often had to spend only 2 or 3 lire per man to get the volunteers to Leghorn. Most committees were able to send just a few men at a time, making an estimate of the total number of volunteers they aided more difficult. Puccioni, *Malenchini*, 137–42, 157–60, 166–71; Puccioni, "Puccioni," *Rassegna Storica*, xvi, 665–84. Mss. in Puccioni family papers; ISR, buste 716, n. 58; 717, ns. 16, 53, 70, 105; 719, n. 3; 720, n. 20. Rendiconti in *Piccolo Corriere*, 23 and 31 December 1860, 6 October 1861.

the Society in the Romagna seemed quickly to become the main agency for aiding Garibaldi. By the end of May some 17 per cent of the separate collections the Society received had come from the Romagna, an impressive figure for so distant an area. Within a month, however, the contributions to Turin began to fall off; and thereafter they steadily accounted for about 12 per cent of the number of contributions and of the total sum of money sent the SNI. The record of this activity is somewhat obscured by the way accounts were kept; for committees in the Romagna tended to list their expenditures in behalf of Sicily among their regular expenses and to treat regular dues as special contributions for Garibaldi. But these figures reflect three important things: the relatively greater poverty of the Romagna and of its municipal governments, the increasing attention there to collecting arms (and purchasing them) in preparation for a move into the Marches, and, after July, the growing split between the National Society in the Romagna and the Central Committee in Turin.

In all, the Central Committee received nearly 60,000 lire from the Romagna although at least half again as much was collected but either sent directly to Genoa or spent locally. Still closely connected to the municipal governments, the Society was able to get most of this money from them though their gifts were not lavish. The Bologna council contributed the significant sum of 20,000 lire after some heated discussion, but this was less than the Society's members had expected; and it caused Forlì to reduce a proposed communal gift from 25,000 to 18,000 lire. The communes of Lugo, Ferrara, and Ravenna each contributed 5,000 lire; Imola's government spent over 2,600 lire making good the debts the local SNI had acquired from its activities of 1859; many towns contributed much smaller amounts. By July some of the tiniest hamlets were doing their share both officially and by private subscription. Yet these impressive municipal gifts to the National Society pale before the more than 4 million lire the Romagna had recently voted for Victor Emmanuel.

The campaign for private contributions was conducted in the Romagna much as it was elsewhere. Lotteries were popular, and the Bologna committee sold hundreds of copies of a song written to honor Garibaldi. The Rimini committee took pride in celebrating the anniversary of their liberation not with "vain dances" but with the kind of fete in which rich and poor alike could take part; elsewhere, concerts by the national guard band proved effective means of raising money. In Bologna tickets were sold to a fireworks display on the anniversary of Solferino; in Forlì and elsewhere there were special appeals to women. The Lugo and Ravenna committees were particularly active.

Merely collecting money never became the primary interest of the Romagna committees. When they exchanged reassuring talk of all the National Society was doing for Garibaldi, they tended to think of volunteers and even direct action of their own. Their bitter comments about the refusal of the nobility to do its part referred to the general political situation as well as to giving money. On the whole, the National Society was confident of its position in the Romagna. The Bologna committee provided its collectors with special identification so the public would not be duped into aiding its competitors. It encountered some hesitance about contributing to any fund of La Farina's, but for the most part the Society's collections in the Romagna were orderly and effective if somewhat unexciting.

As it became identified with aid to Garibaldi, the Society in the Romagna benefited greatly. This identification came slowly; a center so vigorous in aiding Garibaldi as Ferrara did not have an active SNI committee until late in June. During most of May, the Society's men still talked of fusion with Bertanian groups, even occasionally dreamed of winning Mazzini to their program. But by June the competition with Bertani was an accepted fact, and the Society seemed to be triumphing in all the places the Bertanians had threatened to be strong—Imola, Forlì, Faenza, Rimini, and Ravenna. As the Cesena committee boasted, the men of the *Nazione* simply did not have the sympathy of the countryside. Torn by a clash of personalities, the Medicina committee reported that the elections had left their *paese* so disgusted that the SNI had trouble in winning support; but such fears were not common. The Bologna committee soon had more than one hundred members who regularly paid their dues, and committees were growing in town after town.

Brisighella could claim a committee as large as Bologna's; Imola's was even larger. This growth led the Bologna committee to take over active direction of the Society in the Romagna. Complaints continued that the *Piccolo Corriere* was not arriving regularly, and the Romagna committees persisted in expecting more and fuller instructions than Turin ever sent. But they were unwilling to take La Farina's advice on such matters as who should be in their committee. They felt a certain pride in their autonomy, and Casarini's energy made it effective. He subscribed to the reports of the Stefani news agency so the Society could send the latest bulletins to grateful committees, by telegram if necessary, in order to keep them better informed than the Bertanians.

Through Simonetti and others, Casarini maintained close contact with the Committees of Emigration in Bologna and Rimini, a fact which increased the Society's tendency to concern itself with a possible move toward the Marches. Aspirations increased with success. Some suggested a world-wide subscription to purchase ships with which Garibaldi could sail to the Dalmatian coast and sponsor that successful revolution in Hungary which would eventually free Venetia and the Tyrol. There was more talk of establishing mutual aid societies among the workers. Half a dozen committees were enthusiastic about such possibilities, among them Imola's, one-fourth of whose members were artisans or workers. The political complexion of the Society in the Romagna was becoming subtly different.

The Society's apparent confidence was reflected in its propaganda. Old arguments contrasting the policies which had won 8 million Italians their freedom with the failures of Mazzinians were energetically repeated, but stress was placed on all the Society had contributed to Garibaldi. The letter of gratitude Medici received from Garibaldi (thereby denying Bertani's claim to be the General's sole agent) got its widest circulation in the Romagna. Bulletins from the Society in Turin and broadsides by the various Romagna committees, which were distributed by the hundreds, presented the SNI as the great sponsor of responsible action.

Yet by June some dangerous doubts about the Society were beginning to be felt among its own members in the Romagna.

A leader of the committee in Forlì returned from a trip to Turin declaring that the Central Committee there was dormant. Others agreed that the Romagna committees had better meet to discuss their own course of action. The Faenza committee was losing out to the Bertanians to such an extent that it tried to form a joint committee with them. Casarini hesitated before so dangerous a step and sought La Farina's advice, but the fusion took place. Suspicions returned that Bertani was in fact more active than La Farina in behalf of Garibaldi. Two of the most prominent figures of the Imola committee resigned as a result and out of general distaste for the Society's conservatism. Their loss was a serious blow which was only limply explained in a manifesto to the townsfolk. By mid-June Casarini himself said he was not sure that it was as members of the National Society that they were acting.

Having learned to do without precise instruction from Turin and having increasingly diverted their funds and attention to a possible move in the Marches, the members of the SNI in the Romanga were losing their sense of being in a national organization. And with that feeling went some of the need for opposing Bertani. The Bertanians, after all, were also enthusiastic about action in the Marches. The Committees of Emigration now showed themselves anxious to work with both agencies aiding Garibaldi. As the National Society in the Romagna attempted to hold its ground by displaying tolerance toward Bertani and militant vigor in support of Garibaldi, it was moving farther away from La Farina.[11]

[11] The accounts in the *Piccolo Corriere* list donations from Romagna towns which total to about 57,000 lire. Dallolio says at least 90,000 lire was collected in the Romagna; I find references totalling 88,000. Even such towns as Crevalcore and Civitella [di Romagna] voted donations of 250 and 200 lire.

The printed sources for this discussion on the Romagna collection are: Dallolio, *La spedizione*, 45–7, 53–8, 79–85, 91–103, 116–17, 155–58, 169–79, 272–73; Luigi Nicoletti, *Il carteggio del Comitato di Emigrazione di Rimini* (Fabriano, 1925), 411, 457–63, 480–81, 491–92, 635–37, 640–43, 751–52, 802, 834; Maioli, "Ancora della Società Nazionale," *Saggi e documenti*, 118–27; Zampetti-Biocca, *Società Nazionale*, 123; Galli, "La Società Nazionale e Gamberini," *La Romagna*, XVII, 162–64, 175n. About one-half of those in the Imola committee were nobles, landowners, lawyers, or doctors; over a quarter were tradesmen or engineers, the rest artisans and workers.

The broadsides of the Romagna committees may be found among the Buscalioni pamphlets, HCL, and in the MCRB. The *Piccolo Corriere's* reports of the Romagna collection are in the issues of 13 May, 8 and 22 July, 23 and 30 December 1860; 3 February and 27 October 1861 (including, in addition to

From the first, it had been the recruiting and sending of volunteers which had caught the imagination of the Romagnols. The leaders of the Society were suitably outraged at La Farina's stories of Papal agents falsely recruiting, and they took care to see that the drive for volunteers in no way weakened the regular army. But they never doubted the value of gathering and arming as many men as they could; many committees were anxious to divert the funds they collected; some even asked for the return of the money they had sent to Turin in order to use it for this more exciting purpose. Lists were kept of those willing to volunteer, and men with previous military experience were judiciously favored. The form which volunteers signed when they put themselves on the SNI lists required their promise to serve where sent. The Society never lost sight of a possible venture in the Marches; the volunteers, however, made it clear that they wanted to fight with Garibaldi and to do so right away. The pressure they created on the local committees, especially when it seemed that the Bertanians were sending more men, was immense; and the call from Bologna for a specific number of men came too rarely to suit local patriots.

Under Bologna's careful direction, the Romagnols did at least avoid sending many who could not be used in Genoa. The Society considerately took care that its expeditions should not implicate the Government, and it responded to the call from Genoa with impressive dispatch—once in June sending on one day's notice 150 men each of whom had been checked by a doctor and provided with 20 lire in cash. In all, the Bologna committee supervised the sending of more than 500 men, most of them in July. The Ravenna committee sent some 280, many of them directly; Bagnacavallo's committee spent more than 1,100 lire equipping and transporting 20 volunteers; and Comacchio's dealt directly with Genoa to plead that their 70 men be taken. When the *City of Aberdeen* sailed on the evening of July 10–11, a large portion of its 900 men were Romagnols.

---

some of the committees named below, rendiconti from Castel Guelfo and Russi). Other newspaper comment from items among H. N. Gay newspaper clippings, 1856–1927, HCL. Letters in ISR, buste 546, ns. 35 and 36; 555; 716, n. 91; 717, ns. 43, 88; 718, ns. 6, 13, 14, 75; 719; 720, ns. 5, 6, 28. In MCRB the mss. of the Romagna committees are among the Carteggio Casarini, Carte Tanari, and the Posizione Simonetti.

Supply and demand did not often meet so happily. The efficiency of the SNI in the Romagna and the desire to volunteer greatly exceeded the need in Genoa for men. The Society dared not tap the full enthusiasm it helped to promote. This inevitably produced discontent, which increased when some volunteers complained of their treatment in Genoa. Frustration bred distrust. The Forlì and Ravenna committees accused the Bologna committee of sending its own men rather than theirs; and when Casarini explained these matters, he added that the inadequacy of the Society's Central Committee in Turin could be hidden no longer. Each such incident could be explained by the necessity for haste or the sudden breakdown of a ship, but the general view was growing that the National Society itself did not adequately support Garibaldi or use the enthusiasm of its committees.

The separation of the SNI in the Romagna from its Central Committee in Turin was increased by its emphasis on collecting arms and munitions for use in the Marches. It was over a question of aiding the Marches that Garibaldi and La Farina had first clashed in the fall of 1859. Now some felt that failure to go into the Marches in 1860 would produce a discontent more dangerous than the invasion itself. Working closely with the Committees of Emigration, the Society had even smuggled some arms into papal territory. Nearly 2,000 rifles and significant quantities of munitions and other supplies were collected. Rimini, Faenza, and Forlì were, of course, especially active centers in these matters; Simonetti, from Turin, acted as adviser and agent. On occasion, the National Guard served as convenient cover for the shipment of arms, turning them over to the local committee of the SNI on orders from the intendant. The Ravenna committee wanted the Society's plans made public as a means of holding volunteers. This extensive activity was the most exciting in which the Society was engaged, and it gave an added seriousness to all the Society did. La Farina himself had agreed to such preparations. Before leaving for Sicily, he even permitted, at Casarini's cautious request, the spending of funds collected for Garibaldi on arms for the Marches. A little later Buscalioni seemed unaware of or at least hesitant about any plans for the Marches, and the Society's leaders in the Romagna were shocked and disgusted.[12]

In the Marches patriots saw a promise of their own liberation in Garibaldi's rescue of the Sicilians, and they took pride in helping fellow countrymen despite their own plight. These leaders also collected for Garibaldi. But where such things had to be done covertly, the hint of more revolutionary activity to follow was unmistakable. The Commission for Subject Provinces in Florence and the Committees of Emigration in the Romagna both received funds collected in the Marches, but most of their gifts for Garibaldi went through the SNI. The acknowledgment of those donations in either the *Nazione* of Florence or the *Piccolo Corriere* was then eagerly awaited. It was the only receipt they got.

Through the Committees of Emigration the Society appeared to these patriotic leaders as the sponsor of Garibaldi's heroism, and they were informed of Bertani's selfish intransigence in refusing to cooperate with others. Many of them asked for copies of the Society's *Credo* and its other writings. Where access to patriotic literature and even to news was limited, the Society's publications were taken extremely seriously. Its news bulletins and the *Piccolo Corriere* were read with a sensitivity to nuance usually found only in diplomats. The Society was often thought of as better organized than it was and as planning Italy's future in a way it would not have dared. When contributions of a hundred lire or so came from places like Fano or Pesaro, therefore, they were more than an expression of intense patriotism. They were meant to demonstrate the common cause of all Italians, to be a reminder that the Marches were next. They were also, like the steady trickle of men who made their way to

[12] Dallolio, *La spedizione*, 44–6, 84, 92–3, 156–59, 189–99. Maioli, "Ancora della Società Nazionale," *Saggi e documenti*, 115, 120–28. Nicoletti, *Comitato di Emigrazione*, 758–59, 770–71. Buscalioni pamphlets, HCL. *Piccolo Corriere*, 16 September, 23 and 30 December 1860; 3 February 1861. Mss. in ISR, buste 546; 716, n. 3; 718, ns. 7, 8, 13; 719; 720, ns. 5, 6, 7; and in MCRB, Posizione Simonetti and Carteggio Casarini. The ms. of La Farina's letter of 30 May to Casarini in *ibid.*, refers to 100 not 500 rifles, as in Dallolio, *La spedizione*, 115–16. Casarini wrote Tanari, 8 June, saying he had asked Buscalioni for written authorization to use the funds collected for Sicily, and he wrote Ginevri-Blasi, 14 June, saying La Farina had agreed, mss. in Carte Tanari II and Carteggio Casarini, MCRB.

Rimini to volunteer, an expression of a growing confidence in the SNI and the promise it offered for the Marches. The Society's important role there in September and after liberation was prepared in this period and based on the belief that the National Society had done for Sicily what it would do for them.[13]

Farther south, in Umbria and Rome, the National Society had fewer contacts; patriots in these areas tended to be in touch with the Umbrian committee in Florence and with Gualterio. Still, by July the leaders in the key city of Perugia could assure Buscalioni, in answer to his inquiry, that they would be happy to receive orders from the SNI as well. The National Society was gaining revolutionary prestige in central Italy, too. In Sardinia and Malta, as well, there were men to whom the Society sent large numbers of the *Piccolo Corriere* and from whom it received donations to its fund.[14]

There was something of Manin's old vision in the National Society's collections in Europe and America; yet the relatively small amounts donated there stand as a measure of how far the Society had moved from what Manin meant it to be. Bertani received five times as much, the Million Rifles Fund fifteen times as much from outside Italy. It was Garibaldi's heroism more than the National Society's diplomatic caution which struck a European chord. Most of the support the SNI received from abroad depended on personal contacts, such as the three Hungarian officers whom Rasponi knew or an Englishman met by chance on a trip. Gallenga acted as the Society's agent in Great Britain and alone collected more than 1,500 lire, including a large gift from the Atheneum Club. The cause of Italian independence had indeed become respectable. The English, however, were well informed on Italian politics; excited by Garibaldi, they gave far more to the other agencies and almost nothing to the SNI once La Farina had been expelled from Sicily. The National Society's committee in New York, no longer sure of its loyalty to the SNI, nevertheless sent along nearly 2,000 lire, including gifts of 125

---

[13] Nicoletti, *Comitato di Emigrazione*, 473, 521, 574, 586–87, 603, 614–34, 670, 824, 831, 834, 838. Alessandrini, *I fatti*, II, 253, 256. Zampetti-Biocca, *Società Nazionale*, 243, 246–48. Letters, mss., in ISR, buste 718, n. 29; 720, n. 1.
[14] *Liberazione del Mezzogiorno*, I, 404; letters, mss., in ISR, buste 716, n. 10; 717, n. 45; 720, ns. 1 and 2.

lire each from "R. Lowell" and "H. Longfellow." There was evidence of the Society's successful propaganda in the 260 lire collected in Barcelona, the letter from Lisbon suggesting a Spanish legion (and a very Latin sense of history) for the revolt in "Magna Grecia," and the friendly reports of the Society's' activities in two Athenian papers.

In Breslau the German National Society sponsored a petition supporting the resolution in favor of Italian independence which some Prussian deputies had presented, and a member of the Chamber in Bavaria asked to join the SNI. Nearly 1,500 lire was collected in Germany and sent to the Society; most of it came from Berlin (including a gift from the former minister of war of the Roman republic). In Germany and France the fact of the Society itself, as an organization respectable and responsible, aided in the collection of funds. The French Government had grave doubts about these subscriptions and forbade the *Siècle* and *Opinion Nationale* from publicizing the ones they opened. They were allowed, however, to publish letters of gratitude from La Farina, who was too nearly an official figure, perhaps, to be censored. Nearly 1,000 lire was collected in Marseilles, largely from Italian exiles, who then watched the *Piccolo Corriere* closely for their names. The competition with the Bertanians there was as open as in Italy. The largest amounts the SNI received from outside Italy came from the *Siècle* (10,800 lire) and *Opinion Nationale* (6,863.55 lire); old friends of the Society, Henri Martin, Planat de la Faye, and others worked hard to send almost 8,000 lire more. They evoked the memory of Manin and the subscription for the cannon at Alessandria, and there was something of the good old days in the phrases of liberal patriotism they so happily used. The names of many of these contributors were proudly printed in the *Piccolo Corriere*, among them some which express the best of the nineteenth-century idealism of the Risorgimento: a modest gift from "E. Arago"; 20 francs from "Jules Ferry, *avocat*," and a magisterial 100 francs from "Michelet *de l'Institut*." [15]

[15] *Piccolo Corriere*, 27 May; 3, 10, 17, and 24 June; 8, 22, and 29 July; 5 and 12 August; 9 September, 16 December 1860. Letters and memoranda in ISR mss., buste 550, n. 78; 555; 716, ns. 18, 102; 717, n. 55; 718, n. 15; 719, ns. 2, 3; 720, ns. 1, 2, 3, 6. Howard R. Marraro, "Documenti italiani e americani sulla spedizione Garibaldina in Sicilia," *Rassegna Storica del Risorgimento*, XLIV (1957), 39–40. Crämer-Doos, who wanted to join the SNI, was an im-

Even in Italy there was a certain political safety in making one's contribution to the Sicilian campaign through the SNI. The Venetian committee, like many committees to aid Sicily, gave directly to the Central Committee of the SNI. The managers of theaters giving special benefits and of hotels holding special banquets, the Freemasons of Turin or the Chief Rabbi there, probably felt they avoided any dangerous partisan taint by doing the same. There is a hint of political self-interest in the tendency of Government employees whether the railroad workers or *carabinieri* to make their gifts to the Society; and certainly the *Unione Liberale*, the respected *Corriere Mercantile* of Genoa or *Unione* of Turin intended their donations to the Central Committee to stand as a kind of political statement. By the end of May some 15 influential Italian newspapers had announced their support of the SNI's *Danaro d'Italia*.

For a period of several months that fund drive required scores of letters to be written each week and formidable amounts of auditing. Technically, all this fell to the Central Committee in Turin; in practice, the burden was Buscalioni's. With the aid of a few friends, he accomplished most of it. The very success and size of the Society's collection, however, raised further problems. As the number of the Society's committees grew and they became more active, they required more precise directions from Turin. Important questions of policy were unavoidable when committees became concerned in local politics, competed with Bertanians, sent more and more volunteers, or collected arms. Whom the Society aided or how it reported the news went to the very heart of its relations with the Government and of its own policy. But Buscalioni lacked either the authority or the willingness to deal with such problems; at the same time, he was determined, and La Farina supported him, not to share the direction of the National Society even with its most prominent leaders, many of whom as members of parliament were conveniently on hand. Letters whose authors had thought they were urgent went unanswered, and the replies Buscalioni did write

portant member of the *Nationalverein*: Oncken, *Bennigsen*, I, 345, 451. Ferdinand Boyer, "Souscriptions pour Garibaldi en France (1860)," *Rassegna Storica del Risorgimento*, XLVII (1960), 69–74. The New York committee had hoped to equal the $12,356 they collected in 1859, printed fund-raising letter among the Buscalioni pamphlets, HCL.

were vague on policy and full of apologetic accounts of how hard he was working. La Farina could not allow the Society's direction to be shared because he knew that the Society's doctrines, however enthusiastically supported, would offer little guide as to what to do. He could not establish policy in advance because he could not predict what Cavour would do. When its members were more ready than ever before to accept militant leadership, the National Society could not provide it.[16]

The Central Committee had tried to avoid responsibility for volunteers by having the Society's local leaders deal directly with the *Ufficio Militare* in Genoa. But when, at the end of June, Cosenz asked the Society to provide 300 men in a few days, the Central Committee sent out word with dispatch; and the Society responded well. Cressini, who replaced Cosenz at the *Ufficio*, was close to Cortes, a friend of La Farina's, who took an increasing part in the Society's correspondence about volunteers. Communications among Cressini, Cortes, and Buscalioni were frequent, punctuated by occasional telegrams which heightened the sense of urgency. Cressini pleaded with the Society for funds (much of which he got) and occasionally requested men. Yet he must have doubted the Central Committee's enthusiasm for volunteers, because he took pains to argue that the men who would be most helpful in Sicily might prove troublemakers if left at home.

After an embarrassing episode when Bertani succeeded in excluding the Society's volunteers from an expedition to which the Society had contributed, Cressini was careful to report whenever the men sent by the SNI actually sailed. Buscalioni credited Siccoli, who sailed in July, with having worked especially well with the Society. The Central Committee's last large contribution of funds and its last call for volunteers was for the sailing of the *Provence*, on the evening of August 6–7, which had an additional 300 places to be filled. Cortes himself was its leader. The Central Committee had provided Amari with some rifles in June as it had Garibaldi in May, and from May through August

[16] *Piccolo Corriere*, 13, 20, and 27 May; 22 July 1860. Mss. in ISR, buste 382, n. 22; 550, n. 88; 555; 716, ns. 104, 105; 717, ns. 19, 103; 718, n. 33; 719, ns. 8, 18; 720, n. 33. Puccioni, *Malenchini*, 181–82. The Central Committee as a whole did begin to meet often enough that a form for announcing meetings was printed, in Buscalioni pamphlets, HCL.

it helped the *Ufficio Militare* to operate somewhat independently of Bertani. But the Central Committee itself had only been implicated in, without earning direct credit for, that movement of men from Genoa which was the stirring focus of nationalist activity.

The relationship of the Central Committee to the Government of Piedmont was even more uncertain. Amari had from the first doubted that La Farina's statements were a guarantee of the Government's position; but he distrusted Cavour, too. In July the Government withdrew its permission for the maintenance of depots at which volunteers could be collected while waiting to sail; there were then 1,300 men being kept near Alessandria. And it ceased giving volunteers free railroad transportation on their way to Genoa. These measures brought protests from Cressini, who warned of disorders, and from Cortes. But Cressini's insistence that he had avoided politics, like Cortes' plea for the Government's help in such solemn times, suggest that neither the Society's Central Committee nor the *Ufficio Militare* was really close to the Government. In August Cortes asked Cressini if he was sure the Government did not oppose their sailings; when he himself sailed, Cortes was careful to list his men as bound for Athens (via Palermo) in search of work. Cavour claimed that the Government had not only aided the Sicilian venture but would have done more if, after Medici's departure, there had been a center in Genoa with which it could work—but that smacks of an excuse. It took an extraordinary failure on the part of the Society's Central Committee to make such an excuse possible.[17]

Still, throughout the summer the Italian National Society re-

---

[17] The *Provence* apparently carried only 500 men, 100 less than its capacity. *La spedizione di volontari*, 22, credits the *Ufficio Militare* with having sent at least 5,000 volunteers (a note in ms. from the *Ufficio* to the Central Committee in ISR suggests about 4,000 as their total) but gives 13,417 as the total sent, 4,206 by Bertani, and attributes the rest (9,211) to the SNI, the Million Rifles Fund, and the *Ufficio*. Bertani, *Resoconto*, 20, takes credit for sending 20,000 men. It is impossible to disentangle who recruited, paid to send to Genoa, equipped, or paid for the sailing of the approximately 20,000 who sailed.

The information on the Central Committee's role in sending volunteers and its relations with the Government is from: *Piccolo Corriere*, 5 August and 9 September 1860. Puccioni, *Malenchini*, 132–35, 181. Mss. among Carte Morchio, MNRG, and in the ISR, buste 546, ns. 83 and 84; 548, n. 8; 715; 719, ns. 1, 2, 3, 8; 720, ns. 2, 3, 7. Chiala, *Carteggio di Cavour*, iii, 316.

mained closely associated in the public mind with every aspect of Garibaldi's adventure. Suggestions for new ways of raising money (portraits of Victor Emmanuel and Garibaldi on porcelain vases) or for winning the war (a Frenchman's design for a huge warship, a boy's project for the siege of Palermo) were still addressed to the Society. For volunteers, too, the SNI seemed the authoritative center to which a boy could write of his dream of riding with Garibaldi with hope that the National Society might provide a passport, his passage, and a commission. A Venetian doctor offering his services sent his letter to the SNI; so did volunteers complaining of the rank they had been given or families wanting word of a son or husband. To some, the Society did give satisfaction, for Buscalioni on occasion at least passed on these inquiries or pressed a case like that of the two young volunteers from Venice who bore testimonials from the "first houses" of their city.

The Sicilian campaign had made brilliant propaganda for the National Society. The *Danaro d'Italia* provided much of it. No one could fail to be impressed by the *Piccolo Corriere* that summer. Issue after issue contained special notices about gifts from every sort of group and long lists in small print of the donors, sometimes for ten or twelve pages. There were reports of the varied activities of dozens of committees and marvelous instances of enthusiasm. There was the calm notice that the Society spent still more than it received, the deficit being covered by personal obligations assumed by those on the Central Committee. As they became more active, local committees won increased attention from the press, and they took care to advertise themselves with manifestoes and broadsides. The *Piccolo Corriere* gave further circulation to its readers' best patriotic phrases and reported an infinity of their patriotic gestures, from the member of the Society who contributed the royalties from his pamphlet on pellagra (the Society could not, however, agree with him that corn in the diet would prevent the disease) to the beadle who gave what he earned at a church ceremony on the grounds that the love of one's country was also a religion and that Christianity could only gain when its home was out of slavery.

In addition, the Society issued a number of special publications. It was a special supplement in the *Piccolo Corriere* of May

27, entitled *"Inganni,"* which had warned of the dangers to the regular army from desertion and of Papal agents pretending to recruit for Garibaldi. With its authoritative tone, rich with self-satisfaction from having done so much and hints of inside information, it was circulated throughout Italy in hundreds of copies. The Society's news bulletins, so well known in the Marches, stressed its own part in affairs and proved the militance of the SNI with vigorous attacks on the Bourbon and Papal regimes.

A special circular, *"à l'Étranger,"* was issued by the Central Committee in May. It was similar to the announcement of the *Danaro d'Italia;* but, intended for a French audience, it stressed the tyranny of the Jesuits and the international conspiracy of the Church while challenging the French and German liberals to do as much as the English in supporting the cause of national liberty. Not only did the circular contribute to the campaign in France, but it served at home as evidence that the National Society, in addition to being close to the Government, had its own international connections. There was even an edition of it printed in parallel columns of French and Greek. And it was followed by a form letter from the SNI's *Secréteriat pour l'Étranger* asking the recipient to be an agent of the Society in his country. His function would be to combat calumnies against Italy. The offer found a taker in Hungary, who was anxious to express his belief that the destinies of the two nations were intertwined. The project did not succeed with many, but at least the Society became increasingly well known. The *Suddeutsche Zeitung* might express doubt that Italian unity was really in everyone's interest so long as the National Society included Trieste and the Tyrol among its objectives, but even it treated this *National-verein* with some respect and sympathy.[18]

The Italian National Society had achieved new strength and popularity because of a movement it had not started and from its apparent cooperation with Garibaldi. For a moment its old destiny seemed fulfilled; most nationalists, the State, and a revolution were working together. There remained the great division

[18] *Piccolo Corriere,* 13, 20, and 27 May; 3 June; 8 and 22 July; 5 August 1860. Buscalioni pamphlets, Houghton Broadsides, H. N. Gay clippings, and H. N. Gay newspaper clippings, 1856–1927, all in HCL. Ms. in ISR, busta 716, n. 88. Franchi, *Epistolario di La Farina,* II, 317, 320, 380.

with Bertani, but he was notoriously hard to get along with. Then the suspicion grew that Bertani was doing more while the Society's position remained unclear and its leadership weak. Only the slowness in sending and recording earlier contributions and the prohibition against further sailings from Genoa helped to disguise how seriously the National Society was losing ground in August. However much the Society had contributed to the campaign in Sicily—and it was a great deal—it could not hold nationalists together; it could no longer manipulate Garibaldi. And because it now feared him, the Society could not even achieve the militance it had advocated.

Instead, the National Society's achievement was partisan; it had more than any single group kept Bertani from dominating the support for Sicily in the north. Having accomplished this, it made it possible for the Government not to oppose the Garibaldian venture and thus to preserve its popularity; for the Society's actions were taken to be a sign of the Government's intent. If the National Society contributed less than most of its supporters thought it did and with less enthusiasm than its propaganda said it should, it did far more than most Cavourians would have dared. And that kept militant nationalists from having to become revolutionaries. By providing a respectable means of aiding Garibaldi, it had allowed moderates to remain nationalists. The National Society had not brought Cavourians and Garibaldians together, but it obscured their differences until Cavour could pick their battleground.

CHAPTER TWELVE

SCHISM OVER GARIBALDI

(JUNE—SEPTEMBER 1860)

❧ ON JULY 9, 1860, the *Giornale Officiale di Sicilia* announced that, on Garibaldi's orders, Giuseppe La Farina had been expelled from Sicily. The Garibaldians made their meaning clear by ousting two professional spies, currently in Cavour's pay, at the same time. Only a little more than a month before, La Farina had left Piedmont, apparently the very symbol of the cooperation of Government and people in supporting Garibaldi. Now he returned, apparently the cause of a tragic and dangerous split between Garibaldi and Cavour. He had, of course, never quite been either.

Cavour's choice of La Farina is understandable, however unwise. The Piedmontese Minister did not know many Sicilians, and he was indebted to La Farina. Perhaps he really thought La Farina beloved in his homeland; in any case, he sent a shrewd politician and skilled organizer to win another victory. La Farina and the National Society had (from Cavour's standpoint) handled Garibaldi well the year before and seemed able to cooperate with him now. They had made the expeditions from Genoa less threatening to the Government, won Medici and Cosenz to a moderate policy and isolated Bertani. Now, those victories were to be extended. La Farina was sent, Cavour explained, to organize a "regular" government in Sicily (he still worried about Bertani) and to have Mazzini arrested. However one interprets Cavour's statements, clearly his darkest fears were growing.[1]

It is because these fears were reciprocated by the Garibaldians and because, on both sides, they were rooted in real differences of policy, that the sending of La Farina was unwise. The questions now at issue between Cavour and Garibaldi, the role of

[1] Mario, *Bertani*, II, 88–90. Cavour to Ricasoli, 3 June; to A. Mathieu, 12 June; to Persano, 13 June, Chiala, *Lettere di Cavour*, III, 260, 267, 270. For a harsher and much more thorough assessment of La Farina's Sicilian venture, see Mack Smith, *Cavour and Garibaldi*, 37–99.

revolution and the demands of diplomacy, had publicly divided them within the year. Each time, in the disputes over invading the Marches in the fall of 1859, the dramatic failure of the *Liberi Comizii*, the cession of Nice, La Farina had been a leader in the Cavourian triumph. It is only in the context of these real differences of program that the unattractiveness of La Farina's personality becomes important. For his tactics had never been such as to leave his victims unresentful.

Thus there were many ready to predict the failure of his mission, and the news of La Farina's departure was accompanied by an extraordinary flurry of letters to Garibaldi. Bertani, of course, poured forth warnings that La Farina was as dangerous as the aristocracy; and he carefully opened old wounds by sending along a copy of one of La Farina's more intemperate private letters, one written the previous January and filled with harsh comments on the aims of Garibaldi and Brofferio. But it was not just Bertani who wrote; for all who knew Garibaldi seemed to believe in his need for advice and his accessibility to theirs. A number of them now sent it, redundantly demanding that he "beware of La Farina." Pallavicino wrote to insist that the Italian Question must depend on revolution, but he would not even use La Farina's name: as for the man who was coming to Sicily, "I know him," he said with simple bitterness, "and I despise him." [2] It is hardly surprising that Garibaldi, sometimes so gently forgetful, this time greeted La Farina coldly.

From the first then, La Farina and Crispi were engaged in a duel for power; for Crispi, who had primary political authority among the Garibaldians, had also been thoroughly and quite unnecessarily warned against La Farina. Both men had wide connections within the intricate politics of Sicily, and both marshaled every weapon they could command. La Farina, as the man out of office, was particularly free with implied threats and promises and hosts of rumors. His tactics, from backstairs negotiations to organized demonstrations for annexation, were highly disruptive; but they won his friends a brief tour of office while

[2] Bertani to Garibaldi, 1 and 8 June [La Farina's letter had been written to Pietro Monteverde, 18 January 1860]; Cotelletti, 9 June; and Biagio-Caranti, 2 June, to Garibaldi, Curatolo, *Garibaldi, Vittorio Emanuele, e Cavour*, 110–13, 117, 108, 106. Pallavicino to Garibaldi, 3 June 1860, *Memorie di Pallavicino*, III, 583.

earning him new enemies. He remained both too cocky and too conspiratorial; his expulsion was Crispi's final triumph.

La Farina was dealt with so severely partly because of the previous history of the National Society. As they analyzed the disappointments of the last two years, the Garibaldians felt that their nationalism had benefited Piedmont, that their daring and sacrifice had been used to support Cavour's policies. They saw the National Society as the agency which had caused them to be used for ends not theirs, and they even exaggerated its power over public opinion. Thus La Farina's efforts, in Sicily, to enlist public opinion were peculiarly frightening just as his most tactless steps were interpreted as part of some deep Cavourian plot. Significantly, the immediate cause of La Farina's ouster was the reprinting in the *Giornale Officiale* of the claim that the SNI had furnished all the funds for the expeditions to Sicily. And the announcement of his expulsion went to some length to argue that Garibaldi had found the Society more of a hindrance than a help.[3]

The reaction to the expulsion of La Farina was almost universally one of regret, of a feeling that the action had been excessive and in bad taste. The tendency, however, was to criticize La Farina far more strongly. He was the interloper, and for some time word had been coming back to the north that La Farina was causing the most dangerous divisions. Among men anxious not to recognize how far apart Cavour and Garibaldi were, it was tempting to blame this crisis on La Farina's personality. The King had already accepted with indignation a Crispian version of the conflict. And in blaming "all the misfortunes" of Sicilian politics on La Farina, Victor Emmanuel—as he so often did— was representing in simple form an opinion widespread among Italian patriots. Even Cavour had come to doubt that La Farina was an effective emissary, although he maintained some confidence in La Farina's reports despite their throbbing megalomania.[4]

[3] Bertani, 9, 16, 26 June; and Giorgio Asproni to Crispi, Crispi, *I Mille*, 223–24, 234, 237. Amari to G. P. Vieusseux, 10 July 1860, d'Ancona, *Carteggio Amari*, III, 203. Bertani, *Ire d'oltre tomba*, 45. Calvino to Bargoni, 9 July 1860, Bargoni, *Memorie*, 134; and of Giuseppe Piola to Cavour, 10 July 1860, *Liberazione del Mezzogiorno*, I, 318. Mack Smith, *Cavour and Garibaldi*, 88–9.

[4] Bargoni to Calvino, 9 July 1860, Bargoni, *Memorie*, 131; Michele Amari

If Mazzini saw the "triumph" of *his* cause in La Farina's expulsion (the prelude, he hoped, to ousting Cavour), the president of the Italian National Society agreed.[5] La Farina returned to Piedmont certain that he must continue his war against Garibaldi's regime, and he clearly hoped to call on the full force of the SNI to support him. But the Society could not effectively respond for reasons lying in the strength of its doctrine and the weakness of its organization.

For those who thought in the terms made popular by the National Society, the distinction between the policies of Garibaldi and La Farina was too delicate to be understood. In appealing to Italian nationalists the Society's ultimate argument had been that its program was sensible, that it worked. And the Society had been threatened less by the criticisms of Brofferio or the discontent of Garibaldi than the distastefulness of the truce at Villafranca and the cession of Nice. It was then that talk of alternatives to Cavour's policies became effective. Once Garibaldi's expedition to Sicily seemed likely to succeed, the SNI could do nothing but support it.

Indeed, for the men of the Society, Garibaldi's success had raised three questions. The first was, simply, who was doing the most for the national cause? Here, the SNI fared rather well. The suspicion that the Society was inactive had been largely dissipated in May and June. Its fame and skillful propaganda, its far-flung fund drive and the activity of local committees, when added to the fact that the Society had equipped Garibaldi himself, seemed to preserve this practical justification for the Society's existence. The second question was, once revolution was adopted, how could it be limited, as the moderates, the Society itself, and the presence of Piedmontese troops had limited it in 1859? Here again, the fears natural to men in the SNI had quickly subsided. Garibaldi's loyalty to the King was hard to doubt, and

to Count Amari, 3 July 1860, d'Ancona, *Carteggio Amari*, II, 97–8; Amari to Vieusseux, 20 July, *ibid.*, III, 203; Ginevri-Blasi to Simonetti, 26 June 1860, ms. in Carteggio Casarini, MCRB. Carlo La Verenne to Crispi, 1 July 1860, Crispi, *I Mille*, 265; and Victor Emmanuel to Farini, n.d., *Liberazione del Mezzogiorno*, V, 484; the King had not helped by making known his desire for La Farina's recall: *ibid.*, 483n–84n. Cavour to Farini, n.d., *ibid.*, 485; and to Persano, 13 July 1860, Chiala, *Lettere di Cavour*, III, 386. Mack Smith, *Cavour and Garibaldi*, 45, 85–7.
[5] Mazzini to Caroline Stansfield, 26 July 1860, *Scritti di Mazzini*, LXVIII, 231.

the Society's own presence was a further assurance that this revolution, too, would be safe. Bertani himself acknowledged the importance of the regular army, and the Society had won most of Garibaldi's lieutenants to a Cavourian program. In the terms used by the National Society the remaining question was merely political: who was to dominate in Sicily? Disputes over the immediate annexation of Sicily to Piedmont and the tactful consideration of French interests were readily understood as part of the battle for power in Sicily. But for the man whose thought had been molded by the National Society these were questions of means, not ends. The Society's emphasis on compromise among nationalists and on personal sacrifice made La Farina's bitter intransigence look petty. The previous propaganda of his own Society tended to reduce La Farina's attacks on Garibaldi to a personal desire for revenge, a motive it had long denounced as unworthy.

The weaknesses of the Society's organization were also part of its very nature. Committees often suffered from personal conflicts among members as in Sarzana where a new committee was formed in opposition to the old "pseudo-committee"; but increasingly (as in Imola), even these disputes took on some of the tone of the Bertanian attacks on the SNI. The Parma committee had somehow so strayed that La Farina declared it dissolved before leaving for Sicily (but a new one was quickly formed).[6] Still more serious was Vegezzi-Ruscalla's break with La Farina. A philologist with important social connections in Turin, he had served as the Society's foreign secretary until his resignation in June. He complained of La Farina's dictatorial hand and of his greater concern to support the cession of Nice than the revolution in Sicily. And he wrote long letters to the Society's leaders in the Romagna describing the dissension in the Central Committee of the SNI and the incompetence of Buscalioni.

His apparently authoritative reports of the Society in decline

[6] Luigi Dell'Amico to Buscalioni, 2 July 1860, ms. in ISR, busta 720, n. 1. The dissolution of the Parma committee dated 31 May was cryptically announced in the *Piccolo Corriere* of 3 June 1860 (the draft of the announcement was much harsher but no clearer as to the reason for such drastic action, ms. in ISR, busta 555); the issue of 10 June gave the names of new members and that of 17 June announced that the *Unione Liberale* of Parma had dissolved, its members joining the SNI.

fanned the discontent within it. For he pictured it suffering from excessive dependence on Cavour, poor organization and intrigue, losing its important connections in a dozen countries and ignoring promising chances for a revolution in Hungary.[7] Within the Society there was no longer anyone who could challenge or even share La Farina's authority. On hearing the news of La Farina's departure for Sicily, Mazzini was certain that he and Bertani could gain control of the SNI in ten days; other opponents happily watched deep fissures growing, while within the Society itself there was grave concern over the leader's absence.[8]

It was not merely La Farina's energy which was missed. Without his skillful hints, the sense of close connection with Cavour faded somewhat within the Society, and confidence that the Prime Minister had some long-range plan dimmed. Furthermore, it was La Farina who had maintained the illusion that the SNI was tightly organized and highly centralized. Aid to Garibaldi provided a severe test of that organization, and the local leaders of the Society, having believed it to be what it claimed, now found it wanting. Still faithful to the Society, they blamed the lack of central direction and clear policy on La Farina's departure. Loyally, they set about reorganizing.

La Farina had, when the campaign for *Danaro d'Italia* was first announced, named a commission of directors; but its members were meant to provide political tone more than administrative efficiency, and by the end of May few of them were able to devote much time to the National Society. Just before sailing, La Farina called an emergency session of the Society's Central Committee; it was announced that direction of the Society would be left to Buscalioni who, in political matters, would act in agreement with Bartolommei and Manfredi, now prominent Cavourian deputies from Tuscany and the Duchies.[9]

[7] Vegezzi-Ruscalla to Tanari, 16 and 21 June 1860, mss. in Carte Tanari, MCRB; his letter to Casarini, 29 June 1860, is in Teodor D. Onciulescu, "Un assiduo socio della Società Nazionale Italiana e di quella Neo-Latina: il Torinese Giovanale Vegezzi-Ruscalla," *Rassegna Storica del Risorgimento*, XXVII (1940), 257.

[8] Mazzini to Bertani, n.d., *Scritti di Mazzini*, LXVII (Imola, 1934), 385–86; Bargoni to Calvino, 21 June 1860, Bargoni, *Memorie*, 127–28; Simonetti to Casarini, 9 June 1860, ms. in Carteggio Casarini, MCRB.

[9] There were six on the commission including La Farina; Professor Manfredi and Marchese Tanari were both deputies; dott. G. B. Bottero was editor of the

Buscalioni's lack of prestige was recognized from the first. By June 10 he was sending out a circular apologizing for not having done more, although he wrote about as many letters as anyone could, and promising to transmit La Farina's regular reports from Palermo. But to most members of the Society, Buscalioni remained the man whose demands for dues and membership lists had always reflected a kind of bureaucratic selfishness. Many now became aware of a malaise within the National Society; and Bartolommei, who took seriously his role of adviser to the Society, decided to do something about it.[10] On June 19 he sent, over his name, a circular to the major committees of the SNI asking them to send a "delegate plenipotentiary" to a special meeting in Turin and to call on the committees under them to do the same. It was a step without parallel in the Society's history. Some committees, like Guastalla's, elected a special delegate; most merely asked their parliamentary deputy, if he had been a member of the Society, to attend. Bartolommei requested the Tuscan committees to give their deputies the most formal authorization; he, at least, must have had in mind some major reorganization. But little of the sort can have happened at that meeting, held in the Society's headquarters in Turin on June 26. Its members knew too little about their organization to demand a thoroughgoing change. What they wanted in fact was what La Farina had always said they had, and like him, they called for more energy. Having found the National Society somehow inadequate, they called on local committees to recruit more members and to be sure to pay their dues. It was a tribute to the hold the SNI maintained on the minds of its members. The *Piccolo Corriere* was able to report the "marvelous concord" and "unanimity" of the meeting and to praise the "temperance" of the discussion. The implication remained that some fundamental

---

Gazzetta del Popolo; Malenchini was already in Sicily, and Plutino was occupied with the *Ufficio Militare*.

The Central Committee met at 6 a.m. on May 30, apparently in La Farina's home, from the invitation to the meeting in Buscalioni pamphlets, HCL; the announcement of La Farina's departure "to complete his duty" and of arrangements for the SNI appeared in the *Piccolo Corriere*, 3 June 1860.

[10] The June 10 circular and La Farina's report on the devastation of war around Palermo are in the BSMC. Casarini to Simonetti, 26 May 1860, Maioli, "Ancora della Società Nazionale," *Saggi e documenti*, 118. Mario, *Bertani*, II, 86; Bartolommei to Puccioni, 4 June, mss., in MRF, busta 112, n. 2; and 8 June 1860, in the Puccioni family papers.

discontent had not been met. Special instructions, it was promised, would be sent the local committees; but they have strangely left no trace in the archives.

Out of the meeting, then, came evidence of the vigor and loyalty the SNI could claim and some understanding that from now on the Central Committee would deal directly only with the regional centers at Genoa, Milan, Florence, Modena, Parma, and Bologna. This hint of federalism was little more than an acknowledgment of how the Society had come to operate; and La Farina, who would not recognize such decentralization, returned to Turin before there was a chance to test the Society as a genuinely representative body. Buscalioni, defensive about the whole affair, interpreted the meeting as a unanimous endorsement of the provisions La Farina had made on his departure. Buscalioni remained the director of the Society; Bartolommei and Manfredi remained his political advisers with the addition now of Visconti-Venosta, representing Lombardy, and Tanari, representing the Romagna.[11] But the promise implied in those famous names went unfulfilled.

Neither its doctrines nor its organization enabled the National Society to leap to La Farina's aid; and the propaganda of the *Piccolo Corriere* had not even prepared its readers for a break with Garibaldi. Instead, the paper had gone from statements of its cooperation with the General to the bold untruth that it was the committees of the SNI in Sicily which had "the glory of having taken the fortunate initiative." Its committees had fought for forty days "alone" against the Bourbons, but the Society was, its paper declared, too modest to engage in polemics with those who had done nothing. The intolerant note raised some doubts, but not about La Farina's support of Garibaldi. After La Farina's departure, the paper's tone paled a bit. Its denial that the Government might ally with the Bourbons lacked the controlled indignation which had made the Society's public position on Nice effective. While all Italy was celebrating the fruits of action, the

[11] A copy of Bartolommei's circular of June 19 is in the *Carte Morchio*, MNRG. Alessandro Scaravelli to Bartolommei, 24 June 1860, ms. in ISR, busta 717, n. 46; Bartolommei to Puccioni, n.d., ms. in Puccioni family papers. *Piccolo Corriere*, 1 July 1860. Bartolommei to Puccioni, 19 June 1860, ms. in MRF, busta 113, n. 4; Salvoni to Blasi, 29 June 1860, Nicoletti, *Comitato di Emigrazione*, 640–41. Buscalioni to Teresa Bartolommei, 5 July 1860, ms. in MRF, busta 114, n. 4.

Piccolo Corriere called on the Italians of Venetia, Trent, and the Papal States to "persevere in their patient suffering."

Still, the vision of all Italy soon united was maintained. If the paper outrageously exaggerated the enthusiasm of La Farina's reception in Sicily, it did not deny Garibaldi's popularity. The hints at real disagreement between La Farina and Garibaldi over annexation were very gentle; the paper rhapsodically pictured La Farina gaining increased authority and suggested that the General would again prove flexible.[12] Thus the Society's own propaganda contributed to the feeling, when the awful news from Sicily came, that La Farina's expulsion was the result more of some tragic clash of personalities than any political issue on which the Society need take a stand.

With the full force of his personality, La Farina misjudged opinion in the north as he had in Sicily. On his return to Turin, he immediately assumed full charge of the Society; indeed, he had intended, with the improved mail service, to direct it more closely from Palermo. Confident that he was receiving even more support than he had expected, he prepared a pugnacious statement for the next issue of the *Piccolo Corriere*. The National Society, he declared, had been the victim of a contemptible conspiracy conducted by the very men it had defeated in the past. The fault was in part the Society's. It had been too tolerant, remained silent too long out of a spirit of conciliation. The Italian National Society was formally called upon to abandon its claim to represent all nationalists.

With new vigor, the rhetoric once used against Mazzinians was now directed at a somewhat ill-defined group around Garibaldi; the policy of piecemeal annexations was raised to dogma. The correct program for Italian unification must consider the other European powers and the "true conditions" of the Italian provinces, a new note of anti-revolutionary reasoning. It was a stunning statement, which daringly placed the Garibaldians among the "supporters of past failures" who attacked Cavourian success. They demanded, he said, the liberation of all Italy before allowing that annexation which all Sicilians wanted. He would not, he added, stoop to the level of personal attack his enemies used; but he described Palermo as a nest of Mazzinians,

---

[12] *Piccolo Corriere*, 20 and 27 May, 3 and 24 June, 1 and 8 July 1860.

Crispi as greatly disliked, and Garibaldi's aides as using every weapon to discredit Piedmont. This was the regime which had arrested him in the middle of the night with no chance even to embrace the mother who had not seen her son during twelve years of patriotic exile.[13]

Privately, La Farina was less temperate. He wrote the leaders of the Society insisting that the attack had been made not on him but on the SNI. If he dared not tell the whole truth lest Europe and Italy be excessively alarmed, his caution and tolerance must not be mistaken for fear. He did not fear a fight—or civil war. The men around Garibaldi shared a "maniacal hatred" of "Cavour, Fanti, Ricasoli, the National Society." As La Farina watched Depretis leave to undertake the job he had done so badly of representing the Government to Garibaldi, he was confident that Depretis, too, would soon be back. That would be the sign for a complete break between the Government of the King and the filibustering General. The Society was suddenly declared partisan and officially Cavourian as it had never been before. Dramatically certain that a crisis had been reached, La Farina was fond of declaring that he was stripping away his enemies' "hypocritical mask." [14] Perhaps the adjective was too strong, but there were many who felt it was the Italian National Society which was unmasked. Its appeal would never be the same; yet it survived, an indication of the change in Italian politics and a suggestion that the Society's function had never been quite what it claimed.

The National Society, weakened by La Farina's departure for Sicily, was more gravely hurt by his return. For the only time in its history a major schism occurred. It was apparently the Duchess of Bevilacqua La Masa who began the crisis by writing, on July 10, to friends in the Romagna. She reported that La Farina had been the source of myriad divisions among na-

[13] La Farina to Manfredi, 6 July 1860, Franchi, *Epistolario di La Farina*, II, 352; and to Filippo Cordova, 15 July 1860, ms. in ISR, busta 16, n. 22. Buscalioni to Simonetti, 12 July 1860, ms. in Posizione Simonetti, MCRB. *Piccolo Corriere*, 15 July 1860.

[14] La Farina to Bartolommei, 22 July 1860, Franchi, *Epistolario di La Farina*, II, 373–74 (cf. ms. in MRF, busta 115, n. 5); to Gamberini, 18 July 1860, Galli, "Gamberini," *La Romagna*, XVII, 186–87; to Cordova, 20 July 1860, ms. in ISR, busta 16, n. 24. For the changed role the Society assigned the Government, cf. the contemporary statement probably prepared by Buscalioni, ms., *ibid.*, busta 721, n. 8.

tionalists in Sicily, said that Garibaldi was ready to resume the presidency of the SNI, and suggested that the Romagna should lead in bringing this about. Her efforts had immediate effect. The Forlì committee, which had received one of the Duchess's letters, lost no time in endorsing it. Ably seconded by the committee in Faenza, it soon had the wires humming with demands that Bologna call a meeting of the Society in the Romagna. This much had happened even before word had come of La Farina's expulsion from Sicily.

That shock caused further concern for the Society. The Bagnacavallo committee complained of a "change of direction," and Rimini's suggested increased preparation for action in the Marches as the Society's salvation. Only Ravenna, where the Rasponis gave the SNI a conservative and even Bonapartist tone, seemed undisturbed. But La Farina's defense in the *Piccolo Corriere* made even the prudent Simonetti feel that a Romagna meeting was necessary. On July 16 the Bologna committee issued a circular, probably written by Tanari, calling for a meeting on the 21st. It referred to the weakening of the Society in La Farina's absence, to the "calumnies" against him, the tragedy of a conflict with Garibaldi. Each committee was invited to send two delegates to grapple with these difficult considerations of personal honor, the good of Italy, and the future of the Society.[15] To raise such questions was to begin to answer them; the Romagna was turning against La Farina.

Nowhere was the National Society better organized than in the Romagna, and it was there that schism was brewing. Many of the men now demanding La Farina's removal as president had expressed their complete confidence in him within the month. During June many of the Romagnol leaders had nevertheless decided that they must act independently, for there was a suspicion of Buscalioni which verged on hatred, extending even to his "plump, placid, virgin" face. His excessive claims for the SNI in his bulletins to the Marches added to this distrust, and it was

---

[15] Panciatichi [to Tanari?], 12 July (including the letter he received from the Duchess) and 14 July, mss. in Carteggio Casarini, MCRB. Duchess of Bevilacqua to Tanari, in Dallolio, *La spedizione*, 299. Telegrams of Leopoldo Maluccelli and Laderchi to Tanari, 13 July 1860, MCRB. L. Bioni and Ginevri-Blasi [to Tanari?], 15 July; and Rasponi to Tanari, 16 July, mss. in Carteggio Casarini; and note of Simonetti to Tanari, 16 July, ms. in Carte Tanari, II, both in MCRB. A copy of the circular of 16 July is in *ibid*.

increased by Buscalioni's choice for advisers on affairs in the Romagna of men whom Casarini and Simonetti disliked. At the last minute, Festi had tried to reassure Tanari and Simonetti; but La Farina's imbroglio merely confirmed a growing distrust of the Society's leadership. Nor had Tanari forgotten his hope of uniting the two societies, the *Nazione* and the *Nazionale*.[16] The very competition with Bertani, particularly strong in the Romagna, had made the leaders of the Society there especially sensitive to public opinion, and the Romagnols had already shown their enthusiasm for Garibaldi.

Toward the Society itself, its leaders in the Romagna remained loyal. They were frightened by the suggestions of some that the National Society should at long last disband. They were acting to save their Society, without knowing just what they would do. Simonetti even began to wish he knew more of what had happened in Sicily; but from the Romagna to France supporters of the Society had felt that La Farina would have to resign. Casarini and Tanari each wrote him directly, asking that he thus solve their problem. Casarini spoke apologetically of ingratitude and enthusiastically of the need for sacrifice. It was because Garibaldi must be won back to a Cavourian path and because the SNI must be saved that he asked La Farina to wire his resignation before the meeting in Bologna on Sunday. He received no reply.[17] Clearly the delegates to that meeting had

[16] Casarini to Luigi Brussi, 24 May; Rasponi to Casarini, 2 June; Mai to Casarini, 5 June, mss. in Careggio Casarini, MCRB. All express confidence in La Farina—in itself, perhaps, a sign of uneasiness.

The comments on Buscalioni, the resentment of his choice of Berti-Pichat and Carlo [?] Rusconi as advisers, and the reactions to the Society's Bulletins (especially No. 3) are apparent in Ginevri-Blasi to Simonetti, 26 June; Casarini to Tanari, 12 June; and to Ginevri-Blasi, 14 June; Buscalioni to Simonetti, 5 July, and Simonetti to Casarini, 6 July, all in *ibid.*, and Casarini to Simonetti [misdated 10 April but more likely written in July], in Maioli, "Ancora della Società Nazionale," *Saggi e documenti*, 115–17. These letters also suggest that Vegezzi-Ruscalla's denunciations had had some effect, something recognized by Festi in his efforts at a reconciliation, Festi to [Tanari or Simonetti], 12 July 1860, ms. in Carte Tanari II, MCRB.

The Romagnols generally wanted a more major role in the national movement; Bertani's followers there feared *his* delays were the result of some Mazzinian maneuver, Cadolini to Bertani, 6 June 1860, Nazari-Michele, *Cavour e Garibaldi*, 104n–105n.

[17] Simonetti to Casarini, 20 July, ms. in Carteggio Casarini, MCRB; *Emilia* advised the SNI to disband; Pepoli was said to have inspired the attack: Simonetti to Tanari, 18 July 1860, ms. in Carte Tanari II, MCRB. Manfredi felt too close to La Farina to ask for his resignation but thought his own selflessness would lead

already made up their minds: La Farina must go. There was some talk of Depretis as president, more of Garibaldi, supported perhaps by a representative council elected from local committees and sitting in Turin. The sense of crisis deepened as the local committees expressed their demands more rigidly and threats of resignation ricocheted among the Society's members.[18]

Faced with an organized revolt against his leadership, La Farina held firm. He tended to blame Tanari for what was happening, and he wrote his friend Canevazzi a letter which was intended for Simonetti and Casarini as well. As unyielding as ever, his talk of separating "true friends" from false ones and of keeping their banner from being dragged in the mud, could hardly change any minds. He even wrote Minghetti, hoping perhaps to throw his prestige in the balance, declaring that Garibaldi was "drunk with fortune and moved by blind hate." He threatened to publish the names of those who feared to take their stand with the SNI, but the Romagnols were hardly being secretive. The day before their meeting convened, Buscalioni sent a telegram declaring the Central Committee's faith in its president and adding that similar sentiments had come from Florence, Milan, Leghorn, Pisa, Massa, etc.[19] It was too late for such tactics to be effective.

Delegates from ten of the Romagnol committees met in Bologna on Sunday, July 22. After a day's discussion, they were able to issue a statement which the Bologna committee mailed out the next day. It was strikingly like the circular which had invited them there. It declared that La Farina deserved well of the SNI and insisted the Society had done its part for Sicily.

---

to it: Manfredi to Tanari, 15 July, Dallolio, *La spedizione*, 129. Cf. Planat de la Faye to Buscalioni, 28 July, ms. in ISR, busta 550, n. 78. Casarini had been in Leghorn when the Romagna crisis broke and apparently took some sounding of opinion there before rushing back to Bologna. Casarini to La Farina, 19 July, is in Masi, *Casarini*, 122–24; Tanari sent his letter through the intendant, Mayr, who was closely watching the Society's troubles, Tanari to Simonetti, n.d., ms. in Posizione Simonetti, MCRB.

[18] Rasponi, 16 July; Camporesi, 19 July; Giovanni Marchi, 19 July; to Casarini, mss. in Carteggio Casarini, MCRB. Casarini to Pasquale Crecchi, 20 July; Camporesi to Casarini, 15 July; Maluccelli to Tanari, 18 July; Salvoni to Casarini, 19 July, in Dallolio, *La spedizione*, 308–10, 300–306.

[19] La Farina to Manfredi, 17 July 1860, Fermi and Ottolenghi, *Manfredi*, 155; La Farina to Canevazzi [and to Gamberini], 18 July, Franchi, *Epistolario di La Farina*, ii, 362–64. Dallolio, *La spedizione*, 130–31. Buscalioni's telegram, received in Bologna 9 p.m. of July 21, is in MCRB.

Nevertheless, grave recriminations had developed; and those calumnies had undermined La Farina's authority. In the Romagna, the statement added, the National Society had once led the "energetic part" of the populace. Now it was torn between opposing popular opinion by assuming La Farina's personal cause or abandoning him "to the exigencies of circumstances." They were acting for "their own salvation" in declaring that "La Farina can no longer hold the presidency of the National Society." On such reasoning, they voted 6 to 4 to name a new candidate for president and by a vote of 9 to 1 picked Depretis over Garibaldi. If the reasoning of this statement was pained, the delegates themselves had been less certain than they sounded. Four of the committees represented had given their delegates only the vaguest of mandates, and several of those representatives sent somewhat differing reports to Turin.[20]

The *Piccolo Corriere* in its next issue announced the dissolution of the committee in Bologna; the Central Committee in Turin had already circulated a counter-manifesto of its own. Signed by Buscalioni, it pointed up the awkward contrast between the Romagnols' praise of La Farina and their vote to remove him as president. In order to avoid scandal the Central Committee would make no public rebuttal, but it declared the meeting in Bologna to have been a usurpation and promised to disband any committee which supported the Bologna resolution. It added the threat that in each such place a reliable committee would be immediately reconstituted.

The Bologna committee replied in a circular, protesting that they, too, wished to avoid controversy but insisting on their belief both in freedom of association and the principles of the SNI. The fate of the National Society would depend on the replies to Bologna's invitation to its meeting on August 2. The first response came from Bobbio; its committee had, after praising La Farina, unanimously voted to support Bologna. Guastalla's

<hr>

[20] Copies of the July 23 circular are in HCL, MCRB, ISR; it is printed in Masi, *Casarini*, 124–27. Pietro Prampolini, one of the delegates from Ferrara, 25 July [to Buscalioni], ms. in ISR, busta 720, n. 3. Faenza's representatives were told to act as they thought best; Cesena's and Forlì's had even less instruction. Salvoni wrote [Buscalioni?], 1 August, that the Rimini delegates had carried instructions "quite different" from the outcome of the meeting, ms. in ISR, busta 719, n. 3. Tanari sent a copy of the circular with a personal note to La Farina, minute in Carte Tanari II, MCRB.

committee also announced its support of Depretis for president but proved it was still in the SNI by blaming all these difficulties on Bertani. Two other committees of the former Duchies sent similar replies; but of the more than a score who wrote Bologna of their support, all the others were in the Romagna. Civitella's committee explained its position by saying simply that they were always loyal to Bologna, an odd sentiment for members of the Italian National Society.[21]

On August 2 a second meeting took place in Bologna. It was more like a convention this time, and its delegates were now fully aware of the seriousness of their acts. There were 28 delegates from 19 committees. They unanimously agreed, and with some heat, that no committee could be disbanded so long as it adhered to the Society's principles; and then they voted, 13 to 6, to offer the presidency of the SNI to Depretis. A measure to make Garibaldi honorary president was defeated by an identical vote. The majority were determined to escape those "personal issues" which had proved so dangerous. Finally, it was agreed that, until the new office of the presidency was established, the Bologna committee should assume the Society's direction. The schism was complete; it was also only regional.

These deliberations, too, were reported in a circular meant to win further support. Proud of the moderation of their stand, these schismatics managed now to state it with some dignity. Yet, even among them, there were doubts about the constitu-

[21] *Piccolo Corriere*, 29 July 1860. Copies of the Central Committee's circular of 27 July, are in MNRG, HCL, MCRB. Bologna's reply, n.d., is in MCRB. Bobbio's committee felt so strongly they wrote the same thing to Turin, ms. in ISR, busta 720, n. 3. The records in MCRB may well not be complete, but those committees with letters there indicating either that they agreed with Bologna or would send delegates to the August 2 meeting are listed here.

27 July: Bobbio; 28 July: Guastalla; 29 July: Imola, Civitella [di Romagna] (Forlì would vote for them), Codigoro (to send someone if they could), Reggiolo (but no one could come); 30 July: Comacchio (so agreed no need to send a delegate), Saludecio, Castel Bolognese (a special meeting unanimously supported Bologna), Sarsina; 31 July: Brisighella (their stand ambiguous), Budrio (supported Bologna after a special meeting), Medicina (held a meeting in which La Farina was greatly praised but agreed to follow Bologna), Massa Lombarda (voted against La Farina, 24 for Depretis, 15 for Garibaldi; Lugo to vote for them), Bagnacavallo (Ravenna to vote for them); 1 August: Cotignola (Lugo to vote for them), Molinella (unable to send delegate), Montecchio (influenced by attack on La Farina in *La Nazione*), Cesena (taken no stand), S. Agata (Lugo to represent them), Fussignano (Lugo to vote for them), Faenza (insists on Garibaldi for president), Castelnuovo di Sotto. There were, of course, also representatives from Bologna, Ravenna, Rimini, and Forlì at the meeting.

tionality of their act. Those who still leaned toward La Farina sought from Turin some record of how committees outside the Romagna were lining up; and the records of these debates in Bologna were much in demand as local committees explained to their members the necessity for their break with Turin.[22]

The leaders of the Society in the Romagna were worried, too, by La Farina's careful hint that he stayed in office at the wish of Farini and Cavour. It was decided to send the Prime Minister a testimonial and statement of support which Casarini accompanied with a letter of his own, written with embarrassed charm. He apologized for the testimonial's condition, the result of "robust and hardly delicate" Romagnol hands. Then he apologized for his familiarity. Cavour's reply was friendly and reassuring. With a practiced touch he ignored their schism and acknowledged the comfort of their support. Yet he did take care to object to their phrase listing Government and revolution as the two forces for Italian union. One could not properly speak of revolution, the Count suggested, where public opinion was unanimous and a legal government was capable of achieving the desired ends; questions of means, he added, were best left to those responsible for affairs of state.

Grateful to be back in Cavour's respectable company, the Society's men in the Romagna seem not to have pondered his lesson. They had used one of the Risorgimento's traditional phrases; yet Cavour had objected. It was precisely the point around which Manin had conceived his party, the one over which Pallavicino had left it, and the most fundamental of the ones which divided La Farina and Garibaldi. Doctrinal subtleties aside, the letter was something of a coup; and Casarini urged the committees under Bologna to make "prudent" use of it. The Society in the Romagna was managing at least to establish the crucial distinction that, while separated from Turin, it was still Cavourian. Casarini had written Minghetti in detailed caution of the reasons for their schism, and he was upset that Farini con-

---

[22] The circular reporting this meeting was not sent out until August 8; it is reprinted in Masi, *Casarini*, 130–32. Prampolini, 27 July, Salvoni, 1 August; and Laderchi, 21 August, to Buscalioni, mss. in ISR, buste 718; ns. 719, 1 and 3. Gaetano Carboni, 6 August; Ginevri-Blasi, 10 August; Camerani and Laderchi, 13 August 1860, all to Casarini, mss. in Carteggio Casarini, MCRB. Buscalioni may have tried to put off the August 1 meeting, too, ISR, busta 719, n. 9.

sidered it an "irreverent" act toward the Government. But the suspicions in Governmental circles were understandable; the Bertanians themselves had thought that the Society in the Romagna, perhaps with the aid of a few bribes, would defect to them.[23]

The schismatic Society was faced with more concrete problems, too. Its leaders had hoped to inform Depretis of his election as their president with proper protocol, but they could find no one to take the message. Gaspare Finali, a Romagnol and an established Cavourian, had seemed just the man. But he refused, citing his official position and some cutting doubts about the wisdom of their move; Depretis, he suggested, would have no more time to direct the SNI from Sicily than La Farina had had. The delay in telling their president that he had been elected was proving embarrassing; finally, on August 18 the Bologna committee simply wrote him a private letter. They insisted on their loyalty to the Society's old program and spoke again of revolution and Government working together. Depretis, by his very personality, they suggested, symbolized this position. They promised to send a formal delegation later though there is no evidence that it ever arrived. By electing Depretis they had established their loyalty to the Government; he was, after all, Cavour's latest choice as emissary to Sicily. By not really demanding that he serve in the post, they conceded that theirs was a regional movement, not a national competitor of La Farina's. Inaction was the happiest compromise.

If the meetings in Bologna had not established a national organization, neither had they quelled the dissensions within many of the Romagna committees. For those who, like Gamberini, had come to distrust the Society's conservative temper, substituting Depretis for La Farina was not enough. Gamberini complained that those who had consorted with Austrians and priests now paraded as liberals, that he himself was treated as suspect. He joined Bertani's committee. By mid-August the committee

[23] The address to Cavour, Casarini's note, dated August 15, and Cavour's reply, 18 August 1860, are in Masi, *Casarini*, 133–36. Tacconi presented the address to Cavour: circular of Bologna committee (No. 1 of the Comitato Centrale della Società Nazionale nelle Romagne), August 9. Cavour's reply was printed in circular No. 3, August 21, both in MCRB. Dallolio, *La spedizione*, 318–23, 138–40, 329–34. Finali to Casarini, 10 August; Pagano to Simonetti, 14 August; Camerani to Casarini, 18 August; and Casarini to Pagano, n.d., mss. in Carteggio Casarini, MCRB. Cf. Puccioni, *Malenchini*, 173–74.

in Forlì had disbanded, the "best elements," its former president reported, having gone over to Bertani; and the Cesena committee wondered if they and the Bertanians did not really stand for the same thing. For some others, the Government's prohibition on further expeditions to Sicily was a final straw. The Faenza committee, which had never quite contained the explosive personalities which composed it, split between those who demanded that Garibaldi be made president and those who wished to maintain the connection with Turin. By the end of the month, after weeks of wavering and many pleas to maintain Romagnol unity, the committee in Bagnacavallo voted to reunite with Turin.[24]

But in the Romagna most of the Society's committees remained loyal to Bologna, and they continued to meet and to send out letters on their handsomely printed stationery. Although the appeal of the National Society was dimmed when it could not claim to be nation-wide or to reflect the inner thoughts of the Government, in the Romagna it could still claim to represent most reasonable nationalists. The committees talked a bit about establishing a newspaper, and they talked a great deal about the growing signs that there might soon be action in the Marches. The Bologna committee maintained good relations with the committees of the Society in other provinces. The schism had seemed a terrible test of whether the National Society could survive; it proved instead to make less difference than any of its participants expected, a quiet measure of what the Society really was.

The Bologna committee had written to committees throughout Italy, but most of them never replied. The committee in Massa was intransigently Lafarinian, and it told Bologna so. The nearby town of Tresana was more cautious; only one of its seven members could read, it pointed out, which seemed to explain their reluctance to take a stand. Fivizzano's was more sympathetic but felt, in view of what the SNI had done for Sicily, that firing La Farina was at least inopportune. These were areas

<hr />

[24] Dallolio, *La spedizione*, 326–27. Galli, "Società Nazionale e Gamberini," *La Romagna*, xvii, 168, 187–89. Panciatichi, 13 August; Marsilio Nori, 16 August; Carboni, 6 August; Ballelli, 11 and 31 August; Maluccelli *et al.*, 13 August; the Bagnacavallo committee, 20 August; Bubani, 31 August, to Casarini, mss. in Carteggio Casarini, MCRB. Bagnacavallo wrote Turin of its loyalty, 1 September 1860, ms. in ISR, busta 719, n. 4.

in which the Bologna committee had reasonably expected support, but it was Modena's refusal to join in any move against La Farina which made it clear that schism would be limited to the Romagna. The Modena committee was anything but indignant. They courteously suggested that conditions must be different in the Romagna, agreed that Garibaldi must be given every aid and rejected Bologna's conclusions. It was understood that local conditions would determine a committee's political color. Trained to think of national issues only in the broadest terms, most of the Society's members did not feel it necessary to take a stand of their own on the "personal" conflict between La Farina and Garibaldi. Leghorn, for example, had a reputation for being radical; and when Casarini heard that its committee supported Bologna, he hastily wrote to say that his position began with faith in Cavour. Yet the Society in Leghorn was most deeply offended by Garibaldi's denial that the SNI had aided his Sicilian campaign. When it denounced the "diatribe of journals," the Leghorn committee was avoiding judgment, not attacking La Farina.[25]

La Farina encountered a similar reluctance to recognize that any national or institutional crisis had occurred. The Brescia committee, for example, supported La Farina with unusual vigor; but it commented that these "little disappointments" had to be accepted. When Scaramuzza of the important Parma committee wrote of his confidence in La Farina, he made it clear that he was far more concerned that arrangements for volunteers be improved. The Ancona committee, torn by loyalty to the Romagnols yet bothered by rumors of their connection with Bertani, kept requesting more information on the conflict be-

[25] Rasponi, 23 August; and Salvoni, 21 August, to Casarini, mss. in Carteggio Casarini, MCRB. Bologna circular, No. 1, 18 August, *ibid.* There was some effort to bring the Bagnacavallo committee back in line: Masi to Casarini and Casarini to the Ravenna committee, 25 August, mss., *ibid.* Luigi Coccaccini, 6 August; Beghè, 4 August; the Fivizzano committee, 30 July, to Tanari, mss. in Carte Tanari II, MCRB. Giuseppi Basini [to Casarini?], 30 July, ms. in Carteggio Casarini, MCRB. Rasponi to Casarini, 23 August, and minute of letter from the Bologna committee to the one in Leghorn, 27 August, mss., *ibid.* Mengozzi to [Buscalioni?], 16 July, ms. in ISR, busta 720, n. 2. Leghorn's manifesto replying to the *Giornale Officiale* of Sicily is among the Buscalioni pamphlets, HCL. Vegezzi-Ruscalla had claimed that Modena, Parma, and Reggio would join Bologna, and that new committees could be established in Milan and Genoa, letter to Casarini, 26 July, Onciulescu, "Vegezzi-Ruscalla," *Rassegna Storica del Risorgimento,* XXVII, 259.

tween La Farina and Garibaldi—then ruled that no "national interests" were endangered. Careful steps were taken to make sure that the committees in Tuscany would reject Bologna's stand; yet one of the leaders in that effort blandly noted that it would make things easier if La Farina resigned. Many Tuscan committees did go out of their way to endorse La Farina, but the dominant feeling was simply that he defended himself somewhat excessively.

By counting personal friends as whole committees, La Farina was able to publicize impressive lists of those who declared their support for him; but, considering the energy with which he asked for testimonials, the replies were rather sparse.[26] The Italian National Society had offered its members the hope of rising above the pettiness of politics; few were ready to descend. La Farina's clash with Garibaldi had not destroyed the Society, but neither would the Society justify La Farina.

The schism did have some important effects on the Society. La Farina himself was a bit chastened. His first response had been to cry anathema, to rant against Mazzinians, and hint at foul motives (he once suggested the Bolognese were keeping the money they collected for Sicily). But his official response in August was more dignified. It was an exaggeration to declare that four-fifths of the Society's 2,000 committees would rather leave the SNI than abandon La Farina, but he effectively pictured himself as reluctantly remaining on the firing line in order to defend his principles. The attack on him, he argued and not without reason, had been an attack on Cavour. The *Piccolo Corriere* adopted a calmer tone; it denounced Mazzianians rather than Garibaldi. Less was said of Sicilian affairs, and it began publishing the details of the aid provided by the SNI. The Society's statistics, at a time when little was known of what had been done for Garibaldi, were particularly impressive. Along

[26] Mola, 26 July; and Luigi Batturelli and Lucio Fiorentini, 30 July 1860, to Buscalioni, mss. in ISR, busta 720, n. 3. Scaramuzza to Buscalioni, 18 July, ms. in *ibid.* Nicoletti, *Comitato di Emigrazione*, 774–75, 780, 800. Puccioni to Teresa Bartolommei, 12 July, ms. in MRF, busta 115, n. 2; Pelosi to Buscalioni, 8 August 1860, ms. in ISR, busta 719, n. 2. Puccioni, *Malenchini*, 188. For La Farina's requests for testimonials and his claims of those received (including the support of all "honest papers") see Franchi, *Epistolario di La Farina*, II, 367–83. *Piccolo Corriere*, 22 July 1860, listed Milan, Sarzana, Massa, Pisa, Leghorn, Lerici, Scandiano as having given La Farina votes of confidence. The texts were not published, it explained, in order not to add to the debate.

361

with them began to appear the *rendiconti* of the various committees. It was another of those demonstrations, one of infallible appeal to patriots anxious to have their efforts recorded. The paper even found space for talk again of the benefits of unification, of the social and economic reform that would come, of liberty and the constitution. It was soothing to think of the end of all the old abuses without violations of liberty or legality, to be assured that all social questions had natural solutions. When other activities were slowing down, the Society announced the formation of a women's committee to aid the wounded; a romantic view of womanhood and the claims of patriotism were happily interwoven, and at great length, in the paper's pages. By mid-August the first gusts of rumor began to suggest some great Governmental action, the National Society could speak again more firmly about politics in the south without seeming to be opposed to any action at all.[27]

There was also a subtle change in the Society itself. It had been necessary to insist that aid to Sicily would continue, but the situation was at least embarrassing. And the Society's activity in these matters dropped sharply. The Central Committee changed as Vegezzi-Ruscalla dropped out; even Festi felt somewhat estranged. It became, more than ever, a group of La Farina's friends. Vegezzi-Ruscalla's hope that discontent in the Romagna might again make him foreign secretary was foiled, but he was not altogether wrong in declaring that the SNI's foreign connections—even those interesting ones with the German National Society—had largely lapsed.

By late summer there were signs that the Society was contracting a bit in size. Those who ceased paying their dues rarely did so with any declared political intent, but they must have been those who found things dull as expeditions to Sicily ceased, who began to feel uncomfortable with the Society's political position, or who at least did not wish to be in the midst of political controversy. In any case the effect would be the same;

[27] La Farina to Manfredi, 27 July, Fermi and Ottolenghi, *Manfredi*, 156. The SNI's 5 August reply to Bologna is printed in Franchi, *Epistolario di La Farina*, II, 389–93. *Piccolo Corriere*, 22 July, 29 July (the rendiconti began in this issue and continued into 1862), 5 and 12 August; the 26 August and 2 September 1860 issues showed a stiffening on southern affairs.

just as the men now joining the SNI were less likely to be vague patriots happy to have a cause than those determined to oppose what one new member called "democratic infamies." The new commissioner in Bagnone recognized that the political temper in that part of the Lunigiana made forming a committee impossible. And certainly the most recently formed committees tended to be the more vigorous supporters of La Farina. One's view of the *Lafariniani* had become one of the basic measures of Italian politics.[28]

These changes are particularly apparent in the National Society's development in the south of Italy where, before Garibaldi's arrival, its roots were slight. It grew less as a gathering of nationalists seeking a common program than as a group of men, often friends of La Farina's, who were militantly in conflict with Garibaldians. During his brief June in Sicily, La Farina renewed many personal contacts with men who would later be active in the Society; but it was apparently after his expulsion that he determined to make the SNI a primary weapon in the campaign for immediate annexation. And Cordova, who replaced La Farina as Cavour's Sicilian confidant, paid a good deal of attention to the development of the Society. Yet he, like some of the SNI's own leaders in Sicily, seems to have been hesitant about expanding the Society too rapidly or giving it

[28] Luigi Albellonio to Buscalioni, 14 July, and [Buscalioni] to Scaramuzza, 19 July 1860, mss. in ISR, buste 715 and 719, n. 3. Vegezzi-Ruscalla had, of course, the strongest incentive to exaggerate his international connections and the Central Committee's decay: letters to Casarini, 21 and 29 June, 26 and [30 July, printed as n.d., but date on ms. in MCRB], Onciulescu, "Vegezzi-Ruscalla," *Rassegna Storica del Risorgimento*, xxvii, 257–60. Vegezzi-Ruscalla to Festi, 11 and 27 July, mss. in ISR, busta 718. He reported that Nicola of *Espero* and Professor Fenoglio had moved into La Farina's inner circle. The cooling of relations with the *Nationalverein* was due far more to the Germans' fear of French influence in Italy, their reluctance to associate with an extreme anti-Austrian position, and their own nationalist interest in the Tyrol. The efforts of La Farina and Vegezzi-Ruscalla to have men like Bennigsen and Karl Brater serve as representatives of the SNI in Hannover and Bavaria were therefore rebuffed: Oncken, *Bennigsen*, I, 438–40. The *Piccolo Corriere*, 19 August 1860, was still printing Vegezzi-Ruscalla's optimistic reports of German sympathy for the Risorgimento. Gaetano Casani, 2 August; Lepri (Lusignano), 1 August; the Sozagna committee, n.d.; Pietro Zani (Bagnone), 19 August, to Buscalioni, mss. in ISR, busta 719, ns. 1 and 2. Pietro Sbarbaro, then a law student in Pisa and later editor of *Espero*, letter to La Farina, 18 August, ms. in *ibid.*, busta 719, n. 3; La Farina to Sbarbaro, 18 July 1860, Franchi, *Epistolario di La Farina*, II, 364–65. Martini, *Due all'Estrema*, 76–8.

a central role. Emphasis was placed on establishing a network of commissioners rather than full-fledged committees.[29] Perhaps it was impatience with such caution which led La Farina to send agents of his own. Cortes, who led the last expedition to Sicily sponsored by the SNI, was also to be in charge of organizing the Society there. He went about the task in a Lafarinian manner, and Depretis cruelly reminded him that the Sicilian government knew how to use its passports and its jails. Within three weeks, Cortes had, like his sponsor, been expelled from Sicily. The Society's most important role in Sicilian politics had been a ghostly one: it had made La Farina and then Cortes more frightening to their enemies, and it had served as a model to Cordova in his extensive efforts to organize support for annexation.[30]

By September the signs of a Cavourian offensive emboldened the Society somewhat. The *Piccolo Corriere* returned to a harsher picture of Sicilian affairs, stressing the enthusiastic and universal desire there for immediate annexation. It was not above noting how right La Farina had been to see the seriousness of the situation when few others had. Under Mordini's more lenient rule, the Society spread in Sicily, with Palermo, Messina, and Caltagirone developing as its strongest centers. La Farina exhorted his friends to send deputations of local notables with demands for annexation, and the Society's committee in Messina soon circulated a petition which asked for an immediate plebiscite.[31]

[29] The partisan response to La Farina's very name is reflected in Pietro Oliveri, *Episodi della rivoluzione siciliana, rivelazioni segrete sulla vita politica di Giuseppe La Farina e suoi seguaci* (Lausanne, 1865), 37–53. On La Farina's friends, Nota and Gramignani, see Privatera, *Storia di Siracusa*, 451, and Vittorio Emanuele Gramignani (ed.), *Pietro Gramignani, memorie storico-biografiche (1815–1896)* (Palermo, 1898), 25–6. Parlato, *Siracusa dal 1830 al 1880*, 149–56; Conte Cesare di Castagnetto to Cavour, 20 May, *Liberazione del Mezzogiorno*, I, 120. La Farina to Cordova, July and August, mss. in ISR, busta 16; to Giuseppe Natoli, 12 August, Biundi, *La Farina*, II, 540; to *Giunti*, 22 July; to Nota, 2 August; to Antonio Giusto, 23 August; to Gramignani, 19 and 26 August, Franchi, *Epistolario di La Farina*, II, 384, 387–89, 411, 408, 413. Cordova to Cavour, 16 August 1860, *Liberazione del Mezzogiorno*, II, 95–6.

[30] La Farina to Gramignani, 5 August, Biundi, *La Farina*, II, 543–44; to Bartolomeo, 9 and 20 August, Franchi, *Epistolario di La Farina*, II, 399–400, 410. La Farina, 14 August, and Cordova, 16 and 21 August 1860, to Cavour, *Liberazione del Mezzogiorno*, II, 84–5, 95–6, 130. Cordova, Ottavio Lanza and di Torrearsa tried to establish another organization similar to the SNI to campaign for annexation; that, too, was opposed by Depretis: Cordova to Cavour, 4 September, *ibid.*, 240–42. Mack Smith, *Cavour and Garibaldi*, 188–89, 269–70.

[31] *Piccolo Corriere*, 26 August; 16, 23 and 30 September; 7, 14, 21 and 28

It was not until the end of the year, when La Farina returned to Sicily in the King's entourage as a Councillor of State, that the SNI there achieved the kind of organization which La Farina had long claimed for it. At least it was now possible to picture the National Society spreading itself in neat hierarchies across Sicily, where three new editions of its *Credo* were printed.[32] Members of the Society fared well in the new race for public office, and its election committees were important in the new year. Still, the men who led the Society in Sicily were those who, because of their social position, their political views, or their friendship with La Farina would have been politically important anyway. The Society's committee in Palermo was like no other in the SNI in that it could count the city's leading aristocrats among its directors.[33] An organization of men who had already worked together, it institutionalized a political division which was already operative. When the National Society became well organized in Sicily in 1861, it was a club for the victors of a battle bitterly fought in Sicily but won in Turin.

La Farina's second venture in his native island as a leader of the Cavourian position was scarcely less troubled than the first; but when, in January 1861, he resigned his post, he did so with considerably less resentment. The Society was established; he did

October 1860. La Farina to Natoli, 20 September, Biundi, *La Farina*, II, 539; to Giuseppe Ingrassia, 10 September, and to Gramignani, 15 September 1860, Franchi, *Epistolario di La Farina*, II, 417–18.

[32] Two different editions of the *Credo*, published in Messina in 1860, are in the Biblioteca Civica di Catania; one, "2° edizione siciliana," based on the 7th Turinese edition and published in Catania in the Biblioteca Communale di Palermo. They differ from the later Turin editions in that they bring up to date the names of the Central Committee's officers. La Farina's *Sicilia e Piemonte* of 1857 was reprinted as *Una lettera profetica di Giuseppe La Farina*, in HCL; see La Farina to Pisano, 12 January 1861, Franchi, *Epistolario di La Farina*, II, 468–70.

[33] Crispi later conceded abuses by the police under his administration in Sicily but noted that the head of Public Security in Palermo was a member of the SNI: speech of 1 July 1861, *Atti Parlamentari, Camera*, leg. VIII, *Discussioni*, Vol. II, 1687. Gramignani, who held a number of official posts (V. E. Gramignani, *Memorie di Pietro Gramignani*, 42, 59–60), had an important part in personnel matters: La Farina to Gramignani, 4 November 1860, Franchi, *Epistolario di La Farina*, II, 314–15. Natoli was made governor in Messina; Marchese Massimo Montezemolo, in listing for Cavour those "benemerito" of the Government, was careful to include a number of the Society's leaders (Natoli and Filippo Bartolomeo in Messina, Gaetano Deltignoso and Baron Scovazzo in Palermo—who had the added recommendation of being Cordova's cousin—and Campisi in Syracuse), letter to Cavour, 19 February 1861, *Liberazione del Mezzogiorno*, IV, 314–15. Cf. La Farina to Cavour, 3 December 1860, *ibid.*, 12–13.

have some personal following. For the rest of his life he was able to sit in parliament as the representative of Messina. His enemies had lost far more conclusively than he, and he could afford that politician's luxury, the historical view. The troubles in Sicily, the *Piccolo Corriere* explained to its perplexed readers, were all the result of centuries of evil rule.[34]

In the Neapolitan provinces the National Society had never pretended to be strong, and La Farina spoke with Sicilian disdain of the need there to *colonizzare l'italianità*. Like Cavour, he depended on southern emigrants converted in Piedmont to provide safe direction for their homeland. By August Cavour was anxious for a Neapolitan revolution, directed by such men, to help solve his problems with regard both to Bourbons and Garibaldians. It was such emigrants, Cavour's agents and followers, who took charge of the Neapolitan Committee of Order.

The Committee had had some contact with the SNI, and the *Piccolo Corriere* treated it as actually belonging to the Society. United by their fear of Garibaldi and their respectable connections in Piedmont and Naples, these men saw the National Society as having waged elsewhere the battle they fought in the *mezzogiorno*. Their thought had not been molded by the Society's doctrines; they were hardly subject to its discipline. Yet that connection, however tenuous, influenced the kind of propaganda they issued and left a permanent mark on the Society itself. La Farina sent an agent of his own to further the cooperation between the SNI and the Committee of Order; and, aided by funds and arms from Piedmont, the latter established committees from Naples through Calabria. As its title suggests, the Committee of Order found starting a revolution uncongenial

---

[34] La Farina's opponents were organized in Sicily, too: Farini to Cavour, 15 November 1860, *ibid.*, III, 335; the *Associazione Unitaria Italiana* was forming there, ISR, busta 293, n. 58.

Caltagirone made La Farina an honorary citizen, ms. in Biblioteca Universitaria di Messina; an ode to La Farina was published in Messina in 1860; some of the Society's committees published praise of him; the Messina committee and the National Guard, at least, bemoaned his resignation in January, *Piccolo Corriere*, 21 October 1860, 20 January 1861; Montezemolo, 2 January, and La Farina, 7 January 1861, to Cavour, *Liberazione del Mezzogiorno*, IV, 162–63, 185. Emanuele De Marco, *La Sicilia nel decennio avanti la spedizione dei Mille* (Catania, 1908), 97–8. For comments on his unpopularity see Mordini to Farini, 16 November, Giovanni B. Cassinis to Cavour, 24 November 1860, and the views of the King, in *ibid.*, 322–23, 375–82. *Piccolo Corriere*, 3 March 1861.

work; its inability to do so and the tenor of its own conflicts with the Garibaldians became part of the heritage of the National Society.[35] For a brief period it had seemed possible that the *Comitato d'Ordine* and the Garibaldian *Comitato Unitaria* might cooperate, but it soon became apparent to all that they were waging an intricate war using propaganda as their major weapon. For both sides shared La Farina's belief that it was important to reach the isolated population of the south. In its propaganda the Committee of Order clearly allied itself with the SNI, citing it from time to time and quoting its propaganda. By opposing La Farina, it argued, Garibaldi had opposed annexation. The *Comitato Unitaria* directly attacked La Farina as the agent of Piedmontese aggrandizement. The conflict begun in Sicily was carried over to the mainland, and the Committee of Order made annexation its major cry.

It had, however, a far greater fear of revolution than the National Society; like the Society before it, the Committee of Order saw in desertion a way of achieving the effects of revolution without its dangers. The Committee's propaganda was most widely circulated in a small newspaper filled for the most part with bulletins of war news. It told the Neapolitan national guard that there were times when it was honorable to disobey orders; it expressed its rather harsh realism by assuring Bourbon soldiers

[35] La Farina to Moneta, 17 May 1860, Franchi, *Epistolario di La Farina*, II, 322; Puccioni, *Malenchini*, 213; Cavour to the Prince of Carignano, 18 June, to Persano and Villamarina, 3 August; and Persano to Cavour, 6 August 1860, *Liberazione del Mezzogiorno*, I, 216; II, 8–9, 28. *Piccolo Corriere*, 1 July 1860.

Indelli was La Farina's agent: La Farina to del Bene, 6 August 1860, Franchi, *Epistolario di La Farina*, II, 393–94. He also had some contacts in Reggio, letter to Plutino, 7 September 1860, *ibid.*, 416. The membership of the Committee of Order is given with some variations in Zini, *Storia d'Italia*, I², 657; Mario, *Bertani*, 127–28, 133; Puccioni, *Malenchini*, 209n. Some, at least, of the Committee were even in touch with King Francis' minister, Liborio Romano: Salazaro, *Cenni sulla rivoluzione*, 49–50. Reports on the Committee's activity are in *Liberazione del Mezzogiorno*, v, 255–67. The role of emigrants, weapons from Piedmont (500 rifles from Genoa are mentioned), and the frustrating inactivity of the Committees of Order are even clearer in the unsigned, "Memorie sugli avvenimenti compiutisi nell'Abruzzo ulteriore 2° dal 28° giugno al 30 9ᵇʳᵉ 1860," ms. in Luogotenenza generale del Re nelle Provincie Napoletane, Cartella No. 1, AST. Domenico Di Giorgio, "Il 1860 in Calabria e Benedetto Musolino," *Historica*, II (1949), 15–19. The Society's claims for its part in Naples grew with time. The *Piccolo Corriere*, 3 March 1861, p. 19, cited a letter it said Plutino had sent Garibaldi, 9 July 1860, about 400,000 francs and arms and munitions the SNI was sending there and noted a statement in *Movimento* that the SNI had shipped 15,000 rifles to the *mezzogiorno*.

that Victor Emmanuel, as the best of kings, would find them places at their regular rank in his army. Its fears grew with Garibaldi's success; and soon this Committee, whose purpose had been to make a revolution, was arguing that calm was more powerful than any agitation, which would work against the country's interests. It was, the Committee's bulletins announced, profiteers from past tyranny who now tried to stir up the people, so their provocative acts might restore the reactionaries. There were dark references to St. Bartholomew's Day, and the awful prophecy that the last battle of southern liberty might take place in the streets of Naples.

The Committee had become anti-revolutionary, and it failed. In September it was weakly suggesting that love of Garibaldi was after all best expressed by supporting Victor Emmanuel. But its own fear of action and its apparent opposition to Garibaldi discredited it with that portion of the population which cared about unifying Italy. The public clash between Cavour and Garibaldi became necessary when the Cavourians could no longer claim to be supporting a parallel policy of responsible revolution. The failure of the Committee of Order helped to make contempt for southerners a recurrent theme in the thought of Cavourians. And La Farina would long feel the effects of his association with the Committee of Order.[36]

[36] On the relations of the committees see the reports to Cavour from P. S. Leopardi, 6, 14, 31 August; from E. Fasciotti, 8 August, 11 and 25 September; from Alessandro Nunziante, 28 August; from Nicola Nisca, n.d.; from Ruggiero Bonghi, n.d.; and the more optimistic one from Giuseppe Devincenzi (a member of the SNI), 21 August 1860, all in *Liberazione del Mezzogiorno*, II, 23, 79, 186, 44, 279, 365, 179–80, 192, 238–40, 125–27. F. Astengo to Cavour, 8 September, and Edoardo Fusco to Ranucci, 25 September, *ibid.*, v, 264, 324–26. (The effects of all this on La Farina's own position are apparent in his reports to Cavour in *ibid.*, II, 62–3; III, 246, 320; IV, 61, 114–16, 137–38; and in Montezemolo's, *ibid.*, III, 343–45, 356–57.) La Farina to Natoli, 12 August 1860, Biundi, *La Farina*, II, 538; and to Cordova, n.d., ms. in ISR, busta 16, n. 23. Di Giorgio, "1860 in Calabria," *Historica*, 1 (1948), 129–31.

On the propaganda of the *Comitato d'Ordine* see Curatolo, *Garibaldi, Vittorio Emanuele, e Cavour*, 229–31, 247–49; Guardione, *Mille*, 260–61, 312–13; Mario, *Bertani*, 196; Arnò, "Garibaldi, Cavour," *Risorgimento Italiano*, I, 8–9. Some of the fly sheets of the Comitato are in Houghton Broadsides, 820, HCL. Scores of the bulletins of both the *Comitato Unitaria* and the *Comitato d'Ordine* are among the Carte Volante, 822, in HCL. The bulletins of the latter cited here are those of 29 July, 13 and 30 August, 5 and 25 September 1860, and one undated. Some pamphlets of the Committees of Order, including one of a Calabrian committee, are in the BSMC. The *Piccolo Corriere* was, at least on occasion, reaching Naples independently along with other pro-Lafarinian matter, report of San Martino to Cavour, 6 June 1860, ms. in ASR.

The contrast was striking between the failure of the Committee of Order and the confused success of Pallavicino, acting as mediator between the Government and Garibaldi. Appointed the General's prodictator in Naples, but in practice the champion of Cavour's plebiscite, Pallavicino represented the position the SNI once had held. Garibaldi, too, had served as the Society's president; and when the two men seemed at loggerheads over annexation, Pallavicino planned to explain himself in terms of his loyalty to the Society's "former" program. The Society's favorite phrases had become clichés; but for the Marchese they were still vibrant, and he thought in terms of them. They still neatly bridged his loyalties to Victor Emmanuel and to Garibaldi, and they led him where the Society's doctrines had led its members in 1859. Thus this mystic democrat could behave in Naples much as Farini had in Modena. Pallavicino, too, suspended political meetings, subordinated local government, and sought the most favorable formula for the plebiscite. There was an echo of Manin in the Marchese's letter to Mazzini with its painful plea that he leave Naples, because "you divide us."

As the Society itself had once done, Pallavicino was able to act in behalf of Cavour's policy without having to trust the Count. Perhaps La Farina recognized in the Marchese a position he had in the past encouraged; certainly it was that position more than the Society's which enabled the *Piccolo Corriere* to treat the King's entry into Naples as a triumph and to extend again its arrogant forgiveness: "When one is aware of being the nation, one can and must be generous." [37] Such confidence was possible because Piedmont's army was pushing through the Papal States.

[37] Pallavicino did not send his letter to Garibaldi, 4 October 1860, *Memorie di Pallavicino*, III, 612. See *ibid.*, 613–15, 618; Salazaro, *Cenni sulla rivoluzione*, 65–71, 74; Caranti, *Alcune notizie*, 29–31. La Farina to Pallavicino, 21 October 1860, *Memorie di Pallavicino*, III, 638; *Piccolo Corriere*, 14, 21, and 28 October 1860. Carpi, however, is probably treating symbol as fact when he suggests that the important Neapolitan demonstration in behalf of Pallavicino was organized by the SNI, Carpi, "La Farina," *Il Risorgimento*, I, 335.

CHAPTER THIRTEEN

SALVATION FROM CAVOUR

(AUGUST—OCTOBER 1860)

❧ CAVOUR'S DARING decision to invade the Marches restored his dominance of Italian politics; incidentally, it
saved the National Society from imminent decay. The Society's
reliance on Cavour was vindicated, its association with a policy
of action renewed. Cavour may have been driven to act as
much by conflict with Garibaldi and fear of Bertani as desire
for unification; in that sense the Society's participation in the
invasion was an extension of its own battle with the Bertanians.
But for most of the members of the SNI that dramatic invasion
was simply a welcome return to the role they believed they were
meant to play.

This was particularly true in the Romagna, where the Society's earlier conspiratorial tradition had been maintained. Committed to the idea of a revolution in the Marches, the Romagnol
leaders of the Society had tried in May to convince La Farina
that such a project was less dangerous than it seemed. By June
they were frankly acting on their own. They were spurred both
by their connections with the Committees of Emigration and
by the example of Garibaldi's own success. Uncertain how active
the SNI would prove to be, the Committees of Emigration were
careful to make their plans independently; but by the end of
June the organizations had reached an understanding, to which
the Bertanians were privy, about the minimum military preparation necessary before supporting a revolution in the Marches
would be a reasonable gamble.[1]

Late in June Cosenz promised Casarini to come to the aid of
the Marches provided a revolt broke out before he left for Sicily.

[1] Casarini to Simonetti, 2, [10], and 15 June 1860, Maioli, "Ancora della Società Nazionale," _Saggi e documenti_, 122, 115, 127. Casarini to Buscalioni, 4
May, and to [La Farina], 31 May 1860, ms. in ISR, busta 546, n. 35. Casarini
to Ginevri-Blasi, 19 June 1860, ms. copy in Carteggio Casarini, MCRB. Nicoletti, _Comitato di Emigrazione_, 485, 493–94, 519, 525, 627, 635–38, 652. Circular of Committees of Emigration, 30 June, in MCRB; Dallolio, _La spedizione_,
202–207.

And plans then were made, with the approval of at least some representatives of the Government, for a revolt to follow Garibaldi's own landing on the mainland. If the redshirts extended the field of battle, then some Cavourians apparently hoped by their action in the north to regain the upper hand without directly opposing the General. Some of the Society's committees in the Romagna were involved in a wilder scheme for a revolution in the Abruzzi. It was, apparently, La Farina's expulsion from Sicily which changed the Government's view; any revolutionary activity it could not control now looked too dangerous.

In July the Romagnols were suddenly faced with implacable opposition from the Government to any revolt or expedition into the Marches. The Society in the Romagna obeyed, but its break with the SNI left no authority which could ban preparations for the future. These continued; and their schism enabled the Romagnol members of the SNI not only to continue preparations but to remain close to the Committees of Emigration and even to cooperate with local Bertanians, who were equally set on such a move.[2]

Still, the nature of the preparations was changed; for the Society's men in the Romagna were no more capable than its members elsewhere of opposing Cavour. If the excitement and organizing continued, the SNI appears to have stopped collecting arms during July. The nearly 2,000 rifles it possessed at the end of July were those it had gathered by the end of June. Simonetti had purchased 1,000 of them; 400 had come from the town of Faenza. In addition, the Society owned several thousand pounds of gunpowder (but could not make cartridges until it knew the bore of the rifles it would use); and had collected shoes and knapsacks for some 500 men. By the standard of Garibaldi's

[2] Cosenz to Casarini, 25 June 1860, ms. in Carteggio Casarini, MCRB; Zampetti-Biocca, *Società Nazionale*, 141. Alessandrini, *I fatti*, II, 257–58. Casarini to Simonetti, 14 June, in Maioli, "Ancora della Società Nazionale," *Saggi e documenti*, 126; and Dallolio, *La spedizione*, 217–23, 202–207, on the plans for the Abruzzi.

Festi sent Tanari 800 copies of the Society's Bulletin No. 4, explaining that any move in the Marches was fatal, ms., n.d., in Carte Tanari II, MCRB. Buscalioni to Simonetti, 12 July 1860, explaining the Bulletin, ms. in Posizione Simonetti, MCRB. Minghetti to Casarini, 21 July, Maioli, *Minghetti e la liberazione*, 508. Ginevri-Blasi to Casarini, 15 July, ms. in MCRB; Dallolio, *La spedizione*, 375–83, on the continued preparations.

expedition, these were sizable stores; but in terms of what would be needed, they were small.

Not until August, when the Government itself made available some supplies, would the Society be dealing in more significant quantities of weapons. Then, it was able to provide arms for Tripoti, who used them with good effect as Garibaldi's commander in the Abruzzi, and still distribute weapons for local use.[3] By August the Romagnol Society dominated the preparations of all the various patriotic groups. Within the Marches itself the Society's influence operated through the Committees of Emigration which busily exchanged their coded surveys of the possibilities of revolt, their requests for arms, and their mutual encouragement.

The National Society had no comparable influence in Umbria. A comparison of the preparations for revolution in the two areas gives, therefore, an indication of how important the Society's part was beyond the mere stashing of weapons. There were fewer patriotic committees in Umbria than in the Marches, and they seem to have had less regular communication with each other or the Umbrian committees in Tuscany. Furthermore, the leaders of the moderate Umbrian committees had neither regular contact with the SNI nor a position of prominence in Tuscan society. Indeed, there were competing Umbrian committees of differing political hues located there. The moderate Umbrian committee and the National Society in Tuscany were more narrowly Cavourian than their Romagnol counterparts, while Ricasoli represented a more venturesome policy, comparable to that followed by the SNI in the Romagna. The influence of the Bertanians, through Dolfi in Tuscany and through Bertani's own contacts in Umbria, was also greater and more direct than in the Marches. For Umbria, then, the National Society did not come to represent the one most widely accepted program

[3] Some 200 additional rifles were in the hands of the Forlì committee. When on July 23 Casarini listed for Simonetti what was available to them, the only change from June was the inclusion of one-half the National Guard of Cesena. Casarini to Simonetti, Maioli, "Ancora della Società Nazionale," *Saggi e documenti*, 124–27; to Blasi, 14 June, and Masi, 19 June, Simonetti to Casarini, 25 May, mss. in Carteggio Casarini, MCRB; Ginevri-Blasi to Simonetti, 23 June, ms. in Posizione Simonetti, MCRB; Casarini to Simonetti, 10 June (referring to 200 rifles and a project for Ancona), ms. in Carte Tanari II, MCRB. Nicoletti, *Comitato di Emigrazione*, 525, 627, 688, 709. Dallolio, *La spedizione*, 216, 359–60, 385–90, 395–96.

for responsible activity, and Cavour did not work through it for Umbrian affairs as he would for revolt in the Marches.[4]

Instead, he depended upon Gualterio, who established contacts throughout Umbria, stationed himself conveniently at Cortona, and reported directly to the Prime Minister. But Gualterio, like La Farina, was not without his own political ambitions or the concomitant tendency to exaggerate his personal influence. Gualterio succeeded rather well in winning some general direction over the nationalist committees in Umbria. In doing so, he had to combat the Bertanians directly, in contrast to the atmosphere of apparent cooperation in the Romagna and the Marches. As the direct agent of Cavour, he found his task to be more one of discouraging "premature" moves than sponsoring open revolution. The chastening experiences of the Umbrians in 1859, when their efforts at revolt had produced bloody failure, made this easier, as did the fact that Umbria was relatively little touched by the conflict between La Farina and Garibaldi. Patriots there were thus less open to fear that the Government had come to oppose revolution altogether. Given his position, however, it became difficult for Gualterio really to prepare for revolution at all; rather than distribute arms and plans for insurrection, he tended to encourage less dangerous and less appealing policies, such as buying off deserters from the Papal army.

Generally, then, the weakness of the National Society in Umbria hindered Cavour's policy in several ways. It deprived Gualterio of the means for obscuring, at least at the local level, the sharpness of his conflict with the Bertanians. It made it more difficult for him to prevent rash acts without also dampening revolutionary ardor altogether. The National Society seemed, partially perhaps through misunderstanding, to represent a program of revolution. Its advocacy of restraint and postponement

[4] On the organization of Umbrian patriots, see Degli Azzi, *L'insurrezione di Perugia*, 64–72, 87–96, 111; Mario, *Bertani*, 141n. For Ricasoli's policy, note his letters to Ricci (a member of the SNI) in Puccioni, *Ricasoli*, 248–54, 258–59; and Cavour's comment to Gualterio, 8 August 1860, *Liberazione del Mezzogiorno*, 11, 43–4. The need to arrest Giovanni Nicotera weakened Ricasoli's position, however: Puccioni to Bartolommei, 28 August, in Puccioni, *Malenchini*, 219. On the Bertanian efforts, see Degli Azzi, *L'insurrezione di Perugia*, 66, 83–4; the reports of Gualterio, 19 August, and Ricci, 26 August, to Ricasoli, Puccioni, *Ricasoli*, 246, 264; and Gualterio's reports to Cavour, 28 July, 3, 14, 18, and 25 August, *Liberazione del Mezzogiorno*, 1, 403; 11, 10, 80, 105–106, 157.

was therefore less disillusioning than Gualterio's direct instructions which tended to raise the question of whether in fact he would ever give the call to arms. Furthermore, the National Society had a firmly established reputation as Cavour's agent; and the tendency was to interpret its programs in the light of some secret Governmental intent. The response to Gualterio's orders, on the other hand, would be colored by one's reaction to his personality; and his opponents could effectively undermine his authority by suggesting that in a particular matter, at least, he did not represent Cavour at all.[5] When at last the Government did wish a revolt in the Papal States, it got more nearly what it wanted from the Marches than from Umbria.

By the middle of August the *Piccolo Corriere* was predicting imminent war, and La Farina was sending his followers "official" notice that the Government was preparing to act. He maintained a useful air of mystery about exactly what was to happen, hinting sometimes of a move into the Veneto or suggesting that the Government was prepared to save Garibaldi from forces he could not defeat. But he made it clear that the King's Government would "not renounce the right and the duty to be at the head of the national movement." With the promise of action, the Society's old assurance returned; and the *Piccolo Corriere's* tale of the father who stated in his will that he would disinherit his daughters should they marry Austrians recalled the enthusiasm of 1859.

Old ideas regained their appeal, as the Society's paper wrote again of the cooperation of King and people, of revolution and liberty, of unity and the promise of the future. With angry disdain, the failures of the Mazzinians (a term which, in La Farina's mind, included Bertani) were listed all over again to contrast with the procession of victories won by the Society's program. Readers could now be reminded of the debt owed Pied-

[5] Degli Azzi, *L'insurrezione di Perugia*, 73–5, 103ff., on Gualterio's influence. The desire of many for some surer initiative from the Government and of some far more direct contact with the SNI is evidenced in *ibid.*, 79, 86, 109, 123, 67. This last point is supported by Del Trasimino to Buscalioni, 9 July 1860, ms. in ISR, busta 720, n. 1; and Gualterio to Cavour, 24 August, *Liberazione del Mezzogiorno*, II, 141. Gualterio recognized the importance of demands that the Government act: letter to Cavour, 25 August, *ibid.*, 157. On his policies see these letters and those to Cavour written on 28 July, 3, 9, and 18 August 1860, *ibid.*, I, 403–404; II, 10, 50, 106; and his letters to Ricasoli of 9 and 19 August 1860, Puccioni, *Ricasoli*, 256, 246.

mont and her Government, and the politically dangerous ban on sending more volunteers to Sicily was treated as the promise of greater days ahead (as well as an attack on "sects"). At last, the Cavourians were on the march. By the end of the month La Farina could write the leaders of the SNI that on September 8 the Society's committees in the Marches and Umbria would "take the initiative."

If the Italian National Society could only instruct its members at large to "prepare souls" and "strengthen ties," that was traditional, too. Besides, this time Cavour was hardly leaving revolution to chance or to the SNI. As he put it, the Government "is decided not merely to support but to direct the movement." The Society's role would be less great but better defined than in 1859. What was wanted, Farini explained, was the excuse of "little events." [6] Yet the National Society was a popular organization, and the Risorgimento already had its traditions. On August 31 it issued a call to all committees and commissioners to begin enrolling volunteers. It was like the demonstrations of old, except that this time the penalties of the Government's domination were apparent from the first. The call which came late enough to be diplomatically safe risked being domestically ineffectual. The spontaneity of 1859 or of the rush for Sicily could not quite be recaptured.

On September 10 the Society gave somewhat fuller instructions; men between 18 and 35 in good physical condition and with no other military obligations were to be enrolled and presented to the local intendant. The SNI even provided a form on which to list names and essential data. The following day, however, the Romagna committees sent out word that no further volunteers were needed at Rimini. The military events in central Italy had never really depended on another wave of patriotic young men.

Yet La Farina's rhetoric, which characteristically denied the

---

[6] *Piccolo Corriere*, 19 and 26 August, 2 September 1860. La Farina to Puccioni, 17 August, Puccioni, *Malenchini*, 222; to Gramignani, 26 August, and to Poggi, 5 September, Franchi, *Epistolario di La Farina*, ii, 413–14; to Natoli, 15 August, Biundi, *La Farina*, ii, 534; to Cordova, 20 August, ms. in ISR, busta 16, n. 26; to Bartolommei, 3 September, ms. in MRF, busta 118, n. 1. Cavour to Gualterio, 26 August, *Liberazione del Mezzogiorno*, ii, 162. Farini to Ricasoli, 26 August 1860, Puccioni, *Ricasoli*, 267. Significantly, Farini recommended working with Francesco Guardabassi and Simonetti, both leaders of the SNI.

need for "sonorous phrases," was effective; the claim that great events were taking place was clearly true. Some of the committees of the SNI issued local calls for volunteers and seized the chance to print proclamations of their own. Generally, they demanded unity and praised the Government, though some followed the *Piccolo Corriere* in attacking Mazzinians or displayed their misunderstanding of Italian politics by announcing that Cavour and Garibaldi were once again working together. The only party for any Italian who did not wish "to find himself in the ranks of the enemy," argued one such manifesto, was that which supported the Government. Here was the grateful intolerance of a party rescued at the last moment.[7]

Committees complained as always of the influence of the priests, the lack of shoes, and the cost of telegrams; but men did sign up. Some of them may have thought they were going to aid Garibaldi; some hoped to find a career (and a commission) in the army. Already a fairly stable society, northern Italy tended to rely on the National Guard more than volunteers to provide a militia, and the fact of volunteers gave rise again to some political doubts. The volunteers themselves showed the caution of sophistication in their desire to know this time—and before signing up—who their commanders would be and where they would be sent. Some were barely enrolled before their relatives were demanding them back. Yet, even as the veterans of the southern campaign were returning, committees found more men to volunteer for the new venture. One group signed up as a kind of penance for having belonged to their local Bertanian committee—before, they explained, they had realized that it opposed the Government. The towns of the Papal States and along its borders in the Romagna and Tuscany could provide most of the men needed; yet from elsewhere in northern Italy

---

[7] The Society's call for volunteers was mentioned in the *Piccolo Corriere* of 26 August, but the announcement of their enrollment was dated August 31 (a copy of the widely circulated manifesto is in ISR, busta 719, n. 4) and reprinted in the *Piccolo Corriere* of September 2. Copies of the 10 September circular are in *ibid.*, n. 5; Buscalioni pamphlets, HCL; and Carte Morchio, in MNRG. Nicoletti, *Comitato di Emigrazione*, 1101. The proclamations cited here are those of the Oneglia committee, 7 September, Houghton Broadsides, 440, HCL; the Parma committee, 9 September, and the Sissa committee, 12 September, among the Buscalioni pamphlets, HCL. The last two were reported in the *Piccolo Corriere*, 16 September 1860.

the National Society enrolled or aided hundreds of volunteers.[8] The springs of patriotism and ambition and simple hope had not run dry.

The moderate committee in Tuscany and the leaders of the Committee of Emigration in the Romagna began calling themselves the Umbro-Marchigiano committee, a symbol of coordination. On the first of September Farini sent an agent to Florence to confer with Ricasoli and Gualterio, both of whom were also directly in touch with Cavour. Ricasoli, who distrusted the SNI, had extensive funds at his disposal and was eager for action; Gualterio, who had in a sense replaced the SNI, was the hub of an important network of communications among Umbrian patriots. Both men, however, had to deal with members of the Society and at times in effect work through it. With so many yet uncertain lines of authority, it was difficult at so late a date to formulate very precise plans.

Gualterio continued to stress in his instructions the winning of deserters from the Papal army. With more money available, he could even set up a scale of bribes (artillerymen were to be offered more than regular officers); 12,000 lire was the price bid for the garrison, fort, gates, and officers of Perugia. Later Gualterio placed more emphasis on guerrilla tactics: burning bridges, cutting telegraph lines, closing roads. But for the most part it had to be left up to local committees to determine who

[8] Letters to the National Society from committees and members in Bergamo, Genoa, Bodeno, Cuneo, Cremona, Mondovi, Cotignola, and Vercelli, mss. in ISR, busta 719, n. 6; from Bagnoli, ms., *ibid.*, n. 5; from Milan, ms. *ibid.*, n. 7 (Visconti-Venosta and Tacchino helped with the recruitment there). Nicoletti, *Comitato di Emigrazione*, 1069, 1084. It is very difficult to estimate the number of volunteers from outside the immediate area of the Romagna, Tuscany, or the Papal States enrolled by the SNI. A scrap of paper in ISR, busta 719, n. 7, titled "volontari partito al Deposito," lists the following figures: 25 September, 219; 30 September, 54; 3 October, 5; 2 October, 2; 6 October, 44. The fact of its presence among Buscalioni's papers argues that these were the volunteers of the SNI, and the total of 324 men would then become a minimum figure for the number of volunteers. Antonio Colombo, who apparently was in charge of organizing the SNI's volunteers, received 100 lire from the Central Committee for "aid to enrolled volunteers" on September 12, and 1,980 lire more between September 17 and 30; and another 419 lire between October 11 and 18; Cortes received, September 28, 700 lire consigned to the intendant of Vercello for "costs" of volunteers, ms. in ISR, busta 719, n. 11. What costs are being met is not clear, but the total of 3,199 lire would suggest between 300 and 1,000 volunteers on the basis of the committees' previous expenditures for the men on their way to Sicily.

performed which feats and where. Committees were warned not to attempt to capture control of their city unless they were certain of being able to hold out the three or four days before relief could arrive. A revolt in Perugia would be the signal for many lesser places to rise, and by September 5 Gualterio could assure Cavour that three days later a revolt would take place in Orvieto. Detailed instructions, he said, had been sent out and supplies distributed. Some bridges had already been burned. He was confident; he had "done all on a vast scale" to make certain things would go well. But the disadvantages of depending on one person to direct a revolution were implicit both in Gualterio's exaggerations and in his discussion, which immediately followed them, of what position he might be awarded. In Tuscany, then, there was great activity, understandable confusion, and some precise planning; money, weapons, and men were reasonably plentiful. But these Tuscan leaders were themselves often assailed by the gravest doubts; and their responsible caution, with its preference for winning deserters and cutting telegraph lines, hardly created the atmosphere of revolution.[9]

Begun independently of the Government, the preparations for a revolt in the Marches were more impressive. The committees within the Marches had for months interrogated each other as to the possibility of a rising; and if their reports were sometimes gloomy, the tradition of thinking about the problem made planning easier now. Channels of communication among committees and into the Romagna were well established and made more comfortable through a wide use of codes. Unlike the Tuscan-Umbrian frontier, the political division between the Romagna and the Marches had been a formidable barrier for little more than a year. The planners in the Romagna were better informed than those in Tuscany, and they were aided by the hesitant cooperation of Bertanians and the tradition of work-

[9] The meeting in Florence took place either Saturday evening, the 1st, or on Sunday. Gualterio to Cavour, 29 August, 5 and 6 September, *Liberazione del Mezzogiorno*, II, 82, 245–46, 248; and to Ricasoli, n.d. [30 August], Puccioni, *Ricasoli*, 273, and n.d. [31 August], *ibid.*, 274–75, and undated, 278–79. Ricci to Ricasoli, 3 and 14 September, and Ricasoli to Ricci, 15 September, *ibid.*, 277, 280–81, 294; and Farini to Ricasoli, 3 September, *ibid.*, 276. Degli Azzi, *L'insurrezione di Perugia*, 125ff., and 155–61; Puccioni, *Malenchini*, 248, 275. Gualterio also thought of simply misleading the Papal troops with a false telegram.

ing closely with local governmental officials. The support of the Government and the news of activity in Tuscany were further spurs to the Romagnols.

Although he never attempted so tight a control, Simonetti held a position in the planning for the Romagna similar to Gualterio's in Tuscany. The great difference was that Simonetti had long been a leader among the patriots of the Romagna and the Marches. A *marchigiano* and a prince, the president both of the Committee of Emigration and the National Society in the Romagna, with strong official and personal connections in Turin, Simonetti held his position of leadership naturally and could exercise it while leaving a good deal of authority to those working with him. Casarini, the most active leader of the schismatic Society, had conferred with Minghetti about the possibilities of a revolution in the Marches as early as August 16; and Simonetti again coordinated plans with Clementi, Cavour's emissary, early in September.[10] The activity of the Romagnol nationalists during the previous months meant that in planning a revolution now they were not, like Gualterio, suddenly in the position of blowing on the fires they had been attempting to bank.

In the Romagna, then, the last weeks of August saw the speeding up of activities already begun. Telegrams and letters were sent with new intensity; volunteers were recruited and shuttled to strategic posts; new supplies were ordered and old depots transferred. The arms previously collected and those supplied by the Government, several thousand rifles in all, were quickly dispersed. Old plans, particularly those for a move into the mountains around Montefeltre, were brought up to date. Indeed, a meeting of delegates from committees in the Marches had already taken place in Rimini on August 7 for that purpose. Urbino was agreed upon as their first major target. Not that the Romagnols did not encounter snags. The dissension between

[10] Zampetti-Biocca, *Società Nazionale*, 127–28, 134–37, 146, 239–50; Rasponi [to La Farina], 9 June 1860, ms. in ISR, busta 718, n. 13. Dallolio, *La spedizione*, 209–14, 374–75, 404–406. Bruschi to Ginevri-Blasi, 31 May 1860, Nicoletti, *Comitato di Emigrazione*, 531; and to Simonetti, 31 August and 1 September 1860, Alessandrini, *I fatti*, ii, 275–76. Clementi to Cavour, 3 September 1860, *Liberazione del Mezzogiorno*, ii, 220. The Romagna Society's cooperation with the Government thus followed almost immediately on the heels of Casarini's letter to Cavour, of August 15, protesting the schismatic Society's loyalty to the Government and to the idea of revolution.

the National Society and Bertani's Committees of Provision could not always be hidden; for the Bertanians sensed that once again they were to be both used and held in check. Within the National Society, the committee in Faenza maintained its tradition of personal animosities. Almost daily it was found that some plan was less well understood or that some vital store of supplies was less complete than had been thought. And there was delay in getting the Government's permission to use the weapons the Society had collected.

On September 5, the day they received the final instructions for a general revolution on the 8th, the Central Committee of the Marches, in Ancona, replied acidly that for a year it had warned that the Marches lacked the spirit [slancio] for an insurrection, and now "you would pretend that in two days one can prepare and dispose a revolution in every single, sleepy city, where there are but very few men who are bold and have heart." Yet the plans which had been made were not without some solidity, and the growing confusion as volunteers gathered and orders were exchanged produced real enthusiasm. At times, it was almost hard to hold the men back. Those final instructions, which so upset the committee in Ancona, did indeed clearly call for revolution. Everyone was to rise up and move on the capital of his district or the nearest town, where telegraph and postal offices should be captured or destroyed. Once the town was in hand, the revolutionaries were told to establish their own communications, set up a provisional *giunta*, take over the local funds (and keep a strict accounting), then "with brief and energetic words" proclaim their annexation to Piedmont.[11]

---

[11] The documents reflecting the feverish activity, the cry for more weapons (and even ships) and the dissension with the Bertanians may be found in Zampetti-Biocca, *Società Nazionale*, 240–41, 250; and Nicoletti, *Comitato di Emigrazione*, 853–54, 902–903, 913, 946, 964, 1059–74. The difficulties, including the possession of only one map of Ancona, show in *ibid.*, 960, 967, 982–83. The reply of the Ancona committee, by Orsi, is in *ibid.*, 951. Camerani to Casarini, 3 September, ms. in Carteggio Casarini, MCRB. These things and the various plans for a revolt are also discussed in Dallolio, *La spedizione*, 216, 225–29, 359–60, 376–83, 390–94, 408. Pagano was the Government agent who authorized the release of the Society's weapons, *ibid.*, 395–96 (his 19 August letter to Simonetti); and Finali to Casarini, 17 August, and Pagano to Simonetti, 31 August, mss. in Carteggio Casarini and Posizione Simonetti, MCRB. The Bologna committee sent out a circular of 21 August discussing the ban on enrollments but assuring the men of the SNI that the Government was with them. The instructions for revolution, containing 19 points in all, are printed in Dallolio, *La*

September 8 dawned a day of revolution, but a century later it is still not quite clear how much of a revolution actually took place. In Umbria there was some action around Orvieto, and there were a number of other manifestations of patriotic sentiment; but General Fanti complained that the revolt there was *"très peu de chose."* Ricasoli remained a bit more sanguine and continued working hard although he got similar reports. Disappointed, Cavour asked how Italians could hope to conquer independence without sacrifices.[12] He had never really understood the revolutionary's psychology and still had not learned that his determination to prevent revolt when it was inconvenient and to control it when it occurred made revolution less likely when he found it useful.

In the Marches, in Montefeltre and around San Leo, the volunteers fought effectively and with some success. Urbino was taken, but the column which left Rimini to do so had stumbled into itself in the dark. Those volunteers first tasted fire when they shot at each other; Papal troops, it turned out, had been warned of their attack and had retreated to the citadel. Then, when the volunteers arrived in broad daylight, the Papal troops surrendered after some bickering and on the assumption that the Piedmontese were close at hand. The action had not been altogether satisfactory, but it succeeded. If there was disappointment over events in Urbino, the taking of Pergola was a cause for pride. The gravest disappointment was the silence in Ancona.[13] Still, the committees continued sending each other hortatory messages; important territory was won by the volun-

spedizione, 401–404; Simonetti's simultaneous disposition of nearly 2,000 rifles is listed in Nicoletti, *Comitato di Emigrazione*, 872–73.

[12] Cavour to Ricasoli, 10 September, and Ricasoli to Cavour, 9 and 10 September, *Liberazione del Mezzogiorno*, II, 270–71, 267; Ricasoli to Ricci, 26 and 30 November, Puccioni, *Ricasoli*, 323, 325; Mack Smith, *Cavour and Garibaldi*, 229n.

[13] Masi, *Casarini*, 137–40. Report of Bernadino Peger, *vice-bibliotecario* in Turin, to Buscalioni, n.d., ms. in ISR, busta 719, n. 15. Nicoletti, *Comitato di Emigrazione*, 1063–64, 1105; Degli Azzi, *L'insurrezione di Perugia*, 291. C. Solaro (ed.), *Descrizione dell'Asidio del Forte di San Leo sostenuto pei volontari del Monte-feltro* (Turin, 1860), *passim*, esp. 27–33. Giovanni Maioli, "Luigi Mercantini e il suo sogno di liberazione delle Marche (1860)," *Glossa Perenne*, No. 2 (1929), 203–208. Giovanni Maioli, "Il Sarsinate Luca Silvani e l'azione dei cacciatori volontari del Montefeltro," *Studi Romagnoli*, V (Faenza, 1954), 125–50. These ventures and those under the general command of Pierazzoli are the neatest examples in the Risorgimento of the coincidence of Cavour's program with that of the party of action.

teers, and real revolution seemed likely any minute. Telegraph lines were cut (and quickly repaired), and when it was all over, hundreds of men could look back on an honorable part in their liberation.

From a military standpoint, the action of the volunteers and the pallid "revolts" had only the slightest significance. But enough happened to make it clear to Europe that the entrance of the Piedmontese would have popular support. Nor did the lack of flaming revolution quite prove, as Cavour feared, an unwillingness to make sacrifices. The committees had, to be sure, been told to get their weapons from the enemy and to fight with sticks if necessary; but they had also been told to proceed with caution and to pick their moment with care. After waiting until Piedmontese troops were near, excessive daring seemed foolhardy. Nor were there many political incentives for revolt; the kind of political system established would not be affected by the risks taken before the Piedmontese were on the scene.[14]

All the instructions to the patriots of Umbria and the Marches had made it clear that their most important task, whatever else they did, was the sending of addresses, petitions, and delegations demanding immediate annexation to Piedmont. Gualterio had seen to it that some of these were prepared in advance, and the instructions to the Marches specified the brutality of Papal troops as an item to be included in those appeals. Casarini, among the volunteers who arrived in Urbino, immediately began preparing a deputation asking Piedmontese rule, then handed the local government over to his friend Tanari, the King's commissioner, and moved on to do the same at Pesaro. Danzetta, a leading Perugian patriot who headed the provisional government there, circulated a petition among his citizens in favor of Victor Emmanuel and wired five neighboring cities to do the same. These demands poured in from the Papal States, crossing the proclamations of acceptance from Victor Emmanuel

---

[14] Zampetti-Biocca, *Società Nazionale*, 251–57. The issuance of medals, honorary citizenship, and proclamations to Piedmontese troops quickly established the events of September as a source of pride: Masi, *Casarini*, 141n; Alessandrini, *I fatti*, II, 382. The instructions to the committees may be seen in *ibid.*, 302–304; Nicoletti, *Comitato di Emigrazione*, 1002–1105; Zampetti-Biocca, *Società Nazionale*, 251–57. Salvoni wrote Tanari, 17 September 1860, on the importance of subordinating even the volunteers of S. Leo to Cialdini as soon as possible, ms. in Carte Tanari II, MCRB.

and Cavour, which were being distributed by the same people.[15] Something of the atmosphere of popular revolution was achieved after all.

La Farina had been only indirectly involved with the preparations in Tuscany and the Romagna, but what was happening in Umbria and the Marches clearly represented that kind of mass action on behalf of a Cavourian program which the National Society represented. As the success of the operations in the Papal States became apparent, the Society would claim and receive much of the credit. Early in September, however, the *Piccolo Corriere* stressed the perils, particularly the possibility of war with Austria, which Italy faced. Indeed, the Society was prepared to expand its call for volunteers to a general cry for popular action against Austria. Still, if the conquest of central Italy was presented as a victory for the force of opinion, the Society's paper was careful to make clear that it was also a victory by the forces of order. In Turin one did not forget that the threat of Garibaldi had been the spur to action in Papal territory; the policy of nationalism had been adopted in central Italy for a more partisan purpose in the south. And the Society's subsequent role in the Marches and Umbria would be colored by that fact. If its paper could view the Risorgimento as once more progressing along lines the SNI had laid down, the purpose of the National Society now would be to maintain that course.[16]

Few of the patriotic committees in the Marches actually belonged to the SNI or even communicated with its Central Com-

---

[15] Masi, *Casarini*, 140–41; Danzetta's draft telegram to Terni, Rieta, Foligno, Spoleto, Citta della Pieve, 10 September, is in the Archivio di Stato in Perugia, art. 5, fasc. 1. Degli Azzi, *L'insurrezione di Perugia*, 162; Alessandrini, *I fatti*, II, 378–82; Nicoletti, *Comitato di Emigrazione*, 1003–04, 1079; Dallolio, *La spedizione*, 409–10.

[16] *Piccolo Corriere*, 9 and 16 September 1860. The close connection in La Farina's mind between the campaign in central Italy and problems of the south is reflected in his letters to Cordova, 2 and 11 September, mss. in ISR, busta 16, n. 29. The SNI had prepared a galley sheet of a manifesto calling on "Trentini, Veneti, Istriani, Triestini . . . to show Austria that we are Italians." The demand for an Italy, free from the Alps to the sea, was followed by the regular announcement of the enrollment of volunteers. It is probable that it was never published but only held in readiness. The galley sheet without place or date is among the Houghton Broadsides, 440, HCL. Another broadside calling for volunteers, issued by Monti [perhaps Giambattista Monti of Turin], *Commissario straordinario*, n.d., makes a similar call for freeing the whole peninsula, but individual writers of the Society's manifestoes often went beyond the SNI's own careful position; this one ends with a "Viva Garibaldi," in the Buscalioni pamphlets, HCL.

mittee in Turin, but most of them rightly thought of themselves as supporting its program. They were used to accepting the authority of their central committee in Ancona, the members of which had become members of the SNI as well. At the time of liberation, the Committees of Emigration ceased to function; but most of the local committees remained intact and continued to communicate with Ancona. In effect they followed the Ancona committee into the SNI without being aware of any important change.

Frequently, these local committees became the provisional *giunta* for their town acting much like the SNI in Emilia in 1859. They prepared the way for annexation, removing tariffs, preserving order, maintaining a sober government, and issuing proclamations designed to keep morale high. Within a matter of days, they were sending out the most official government documents, carefully marked with the committee's new stamp —the Cross of Savoy. When Valerio arrived as the King's commissioner, these same committees greeted him and seized the occasion to create a demonstration which would make a good impression. The men of the SNI soon gained importance with Valerio's regime. The Society became, as he himself later confessed, "a kind of state within the state." Many of those who were Valerio's immediate subordinates had been active in the SNI or the Committees of Emigration. Such men knew and tended to trust those who had been active in the local committees. Crediting them with having maintained order during the interregnum, Valerio consciously favored them. At first he used them as a quick and efficient way of making his policies generally understood. Many of them he appointed to administrative posts; and as they in turn recommended their friends for other jobs, the members of the local patriotic committees tended to become the new bureaucracy. More than in any other province, the Italian National Society became the governing party.[17]

[17] The best opportunity for studying in detail the way in which members of the SNI assumed and kept local administrative posts is in Zampetti-Biocca's documents on Camerino, *Società Nazionale*, 258–62, 278, 295. (The local Society even sent Ancona a critique of the operation of the tobacco plant by the Capuchin fathers.) Examples of recommendations for jobs and of the Society's particularly important role in arming and directing the National Guard are in *ibid.*, 279–80, 269–70. Salvoni wrote Tanari, 16 September, and Simonetti was still writing him on 15 December, about these matters, mss. in Carte Tanari II,

The Ancona committee maintained its tradition of ornate rhetoric, warning of threats to the new order from priests, bad habits, and the *tristi*. With its prodding, the Society in the Marches continued to grow. Committees of the SNI spread from the villages to hamlets, announcing themselves and commenting on local affairs with a kind of official tone. Devotion to Valerio's regime was apparently the prime qualification for new members. Some of the local committees, and the Ancona one itself, were now regularly in touch with the Central Committee in Turin; but the Society in Ancona wished to preserve a certain autonomy as the central committee of the Marches, a title it never surrendered. In some towns nearer the border there was a desire to maintain the connection with Bologna, but the committees in the Marches never acknowledged the Society's schism, and the blandishments of the Romagnols were resisted. Casarini came to suspect the Society in the Marches of the sin of regionalism, and Tanari saw in its attitude an unpleasant parallel to the pretensions of Tuscans.

By the fall the SNI in the Marches was well organized, adept at advertising itself and the Society's past achievements. It extended formal thanks to the SNI elsewhere for help in liberating the Marches but made Simonetti one of its own members; and, in a local imitation, sponsored a collection to which the Government itself contributed for a monument to Leopardi, the Marches' great poet.[18] The Society was far less successful in

---

MCRB. Valerio's reliance on the SNI is discussed in Lorenzo Valerio, *Le Marche dal 15 settembre 1860 al 18 gennaio 1861, relazione al Ministero dell'Interno del R. Commissario Generale Straordinario* (Milan, 1861) [reprinted as a pamphlet from *Politecnico*], 10, 15–16, 19, 60, 62. Salvoni and Tanari, leaders of the SNI in the Romagna, were commissioners, respectively, of Fermo and Urbino-Pesaro. It was they who, at Valerio's instruction, drew up the list of the evils of the old regime: Act No. 44, 10 October 1860, *Raccolta ufficiale degli atti del R. Commissario Generale Straordinario nelle Provincie delle Marche* (Ancona, 1860–61). For Valerio's policy of keeping the *giunte* in power (and the importance of members of the SNI in the Municipal Commission in Ancona) see *ibid.*, Act No. 20, 30 September. For example, Giulio Paradisi, Mariano Ploner, Cesare Marinelli, Gennesio Ninchi, G.B. Ionni, Luigi Sturani, Alippi, Gatti, Adolfo Spada—all of whom were assigned important posts—were members of the SNI, *ibid.*, Acts Nos. 101, 138, 429, 559, 22, 698, 216, 181, 444, 18, 19.

[18] The Ancona committee's proclamation of 30 September is printed in Alessandrini, *I fatti*, II, 380–82; the longer one of 18 October is in pamphlet form in HCL; that of 14 November is cited in Zampetti-Biocca, *Società Nazionale*, 279. For the extraordinary spread of the SNI see *ibid.*, 178–80, 263–69; proclamation of the Urbania committee, 25 September, in MCRB. The Fano and

Umbria. The leading patriots of Perugia, now the administrators on whom the Government poured its favors, were members of the Society. But they were men of such prominence that their position in no way depended on that association. Such men were more susceptible than the Society's men in the Marches to the widespread distrust of La Farina. Sympathetic to Bologna's position, they felt that at least the SNI needed some new program. But for the moment, the SNI did not seem very important to Umbria. The royal commissioner there was Pepoli, who had had his own troubles with the Society in his native Bologna. Under his rather highhanded rule, there was no place for the SNI in Umbria comparable to the one it held in the Marches.[19]

The plebiscites, to be held in the Marches and Umbria on November 4 and 5, would be the real test of the Society's popular influence there. It rose to the challenge with vigor, for universal suffrage still held its terrors. The priests, Simonetti said, were threatening peasants with excommunication if they voted; the landowners were obliging them to vote. The various local committees produced scores of proclamations, and in all of them fear of the Church was dominant. A vote for annexation was a vote for Christianity, Camerino's committee reasoned, since religion would benefit from a decline in clerical intervention. Abstention, Urbino's committee warned, was the way of those "without heart, without family, without religion" who placed "earthly cupidity" before "celestial good." But there were appeals also to the simple dream of plenty which was so much a part of the Risorgimento. The Ancona committee explained to the "poor artisans and oppressed peasants" that from their free

---

Sinigallia committees were most anxious to remain tied to Bologna: letters from the committees of Urbino, 23 September (when the SNI was organized there, Cesena had sent them the *Credo*); and Sinigallia, 12 and 18 October and n.d., November (from Montanari) to Casarini, mss. in Carteggio Casarini, MCRB. Simonetti, 1 November, Tanari, 26 October, to Cassanini; the Orsi brothers, 1 December, to Casarini, and Casarini to the Ancona committee, mss. in *ibid. Raccolta ufficiale degli atti nelle Marche*, no. 309, 3 November 1860.

[19] Bruschi, n.d., to Casarini, ms. in Carteggio Casarini, MCRB. Pepoli proposed the nomination of five Perugians to be *cavalieri* (Zeffino Faina, Guardabassi, Danzetta, Bruschi, and Tiberio Berardi)—all of them had been leading nationalists before liberation, all were now officials in the Government or the National Guard, and all were members of the SNI: letter to Cavour, 22 October 1860, *La Questione romana negli anni 1860–61* (Bologna, 1929), I, 62. The position of a Cavourian party in Umbria was made more difficult by the embarrassing surrender of Viterbo.

vote would come lower taxes and "so many sources of material and moral prosperity." Everywhere, flourishing commerce and the protection of the poor were the visions evoked; Victor Emmanuel's goal, announced the Osimo committee, was "the wealth, the will, the industry, the commerce, in short the happiness of his subjects." Landowners were called on to enlighten their peasants, for, they were reminded, annexation was the way of order, a "conservative task."

In preparing for the voting itself, the Society in the Marches followed the techniques developed by the SNI in the Romagna the year before. The cities were to lead the way for the countryside. Bands would start playing the day before the voting was to begin; the towns were to be illuminated and campfires built across the countryside and on the hilltops. The word, "annexation," should be displayed "on the hat, the arm, and the chest" of every citizen. Suitable slogans ought to cover every building. Artisans "in festive attire" could proceed to the polls behind their most respected leaders. But it was on the landholders that the burden of assuring unification fell most heavily. They were not only to instruct their peasants (aided by doctors and pharmacists) but to lead them to the polls exerting "every influence" after having "gladly" entertained them in their houses.

If all this was done, the Society was sure that the Marches would, like the other provinces of Italy before them, give Europe cause to marvel at their unanimity. Much of it was done; and if the total vote was not great, there was certainly cause to marvel at its unanimity. With somewhat less organization, similar steps were taken in Umbria. The Perugian committee of the Society, often neglecting to identify itself with the SNI, issued similar instructions. Indeed, it was its hope that someone would call on each voter in every parish explaining the "appropriateness and utility" of voting for annexation. When it was all over, they announced with pride and relief the disproof of that "calumny that we are not worthy of modern civilization." The *Piccolo Corriere*, in giving the SNI due credit for the outcome of the plebiscite, reported ecstasy throughout the Marches and Umbria—a sentiment it understandably shared.[20]

[20] Simonetti to Casarini, 1 November 1860, ms. in Carteggio Casarini, MCRB. The proclamations of the Ancona, Urbino, and Osimo committees are in Ales-

From July to November of 1860, Italy had weathered the gravest of crises; during that period, the Italian National Society seemed on the verge first of destruction and then decay only to emerge with its organization somewhat better defined, its composition and purpose significantly altered. La Farina's inability to make the SNI serve as the instrument of a nation-wide attack on Garibaldi established that it had never been and could not be a monolith capable of following a detailed or subtle "party-line." Yet that fact made schism less devastating (except perhaps to La Farina's prestige) than was feared. At the same time, the Society's Central Committee had become still more frankly a mere extension of La Farina; the efforts to make the SNI genuinely representative had come too late. But the effects of this, too, were softened by the lesson La Farina learned; the Society could not afford to abandon its claim to represent all true nationalists. Even the angularity of La Farina's personality had proved to be something of an advantage; for it helped to obscure for many the depth of the antagonism between the policies of Cavour and Garibaldi. Still the Society's importance as an organization had, as much as Cavour's own political position, been saved only by Cavour's daring—and his success. No one to whom the Society's pragmatic arguments had ever appealed could fail to be impressed by such success.

The march of the Piedmontese through the Peninsula overshadowed still more the issues that divided Italians. That popular sentiment and governmental policy were once again in phase was much more important to most nationalists than that they were joined only on Cavour's terms. Because the National Society seemed to many the agency of that cooperation, it escaped some of the taint of its association with the Neapolitan Committee of Order. Only the most fretfully observant would worry for long about how real the revolutions in the Papal States had been or what role they would have been permitted whatever their strength. Only an ideologue would let concern for the

---

sandrini, *I fatti*, II, 387–93; of Camerino in Zampetti-Biocca, *Società Nazionale*, 271–72. They were serious about the fires: see Bianchi to Filippo Bettacchi, 30 October, *ibid.*, 270. The detailed instructions of the Ancona committee are printed in *ibid.*, 184–85; they reached clear to Bologna, where a copy is in MCRB. Three proclamations of the Perugian committee, the last on November 9, are in the Archivio di Stato, Perugia, art. 5, fasc. 1. *Piccolo Corriere*, 11 November 1860.

nature of the plebiscites or the size of the vote lessen his pleasure in their outcome. But if the National Society seemed again the agent of popular action, it had regained that status at the price of moving from support of Cavour to subordination to the Government. The SNI in the Romagna would not make that shift. In Sicily the National Society had become the organization of the most vocally anti-Crispian, annexationist party. In both Sicily and the Marches it had become the governing party. Indeed, the National Society, with active members throughout Italy, was now less the embodiment of nationalist sentiment than a formal political party—and one which enjoyed a party's greatest asset, friends in power.

V ❖ POLITICS IN A NEW NATION

CHAPTER FOURTEEN

THE SOCIETY SEEKS ITS PURPOSE, I

(NOVEMBER 1860—JULY 1861)

✤ ITALY WAS MADE. Rome and Venetia were not yet part of it, but the Marches, Umbria, and the Bourbon Kingdom had been annexed. From the Alps to Sicily there was one Italian state, under one King, with one constitution. And Cavour was again in control. Characteristically, he sought the symbol of his triumph and the stable base for his future power in a new parliament. The first elections of the Kingdom of Italy were equally important to the SNI. The chance to vote throughout the nation was the clearest gain of unification, the elections an opportunity to beat the Bertanians. Campaigning was what the Society did best.[1] Late in December its Central Committee declared that the SNI again had a vital role to play.

As in the year before, the Society cooperated with the *Unione Liberale* of moderate deputies; but the only organized, national electoral effort was its own. The choice of candidates was still to be made locally, but the Society's Central Committee coordinated this effort more actively than in the past. La Farina advocated selecting "honest men of secure principles," but his standards were not unrealistically high. They need not be "great orators" nor have "high intellects." It was crucial only that they "not compromise with disorder, with anarchy, with corruption."[2]

Local committees sometimes combined with other groups,

[1] Casarini listed its role in elections first among the services the Society could still perform: letter to Gioacchino [Rasponi or, perhaps, Pepoli], 24 November 1860, ms. in Carteggio Casarini, MCRB. From the Marches to Carrara the Society participated in local elections, campaigning and naming slates of candidates in which they did not forget their own members. Zampetti-Biocca, *Società Nazionale*, 198–201, 279–81; Russi manifesto of 1 November 1860 in HCL; report from Carrara, 1 November 1860, in ISR, busta 719, n. 7.
[2] The Central Committee made its decision at a meeting on December 21, the day after deputies of the *Unione Liberale* met in Boncompagni's home, a meeting attended by Rattazzi and by Buscalioni, representing the SNI. Vegezzi-Ruscalla, 20 December 1860, to Festi, ms. in ISR, busta 718, n. 82; *Piccolo Corriere*, 23 December 1860. La Farina to Giusti, 18 January 1861, Franchi, *Epistolario di La Farina*, II, 470.

393

sometimes directly and enthusiastically undertook their new tasks.[3] The selection of candidates was made most elaborately in the Marches where a special convention of the National Society met in Ancona and picked candidates for 17 of the area's 18 seats. Everywhere choices were weighed with care, quite subtle matters often determining the decision.[4] Even where one seat represented several different towns, the Society usually persuaded the politically influential to agree to a single moderate candidate. Occasionally the Society's local leaders became candidates, but the tendency was to prefer men of wider fame. The Society still conceived of its cause as broader than its own organization.[5]

[3] The Bologna committee presented a special 14-man election committee of noted names as in itself an electoral program: broadside of 17 January 1861 in MCRB. Special committees were also quickly announced for Monte San Savino, 3 January, ISR, busta 717, n. 82; Perugia, 16 January, *ibid.*, busta 717, n. 63, and letter of Bruschi, n.d., in Carteggio Casarini, MCRB; Parma and Piacenza, *Piccolo Corriere*, 20 January 1861; Lodi, 31 January, ISR, busta 718, n. 82. With rare delicacy Pistoia hesitated to form an election committee because their president was a likely candidate; Correggio could not until it learned the boundaries of its electoral district, letters, mss. of 20 January 1861, in ISR, busta 716, ns. 58 and 92.

[4] The Ancona convention of January 16 was attended by 60 delegates: manifesto of 19 January in MCRB; Bellini to Tanari, 22 January 1861, ms. in Carte Tanari II, *ibid.*; Zampetti-Biocca, *Società Nazionale*, 202, 285. The 18th seat was Macerata's where there was already an election committee considering a number of candidates, all of them leaders in the SNI.
Some of the choices which were apparently the result of particular deliberation were Guastalla's of Ribotti, Rapolano's of Bianchi, Reggio's (1st college) of Cialdini, mss. in ISR, buste 718, n. 4; 717, n. 52; 720, n. 9 Monte San Savino selected Poerio, *ibid.*, busta 717, n. 82; and Camerino chose Valerio with little difficulty, Zampetti-Biocca, *Società Nazionale*, 282. Parma found it hard to pick Cusconi over Prosperi, ms., ISR, busta 718, n. 44. Torrita was pleased with its rather late choice of Celestino Bianchi, ms., ISR, busta 719, n. 93. Lugo settled on Gherardi although some preferred Manzoni, ms. Masi to Casarini, 27 January, Carteggio Casarini, MCRB, and ms. in ISR, busta 717, n. 14. Rimini was torn between Beltrami and Rasponi, although Camporesi felt both were too successful to deserve much sympathy, letter to Casarini, 17 January 1861, ms. in Carteggio Casarini, MCRB.

[5] Vignola accepted the choice of Malmusi, made by the Modena committee, ms. in ISR, busta 715, n. 85. Massa and Carrara supported Domenico Cucchiari, but after considerable discussion, mss., *ibid.*, buste 719, ns. 8 and 9; 716, n. 14. Reggio's choice of Giuseppe Torelli was accepted in Scandiano only after a special meeting where it was promised that Vegezzi-Ruscalla, whom they wanted, would be their second choice, mss., *ibid.*, busta 720, n. 9. The Soragna committee wanted Minghetti, but Borgo San Donnino and Busseto, moved by more than politics, insisted on supporting Giuseppe Verdi who defeated Minghetti in the election, mss., *ibid.*, buste 715, n. 106; 716, n. 15.
The committees in Pistoia and Bagnacavallo nominated their own presidents, Bartolomeo Cini and Beltrami, ms., *ibid.*, busta 716, n. 58, and broadside of

Absorbed in politics, the committees of the National Society busily assessed local conditions and estimated the strength of their candidates. The choice of the Pontremoli committee was hailed as the first victory for liberals there since the revolution, though it was conceded that the "alienation" produced by "Turinese aristocrats" and Piedmontese troops made the election of their man uncertain. In Sarzana the committee's brief soundings showed an indifference to Bixio, so they made Admiral Persano their candidate, confident that his fame would rout the Mazzinians. From Busto Arsizio La Farina was told that all "good men" favored his candidacy but that the neighboring towns were uncertain; he was advised to run for some safer seat as well. Simonetti may have worked out with Cavour a list of candidates for the Romagna, but even the Prime Minister could not always get the Society to accept the man he wanted. Often conducted on a scale out of proportion to the size of the electorate, the campaign belonged to the local committees. Only a few needed instructions from the SNI's Central Committee.[6]

If there was a second ballot among the leading candidates or a vacated seat, the Central Committee might well be expected to suggest a candidate. Pressure from Turin forced the Lucca committee to abandon, on the second ballet, a man better known locally in favor of Vegezzi-Ruscalla, who lacked a seat. When their candidate opted for another seat, the committee in Aosta accepted Turin's nominee though they had no time to make sure he favored teaching French in the local schools, the liveliest issue there. The loyalty of the Camerino committee was severely tested when, after Valerio chose another seat, his unknown

23 January in *ibid.*, busta 719, n. 19. But Pavia's choice of a member of the SNI, Mai, was apparently prompted primarily by the difficulty of finding someone to run against Benedetto Cairoli, *ibid.*, busta 717, n. 8.

[6] Pietro Zani of Bagnone wrote Buscalioni about Pontremoli, 21 January 1861, ms., *ibid.*, busta 718, n. 95; Mazzi wrote from Sarzana, 21 January, *ibid.*, busta 717, n. 48; Ambrosio Crespi wrote La Farina from Busto Arsizio, 14 January, *ibid.*, busta 716, n. 1. Simonetti wrote Cavour, 21 [January 1861], that all their candidates had been accepted, ms. in Carteggio Casarini, MCRB; Chiala, *Carteggio di Cavour*, IV, 146 and 146n, indicates a candidate Buscalioni did not support. Casarini offered, 10 December 1860, to pick a candidate for Rimini, ms. in Carteggio Casarini, MCRB; La Farina passed on 5 candidates being considered in Sicily: letter to Gramignani, 11 January 1861, Franchi, *Epistolario di La Farina*, II, 471. Prosperi, in Ferrara, waited for La Farina to inform the *sindaco* of the Society's final choice, letter of 2 April 1861, ms. in ISR, busta 718, n. 7.

brother was pressed upon them. Cesare Valerio emphasized in his election statement that he had supported his brother since adolescence, but the ambiguity of his last sentence must have been depressing: "This is my life—a life silent and obscure but one, however, which expresses what I think and desire." Nevertheless, he won his seat, and the local committee reported happily that he had defeated a candidate with clerical support.[7] Still, the powers of the Central Committee were limited. When, for reasons still unknown, it advocated support of Brofferio, whom most members of the SNI saw as the leader of the "reds," the instructions were received with astonishment and disbelief. If the Society was thinking of such subtleties as a kept opposition, its committees lacked the flexibility to make the necessary sacrifice.[8]

The preference for choosing some famous figure as one's candidate meant that many of those the Society elected felt no particular loyalty to the SNI. The fact remains that when the new Chamber met, 110 deputies were prepared to sign a broad program drafted by La Farina; and the *Piccolo Corriere* could claim over 100 of the new deputies as members of the SNI.[9] The parliamentary majority which gathered in 1861 was the basis of that "Old Right" which would dominate Italian politics for more than fifteen years, and the Italian National Society

[7] Homodei to Buscalioni, 18 March 1861, ms., *ibid.*, busta 716, n. 93. Domenico Carutti was the man named for Aosta, letters, ms., *ibid.*, busta 717, n. 11, and busta 716, n. 57. Zampetti-Biocca, *Società Nazionale*, 288; Angelucci to Buscalioni, 15 and 30 March 1861, ms., *ibid.*, busta 715, n. 9; Buscalioni was involved with the choice of Cesare Valerio from the first, telegram to Matelica, 5 February 1861, *ibid.*, busta 720, n. 13.

[8] Buscalioni's wire in behalf of Brofferio, meant for Giuseppe Brisetti in Castellarano (the seat in question was that of Castelnuovo nei monti), *ibid.*, busta 720, n. 13, was missent—by a dispatcher apparently not yet familiar with the towns of united Italy—to Correggio, which though baffled offered to do what it could: letter, 3 February 1861, *ibid.*, busta 716, n. 92. It was then sent by mail to Reggio whose committee was clearly relieved to receive it too late: letter, 2 February, ms., *ibid.*, busta 716, n. 32. A similar wire was sent to Lodi where Ghisalberti assumed it had been forged, letter, ms., 3 February 1861, *ibid.*, busta 716, n. 63.

[9] The program attacked the idea of regional organization: Biundi, *La Farina*, II, 152–53, *Piccolo Corriere*, 3 February 1861. Zini, *Storia d'Italia*, II², 1122, attributes the air of intolerance surrounding the majority to the SNI. The Central Committee served as a kind of election headquarters: G. B. Giustinian to Buscalioni, 28 January 1861, ms. in ISR, busta 548, n. 39. A list of senators, apparently those connected with the Society, is in *ibid.*, busta 179, n. 22.

had a major part in choosing and electing a third of that majority.

The Society spoke the promise of Italy, disguising the fact that only a tiny fraction of the population was enfranchised as naturally as it overlooked the two-thirds whose illiteracy made such propaganda useless. It helped make the election a national event while teaching Italians the importance of parliament and of the right to vote. It made Italy appear more united by using similar slogans everywhere, and it assured Italians of the national intent of Cavour's program. The outcome of the elections it hailed as the vindication of its whole history, a victory as important to the Risorgimento as those on the battlefield.[10] The Italian National Society seemed about to become Italy's first national political party. A study of the Society's growth or decline in the various provinces from mid-summer 1860 to mid-summer 1861, from just after Garibaldi's expedition to shortly after the death of Cavour, suggests that many felt the need for such a party.

Wherever Cavourian policies seemed threatened, the Society prospered. It even began to grow in Umbria. After liberation, the leading patriots of Perugia were too secure in their prestige to feel great need for the National Society; and those who resented their dominance were unable to activate the committee there. But by July 1861 amid talk of the need to influence the working class, the committee of the SNI was re-established. Committees were formed or re-formed elsewhere in Umbria, too, in Fuligno, Spoleto, and Gubbio. They felt the traditional spurs of politics, fear and resentment and ambition. The dangerous influence of the clergy, discontent with Pepoli's policies, and the pressure of unemployment sponsored this new activity as

[10] Election proclamations of the committees in Parma, Perugia, Medicina, and in Bagnacavallo and Modena are printed in the *Piccolo Corriere*, 13 and 20 January 1861. Manifestoes on behalf of candidates from the Trentino are among the Buscalioni pamphlets, HCL. Other proclamations of the Perugian committee, n.d. and 21 January, are in MCRB; those of Ferrara, Rimini, and Camerino are in Zampetti-Biocca, *Società Nazionale*, 198–201, 283–84; those of Parma, Legnano, Vignola, and Messina are in ISR, buste 720, ns. 4 and 9; 719, n. 19. The victory claims are in the *Piccolo Corriere*, 3 February 1861, and La Farina to Gramignani, 1 February 1861, Franchi, *Epistolario di La Farina*, II, 472. La Farina himself was elected in Messina's 2nd college where 896 men were eligible to vote; 682 voted, 369 of them for La Farina.

much as the desire to serve and regain the enthusiasm for a national cause whose victory seemed incomplete and perhaps even endangered.[11]

In the Marches scores of the Society's committees were active at the time of the plebiscite; but by the end of the year their early position as an adjunct to government was fading. With the loss of its political function, the Society in the Marches lost much of its vigor. The SNI's conventions held in Ancona in mid-January and again in March were already in part an effort at revival. The plan adopted in January was for a Society of inspectors and squads, with interlocking committees to fit each administrative unit. The Society sought the *esprit* of a vast semi-secret network.

One of its committees was so successful that it could denounce in print the misanthropy of any who had not joined; but most were at a loss as to how, beyond remaining in existence, they might alleviate that backwardness of the Marches which they lamented. Some committees collected funds for a present to Garibaldi; some were shocked to find themselves involved in polemics with the opponents of the SNI from other parts of Italy. But the Society's difficulties in the Marches went beyond doctrinal confusion; the goals established at the Ancona meetings were both impossible and vague. By May the Ancona committee, weakened by the death of Alessandro Orsi, was still hoping for the Society's organization to blanket the Marches, talking of the "revolution of order" just achieved, admitting it had done little in Ancona itself, and suggesting for a patriotic activity, the honest administration of funds.

In the spring of 1861 the Society in the Marches was quiescent; then in the summer there was a new spurt of activity as local committees re-established direct contact with Turin, complain-

---

[11] Gualterio's influence in Umbria and his doubtful relations with La Farina also retarded the Society there; Monti was a leading resenter of the influence of Bruschi, *et al.* La Farina was, characteristically, in touch with all three, on occasion even showing them each others' letters. C. B. Monti to Buscalioni, 16 and 22 January, 14 July 1861, mss. in ISR, busta 717, ns. 63 and 64. Carlo Luzi (Spoleto) to Buscalioni, 27 July and 29 August 1861, including a broadside, mss., *ibid.*, buste 717, n. 14; 719, n. 22. Letter from Gubbio, n.d., ms., *ibid.*, busta 720, n. 12. Bruschi to Buscalioni, 28 June and 9 July 1861, *ibid.*, buste 717, n. 65; 720, n. 11; the Perugian committee wished the title of central committee for Umbria.

ing either that Ancona was dictatorial or inactive. Anxious to prevent another schism, La Farina had been solicitous of these local committees since the arrival of the Piedmontese; and they were clearly flattered. The newly active committees often published proud accounts of their former activity (the SNI was already something of a veterans' organization), but it was as part of a national party that they found their purpose. They were obviously delighted to have a direct line to Turin, to learn of the Government's plans and to inform it of their peculiar problems. When one needed to tell his deputy there were still too many clericals in the government, it was useful to be in the SNI. It might also be useful when one hoped "for the common cause" to get that vacant librarianship in Matelica.[12]

The Society's position in Sicily was similar. Its organizational ambitions remained far from fulfilled, but it was generally recognized as a political force in Sicilian affairs. When La Farina returned to Sicily in December 1860, the Society there benefited from his proddings and developed the hardened militance of a party under attack but in power. More than 200 of Messina's citizens attended a meeting of the Society held at the university; the Catania committee was as large; and the Palermo committee, which was larger, not only followed other committees in sending its greetings to the King but published a new *Statuto*. To be sure, its fulsome plans for committees and subcommittees to fit each administrative unit and its provisions for every contingency re-

[12] For the activities of the Ancona committee see the documents in Zampetti-Biocca, *Società Nazionale*, 207, 279, 281, 290–95; its long statement of 20 May 1861 was published as a pamphlet, in HCL. Fano published a long history of its activities in March 1861, in HCL; cf. Alessandrini, *I fatti*, II, 61–9. Pergola's attack on misanthropy and its polemic with the *Unità Italiana*, 1 March and 15 July 1861, are in ISR, busta 719, ns. 19 and 21. A broadside of Mondolfo's, promising more public works, 10 March 1861, is in *ibid.*, busta 719, n. 19. Gerolamo Orsi to Simonetti, 6 November 1860, ms. in Posizione Simonetti, MCRB.

Iesi preferred to remain in touch with Bologna: letter of 5 June 1861, *ibid.* Loreto tried it both ways: letter of 5 June 1861, *ibid.*, and 22 July 1861, to Buscalioni, ms. in ISR, busta 718, n. 66. Committees in Osimo, Treja, Montalboddo, S. Angelo, Pontano, Monovalle, and Aspra wrote Turin during June and July 1861, *ibid.*, buste 720, ns. 10 and 11; 715, n. 22; 716, ns. 2 and 88; the last three had commissioners newly appointed from Turin. The largest of these committees was Ascoli's, which claimed 100 members in 1861 when it broke entirely with Ancona and dealt directly with Turin, *ibid.*, buste 718, ns. 69 and 70; 720, n. 11. Angelucci of Matelica wanted the job, letters of 24 January, 30 March, 5 and 18 April 1861, mss. in *ibid.*, busta 715, n. 9.

sulted less from past experience than from the hothouse of ambition.[13] If committees were never so large as their leaders thought they should be, new ones were steadily being formed; the SNI was well enough organized in Sicily to earn Mazzini's envy. There, too, it was the national political connection which gave the Society life and endowed local issues with larger meaning; its members were quick to report administrative failures or an unsatisfactory judge.[14]

Nowhere in this period was the Society more active or larger

[13] On the Messina meeting of 2 December, see H. N. Gay newspaper clippings, 1856–1927, HCL, and the *Piccolo Corriere*, 13 January. The issue of 27 January 1861, reported a meeting there at which La Farina spoke; he put the attendance at 800 in a letter to Cavour, 7 January 1861, *Liberazione del Mezzogiorno*, IV, 185. Its electoral proclamation, the same month, is in ISR, busta 719, n. 19. *Piccolo Corriere*, 20 January 1861, said more than 200 men were members of the Catania committee. *Ibid.*, 16 December 1859, listed committees in Caltagirone, Castrogiovanni, Catania, Leonforte, Messina, Palermo and Syracuse. Mistretta had reported 9 wishing to join its committee, 1 October 1860, and a total of 35 members in January 1861, ms. in ISR, busta 720, n. 8. Caltagirone's committee had in effect announced its formation by addressing the King: letter of Ingrassia, 16 November 1860, *ibid.*, busta 719, n. 7; *Piccolo Corriere*, 8 November.

The Palermo committee included Marchese Rudini, Father Lanza, S. Elia and Martino Scalia on its Consiglio Direttivo. Principe S. Elia was president; Barone Rocco Camerata Scovazzo was vice-president and a principal organizer. Four of the five who signed the special edition of *Il Regno d'Italia*, 6 September 1860, demanding annexation, became *socii promotori* of the SNI in Palermo. The November announcement for a new Society, in the Biblioteca della Società Siciliana per la Storia Patria, may be that of the SNI; Gramignani's rendiconto, in the *Piccolo Corriere*, 7 July 1861, makes it clear the Society was not well established in Palermo before November. The Palermo committee's petition to the King, 5 December (over 100 lire was spent for 2 banners presented to His Majesty), is reported in H. N. Gay newspaper clippings, 1856–1927, HCL; its broadside listing members, 9 January 1861, is in ISR, busta 719, n. 19. The meeting of the Palermo committee, the speech of Baron Rocco Camerata Scovazzo, and the lengthy *Statuto* were printed as a pamphlet, among the Buscalioni pamphlets, HCL.

[14] La Farina to Gramignani, 29 April and 19 May 1861, Franchi, *Epistolario di La Farina*, II, 483, 487; "D" is probably Daita. *Piccolo Corriere*, 3 April 1861, claimed 48 committees in Sicily and new ones spreading to the smallest communes; Mazzini to Felice Casaccia, 12 January 1861, *Scritti di Mazzini*, LXX (Imola, 1936), 288. Messina's committee was stirring itself; Palermo's promised to get better organized, letters, ms. in ISR, buste 720, n. 10; 716, n. 78. When Montezemolo desired to confer with the leaders of the various parties, he was careful to include a number of men of the SNI: letter to Minghetti, 11 April 1861, *Liberazione del Mezzogiorno*, IV, 440. The Mistretta committee complained about the judge, 7 July 1861; the one in Aggira had 30 members, ms. in ISR, busta 720, ns. 11 and 12. Guardione, "Società Nazionale in Sicilia," *Il Risorgimento Italiano*, V, 901. Pagano wrote Buscalioni reporting on conditions in Sicily and noting when the president of the SNI in Catania got a government job, 5, 10, and 14 January 1861, ms. in ISR, busta 717, n. 92.

than in the former Duchies; there, too, it developed as a reaction to the forces threatening it. La Farina's break with Garibaldi had so affected the SNI there that by August its committees were once again simply being replaced by new ones. The new members were militants, fearful of the local strength of the "red Bertanians," anxious that the Society take a strong stand against its opponents. A new committee was established in Modena in November; the committee in Parma rose to over 800 members and formed some 20 other committees in neighboring towns; the Reggio committee appointed commissioners in the areas surrounding it and issued intransigent manifestoes. In Vignola and Soragna extra copies of the Piccolo Corriere were distributed. Throughout the Duchies the concern for propaganda, for combating the visible enemy, was the strongest in the Society.

In the traditionally radical area of the Lunigiana where Bertani had significant following, a number of large committees were formed. Here, as elsewhere, the committees talked of national issues in local terms and reacted to local problems in national terms. The Carrara committee wrote with pride, and at length, of its past contributions to the Society, but when the court was moved to neighboring Massa, the committee in Carrara disbanded. The committee in Massa went on unmasking "pseudo-liberals," reporting when a railroad job went to a man friendly with Jesuits or when a government official was rumored to have donated to the Danaro di San Pietro. In the Duchies the Society's greatest activity was in the fall of 1860 when the Bertanians seemed most threatening, but its large committees remained active in 1861.[15]

[15] Piccolo Corriere, 16 September, 14 October and 18 November 1860. Letters, ms. in ISR, buste 718, n. 45; 719, n. 3; 720, n. 2, and letter to La Farina, 29 June 1861, ibid., busta 715. Like most of the committees in the Duchies, the one in Piacenza grew out of the collections for the Sicilian campaign, but it experienced great difficulty in getting organized in the SNI: Manfredi, 4 September; Luzzardi, 5 September; and Biancani, 8 September 1860, to Buscalioni, ms., ibid., busta 719, n. 5. Piccolo Corriere, 30 December 1860. Guastalla's beginnings were the same, but its committee folded briefly: Piccolo Corriere, 18 November 1860, letter, ms., n.d., in ISR, busta 718, n. 47. The manifestoes of the Reggio committee were printed in the Piccolo Corriere, 21 October 1860 and 31 January 1861; the reorganization and appointments of commissioners are mentioned in a letter of 14 January 1860, ms. in ISR, busta 720, n. 9. There were also committees in Soragna, Busseto, Sissa, Borgo San Donnino, Fiorenzuolo [d'Arda], and Correggio, mss., ibid., buste 715; 719, ns. 1 and 3.

Modena's proclamations are printed in the Piccolo Corriere, 7 and 14 October,

In contrast, where the National Society had long been relatively well organized, in the Romagna and Tuscany, it experienced a general decline in the year following Garibaldi's expedition. By invading the Marches, the Government had considerably raised its prestige as well as the Society's in the Romagna. There was recurrent talk there that the schismatic Society might return to the fold. Willing to overlook past unpleasantness, La Farina even made some effort to go on as though nothing had happened by publicizing Romagnol manifestoes and asking for the names of those who should receive the *Piccolo Corriere*. Many of the Society's members in important cities were tempted; but for some, and especially for its leaders in Bologna, too much had been at stake in their schism.

They hoped at first that Ancona would join them in applying pressure to replace La Farina. That failed, and they viewed with distaste La Farina's performance on his return to Sicily. He represented the division of parties; his name evoked antagonisms; and, true to the Society's old program, its leaders in the Romagna wished to avoid such divisions.[16] They were unwilling to accept the animosities that go with partisanship; they would not be a

---

18 November 1860; Vignola's committee to Buscalioni, 24 January 1861, ms. in ISR, busta 715, n. 84. The problems of Massa and Carrara are discussed in letters from September 1860 (when the Massa committee was reorganized) to April 1861, mss., *ibid.*, buste 719, ns. 5, 7, 8; 715, n. 60; 716, n. 3; 718, n. 92. There were also committees in Castelguelfo di Garfagna, Fivizzano, Pontremoli (it had no committee in July, was up to 143 members in October, and down one-fourth in December), Calice, Finale, and Tresana (this last is typical; its membership sank from 20 to 6 in August, but then it began to grow again), mss. regarding these committees in ISR, buste 719, ns. 3, 5, and 8; 720, ns. 1, 2, and 10; 721, n. 8. Because they were active in the fall of 1860 these committees account for a large number of the rendiconti of aid to Garibaldi in the *Piccolo Corriere*, 23 September, 9, 23, and 30 December 1860; 20 and 27 January 1861.

[16] Buscalioni to Casarini, 5 and 25 October 1860; and Casarini to Simonetti, 25 October (still dreaming of the Romagnol society's connections with the rest of Italy); to Montanari, 25 October; to Tanari, 15 November (mentioning Pallavicino as president but suggesting it is better that the Society sleep); to Gioacchino [Rasponi], 24 November; to the Faenza committee, 20 November; draft to a new committee, n.d.; to Giovanni Paolucci, 10 December 1860; Simonetti to Casarini, 27 October and 1 November; and Tanari to Casarini, 26 October 1860, all mss. in Carteggio Casarini, MCRB. Simonetti to the committees in Iesi and Loreto, 5 June 1861, mss. in Posizione Simonetti, *ibid.* Also Rasponi, 29 September and n.d., and the Faenza committee, 20 November, to Casarini, mss. in Carteggio Casarini, *ibid.* The proclamations of the Bagnacavallo, Ravenna, Forlì, Ferrara, and Russi committees were printed in the *Piccolo Corriere*, 23 September, 7 October, 18 November, and 9 December 1860. Dallolio mentions the Government's greater prestige, *La spedizione*, 174–76.

party. Their attitude was fatal to the Society there. As it became clear that there would be no imminent move into the Veneto and talk of extending the Society to Istria died, the schismatic society in the Romagna grew more quiet.

A few committees contributed to a monument for Garibaldi; there was a significant stir at the time of the elections. The Society aided local emigrants and helped some members find government jobs. Anxious for some political peace, however, the leaders of the SNI found it in encouraging the Society's "peaceful sleep." Simonetti could return now to his estate in the Marches; Tanari was one of the Government's commissioners. Proud of their independence, they would not dedicate themselves to a single ministry. One of their last acts in the name of the Society in the Romagna was to send a letter to the Prussian deputy who had introduced that motion in the Diet on behalf of Italian independence. It was a gesture which deepened no divisions; the Romagnol Society would undertake nothing more daring.

When some men presented themselves to volunteer, the SNI suspected *vagabondaggio*. Those in the Romagna who worried about the growth of radicalism were more tempted to return to a connection with Turin. After a long debate, nearly a dozen committees in the smaller towns, anxious perhaps to have their moment in national politics, did renew that tie. They then could send on their complaints about the schools, the allocation of jobs "with Papal astuteness," the state of hygiene, or the character of their *sindaco*. Some other committees continued to meet and to receive the *Piccolo Corriere*, but by the summer of 1861 the most active and best organized branch of the SNI had ceased to count. To be above the divisions of domestic politics but without a national organization had lost its meaning. Inspired perhaps by proximity to the Marches, the Rimini committee continued to publish patriotic rhetoric, but its nearly sacrilegious hymn to Victor Emmanuel and its endless epigraphs to Farini and Cialdini were already efforts to recapture the past.[17]

[17] Paolucci, 7 December, and Simonetti, 24 December, wrote Casarini clearly wishing more had been done for the elections; Pescanti wrote Simonetti, 5 December, about Istria; Demetrio Mazzini, president of the committee in Fossignano, thanked Casarini, n.d., for his railroad job. The Imola committee hoped to avoid further losses of members by contributing to Garibaldi's monument:

The Society's development in Tuscany during this period was the obverse of that in the former Duchies, with results similar to those in the Romagna. As in the Duchies, some Tuscan collection committees had drifted into the SNI as late as the fall of 1860; but most of the Society's committees in Tuscany had been active throughout the year. It had grown there as a Cavourian party, and only a few committees were rent by La Farina's expulsion from Sicily. Thus the Tuscan Society experienced a relatively steady growth into the fall; and its committees, like those in the Duchies, were dutiful about filling the *Piccolo Corriere* with their proclamations and *rendiconti* in the winter of 1860.

As in the Romagna, however, local committees tended to correspond with their provincial central committee rather than with the one in Turin; and La Farina could never establish a sense of urgency among the Society's members there. They did not feel that the moderates held power precariously. Generally, the SNI encountered good will, but the lack of enemies made dues harder to collect—or to justify. Some committees began excusing certain members from paying their dues; a member in Empoli asked to be made a commissioner so he would not have to pay for the *Piccolo Corriere*. Indeed, membership in the Society meant primarily subscription to a newspaper; and the irregularities of its delivery were the SNI's greatest handicap. Too Cavourian to be threatened by schism, too much under the sway of Ricasoli to be narrowly Cavourian, the Florentine committee grew silent toward the end of 1860. Tuscan affairs were firmly

Scarabelli to Casarini, 20 December. Rimini contributed, too: Paolucci to Casarini, 14 December; Imola worried about the volunteers, 14 January 1861, and Casarini warned a number of committees against them, mss., all in Carteggio Casarini, MCRB. Dallolio, *La spedizione*, 177, gives June 1861 as the date of the demise of the Bologna committee; a note of Buscalioni's, 25 July 1861, says there is no committee of the SNI there, ms. in ISR, busta 720, n. 12. But see note 33 below and note 16 above.

Committees in Bagnacavallo, Medicina, Ferrara, Bondeno, Fusignano, Russi, Cotignola, Montiano, San Giovanni in Persiceto, and Cesena rejoined the national SNI by June 1861, from mss. in ISR, buste 716, ns. 29 and 75; 61, n. 36; 719, ns. 5, 6, and 7; 720, ns. 4, 9, and 11. Russi's complaints (or perhaps only Aristide Farini's) were published in a manifesto so strong it included the SNI in its censure, 28 February 1861, in Buscalioni pamphlets, HCL. Cesena's agonized decision raised all over again the question of whether Garibaldi would return to the SNI: letter of Silvani, ms. in ISR, busta 716, n. 29. Rimini's hymn, 2 June 1861, is in *ibid.*, busta 719, n. 2; its epigraphs in Nicoletti, *Comitato di Emigrazione*, 1109, 1115.

under moderate direction; the National Society was not needed. In towns nearer the Duchies, such as Pistoia, or where a particular leader was energetic, a committee might become quite large; but by 1861 only the earnestness of a few individuals kept the SNI alive in a number of Tuscan towns.[18]

In Lombardy and Piedmont the Society was almost extinct. The elections and the sending of volunteers to the Marches had prompted a few manifestoes. Occasionally, a commissioner would be moved to announce to the public his responsibility and his loyalty to the monarchy. But the more common tone was to be found in the mayor who reported that he had no time left for the Society or the commissioner who explained that the peasants never read political journals although he promised to search in some other towns for someone who might join the Society. In the north the political goals of the Italian National Society seemed essentially accomplished.[19]

[18] The proclamations of the Pistoia, Lucca, and Cortona committees are in the *Piccolo Corriere*, 7 and 21 October, and 14 November; the Cortona one, referred to in *ibid.*, 16 September, was dated 30 August and is among the Buscalioni pamphlets, HCL. The most important rendiconti printed in the *Piccolo Corriere* in this period are those of Lucca, 20 January and 6 October 1861; Pescia, 23 December 1860; Florence, 25 November 1860.

La Farina wrote Rizzari, 17 August 1860, Franchi, *Epistolario di La Farina*, II, 406–407, suggesting Pisa correspond directly with Turin; he made this a general instruction in the *Piccolo Corriere*, 28 October 1860. Sinalunga's was one of the committees that grew out of the collections for Garibaldi, *ibid.*, 7 July 1861. The Pescia and Lucca committees may have had to re-form as an effect of La Farina's expulsion from Sicily, *ibid.*, 22 July 1860, but Puccioni attributed the trouble there to Turin's laxness in answering correspondence: letter of 29 July to Buscalioni, ms. in ISR, busta 720, n. 3. Pistoia had over 120 members in August 1860 and, a revived committee, still had about 100 in January 1861, ms., *ibid.*, buste 719, n. 3; 716, n. 58. La Farina promised Puccioni, 6 September 1860, to have the *Piccolo Corriere* sent regularly and Pagano seconded it, ms. in Puccioni family papers.

When the Pescia committee learned the *Piccolo Corriere* would be mailed directly to *socii* they felt absolved from collecting dues: letter of 31 January 1861, ms. in ISR, busta 717, n. 8. The Torrita committee hailed a monthly paper but lost 3 members in April, 5 more in June, and absolved 10 from paying dues: letters, mss. in *ibid.*, buste 717, n. 93; 720, n. 8. San Sepolcro gave up collecting dues in September; no members could be recruited in Terra del Sole in January; Rapolano had had 20 members who preferred to be commissioners, but Monte San Savino's committee started appointing some from there all over again in January; Empoli's commissioner wrote 26 January 1861, mss., *ibid.*, buste 719, n. 4; 716, ns. 77 and 35; 717, n. 52. *Piccolo Corriere*, 6 January 1861.

[19] The *Piccolo Corriere* published the manifestoes of committees in Lodi and Milan, 7 October; Oneglia, 23 September and 4 November; Novi, 14 October 1860. The latter, dated 6 October, is in Houghton Broadsides, 440, HCL. The enthusiasm of the commissioner there led to the winning of some 30 *socii*: letter

Elsewhere, the Society had a few committees. There was at least one large committee in the Abruzzi. In Naples, despite connections with the Committee of Order and some stalwart local effort, the SNI found it almost impossible to get established. It had a correspondent on Elba, who complained that his island had no representative of its own, and someone who printed its propaganda in Malta. In New York there was only one member of the old committee who still wished to receive the *Piccolo Corriere*. The SNI was, however, establishing promising connections among Italians in Greece. Only where the National Society found a place in lively local politics did it do well.[20]

The erosion of political battle had given the Society the narrower outlook of the normal party; it had then taken effective part in nation-wide elections. Like a political party, it had exercised a kind of natural patronage, as many of its leaders slipped into the new bureaucracy which spanned the Peninsula. Now there was some pressure to make it a deliberate instrument of patronage. The very nature of the new Italian state would be determined by the kind of men who acted in its name, and providing the state with a politically reliable staff became a common preoccupation. La Farina often encouraged members of the SNI to believe he could find them jobs or assure their advancement. And many of them clearly hoped that they had earned an attractive post. The complaints which local committees forwarded to Turin centered heavily on questions of personnel, and the in-

---

of 3 February 1861, ms. in ISR, busta 720, n. 9. Oneglia's committee was stimulated by the electoral activity, *ibid.* Trecate got a new committee: letter of 19 February 1861, ms. in *ibid.*, busta 718, n. 18. The more pessimistic reports came from commissioners in such places as Zenevedo, Azeglio, and Germignaga, mss., *ibid.*, buste 719, ns. 3 and 4; 700, n. 10. The Society depended heavily on the personal friends of its leaders: D. B. Bottarella to Festi, 20 July 1861, and letter of Homodei, mss., *ibid.*, buste 715, n. 59; 716, ns. 93 and 95. Some effort was made to keep the Genoa committee alive, ms., *ibid.*, busta 719, n. 7.

[20] The committee in Castelli had 48 members: mss. in ISR, busta 720, n. 12. The Committees of Order were still active in the *mezzogiorno*: report of Ricciardi, in *Liberazione del Mezzogiorno*, v, 255; Saverio did later join the SNI. On the difficulties of forming an SNI committee there see La Farina to del Bene, 23 and 28 June, and del Bene to La Farina, 19 May 1861, Franchi, *Epistolario di La Farina*, II, 485–86, 492; and 19 June 1861, ms. in ISR, busta 716, n. 10. Pezzalato wrote from Elba, 29 January 1861, ms., *ibid.*, busta 717, n. 11. The Malta propaganda, dated 18 March 1861, is in *ibid.*, busta 719, n. 20. Botta was the one loyal New York member: letter of 21 January 1861, ms., *ibid.*, busta 545, n. 69. The *Piccolo Corriere*, 7 October, 9 and 26 December 1860, boasted of its Greek connections.

secure position of much of the middle class added poignance to the Society's political desire that power in a new Italy be wielded by true nationalists and real liberals.

The hopes which underlay these petitions and complaints to the SNI were doomed to frustration. The Society could not enunciate any general public criticism of the Government; it lacked the power consistently to affect the Government's decisions in private. That lack of power stemmed in part from the fact that the Society was reluctant to consider itself (and therefore to behave like) a mere party. It resulted, too, from the nature of Italy's constitutional system which left little place for a permanent party. Even the SNI had never included among its members the real directors of the Government. As a party within parliament, the National Society could look to approximately one-third of the Government's majority as its base. But the SNI had avoided precisely those specific issues with which parliament was most concerned; within the Chamber, the members of the Society could not even be sure they would agree. Indispensable in making the Cavourian majority appear to reflect the nation, the Society could not separate itself from that amorphous majority within which it was lost. It had appealed effectively to the literate third of Italy, but most of them were too poor to vote. Once unification was achieved, once a centralized administration and the Piedmontese franchise were put into practice, there was hardly room for the National Society as a political party.[21]

Still, the Society nevertheless maintained the façade of a

[21] Pallavicino was never more resentful of Cavour than over the latter's failure to follow his recommendations for jobs: letter to Cavour, 1 December 1860, *Memorie di Pallavicino*, III, 656, and Cavour's reply, 4 December, ms. in MNRT. One of La Farina's primary concerns in Sicily was the filling of bureaucratic posts: letter to Gramignani, 4 November 1860, Franchi, *Epistolario di La Farina*, II, 435–36. He himself did not exclude reactionaries although it is not clear that the same amnesty was extended to Bertanians.

Minghetti wrote Farini, 1 November 1860, on behalf of Armelonghi: *Liberazione del Mezzogiorno*, III, 252; La Farina claimed to have an eye out for Manfredi's advancement: letters of 2 March and 24 September 1861 and 16 May 1862, Fermi and Ottolenghi, *Manfredi*, 165n, 166n, 177n. La Farina to Cavour, 3 December 1860, *Liberazione del Mezzogiorno*, IV, 12–13; Salvoni to Tanari (on behalf of Niccolini), 16 September 1860, ms. in Carte Tanari II, MCRB. Other examples, not previously cited, are in mss. in ISR, buste 717, ns. 7 and 82; 719, n. 5.

Cavour was fond of the phrase "national party" but always used it to suggest a body of moderate, nationalist opinion. See his letter to Shaftsbury, 22 September 1860, *Cavour-d'Azeglio*, II², 126.

vigorous organization. The *Piccolo Corriere* was filled with news of local committees, their manifestoes and accounts of funds contributed to Sicily, their current news and the histories of their past deeds. The paper itself painted a vivid picture of the Society's part in the Risorgimento, of how, against great odds, it had molded Italian opinion, outwitted the police, engineered the revolutions of 1859, made the Sicilian expedition possible, and led the uprisings in the Marches. The paper claimed thousands of members for the SNI in the fall of 1860; the Central Committee announced the formation of 29 new committees and the appointment of 186 new commissioners in December alone. The *Piccolo Corriere* gave its own circulation at 10,000, huge for the Italy of its time, and declared that more than 100,000 copies of the Society's pamphlets had been distributed, including the several editions of its *Credo*.[22] All of these claims were exaggerated or hid some less pleasant truths, but they left the impression of the SNI as an association of continuing strength.

The changes which took place within the Society in the winter of 1860/1861 reflected some serious weaknesses. In December La Farina went again to Sicily, this time in a frankly official capacity; and the Society was once more left to Buscalioni. Its officers were all men of little independent note; and although the greatly expanded Central Committee now included a number of deputies, the Society lacked firm direction. The Central Committee took to meeting more often and called for general meetings of representatives from all committees in December 1860, and March and June 1861. But none of these meetings won for the Society the political power or the monolithic organization to which it apparently aspired.[23]

[22] The new committees are mentioned in the report of the 21 December meeting of the Central Committee, *Piccolo Corriere*, 23 December 1860. The other claims are in the issues of 7 October 1860; 6 and 27 January; 3 March 1861, p. 19. Committees were encouraged to send their rendiconti as a demonstration, *ibid.*, 11, 18, 25 November 1860. The accounts of the Million Rifles Fund and of the *Ufficio Militare*, published in the *Corriere Mercantile*, were republished in the issues of 3 March, 12–19; 3 April 1861, 25–7.

[23] Ermanno Buscalioni was treasurer; dott. Fenoglio, foreign secretary; Vitale Marenda, the paper's director from 2 December on. The *Piccolo Corriere*, 4 November 1860, told members once again to correspond directly with Buscalioni. Some 51 members attended the 21 December meeting of the Central Committee at which prof. Felice Daneo and Apollo Sanguinetti, a deputy, acted as secretaries, *ibid.*, 23 December; Vegezzi-Ruscalla to Festi, 20 December 1860, ms. in ISR, busta 718, n. 82. The main business of the meeting was probably the planning

In October the Society announced that starting in 1861 the *Piccolo Corriere*, instead of being mailed in large packets to the committees, would be sent individually to each member who must pay quarterly in advance. Since most committees had drastically lowered dues and often been lax in collecting them, this added new stringency to membership in the SNI. The blow was softened somewhat with the institution of a new category of membership which in effect lowered the minimum dues to 25 *centesimi* a month. The whole measure proved difficult to effect, and committees were soon allowed to make special arrangements of their own.[24] Faced with a heavy debt, the Central Committee announced that the *Danaro d'Italia* would be continued; but the response was only the barest trickle of money.

In November the *Piccolo Corriere* appeared on cheaper paper, and in March it was announced that the Society's famous weekly would become a monthly. The reasons for the change were not all financial; it made sense to point out that now news traveled freely in Italy and every city had its dailies. The *Piccolo Corriere* would devote itself to longer articles on its own affairs (the Society was becoming obsessed with its past) and on important current problems.[25] The new paper, in essentially the same for-

---

for the coming elections. Delegates to this meeting and to that of 13-14-15 March 1861 were invited from all committees, but the announcements hardly gave time to send anyone other than someone, such as a deputy, already in Turin: *Piccolo Corriere*, 16 December, circular of 12 March 1861 in ISR, busta 719, n. 20. Another meeting was called for June 10, 1861, circular in *ibid.*, n. 21.

[24] The paper was to be sent members who had paid the first quarter's dues by December 15. A *socio promotore* still paid an initiation fee of 20 lire and 5 lire a month; the *socio ordinario*, first class, 5 lire on entrance and 1 lira a month. The new category was the *socio ordinario*, second class, who paid a 1 lira initiation fee and .25 lira a month. The latter got one copy of the *Piccolo Corriere*; the other two classes of members, 6 and 2 copies respectively. They were expected to give their copies to those too poor (or too little interested?) to get any. Local committees were to keep the initiation fee and one-half the dues: from the *Piccolo Corriere*, 21 October 1860. The measure, however, was approved at the 21 December meeting with the provision that committees could work out other arrangements, *ibid.*, 16 and 23 December 1860. This was all sent out in a circular on 15 January, copy in Carte Morchio, MNRG; the December 15 deadline had gone by the board. The Central Committee, in the meantime, had been trying to get the names of members from the local committees.

[25] The debt announced at the 21 December meeting was divided—17,893.58 lire charged to 1860, 70,564.63 to 1861: *Piccolo Corriere*, 23 December 1860. Pleas for continued contributions to the *Danaro* were contained in *ibid.*, 23 and 30 December 1860, 6 January 1861. From 18 December to the list in *ibid.*, 3 February, only 16,069.26 lire was received, 7,500 of which was the gift from Stockholm (see below). Both Buscalioni and La Farina were personally in debt,

mat, made an attractive magazine of two dozen pages; but the deeper difficulty of the Society's position became apparent when, by the May issue, even the new monthly was becoming repetitious.

The Italian National Society was in trouble. Its organizational difficulties were serious; it had not established its place as a political party, striving instead to maintain its claim to be Italy's great mass movement. That claim required popular demonstrations like the contributions to the cannon at Alessandria in 1856 or the movement of volunteers in 1859 or the aid to Garibaldi in 1860. Although it tried, the National Society could not stage such a demonstration.

One effort was a subscription for a medal in honor of La Farina. The Risorgimento was being commemorated long before it was completed, and in the fall of 1860 there had been a flurry of monuments to Garibaldi and testimonials to dozens of others. The suggestion that the members of the SNI subscribe to a medal for their president was meant to prove the Society's vigor, remind Italy of its achievements, and perhaps put La Farina on a plane of popularity with Farini and Valerio, if not Garibaldi. Large contributions were expected, and many were received. But some members saw that the Society was toasting itself. La Farina, who personified the narrowly political aspect of the SNI, was hardly the subject for a mass demonstration of popularity. In March a banquet was held, and La Farina was given a gold medal with an inscription more restrained than most. The whole affair had cost a good deal more than was contributed. As a demonstration, it was a failure.[26]

---

and La Farina listed the SNI dues owed among his credits, but perhaps for funds he had advanced the Society—its accounts were not very carefully kept, from notes, mss. in ISR, buste 719, n. 98; 721, n. 8.

The *Piccolo Corriere* began with the 23 September 1860 issue appearing on colored paper, which may have been cheaper; that used for the issues from 11 November clearly was. There was no paper between 3 February and 3 March 1861, the first *Bollettino Mensile* of the SNI; p. 11 contained the fuller rationale. Most committees seemed to favor the change, although Massa commented that the paper always came so late and with too few copies, so that it did not matter whether it was weekly or monthly, ms., 11 March 1861, in ISR, busta 718, n. 92.

[26] The idea for the medal was Ottavio Mazzi's, the Society's loyal member in Sarzana; it was announced in a circular of 20 December, containing the inscription ("Il gran concetto dell'*Immortal* Manin, veniva raccolta e messa in opera con cura instancabile, e con abnigazione piutosta unica che rara, dall'impareggia-

The Society fared rather better at the unveiling of a monument to Manin a few days later. French friends of the Society attended in significant number; La Farina, who was on a special parliamentary delegation, gave an address; and the occasion was well received in the press. But it was only the Society's past that was honored.

The National Society came closer to capturing the popular imagination through its Feminine Committee, a kind of ladies' auxiliary organized to aid wounded veterans. The women visited hospitals, made up bandages, and collected large sums of money through public subscriptions and lotteries. This was the kind of purely patriotic demonstration which recalled the visions of sacrifice and unanimity on which the Society had flourished. Soon the women had an office of their own and were aiding those whose wounds, for special reasons, were not classed as war injuries. In the search for needy veterans they extended their charity to Naples. By April 1861 they were as widely known as, and probably more widely admired than, the SNI itself.[27] A

bile cittadino GIUSEPPE LA FARINA.") and promising a copy of the medal to all who contributed 50 lire or more: the circular is among the Buscalioni pamphlets, HCL, and in ISR, busta 720, n. 8. Some contributions came from outside the Society, *ibid.*, busta 717, n. 50 (and some criticism from within, *ibid.*, n. 82); but the dinner held on March 19, La Farina's *onomastico*, cost 580 lire, the design and stamping of the medal, 553.32. Some 36 copies were made at 2 lire each, but only 358.20 lire had been contributed by April. Professor Daneo spoke at the dinner; Francesco Matraire designed the medal, mss., *ibid.*, busta 720, ns. 8 and 10; *Piccolo Corriere*, 3 April 1861. La Farina was, of course, touched and proud, letters to Torti, 18 March, to Mazzi, 20 March and 3 May 1861, Franchi, *Epistolario di La Farina*, II, 477, 481, 484.

[27] The monument to Manin was unveiled March 22, 1861: *Piccolo Corriere*, 3 April 1861. The Society had helped collect funds for it: circular of the Central Committee, n.d., in the Buscalioni pamphlets, HCL. The same issue of the paper also supported the subscription for the King's crown. The ladies' committee was established in September 1860, by some 30 ladies of Turin: circular of 15 September 1860, in Buscalioni pamphlets, HCL. Their activities were proudly reported in the *Piccolo Corriere*, 23 December 1860, 6 January (when a regular column of their "Cronaca" was begun), 20 January and 3 April 1861. They planned to print 100,000 tickets for their lottery, received 1,000 lire from the King, made gifts to the state's seven military hospitals and gave Cialdini 4,000 lire for the wounded of Gaeta. Professor Daneo served as their treasurer, and they had a representative on the SNI's Central Committee, ms. in ISR, busta 716, n. 50. When they presented a Signora Termelli of Bologna with a medal, their demonstration was oversubscribed. Committees of the SNI itself were also engaged in aiding veterans, *Piccolo Corriere*, 30 September 1860, and the reports from Pescia and Piacenza, in November and December, mss. in ISR, busta 719, n. 7.

demonstration based on the patriotic energy of Italian women was, however, too safely apolitical to add much to the Society's vitality.

The SNI sought to embody the nationalist cause in ways that it had found successful in the past. Among these were its connections with friends of Italy elsewhere in Europe and the promise its existence implied of winning the Veneto and Rome. The *Piccolo Corriere* advertised popular sympathy for Italy from Spain to Greece. It renewed its interest in good relations with the German National Society (and some committees even joined the brother organization). To honor the French press Flavin was presented with a statue by the Society's favorite sculptor. It represented the dawn of Italy, scattering flowers and carrying the national banner, and Flavin proved his sympathy for the Italian cause by promising to keep it in his home. From Stockholm the Society received a gift of 6 cannons and 7,500 lire for aid to the wounded.[28]

If the National Society could claim to represent Italian nationalism abroad, it also meant to stand for the completion of unification at home. The Central Committee of the SNI had always been close to the Venetian committee in Turin and actively interested in the Trentino. Many Venetians looked to the Society to aid in their liberation, and some of its committees were anxious to prepare for new action there. In December it had seemed to foresee a diplomatic solution to the Venetian question; but by June 1861 the *Piccolo Corriere* was warning that the Veneto could be acquired only through war. It came to paint a black picture of Austrian brutality and a stirring one of Italian patriotism from Verona to Trieste, but there was little promise of action left in its praise of the Venetians' "dignified

[28] *Piccolo Corriere*, 24 February; 3 March, 7–9; 5 May 1861, 49–50. The common interests (and enemies) of German and Italian nationalists were frequently stressed, *ibid.*, 25 November; 9 and 16 December 1860; 13 January; 3 March, 9–11; 5 June 1861, 75, 81–91. The Massa and Carrara committees joined the German society, accepting its Eisenach program; *Der Bayerische Landbote*, 12 June 1861, spoke of the possible union of the two societies, in H. N. Gay clippings, HCL; the Society issued a special proclamation to the German society, 30 January 1861, in ISR, busta 720, n. 4.

The statue, also by Matraire, is discussed in Luigi Fontana to Festi, 10 March 1861, *ibid.*, busta 716. The Stockholm gift was reported in the *Piccolo Corriere*, 11 November 1860.

calm, noble disdain."[29] The Society had no program for the Veneto.

The National Society could claim to be much more active in Rome through the independent though affiliated *Comitato Nazionale* there. The CNR gave the Piedmontese some military information and indulged in some subversive activity, but it was markedly moderate, hesitant to promote even street demonstrations. Its aim was to remind Italians of Rome and to convince the world of the Roman desire for unification. Its favorite technique was collecting petitions—petitions to Cavour, to Victor Emmanuel, to Napoleon III. The dramatic efforts of the Papal police to stop those petitions and the committee's own boast that it need count only the signatures of literates were used as evidence that it had support in all levels of Roman society. The thousands of signatures collected were impressive, and the *Piccolo Corriere* reported this activity with paternal pride in the restraint as well as the nationalism it displayed. For Rome, too, the SNI offered an effective appeal to sentiment without a program.[30] The National Society was no more willing to organize Italians to act in behalf of the subject provinces than it was able to organize them in behalf of La Farina.

Its part in insurrections and elections over, the Italian National Society, not quite a political party and unable to find a program of mass appeal, suffered a sudden shock when Count Cavour died. No group had more cause to bemoan his passing. The poli-

[29] The *Comitato Politico Veneto* was frequently in touch with the SNI from July to October 1860, particularly with regard to volunteers for Sicily, mss. in ISR, busta 715. The *Comitato Trentino* was really an adjunct of the SNI, *ibid.*, buste 718, n. 2; 721, n. 8. The Society had a commissioner in Verona, ms., *ibid.*, busta 720, n. 12; a delegation of Venetians called on La Farina asking the Society's help, Vegezzi-Ruscalla to Festi, 8 November 1860, ms., *ibid.*, busta 718, n. 82; the Venetian ambitions of local committees, in addition to those of the Romagna, show in Homodei's letters of 5 and 20 September, and Piacenza's rendiconto of 10 December, ms., *ibid.*, buste 716, n. 95; 719, n. 8; the December meeting of the Central Committee was informed of the Society's discussions with the Venetians: *Piccolo Corriere*, 23 December 1860. The comments cited on the Veneto appeared in the issues of 25 November; 2, 9, and 16 December 1860; 20 January and 5 June 1861.

[30] Zini, *Storia d'Italia*, i², 1120–25; Leti, *Roma e lo Stato pontificio*, ii, 209–11. CNR to Pepoli, 6 October 1860, *Liberazione del Mezzogiorno*, iii, 51; *Cavour-Salmour*, 311. The CNR's claims for its petitions, June 1861, to Lorenzini, are in ISR, busta 293, n. 77. *Piccolo Corriere*, 16 December 1860; 27 January and 5 June 1861.

cies of the National Society had been his, but now it would be hard to know Cavourian policies without Cavour. The assurance that the Society was important had been its closeness to Cavour. The ring of authority in its propaganda had been the hint that it shared his secrets. His past success had been the greatest guarantee for Italy's future. Everywhere some of the confidence in the new Italian state departed with Cavour. Out of grief made more genuine by fear, the men of the National Society helped Italy to mourn. They published black-bordered lamentations for their Moses. They wrote special hymns. In town after town they led shuffling funeral processions; and, Italians as well as anticlericals, they sponsored requiem masses in the local churches. Within the eulogies the note of reassurance grew. Italy would be all right; she had still her King, her army, other able men. A people who wept together must be united after all. It was possible at last to be emotional about Cavour; he had never been so popular. Suddenly, the National Society was part of a national demonstration after all. As it promised that Cavour's memory would live, his lessons learned, his policies pursued, the SNI was renewing its sense of purpose.[31]

It was almost as if the National Society was beginning again. On June 14, 1861, the Central Committee issued a four-page circular stating the Society's purposes.[32] Largely a paraphrase of its doctrines of 1857, the circular stressed the importance of election committees and spoke more clearly of the need to "inspire in the ill-instructed populace love of order and of liberty, of the Royal House of Savoy and of the Great Italian Fatherland. . . ." To do all this, the Society needed more discipline and more members, although the circular boasted with suspect

---

[31] A number of local committees' manifestoes on Cavour's death are in ISR, busta 719, n. 21. The impressive subscription of the Roman committee for a monument to Cavour, complete with receipts and the promise that, unlike Cavour, Peter would have no successors, is in *ibid.*, busta 546, n. 59. Pesaro's manifesto is in Posizione Simonetti, MCRB. The *Piccolo Corriere*, 5 June 1861, devoted pages to an obituary by Pettrucelli, comments of their own and from the press of Italy, France, Britain, and even from some Hungarians. Camerani wrote Casarini from Ravenna, 9 June 1861, of the need to fill the breach; and Gramignani described the obsequies in Palermo as a "triumph" for the SNI, letter of 27 June 1861 [to La Farina?], ms. in ISR, busta 716, n. 84.

[32] The circular signed by La Farina as president and Buscalioni as secretary-general is in *ibid.*, busta 720.

symmetry of 454 committees and 4,500 commissioners. This was its call to action.

The Society took comfort in the fact that its principles were those of the parliamentary majority. It proposed to make the *Piccolo Corriere* into a daily while maintaining its qualities as a "moral and political catechism." It would circulate thousands of copies of Cavour's parliamentary speeches so the new provinces might savor the policies which had given the old ones their hegemony. It promised a "popular manual" taken from Cavour's writings. Thus his faith in Italy, declared the SNI, would remain a living faith; the Society would in effect be his church. It was a stirring appeal, and it won a wide response. Nearly everywhere there was a marked revival among the Society's committees in June and July. Sharing the sense that they must all help to fill the breach left by Cavour, the members of the SNI showed new energy. The Society's man in Naples reported bitterly that most people there had received the news of Cavour's death with joy or mere coldness, but he was ready to make another effort at establishing a committee. In the Romagna the members of the schismatic society felt the tug of Turin as never before, and a special agent came from the capital to arrange a reconciliation between the two branches of the SNI. The talks collapsed when it became known that the new Government thought the National Society at best an embarrassment.[33]

The Government's attitude might well prove fatal to the Society. Ricasoli's dislike of the SNI was deep-rooted. La Farina

---

[33] Del Bene to La Farina, 19 June 1861, ms. in *ibid.*, busta 716, n. 10. The Romagnols abandoned the idea of supporting workers' societies and agreed to the dissolution of their central committee. Although some felt the SNI in the Romagna should remain active until Venice and Rome were acquired, it was not heard from after the fall of 1861. Circular of Casarini to 10 Romagna committees, 9 June 1861; Simonetti, 12 June; Tanari, 22 June; Masi, 9 July; and Rasponi, 10 July and 7 August, to Casarini, mss. in Carteggio Casarini, MCRB. Bregati Bellini was the agent, and his mission is described [by Casarini] in a letter to Rasponi, 11 July, and a circular to the Romagnol committees (in which he suggests Cavour had sent Bellini), n.d. [July 1861], mss. *ibid.* Bellini [to Simonetti?] from Turin, 19 July 1861, ms. in Posizione Simonetti, MCRB. Cesena's committee was particularly anxious to remain active: letters of 14 September and 8 November (which imply that a meeting of the Romagnol SNI was scheduled for September) and circular of the Bologna central committee (perhaps its last), 6 October 1861, mss. in Carteggio Casarini, MCRB.

had complained of it in 1859, and it had remained apparent in 1860. When in October 1861, Ricasoli, as the new Prime Minister, received two confidential reports regretting the Society's role in politics, he was, in the way of all bureaucracies, being told what he already knew. One report was on Sicilian affairs, and it found the island's great misfortune to be the political division which resulted from the antagonism between Garibaldi and the SNI.

The Society, it explained, had attracted the "most pacific, most temperate, most tranquil" men, men of the upper classes who would have been content with any enlightened despotism. At the same time, and in the manner of all sects, the Society had collected many ruffians (*accoltellatori, facinorosi, mal affare*) who then scandalously won positions in government. The prestige of the Government had been hurt, and the abler men in the Party of Action, which had deeper roots in the country, were pushed into opposition. The report suggested that it would be necessary to continue governing through the lifeless minority of the Society (using administrators from other parts of Italy), but it hoped these ties could soon be broken so that good men regardless of party might be employed.

In the same month a report on the Marches took a similar view. The Society's role through the period of the invasion was praised; but its leaders now, the report complained, were men of lower caliber. The Society's committees, without a function, had sunk in apathy; yet they continued to influence the government by claiming to speak for the people. The SNI was thus a potential threat to the Government which it would do well to destroy.[34]

The National Society was paying the price of having advertised too well its conspiratorial prowess and its political influence. The leaders of the Government itself were now added to all its old enemies. Yet despite the Society's other weaknesses, its leaders remained determined to keep it alive; and they succeeded.

---

[34] Cav. Pantaleoli reported to Ricasoli on conditions in Naples and Sicily. In the Naples report, dated 8 October 1861, he significantly made no reference to the SNI, ms. in ASR, Ricasoli, 1.17.b-1. Sections xi and xii of his report on Sicily, dated 10 October 1861, refer to the Society, ms., *ibid.*, 1.17.b-2. The report on the Marches, dated 23 October 1861 and by "C.T.," deals with the National Society in sections iv, 3 and vi, ms. in *ibid.*, 2.17.i.

Their reasons for doing so and the reasons for their limited success cast an important light on the Society's whole history. There were many in Italy who agreed with Ricasoli's agent. To them, the National Society appeared a dangerous sect, an organization which connived for power, a threat to regular government, a source of bitter dissension. La Farina was as intensely disliked as any man in Italian politics. The maintenance of the SNI seemed to many the result of mere ambition.

But if the National Society was feared, it was driven on by fears of its own. It feared the influence of the priests, especially in the countryside; and the Central Committee had received scores of reports attributing local political evils to their power. In the view of the Society, priests were opponents of the regime, men outside the state, now taking advantage of liberty to wage a subtle war against Italy. When priests failed to take part in national celebrations, the Society was outraged; and it in turn attacked these "sons of ambition and deception" with their "simulated rites" and "vain pomp" who ignored the true religion of the heart.[35]

And the Society feared the Bertanians. It found them indistinguishable from Mazzinians, advocates of war with France, armies of place-seekers attacking the public till, enemies of the new order. The Society repeated every slander against them— that Bertani had ordered Garibaldi's men to fire on the troops of Piedmont, that he was guilty of peculation on a grand scale. The propaganda of the National Society thus did much to increase the deep cleavage that already marked Italian politics and to defeat the efforts of men like Pallavicino (using Manin's slo-

[35] Even the clerical *Armonia* accused the SNI of being more a threat than an aid to the Government: *Espero, Il Piccolo Corriere d'Italia*, 18 February 1862. Scores of examples could be cited of the hatred held for La Farina; the epigram that Fulton discovered steam [sic], ". . . La Farina invented the art of animalizing men" is fairly typical: Oliveri, *La Farina*, 32–3. This feeling, which included the SNI, was likely to show itself over any issue: *Proemio alla orazione detta in sua difesa di F. D. Guerrazzi davanti la corte regio in Firenze . . .* (Milan, 1861), 39–40. The Society's anticlericalism broke out strongly in the *Piccolo Corriere*, 20 November 1860; 5 June, 91, 96; 7 July, 117–18; 19 November 1861; *Espero*, 18 October 1862. It was, however, not often so bald as in the attack on the Pope who dared not leave the spot where Peter "cast the first stone of an edifice already used up by the ambition and the cowardly brutality of a degenerate priesthood," *Piccolo Corriere*, 3 April 1861, 24, or in the story of the sales of blessed salami, *Espero*, 4 April 1862. A clerical-Mazzinian alliance was a common nightmare, Zani to Buscalioni, 21 January 1861, ms. in ISR, busta 718, n. 95.

gans) or Ricasoli (with simple disdain) to heal this wound. Yet the Society, anxious that Italians agree, was terrified by this very division. It watched with horror as Bertani skillfully defended himself and maintained his Committees of Provision as a competing society with its own propaganda and electoral ambitions.[36] The National Society was sustained in part by the belief that Italy's union was extremely fragile, that it might at any moment be undone by the machinations of its enemies, by war or subversion or simple anarchy.

Attached to these fears was the simple belief that united Italy required a different kind of citizen. Revolution bred heroes but not regular soldiers, the *Piccolo Corriere* explained; and heroes were moved by false dreams and excessive faith in themselves. More steadfast and milder civic virtues were needed now. It was in these terms that the National Society defined its functions; it was to create the proper kind of citizens and make them dominant. When the SNI harked back to its successes and exaggerated its role in the great moments of 1859 and 1860, it was not merely advertising itself but attempting to make the modest virtues it extolled as important and exciting as those Garibaldi represented, while trying to combat any decline in the sense of urgency.

By simple translation, the Society used the arguments once meant to make monarchy acceptable to republicans to make the Italy of the 1860's acceptable to all nationalists. The Society's

[36] *Piccolo Corriere*, 16, 23, 30 September, 7 and 14 October 1860, 13 January 1861; Sissa proclamation "Ai purissimi . . ." [1861] in HCL; letter of Arrivabene, 4 February 1861, ms. in Carte Morchio, MNRG. Pallavicino to Garibaldi, 19 December 1860, *Memorie di Pallavicino*, III, 658–59; to the Council of Ministers, 31 March 1861, ms. in ISR, busta 46, n. 26; to Ghiron, 1 January 1861, ms., *ibid.*, busta 1, n. 26. The Million Rifles Fund avoided a joint accounting with the SNI out of concern, it said, for Garibaldi's feelings: Cressini to Buscalioni, 2 October 1860; Cressini to Cortes, 11 December 1860, and Pagano to Buscalioni, 26 December 1860, mss., *ibid.*, buste 719, ns. 12 and 8; 546, n. 85.

More than two dozen of Bertani's committees sent their protests against claims of his dishonesty before December; some 63 delegates attended the meeting of his association in Genoa in January 1861, where Guerrazzi and Brofferio spoke and Garibaldi was elected honorary president of the *Comitati per Proviredimento* for Venice and Rome: *Calunnie e Proteste* (Genoa, 1861) and the Bertanian *Resoconto*. The moderates generally were showing some panic: see Farini to Cavour, 15 November 1860, *Liberazione del Mezzogiorno*, III, 335. But Mazzini, who still thought of himself in the thick of battle against the Society, would remain less impressed with Bertani's organization, letters to Clementia Taylor, 14 January 1861, and to Vincenzo Cattoli and Malucelli, 8 December 1861, *Scritti di Mazzini*, LXX, 300; LXXII, 117.

first lesson was that things were going well; time, not agitation, would right any remaining wrongs. The old cry for sacrifice now included the sacrifice of criticism. For the Society's second lesson was that tranquillity and order were Italy's greatest needs, the man who could wait her best citizen. The revolution was over; its consolidation the real, and more difficult, task. The greatest achievement of unification was domestic peace, and it would bring the Risorgimento's other benefits.

The task of the SNI was primarily educational; people unused to freedom must be taught not to abuse it, not to expect too much. This was what the National Society meant when it insisted that its mission was not fulfilled. When it lamented that Italy was still not wholly united, it referred less to the absence of Venice and Rome [37] than to the fact that there was still disagreement among Italians. For those who held them, such attitudes made the SNI seem essential to Italy's well-being even when they did not define just what the Society would do.

[37] *Piccolo Corriere*, 9 December 1860; 1 September; 10, 27, and 29 October; 16 December 1861. Proclamations of committees: Norcia, in *La Discussione*, *Piccolo Corriere d'Italia*, 11 January 1863; Parma, 9 September 1860, Novi, 6 October 1860, Sissa, 1861, in HCL; Messina, 18 January 1861, in ISR, busta 719, n. 19; Ancona, 14 November 1860, in Zampetti-Biocca, *Società Nazionale*, 275–76, and May 1861, in HCL. Bruschi to Buscalioni, 9 July 1861, ms. in ISR, busta 720, n. 11. The committees in the Marches, especially in the smaller towns, had a certain Mazzinian taint in their talk of brotherhood, spiritual mission, etc. Note Pesaro's declaration, 21 July 1860, in Nicoletti, *Comitato di Emigrazione*, 755–56. The word "unification" in the Society's slogan had now come officially to mean the Cavourian achievement of union, province by province, in contrast to the Mazzinian desire for unity all at once. See Chapter Three, note 40. Crispi taunted La Farina with the change: *Atti di Parlamento*, *Legis.* VIII, *Sess.* 1863–64, *Camera, Discussione*, I, 490 (20 June 1863). Pallavicino thanked Salazaro for the rebuttal La Farina did not make, letter, 16 July 1863, ms. in ISR, busta 9, n. 3.

CHAPTER FIFTEEN

THE SOCIETY SEEKS ITS PURPOSE, II

(AFTER THE DEATH OF CAVOUR)

✦ CONVINCED of its importance, the National Society met the crises of the years from 1860 to 1863 with a developing doctrine of its own; it was a view born of political concern which came close to being a denial of politics. The Society had frequently attacked Garibaldi's fondness for dictatorship (and exaggerated it). Genuinely attached to a parliamentary system, it insisted that as Italians became used to the ways of freedom, utter confidence could be placed in parliament. But that admiration of parliament was used to justify an opportune insensitivity to the environment of political freedom. The SNI was unembarrassed by its willingness to exclude its opponents from the normal guarantees of a free society. Restrictions on the press, on the right to office, on the freedom of Italy's "enemies" could not endanger liberty because parliament by itself was freedom's "holy ark." The nation *had* been heard from in the blood of its soldiers, in the plebiscites, and through its representatives in parliament.

The Society opposed criticism of present conditions in Italy not merely because such criticism, like the spreading of bad news, was an unpatriotic undermining of the state. In a parliamentary regime any errors were the fault of the people, of those who criticized; while criticism, by weakening the institutions of liberty, hurt liberty itself. If changes were needed, let the critics elect new deputies (but the conditions needed to make this a possibility were ignored). In a parliamentary system, the Society conceded, an opposition was necessary; but such opposition should not be that of a party. The SNI meant by this that opposition should exist within parliament but not extend itself into the country; it should not be systematic, that is, consistent and ideological.[1] For the National Society, then, parliament be-

[1] *Piccolo Corriere,* 1 September, 1 and 6 October, 12 and 29 November, 2, 13, and 17 December 1861; *Espero,* 14 February, 5 and 18 April, 30 October

came a kind of buffer between the people and their government. Disagreement, they felt, should take place within its safe confines. This could lead at times even to the suggestion that politics should be left to the experts.

The men of the Society wanted reform, but they wanted it safely led by the state; and the changes they hoped for were those the state could bring about. They wanted the technical changes necessary to a modern society, in provisions for trade and railroads, in education and the administration of justice. As pragmatists, they looked within government to the place where things were done; they were obsessed by the problems of bureaucracy. There was some self-interest in this, for the Society's members viewed themselves as belonging to a new and deserving governing class. They never sounded so radical as when they talked of the changes in personnel necessary if Italy was to prosper; then even they could speak of the need for purges.

The emphasis on administration was useful in another way. If things did go wrong, it was evidence of errors by men in office not of anything lacking in the system itself. The bureaucracy became the focus of the Society's traditional concern that the state be strong. Domestically, strength meant that the procedures of administration would be orderly and regular, unified and consistent, prompt and just. This was the means of achieving reform while assuring order (by avoiding politics). Here lay the one strong element of utopia left in the Society's thought. Its vision contained few limits to what administration could accomplish. Even some of the burdens normally assigned the representative process would be met by bureaucracy. There people and government would meet in daily contact and conflicts between local and national interests would be resolved practically, one by one.

Liberal enough to hope the bureaucracy would be kept small and the cost of government low, the men of the Society had largely lost the liberals' emphasis on the individual.[2] The SNI

1862; *Discussione*, 3 January 1863. Proclamations of Sissa committee, 12 September 1860 and 1861, HCL. "Poche parole aggiunta . . . ," ms., ISR, busta 721, n. 8. The moderates generally had trouble in justifying parties.

[2] *Piccolo Corriere*, 1 September; 19 and 29 October; 3, 4, and 26 November; 18 December 1861; *Espero*, 28 March; 15 and 24 April 1862. Norcia proclamation in *Discussione*, 11 January 1863. In addition, the Society's paper published two long series of articles on the organization of the state: *Espero*, 21–27 January 1862; 17, 20, 29 September; 1, 16, 20 October 1862. Giuseppe La Farina,

bore the scars of its experience. It found ignorance and interest at the base of most political attitudes. This made it hard to respect one's opponents. The *Piccolo Corriere* was needed to inform that majority of men "who neither think nor feel" about the problems of a new society. But the SNI was not overly hopeful. If the idolators of princes had ruined the governments of divine right monarchy, the idolators of the people threatened to do the same to a representative regime. Italy's unification, the Society conceded, had been supported by the timid who feared war or revolution, by merchants who wanted to improve business, by landlords who wanted to collect their rents again. Only the national party had wanted Italy. Sometimes the Society threatened to reveal who had refused to join it in more difficult days.

Seeing itself as the conscience of the country, the SNI accepted the difficult role of the moderate, of the party in the center. While admitting that the elevated classes seemed most able to play such a part, it hopefully insisted that the Italian genius generally was for the practical (its examples from the Romans through Machiavelli were notable for their omissions). In any case, the National Society placed its hope in institutions not human nature. The patriot would obey the law both as an expression of his faith in *Statuto* and King and because he knew that it was more important that such laws exist than that they be perfect. That was the truth which made criticism ungrateful, beside the mark, and dangerous. More than ever the Society's propaganda looked to the King. The cause of the crown, the *Piccolo Corriere* explained, was identical with the liberty of the people; there was no need to worry about liberty. As the symbol of concord, above daily disagreements, the monarchy became increasingly precious to the SNI; it shrewdly recognized that the King was far more a popular figure than many elected representatives.[3]

Sulle presente condizioni d'Italia (Turin, 1862), a publication of the SNI. La Farina to Gramignani and to Giunti, 14 July 1862, and to Gaetano De Pasquali, 8 October 1862, Franchi, Epistolario di La Farina, ii, 519, 526, 528. Bonghi, Partiti politici, 22, notes the bureaucracy was ancillary to the ruling class. Even Pietro Sbarbaro, an ardent supporter of La Farina and liberal economist of some note, recognized La Farina's lesser concern for individual liberty, Mazza, Sbarbaro, 37.

[3] La Farina, Sulle presente condizioni, 9; La Farina to Mazzi, 8 March 1861,

Shortly before he died, Cavour had stood in the comfortable semicircle of the Piedmontese parliament to speak to the deputies of how they had conspired together. The Italian National Society, he added, had provided him with companions all over Italy. Now the Prime Minister would conspire with 26 million Italians. Cavour had at last acknowledged the Society which had been so dedicated to him. He did so after it had ceased to be a force for conciliation or a center of agitation, but once again he found the phrase to express its aims. It would conspire with the Government which conspired with all Italy; the hint of desperate action, the promise of secret plans, and the security of responsible government could still all be enjoyed at once.

Despite the death of Cavour and Ricasoli's contempt, the SNI would support the Government of Italy. It would do so in its propaganda and through the parliamentary influence La Farina could wield. And the two, propaganda and parliamentary maneuver, would be kept largely separate. La Farina would support any ministers so long as the defense of order and free institutions was at stake. The Society had long seen those questions in most issues facing Italy. Its leaders could not now lose their slowly matured sympathy for the problems of men in power.

La Farina himself was fond of power, and in parliament he was convinced he had it. If—even with the more than 100 deputies he claimed as members of the SNI—he could not win great favors from the Government, he enjoyed the thought that he could overthrow it. With his friends outside parliament as well, La Farina acted like the head of a party, advising them on general policies or the chances of promotion, commiserating with them when attacked.[4] Yet La Farina's political authority was only in-

---

Franchi, *Epistolario di La Farina*, II, 476. Carrara proclamation, *Piccolo Corriere*, 4 November 1860; *ibid.*, 11 October 1861; 5 June 1861, 73; 1, 13, 20, 26, 31 October 1861. The Risorgimento was viewed as that cooperation of popular forces and government which began with the "martyrdom" of Charles Albert: *Espero*, 19 May 1862. The emphasis on the King is notable in *ibid.*, 11 and 27 August 1862; proclamations of the committees in Parma, 9 September 1860, and Fano, March 1861, HCL; in Rimini [spring 1861] and Torrita, January 1861, ISR, buste 719, n. 20; 720, n. 13.

[4] *Piccolo Corriere*, 3 April, 34–8; 7 July; 1 September 1861; *Espero*, 26 July 1862. Pallavicino was sure La Farina just wanted a cabinet post: letter to Ghiron, 24 October 1862, Leti, *Rome*, II, 210n; but the accusation was a common one. See Braglia to Buscalioni about Pallavicino, 12 October 1863, ms. in ISR, busta 715, n. 63. La Farina to Francesco Oglialoro, 4 May 1863; to Onofrio De Benedetto, 27 July 1861; to Del Bene, 1 November 1861; to Enrico Falconcini, 15

directly a product of the SNI. The Society had won him fame and association with Cavour. It gave him a useful relationship, though not necessarily that of leader, with the many deputies who had belonged to it or been aided by it. La Farina's real following, however, quickly became a more personal one, these followers then tending to associate more actively with the SNI. The belief in the Society's strength and the fact that it controlled a newspaper made following La Farina attractive. Years of propaganda made doing so natural for many.

La Farina and the National Society, then, supported Ricasoli's ministry (June 1861 to March 1862); but their support was temperate. They argued that he was the only man for the moment, that his administration should be given time to prove itself, that the policies of Cavour would be continued. Underneath these statements there began to appear by the fall of 1861 a current of discontent. The Government was repeatedly warned not to hold back from strong action because of technical legal scruples, not to worry about popularity. La Farina feared that Ricasoli relied on the wrong men; and by December the warnings against "weakness" were almost ominous. By weakness, La Farina meant Ricasoli's tolerance of the Committees of Provision, whose meetings in Genoa in December were stirring demands for action on behalf of Venice and Rome. Worse yet, the tone they took was increasingly democratic. By the end of the month the Society's paper cautiously mentioned the possibility of a Rattazzi cabinet if Ricasoli would not remake his; in February it assured its readers that Italy could survive a change of government and noted that Ricasoli was having a bad time in parliament.

At the end of the month some 60 members (including some deputies) attended a meeting of the Society's Central Committee where La Farina spoke about the political situation. Apparently, it was agreed there to withdraw support from the Government and to let La Farina decide whether to try to bring it down. On March 2 Ricasoli resigned. He had been undone by complex intrigues between the Court and Rattazzi and by intricate con-

March 1863; to Bartolommeo, 1 April 1863; to Crespi, n.d.; to Terasona, 10 and 20 September 1861, Franchi, *Epistolario di La Farina*, ii, 548, 497, 508, 592, 544, 498, 502, 527.

flicts, both personal and regional. But the specific issue which led to Ricasoli's resignation was the one La Farina had picked, the Government's attitude to the Bertanian committees. La Farina was widely accused of having played the decisive part in the Government's fall, something he denied in public and claimed in private.[5] The Society's power in parliament had never been greater.

It took a quite different stand toward Rattazzi's government (March to December 1862); his first speech was hailed in the Society's paper as a great day for Italy. The program of the majority would remain the basis of any government. Rattazzi was praised for being more energetic, and there was some suggestion of why the SNI had turned to him in its complaint that Ricasoli had been expected to remake his cabinet but refused, that he had gotten into trouble by depending too much on men of the old regimes whereas the new government paid more attention to the liberal party in its appointments. It would have been no service, the reasoning ran, to support a government once it was weakened.

La Farina had used the weapons at his command in a complicated parliamentary maneuver which strengthened his reputation as a manipulator and a figure of power. Crispi's charge that Rattazzi was a member of the SNI had at least symbolic merit. And early in March La Farina led a meeting of deputies which sought to establish the nucleus for that firm majority without which, it was explained, the initiative of Cavour would have been lost. Some 40 deputies joined in the new program (far fewer than had been willing to support La Farina's general statement in February 1861). With the somewhat conflicting explanation that even Cavour changed his direction at times and

[5] *Piccolo Corriere*, 7 July; 12, 15. 28 October; 4, 9, 11, 13, 26 November; 15, 17, 30 December 1861; *Espero*, 14, 16, 18, 24–28 February; 2–4, 9 March 1862. La Farina to Gioacchino De Agostini, 20 September; to Giusto, 20 October, Franchi, *Epistolario di La Farina*, II, 504, 507–508; to Gramignani, n.d., Biundi, *La Farina*, II, 543. *Atti del Parlamento, Legis.*, VIII, Sess. 1861–62, *Discussione*, III, 1378–89. *Assemblea della Associazioni Liberali, Comitati di Provvedimento e deputati dell'opposizione* (Genoa, 1862). That only about 8 of the delegates to this conference had ever been in the now crumbling National Society suggests how effectively the Bertanians had been isolated. Ricasoli must in fact have watched the Bertanians with some concern, ms. in ASR, Ricasoli, 1.4-d. Carpi, "La Farina," *Risorgimento*, I, 337–39.

that there really was no fundamental difference between the Ricasoli and Rattazzi ministries, the Society launched its full support of the new Government.

The old threats continued from those demanding some dramatic step toward Venice and Rome. The Society's paper praised the Government for its firmness in using troops against the demonstrators in Bergamo and Brescia. But the dream of doing what the National Society said it once had done would not die; an Emancipation Society replaced Bertani's committees as the organs of the Garibaldian demand for action. The furor continued. By August 1862 Italy was on the road to Aspromonte where, at the end of the month, a frightened government's troops wounded Italy's greatest hero to prevent at the last minute his attempting what both wanted and neither could accomplish. There would be no expedition against Rome. The National Society called itself Cassandra for having foreseen the danger since July of 1860, but it insisted that the Government was not implicated in Garibaldi's venture. And after the frenzied warnings of August, the reports in its paper became almost strangely calm. The Garibaldian prisoners were being well treated; Italy had been saved; the great majority was solidly behind the Government; the *meridionale* was grateful for the state of siege.

La Farina's importance to the Government had grown greatly, and in October he published a pamphlet, *Sulle Presente Condizione d'Italia*, which bore the label of the SNI and was sent to all its members. In it he argued that Garibaldi's cry of *"Roma o Morte"* was a declaration of war on France, that what Italy really needed was a period of consolidation and quiet. Italy's strength not filibusters would win Rome. He painted in contrast a thrilling picture of the Society's steady nationalism, and then argued at length on his favorite theme, the desperate need for extensive administrative reform. The pamphlet represented at their best the Society's realism, its theoretical liberalism, its national pride, and its sense of diplomacy.

But it was too much the work of a partisan whose past made his intent suspect. It relied too much on bureaucracy and treated fundamental political issues as those of mere organization and sound administration. It left the Risorgimento with little emotional or ideological appeal beyond the hope of future peace and bland prosperity supported by stable institutions. It was every-where viewed as La Farina's bid to become Minister of the In-terior, and the campaign waged in the Society's paper (and in the press generally) supported that view. Columns were filled all over Italy and France with reviews of the pamphlet, and for a period of two weeks *Espero* was able to quote at length from favorable reviews in nearly 40 papers. Comments that La Farina would make a fine minister were carefully included with a note that it was not yet time to bring that up. La Farina's hopes must have been high.

When the Chamber convened after the tragedy of Aspro-mente, the Society's paper fervently insisted that Rattazzi must be sustained; and, although it had usually ignored them in the past, it referred openly to some of the personal rivalries and am-bitions which made Italian politics so perilous. Even at the last minute, when the Government was clearly doomed, La Farina made a valiant effort to save it. In proposing a neutral order of the day to replace one prejudicial to the Government, he created a sensation by telling a story. Once, after Garibaldi had attacked Cavour in the Chamber, the Count had turned to La Farina to declare that if war broke out tomorrow he would put his arm around Garibaldi and say let us see what they are doing in Verona. Concord between the constitution and revolution, La Farina pleaded, was the basis of the Risorgimento. When things slowed down, one side cried "anarchy" against the other which shouted "reaction" in return. With something of the Society's old voice, he asked for calm; with the politician's skill, he sug-gested that Rattazzi would remake his ministry to better repre-sent the majority.[6] But, the Government, too badly discredited, lost.

[6] *Piccolo Corriere*, 30 December 1860; *Espero*, 28 February, 4, 9, 24 March 1862 (comments on Ricasoli's fall). *Ibid.*, 8, 10–11, 14–15, 26–27 March; 19 June; 3 July 1862 (support of Rattazzi). The SNI remained greatly concerned with the Committees of Provision and the Emancipation Society, *ibid.*, 18–19, 26 March; 7 April; 17–18, 21 May; 3 June; 26 August 1862; *Discussione*, 28, 30 December 1862. *Espero*, 23–31 August; 2–4, 8, 10, 16–17, 24 September (the comments on Aspromonte). *Civiltà Cattolica*, never prone to make nice distinc-tions among opponents, had, from the first, seen the SNI behind Garibaldi's maneuvers, 28 June 1862, ser. 5, III, 115. La Farina, *Sulle presente condizioni*, *passim*, and the campaign for it in *Espero*, 16–18, 20–24, 27–28, 30–31 Oc-tober; 3, 10–11, 22 November 1862. The French press was, of course, especially kind. There were also widespread rumors that La Farina was to be rewarded with

With the fall of Rattazzi, the National Society returned more strongly to its hope for a great and permanent majority of all who had supported Cavour. Then, the Government would have the authority it needed. The SNI did its part by supporting the Government formed after considerable difficulty under the nominal leadership of Farini. From the standpoint of the SNI, the new cabinet, really Minghetti's (December 1862 to September 1864), never realized the full authority it needed; and the complaints about internal administration, the lack of Cavour's forcefulness, and the injustice of Rattazzi's defeat would continue to echo in its paper.

Peruzzi, the anti-Piedmontese Tuscan, and Minghetti, who had advocated a regional organization of Italy, were the two leading figures of the Government; the Society had strong doubts about both. In December La Farina drew up, in conjunction with some other deputies, a five-point program which won the support of some 60 members of the Chamber. In addition to the usual La Farinian call for order and liberty, it took a stand against any regional organization and asked for stronger, local, administrative authority. The Society's paper hailed this as the first step toward that firm majority and that new party of principle for which it had been calling. The program made La Farina one of the most powerful figures in the parliament, and he frequently boasted of his hold on the new cabinet.

The Society's paper was now officially directed by La Farina's parliamentary group; the SNI had become a bloc within the Chamber. By May 1863 when Minghetti was officially Prime Minister, this group was moving closer to the Government. When the Government suppressed a democratic meeting ostensibly held for the hoary cause of Polish freedom (at Sampierdarena, the site of one of Italy's few large factories), La Farina and his followers became open ministerialists at last. Their program, it was recalled, had always been the "most ministerialist imaginable"; and La Farina won cheers from the Chamber

---

a mission to Greece, *ibid.*, 28 October 1862; *Corriere delle Marche*, 29 October, H. N. Gay clippings, HCL; *Indépendance Belge*, 6 November, ISR, busta 720, n. 16. *Espero*, 5, 16, 18–19, 22, 27, 29–30 November; 3 December (on the hope of saving Rattazzi). La Farina to Homodei, 14 September, and to De Pasquali, 8 October 1862, Franchi, *Epistolario di La Farina*, II, 525, 528. Biundi, *La Farina*, II, 164.

with his references to reconstituting Cavour's old majority. He himself had been moving closer to Depretis in a pale imitation of the *connubio*, and at the new parliamentary session in May, La Farina's importance was officially recognized with his election to one of the Chamber's vice-presidencies. He died a few months later, but his followers would continue acting as a group although hard-pressed to explain just why—except that they were a party of principle, the principle of the majority first of all.

Within the Chamber of Deputies the Italian National Society had assumed a life of its own as La Farina's personal following. It was able to contribute substantially to that firm majority which was the basis for the strong government in which it believed. Unable to draw significantly on support outside the Chamber, it had operated more as a faction than as a party, and it had lacked the numbers to guarantee any cabinet position. The Society could not quite push any government to that vigorous administration, that strong hand, for which it cried. Indeed, the goal itself, which ignored the political forces and social realities of Italy, was probably a chimera, significant more as a commentary on the view of politics which the SNI had come to hold.

The Society had been effective, however, in demanding increased restrictions on the political activity of the left. In its campaign against such activity by workers' societies, by the Emancipation Society, by the workers at Sampierdarena, it played on all the fears of the moderates. And the existence of the SNI itself was always an issue in these discussions, used by its supporters to show that plenty of political freedom remained. It is a crucial point in Italian history that the National Society's narrow view of legality, its elimination of social questions from the realm of political debate, its feeling that the disenfranchised could be allowed only the most restricted voice in political matters became the policy of Italy's authorities.[7]

[7] *Espero*, 3, 6, 12 ,14, 18 December 1862; *Discussione*, 23–25, 27–30 December 1862; 2 and 21 January 1863, 29 July 1863. La Farina to Torti, 31 May 1863, Franchi, *Epistolario di La Farina*, II, 544. The meeting of 13 December was announced in a circular of 15 December, in Buscalioni pamphlets, HCL; this political group is discussed in *Espero*, 21 December 1862; *Discussione*, 1 Janu-

The Society's important part in Italy's parliamentary life remained well insulated from its members at large. Their knowledge of it, aside from a few circulars and pamphlets and what they heard elsewhere, came from the Society's newspaper, whose voluminous political reporting was striking for its omissions. The edifying view of parliament presented there included very little of the jealousies and factions which troubled these years. Instead, parliamentary affairs were reported with a self-conscious dignity approaching that used to describe the workings of the judicial system. To be sure, the Society's paper supported its general program with long articles on Italy's administration which rose at times to charges of laziness, dishonesty, and corruption. It opposed any regional system with vigor (the source of civil war and "Lincoln's barbarism"); it denied that "Piedmontism" was an issue at all. It decried the recriminations against the new Italy and presented a generally sanguine view; even the seriousness of brigandage was, it claimed, being exaggerated. It stressed the gains of unification, especially economic ones, while admitting that it would be some time before they were felt. Foreign relations were also seen as satisfactory; and a good deal of effort was spent in insisting that Louis Napoleon was anti-Papal and that British opinion was highly sympathetic to Italy.[8]

---

ary, 3 May, 2 June, 21 and 30 September 1863. La Farina to Luigi Florio, 21 April, and to Oglialoro, 4 May, and memo to Peruzzi, 7 March 1863, Franchi, *Epistolario di La Farina*, II, 545–46, 548, 541. La Farina had organized opposition to Minghetti's regional plans before: letter to Bartolomeo, 2 April 1861, *ibid.*, 481. On the debate on political associations, see La Farina to Oglialoro, above; *Atti del parlamento, Legis.*, VIII, Sess. 1861–62, *Discussione*, X, 6613–26; sessions of 16, 17, 19, 20 June 1863, *ibid.*; Sess. 1863–64, I, 449–61, 467, 490–91. La Farina was elected vice-president with 137 votes, Cantelli got 138, Poerio 195, and Cassinis was elected president by 166 (La Farina got 1 vote), *ibid.*, 2. Aldo Romano, *Storia del movimento socialista in Italia*, I (Milan, 1954), 80–8. Bancheri, *Rattazzi*, 27. A contemporary cartoon [1863] depicts La Farina's shock at not being a minister after Buscalioni has called him to office several times, by "Marco," in HCL.

[8] *Piccolo Corriere*, 26 August and 23 December 1860; 5 June (p. 14), 7 July (pp. 99–101), 7 September; 2, 4, 7, 10, 27 October; 6, 9, 22, 24, 30 November; 11, 21 December 1861; *Espero*, 13 May, 7 July 1862; *Discussione*, 5 January, 13 March, 5 May, 8 June, 23 August, 29 September, 20 October 1863. On Napoleon, *Piccolo Corriere*, 24 October 1861; *Espero*, 27 January, 9 February, 14 September 1862. The debate in the House of Commons on 11 April 1862 was reported in *ibid.*, 16 April 1862; and, with that of 8 May, printed as a 58-page pamphlet of the SNI: *La questione romana alla Camera dei Comuni in Inghilterra* (Turin, 1862), giving speeches of Gladstone, Palmerston, Leyard, and

But on the specific issues around which parliamentary coalitions revolved little was said. The paper indulged with some frequency in polemics against its public opponents, but those who depended on it alone could not always be sure just what the conflict was about. Rarely, then, did the organ of the SNI seek general public support for its specific parliamentary position. The attacks on the burgeoning mutual-aid societies among the working class were a significant exception. Their functions of assistance and education were praised, but their dabblings in politics were deplored. The paper warned of the "hypocritical monarchists" who used them for radical ends; it printed long essays arguing with liberal precision that these societies should spend their time instead in gathering better actuarial tables. When the societies, as many of them did, refused to participate in politics or sent testaments of loyalty to the King, they won great praise, as did the Government for suppressing those which were not so cautious.[9]

With regard to mutual-aid societies the SNI's members were enlisted for a precise stand on quite specific issues and encouraged even to form and support the proper sort of workers' societies. But beyond this, the SNI was attempting to mold opin-

Disraeli complete with cries of "here, here." It was distributed free to Espero's subscribers on June 1. British sympathy for Garibaldi was seen, however, as Machiavellian, Espero, 13 August 1862.

[9] The personal fury of these polemics shows especially in the exchange with Stampa: Espero, 22 September 1862. The Society's paper had, of course, taken stands on many specific issues, such as the danger of too many pardons in the south: Piccolo Corriere, 25 November 1860; the need to abolish the lieutenancies: ibid., 8, 10 November 1860; the correctness of Cialdini's caution in accepting Garibaldians into the army: ibid., 5 May 1861, 52–4; and in contrast, the propriety of absorbing the Bourbon army into the Piedmontese ranks: Espero, 22 March 1862; the banning of French in the schools of the Val d'Aosta: Piccolo Corriere, 22 November 1861; the confiscation of Church lands: ibid., 16 December 1861; or marriage as a secular ceremony: Discussione, 15 July 1863. But none of these so defined a party position, were so recurrent, or prompted such extensive analysis as the workers' societies: Piccolo Corriere, 10, 12, 19 October (on the contentment the SNI produced among Perugian workers); 9, 11, 15 November 1861 (the SNI played an active part in behalf of the Asti Congress against the Florentine one); Espero, 22, 23 March; 26 April; 2 May (a long article by Sbarbaro); 24 August; 13, 15, 16, 24 September 1862. These attacks were connected with suggestions that Aspromonte was Garibaldi's revolt against property, 30 August 1862, or warnings that democracy necessarily led to socialism, 11 December 1862. On these workers' societies and their congresses, see Richard Hostetter, The Italian Socialist Movement, 1 (Princeton, 1958), 50–69. In 1858 the National Society had been more sympathetic to political activity of workers' societies in behalf of the SNI itself, ibid., 36.

ion without defining what one did with opinions besides hold them. Its members were encouraged to support the railroads and the building of highways, or to favor improvement in education (although it was added somewhat irrelevantly that the education which produced a generation of Cavours, Balbos, and Ridolfis could not be so bad). The Society's members were encouraged to do all they could to extend their own liberal vision, to establish night schools perhaps, to help eradicate superstitions or to aid programs for improved sanitary services and the building of public lavatories. Even with this rather literal approach to social engineering, the members of the SNI were expected not to usurp any functions properly the Government's.[10] For most of its members, belonging to the Italian National Society had come to mean an occasional meeting of the local committee and a subscription to a newspaper.

The subordination of the National Society to a newspaper may have been deliberate; it had come about in October 1861 when the *Piccolo Corriere* had become a daily, a project first discussed shortly after Cavour's death. No longer a monthly, the Society's paper concerned itself less directly with the affairs of the SNI and with formal statements of its position. Rather, its views were now reflected in the traditional ways of a partisan paper. The change had also meant an increase in dues for most members, something which brought strong protests from many committees though few reacted with the vigor of Lucca's which pled with its deputy to prevent the increase. The recently established category of *soci ordinarii*, second class, who paid only 25 *centesimi* a month, would now receive only the paper's Sunday edition—a weekly review of the news which contained most of the items about the Society itself. A number of devices were worked out for easing the financial burden, and

[10] The obligations of liberty included helping to draw up plans for railroads, joining the National Guard, and urging the Government to sponsor scientific congresses, etc., but not attempting such tasks as the collection of statistics on economic and social matters: *Piccolo Corriere*, 3 March, 11–12; 3 April, 19–22, 28–9; 26 August, 19 December 1861; *Espero*, 16 February 1862; *Discussione*, 8 May 1863. Their desperate need for something to do must have been quite obvious; one Enrico Grimala Lubansky of Barcelona wrote from Sicily suggesting they could collect money to build some fortresses there, *Espero*, 28 April 1862.

by the end of the year the *Piccolo Corriere* appeared to have prospered as a daily.[11]

In January 1862 the dominance of a newspaper over the Society was extended when the *Piccolo Corriere* combined with an established Turinese daily to become *Espero, Il Piccolo Corriere d'Italia*. The name of the National Society disappeared from the masthead, although it left its traces in the two words, *Indipendenza* and *Unificazione*, which remained. La Farina claimed no official connection with the paper, although that fact merely enabled it to be less lofty in the tone with which it supported him and defended the Society. The news of the SNI continued to appear in the Sunday bulletin.

The paper was in effect becoming the Society; it assumed the normal operating expenses of the SNI, membership in which came to be thought of as daily or weekly according to the copies of *Espero* one received. Its circulation was relatively large (an average of 3,800 copies daily and 4,800 on Sunday in the spring of 1862); but rates were increased slightly in May, and by June circulation had dropped about one-sixth. *Espero* operated with a daily deficit until August when a careful paring of expenses put it in the black. By the fall of 1862 it, too, was apparently a success. It was also increasingly just another newspaper, dependent primarily on its sales in the streets of Turin, printing more local and commercial news in addition to political and

[11] Bellini wrote Simonetti, 19 July 1861, that it had been decided at the Central Committee's June meeting that only a journal would be left of the SNI, ms. in Carteggio Casarini, MCRB. *Piccolo Corriere*, 7 July 1861, 97; 1 September 1861. The dues of *socio ordinario*, first class, were raised from 1 lira to 1.25 lire a month. Committees, it was suggested, could subscribe to one copy of the paper (for 1.25 lire a month) or 4 copies (for 5 lire) and a group could even combine to subscribe to one Sunday copy at the rate for ordinary members of the second class, .25 lira a month. Members were to agree to take the paper for two years; non-members to pay 1.60 lire a month for the daily.

Complaints and queries came from Parma, 29 June; Soragna, 14 July; Massa, 29 July; Sarzana, 29 June 1861. Some, like a member from Bagnacavallo, hailed the daily but regretted they could not afford it (Bubani, 28 June, explained that his brother had inherited all their money), mss., ISR, buste 715, n. 83; 716, ns. 16 and 13; 717, n. 48; 715, n. 66. Lucca wrote to Telotti, their deputy, 2 July 1861, ms., *ibid.*, busta 715, n. 2; but they were making a similar complaint to Buscalioni, 25 February 1862, ms., *ibid.*, busta 716, n. 72. The *Piccolo Corriere*, 20 November 1861, appeared in a larger format to handle the news of the parliamentary session after explaining, 18 November, that the zeal of the Society's committees and commissioners had made this possible.

official items. In December it combined with the relatively new daily, *Discussione*, to become *La Discussione, Piccolo Corriere d'Italia*. With a larger format, more expensive printing (and more advertising) this paper carried the Society's views in 1863 and 1864. Directed by La Farina's parliamentary group, its news of the National Society was still more consistently relegated to the inner pages of the Sunday edition.[12]

The Italian National Society had failed to become a national political party; it had been unable to create the broad demonstrations it wanted, unwilling to sponsor those that had appeal. Politically, it had become a parliamentary faction; organizationally, it was little more than a newspaper. Defeated by its own ideas, it could find for itself little place in an established Italian state. Yet, measured in terms of the numbers of its mem-

[12] *Piccolo Corriere*, 19 January 1861; *Espero*, 20 January and 22 December 1862 (its first and last appearances as the Society's paper, a lifetime so nearly that of Rattazzi's ministry as to cast doubt on *Espero*'s denial, 29 October 1862, of receiving a subsidy from any minister); *Discussione*, 22 December 1862. The *Piccolo Corriere* was printed at the offices of *Espero* from 14 January 1862 on; the *Typografia Amaldi* had tried to get the Society's printing in the fall of 1861: letters to Festi, ms. in ISR, busta 715, n. 15. *Espero* adopted a new type face with the 1 April 1862 issue and announced new rates (1.75 lire a month for the daily; 9.50 lire for six months) in the 19 May 1862 issue, probably the time when rates for a *socio ordinario*, first class, went up to 1.50 lire a month. La Farina's statement that he neither owned nor in any way directed *Espero*, although it represented the opinions of the SNI, appeared in the 10 June 1862 issue. One sign of the continuity through the three papers was the relentlessly regular appearance of La Farina's novel, *Gli Albigesi*, as a serial right through to its conclusion in the 25 December 1862 issue of *Discussione*. Form for commissioners, n.d. [1862], in HCL and ISR, busta 719, n. 13. *Discussione* ceased printing on December 16, 1862, with *Espero* sent to its subscribers until their combination on December 22. It immediately began promising its enlarged format of 1863.

The circulation of *Espero* was kept as daily totals for the previous week; weekly circulation declined from 33,140 [in late April] to 22,129 for the week ending July 19, the last figure available. Some 1,400 members of the SNI were subscribers; there were also 82 subscriptions in Turin and 28 abroad. Thus most sales must have been on the streets. The deficit for the first quarter of 1862 was 21,147.99 lire, and by July the treasury was apparently dry as the deficit reached 28,000 lire. Expenses included salaries to Festi, Rapetti, and Sbarbaro, a few loans to friends, and aid to widows in addition to the usual office expenses. From January to May the paper painfully calculated its losses at 104.84 lire a day or 3,147 a month. Thereafter, they declined to 2,280 lire for April–May; 626 in June; 201 in July; with the August 16–31 period reflecting a profit of 756.10 lire. The over-all deficit had fallen to 14,000 lire then. Scraps of *Espero*'s accounts in ISR, busta 720, ns. 15 and 17. The rumor that the paper was seeking merger was denied, 1 June 1862. On November 18, *Espero* began publishing a second edition at 6 p.m. containing the parliamentary debates of the day.

bers, it had continued in 1862 and 1863 to exist and, in places, to grow. The Central Committee continued to meet and to discuss the SNI's affairs, striving to keep it alive. Its newspaper helped by insisting that the Society was prospering; even in 1863 it claimed "incessant growth." Toward the end of 1861 there had been something of a membership drive, and both La Farina and Buscalioni issued lengthy instructions to the Society's committees. But these were unmistakably quotations from the past; all who could write, teach, or spend money were called on to pull together, but the initiative for that would clearly have to come from the local committees. Those who still wanted La Farina's hints of inside information were told the Society had nothing to communicate that was not in its paper. Except for occasional pamphlets, that proved to be essentially true. If the Society continued to have several thousand members, it owed them to something else.[13]

Some committees were able on their own to find suitable things to do. Their very establishment would justify a broadside on the importance of sowing the seeds of liberty and teaching civil wisdom. Later, they could, like Diamante's committee,

[13] *Piccolo Corriere*, 10 October and 18 November 1861; La Farina's instructions appeared in the 29 December issue and again on 1 January 1862 along with Buscalioni's 14-points printed on a single sheet so they could be distributed separately. *Discussione*, 18 January 1863. An agent even toured the Romagna selling subscriptions to *Espero* and talking of revival of the SNI: Paolucci [to Casarini], 7 December [1861], ms. in Carteggio Casarini, MCRB. At the Central Committee's meeting on 27 February 1862, deputy Cosimo Ara reported on the most active committees and talked of the SNI's part in elections. In addition to the pamphlets *Questione Romana* and *Sulle presente condizioni* (whose fulsome claims for the Society were among its most controversial contents) which were distributed in June and October respectively, two pamphlets not bearing the SNI label were sent to subscribers. These were Rattazzi's speech in defense of his ministry in November and Boggio's *Una pagine di storia* in December. The 1,400 members of the SNI who subscribed to *Espero* included 39 *soci promotori*; 1,222 *soci ordinarii*, first class; 139 *soci ordinarii*, second class —the figure remained constant through July, ISR, busta 720, n. 17. There is a cryptic reference in these accounts to "3M [3,000] soci," and certainly many more men must have thought of themselves as members than actually subscribed to the paper; there is a reference there also to a "normal diminution" in number. La Farina's claim of 14,000 members was apparently an excessively round multiplication of the number of subscribers: letter to Terasona, 10 September 1861, Franchi, *Epistolario di La Farina*, II, 502; letters to Giunti, 18 September 1862, and to Mazzi, 1 January 1863, *ibid.*, 526, 532–33.

publish a denunciation of Cardinal Antonelli (in which even some *clero liberale* joined) or attack Papal rule in general, or start a subscription for the victims of brigandage. Urbino's committee expressed its love of order in a special proclamation of gratitude to the local unit of *bersaglieri*. Having published on most of these subjects, Grottamare's committee returned to a promise to promulgate the *Credo* of the SNI[14] Often, the recounting of past exploits was enough to establish a committee's or an individual's importance, in itself a comfort for men who had not since risen to higher honors.

The anniversaries of more public events provided even greater opportunities for action. The committee at Conversano in Apulia sponsored a requiem mass on the anniversary of Cavour's death with a Bishop officiating and many of the clergy and the National Guard attending. The committee in Amelia, Umbria, celebrated the anniversary of unification by distributing charity, a technique frankly borrowed from their clerical enemies; the committee of Afragola, near Naples, brought off a grand celebration complete with a parade in which the mayor and council took part. The Pergola committee chose to celebrate the anniversary of the Piedmontese entry into the Marches; and the Messina committee, carefully selecting the one thing Garibaldi did not do, celebrated the anniversary of the fall of the Bourbon citadel there. At times, the committees of the SNI even went beyond such commemorative activity to sponsor a reading room for adolescents or pay the teachers of a night school. One committee gave a testimonial to their deputy for his firmness during the Aspromonte crisis: another, in Castellana, Apulia, wrote at length of its general plans to educate the public and announced its specific plan to build a shooting range.[15]

[14] Manifestoes of the committees of Spoleto, 29 November 1861; Fuligno, 1 September 1861, ISR, busta 719, n. 22; Assisi, *Piccolo Corriere*, 14 January 1862; Diamante, 5 March 1862 (44 "notables" and some officers of the National Guard joined the 7 "liberal" priests), ISR, busta 720, n. 14; Centorbi, *Espero*, 22 March 1862; Matelica [1862], ISR, busta 719, n. 24; Grottamare, 19 July 1862, in *ibid.*, busta 720, n. 15, and *Espero*, 12 October 1862, *Discussione*, 8 February 1863; Narni, *ibid.*, 25 January 1863; Urbino, 27 August 1862, *Espero*, 27 August 1862. The committee in Augusto, Sicily, informed the Government of the virtues of the local harbor with the enthusiasm of a chamber of commerce, Mariano Gabriele, *Da Marsala allo Stretto.* (Milan, 1961), 231n–32n.

[15] Reports of the Norcia committee, 5 January 1863, ISR, busta 720, n. 16, *Discussione*, 1 and 11 January, 3 March 1863. Antonio Iachelli Vecchio credited

In 1862 and 1863 the nature of the National Society had changed; its strength no longer rested primarily on its committees, although there remained some of surprising size. As the Society had come to represent an attitude and had been subordinated to its newspaper, its commissioners had become the core of its organization. Named by the Central Committee to recruit enough members to form a local committee, the commissioners more often nominated their friends to become commissioners in turn. The National Society spread during these years in sudden little spurts, reaching into places where it had never been represented before. A minimum of organization was involved; sometimes the commissioners had quite ephemeral effect, but most of the Sunday issues of *Espero* and *Discussione* carried lists of their names.

The word of the SNI was being carried where it had not been clearly heard. The Society claimed, of course, to be the same; it could even boast of a vigorous committee in Athens and another in Buenos Aires, and it reported fondly on the activities of the German *Nationalverein*, although the question of the Tyrol stood as firmly between the two societies as between their countries.[16] The fact remained that even in those parts of Italy where the SNI had once been strong it had now nearly disappeared.

In Lombardy-Venetia the Society had perhaps a score of commissioners in the areas of Bergamo and Cremona; it claimed a committee in Trieste, and it cooperated with the Venetian committee (in Turin) in opposing Austrians and "reds"; but even the anguish of the lost province was not much of a spur

himself, 11 March 1862, and his brother, the canon, for the outcome of the plebiscite, ms. in ISR, busta 716, n. 95. Ing. Mai's recounting of activities in Pavia, 16 October 1863, is a valuable historical source, *ibid.*, busta 717, n. 20. Reports of the committees in Conversano, *Espero*, 29 June 1862; in Amelia, *ibid.*, 15 June 1862; in Afragola, *ibid.*, 8 June and 15 July 1862 (good relations with the mayor and the National Guard did not last); Pergola, *Piccolo Corriere*, 7 September 1861; Messina, *Espero*, 10 and 19 March 1862; Macerata, *ibid.*, 6 July 1862; Diamante, *ibid.*, 31 August 1862; Castellana, *ibid.*, 26 January 1862.

[16] The reports on the Society were quite thin in *Espero* from August to December 1862. On the *Nationalverein*, *ibid.*, 28 February and 14 March 1862. Niccola Loviselli of Athens was a devoted follower of La Farina and leader of the SNI there; as director of *Il Corriere Italiano in Grecia*, he made it an organ of the Society: ISR, busta 555, n. 17; *Espero*, 24 August and 21 September 1862 (on the Buenos Aires committee, founded March 1861).

to the SNI north of the Po.[17] In Tuscany the impressive organization Piero Puccioni had led was no more. In 1863 a commissioner was named for Pescia which had a large committee two years before; by 1862 only Lucca, Monte San Sevino, Pistoia, and Rapolano had sizable committees, though these were among the largest in the north.[18]

In the former Duchies the Society's fate was slightly better; a sudden burst of activity in 1862 by commissioners in the area of Parma led to the formation of a score of committees with a total of 180 members. But in Massa the Society had long since been reduced to one man; honesty forced him to strike from his printed stationery his title, president of the committee. Fivizzano's committee dwindled each year, but a hardy 9 of its members remained in 1864. Much the same was true of the once vigorous committees of Pontremoli and Reggio; few others remained by 1863.[19]

---

[17] The statistics on membership in this chapter are, unless otherwise indicated, compiled from the lists of actual names in *Espero, Discussione*, and the printed broadsides in ISR and HCL. When a committee simply gave a figure for its own strength, that is noted; when one is mentioned with no figure for its membership, it means that the evidence of activity is certain but the number of its members too doubtful to include here. The totals, then, should be considered simply as estimates; there is no way of proving their accuracy or completeness, except that on the one hand printing the names of men who did not exist or were not in the SNI would be dangerous and on the other, committees or commissioners who did not get their names in print were probably not very effective.

There was a committee of 9 in Casalbuttano. Mazzini believed that his plans for the Veneto were winning over the SNI: letter to Cesare Bernieri, 21 December [1862], *Scritti di Mazzini*, LXXIII (Imola, 1936), 277. Certainly, Festi's contacts in the Trentino kept some interest in the Society and hope for action alive there: Monga to Festi, 3 and 14 April, 11 June, and 30 September 1863, mss. in ISR, busta 717, n. 61. On relations with the Venetian committee: Alberto Cavalletto to Buscalioni, 27 February 1862, *ibid.*, busta 546, n. 44; *Espero*, 27 March, 26 June, 12 September 1862.

[18] In 1862 there were still a number of members in Pescia, but dues were getting harder to collect: Neri to Buscalioni, 27 December 1861 and 2 March 1862, ms. in ISR, busta 717, n. 79. Lucca had 82 members in February 1862 but had lost 10 by June; Rapalano's committee fell from 27 to 21 in the same period. Monte San Savino had 51 members; Pitigliano's 28 in 1861 are not heard from again. Pistoia had 43 in 1862 (and Scove, 4: P. Occhini to Buscalioni, 30 March 1862, ms. in ISR, busta 717, n. 82).

[19] Dell'Amico to Buscalioni, 29 June 1861, ms. in ISR, busta 716, n. 14. Fivizzano had 37 members in 1860, 28 in 1861, 9 in 1864. Pontremoli's 43 at the end of 1860 were 29 in 1862, when Calice still had 25. Reggio had 59 members in the first quarter of 1861, 52 in the second, 45 in the third, 30 (few of whom paid their dues) in the fourth and 18 in the first three months of 1862. Garfagnana's 60 members at the end of 1861 leave no trace thereafter;

In the Romagna a few loyal committees remained into 1862, but the tone for the province was set by the committee of Montiano which met in December 1862, unanimously agreed on the Society's principles, and announced its dissolution. And in Russi, Aristide Farini who had been loyal to La Farina through the trying years of schism finally gave up in 1863; he could only suggest they might try his uncle in Macerata.[20] Yet in some parts of Italy the Society held its own or even gained ground during this period. There was little activity in Piedmont in 1862, but the following year more than 100 new commissioners were named. The Society had never been better diffused throughout the province it so admired.[21] The pattern in the Marches was somewhat different. The tendency in 1862 was for commissioners to establish small, new committees (some 20 committees of 85 men were named), but the older ones which survived there were among the more active of the SNI. Members continued to complain, however, about the clerical superstition of mountain folk; and the habit remained of confusing the National Society with older, more secret, and more radical Mazzinian groups. By 1863, in the Marches, too, the Society spread primarily through new commissioners, an impressive number of whom, 65, were appointed.[22]

Soragna's committees, however, apparently stayed at about 16 members from 1860 into 1862. Ligonchio had a committee of 5.

[20] Medicina had 71 members late in 1861; Sant'Agata Bolognese, 17; Bagnacavallo's committee was still active, but we have only the names of the 8 who signed their manifestoes. Concordia still had 4 members in 1862; a new committee of 3 was established in San Giovanni in Persiceto, and a commissioner in Brisighella set up a committee of at least 7 members which took over the small treasury left by the old one. Cesena's committee was still helping a workers' aid society in 1862. August Ferri (Montiano, the committee there had 23 members in 1861), 28 December 1862, and Farini, 5 May 1863, to Buscalioni, mss. in ISR, busta 716, ns. 31 and 26.

[21] Novi Ligure and Cuneo, where a dozen or more commissioners were appointed, were the areas of most SNI activity in 1862. Ermanno Buscalioni, of the Central Committee, appointed many of these commissioners, and his personal contacts were undoubtedly important.

[22] Avv. Murri, 23 July 1861, and Leopoldo Santangali, 29 November 1861, to Buscalioni, mss. in ISR, buste 717, n. 76; 720, n. 12. Ibid., buste 717, n. 68; 720, ns. 14 and 15. Pergola's committee had 110 members in 1861; the number had probably shrunk in 1862, but the committee remained active as did committees in Castignano (19 members in 1862) and Grottamare (6 members) and new ones in Matelica and Gobbi. The committee of Ascoli [Piceno] which had more than 100 members and a new slate of officers in 1861 did not survive into 1862, mss. in ISR, buste 720, n. 11; 717, n. 94; 718, n. 29 (Tolini misdated his own letter here as 1861 instead of 21 January 1862); but

In Umbria, which had not been particularly hospitable to the National Society until the time of Cavour's death, the Society continued to grow, first around Perugia, and then throughout the new province. Some 10 new committees with 69 members were founded in 1862, and older ones often became somewhat larger, taking their association with workers' societies or their part in elections quite seriously. Not until 1863 did the membership there begin to decline as it had elsewhere.[23] In Sicily the Society was not able to maintain the membership it boasted in mid-1861, and 1862 was a period of consolidation and reorganization. But more than anywhere else, the SNI in Sicily had committees in the major cities as well as in the smaller towns, and the appointment of 70 commissioners in 1862 and 1863 meant that the Society maintained connections throughout the island even if its organized membership declined.[24]

In the Neapolitan provinces the National Society made sensational progress. Some activity in the Marches and Umbria spilled on into the Abruzzi, and supporters of the Society there had established 7 committees and claimed 160 members in 1862. The small town of Paglieta had 61 members (their citizens, it was explained, had always been unusually zealous nationalists), and a committee was established in Limosano in

a new committee of 7 replaced it and 6 committees totaling 22 members were established in neighboring towns in 1862. In 1862 Monalto had 16 members; Force, 8; Amandola and Chiaravalle, 6; Macerata and Marano [Cupra Marittima], 5; Ortezzano, 4; there were many other smaller committees, at least 7 of which had 3 members. In some cases these figures may, however, indicate only the number of officers who, as a body distinct from the members, were often called the committee. Vincenzo Panichi of Matelica was the most active commissioner in the Marches.

[23] Some 5 or 6 commissioners were named in 1862, ISR, buste 716 n. 2; 720, n. 14. Perugia, Spoleto, Fuligno, and Assisi (with 7 members) had committees in 1861–62. Urbino had 12 members; Todi, 16, Nereto and Orciano, 6 in 1862. The committee in San Gemini grew from 10 to 15 members; in Preci, from 5 to 19; in Narni, from 6 to 12 in 1862. The dues paid by Norcia suggest its committee declined from about 17 members in 1862 to 11 in 1863: ISR, busta 720, n. 16. Amelia's committee disbanded in 1863, *ibid.*, busta 720, n. 17.

[24] In mid-1861 the Society claimed over 700 members in Sicily; the committee in Palermo had 78 members, that in Messina 29 with another 150 in the surrounding area. Seven new committees with 68 members in all were announced in 1862 when the SNI was active in Lentini and Palagonia as well as Catania and Palermo (with a committee of 10 in Monreale). Centorbi's committee had 22 members in 1862 (reorganized in November); Caltanisetta's, 15 or 17; Syracuse's, 12; Messina had a new reduced committee of 9; Francoforte, 4. Some 20 commissioners were appointed for Sicily in 1862 (13 for the area around Palermo) and 50 more in 1863.

the Molise. In Apulia there was a committee of 70 members in Conversano and one which claimed 180 in Castellana. Even in Naples, where Claudio del Bene had struggled to found a committee through 1861, a committee of 7 members was finally established in 1862, only to collapse at the end of the year (because the *"tristi"* were too strong); but there were a few committees active in Calabria. Nearly 50 commissioners were appointed in the Neapolitan provinces in 1862, and they must have done their work well. For some 500 more, divided about equally between the Abruzzi and Apulia in the east and from Naples through Calabria in the west, were appointed in 1863. The lists of their names and their towns, many of which had probably never before been set in type north of Rome, were so long that the Society's paper was sometimes six months behind in printing them. *Espero* took special pleasure in these successes in the *meridionale*; they were surprising enough to force a denial that local officials required citizens to join the Society.[25] In its last year the Society had become more nearly nation-wide than ever before in its history.

These hundreds of commissioners cannot be taken as evidence of any great organizational strength, but in joining the SNI they did accept its ideas. Often they were men of some importance in their neighborhood; occasionally, they must have wielded great influence.[26] They spread the Society's newspaper and pam-

[25] In the Abruzzi there were committees of 9 at Cellino, of 7 at Torricella [Sicura] and at Civitello del Tronto, of 6 at Noreto, of 5 at Forcella, and of 4 at Montenerodomo. Pietro Alfieri was the most active commissioner. Limosano's committee grew from 9 to 12 members in 1862. Near Naples there were committees in Salerno; Afragola, with 5 members; and Diamante, with 3. Fenocchio had greater success as a commissioner (letters, ms. in ISR, buste 721, n. 8; 716, n. 28), than Del Bene in Naples (letters of 25 February and 19 December 1862, ms., *ibid.*, busta 716, n. 10). Commissioners were especially numerous around Bari: *Espero*, 25 May and 5 September 1862, denying *Diritto's* charge of Governmental influence. If there was such pressure, it was certainly uneven. The subprefect for Afragola viewed the SNI as an undesirable *"consorteria,"* and the authorities in Palagonia, Sicily, ignored political distinctions in disbanding both the *Società Emancipatrice* and the SNI.

[26] Becoming a commissioner of the SNI was viewed as a political act; and those who disagreed with it refused, a great many to the commissioner who first named them, some directly to the Central Committee: letters, mss. in ISR, buste 717, n. 38; 720, n. 15. The Society's commissioner in San Pietro Avellana, Molise, who was also the village priest, must have had unparalleled authority. Few of the members of the SNI in 1862–63 appeared to have hoped for any personal benefit from Turin; Luigi Bobbio in Castignano did want a Governmental post; the committee in Messina hoped to have an important member

441

phlets and encouraged local manifestoes of similar tenor. Even in 1862 and 1863 the Italian National Society must have been well known in most of Italy and still viewed as something of a political force. With no program of action and a tendency to isolate politics from the masses, the SNI was dying out in those parts of Italy where politics were best organized and most vigorously conducted. It retained a slight hold among militant Cavourians in Tuscany and the former Duchies and was somewhat stronger in the still more bitterly divided political atmosphere of Sicily. It held on in the Marches, where fear of the Church was strongest. Its spread in Piedmont may indicate a late growth of national sentiment there, but it probably reflects the fear that Piedmont was losing its pre-eminence in Italian affairs. A rigidly Cavourian policy was the best defense against this loss as it was against the politicization of the workers' movement.

Well over a thousand men joined the National Society, more than half of them from the south, after it had ceased to find anything new to say. This was precisely its appeal. By quoting itself, the SNI offered a kind of belated chance to participate in the Risorgimento. The Society had moved from the center to the political periphery of Italy, from the great cities to the smaller towns, from the north to the south. This was the last function the Society served, but it had been one of its most important all along.

The Italian National Society gave the frightened but hopeful men of Italy's middle class, men not quite rich enough or influential enough to have a direct and important role in affairs, some part to play. It had allowed them to join their betters in attacking much of the aristocracy and clergy without risking radicalism. It had offered a path to apparent participation in the mainstream of Italy's political life, a path which the social and political realities of unified Italy largely closed. Most of its members did not, after all, wish to do much; they just wanted to feel that they belonged in a new Italy.

In the south it was men such as these but more isolated and in a more precarious position who, once unification was achieved,

---

who was a judge transferred back to their district and promoted, letters, mss., *ibid.*, busta 720, ns. 14 and 17.

began to feel more strongly the tug of nationalism. To that sentiment they attached their hope for a society of liberty and order, where good men like themselves would run the government. They knew that to achieve this attitudes widely held would have to change. The National Society with its emphasis on propaganda, its prestige from past action, and its promise of domestic peace offered a way into the Risorgimento. As these latest members of the SNI distributed *Espero* or *Discussione* or explained the workings of parliament, the promise of unification or the need for order, they were doing on an immediate and local level what Manin and Pallavicino had attempted years before.

Appropriately, the most active committee of the SNI at the end of 1862 was the one in Cagliari. A commissioner had been appointed for Sardinia in January, but only toward the end of the year did he announce his hope of spreading the Society throughout the island. His claim that Cavour had declared the SNI to be his most useful auxiliary and that the Society now had 25,000 members did not impress the island's leading paper. It denounced the National Society as a sect which served only as an excuse for Bertani's society and as a device for winning La Farina a cabinet post. Sardinia should not, it snarled, "embrace a corpse." The vigorous replies from the Society may have helped to arouse some interest; for in November the first meeting of the SNI in Cagliari was well attended.

Particularly concerned to combat the "red party" which he saw growing around him, the Society's commissioner made his public appeal in terms of the exciting progress taking place all over Italy. Sardinia, he said, had sacrificed much for unification and must now organize to benefit from it. He found a specific issue in the bill then before the senate for building a railroad on their impoverished island. On this measure, dealing with the very symbol of progress and touching very immediate interests, the Society won wide support. Public meetings were held and telegrams sent to Sardinia's senators. The Society's paper filled pages with accounts of these successes; and when the measure was passed, the men of the SNI were the heroes of the crowd during a night of celebration. The festivities ended, everyone was careful to add, in perfect order—the Society's final success. A year later, the SNI had spread to only one member in Sassari:

but it had had its moment even in Sardinia.[27] The Society had given local Cavourians the sense of being in the thick of Italy's political battles. It had, in terms of quite immediate gains, dramatized the benefits which unification—and political restraint—might bring.

The new breath of life in the Society was already growing faint when, on September 5, 1863, *La Discussione, Piccolo Corriere d'Italia*, announced that "a great misfortune has struck our country." Giuseppe La Farina was dead. To his followers, he seemed now to have been a part of Italy's destiny, the man who had shared the "secret" of Cavour's policy, who had been "the organ by which Cavour spoke to the peoples of the Peninsula." His death found him for many the symbol of a happier era, already passed, when Italians were unanimous and governments directed revolutions. Even those who opposed him could praise what he had meant to represent. The propaganda which had absorbed so much of La Farina's talent and energy was rising in retrospect to the level of myth. His funeral was attended by his friends, personal and political, by senators and deputies, by representatives of the Freemasons and of those good workers of Piedmont who kept their mutual-aid societies out of politics, and by all the ministers of the Government. Yet this was hardly enough; readers of the Society's paper were reminded to visit the cemetery,[28] and the Society decided to sponsor another memorial service to be paid for by subscription. A volume of his letters would be published and then a biography.[29] In October

[27] *Piccolo Corriere*, 3 January 1862; *Espero*, 23 November; 7, 14, 21, 28 December 1862; *Discussione*, 18 January 1863. F. de Lachenal was the commissioner; his circular of 14 November 1862 is in ISR, busta 555, that of 19 November in the Buscalioni pamphlets, HCL. Lachenal to the local paper, 15 November, in ISR, busta 550, n. 5; to La Farina and Buscalioni, 27 January and 6 December 1862, 8 November 1863, mss., *ibid.*, buste 716, n. 100; 620, n. 16. The relevant items in the *Gazzetta del Popolo*, Cagliari, 4 and 9 December 1862, are in H. N. Gay clippings, HCL.

[28] *Discussione*, 5, 6, 7, 16 September, 2 October 1863. Clippings of obituaries of La Farina (all favorable to him and ones probably selected for reprinting in the SNI's paper) are in ISR, busta 553, n. 43, and H. N. Gay clippings, HCL. Peruzzi, who was ill, was the only minister who did not attend the funeral: Biundi, *La Farina*, II, 177. *Discussione*, 11 December 1863, hoped to please its readers by printing an ode La Farina had written in 1848; it was on the opening of the Lucca-Pisa railroad. One member wrote Buscalioni in grief asking for pictures of La Farina, ms., 11 September 1863, ISR, busta 718, n. 56.

[29] *Discussione*, 27 September 1863. Sbarbaro hoped the Society would purchase his brief biography of La Farina: letter to Buscalioni, 17 September 1863,

it was decided to construct a monument to La Farina in Turin, and the Society's committees and commissioners were called on once again to begin collecting contributions. It was the National Society's last demonstration. Its sponsors included many men of note from beyond the Society itself, but those who responded were largely the faithful of the SNI. From all over Italy the money came, sparsely and in small amounts; but the Society's paper could once more print lists of patriotic contributors. By March 1864, nearly 1,300 lire had been received.[30]

To properly mourn La Farina the National Society was necessary. Count Alfieri, a leading parliamentary follower of La Farina and editor of *Discussione*, was determined that the SNI should be maintained. They possessed, he suggested, a "complete political system," by which he apparently meant the cooperation of deputies, newspaper, and Society as much as the ideas they shared. By mid-September he was attempting to reestablish La Farina's parliamentary group and bringing pressure on Buscalioni not to leave the National Society without direction. On September 26 its Central Committee met.

The subscription for La Farina's monument was the only publicly announced result of the meeting, but the friends of La Farina were determined to use the legacy he left in the SNI—

---

ms. in ISR, busta 551, n. 43. But La Farina's friend, Vincenzo Gallina, was to write a full-scale one: letters to Buscalioni, December 1863; 2 and 21 January 1864, mss., *ibid.*, busta 718, n. 56. The idea for the published letters was Mazzi's, 12 October 1863; a committee of Ara, Giunti, and Buscalioni planned to edit them. The recipients of La Farina's letters showed, however, a greater sensitivity to their political explosiveness: Duca di Cesarò, 27 October; Giusti, 29 November; Gualterio, 28 October; Lachenal, 3 November 1863, all to Buscalioni and draft of his request for the manuscripts, mss., *ibid.*, buste 717, n. 48; 720, n. 17; 716, ns. 18 and 99; Fermi and Ottolenghi, *Manfredi*, 173*n*. Franchi took over the editing but apparently gave up: Luisa La Farina to Buscalioni, 1 July 1864, ms., *ibid.*, busta 716, n. 100. By 1867 Franchi had taken it up again. Selmi, *La Farina*, 26, said Buscalioni would write a history of the SNI. For the second memorial service, 36 men were listed as having contributed 122 lire; they included 11 deputies, 4 senators, and the Minister of War, *Discussione*, 21 September 1863.

[30] *Discussione*, 8 October; 24 and 30 November; 6, 20, 28 December 1863; 1 February and 6 March 1864. Some 228 donors were listed, most of them from towns in which the SNI had recently active committees, although many besides its members contributed. A total of 1,297.03 lire was contributed. The circular announcing the subscription, 6 October 1863, is in the Buscalioni pamphlets, HCL; it was signed by 7 deputies and 2 former deputies, the former Minister of Education, the Buscalioni brothers, Selmi, and Giunti. The printed forms for the subscription are in ISR, busta 548, n. 66.

a group of deputies and a doctrine. Personal ambitions and a direct interest in the welfare of the Society's newspaper may have helped them to their decision, but they were moved by the Society's principles as well. Most of the reasons used in the past to explain the importance of the SNI seemed as valid as ever in the discontent of 1863. La Farina's death itself added to his followers' fears of the political apathy of good men. They believed they represented a majority of informed Italians; for that very reason the Society was needed to combat the majority's overconfidence and lack of cohesion.[31]

In October, then, Buscalioni sent out another circular calling on the men of the Society to act with new vigor while asking, apparently, if they did not think the SNI should be maintained. For the next month their replies came in—occasionally still on elegant stationery—making it clear that something more than a circular would be necessary to preserve the National Society. One suggested the lowering of dues to attract artisans and workers. Another warned against the promiscuous appointment of commissioners; too many "Reds and prisoners" were among those named. There were the old requests for more frequent correspondence with Turin and for more specific instructions. There was the suggestion that the Society campaign for railroads in the Abruzzi. Most of those who bothered to reply were willing to try again, but few were sanguine.

Two men in Lucca promised to revive the Society there, but by the end of the year they were tired of paying out of their pockets for others' dues. Apathy and the mania for criticism were the difficulties in Ferrara, one member wrote. Another reported that his area of the Marches was reactionary; he would

---

[31] *Discussione*, 15, 21, and 27 September 1863. Alfieri's circular to the deputies who signed La Farina's program of December 1862, was dated 17 September; Professor Felice Daneo wrote Buscalioni at Alfieri's request, 17 September 1863, ms. in ISR, busta 716, n. 8. Buscalioni may have been elected president of the SNI at the September meeting or soon thereafter: Maineri, "Buscalioni," Carpi, *Risorgimento*, IV, 670–71. The loyal Mazzi expected him to be: Mazzi to Buscalioni, 12 October 1863, ms. in ISR, busta 717, n. 48; but Giovanardi in San Giovanni di Persiceto hoped for an election by representatives of the committees, the old Romagnol wish: letter of 31 October 1863, ms., *ibid.*, busta 720, n. 17. The *Gazzetta di Messina*, 22 October 1863, lamented the dispersal of the SNI in commenting on the election to fill La Farina's seat, in H. N. Gay clippings, HCL. Gualterio wrote Buscalioni, 28 October 1863, on the dangers of apathy, ms. in ISR, busta 720, n. 17.

still keep trying although, despite his past services, the Government had never rewarded him well. The sense that the Society was needed and that the Government deserved support was strong among these last supporters of the SNI, but many of them had the tone of malcontents as they complained of those who got the jobs (just what was the Society's influence with the Government, one pointedly asked). The mixed motives which now sustained the Society show in the doctor who hoped, through the SNI, to help defeat the reactionaries who were gaining in the former Papal States, to get his pamphlet on hygiene published, to be able to move his practice to Rimini, and to have a friend promoted in the National Guard.

By mid-1864 the National Society was near extinction. Its most active committee was at Diamante, in Calabria, where another anniversary of unification was celebrated. Jointly planned by the Society and local officials, the ceremonies included a review of the National Guard, a meal for the poor, and a dance. At mass, the priest preached, with a bust of Victor Emmanuel beside him, on the superior claims of nationalism over those of divine right. The Society in 1864 enjoyed no greater success.[32]

Real effort was made to keep the Society alive. Commissioners were being appointed in May 1864; and the Central Committee met with new frequency. *Discussione* enlarged its format and proudly announced the purchase of a new steam press. The men of the Society defined their position as "liberal conservative" now, but their paper daily maintained the views the Society had made famous, with two slight changes. There was more talk

[32] To Buscalioni from Vincenzo Panichi (Ascoli-Macerata), 4 and 19 October, 27 November 1863, mss. in ISR, busta 719, n. 94; from Lovitelli (Potenza Picena), 5 and 21 October, 8 December 1863, *ibid.*, busta 717, n. 9; from Raffaele Angelucci (Matelica—he now advocated establishing a library; he had wanted the SNI to get him a librarian's job for years), 14 September 1863, *ibid.*, busta 715, n. 9; from Prampolini (Ferrara), 14 January and 4 March 1864, *ibid.*, busta 718, n. 6 (he was announced as a commissioner in *Discussione*, 24 January 1864); from P. Sandini (Grosseto—noting simply that he had not been president of their committee for years), 30 December 1863, ISR, busta 718, n. 56; from Bichelli (Montefalco), 31 May 1864, *ibid.*, busta 715, n. 4; from Sinibaldi (Lucca), 26 October 1863, *ibid.*, busta 718, n. 56; from Giorgi (Lucca), 15 January 1864, *ibid.*, busta 716, n. 73; from Alfieri, 19 October 1863, *ibid.*, busta 545, n. 7; from Clementi (Fenestrelle), 14 November 1863, *ibid.*, busta 715, n. 99. The doctor lived in Treja: letters of 19 and 28 July 1864, *ibid.*, busta 717, n. 2. The report on Diamante, 7 June 1864, is in *ibid.*, busta 720, n. 18.

now of a reconciliation between Italy and Catholicism; moderates, unlike radicals, it was explained, recognized religion as the source of morality. And there was more open admiration, in 1864, for Louis Napoleon. Its whole position, *Discussione* airily explained, was defined in the political concepts of Napoleon III, the policies of Cavour, and the program of the SNI. But such disparate strands were hard to hold together except in metaphor: the Emperor conducted the great European symphony; they wanted Italy to play first violin.

Even this fondness for the Second Empire was put to use, for Alfieri wrote Napoleon, who replied to the *Société Nationale*, noting their common mission. When the Emperor was the victim of still another attempted assassination, the Society wrote of its concern and got a second sympathetic answer. Widely reprinted in Italy and France, it made excellent propaganda. *Discussione's* readers were also informed that joining the Society had been the great Manin's last act, that Garibaldi in 1858 had declared that the SNI "is Italy, it is the entire nation." Even La Farina's instructions to the Society on its refounding in 1859 were reprinted, and a special supplement of the paper gave a triumphant account of the Society's history, which served at least to establish the predawn meetings of Cavour and La Farina as part of the lore of the Risorgimento.[33]

The Society was tempted to try influencing the Government and to toy with visions of almost Mazzinian action. But its pleas for unity and patience, for a calm and isolated politics, for con-

[33] From 1 January to 27 May 1864 (the last copy I found) *Discussione* announced the establishment of 3 committees (Montemarciano and Treja, Cuneo, Crema) and 22 commissioners (8 for Piedmont, 5 in the Marches, 4 in the Molise, 2 each in Calabria and the Romagna, 1 in Sardinia). The Central Committee, apparently scheduled to meet every fortnight, actually met January 8, February 17, March 30, 1864. The paper's issue of 16 October 1863 introduced the new format. *Discussione*, 2, 4, 22, 29 October; 15 and 22 November; 13 and 18 December 1863; supplement to *Bollettino Settimanale* No. 42 (18 October) issued 23 October 1863. L. M. Billia, *Dopo un anno* (pamphlet from *La Sapienza*, July–August 1886), 5, suggests Buscalioni shared Count Carlo Alfieri's hope for a reconciliation with religion. Maineri, "Buscalioni," Carpi, *Risorgimento*, IV, 671, sees him as hoping for a reconciliation with the party of action, too.

Napoleon III to M. le Comte [Alfieri], 25 November [1863] and Alfieri to Buscalioni, 13 January 1864, mss. in ISR, busta 575, n. 7. Alfieri wanted the reply distributed by the Government to all prefects, but Spaventa refused. Napoleon's second letter, 28 February 1864, was reprinted in a number of papers in *ibid.*, busta 555, and H. N. Gay clippings, HCL.

fidence in the vague promises of progress no longer seemed relevant to the problems, the real divisions, and the deep disappointments of Italian life. They could not support an organization. In 1864 the National Society collected only 218 lire in dues.[34]

Since 1862, in fact, the Society had become less famous than two organizations once viewed as its subsidiaries. The women's committee of the SNI in 1862 staged a magnificent lottery for aid to wounded soldiers which netted more than 20,000 lire from all over Italy. The Society's paper proudly reported the women's activities, and its leaders remained directors of the Feminine Committee which soon had 15 sub-committees of its own throughout Italy. With contributions to the Greek revolution and aid to the victims of brigandage, the women even touched lightly on political issues. The National Society itself contributed, offering for lottery objects which demonstrate its deep grounding in the tastes of the time. Its donations included two alabaster obelisks, a "Chinese Gypsy" dress with silver medallions, four busts of Garibaldi, and a porcelain vase in the shape of an artichoke.

The ladies' pure purpose, and perhaps their tenacity, caused their committee to outlast its parent. In 1866 they refused to join similar groups in order to keep "the name and the traditions of the Great Italian National Society, that did so much for the unity of the fatherland." The challenge of the Austrian war they met with a varied display of feminine vigor, and the Society's old dream of concord was never more nearly realized than when these ladies made bandages and saw that at the soldier's bedside there was "a woman who smiles, who recalls a mother and a distant sister, and who lightens with little gifts

[34] Buscalioni to the ministry about promotions in the guard at Urbino, 19 December 1863, ms. (his draft), ISR, busta 720, n. 17. Note on plans among Kossuth, Spaventa, and the King for war against Austria in case of revolution in Hungary, ms., *ibid.*, busta 720, n. 18. On occasion, Buscalioni asked how many volunteers an area might provide in case of war: *ibid.*, busta 715, n. 111; Fermi and Ottolenghi, *Manfredi*, 174. The accounts for 1864 are in ISR, busta 720, n. 19. The Feminine Committee deposited 2,688.98 lire with the Central Committee, apparently repayment for an earlier loan (Cortes repaid a loan of 100 lire). The figures of identical office expenses for the two committees suggest they split this overhead; the Society's rent for one quarter was paid by the Neo-Latin Society. Apparently the 200.73 lire remaining in the treasury, 4 December 1864, were transferred to Buscalioni.

the pain of the resting warrior." For these women, as for the National Society itself, the things they could do were painfully less than the patriotism which prompted them. After the war, there were no more soldiers to visit; and there were complaints that they overcrowded rooms and overtired patients. They extended their aid to orphans and decided, as the SNI so often had, that because Italy was not yet united they could not disband. After a few internal squabbles of their own, they came forth with a magnificent new constitution in 1869.[35] The name of the National Society was preserved until the capture of Rome crowned the Risorgimento.

The National Society was also being overshadowed by the *Comitato Nazionale* in Rome. The connection between the two was still tenuous; but the Society claimed the Roman Committee as one of its own, and the Society's newspaper regularly pictured the Committee suffering from Papal harassment, maintaining its responsible moderation, "keeping alive" the best traditions of the SNI. Taken by contemporaries to be more closely connected than they were, the two organizations did represent similar policies; and the Society consistently defended the Committee, a frequent subject of dispute in the north.[36] The Com-

---

[35] The lottery of 18 June 1862 netted 23,355.55 lire by selling tickets at .50 lira for 1,248 items! Daneo, Cortes, Buscalioni, Cora, Selmi, Giustinian were among the directors of the Feminine Committee. The 4,000 lire it gave the Greeks came from other funds: *Espero*, 5 January, 17 and 20 July, 11 November 1862; *Discussione*, 3 and 8 February 1863. The committee achieved something the SNI could not in keeping a Pallavicino a member: Anna Pallavicino Trivulzio to Buscalioni, 13 December 1864, ms. in ISR, busta 550, n. 45. It had an office in the Palazzo Madama during the war in 1866 and apparently over 30,000 lire left in its treasury afterward. The account in *Gazzetta di Torino*, 5 November 1867, H. N. Gay clippings, HCL, indicates only 1,825 lire spent on charity from May to September that year; but the committee's funds were nearly exhausted by 1869. See note 42 below. Some of the Committee's accounts are in ISR, buste 720, ns. 19 and 20; 555; its funds were formally combined with the SNI's in August 1866. Nicomede Bianchi, as president, called for a November meeting to discuss continuing the Committee in a circular of 24 October 1866, *ibid.*, busta 717, n. 56; Teresa Turò Caleagro to Buscalioni, 7 December 1866, ms., *ibid.*, busta 718, n. 75. *Catologo degli oggeti offerti per la lotteria a benefico dei feriti nelle guerre italiane* (Turin, 1862). Comitato Femminile pei Soldati Feriti, untitled printed report dated 12 July (Turin, 1866). *Relazione sull'andamento del Comitato Centrale Femminile della Società Nazionale Italiana durante la guerra del 1866*, dated 11 November (Turin, 1866). Comitato Femminile della Società Nazionale per Soccorso ai Feriti nelle patrie guerre, *Statuto Organico*, dated 21 January (Turin, 1869).
[36] The formal connection between the *Comitato Nazionale* and the SNI cannot have been very close: the Committee seems never to have used the title of the SNI; the documents in the Archivio Checchetelli, ISR, busta 186,

mittee called on Romans to absent themselves from Easter celebrations (and then reported they had); it launched tricolored
boats in a park pond and joyously described the "first naval en-
gagement" of the Papal forces. To men even slightly to the left
in the north, the Roman Committee was distastefully tame; to
Garibaldians it was, like the SNI, a "narcoticizer" of the people.

In Rome itself a battle raged between the Committee and
the Party of Action which culminated in the Committee's capture and destruction of the clandestine press on which *Roma o
Morte* was printed. The act was widely denounced in the north,
but the Society's paper defended it, using such words as
"honest," "just," and "provident." It was the prevention of the
dangerous division between committees which had so hurt
Naples; there could hardly be a question of freedom of the
press when Rome itself was not free. Even for those who followed politics fairly closely in 1863 the attitudes of the SNI
were probably represented more by the Roman Committee than
by the Central Committee in Turin; and the former would continue well after the Society had died, still calling on Romans to
wait their liberation with a calm worthy of Victor Emmanuel.[37]

The Feminine Committee, with its sentimental patriotism,
and the Roman Committee, with its hint of restrained subversion, were more like the SNI of 1859 than was the Society itself
in 1863. And they were winning wider fame. If their Society

ns. 44, 50, 54, 62, give no evidence of a connection; neither do any of the copies
of the Committee's papers, *Cronaca Romano* and *Don Pirlone Redivivo*, in
BSMC. The *Cronaca*, a monthly, does not mention La Farina's death in its
26 September 1863 issue. On the other hand, *Espero* and *Discussione* consistently referred to the Committee as part of the SNI and often put news of it
in the columns devoted to the Society without claiming any direction over the
Committee. There was some slight contact between some of the SNI's committees and the Roman Committee; by 1862 Gualterio and Coccaneri, one
of its leaders before his exile, apparently viewed *Espero* as the Committee's
natural organ in the north. Letters of Tanari (one to Checchetelli, 20 February
1863), mss. in ISR, busta 186, ns. 55 and 62; Gualterio to Coccaneri, 26 March
1862, ms., *ibid.*, busta 402, n. 10. Leti, *Roma*, II, 209–11; Zini, *Storia d'Italia*,
I², 1120–25.

[37] *Espero*, 2, 22, 25 July; 2, 12, 13 August; 8, 21, 28 September; 18 and 19
October 1862. *Discussione*, 24 and 27 February; 10, 22, 26, 27 June; 6, 8, 20,
22 July; 15 and 30 August; 8, 9, 12 (claiming priests supplied the party of action with a new press), 16, 29, 30 September; 7, 9, 21 October; 6 December
1863. *Cronaca Romana*, 25 July 1863 and issues of 1865. Proclamations of the
National Committee, 1 June 1865, and attacking it, by the Papal Government,
12 April 1863, and the *Comitato d'Insurrezione*, December 1867 in Houghton
Broadsides, Papal States, 1859–71, 710, HCL.

was failing, its leaders apparently reasoned, then another one was needed. In February 1864 they proposed transforming the SNI into an *Associazione Liberale Italiana*. Perhaps they felt the years had won the old Society too many enemies, and they made a conscious shift in the use of the word liberal. The general program and organization for the proposed Association were essentially those of the National Society, and the changes are therefore a suggestion of what these men felt was going wrong with the SNI. Membership in the Association would be open to everyone, not automatically as in the Society but by the secret vote of local committees; the fraternal bond would be tighter. Further, the Association would have a marvelous number of officers who would be subordinate to a general assembly which would meet once a year; the Association would be representative as the Society had not.

More important, the new Association would be frankly political, its primary purpose the nomination of candidates in local and national elections and the sending of reports to Turin on local conditions. From across the Peninsula the score of men still actively loyal to the National Society responded enthusiastically. The hint of political power excited them; the promise of establishing a connection between national politics and local problems filled a need they felt. Despite a published *Statuto*, a further circular, and a lowering of dues, however, the required 100 members never joined; the assembly of the Italian Liberal Association appears never to have met.[38]

[38] The circular of 12 February 1864, signed by Americo Barbieri and asking for replies to Buscalioni, is in ISR, busta 720, n. 18. *Discussione*, 1 November 1863, had noted the formation of an *Associazione Unitaria Costituzionale* in Naples dedicated to the program of Cavour and asked why they did not "join the rest of the nation" in the SNI; such things probably spurred the formation of a new society. Replies came from Lachenal (now in Casale), 27 February, ms., ISR, busta 716, n. 99; from Mazzi (Sarzana), 27 February, *ibid.*, busta 717, n. 48; from Lovitelli (Potenza Picena), 24 February, *ibid.*, busta 719, n. 9; from Angelucci (Matelica), 23 February, *ibid.*, busta 715, n. 9 who went ahead (letters of 24 April and 17 May 1864) recruiting members. Lucca's defunct committee heard of the Association from their deputy and thought they might revive, *ibid.*, busta 717, n. 2. From Milan came a flurry of reports worrying especially about the meetings on behalf of Venice—too much like the ones for Poland, they feared: 21 February, 5 and 27 March, 19 June, 20 November 1864, *ibid.*, busta 720, n. 19. Scandiano complained of the number of towns to which a *sindaco* had not been appointed: 26 February, *ibid.*, busta 715, n. 62. Catania noted the depth of local ignorance and Braglia thanked Buscalioni for the aid in getting a job as stationmaster: 15 March and 27 July 1864, *ibid.*,

Even while that Association was being outlined, some in the National Society were looking in the other direction toward the Society's old call to some higher unity above the dullness of domestic politics. In March 1864 they published the program for a *Società Internazionale Neo-Latina*. Its immediate goals were nothing less than a tariff union with common weights, measures, and passports for the five Latin countries of Europe. For a brief period they even managed to publish a weekly paper. The nationalism of the SNI showed its deeply Mazzinian and racial roots in the Neo-Latin Society. And although the two organizations never formally merged, the same men led both; and some of the SNI's members responded to this new project out of their old yearning to be in an active organization.

Indeed, all these men displayed a kind of post-operative shock. The dramatic moments of the Risorgimento had passed, but they could not let go of the dreams that drama had fostered, the demands for their plans and their energy it had made, the sense of their own importance it had given. Building on the National Society's attachment to the House of Savoy, the Neo-Latin Society stressed the connections of that House to the thrones of France and Portugal and foresaw a Prince of Savoy on the Spanish throne. But royal in-laws can be as awkward as any others; Prince Jerome's presidency of the Neo-Latin committee in Paris was seen as a mixed blessing by the parent committee in Turin. The disagreement over him led to the dissolution of the Neo-Latin Society.[39]

---

busta 716, n. 84. Only from Taranto, 30 March, and Cassepolombo, 29 May 1864, were there signs of coolness to the idea, *ibid.*, busta 717, ns. 44 and 56.

A draft of the *Statuto* in ISR, busta 720, n. 12 and its printed version in Buscalioni pamphlets, HCL. A circular of 9 April [1864] calling a meeting may have been on behalf of the Association; one on 1 August 1864 announced 100 members as the number necessary before the Assembly met and lowered dues to .60 lira a month. A *Programma* of 1865, talking of the need to be militant and progressive (conservatism is impossible while Italy is still in revolution) was—judging by format, type face, etc.—probably the Association's, all these among the Buscalioni pamphlets, HCL.

[39] *Discussione*, 11 March 1864, announced the new society and said the idea for it came from the favorable reactions of the Latin countries (in contrast to the British and Germans) to Napoleon's suggestion of an international congress. The *Statuto* of the Neo-Latin Society, 19 March 1864, is in the Buscalioni pamphlets, HCL; it provided for five-man committees and a central committee in each country. The *schede*, 1 March 1864, ISR, busta 720, n. 18, providing for dues of .60 lira a month (.20 for artisans) is probably for this society. Vegezzi-Ruscalla remembered their paper as having lasted 4 months; in any

The floundering of these two new societies had helped to make it apparent that the National Society, too, was finished. By the middle of 1864 even *Discussione* was faltering. A few members complained that their paper no longer came; some wondered if or why the Society had ceased to exist or how they could explain it to "our few friends"; but only one cared enough to cry, "you have abandoned us." On December 26, 1864, the Central Committee of the Italian National Society announced its end; because of the decision to move Italy's capital from Turin to Florence, provided for in the September Convention with France, the full powers of the Committee were being turned over to Buscalioni.[40] The SNI still could not quite admit its end, but it was down to one man. Given life by Cavour's success at the Congress of Paris in 1856, it recognized its own

case, its second number earned a rebuke, 21 March 1864, from the Minister of Public Works, *ibid.*, busta 715, n. 9. Isopescu gives 16 January as the date of the first meeting of the society's directors. From April 10 to July 10, 1864, the Neo-Latin Society paid the rent for the SNI's office, ISR, busta 720, n. 19.

Cordova, La Farina's close friend, was elected president; Vegezzi-Ruscalla, Buscalioni, Festi, and Alfieri (4 of its 5 vice-presidents) as well as Ara and Giustinian, who were active in it, had been on the Central Committee of the SNI. Tecchio, Sineo, and Cesare Cantù, who were also involved, represented somewhat different camps. Castelar was president of the Spanish committee. Vegezzi-Ruscalla was particularly interested in Rumania, Buscalioni in Iberia; but Vegezzi-Ruscalla's article, "Dalla facoltà assimilatrice delle stirpe latina," in *Rivista Contemporanea*, November 1857 (published later as a pamphlet) had expressed admiration for the Latins in general which had won great praise in the *Piccolo Corriere*. Letters of support from the National Society reached Buscalioni from Brescia, ms., ISR, busta 720, n. 18, from Ascoli, 8 May, and Matelica, 27 July 1864—but the lonely Angelucci by 1866 was ready to join the committee for aid to the wounded, letter to Buscalioni, 9 June 1866, mss., *ibid.*, busta 715, n. 9.

Lorenzo M. Billia, *La Lega Filellenica e l'ideale politico di Carlo Michele Buscalioni* (Turin, 1885), 4 (apparently an 8-page offprint). Claudio Isopescu, "La Società Internazionale Neo-Latina di Torino (1864) e i Romani," *Atti del XXIV Congresso di Storia del Risorgimento* (Rome, 1941), 324–29, 332–36. Maineri, "Buscalioni," Carpi, *Risorgimento*, iv, 672. Marcu, "Vegezzi-Ruscalla," *Giornale di Politica e di Letteratura*, ii, 614–15. Onciulescu, "Vegezzi-Ruscalla," *Rassegna Storica del Risorgimento*, xxvii, 255, 262.

[40] The latest issue of *Discussione* I have seen is that of 27 May 1864. Niccola Bernardini, *Guida della Stampa periodica italiana* (Lecce, 1890), 682, says only that 1864 was its last year. The April 15 issue said Alfieri was no longer director, a sign of significant change; D. F. Botto was announced as his replacement in the April 26 issue. Letters of Angelucci, 24 May and 26 June; of Lovitelli, 6, 10, and 19 June; of Cortes, 27 October; of Sinibaldi, 23 December 1864, and of del Bene, 13 January 1865, mss., ISR, buste 715, ns. 9 and 110; 717, n. 9; 718, n. 56; 547, n. 23. The Central Committee's announcement, handwritten on embossed stationery and signed by 8 of its members, is in *ibid.*, busta 720, n. 19.

demise in the awkward treaty of 1864. It had striven to make provincial Turin the country's capital and seen in Piedmont the model of a mighty nation, but it could find no place in the state now formed; it had less relevance for the nation that would be ruled from Florence.

The Society which had been so much a part of Italian political life existed now in echoes. When in 1865 the monument in Turin to La Farina was unveiled, the still active women's committee was represented by Signora Elliot, the British Ambassador's wife; and Buscalioni spoke for the Society. If some newspapers, while admitting that the SNI had paid for the monument, were so unkind as to comment that the work had been done for nothing and a grander monument was planned in Florence, the event itself was enough to revive talk of a union of all liberal associations.[41]

When war with Austria broke out in 1866, there were those who regretted that the Society had not risen to play its part of 1859 and 1860. It was less satisfactory to have the Government collecting subscriptions and enrolling volunteers. Yet, through the women's committee, the Society made large contributions, and the army was given those 6 cannons which the Society had gotten in 1860 from some admirers in Stockholm. The Minister of War responded by expressing his gratitude in the eulogies of an epitaph recalling, as few ministers had cared to in its livelier days, how much the National Society had done.[42]

There was even another good manifesto left in the Society; in 1867 something called the Comitato Centrale del Trentino of the SNI published a broadside lamenting that the Tyrol had

[41] The unveiling was on February 17, 1865; Opinione and Gazzetta di Milano, 18 February, among clippings in ISR, busta 553, n. 45. The Florentine monument referred to in the latter was a parliamentary project completed in 1884; Alfieri was on the committee for it: Biundi, La Farina, II, 177. The occasion in Turin was apparently enough to cause one last meeting of the Central Committee, notice, dated 11 February 1865 and sent to senator Aradi, in Buscalioni pamphlets, HCL.

[42] Carlo Della Noce to Buscalioni, 21 May 1866, ms. in ISR, busta 716, n. 14. Some 1,000 lire was given the Minister of the Marine and 30,000 to the Minister of War for aid to the wounded. The accounts are unclear, since Buscalioni kept the funds for both the SNI and the Feminine Committee until just this period, but it may be that only 371.40 lire of these sums was from the SNI itself, see notes 34 and 35, above. The Minister of War to Buscalioni, 27 July 1866 (replying to a note of Buscalioni's, 23 July), ms. in ISR, busta 555; receipt from the Ministry of Marine, 9 August 1866, ibid., busta 719, n. 20.

not come to Italy with Venice. It ended sensationally with another letter from Louis Napoleon who agreed the Tyrol was
Italian but limply suggested good fortune and good relations
with Austria as the means of getting it. At least a monument
to Manin could at last be built in Venice, nearly twenty years
after he had been forced to leave; and there was just enough
of the National Society left for a donation in its name.[43] It could
have had no more fitting tomb.

The continuance of the Society after Cavour's death had
been the result less of its political program than its members'
psychological need. Middle-class men of uncertain standing in
their communities, they were frequently at odds with their
environment. They were a minority in that society while having
to believe they represented a majority in the country at large.
From town after town they wrote with indignation of the
aristocracy and with fear about conspiracies among the radicals
and the clergy. Belonging to a national organization offered
important support. As the Society, paralyzed by its own doctrine
and by the narrow base of Italian politics, weakened, they sought
that support in other societies, most notably Freemasonry. The
members of the SNI had seen themselves part of some vast but
vague program which moved on the forces of history. They had
persisted in their letters and even in their letterheads, in pretending, as if by tacit agreement, that they were better organized
than they were. But the Masons did all these things better while
providing greater fraternal comforts and the excitement of secrecy. In its nationalism, its anticlericalism, its close ties to
France, and its international organization, Masonry met and

[43] The manifesto, dated Trento, 24 February 1867, is in the Buscalioni pamphlets, HCL; Napoleon's letter "to one of the most illustrious members" of
the SNI was dated 24 August 1866. The *Nazione*, 19 March 1867, printed the
letter Napoleon replied to. A rather humble letter, it referred to the teachings
of Cavour and La Farina, spoke of natural frontiers and somewhat inaccurately
described the alliance with France as part of the Society's *Credo*. The paper
also reported the Society's publication of the reply which first appeared, it said,
in the *Correspondence Bullier* and had distressed the *Neue Frei Presse* and
puzzled the *Indépendance Belge*. All this, plus Napoleon's letter of 28 February 1864, was reprinted as a broadside, in ISR, busta 555, the last pertain-
ing to the SNI. Fermi and Ottolenghi, *Manfredi*, 174–75, say Festi had written Napoleon, 27 July, for the "Trentino Committee" and Alfieri, 30 July 1866,
for the "Central Committee of Florence." The letter in *Nazione* sounds like
Alfieri; the Trentino was a particular concern of Festi's.

Adriano Rocca, 23 January 1867, to Buscalioni, ms. in ISR, busta 553, n.
28, reporting that Manin's son and cousin were pleased by the gift.

outbid much of the appeal of the National Society or the Neo-Latin Society.

It is hardly surprising, then, that the leaders of the Italian National Society were leaders in the growing Masonic movement as well. La Farina had been a founder of one of the lodges in Turin and an active Mason. Buscalioni, important in another lodge, had been on the Masonic Grand Council in 1861. At the time of La Farina's death, Buscalioni was in France on Masonic business, apparently connected with a serious division in Masonry there. By 1864 he was a dominant figure in Italian Masonry where he combated but also contributed to the same schisms that embittered Italian politics. Although it traced its nationalism to the twelfth century, Freemasonry found it no easier to encompass Cavourians and Garibaldians than the National Society. The Neo-Latin Society even more than the SNI showed the influence of Masonry; and Cordova, the president of one, was the Italian Grand Master of the other.

For the period before the war of 1859 there is no evidence of any consistent connection between Freemasonry and the SNI; but after the war, when the lodges began to be nationally organized, that connection grew. By 1862 the newspaper of the SNI was carrying occasional news items about the Masons, merely announcing a meeting or making them sound like the Society itself; for they were described as no longer secret, above politics, and against social divisions. The paper gave relatively frequent mention to the recognition Italian Masonry had won from France and Portugal, the Ionian lodges, and those of England. When Crispi and his supporters threatened Italian Masonry with a schism, supposedly over questions of ritual, *Espero* publicly took sides against the Society's old enemies.

By 1862 the letters written to Buscalioni by members of the Society occasionally contained Masonic symbols; and in the next two years those signs of Masonry grew more common. La Farina's Masonic obituary may have been roughly correct when it said that the Masons of the northern provinces "were selected from among the members of the National Society." [44] There could have been no better place to look. As the Society failed to become a modern political party, it lost old members and

[44] See Chapter Eight, notes 90–94. Ernesto Nathan, "Della Massoneria e dei suoi fini," *Rassegna Contemporanea*, VII (1914), 211, associates La Farina's

gained new ones who were anxious to prove their patriotism. Once that was done, they found the attitudes represented by the SNI now maintained, without embarrassing attachments to the specific deeds of Cavour or La Farina, and with greater color, in Freemasonry.

For the thousands of men who joined it from 1856 to 1864, the National Society must have represented, however briefly, their high hopes for their country and for themselves. For many, the memory of that optimism and that faith would be as hard to escape as the realities which undermined it. The men who had been the Society's leaders were disappointed that winning Rome did not lessen domestic division and shocked when a Savoyard prince did ascend the throne of Spain—only to fail. Yet they could not cease trying, through organizations, to find a way to their vague goals.

In foreign affairs they sought, in the manner of the pan-Slav or pan-German movements, to assemble sentiment into force. They established societies for Franco-Italian understanding. They formed a Greco-Latin Society, whose hopes were destroyed at the Congress of Berlin; they changed it to a Philhellenic organization, whose confidence in Balkan nationalism was shattered by the Greeks' battles with their neighbors.[45]

---

trip to Sicily in 1860 with Masonry. Most of the men of the Marches and Umbria mentioned as Masons in Leti, *Carboneria e Massoneria nel risorgimento*, 309–54, were, however, also in the SNI. Luzio, *Massoneria e il Risorgimento*, I, 288–305, 323–42, 350–51; II, 1–73. Colombo, "Per la storia della Massoneria," *Rassegna Storica del Risorgimento*, I, 53–89; Patrocco, *Documenti su Garibaldi e la Massoneria*, 20–9. Maineri, "Buscalioni," Carpi, *Risorgimento*, IV, 657, 671. Alfredo Grilli, "Imola nel giugno 1859," *Risorgimento e Farini*, I (1959), 155, is typical of those who have found local connections between the SNI and the Masons, but he sees the latter and Young Italy as having founded the SNI in Imola!

Piccolo Corriere, 24 December 1861; *Espero*, 23 March; 28 June; 1, 11, 16, 18, 20 and 29 July; 3, 7 and 27 August; 7 and 23 October 1862. La Farina to Terasona, 7 August 1862, Franchi, *Epistolario di La Farina*, II, 552; and Mazzi, 12 October 1863, Panichi, 8 May 1864, Lachenal, in 1864, to Buscalioni, mss. in ISR, buste 717, ns. 48 and 94; 716, n. 19. (Garibaldi's letters were filled with Masonic symbols, too, ISR, busta 49, ns. 29, 30, 31.)

Carlo Salvadori, "Alla cara memoria del fr.·. Giuseppe La Farina," *Bollettino Officiale del Grande Oriente Italiana*, n.d. [an excerpt, 1863 or 1864], 243–47. *La Genesi dell'idea Mass.·. nella storia d'Italia, discorso pronunciato dal G.·. S.·.* etc., 23 November 5861 [1861]; and two other statements of Masonic nationalist doctrine in 1861, "Programma Masonico adottato dalla Mass.·. Ital.·." etc. and "A.·.G.·.D.·.G.·.A.·.D.·.V.·.," Grand Council at Turin, 29 May, all in HCL.

[45] Interest in such societies was, of course, hardly limited to Italians. Sir Charles Dilke belonged to the Greco-Latin one; the Archbishop of Corfù and

On the domestic front, too, they saw in the possibilities of association a means of teaching civic virtue and creating an atmosphere of agreement. Again and again, and with an infinite variety of meanings, they would warn liberals that in this time of crisis they must get together. Their Reform societies, Liberal Progressive or Democratic associations could still sound alike no matter how different their ends and then similarly peter out. Pallavicino never lost hope for a "great national party," and he tried for years to build one around Garibaldi as he had earlier tried to do around Gioberti and then around Manin.[46]

Through such associations these men sought the popular following that would provide a path to political influence. They would not see that Italian politics were based on a social stratification and a political system in quarantine from most of society which made their ambitions impossible. Their failure was the more poignant because they now recalled the National Society as having achieved what they could not only a decade or so later.

Yet the Society itself remained a subject of the very controversies it had abhorred. There were many who remembered it, and some of its members, with strong distaste. The publication of La Farina's letters in 1869 led to lawsuits and to Bertani's

---

Victor Hugo joined the Philhellenic one—Buscalioni was president of its Turin chapter. Maineri, "Buscalioni," Carpi, *Risorgimento*, IV, 657, 672–74; Billia, *Lega Filellenica*, 4–7; Marcu, "Vegezzi-Ruscalla," *Giornale di Politica e di Letteratura*, II, 605; Onciulescu, "Vegezzi-Ruscalla," *Rassegna Storica del Risorgimento*, XXVII, 256.

[46] Buscalioni was at least actively interested in an *Associazione Italiana per l'Educazione del Popolo* (1866), ISR, busta 720, n. 20; a Franco-Italian League to correct misstatements about either country in the press and thereby lead to world peace (n.d.); an *Associazione Reformatrice Italiana* (1866); an association of members of the parliamentary left who supported the monarchy (n.d.). With Daneo he was among the 12 directors of the *Associazione Liberale Progressista di Torino* (1879), all in HCL. His Latin dreams led to his becoming Argentina's commercial agent in Italy and his experience as a publicist to his becoming head of the Italian news service *Agenzia Stefani*. The Minister of the Interior could be confident he would understand the need—for the sake of public order—to let prefects decide on the publication of bad news, note, n.d. [1866?], ms. in ISR, busta 719, n. 8.

Pallavicino was president of the *Associazione Democratica Italiana* (1865) and a member of the *Comitato Centrale per Concorso alla Insurrezione Romana* (1867), ISR, busta 490, n. 4. Pallavicino to Count F. Lineta, 24 August 1864, ms., *ibid.*, busta 1, n. 25; 4 December 1861, 13 and 25 January 1862, ms. in MNRT. Salazaro, *Cenni sulla rivoluzione*, 117–20. Pallavicino, *Il Giornale Il Diritto e Giorgio Pallavicino* (Turin, 1863) and *Non Disarmo!* (Turin, 1866). With that mixture of admiration and condescension with which he was often treated, Garibaldi was made honorary president of literally scores of societies for all sorts of purposes, local and national.

brilliantly titled pamphlet, *Ire politiche d'oltre tomba*, to which General Türr replied in a pamphlet reprinted as late as 1903.[47] With the passage of time, however, the threads of the Risorgimento did seem to draw together. Many an old patriot told of his part in the Italian National Society. And had not that Society somehow combined the ideas of Gioberti and Mazzini with the policies of Cavour and the heroism of Garibaldi? The National Society never brought Italians to that unity which it espoused, but it stood in retrospect as evidence for another generation that Italians had at least once been united in a common cause.[48]

In May 1915, the senate of the Kingdom of Italy, in preparation for war, granted their King extraordinary powers, just as their ancestors had done two generations before in a smaller senate. After the vote was recorded, the president of the senate rose to give a kind of benediction to the day's work. He was Giuseppe Manfredi, who had in 1859 been president of the committee of the *Società Nazionale Italiana* in Piacenza; and there was an echo of the SNI in that old voice as, to the cheers of his colleagues, he cried, ". . . Spirits of the great men of our Risorgimento, come down and propitiate our fates." [49] The Society left its traces in the whole history of Italy's liberal monarchy.

[47] The questions of how much and with what spirit the Society aided Garibaldi's expedition remained the central subject of dispute about the Society, breaking out on occasion in parliament, session of 17 June 1863, *Legis.*, VIII, *Sess.* 1863–64, *Camera, Discussione*, I, 453. Garibaldi never forgave the Government's sequestration of his arms or the SNI's bad muskets. But La Farina's death did not soften the judgment of Massimo d'Azeglio, letter to Torelli, 5 September 1863, *Miei ricordi*, 168–69.

[48] Manin had died in time to win quick acceptance as one of the Risorgimento's heroes. In praising La Farina, Cordova was careful to associate them: commemorative letter in many copies, 26 November 1866, to Prof. Lizio Bruno in Biblioteca Universitaria, Messina. Pallavicino was anxious to keep his connections with Manin and the latter's part in the SNI well known, *Non più indugi* (Turin, 1863), 45–6, *Discussione*, 18 October 1863, supplement to *Bollettino Settimanale* No. 42 replied with the Lafarinian version of the Society's history. On Pallavicino's death in 1878, it was his part in the SNI that was most warmly remembered: obituaries in H. N. Gay clippings, HCL. Manfredi published his reminiscences of the Society beginning in 1904: Fermi and Ottolenghi, *Manfredi*, CLXIIff. Maineri, "Pallavicino," Carpi, *Risorgimento*, I, 366. Minghetti to Pasolini, 25 September 1866, *Carteggio Minghetti-Pasolini*, IV, 139.

[49] *Atti di Parlamento, Legis.* XXIV, *Senato, Discussione*, II, 1854 (21 May 1915).

✤ CONCLUSION

A GENERAL CONCLUSION

I

✦ STUDY OF THE Italian National Society lends support to two views of the Risorgimento favored in much recent scholarship. The unification of Italy never won the active support of more than a minority of the population. The achievements of the Risorgimento resulted in large part from the coincidence of interests and programs normally quite divergent.

The illusion that by mid-century nationalist sentiment had struck deep roots into Italian society was in part the deliberate creation of nationalist propaganda. It was given wide currency by sympathetic French and British commentators who tended to overlook the smallness and insecurity of Italy's middle class; and it was adopted by the next generation of Italians who sought to make of the Risorgimento a model for subsequent Italian political life. The Risorgimento came closest to being a mass movement when the solution for particular and local discontents was sought through unification. But demands for reform and the cry of nationalism were often loosely and sometimes only transiently associated; the strength of the association varied with time, place, and class. Those who made unification their primary political goal, one worth achieving at almost any price, remained a relatively small group.

Three other points should be added to this view. First, the men of the National Society themselves rarely forgot that theirs was a minority position. Second, the Society's history suggests that even in the north that minority was smaller than most accounts suggest. Third, Italian nationalism was not so simply a sentiment of the middle class as historical terminology often implies. It was Italy's liberal aristocracy which set the dominant moderate tone of her nationalism; the middle class was more one of professional men than entrepreneurs, and its members did not lose their respect for the liberal aristocracy which shared their aims.[1] Thus Italian nationalism made its most successful

---

[1] Talcott Parsons has suggested rationality, functional specificity, and universalism as characteristics of a professional bourgeoisie; these categories provide a tempting analogy to the National Society's concern for practical means

appeal when it transcended immediate class interests, as the National Society did before its break with Garibaldi. The national movement needed all the support it could get, from literate artisans to enlightened aristocrats.

The disparate groups which supported the Risorgimento have long been recognized and listed; there were, among others, agrarian reformers, urban leaders, Mazzinian idealists mellowed with middle age, and Piedmontese nobles cherishing traditional ambitions for their state's expansion. The fact that such varied interests seemed for a moment to meet has made it difficult, however, to write of Italian unification without making it seem to have been inevitable. But to do that causes one to miss a simple, crucial fact—contemporaries had no such confidence. Even while claiming to have all the forces of history on their side, the men of the National Society were aware that unification was contingent on the maintenance of a delicate political balance. Such awareness explains much of the Risorgimento: the caution of its leaders was rooted in their realism as much as their conservatism; they were willing to compromise so much of their earlier programs because even after 1860 they would not be certain that Italy was lastingly unified. They talked so much of vigorous action while fearful of taking it not merely as psychological compensation but because they learned to disguise their differences in the hope that events would resolve them.

Now, to this view three other points should be added. First, even in 1859 and 1860, the Risorgimento was not just a movement to unify Italy but a battle to determine what united Italy would be like. This the National Society helped to hide. Italy had come so close to winning freedom in 1848 that compromise afterward seemed worthwhile to assure a victory but barely missed. Yet everyone really knew that the events of 1859 and 1860 would in effect determine the terms of the compromise to which they had already agreed. Second, the Risorgimento was thereby given new momentum while stripped of some of its most important content. Third, moderate nationalists were in fact more cautious than they need have been. These last two

and limited goals, its tendency to leave political decisions to the experts and to seek administrative solutions to political problems, and its readiness to find a model for Italy in the industrialized states of Western Europe.

sentences explain most of the recriminations which have followed Italy's unification.

The coalition of Italian nationalists seemed a momentary one dependent for its cohesion on apparent success. At Villafranca, when French influence was too apparent, and in 1860, when Garibaldian policy was too independent, the Cavourians saw their own influence endangered and unification itself threatened. Unable to afford failure in any test of power, they tended increasingly to make the simple control of power a primary goal.

Taken together, these points suggest some conclusions about mid-nineteenth-century nationalism as a whole. Insofar as politics was the public battle of ideas and interests, then nationalism was a denial of politics. For in stressing the values of unity, loyalty, and duty, nationalism saw political dispute as a source of weakness. It denied that there was conflict in the true interests of classes, groups or regions. The effect of nationalism was therefore inherently conservative in that it provided reason for supporting anyone thought to wield the power of the state effectively in behalf of national unity and strength, Disraeli or Gladstone, Napoleon III or Bismarck. Since order and unity, the cry of the political conservative, are essential to a strong state, and since, to the nationalist, most worthy ends required that strength, the nationalist was always tempted under pressure to move toward the political right, to sacrifice liberty to unity, discussion to authority, ends to means.

Yet the origins of nationalism were usually liberal and reformist; for everywhere it was a demand for change, the doctrine of the modernizers who, while they had too much to lose to want a social revolution, were self-consciously aware that theirs was an "underdeveloped" country. Nationalism could make its denial of politics effective because its ends were so clear, so easily defined in the model of the modern state. For the French that model had been England; for the Italians it was England and France. Italian nationalists were usually liberals, but their liberalism was primarily an admiration for the achievements of the liberal state. Because their model already existed, they looked directly to it, anxious to achieve an efficient bureaucracy, a responsible government, a progressive economic structure, all based on accepted and universally applied laws. Nationalism was a program to obtain these things quickly, not to evolve toward them but, if necessary, to superimpose them. The hurry to achieve these goals where nationalism itself was seriously opposed made a doctrinaire concern for means appear pedantic and unrealistic. Italian nationalists needed nothing so brutal as cynicism to justify "postponement" of controversy or the choice of practical means, though often this meant whittling away at the practices necessary to viable liberalism.

II

Whether universally valid or not, such generalizations do help to explain the history of the Italian National Society. It grew from the desire to make of public opinion a useful political force, and that remained a primary purpose. Initially, a movement to unite the molders of opinion, it claimed little more than that unification was possible and that Piedmont might lead in bringing it about. With a lawyer's liberalism, Manin asked for agreement in the name of nationalism. He did not have the direct success he expected. There were not many influential men in Italy who shared the simple assumptions about progress and the benefits of the modern state and civic virtue which made his vague program vibrant. The men to whom he addressed himself were, most of them, exiles in more than one sense, essayists out of office, who were listened to primarily because they had briefly held power.

Pallavicino insisted that theirs, more than a movement to unite leading nationalists, was a movement of mass opinion in support of Piedmont. The National Party made a sharper break with the tradition of 1848. To the appeal of sentiment, the promise of military force was added. This more practical program focused on socially stable Piedmont and won a firmer following. But Pallavicino still hoped to create an unwieldy shadow cabinet of radicals to bring pressure on Cavour. Such independence proved impossible. The National Party had jettisoned too much to win men with radical visions of a good society; it needed some promise of political power to attract other nationalists; it needed more supporters than Italy could provide to garner power.

Primarily a movement of propaganda before 1858, its failure to establish itself as a movement of opinion led to its establishment as an organization, the National Society. With less interest in the prestigious leaders of 1848, La Farina led the Society to recruit nationalists of more local influence to an organization which combined explicit support of Piedmont with the promise of restrained direct action. The National Society prospered. Following Piedmont meant accepting monarchy and a path to modernization which did not open dangerous social divisions or new disputes. Even this program won a limited number of active adherents, but they were enough to be significant.

With its re-establishment in 1859 and particularly after Garibaldi's resignation, the SNI became an organization of Cavourians. Its strength lay among those of the middle class who rejected the Bertanians as "reds" but who by themselves would not have found a place in Italian politics. Even for them, its appeal included the promise of direct and heroic action. Garibaldi's expedition to Sicily was therefore essential to the Society's vitality, and La Farina's expulsion from Sicily nearly fatal.

By the fall of 1860 the National Society was becoming a political party of those who readily accepted all the Cavourian compromises and asked only a part for themselves in the regular politics of united Italy. Then the elections perfectly met the Society's needs. Rent by schism, the Society gained in militance; for its remnant was clearer as to what their tasks were. The Society became increasingly narrow and intolerant as it sought its place in politics. But, having elected their betters to the Chamber, the little men of the National Society were no longer needed. There was no place even for the pretense of mass politics in united Italy, no use for a national political party. In its last years the Society became a faction within parliament and a limp collection of discontented Cavourians outside it. In Buscalioni the Society had the bureaucratic administrator who could have held together a non-political organization, the earnest secretary who could have succeeded with a political party. The SNI was neither.

Joining the National Society was the simplest and safest way of expressing a desire for Italian unification under Piedmont. Yet the Society was never strongly organized in Piedmont, where such feeling was not so vigorous that it required anything beyond restricted representative government. The SNI was more vital there than elsewhere only in 1863 when retroactive Cavourianism became a form of regional self-defense. If nationalist sentiment was great in Lombardy, the need to subordinate local programs to Piedmont's was less appealing. The Society was never very strong there. In the discontented Duchies the SNI did much better, but there it suffered its greatest failure in 1859 in Parma. And it was better organized in 1860 and 1861 when the tradition of discontent made the Bertanians a threat. On the whole, the National Society fared extraordinarily well in Tuscany, where a liberal aristocracy kept nationalism from being radical and a separatist tradition made nationalist propaganda necessary. In the Romagna the Society became most nearly what it generally meant to be, but there it developed a vitality which made it suspicious of Turin and local roots which led to independent policies and to schism. Elsewhere, the National Society was always the haven of a self-conscious minority, fearful of its isolation; it became the refuge of men who sought by association with a strong government—once it ruled over them—protection against conditions at home.

In broad social terms, the Society placed nationalists of the middle class effectively in the tow of the gentry and upper-middle class. Its own history reflects Italy's class structure. The great nobles, even when nationalists, remained suspicious of the effort to appeal to the masses; peasants and artisans could rarely find an important place in the SNI even if they were literate or had a lira to spare. Its committees were most influential when liberal aristocrats and professional men were dominant. They were more suspect, more controversial, and ran into conflict with the authorities when composed of the personally ambitious men of the middle class, whom La Farina tended to typify and from whom he often won personal loyalty.

Locally, the Society's success depended more on the social connections of its leaders than on any other aspect of its organization. Wherever the new regime became well established, the SNI tended to lose its appeal for the gentry. Then, in the years from 1861 to 1863, the Society showed more clearly its base among the bureaucracy and the National Guard, among local political figures in small towns, in areas (like the Marches or Naples) uncertain of their part in national affairs or (like the border towns) more aware of the connections between international and domestic politics. Disdained by most of the major leaders of Italian political life, the Society held a position in the middle, between them and those beneath them who shared their fears about the masses. The Society lived by its claim to have connections with those in power and to have power itself through its large following. When those claims lost their credibility, the Society died. It never lost its fear of the fickle mob; it never ceased to seek social unity.

Such social deference, the great regional differences in Italy's political life, the nature of the National Society's ideology, the fact that it rarely had a program of specific action, all this meant that the SNI could not be tightly organized or disciplined. It had every reason to maintain the appearance of carrying out Cavour's orders, and often there was a great willingness to do so; but the National Society was ill-suited to so precise and subtle a task. For all the intricacies of his policies, Cavour had few orders to give. The National Society was less well organized and apparently won less widespread and vigorous support than the German *Nationalverein* which was modeled on it. Both organizations attempted to straddle controversial political and social questions (and were torn by the latter, which were much sharper in Germany). The SNI may even, like the German society, represent something of a transition between the middle class's awareness of its growing power and its organization for real political struggle.[2] But the German organization represented a more developed politics. For all of its advocacy of Prussia, the *Nationalverein* was never so close to nor so dependent on the Prussian Government as was the SNI on Piedmont. In unified Germany the *Nationalverein* would foster a national political party as in Italy the National Society could not, although respect for the reality of power eroded the liberalism of both groups in strikingly similar ways.

The National Society's greatest success was its propaganda, the most pervasive expression of the ideas of the "high" Risorgimento. Its doctrine represented the delicate balance of forces which came about in 1859; yet it was dependent on events, the shadow of war, and the shining promise of Piedmont's army, to make its call really appealing. After 1859 it could never recapture

[2] Leonard Krieger, *The German Idea of Freedom* (Boston, 1957), 413.

the old ring. It would continue to have meaning primarily for those who were themselves nationalists in areas where nationalism seemed threatened, where, in short, conditions were more nearly like those of prewar Italy as a whole. The Society's program of compromise never lost its borrowed air. The appeal and necessity of nationalism as a natural sentiment was largely assumed.

If great benefits were promised from unification, they were mostly palpable and institutional ones, befitting practical men. The Society's liberalism was largely implicit; there was little talk of natural rights. Thus the Society lacked the ability of Jacobins or Communists to maintain a religious fervor, although it could appeal to fervor which preceded it. Its tone was proudly that of a "mature" political party like those of England or France, which may be why English and American writers have usually treated it so sympathetically. But in a country where little of the political system was yet determined, such mature restraint had its disadvantages. The connection between specific issues and general programs was too often unclear or simply ignored. From its emphasis on realism and force, on compromise and the postponement of controversy to its belief in a liberal parliament and economic progress, its ideology became a fundamental part of Italy's political heritage. Much of what happened, however, was not what the Society had predicted. Self-preservation required it increasingly to devote energy to the defense of the recent past. There was even something in La Farina's claim that the SNI suffered from an excess of tolerance; it lacked a theoretical base from which to reject the programs of its opponents. No matter how many single victories were won for the Society's position, essentially the same issues would have to be fought out over and over.

The National Society's greatest action was its part in the interim governments of central Italy from the outbreak of the war in April 1859 to annexation. Yet those deeds which did so much to determine Italy's unification came when the Central Committee was dissolved and the Society itself had little leadership. The fortunes of war created the political vacuum which the men of the Society could decently fill without the threat of revolution. It was the temporary failure of Cavour's program which gave these Cavourians their chance. They then needed only short-range policies which followed easily from dependence on Piedmont. Otherwise the Society could rarely initiate political action, for it was stymied both by its support of a government in which it did not share power and its lively, practical fear of disorder.

Rarely able to issue the call to action it spoke of so often, the Society could not abandon the word revolution; its desire for rapid modernization and the weight of Western tradition would not let it. Most of its members believed in revolution—so long as it was not foolhardy, did not risk offending Piedmont or the Powers, would not open up a social abyss or risk serious violence. The restraint of the "revolutions" of 1859 may have made Italian unity possible. They were the epitome of what the Society desired. Never again would it come so close to experiencing the world of which it wrote. Garibaldi's venture in Sicily became frightening; the revolts in the Marches in 1860 accomplished too little to be satisfying. Faced with the possibility of revolution, the Society always found itself preferring the discipline of regular forces. Its dark view of human nature made military desertion seem a more probable and a safer way of weakening the enemy in 1859 in the north, and in 1860 in Naples and Umbria. Faced with the desire to act, it most often called first for calm. Through most of its history the Italian National Society was simply embarrassed by enthusiastic members who asked for instructions as to what to do.

The Society's greatest popularity came with Garibaldi's expedition to Sicily, which seemed once again to tie together surging popular sentiment and the Government's policy, to raise the Risorgimento above selfish interests and the pettiness of politics. The drama of heroism stirred hopes the Society's doctrines could not touch. Yet that expedition represented a risk the Society could not have sponsored, and it led to the sharper definition of the differences in nationalist programs which the Society had striven to hide. In collecting money, the Society found the perfect demonstration, one more stirring than cannon for Alessandria, less obvious than a medal for La Farina. Here was something all could do, an appeal to patriotism few would resist. And the SNI was clearly more concerned that all contribute than with how much it received, more concerned with the demonstra-

471

tion than with aiding Garibaldi. As the redshirts moved across Sicily, the National Society touched more deeply into Italian society than at any time in its history.

Its greatest power was exercised in the Marches in 1860, not because it was best organized there or had its greatest following but because an uncertain new government chose briefly to make the Society its agent. But if a whole organization can achieve self-fulfillment, the National Society did so with the plebescites. The liberal act of voting became a demonstration of unanimity. Political campaigning became the most direct and simplest way of educating the masses and leading them to safety. For a moment, politics turned on a slogan of the SNI.

The Society missed its greatest opportunity—the chance to become liberal Italy's first political party. Although it became one in fact, it could not accept that role. Its ideology allowed no admission that the SNI was a party, for its doctrines of a homogenized nationalism could not justify consistent political differences among nationalists of good will. Both the SNI and the Bertanians led their followers to disillusionment in the 1860's. Bertanian opposition could never undo Cavourian policies. The Society was not a path to lasting power for many who could not have achieved it anyway. Because the Risorgimento seemed incomplete and Italy's gains not yet securely held, the SNI believed it still had a place in politics.

Insisting that it represented the majority of Italians, the Society in parliament became lost in the Government's majority. A glimpse of power kept it alive as a political group in the Chamber, but real effectiveness there would have required a willingness to act as a party and to appeal beyond parliament to society as a whole. By precept and temperament, however, the men of the National Society were dedicated to making politics less controversial and even less public. Instead of seeking wider support, the unified state became more isolated from society as a whole, the province of an earnest but narrow ruling class. The SNI had already fulfilled its function. When the policies of Piedmont had required for their success something like the support of mass opinion, the Society had thrived. As the issues of Italian political life became more specific and less general, it found little it dared to say. When Italy's institutions were established, her political procedures made regular, and participation in them opened to a small segment of the population, the Society had nothing more to do. Since this was the very system it had supported, the Italian National Society had to die quietly.

I I I

Without the National Society, or some agency to accomplish what it did, Italy could hardly have been united in the middle of the nineteenth century. This proposition can be roughly tested even in the concrete realm of the events themselves. Would Piedmont have been willing to run such risks without the assurances the Society and its propaganda provided that she had a following throughout the Peninsula? Would Cavour's dispassionate designs have been sufficiently trusted outside Piedmont to prevent dissension to the point of disaster in 1859 and 1860? Would the war of 1859 have been clearly enough a national one to hold France in check and to keep British sympathy? Would revolution have spread so far so safely? Would the provisional regimes of 1859 have gained so easily the aura of popularity? Without the appearance of agreement the Society presented, could Garibaldi have been used effectively by the moderates or Cavour have triumphed over him? Would the plebescites have been risked or the elections so open as they were? It seems unlikely.

Certainly, Italian unification without the National Society would not even have seemed a national experience shared by patriots everywhere. The Society allowed thousands of politically conscious Italians who would otherwise have felt excluded to have a part in making Italy. Without its guidance, their desire for change might have erupted in isolated bursts, been dissipated and lost as a political force.

It gave Cavour invaluable aid by providing apparent popular sanction for his policies, while at the same time serving as the guarantor to nationalists of Cavour's patriotic intent. The SNI may even have acted as something of a pressure on Cavour, pushing him to a more nationalist policy; certainly it provided him with a useful justification abroad. If Cavour seems not to have

473

relied very heavily on the Society, its effects are apparent in his expectation of greater popular sacrifice than there was in central Italy in 1859, in Naples and the Marches in 1860.

The desire for a unified nation, an abstraction only tenuously attached to more specific programs, became the central theme of Italian political life. If the changes unification brought benefitted primarily one fraction of Italians, that was disguised as a few became the voice of a nation.

The National Society stood as the most striking evidence contemporaries had that Italians did want unification—evidence which its propaganda made more impressive. More than 4,000 men, perhaps twice that number, joined the Society from 1857 to 1864.[3] This means that nearly everyone in Italian life who could vote or could influence those who voted must have had some contact with the SNI, some exposure to its ideas; a sizable number of the politically significant were moved to join the Italian National Society. It was largely in the Society's terms that the Risorgimento was understood by the respectable core of Cavourians who were indispensable to its success.

The National Society was an expression of the way in which they learned to relate their concern over local restrictions and injustice, their regional, political, and social resentments, their personal ambitions and aspirations to a national program valid

[3] My own list of the Society's members has 4,270 names. I have included in it names printed in the *Piccolo Corriere* or on local manifestoes and explicitly listed as members, names on membership lists sent to Buscalioni, names of those who wrote letters on the letterhead of the SNI or who are clearly considered members in such letters, and names listed with some evidence in regional studies of the Risorgimento. This figure does not include the number of members a committee claimed if the names themselves have not been found nor does it include those whose membership in the SNI has simply been assumed by contemporaries or by historians.

The figure of nearly 4,300 members remains only a guide to the size of the Society. Many of those listed may have forgotten within a few weeks that they ever joined or may never have been active members. Evidence of membership remains incomplete, and as many as 8,000 men may have paid dues at least once. Nearly 1,400 of those in my list are from south of Rome, suggesting that the membership records for that area, being later, are more complete but less meaningful. More than 1,000 of these names are from Tuscany, the most for any province; yet there may well have been more members in the Romagna, where some committees sent to Turin the names only of their officers. In trying to disentangle the names of those in the Marches who belonged to other patriotic committees from those actually in the SNI, I may have been too severe. Finally, not more than half this total belonged to the Society at any one time, even in 1860–61, the period of its largest membership.

for Italy as a whole. The great demonstrations in which the Society was involved reflect this growing sense of connection between the policies of Cavour and the sentiments and interests of local patriots. The contributions for cannon at Alessandria were relatively safe and simple testimonials of patriotism and confidence in Piedmont. The movement of volunteers required greater enthusiasm and cut more deeply into the layers of society; it showed that the Cavourian program for unification was becoming more widely accepted and better understood.

Because such a demonstration might develop a political tone of its own, both the Government and the Society reacted to it with some ambivalence. More even than those closest to Cavour realized, the price for Piedmont's sacrifices would be Turin's careful supervision of the Risorgimento. Step by step, the National Society supported and helped to justify that supervision. With more at stake, the revolutions of 1859 and the elections and plebescites which followed were also treated as demonstrations. A way had been found to coax and to display popular enthusiasm which did not endanger Cavour.

If in 1860 the Society helped make the divisions in Italian politics deeper than they need have been, that was largely a result of the SNI's great accomplishment in the dangerous years before of having made Italians seem more united than they were. If the Society acted with hesitance, it had acted in time to prevent men more radical from pre-empting the field. The volunteers of 1859 and the revolution of central Italy kept a moderate tone. The Garibaldians were dissuaded from attacking the Papal States in 1860. One of the Society's great contributions was the things it did not do, the calm it maintained and the patience it encouraged. With its help, those who could unify Italy were not afraid to do so. And Italians were taught to see their national aspirations in the context of international affairs.

The Society served as a crucial link between the enthusiasm of thousands and the caution of Cavourians. When unification with order seemed possible, the moderates could afford to be nationalists and nationalists could accept moderation. The compromise Manin had urged was nearly achieved. The Society was loosely organized while appearing to be highly centralized and its program was broad and general while apparently reflecting Cavour's most secret intent. But confusion over what the Society was and claimed to be, what it had done and meant to do aided it in holding together diverse interests and pointing them to the one goal: unification. The National Society made possible the transition from division and oppression to unity under a stable and representative regime. It did so in part and without calculation by encouraging aspirations bound to be frustrated. That transition achieved, the SNI had little to offer the new state.

And all of this was accomplished while the promise of modernization was still held aloft and the belief in parliamentary institutions was maintained. For the surrender to *Realpolitik* was never complete, never quite raised to the level of overriding principle. The Society continued to advertise the benefits of a liberal society even when violating its practice, and it marshaled for the new state many supporters who were ready to accept the responsibility as well as the benefits of a place in the new bureaucracy.

I V

The Italian National Society contributed in innumerable ways to Italian unification, by the fact of its existence, by its policies and propaganda, and by hundreds of the deeds of committees and members. The history of that Society, of its compromises and confusions, its hesitant beginnings and inevitable decline, suggests what a precarious attainment that unification was. The study of the SNI explains something, too, of the difficulties united Italy has had to meet.

In its advocacy of unity, the Society had adopted a good deal of the Mazzinian dream of Italy's greatness. By divorcing that dream from much of the moral content Mazzini had given it, the Society helped make strength and prosperity seem almost automatic benefits of unification. Disillusionment was inevitable. Using phrases of Mazzinian fervor, the Society foretold too great a change while opposing fundamental social or economic innovation. Nationalism was given a religious cast which often made politic caution seem craven and selfish. Having left it to successful action to fill out its doctrine, the Society found its program sounding hollow and incomplete because the kind of action its propaganda implied had rarely taken place. During these years of the Risorgimento, events themselves were often disappointing. Even the cautious could feel chagrin over Tuscany and Sicily in 1859, Naples and the Papal States in 1860. Whenever it seemed to be losing ground, the Society would speak again of dramatic action. Like much it said, such talk built into the process of unification itself a reminder of how much remained to be done and some doubt as to the popularity of what had happened.

Even when they were shrewd analysts of local conditions, the members of the Society tended to believe their own propaganda and to think the spirit of cooperation and enlightenment were taking root elsewhere in the Peninsula. Having tasted the dream of unity, of common interests and shared opinions, they were reluctant to part with it; and they found the disagreements natural to any free society a sign of some decay. As the followers of Cavour became more secure, they became more intolerant and more resentful of their opponents. Having so long ignored the differences among nationalists, they were not prepared to accept the differences between north and south, city and town, artisans and aristocrats. They never gained enough confidence not to wish for the postponement of controversial issues until administrative processes had settled them. Instead, political dispute tended to renew their old distrust of politics. The neat power of a single national party haunted them, but they looked to the state, not to the process of debate and compromise, to solve problems which they saw as administrative rather than political. Principled disagreement was too easily explained as the avarice of men who would not sacrifice for the nation. The Society's followers would find a disappointing lack of vigor in all Italy's governments.

The Society's proud realism left its followers too painfully aware of dependence on foreign powers. Interest in Great Britain and France had shifted from the sympathy of liberal public opinion to the diplomatic necessities of those states. After unification, the Society's successors would at times irresponsibly reject outside aid and advice, while Italy's history increased their inevitable temptation to find in diplomatic triumphs a counterweight to domestic disappointment. The myth the Society had

477

sponsored of a highly organized, secret, and extralegal conspiracy as an aid to Governmental policy would lead other governments to yearn for such support. Its emphasis on success as the justification of its program put few restraints on the tactics a government might consider. The belief that the Government and revolution had cooperated in 1859 embarrassed Cavour in 1860 and all of Italy at Aspromonte in 1862. To be right in such cases, Pallavicino complained, it was necessary to succeed. Limits on the means to success were further undermined. Cavour's greatness was not forgotten, but he was remembered too simply as Machiavellian.

The National Society had made it clear that public opinion could be mobilized to support the state without allowing the masses a voice in determining policy, a lesson politicians were bound to learn too well. By confusing unity with unanimity, the Society had injected an impossible and dangerous goal into Italian politics, a standard which left its followers thinking Italy even weaker than she was. Their fears, increased by the acquisition of the South, had made the Society more conservative and intolerant. It had favored the exclusion of the Bertanians from respectable political life; yet that embryonic left was not very radical. Most of its supporters were, as the evolution of Depretis and Crispi shows, susceptible to the restraints of office, willing to compromise after all. Those who did not accommodate were isolated, and Italy unnecessarily lost their humane influence.

Garibaldi might advocate an international arbitration league or rediscover his youthful shock that the Pope was not a Christian, but he could find no place in the real political life of Italy. Yet both Bertanians and the SNI needed Garibaldi, not merely because he was a dashing hero, the personification of quick action and direct solutions. More important, he was the symbol proving that the people had a part in Italy's resurgence, that patriotism was not self-serving. Whatever the political quality of his judgment, Italy could ill afford to deny the symbol.

The activity of the SNI in 1861 shows that a somewhat broader political life was safely possible in Italy, but with the death of Cavour, the Society's old call for compromise lost its last vitality. It had come to rest at simple acceptance of the *status quo* and of the state. Pallavicino's simple dogmatism was treated with condescension by the practical men of Government. But he was right to be shocked and hurt by the intolerance Italy's leaders showed, and there was merit in his wish that the Government be frankly nationalist and decently liberal. His historical significance lies, however, less in his insight than in his confusion. He personified the dilemma of Italy's nationalist reformers, and for all his faith in Italy, his honest and sentimental liberalism, he could find no path for Italy very different from the one on which her leaders took her. The man who had corresponded so enthusiastically with Gioberti and Manin (and who had worried them both about his poor health) lived long beyond them to correspond in his later years with Vilfredo Pareto about the dangers of universal suffrage.

The history of the Italian National Society suggests how very difficult it was to achieve unification as well as what it cost to do so. The Society both aided in that achievement and made men more willing to pay its price. If, almost naïvely, it reminded Italians of how much more they once had wanted, that was because the National Society had always meant to be liberal. Even Pallavicino came to understand this. He lamented in 1875 that the work of the *Società Nazionale Italiana* had been forgotten, but he added confidently that "posterity will render it justice. We have in fact arrived at the unity of Italy under a monarchy. Certainly, we would have gotten there with a republic, and in a worthier way; but when? Perhaps in a century, and perhaps in a still longer time." Even an American who had expected better things from Europe could accept that, with Yankee resignation and poetic grandeur, as God's "sterner plan."

A NOTE ON SOURCES AND OF
ACKNOWLEDGMENT

✤ THE BIBLIOGRAPHY of this study is in the footnotes, but some further guide to the provenance of the primary sources may be useful. Published letters and memoirs offer rich material for the study of the Risorgimento; three such collections, less famous than many others, are particularly important for the history of the National Society: B. E. Maineri (ed.), *Daniele Manin e Giorgio Pallavicino, epistolario politico* (1855–57) (Milan, 1878); Ausunio Franchi (ed.), *Epistolario di Giuseppe La Farina* (2 vols., Milan, 1869); *Memorie di Giorgio Pallavicino*, Vol. II edited by Anna Koppmann Pallavicino (Turin, 1885) and Vol. III edited by Anna Pallavicino d'Angrogna (Turin, 1895). Unfortunately, the editors of all these volumes were moved more by admiration for the men whose documents they printed than by the historian's cruel wish to know all.

Maineri's omissions are probably not terribly important, although his sensitive use of the asterisk leads to an overly convivial picture of the movement's early years. Manin's letters still exist in manuscript, and a comparison with them shows that Maineri deprived us of more spice than basic content; for Pallavicino no such comparison can be made, however; and since he was the more outspoken correspondent, his letters suffer from more frequent deletions. Pallavicino's *Memorie*, a potpourri of documents he left behind, provide little detail on any single matter but offer important evidence as to his views. Franchi's edition of La Farina's correspondence is marred by the unmarked omissions of whole letters and significant passages. The volumes themselves were almost a political tract, and Franchi only obtained the letters he used by promising the "most severe observance" of propriety and regard for all those involved (letter to Daniele Morchio, 15 June 1867, ms. in Carte Morchio, MNRG). This most important of published sources on the SNI must be used with particular care.

The numerous articles of Giovanni Maioli, like the articles and the book of Alberto Dallolio and Ernesto Masi, contain scores of important letters and documents on the Society in the Romagna. The studies of Sergio Camerani and Mario Puccioni similarly provide a very useful sampling of the sources on the Society in Tuscany, and indeed, many of the letters Puccioni quotes have since been lost. Alessandrini and Nicoletti have provided huge compilations of documents on the SNI in the Marches, but their confusion of the National Society with other groups which favored unification with Piedmont makes these printed sources almost as dangerous as they are helpful for the history of the National Society.

Although there are hundreds of printed works important for this study, it must, then, rest largely on sources which have not been edited. The repositories most frequently cited in the text have been given abbreviations there and are listed alphabetically here:

ASF. Archivio di Stato, Firenze.

ASR. Archivio di Stato, Roma.

AST. Archivio di Stato, Torino. The leavings of bureaucracy are always uneven, but the Florentine archives contain a few useful reports from the rather inept Granducal police. The Roman archives have a few scattered references to the Society in addition to the reports sent Ricasoli on the SNI in the Marches and Sicily. The archives in Turin contain reports to Cavour on political conditions in Tuscany and the Romagna which, for the latter, establish important connections between the Society and government.

ISR. Istituto per la Storia del Risorgimento. This well-organized collection in Rome is by far the most important single archive for the history of the National Society. In addition to hundreds of relevant documents and broadsides scattered throughout the collection, it contains the papers of Buscalioni, a gift from H. Nelson Gay. Buscalioni's papers are certainly not complete, but they include about 2,000 letters to and from members of the SNI, most of them written after 1859.

MCRB. Museo Civico del Risorgimento, Bologna. Nearly 1,000 letters and documents about the Society in the Romagna are among the papers of Casarini (by far the largest grouping),

Simonetti, and Tanari (which contain relatively fewer on the Society).

MCV. Museo Correr, Venezia. The Manin documents here contain some letters of importance for Manin's later years.

MNRG. Museo Nazionale del Risorgimento, Genova. The papers of Morchio, the secretary of the Society's committee in Genoa, provide a good deal of information on the SNI there as well as copies of some circulars from the Central Committee; unfortunately, such treasures are not common.

MNRT. Museo Nazionale del Risorgimento, Torino. In this collection there are hundreds of letters important for the early years of the PNI and SNI, particularly those to Pallavicino, a great many of which have never been fully or correctly published.

MRF. Museo del Risorgimento, Firenze. This collection contains the Bartolommei letters, including many to Teresa Bartolommei most of which have, however, been assimilated into secondary works.

Equally important are the publications of the National Society and its various committees; a number of libraries are significantly rich in these:

BCT. Biblioteca Civica, Torino. Next to the HCL, the best collection of the publications of the PNI and SNI is here.

BSMC. Biblioteca di Storia Moderna e Contemporanea. This library in Rome has a good many relevant pamphlets and newspapers, including some on the CNR and the Neapolitan committees not available elsewhere.

HCL. Harvard College Library. The printed materials on the Risorgimento collected by H. Nelson Gay were all sold to Harvard, which already had a strong collection in Italian history; the result is a library unequaled in this field. The most nearly complete collection of the pamphlets of the PNI, SNI, and of the local committees is here. Buscalioni's pamphlets, bound as one volume in the Houghton Library, contain the largest group of the Society's circulars and membership forms. In addition, Gay's newspaper clippings and the regional collections of newspapers, pamphlets, and broadsides in both Houghton and Widener libraries are invaluable. The Harvard Law School library also contains important collections of proclamations.

ISR and MCRB. In addition to the manuscripts mentioned

above scores of the Society's broadsides are scattered through these two collections.

MNRM. Museo Nazionale del Risorgimento, Milano. The famous Bertarelli collection here is relatively rich in pamphlets relating to the Society.

It has become almost a tradition in Risorgimento bibliographies to lament the disappearance of copies of the Society's newspaper and the necessary reliance instead on the somewhat sparse selections in Ausunio Franchi (ed.), *Scritti politici di Giuseppe La Farina* (2 vols., Milan, 1870). It is, however, possible to assemble a nearly complete file of the Society's newspapers; and this study would have been impossible without it.

Il Piccolo Corriere d'Italia. A weekly. The issues of 21 December 1856 to 11 January 1857, 25 January to 8 February 1857, 12 April to 24 May 1857, 19 July to 1 August 1857, 4 October to 29 November 1857 are in HCL. The issues of 1858 (except for those of 10 and 31 January) and of 1859 until it ceased publication with the edition of 18 April 1859 are in MNRG.

The issues of 1 November 1859 (when it resumed publication) through all those of 1860 to 3 February 1861 (when it became a monthly), the monthly copies of March, April, May, June, July 1861 (when the paper suspended publication), and the daily copies of 1 September 1861 (when the paper resumed in its new format, although the next issue was that of 1 October 1861) to 19 November 1861 are complete in HCL.

Espero, Il Piccolo Corriere d'Italia. A daily. The copies of *Espero* from 20 November 1861 to 18 March 1862 are complete in HCL. The copies from 19 March 1862 to 20 December 1862 (when *Espero* ceased) are complete in MNRM.

La Discussione, Piccolo Corriere d'Italia. A daily. The copies from 21 December to 31 December 1862 are complete in MNRM. From 1 January 1863 to 31 December 1863 they are complete in MNRT. From 1 January 1864 to 27 May 1864 they are complete in MNRM.

✧

One of the great rewards of scholarship lies in the fraternity of scholars. As the preceding notes suggest, my debt to librarians and archivists is particularly heavy. From directors to clerks, their interest and understanding was matched by boundless patience—in Italy for the accented foreigner hopefully prying into their past, in this country for the esoteric demands of a regular customer. In addition to the staffs of the institutions mentioned above I am particularly grateful to those who helped me at the national libraries of Florence, Rome, and Palermo, at the university library in Messina, at the archives in Marseilles, at the Bibliothèque Nationale, and at the British Museum, and to those at scores of other places where anticipated treasures did not exist, who carried their assistance to the point of sharing my disappointment.

Funds from Harvard University, the Woodbury-Lowery Travelling Fellowship; from the United States Government, a Fulbright grant; and from Princeton University, the Faculty Research Fund, made this work possible. To all those involved in these acts of faith I am grateful.

From Italian scholars I have received a good deal of encouragement, useful advice, and often quite extraordinary assistance. I wish particularly to thank professor Eugenio Artom, professor Luigi Bulferetti, dott. Sergio Camerani, dott. Arturo Codignola, professor Alberto M. Ghisalberti, signorina Emilia Morelli, the late professor Walter Maturi, and the late dott. Giovanni Maioli. The Marchesa Luini and the Puccioni family in Florence were very helpful; Mrs. Marion Swann Miller and Mr. Denis Mack Smith have offered their expert's knowledge with a friend's good humor. The prize committee of the Society for Italian Historical Studies provided great encouragement and three of its members, Professors Shepard B. Clough, Kent Roberts Greenfield, and A. William Salomone, added very helpful comments on the first half of the manuscript in an earlier form. Professor Dante L. Germino of Wellesley and several of my colleagues at Princeton, Professors David D. Bien, Gordon A. Craig, Robert R. Palmer, and Joseph R. Strayer, have also read parts of the manuscript with kindly discernment. Professor Crane Brinton would be surprised to know how much he has aided me by both his criticism and encouragement and in the development of my own judgments. From my earliest research in Italian history to the completion of part of this manuscript, the late professor Donald C. McKay was my most conscientious counselor and severest critic. My own sense of loss at his death is heightened now by the regret that he could not see this tangible return on his investment of enthusiasm and concern. Finally, one need not declare his conjugal gratitude in print; but there is no more important fact in the history of this book than that my wife has so intelligently and steadily edited, typed, collated data, and helped with the digging in the archives while keeping her balance and mine.

To name these people is not to implicate them; their generosity has hardly lessened my responsibility.

INDEX

M.